Sentencing and Punishment

Sentencing and Punishment

The Quest for Justice

Second Edition

Susan Easton and Christine Piper

OXFORD
UNIVERSITY PRESS

OXFORD
UNIVERSITY PRESS

Great Clarendon Street, Oxford OX2 6DP

Oxford University Press is a department of the University of Oxford.
It furthers the University's objective of excellence in research, scholarship,
and education by publishing worldwide in

Oxford New York

Auckland Cape Town Dar es Salaam Hong Kong Karachi
Kuala Lumpur Madrid Melbourne Mexico City Nairobi
New Delhi Shanghai Taipei Toronto

With offices in

Argentina Austria Brazil Chile Czech Republic France Greece
Guatemala Hungary Italy Japan Poland Portugal Singapore
South Korea Switzerland Thailand Turkey Ukraine Vietnam

Oxford is a registered trade mark of Oxford University Press
in the UK and in certain other countries

Published in the United States
by Oxford University Press Inc., New York

British Library Cataloguing in Publication Data

Data available

Library of Congress Cataloging in Publication Data

Data available

Typeset by Newgen Imaging Systems (P) Ltd, Chennai, India
Printed in Great Britain
on acid-free paper by
Ashford Colour Press, Gosport, Hampshire

ISBN 978–0–19–921810–3

1 3 5 7 9 10 8 6 4 2

OUTLINE CONTENTS

DETAILED CONTENTS

PART A Sentencing Principles and Policies

3 'Just deserts': developments in retributivist sentencing 72

4 Utility and deterrence 111

5 Risk and danger 140

6   Making amends   173

7   Mitigating the sentence?   209

8   Treating children differently   237

PART B Punishing Offenders

11 Experiencing imprisonment   338

12 Just punishment in the community   388

PREFACE

We began the Preface to the first edition of this book with the following statement: 'Sentencing and punishment are currently high-profile policy issues: proposals for new procedures, criteria, and punishments make headline news and generate debate at all levels of public and social life. This policy area is also complex and volatile: legislative change is frequent and recurring, and issues of criminal justice practice and administration are continually in the public domain.' The last three years have been no exception and further change has recently been debated in Parliament in the form of the Criminal Justice and Immigration Bill (now Act). The Criminal Justice Act 2003, which was just coming into force three years ago, is now mostly in place and the Sentencing Guidelines Council has not only been established but has produced a large quantity of consultation and guideline documents.

What, unfortunately, is not new is the increasing use of custody with several well-publicised crises over the last three years and the decision to address the problems of crime and disorder by building yet more prisons is not one we welcome. So we are delighted that Oxford University Press has reproduced on the cover of this second edition Vincent van Gogh's famous picture *The Round of Prisoners*, also known as *The Prison Courtyard*, of prisoners walking aimlessly and pointlessly in a circle in the exercise yard at Newgate Prison. We have also quoted at the beginning of Chapter 5 a recent commentator who has pointed out that, on current estimates, the global population of prisoners forms 'another "round", another circular view' and that 'such a number could go twice round the world' (Rivera Beiras 2005: 167). We hope this book will contribute to the debate on how best to counter the futility of incarcerating an ever larger proportion of the population.

Sentencing and punishment are, then, by no means merely academic matters: policy and practice impact on actual and potential victims of crime if they fail to prevent or limit reoffending, they affect the offender and his or her family and friends, and also lead to a large expenditure on courts and prisons: the effects may be far-reaching indeed. Further, these are topics where there are strong personal and popular feelings about what 'should' happen, and how 'justice' should be done. Policy and practice in this area are also contingent on, and influenced by, a very wide range of factors. Political, social, and economic issues are not only of great importance in the broader development of penal policy, but are also relevant to the particular circumstances of individual offenders and their experience of punishment. For this reason, we have included more material on sentence impact, prisoners' rights, and the equality/difference debates. We have also again included two chapters on the state's responses to children and young people who offend as they increasingly face similar processes and punishments.

All these themes and issues have contributed to our strong interest over many years in sentencing and punishment and in teaching in this area. Our different academic backgrounds and interests have allowed us, jointly, to synthesise a wide range of theoretical, philosophical, and practical issues raised by developments in sentencing and punishment. The thread which runs through our interests—and also this book—is the focus on different notions of justice in sentencing and punishment which have been theorised historically and, consequently, on principles of fairness, equality, and the quest for justice.

This wide range of influences on sentencing and policy, and the fluid state of sentencing law and policy do, however, lead to problems when writing a book in this area. We have, therefore, had to make choices about coverage, about themes, and about the organisation of material. We would have liked to include more comparative material. We have referred to other jurisdictions where possible but clearly a fully comparative approach would require substantially more discussion than is possible here.

We strongly believe that penal theory, penal policy, and sentencing law should be discussed together and not addressed separately. The first part of our book, therefore, considers the classical justifications for punishment, and also the more recent restorative justice theories, in conjunction with a review of relevant policy and law. The second part of the book focuses on the practice of punishment but again relates the information to policy, theory, and matters of principle.

As with all books, our material will not be up to date on the day of publication. This book reviews law and policy up to the end of March 2008, although minor amendments relating to the passage of the Criminal Justice and Immigration Act 2008 were made at proof stage. The Online Resource Centre will direct readers to subsequent changes. However, this book is not simply a summary of sentencing law: it is essentially an examination of the issues that arise when we try to justify, choose, and impose punishment. These issues—which are an integral part of the quest for justice in dealing with offenders, victims, and the wider community—are not contingent on time and place and will continue to be important whatever are the next developments in sentencing and penal policy.

We would like to thank the editorial and production staff at Oxford University Press, particularly Tom Young, Joanna Godfrey, Naomi Clark and Matthew Baldwin, for their support and we are very grateful to our families, especially Alan and Esmond, whose weekends and Easter holidays have been severely disrupted by our commitment to finish this edition on time.

We have also benefited from the comments of reviewers and readers of the first edition. In particular we have welcomed the comments from judges in other jurisdictions, including Mr Justice Gilles Renaud and Judge David Stutzman.

Susan Easton
Christine Piper
26 May 2008

ACKNOWLEDGEMENTS

Grateful acknowledgement is made to all the authors and publishers of copyright material that appears in this book, and in particular to the following for permission to reprint material from the sources indicated:

Extracts from Crown Copyright material are reproduced under Class License Number C01P000148 with the permission of the Controller of HMSO and the Queen's Printer for Scotland.

The Audit Commission for Chart: Exhibit 2, 'The Youth Justice System' in *Youth Justice 2004* (Audit Commission, 2004).

Centre for Crime and Justice Studies for Fig. 2, 'Sources of the mediation movement and their objectives' in T. Marshall, 'Seeking the Whole Justice' in S. Hayman (ed.), *Repairing the Damage: Restorative Justice in Action* (ISTD, 1997).

Mennonite Central Committee for Appendix: 'Paradigms of Justice Old and New' in H. Zehr, 'Retributive Justice, Restorative Justice', *New Perspectives in Crime and Justice*, Vol 4 (MCC Office of Crime & Justice, 1985).

NACRO for Chart: 'Convictions for Murder 1989–1999' in *Youth Justice Briefing: The Grave Crimes Provision* (NACRO, 2001) and Chart: 'Sentences under section 91 1980–2002', in *Youth Crime Briefing: The Grave Crimes Provisions and Long Term Detention* (NACRO, 2004).

Every effort has been made to trace and contact copyright holders prior to going to press but if notified, the publisher will undertake to rectify any errors or omissions at the earliest opportunity.

GLOSSARY

Anchoring point the level at which punishment is set.

Attorney General the principal law officer of the Crown who is responsible for the Crown Prosecution Service.

Autopoiesis a biological term used to refer to a socio-legal theory which analyses communications within systems such as law.

Bifurcation in relation to youth justice denotes a two-pronged policy whereby the majority of offenders are diverted from prosecution and the minority are prosecuted and punished.

Cardinal proportionality non-relative proportionality where the overall level of punishment is addressed.

Cautioning plus a form of cautioning (official warning by the police) which included voluntary participation by the young offender in a preventative programme.

Censure the process of public denunciation and reproof of an offender's criminal behaviour.

Contestability the opening up of the market to new providers of goods and services, for example from the voluntary sector as well as the private sector.

Culpability blameworthiness in relation to criminal wrong-doing.

Deterrence using punishment to deter the general public from offending (general deterrence) or to deter offenders from reoffending (special or individual deterrence).

Discretion the power of the sentencer or other official to make a choice of processes or outcomes available.

Doli incapax a Latin phrase meaning 'incapable of wrong'. Currently this refers to children under 10 years of age in English law.

Felony formally (until 1967) an offence more serious than a misdemeanour.

Governance governance has different meanings in different contexts. It refers generally to the exercise of power more widely than that covered by the term 'government'.

Incapacitation preventing reoffending by removing offenders from society through the death penalty, imprisonment, or other means.

Indictable offences an offence that may be tried on indictment, that is, by jury in the Crown Court. Some indictable offences are triable either way (see below).

Just deserts the term used to refer to punishment calculated in relation to the culpability of the offender. It is an outcome justified on retributivist principles.

Less eligibility the principle developed originally in relation to the Poor Law, that conditions inside prison must be worse than outside prison for the deterrent effect to operate.

Misdemeanour formerly (before 1967) any of the less serious offences.

Moral panic a term used to denote a theory developed to explain the way an incident triggers a generalised and disproportionate public concern about a social issue or penal policy.

New Managerialism using strategies and techniques from the private sector in the management of punishment in the public sector, focusing on the most efficient use of resources, for example, using Key Performance Targets, Key Performance Indicators, and league tables.

New Penology an approach which is concerned with risk management, using actuarial data to predict and manage risk, and which focuses on categories of offenders rather than individuals.

Normalisation in the context of imprisonment, using the same standards in prison which are applied to the lives of offenders in the community as far as possible, within the constraints required by imprisonment, so that prisoners are able to lead as normal lives as possible apart from their loss of liberty.

Ordinal proportionality an amount of punishment which is proportionate to culpability in terms of parity between offenders committing offences of similar gravity, and such that the relative severity of punishment reflects the seriousness-ranking of offences.

Out-sourcing the management technique of tendering part of an organisation's work or services to an external provider.

Paramountcy principle in law relating to children this refers to the principle that the welfare of the child shall be paramount in the making of decisions about the child's upbringing.

Parsimony principle using the most economical means of punishment, to impose the least severe punishment necessary to achieve the objective of crime reduction.

Populist punitiveness the increased punitiveness of governments to attract public support.

Prisonisation the forms of adaptation of individuals and groups to prison life.

Privatisation the transfer of state functions or services to the private sector.

Protective sentencing sentencing with the aim of reducing the likelihood that the offender will cause harm to the public by offending in the future. The form such public protection takes may be incapacitation through imprisonment.

Prudential disincentive a penalty which is designed to deter an individual from offending.

Quantum the amount of money awarded as compensation or imposed as punishment.

Racism exclusionary practices based on assumptions about racial hierarchies, which see the qualities of social groups as fixed.

Rehabilitative ideal using treatment and training in custody or in the community to rehabilitate individuals so that they can contribute to society.

Restorative justice an approach to crime and disorder which focuses on the restoration of harmony between the victim, the offender, and the community.

Retributivism the theory of punishment which links punishment to the desert of the individual and which matches the severity of the punishment to the seriousness of the crime.

Ring-fencing specifying a proportion of a budget which can be used only for particular purposes.

Summary offences offences that can only be tried before magistrates. Most minor offences are summary offences.

Three Strikes laws mandatory minimum sentencing schemes in the United States aimed at repeat offenders where the third sentence mandates 25 years to life in prison.

Triable either way offence a crime that may be tried either as an indictable offence or as a summary offence.

Utilitarianism a philosophical approach which sees individuals as motivated by the pursuit of pleasure and avoidance of pain and uses this to devise policies which maximise the greatest happiness of the greatest number.

Utilitarian theories of punishment the use of punishment to reduce or prevent crime through deterrence, incapacitation, and rehabilitation.

White-collar crime non-violent crime committed for financial gain in commercial situations or in relation to personal finances.

TABLE OF STATUTES

TABLE OF CASES

TABLE OF EUROPEAN LEGISLATION

TABLE OF INTERNATIONAL TREATIES
AND CONVENTIONS

PART A

Sentencing Principles and Policies

1

New penology and new policies

SUMMARY

This chapter focuses on key questions in penal policy. It also considers the principal factors which shape the development of penal policy, notably political imperatives, economic influences, penological and criminological principles, and the influence of public opinion. We review developments over the last two decades to highlight significant trends and problems. We conclude the chapter by focusing on the **governance** of sex offenders.

1.1 Introduction

1.1.1 Our approach

Our approach is to identify what counts as 'justice' in the context of sentencing and punishment, and why. We will therefore examine the ways in which Parliament, judges, and magistrates and criminal justice professionals seek to justify, impose and implement policies which convey particular answers to these fundamental questions about sentencing and punishment. So we are not concerned only with what 'the law' says about sentencing and punishment, but why the law has developed and whether it can be justified on the philosophical principles underpinning punishment. We are also concerned with what happens when the sentencing outcomes are put into practice: what is the experience of punishment like, what issues do these various penalties raise, do they achieve their intended results?

To understand how the state punishes, we will consider the relevant sentencing law, the policy guidelines, professional guidance, including national standards, and what we know about their implementation. Our interest lies not simply in 'how much' punishment, but also in wider questions about the range and types of punishment. In scrutinising why we punish we will discuss the 'answers' in two ways: first by analysing the political, policy, and pragmatic reasons and second, by focusing on penology—the study of the reasons and justifications underpinning the practice of state punishment. These two questions, the how and why, are linked. The policy reasons or penological justifications for state punishment may determine how the offender is treated. For this reason, each chapter in this book will integrate discussion of policy and theory with analysis of sentencing law or punishment practice.

This chapter will begin this project by reviewing key questions and concepts in penal policy and the major factors which influence its development. Chapter 1 will also look at the emergence, at the end of the twentieth century, of the '**New Penology**' in criminology and of a rights-based jurisprudence in law, and will explore some of the issues this raises in relation to recent sex offender legislation. At the end of this chapter, we will include a sentencing exercise, the aim of which is to encourage reflection on the practical outcomes which flow from adherence to one or other justification. Chapter 1 will look only briefly at penological theories; Chapters 2 and 3 will consider in more detail one of the classical justifications for punishment, **retributivism**, whilst Chapters 4, 5 and 12 will focus on **deterrence**, risk management and rehabilitation which reflect the other main justification of punishment, namely **utilitarianism**. Chapter 6 will focus on the more recent thinking in relation to **restorative justice**.

1.1.2 **What is punishment?**

We first need to consider what is meant by punishment. Punishment can be distinguished from other forms of pain or suffering such as a painful treatment for a medical condition where the harm is not an expression of moral condemnation, and not a response to our misdeeds. Punishment rests on moral reasons, the expression of moral condemnation, in response to rule infringements. Indeed, Feinberg (1994) refers to **censure** or condemnation as the defining feature of punishment. What distinguishes punishment, says Feinberg, is its expressive function: 'punishment is a conventional device for the expression of attitudes of resentment and indignation,... Punishment, in short, has a *symbolic significance* largely missing from other kinds of penalties' (Feinberg 1994: 73). A penalty in football is not comparable to imprisonment in terms of public reprobation. Punishment is 'a symbolic way of getting back at the criminal, of expressing a kind of vindictive resentment' (ibid: 76). Condemnation or denunciation, he says, conjoins resentment and reprobation.

The criminal law distinguishes between regulating and punitive statutes, often imposing strict liability in the former case. But in practice the line between regulation and punishment may not be so clear-cut which can cause problems. For example, in the United States there are constitutional safeguards for those facing punishment which are not available if the measure is construed as a regulatory activity. So if a repressive act is defined as non-punitive, then the individual will be in a worse position. Feinberg gives the example of the case of *Flemming v Nestor* (1960). Here an old-age pensioner was deported and then deprived of his social security benefits, because of his membership of the Communist Party for four years during the 1930s, yet the US Supreme Court held that the loss of benefits was not punitive, but simply incidental to the regulation of an activity. In European Convention jurisprudence there are similar arguments about what constitutes punishment in relation to Article 7 of the Convention. In *Gough v Chief Constable of Derbyshire* (2001), for example, the Court held that a football banning order was not a penalty for the purposes of Article 7. Similarly, the European Commission of Human Rights held that the sex offenders' registration scheme did not constitute a penalty in *Ibbotson v UK* (1999). A similar approach was taken by the House of Lords in relation to anti-social behaviour orders (ASBOs) in *R (McCann)* [2003] where their Lordships held that an application for an ASBO was a civil and not a criminal matter as they are designed to prevent behaviour rather than to punish, do not appear on criminal records and do not immediately entail imprisonment.

A key feature of punishment is that it rests on a moral foundation, expressing a moral judgement. It is reflective and based on reasons. A further distinguishing feature of punishment is that it stems from an authoritative source, usually the state. Suffering consequent upon misdeeds is not punishment unless those who inflict it have authority over the offender. If we imagine that a murderer chased by the police crashes his car and dies before he can be tried, he has not suffered punishment but escaped it. Even if we conceive of misfortune befalling a person who commits a bad deed, as 'God's punishment', we are still conceiving of punishment as derived from authority.

Although our focus in this book will be on state punishment, of course punishment may also be informal in so far as it is imposed outside the formal criminal justice system. Informal justice developed as an alternative to state-centred methods of dispute resolution as the parties sought to recapture conflicts from professionals (see Christie 1977; Abel 1982; Matthews 1988; and Chapter 6). An extreme form of informal justice would be vigilantism and state punishment is usually seen as a necessary means of avoiding the excesses of unrestrained popular justice, by satisfying the public's demands for punishment.

1.2 Understanding penal policy

1.2.1 Key questions

The question of why some acts are criminalised and not others, and why society deals harshly with some wrong-doing but lightly with others, is much debated in criminology. But when we consider this in relation to penal policy, a fundamental issue is why punishment is seen as an appropriate response to a specific event or mode of behaviour. This entails asking three questions:

- first: what particular response is made and why?
- second: if the response is penal, which particular penal option is selected?
- third: what is the particular level of penal response?

These three dimensions of penal policy, what to punish, how to punish, and how much to punish, will shape policy outcomes and while this book will focus principally on the last two, the first is still important as it sets the scene for the latter two elements.

In looking at the first question, we might ask why the response is punitive, rather than taking some other form, such as social assistance or a medical response. The offender might be seen as a wicked person who should be punished, or as a sick person requiring treatment, or as an inadequate individual whose criminality is the result of social deprivation and who needs social welfare policies to address that problem, as well as appropriate crime-prevention strategies. So, in some societies, such as Stalinist Russia or modern China, wrong-doing may be met with a medical response, using medical incarceration for political dissidents. Or, currently, the unruly behaviour of children might be controlled through drugs such as Ritalin which is popular in America and the UK. Experiments have also been conducted using vitamin supplements on young offenders at Aylesbury Young Offenders'

Institution in England, with positive results on behaviour in that the group receiving vitamins committed fewer disciplinary offences than the group given placebos (see Gesch *et al.* 2002).

So the punitive response is only one of several possibilities and each response will rest on a particular model of human behaviour. In practice we may find a combination of policies and strategies, depending on the type of offence and offender and on the political climate. Political pressures may also shift the reaction to crime and disorder from a penal response to a military response. Examples of this approach would be the use of troops to deal with sectarian conflict and disorder in Northern Ireland and in response to strikes in the UK and of course, in recent years, military responses have dominated the United States' fight against terrorist crime. However, it is conceivable that, in other contexts, pressures on governments might engender a move away from penal and punitive responses to a welfarist response, to address problems in communities by supporting disadvantaged groups and promoting social inclusion. So we may find a variety of strategies depending in part on pressures on governments.

Secondly, in terms of the particular type of response made through penal policy, a number of options may be available, from educational programmes, such as driver education or anger management, through to extreme punishments such as execution. Thirdly, in reviewing penal policy, we should consider the level of response via penal policy, in other words, how long is the sentence of imprisonment, how heavy is the fine, and how firmly is the response enforced.

1.2.2 Equality, fairness and justice

Understanding penal policy also requires a focus on equality and fairness, particularly if some groups are selected for harsher punishment or if apparently neutral policies have differential impact. The concern with equality of impact in the late 1980s and the 1990s focused on disparities in sentencing (see Chapter 10), as well as on direct and indirect discrimination. This was also reflected in changes in the criminal law itself; for example, the Criminal Justice Act (CJA) 1991 made racial motivation an aggravating factor in assaults, and s 95 of the same Act imposes a duty on the Secretary of State to publish information considered expedient to enable those involved in the administration of criminal justice to avoid discriminating against any person on the ground of race, sex, or any other improper ground (see Chapters 10 and 11). The principle of equality has also entered penal policy debates on the impact of apparently equal punishments imposed on individuals who are not equal. Examples of potentially unjust punishments would include fines which are unrelated to means, or the impact of punishment on people with particular medical conditions, for example those offenders who are mentally disordered (see Chapter 7, section 7.4). Policies may also indirectly discriminate against certain groups, such as women with children, or directly discriminate if there are problems of bias in the imposition of punishment (see Chapters 10 and 11).

Injustice may, then, operate at each of the three levels we have identified, in terms of what is punished, how an offender is punished, and how much an offender or offence is punished. Hudson's experience of sitting in courts in the 1980s and early 1990s gives a picture of disparity and variability in offences leading to imprisonment, but consistency in vulnerability to custody of the homeless, the mentally ill, and the unemployed. Using the examples of burglary and racial harassment, she argues that 'sentencing patterns reveal a vast difference between serious crimes and crimes taken seriously' (Hudson 1993: 77). For Hudson, contemporary penal practice does not satisfy standards of social justice and fails to deliver criminal justice as fairness and equity to offenders: we should treat like offences similarly and should not penalise people for what/who they are but only for what they have done. Moreover, the selective use of community punishments may increase inequalities. She argues that 'penal policy has its ultimate justification that it contributes to social justice' (1993: 12) but acknowledges that 'commensurate punishment is not always the "just" solution; there are occasions when not to punish might be just' (1993: 13). Significantly, she sees penal policy—actions taken by political actors concerning selection of goals and means to achieve them—and social policy—usually referring to the provision of welfare goods and services—as linked. In practice they deal with the same client groups and are influenced by the same ideological movements and the same socio-economic contexts and there are similarities between policies towards offenders and the mentally ill. Examples would be the deinstitutionalisation of the mentally ill into community care, the transcarceration from hospitals to prisons, the falling numbers in mental hospitals and the criminalisation of mental disorder, the increasing use of imprisonment, the declining influence of psychiatry, the rise of the market, and the decline of welfare support.

Of course the notion of justice is not clear-cut: like 'rights', justice is a slippery concept which has been used by both right and left to embody aspirations and to legitimise policies. Justice was stressed by the Woolf Report (Woolf and Tumim 1991) as one of the key principles which should govern the treatment of prisoners (see Chapter 9). A sense of injustice, it argued, was an important contributory factor in the prison riots of 1990. 'Justice' has also been a key strand of New Labour policy, expressed in the White Paper *Justice for All* (Home Office 2002a), which said the government's aim was to 'narrow the justice gap' by which it means reducing the gap between the number of crimes reported to the police and the number of offenders brought to justice. *Rebalancing the Criminal Justice System in Favour of the Law-Abiding Majority* (Home Office 2006a) stressed that people want to see the system 'delivering justice—with fairer sentencing and fewer occasions when the system seems to let the offender off the hook' (ibid: para 2.2). In a recent strategy document the Home Office also describes its role as 'supporting the efficient and effective delivery of justice' (Home Office 2008: 2).

Justice embodies notions of fairness to all members of the community, including victims and offenders, and striking a balance between their competing interests is the cornerstone of current criminal justice policy. But it also assumes a consensus on what constitutes justice, and achieving justice in terms of improving conviction rates, for example, may create injustice for particular individuals or groups. What is construed as fair treatment means different things in different theories of social justice,[1] but its construction also depends on how punishment is rationalised in the different theories of punishment which moral philosophers,

---

[1] For discussions of notions of justice see, for example, the following texts: Campbell (2001) and Rawls (1971) for a liberal concept of justice; Rhode (1989) and Heidensohn (2006) for feminist standpoints; Nozick (1974), for an individualist approach.

penologists, and criminologists have developed, notably the classical theories of retributivism and utilitarianism. By retributivism is meant the approach which links punishment according to the desert or **culpability** of the individual and which matches the severity of the punishment to the seriousness of the crime and the culpability of the offender. By utilitarianism is meant the approach which sees individuals as motivated by the pursuit of pleasure and avoidance of pain and uses this to devise social and penal policies to promote the greatest happiness of the

greatest number. Punishment, on this approach, is used to prevent offending and reoffending through deterrence, **incapacitation**, and rehabilitation.

Consequently, determining what constitutes the justice of a particular punishment requires a decision on the theory of punishment to be deployed: just punishment from a retributivist standpoint might seem unjust from a utilitarian perspective and vice versa. As we shall see later, preventive detention may be justifiable if the interests of the wider society are given priority over individual rights but this raises problems for retributivism.

The dominant concept of justice may be only one of a number of key factors to consider in identifying the influences on modern penal policies: others might be ideologies, such as laissez-faire liberalism, which is essentially individualistic and construes society as a collection of egoistic individuals in which the state's role in economic and other spheres is minimal, and communitarianism, its opposite, which focuses on interdependence between citizens within the social framework, mutual obligations, trust and group loyalty (Etzioni 1993). Other influences on penal policy which may be significant are political and economic factors and the role of public opinion. So a recurring theme in the following discussions will be the justice and injustice of punishment in the political and economic context in which decisions are made and policies formulated.

1.2.3 **Human rights**

Human rights have implications for both the theory and practice of punishment in justifying specific punishments, in assessing the justice of punishments, and in improving standards in penal institutions. Human rights instruments are, then, a key mechanism for achieving just punishment and rights are themselves an important element of many theories of punishment. For example, natural rights are a significant dimension of retributivist theory, which recognises the right of the offender to be treated with respect as an autonomous human being. Rights have therefore provided a way of criticising the penal system in the UK which has been strongly influenced by utilitarianism, an approach which has been criticised for its failure to acknowledge the rights of the offender and for sacrificing the individual's rights for the wider public interest (see Chapter 4, section 4.4.3). Rights also have implications for issues such as the interviewing and detention of suspects before trial, the treatment of remand prisoners and the granting of bail, the defendant's right to a fair trial, the right to be presumed innocent, the treatment of witnesses, preventive detention, the right to be released when one's sentence is served, and

the right not to be subject to unfair or discriminatory treatment. These principles may act as a control on judicial **discretion** and inhibit disparities in sentencing. Rights also extend to victims of crime and help shape policy on their role in the criminal process, on their entitlement to redress. These issues will be considered further in subsequent chapters in relation to the principal justifications of punishment and to sentencing policy and practice.

Rights have an important function in protecting prisoners from the excessive zeal of their keepers and, if prisoners retain fundamental rights as human beings while serving their sentences, this will help to ensure that they are treated with dignity. A system of punishment which respects human rights will have more legitimacy than one which rides roughshod over them, particularly as utilitarian arguments have failed to protect prisoners. Rights are therefore crucial to penal theory and practice and, while rights may be limited when rights are infringed, the state's justifications for doing so need to be interrogated. A rights standpoint is an important critical tool for assessing systems of punishment, providing a check on powerful regimes, and on **populist punitiveness**. The term 'populist punitiveness', coined by Bottoms (1995), refers to the increased punitiveness of governments which they believe will appeal to the public and which has been used to justify increases in sentence severity.

For penal reformers, rights are seen as a way of achieving reform, although not all radical reformers share a commitment to a rights approach. Some Marxist theorists of law, who believe the rule of law may mask social injustice, are suspicious of rights because they are essentially individualist rather than collectivist, abstracting the individual from the historical and social context, and because they fail to deliver substantive justice (Easton 2008a).

There are, of course, problems of defining rights in jurisprudence. There is a huge body of literature with disagreement over what rights mean and what they entail, what should be included within their scope, and who possesses them. For Dworkin (1977), the right to equal concern and respect is paramount, while others have broadened their concern to include social rights (Marshall 1950, Titmuss 1968, Burca and de Witte 2005), and some see rights as a means of satisfying human needs (Campbell 1983). But they share a conception of fundamental rights as existing beyond positive law, that is, formal, black letter law in cases and statutes. Rights are entrenched and occupy a privileged position, protecting the individual from the state and protecting the weakest individuals from the majority. For Dworkin (1977, 1986), rights trump utility and, whilst rights may be limited if they conflict with competing rights, the circumstances in which this may occur are carefully drawn and more narrowly defined than on classical utilitarian models. Rights theorists argue that rights apply to all equally: even the worst offenders, such as war criminals, have procedural rights, for example, to take part in their trial, and, when convicted, to non-degrading punishment. Because rights are universal they have a crucial role to play in the practice of punishment and apply to all offenders and ex-offenders: the mark of a civilised society is to respect the rights of all.

Rights have implications across the criminal justice system and at all stages of the criminal justice process, but we will be particularly concerned with the impact of a rights jurisprudence on the experience of custody. Due process and substantive rights have implications for the treatment of prisoners. For example, they can achieve fairer treatment in the context of disciplinary procedures and decision making over issues such as segregation and transfers, but also in terms of substantive rights to food, exercise, and time unlocked. The European Convention on Human Rights had a considerable impact in improving prisoners' lives in the UK long before the Human Rights Act 1998 was passed. Following key decisions the

UK has had to change secondary legislation, including the Prison Rules as well as Prison Service Orders, to comply with the European Court of Human Rights' judgments and English judges have followed, for the most part, the recommendations of the Strasbourg court. These issues will be considered in relation to imprisonment and prison policy in Chapter 9, section 9.6.

1.3 Influences on penal policy

What is seen as an appropriate response to crime—the type and level of response—may reflect political and ideological principles. Ideologies are chains of interrelated ideas, the principles underpinning penal policies. For example, laissez-faire liberal ideology, which was in the ascendant during the Thatcher period, has had an enduring resonance and is reflected in **New Managerialist** approaches to the criminal justice system, including the **privatisation** of prisons and a concern with efficiency and economy of punishment, while welfarist ideologies have declined since the 1980s, although New Labour has tried to chart a path, or 'Third Way', between them (see Giddens 1998, 2000).

1.3.1 Political imperatives

The political dimension raises questions about power; how much power a government has to implement policy. With a large majority in the House of Commons when it first came to power, the New Labour administration was in a strong position to enact its legislative programme although it subsequently met opposition from the House of Lords on issues such as fox hunting and jury trial. A weaker government may have to rely on the support of opposition parties or powerful interest groups to gain acceptance for a particular policy.

Currently, however, there is a large measure of consensus between the main political parties on law and order policies, and it is unlikely that a party would adopt a 'soft' policy on crime because of the perception that public opinion would be hostile (see section 1.3.3). Underpinning the apparent public desire for tougher criminal justice policies is a mistaken public belief that offending is on the increase. In the 2002 British Crime Survey (BCS), the numbers who believed crime was getting worse rose from 56 per cent in 2001 to 71 per cent in 2002; similarly, three-quarters of those questioned by the BCS in 1996 thought crime had increased, as did 59 per cent in 1998 and 67 per cent in 2000. Yet crime rates actually fell by one-third and violent offences by 36 per cent in the period 1995–2001, with a further fall of 9 per cent in 2002, and the latest figures from the British Crime Survey (Nicholas *et al.* 2007: 15) show that, since peaking in 1995, overall crime has fallen by 42 per cent, violent crime by 41 per cent, and domestic burglary and thefts by more than a half (59 and 61 per cent respectively). Recorded crime figures showed a similar trend. Comparing 2005/6 with 2006/7, the BCS found an increase of 10 per cent in vandalism, but violent crime was stable, while recorded crime figures showed a 1 per cent fall in violence, a 7 per cent fall in sexual offences and a 3 per cent increase in robbery (ibid: 16). Of course, rates of victimisation are not uniform with some groups, individuals and residents of particular postcode areas being at greater risk than others. The Carter Report (Carter 2007) refers to polls showing that 65 per cent of the public think that crime is increasing, 79 per cent think sentence lengths should not be shortened, and 57 per cent think that the number of people sent to prison should not be reduced (ibid: 6).

The entrenched belief that the public is punitive makes it difficult for governments to win support for reductionist policies. The government's awareness of this became clear in the debate in the winter of 2002 when the Court of Appeal in *R v McInerney, R v Keating* (2002) issued new guidelines for domestic burglars, under which a domestic burglar who previously would have been sent to prison for 18 months or less should in future receive a community sentence (see Chapter 3). The Court acknowledged the need to promote public confidence in the criminal justice system, the costs of different sentences and their relative effectiveness in preventing reoffending, prison overcrowding, and the limits on what the Prison Service could achieve in rehabilitating a prisoner during a short sentence, in comparison with positive evidence of results achieved by punishment in the community. For a low-level first-time burglar and some second-time burglars, a community sentence was deemed appropriate, provided action could be offered to address the underlying criminal behaviour and other problems such as drug addiction.

However, this guidance, supported by Lord Irvine, the Lord Chancellor, who agreed that prison should be a last resort, led to criticism in Parliament and in the press. It was criticised by the then Home Secretary David Blunkett and also by the then Metropolitan Police Commissioner (Sir John Stevens) as well as by the Police Federation who expressed fears that the guidelines would give a green light to burglars who had not yet finished their Christmas shopping! Lord Woolf later said that he had been misrepresented and the charge in the press that the Government was 'going soft on burglars' was vehemently denied by the Prime Minister,[2] who stressed that imprisonment should be given for repeat offenders regardless of the problems of prison overcrowding.

This episode also highlights the difficulties facing the government when the political need to pursue policies and practices deemed by the public as legitimate conflicts with economic imperatives. Which priority 'wins' may depend on whether the policy would be implemented early or late in the government's term of office. Public opinion is a crucial pressure on the government at election time as parties try to capture floating voters, but may also be a significant force between elections at party conferences and in the constituencies. So political expediency may lead to the decision that it is not worth implementing an unpopular policy even if it saves money or, conversely, may implement a popular policy which imposes huge financial costs. An example of the latter would be the strong commitment of the governments of the 1990s to prison building and expansionist programmes, which were very expensive, but were intended to show to the public that they were taking their concerns on crime seriously. On the other hand, the government may negotiate these conflicts by trying to formulate policies which appear to protect the public while reducing costs: an example would be risk management which can reduce costs by focusing on those posing the highest risk of serious harm to the public. Certainly, since 1990 the key policy aim of public protection has been reflected

[2] In Prime Minister's Questions, House of Commons, 8 January 2003.

in the CJA 1991 and in subsequent legislation and developments, including the establishment of Multi-Agency Public Protection Arrangements (MAPPAs). There is a legal requirement on the police, probation, and prison service in each of the 42 areas of England and Wales, to establish arrangements to assess and manage risks posed by sexual and violent offenders, to review and monitor these arrangements, and to publish annual reports.[3]

Another policy scenario is that a government may find it is unable to relinquish a policy because it is so popular. For example, in the United States it may be politically damaging to retreat from the death penalty, when a large majority of the population support it and candidates try to exceed each other in their zealous commitment to it. Governor George Ryan of Illinois waited until he was retiring from office in January 2003 before commuting the death sentence for all 167 prisoners on death row in the state at that time. In the UK Home Secretaries have been heckled in the past at party conferences if perceived to be weak on law and order, and crime has been a recurring key election issue in party manifestos. Powerful interest groups may also affect policy regardless of which government is in power, and in the UK the Police Federation exerts a strong influence, competing with those working with offenders such as NACRO and the Prison Reform Trust. When the Government is pursuing a policy of 'rebalancing' the criminal justice system in favour of the law-abiding, then the relative power of groups representing the public may be an important factor in policy initiatives.

Negotiating public opinion may be particularly hazardous for the government when it is difficult to gauge public opinion. During a period of anxiety over prison escapes and security in the mid-1990s when the Conservative government was under strong pressure to deal firmly with prison security, a press report of a woman shackled during childbirth led to public outrage: the government misjudged the mood of the public and was forced to modify the policy.

One particular policy technique is that of diverting attention by blaming individuals for crime or targeting and demonising particular groups such as sex offenders (section 1.6) in order to defuse hostility to the government over crime and disorder. There are also examples from the recent past of how dysfunctional and anti-social families, juveniles, single-parent families, and truants have been selected as criminogenic categories (see Day Sclater and Piper 2000). Professional failures, for example of social workers and teachers, have also been highlighted for criticism.

1.3.2 **The costs of punishment: economic influences**

Penal policy can be seen as the result of a negotiation between the desire to sanction a moral code and the problem of limited resources to do so. Economic factors may be much more influential than penological theories and there may be conflicts between the Treasury and the Home Office over penal policy. The option which may best satisfy the public, namely imprisonment, is also the most expensive in terms of staffing and capital costs. The view that 'Prison Works' famously expounded by Michael Howard, the former Conservative Home Secretary, is very costly to implement. So a society has to negotiate both the amount of censure and

---

[3] See Wood and Kemshall (2007) for a review of the workings of these arrangements.

the amount of punishment it can afford to incorporate into its penal policy. Some popular policies have proved massively expensive, as in the case of the '**Three Strikes**' legislation found in many states in the USA including California and Washington. These are mandatory minimum sentencing schemes aimed at repeat offenders, where the third sentence mandates 25 years to life in prison.

Crime and punishment are costly in financial terms, to individuals who pay increased insurance premiums and to the public whose funds are used to finance law enforcement and punishment. As this is a substantial economic burden, inevitably costs are a significant influence on penal policy. Financial concerns became increasingly important in the 1990s, not just because of the ascendancy of New Right ideologies, but because increased punitiveness was reflected in prison expansion which led to substantial cost increases. When the Royal Commission on Criminal Justice was set up in 1993 to examine the effectiveness of the criminal justice system in England and Wales in securing convictions of those guilty of criminal offences and acquittals of the innocent, its remit included having regard to the efficient use of resources (RCCJ 1993). These economic pressures posed real problems for governments in the 1990s—and now again at a time of threatened recession—with the need to respond to the public's demand to reduce crime and to make society safe, but also to cut taxes.

The cost of processing offenders is potentially enormous if expensive penal options such as custody are freely used, so one way of negotiating this conflict has been to represent community penalties as punitive in order to win public support for them. Cost effectiveness, or Value for Money, the allocation of scarce resources in the most efficient way, has become an increasingly important criterion for evaluating penal policy in recent years and we find in the Halliday Report (2001) an emphasis on assessing the costs and benefits of specific measures. Although the origins here are in New Right theory, as reflected in the Citizen's Charter, the quest for economic efficiency was adopted by New Labour and has permeated the public management of a wide range of institutions. All public sector institutions and agencies have to justify their spending with transparent and comparable measurable results. The focus on value for money is a key feature of the New Managerialist approach, reflected in the New Public Management. This approach applies methods from the private sector to the public sector, incorporating a concern with the efficient use of resources, the use of Key Performance Indicators, transparency, a move towards performance-related pay, a stress on competition and **contestability**, that is opening up the market to new providers of goods and services, and the use of incentives regardless of the type of organisation, targets, and league tables comparing levels of efficiency. New Managerialist policies have been applied to Probation, the Police, and the Prison Service, to ensure the best use of resources. Further measures to cut costs include a policy of privatisation of entire prisons or selected services within prisons or in the context of community punishment, and making greater use of voluntary organisations where appropriate.

When deciding *what to punish* some offences may be uneconomic to punish, such as minor infringements or minor drugs offences which may exist on the statute book but not be enforced. Other offences, such as counterfeiting of notes, may need strong sanctions because they will destabilise the economy. Although the criminal law incorporates a moral code, that is, value judgements about expectations of behaviour, there will always be grey areas, particularly in relation to issues such as sexual behaviour and recreational drug use. In terms of *how to punish*, clearly a community sentence is cheaper than a custodial sentence, while the death penalty may also be cheaper than life imprisonment, although of course this would depend on how the calculation is made; for example, whether collateral costs of appeals and reviews are included within the calculation.

In terms of *how much to punish*, a heavier sentence is more expensive than a lighter sentence, although it may offer more opportunities for rehabilitation which may, in the long term, cut the costs of crime. So when we talk of the 'prison crisis', it is not only a question of physical conditions or overcrowding or disorder, but also a fiscal crisis, with the burden of prison building falling on taxpayers, diverting funds from other essential public services. As it is a labour-intensive mode of punishment, the largest running cost of imprisonment is labour, although prison officers are not a very highly paid group. These costs escalated in the 1990s as the prison population increased dramatically, from 45,636 in 1990 to 64,600 in 2000. By 2000 the annual cost was in excess of £16 million. In 2006–7 the average cost per prison place was £28,734 and the average cost per prisoner was £26,737 so with a prison population in excess of 80,000 this represents a cost of over £22 million (HM Prison Service 2007a). In addition to running costs, there are capital costs of building prisons and indirect costs, such as welfare support for dependants affected by the imprisonment of the breadwinner, and costs to the economy with the loss of productive labour and associated revenues.

1.3.3 The influence of public opinion on penal policy: a known unknown?

Public opinion is a key variable in shaping the response to crime and disorder. Indeed, many would argue that public opinion on law and order has been the major influence on penal policy and particularly on levels of punishment since the 1990s. Public opinion may be expressed through electoral choice, public opinion polls, focus groups, or sometimes by direct pressure on sentencers. Judges regularly receive letters from disgruntled members of the public complaining about sentences, mostly because they are seen as too short. Magistrates who undertake the bulk of sentencing see themselves as dispensing popular justice, as representatives of the public, and believe that they should respond to public opinion (Brown 1991), although many members of the public complain that judges and magistrates are out of touch with what the public want.

GLOSSARY
g

Public opinion can be orchestrated to win support for policies, and public opinion and **moral panics** about particular crimes can be fanned by the media. Since the late 1980s the public mood in Britain has been more favourable to punishment as the main response to criminal behaviour. New Labour and past Conservative governments have both responded to and, arguably, encouraged the punitiveness of the public. However, Johnstone (2000) argues that what is distinctive about New Labour's approach is that it has imposed a duty on the public to actively participate in crime reduction but, by denying genuine participation in penal policy decision making, has made an emotional and vengeful reaction by the public more likely.

As we saw in relation to political imperatives, public opinion is important in the sense that, for a criminal justice system to be effective, it must have legitimacy in the eyes of the public. This creates a conflict for professionals in a number of areas of the criminal justice system in that agencies such as the police have to be accountable to the public, yet may feel frustrated by the conflicting pressures to control crime while following rules and procedures designed to safeguard civil liberties. This conflict is reflected in efforts to strike a balance between civil liberties and crime control in the Police and Criminal Evidence Act (PACE) 1984, in the Report of the Royal Commission on Criminal Procedure (RCCP, 1981) which preceded it, and was recognised by the Royal Commission on Criminal Justice in its Report (RCCJ 1993). These tensions may also be reflected in 'noble cause corruption' as the police search for ways to neutralise the constraining effects of PACE. It may also be difficult to retain public support when the avowed aims of penal institutions and the criminal justice system are not fulfilled, if crime increases and the system of punishment seems to be ineffective. The Government's current emphasis, expressed in the document *Rebalancing the criminal justice system in favour of the law-abiding majority: cutting crime, reducing reoffending and protecting the public* (Home Office 2006a), is to strike the right balance between the needs of the law-abiding majority, including victims and witnesses, and avoiding privileging the offender over the victim (ibid: para 2.9).

The government's populist punitiveness is problematic because it reinforces the view that crime can be controlled through punishment and leads to problems when harsher punishment does not succeed in controlling crime, as Brownlee notes (1998a). Once the government pursues the punitive route it may find that the public is never satisfied and that the demand for punishment exceeds the supply of punishment.

Moreover, by reacting strongly to the perceived public concerns over crime, governments may, ironically, increase the public's punitiveness. In any case, it is arguable that measures to control crime will not work without attacking deeper social causes and hence the problem of social exclusion needs to be addressed (see Young 1999, Byrne 2005).

The Labour governments have been very concerned to promote public confidence in the criminal justice system, to stress the need to evaluate the cost effectiveness of different sentences, to achieve more consistency in sentencing, and to introduce stronger punishments for repeat offenders. Section 80 of the Crime and Disorder Act 1998 required the Court of Appeal to consider producing sentencing guidelines where there are none, and to review existing guidelines, and this initiative was taken further in the CJA 2003 (see Chapter 2). As we saw earlier, in relation to new guidelines for burglary, this has led to conflict with, and splits within, the judiciary over the desirability of custodial sentences.

One problem already alluded to is how to identify accurately the public's opinion on issues of crime and punishment. We cannot infer it just from the headlines of the popular press, for the media may shape public opinion as well as simply reflect it. Most of our knowledge of public opinion comes from the British Crime Survey (BCS) and similar social scientific research. Identifying attitudes to sentencing may also be problematic in so far as reports of attitudes to sentencing may reflect the methodologies used, as Hutton (2005) has argued. If more information is given in the scenarios presented to respondents, then a more lenient response may be elicited. The BCS confirms a high level of fear of crime, although this does not necessarily correlate with the actual risk of victimisation. The public also want strong penalties for violent crimes, but may be willing to accept the decreased use of imprisonment for some crimes and do not object to community punishment for lesser crimes.

Public opinion does impact on legislation but while it may reflect genuinely deeply felt anxieties, it might also be based on inaccurate views and information. Using data from the 1996 British Crime Survey which involved 16,348 respondents, Hough and Roberts (1998) found that the public in England and Wales displayed widespread ignorance about crime levels, overestimating crime levels, particularly for violent crime—especially in relation to mugging, rape, and burglary—and underestimating the severity of the criminal justice system in dealing with crime. They also found that the British public are not necessarily excessively punitive, but are often ill-informed about sentencing and, once aware of the levels of sentencing, are more willing to accept them and the public seem unaware of the increased use of imprisonment in recent years. Hough and Roberts found that the most ill-informed members of the public were readers of the popular press.

Mattinson and Mirrlees-Black (2000) found similar attitudes expressed by respondents in the 1998 British Crime Survey: 8 out of 10 thought sentences were too lenient, as in 1996, and 59 per cent of the sample thought recorded crime had risen between 1995 and 1997 whereas it had actually fallen by 10 per cent. They found that there was still a tendency to overestimate the amount of violent crime and underestimate the use of custody for the serious offences of burglary and rape. Yet, whilst they wanted custodial sentences for persistent offenders, respondents did not necessarily support more prison building: they wanted to punish some offenders in ways which were cheaper than prison but tougher than probation. Interestingly, when the respondents were given a sentencing exercise to undertake, they were more lenient than the sentencing guidelines and there was no evidence that being a recent victim increased the punitiveness of their sentencing. This accords with earlier research which suggests that victims are no more punitive than the average person, and may want redress or compensation rather than harsh punishment (see Kelly and Erez 1997). They also found little change in public confidence in the criminal justice system since 1996.

A key objective of current government policy is to reduce crime and fear of crime and thereby to promote confidence in the rule of law. But the public's views on sentencing come in part from the media and the media tends to focus on erratic sentencing rather than dull sensible sentencing, and on grisly violent crimes rather than routine everyday crimes. American and English crime and police television series tend to concentrate primarily on violent crime rather than crimes like 'twocking' (taking a vehicle without the owner's consent), even though such crimes are far more significant in terms of numbers. The press have also highlighted those cases where dangerous offenders have been released without appropriate supervision and have reoffended, heightening public anxieties. For example, Anthony Rice was convicted of murdering Naomi Bryant in 2005 while released on licence. A subsequent report was very critical of cumulative failings which meant that the risk of harm was not properly assessed or dealt with (HM Inspectorate of Probation 2006a). It is important that information made available to the public is accurate as the public's views on sentencing are shaped partly by the information available.

Recent British Crime Survey findings suggest a continuing fear of crime but again the fear of crime did not correlate with actual risk of victimisation or levels of crime. Since the mid-1990s the risk of victimisation and the crime rate have fallen (Nicholas *et al.* 2007: 15). The BCS for 2006/7 found that a relatively high proportion of people believe that crime has risen both nationally and in their local area (ibid: 110) and that women, older people, members of ethnic minority groups, and readers of the tabloid press, were most likely to believe that there were high levels of crime (ibid: 15). However, it is clear that whether justified or not the public are experiencing a fear of crime and that the public do display both punitiveness and at the same time a willingness in some cases to consider alternative approaches. Research by Hough and Roberts (2005) on public attitudes to young offenders found a number of misperceptions but at the same time a willingness to consider non-custodial options where there had been 'restorative steps', for example where offenders had made efforts to apologise to victims.

Any reductionist policy on the part of governments has to address the issue of communicating to the public the effectiveness of alternatives to custody, the economic and social costs of custody, and also the actual levels of sentencing in cases of serious offences to assuage public concerns and to enhance confidence in the sentencing system. These issues have been addressed in some recent policy documents including the Carter Report (Carter 2003), the Consultation Paper, *Making Sentencing Clearer* (Home Secretary *et al.* 2006) and *Rebalancing the Criminal Justice System* (Home Office 2006a).

1.3.4 Policy effects: prison expansion

The prison population has increased since 1993 for a number of reasons, including the actual number of cases going through the courts and the increase in the custody rate. The number of cases processed was affected by demographic factors, namely an increase in numbers in the crime-prone age groups, and by the impact of drug-related crime. The custody rate in the Crown Court, that is the proportion of the total number sentenced who received a custodial sentence, rose in the period 1992–2005, from 44 to 60 per cent (Home Office 2007a: 14) and the average custodial sentence length (ACSL) for adults in the Crown Court increased from 20.8 in 1995 to 25.9 months in 2005 (ibid). Offenders convicted for relatively serious crimes were given longer sentences and tariffs for particular crimes also increased. The largest growth was in the proportion of inmates who are serial recidivists, that is, offenders who have several previous convictions. Imprisoning offenders who in the past would have received community punishment and giving longer sentences to those who would previously have gone to prison have added to the prison population. There has been an increase in the numbers of prisoners defined as 'serious' and as presenting a risk to the public, and a new sentence of Imprisonment for Public Protection (IPP), which have inflated the prison population. Also, some offences now carry longer sentences as a result of changes in sentencing law and guidance. For example, Schedule 28 of the Criminal Justice Act 2003 raises the maximum penalties for drug-related offences, in some cases from 5 to 14 years. The CJA 2003 has also raised numbers further as magistrates' powers of sentencing have increased to 12 months.

In 1995 the prison population passed 50,000 for the first time (Home Office 1996b); by 2002 it had passed the 70,000 total; by the end of 2006 it had reached 80,000 and it stayed over 80,000 during 2007, reaching a record high of 82,180 on 29 February 2008.[4] On 6 June 2008 it was 82,791. The latest prison population projections for 2014, based on current sentencing trends, published in 2007, indicate that the lowest figure will be 88,800 and the highest figure 101,900, so the current high levels are clearly expected to prevail for some time, despite attempts to curb the population (Da Silva *et al.* 2007).

The expansion has also arisen during a period in which more emphasis has been placed on retributivism yet, as we shall see in Chapter 3, in some other societies retributivist-based sentencing systems have prevented excessive punishment.

The expansion of the prison population may be affected by legislative changes, increases in crime detection, using techniques such as DNA, an actual increase in the numbers of police, and the new National Standards for enforcement of breaches of community penalties whereby Probation Officers are now required to start breach proceedings after a second failure rather than the third specified under the 1995 Standards (see Home Office *et al.* 2000). One factor contributing to the growth in the prison population over the past ten years is the 'greater number of offenders recalled to prison for breaking the condition of their licence, reflecting legislative changes in 1998 and 2003' (Da Silva *et al.* 2007: 4; see also HM Inspectorate of Prisons 2005b). The release rate of the Parole Board also declined in 2006/7 and the numbers released on home detention curfew fell, suggesting a more 'risk-averse' approach (Parole Board 2007).

Recent changes, for example in relation to the discount for a guilty plea, as well as changes in sentencing guidelines may also further inflate the figures in future. Although it is difficult to make firm predictions because there are a number of variables involved, it seems very unlikely that the current high levels of the prison population will decrease significantly in the near future.

A number of explanations have been given for the increased use of custody in recent years, including the increasing importance of allowing public opinion, and specifically the perceived punitiveness of the public, to play a greater role in penal policy, which has been reflected in a number of specific sentencing provisions. More weight has been given to persistence in offending so that repeat offending has been treated more severely, more weight has been given to 'seriousness' in offending with a corresponding reflection in punishment and more emphasis has been given to protecting the public from violent offenders and sexual offenders with a corresponding increase in the number of prisoners serving indeterminate sentences. As well as the increase in the number of prisoners returning to prison for breaching the terms of their licence, we have a much wider range of orders, both civil and criminal, breaches of which are punishable by imprisonment. Breaches of civil orders, and particularly anti-social behaviour orders, have become such a significant factor in the increasing use of custody that the Sentencing Advisory Panel (SAP) has now issued a consultation paper on this issue (SAP 2007a).

The combination of these factors means that more pressure is exerted on the prison population and that more offenders are returning to prison following a period in the community. The implications of this expansion on the prison regime and the problems generated by overcrowding will be considered in Chapter 9. Already, the expansion has meant that increasingly police cells have been used

---

[4] All figures from HM Prison Service Prison Population Statistics.

to house prisoners as well as, on occasion, courtroom cells and, for a period, a prison ship, *HMP Weare* was moored off Portland in Dorset. *HMP Weare* was sold in 2005 but it is possible that a prison ship could be used again if a suitable vessel is found.

In July 2006 the then Home Secretary, John Reid, announced plans for 8,000 new prison places as part of a package of measures 'to protect the public and further rebalance the criminal justice system in favour of the law-abiding majority ' (Home Office 2006b). Almost a year later, on 19 June 2007 he announced that an additional 1,500 places would be provided and two more prisons would be built. A new prison, HMP Kennett, opened in February 2008 on Merseyside. In addition there are building programmes under way to expand the available accommodation within many existing prisons. The Government also plans to build three 'Titan' prisons.

The UK now has one of the highest incarceration rates within Western Europe at 148 per 100,000 of population, compared with 85 in France and 93 in Germany (ICPS 2007). This is surprising in so far as the UK has a far wider range of non-custodial options than most other Western European societies. Sentencing levels are also higher in the UK than in some other European societies, as evidenced, for example, by a comparative study of sentencing of burglars in England and Wales and Finland (see Davis *et al*. 2004).

These rising figures for incarceration were fuelled by increases in both short and long prison sentences in the 1990s. The message of the Halliday Report and of the government in 2001 was that persistent offenders should get harsher sentences and that breaches of community orders should be punished with custodial sanctions. So the expansion of custody cannot therefore be attributed solely to sentencers: the sentencing framework within which they operate is, we shall argue, potentially more punitive and the Guidance is more prescriptive (see Piper and Easton 2006/7). The implications of these specific changes in sentencing law will be considered below in Chapters 3 and 5.

The problem is how to 'sell' to the public a reductionist policy, that is, one committed to the aim of reducing the use and extent of imprisonment. A modest decarceration programme or expanded use of alternatives needs to take seriously the public's fears of crime and to contest the public view of the courts as 'soft'. To do this the public need accurate information about crime levels and sentencing decisions and policies. For this purpose, Halliday (2001) proposed putting sentencing guidelines online for the public to access and this has now been implemented. The public also have to be convinced that alternatives to custody will be effective and to be aware that the greater use of imprisonment will only marginally affect crime rates: a 25 per cent increase in custody may lead only to a 1 per cent fall in the crime rate (see Tarling 1993: 154). However, when asked to undertake sentencing exercises, the public may be less punitive than sentencers (see Mattinson and Mirrlees-Black 2000 and also section 1.3.3 above). So the government needs an accurate measure of public opinion otherwise it may overstate the public's punitiveness when the public is selectively punitive on some crimes but not others.

Hough *et al*. (2003) argue that it is necessary to widen the awareness of those who sentence as well as the public, particularly in relation to the advantages of using non-custodial penalties, including fines. But changes in sentencing law and practice and changing public attitudes to crime and punishment will not succeed in reducing prison numbers without the political will and commitment to a reductionist policy. The relationship between political and economic factors is therefore complex, fluid, and indeterminate. While they may sometimes bolster each other, they may also conflict.

1.4 The influence of theory on penal law and practice

1.4.1 Principles from criminology and penology

Penological principles also shape the development of penal policies. These principles are the justifications of punishment and include retribution, deterrence, rehabilitation, social protection, and, more recently, the restoration of social harmony, which will be discussed in Chapters 2–6 and 12 below. Together they constitute the store of knowledge regarding what is, theoretically, the best response in dealing with offenders. Because theorists from opposing traditions may agree that punishment is necessary, but differ in their views of what is the best response, the type of punishment may depend on which theory, which purpose of punishment, is implicit or explicit in policy. It may also depend on which philosophical ideas underpin the chosen punishment, for example whether individuals are seen as autonomous or possessing free will, or whether their actions are determined by the surrounding environment or genetic make-up.

Retributivism punishes according to **just deserts** which assumes a free choice by a rational person who chooses how to act, while a utilitarian approach may use rewards and punishments to channel behaviour into desirable ends and adjusts the social context to change the individual's behaviour, using treatments and therapies to rehabilitate the offender. Another perspective which has strongly influenced penal policy since 1990 is the New Penology which draws on New Managerialist and actuarial techniques to manage the risk of offending and reoffending.

Compared to political and economic factors, the influence of penology and criminology is limited. However, the economic climate may favour the rise of a particular justification of punishment and particular criminological theories may also be appropriated by governments to legitimise a particular policy. For example, 'left realist' criminology, which developed in the 1980s, has been used subsequently to legitimise strong law and order policies and to justify increased punitiveness in the interests of public protection. This theory takes crime seriously, while linking crime to class inequality, and focuses on both crime and the social reaction to crime (see Lea and Young 1984). It recognises crime as a serious social problem, in particular for working-class communities, and demands action accordingly. These criminological ideas have now been incorporated into mainstream government thinking on crime and New Labour has used left realist criminology to justify actuarial criminal justice policies.

1.4.2 The New Penology and risk management

Actuarial justice uses technology and statistical calculations to enhance the risk management of high-risk groups. This approach has been described by Feeley and

Simon (1992) as the New Penology and it embraces both a theory and practice of punishment. In the New Penology, crime is seen as normal and the best we can hope for is to control crime and risk through actuarial policies and technocratic forms of knowledge, internally generated by the penal system (Simon, 1998).

This approach focuses on categories of potential and actual offenders rather than on individuals, and on managerial aims rather than rehabilitation or transformation of the offender. It can be seen as a reaction to the decline of rehabilitation and to the 'nothing works' pessimism of the 1980s. Risk—the core concept of the New Penology—is no longer calculated on personal knowledge of particular individuals or by in-depth clinical judgements: risk is seen as distributed unevenly across categories of offender (see Chapter 5). A biographical study such as Clifford Shaw's *The Jack-Roller* (Shaw 1930) in which the offender's detailed life-history is given in his own words, supplemented by reports from his probation officer, is therefore far removed from the experience of modern probation practice.

While there is a *potential* conflict between the New Penology (which treats crime as a normal fact of life to be managed, using technological tools) and populist punitiveness (which sees crime as abnormal, to be eliminated, through for example, zero tolerance), the two may converge in a common focus on incapacitation as a way of managing risk and removing persistent offenders from society. In the New Penology approach, prison is used to warehouse offenders at high risk of reoffending and, because managerial cost concerns are crucial, prison will be reserved for the highest risk categories. Actuarial justice provides a means of selecting the target population to be incarcerated. However, its cost-cutting impetus may also come into conflict with the populist demands for an expansion of punishment.

The New Penology has been a significant recent influence on penal policy both here and in the United States. It is both an influence on current policy and also itself a policy approach. A concern with risk management has diffused through the key agencies of the criminal justice system and has been a significant feature of public concern, particularly in relation to dangerous offenders. However, the implementation of New Penology has been uneven across the criminal justice system, meeting with resistance from probation officers at the point of working with clients while being well-established at the central level of policy making and at the Home Office. Managing risk in the community and on release from a custodial sentence has been a major challenge for criminal justice professionals and this has been increasingly seen as a joint enterprise involving cooperation between agencies, as we shall see, in relation to sex offenders and dangerous offenders.

1.4.3 Classical theories of punishment

The principal justifications of punishment are closely associated with distinct philosophical traditions or schools. Both retributivist and utilitarian theories have a long history. Retributivism was influential in late eighteenth- and early nineteenth-century philosophy, and was revived in the 1970s and 1980s in the United Kingdom and the United States (see Chapter 2). It is strongly associated with the

German idealist tradition, particularly the work of Kant and Hegel, which focuses on the role of ideas in the construction of reality and sees reality as mediated through consciousness.[5] The rival tradition is utilitarianism which includes the justifications of deterrence, social protection or incapacitation and rehabilitation associated with the English philosophers Bentham (1789) and Mill (1861) but also derived from the work of Beccaria (1767).

Retributivist and utilitarian theorists both accept that punishment may be justly inflicted but differ in their views of what constitutes the justice of a particular punishment. Both seek to limit the use of discretion in sentencing in favour of a more rigorous principled approach and both address the issue of proportionality but from quite different standpoints. Consequently both see a link between punishment and the seriousness of the offence by upholding the idea that custody should be reserved for the most serious offences. However, the utilitarian does so because it is hoped this will prevent the commission in the future of those offences which are most harmful to the public. So it is important to find the optimal level of punishment, to prevent offenders from reoffending, to deter the general public, and to protect the public from future offending by incapacitating individuals who threaten society. So there is scope on this theory for preventive sentencing. However, the aim in devising punishments is to prevent future offences with minimal expense, so utilitarians would not favour excessive or harsh punishment unless there are clear social benefits which result from that punishment. Punishment can also be used to rehabilitate the offender so that he can make a useful contribution within the prison community and on his return to the wider society.

Neither approach can be seen as purely theoretical as each has had a strong impact on penal policy in recent years. What is interesting is that although these theories are strongly opposed to each other in certain key assumptions, in practice they may both be incorporated in the same piece of legislation. The main provisions of the Criminal Justice Act 1991, for example, were based on a version of retributivist philosophy, but parts of that Act and subsequent legislation reflect utilitarian principles. Similarly, individuals may hold, for example, strongly retributivist views on violent crimes but take a more utilitarian approach in relation to lesser offences.

On the retributivist approach, just deserts equates to determining a sentence which is proportional to culpability so that offenders receive what they deserve for what they have done. There is no concern with the future effects of the sentence but rather with a just response to wrongdoing. On retributivist theory, justice demands that the perpetrator of the offence suffers punishment, regardless of the effects the individual's suffering may have on himself or others. Justice is served only if the offender is made to suffer. Using the metaphor of balancing scales, justice is satisfied when the scales are evenly balanced, between the offender's actions and the level of punishment. In completing the term of punishment, the offender pays and cancels his debt to society. Chapters 2 and 4 will explore in more detail the foundational writings of the retributivist and utilitarian approaches and the problems they raise, and we have inserted at the end of this chapter an exercise which you might wish to do. It makes very clear the difference that the application

---

[5] For further reading on German idealism, see, for example, Lukács (1975) and Armstrong Kelly (1969).

of principles makes to sentencing outcomes. Next, however, we will focus on just deserts.

1.4.4 **The influence of 'just deserts'**

One major influence on penal and sentencing policy has been a particular retributivist idea of 'just deserts'. Prior to 1991 its influence was not clear. The CJA 1991 was a piece of legislation which was heralded as marking 'a sea change in the philosophy and practice of sentencing' in the UK (Henham 1995: 221) because it imposed a new constraint on the courts' discretion—that of a presumptive sentencing rationale. In the 1990 White Paper the Government announced its intention to establish 'a new and more coherent statutory framework for sentencing' (Home Office 1990a: para 1.5): 'The aim of the government's proposals is better justice through a more consistent approach to sentencing so that convicted criminals get their "just deserts". The severity of the sentence of the court should be directly related to the seriousness of the offence' (ibid: para 1.6). A general aim of sentencing on retributivist principles was not, however, invented in 1991. The Streatfeild Committee in 1961 said that 'sentencing used to be a comparatively simple matter. The primary objective was to fix a sentence proportionate to the offender's culpability', the assumption being that practice had changed with the increased use of rehabilitative, community-based measures.

In the period before 1991 sentencers could freely choose to sentence on one or more principles or mix retributivist and utilitarian reasons in any particular case (Sargeant 1974). Nevertheless there emerged a 'tariff system' under which sentencers could use a normal range of sentences and choose what was proportionate to a particular level of offence gravity (see Cross 1981: 167–73) but they could also choose not to impose a tariff-based sentence but, rather, one based on the needs of the offender. The latter decision was referred to as the primary decision and if individualised measures were chosen rather than the tariff, the assessment was of the offender's suitability for a form of treatment (see Henham 1995: 221–2).

The significance of the provisions in the CJA 1991 was, then, that they statutorily imposed on judges and magistrates 'just deserts' as the presumptive rationale. The 1991 Act imposed levels of seriousness as 'hurdles' to the three main levels of punishment. Consequently, the sentencing decision-making process had to focus first on basic elements of a just deserts approach—the calculation of seriousness and the consideration of a sentence proportionate to it (see Chapter 2). This is not to say that all sentencing provisions in the 1990s were consistent with this rationale, given the existence of the provisions in the 1991 Act justifying custodial sentences on the basis of protecting the public, and the form of cumulative mandatory sentences added by the Crime (Sentences) Act 1997 (see section 2.3.3 below) which were explicitly excluded from the just deserts approach (Powers of Criminal Courts (Sentencing) Act (PCCSA) 2000, ss 79(1)(b), 34(a), and 127). A similar shift occurred earlier in the 1980s in the United States, when there was a shift from an emphasis on rehabilitation towards retribution. This persisted in the 1990s but came under threat from the increasing focus on incapacitation (see Chapter 5, section 5.2.3).

This basic question of sentencing rationale—with its long history in classical theory—is still currently high on the policy agenda and the subject of academic critique. In particular the recent changes have raised the fundamental question of 'why punish?': to impose the burden of punishment on offenders there needs to be a good reason. Section 142(1) of the CJA 2003, despite the continuance elsewhere in that Act of retributivist criteria for the use of different levels of sentence (see Chapter 3), imposes a varied—and potentially inconsistent—list of 'purposes of sentencing' to which the courts must 'have regard': the punishment of offenders, the reduction of crime (including its reduction by deterrence), the reform and rehabilitation of offenders, the protection of the public, and the making of reparation by offenders to persons affected by their offences.

Justifications are central to sentencing and they are also central to the legitimacy of policy. As we have noted, if sentencing policies are to be justifiable to the electorate they must be capable of being supported by reasons, to justify the actions—or failure to act—of sentencers and the costs of punishment imposed on society.

1.5 Penal policy: conflicts and ambiguities

We have identified a number of key influences on penal policy which we will now consider in relation to the development of penal policy in the UK in the late twentieth and early twenty-first century, and, more specifically, in relation to the governance of sex offenders. The present government is committed to substantial reform of the criminal justice system, to remove inconsistency in sentencing and to target persistent offending and to improve cooperation between different agencies. The government has already moved towards its aim of a centralised criminal justice system by unifying the separate probation services into a National Probation Service for England and Wales under provisions in the Criminal Justice and Court Services Act 2000, and by conjoining the Prison and Probation Services into the National Offender Management Service in 2004.

1.5.1 Policy trends in the late twentieth century

If we consider the broad shifts in penal policy in England and Wales in the period after the Second World War, we can identify a number of important trends, a major thread being the changing fortunes of the **rehabilitative ideal** with its optimism that the offender could be reformed. As we shall see (Chapter 12), the rehabilitative ideal was reflected in the development of community penalties to operate as alternatives to custody and the treatment approach had gained ascendancy by the 1960s, with a further order, the community service order, introduced in England and Wales in 1972 (see Powers of Criminal Courts Act 1973, s 14, as amended by CJA 1991, s 10, then governed by PCCSA 2000, s 46). However, the increase in crime and evidence of recidivism in the 1970s and early 1980s cast doubt on the validity of this approach and its use declined in the 1980s and 1990s (see Chapter 12). Yet, while much is made of the decline of the rehabilitative ideal, it has in recent years received further support, albeit prompted primarily by pragmatic cost considerations. It survives in the Probation Service and in offending behaviour programmes (see Chapter 12); it is also found in the Halliday Report (2001) and of course has remained a major influence on penal policies in some other European societies, including the Netherlands (see Downes 1988, Tak 2003).

In contrast to the focus on rehabilitation, the 1990s were marked by an increased use of punishment and incapacitation, with both the Conservative and Labour administrations tending to focus on punishment rather than crime. Priority was given, by the CJA 1991, to the retributivist principle of just deserts as the primary principle of sentencing, whereby the focus is on proportionate punishment rather than treatment or deterrence *per se*. The increased concern with incapacitation became evident in the electronic monitoring and curfew provisions in the Crime and Disorder Act (CDA) 1998 (now consolidated in ss 37 and 38 of the PCCSA 2000; see also CJA 2003, ss 204 and 215) and through prison expansion, whilst a trend of making alternatives to custody more punitive—or at least appear so—developed. Policies in the 1990s also revealed a continuing acceptance of managerialism, increased concern with safety and justice for victims, and a commitment to speed up the criminal justice process, to shorten the period between arrest and trial.

Despite the New Labour rhetoric of being tough on crime, tough on the causes of crime in the 1997 election, punishment and the reduction of opportunities to commit crime received considerably more attention than the causes of crime. So we find a continuity between the previous Conservative administration and the following Labour government reflected in similar approaches to increasing punishment. The continuing focus on punishment is reflected in legislation such as the Crime (Sentences) Act 1997 ss 2–4 (consolidated in the PCCSA 2000, ss 109–111) which was enacted by the outgoing Conservative government but retained by New Labour. These provisions empower the courts to pass a life sentence for those convicted of a second serious offence (now repeated), seven years for a third Class A drug trafficking offence, and three years for a third domestic burglary, unless the court is of the opinion that it is unjust to do so. New Labour then, is committed to the view that crime can be controlled through punishment and this was a strong theme in both the 1997 and 2001 general elections.

There is now a substantial quantity of new legislation on sentencing and punishment, including the CDA 1998 which introduced new penalties for young offenders and new measures such as curfews, anti-social behaviour orders and sex offender orders. A wide range of new criminal offences was created by the Sexual Offences Act 2003. In the 2005 general election the Labour Party's emphasis was on dealing with anti-social behaviour, promoting the Respect Agenda, using the criminal justice system to protect the public and focusing on crime in local communities. Similarly, the Conservative Party manifesto focused on tackling anti-social behaviour, restoring respect and discipline, and making communities safer, but also promised an increase in police numbers and 'honesty in sentencing', ensuring that offenders serve the full custodial period of their sentences. The Liberal Democratic Party also favoured more police recruitment, dealing with anti-social behaviour, and preventing reoffending but also more emphasis on tougher community punishments as an alternative to prison. The differences in approach are clearer on the issue of terrorism. At the election, three months before the bombings on 7 July 2007, terrorism was a less prominent issue than it is now and the Labour manifesto just briefly referred to tackling terrorism and finding ways to move forward in the fight against terrorism and its causes. For the Conservatives the fight against terrorism was a high priority with an emphasis on a coordinated response, robust anti-terrorist laws and the appointment of a Minister for Homeland Security, while the Liberal Democrats' approach in contrast emphasised the need to repeal the Prevention of Terrorism Act and to bring anti-terrorism law within the ambit of the ordinary criminal law and its procedures. The party was also strongly opposed to identity cards and expressed concern at using the fight against terror to justify the undermining of civil liberties. Since then there has been greater emphasis on strengthening counter-terrorist measures and a number of new powers to deal with this issue, including a new Counter-Terrorism Bill introduced in the 2007–8 Parliament. There have been over 50 law and order measures since Labour came to power and their enthusiasm for new law and order measures remains undimmed. In the 2007–8 Parliamentary session there are bills in progress on Serious Organised Crime, and the Criminal Justice and Immigration Act 2008 which covers a wide range of offences and sentencing issues received Royal Assent in May 2008. The new Act reflects the increasing overlap between issues of immigration and crime as the Government responds to criticism over its handling of the issue of crimes committed by foreign nationals. The Government is also reviewing the Police and Criminal Evidence Act and further modifications are possible here.

Labour has effectively 'stolen' the law and order issue from the Conservatives, seeking to make Labour the party of law and order, while also accepting the need to control public spending and to make the penal system efficient and accountable. The concern with law and order and the importance of punishment as a political issue increased substantially in the 1990s and since, compared to the 1980s: even in the Thatcher era there were significant advances in the protection of the accused's due process rights, principally in PACE.

When the government uses 'punitive rhetoric' to win support for its policies it is a double-edged sword because, if the public then favours punitive and expressive custodial measures, it imposes substantial economic burdens yet, as we have noted, the government is under pressure to cut costs. One government technique is to shift the burden for crime prevention to the individual by giving the message that we are all stakeholders in society: the individual and community should take responsibility for safeguarding their homes and property, through better security, neighbourhood watch schemes, by not inviting crime, and by reporting crime. The same messages have been given in relation to 'youth' crime in the Audit Commission's reports, *Misspent Youth* (Audit Commission 1996, 1998) which focused on the effective use of resources, and in the White Paper, *No More Excuses* (Home Office 1997a), which was explicit in placing responsibility on parents and the young offender (see Chapter 8).

The current concern with economic issues may also reflect the continuing influence of New Right ideology, despite a change of regime, and the New Public Management intermeshes ideologies with economics, but this may also generate conflicts as the ideology itself contains tensions. For example, New Right ideology prioritises law and order as a legitimate governmental function but is also committed to minimise costs as part of its economic individualism. In the Thatcher/Reagan era of the 1980s and 1990s, as working-class support for welfare dramatically declined, this created a climate in which increased punitiveness could flourish and collectivist welfarist solutions to social problems were abandoned. At the same time, this punitiveness was also a genuine response to fear of crime and an expression of individualism applied to law breaking rather than simply manufactured by the media.

Trends in the past 20 years, then, have seen the emergence of law and order as a key political issue and an increase in punitiveness on the part of both governments and the public. In the 1990s these shifts were reflected in a commitment to the expansion of prison building and tougher community punishments. We also saw the development of a bifurcatory policy in the distinction between ordinary petty and serious persistent offenders, with a focus on community punishments and restorative justice for the former, and increased use of custody for the latter, although in practice the lines have not been drawn so clearly. This distinction between minor and serious offenders which was embodied in the 1991 Criminal Justice Act has been a continuing feature of penal policy since the early 1990s and extended by the 2003 Criminal Justice Act which sought to ensure that community sentences aimed at rehabilitation were used for the majority of offenders with long custodial sentences for serious offenders. Current policies also distinguish sharply between 'normal' offenders and high-risk offenders (see Chapter 5).

Concern with value for money has loomed large since the late 1980s and encouraged the introduction of privatisation and New Managerialism within the state sector. On the other hand, there was much more concern with the rights and needs of the victim, and the Woolf Report in 1991 led to a substantial improvement in the physical conditions and quality of life in prisons (see Chapter 11, section 11.4.2). With the incorporation of the European Convention on Human Rights in 1998 human rights issues have also assumed increasing significance in penal policy (see Chapter 9, section 9.6).

1.5.2 Policy documents 2000–2003

The new century saw the publication of several major policy documents relevant to our focus on sentencing and punishment which provide evidence of the continuing importance in policy of the factors outlined above. First, the White Paper, *Criminal Justice: The Way Ahead*, published in February 2001, affirmed the Government's commitment to funding another 2,660 prison places and committed an extra £689 million for the Prison Service over the next 3 years, £21 million of which was to be used to prevent reoffending. The White Paper aimed to reduce both crime and fear of crime, and so also reduce the social and economic costs of crime. It argued that the criminal justice system has to be effective in preventing offending and reoffending and efficient in the way it deals with cases, to be responsive to victims and the community and to dispense justice fairly and efficiently, promoting confidence in the rule of law.

Similarly, the Halliday Report, *Making Punishments Work*, published in July 2001, referred to the need to increase public confidence and reduce crime. It advocated more research on the costs and benefits of particular sentences and proposed a duty on the Secretary of State to disseminate information about the effectiveness of sentencing as well as its costs. However, the Halliday Report was more specific about the aims of sentencing, arguing that they should cover crime reduction, reparation, and punishment. This has echoes of the policy floated in the Green Paper of 1988—but not incorporated in the CJA 1991—which stated that every community penalty should have three elements: the deprivation of liberty, action to reduce offending, and recompense to the victim or community (Home Office 1988a: para 1.5). The Halliday Report (2001) argues that to do this we need to clarify what is effective, particularly in relation to short sentences, we need clear guidelines to achieve sentence consistency and for previous convictions to be reflected in sentence severity for persistent offenders. It advocates a statutory Penal Code and guidelines on seriousness of the offence, aggravating and mitigating grounds, and the impact of previous convictions. It also recommends closer collaboration between sentencers and other criminal justice agencies to achieve 'seamless sentencing', with the utilitarian aim of informing sentencers about what works in reducing reoffending and making them aware of the availability of different programmes and their suitability for different types of offenders.

Both the above policy documents also reflect the rise of actuarial justice: the acceptance that crime will not be eliminated and all we can do is manage the risk, limit the impact of crime, and promote efficient, cheap methods of crime management and diversion. The White Paper, *Criminal Justice: The Way Ahead* focused on finding cost-effective measures, while the Halliday Report (2001) emphasised assessing the costs and benefits of particular punishments and using risk-assessment criteria when selecting appropriate custodial and non-custodial sentences. It also recognised the need to improve public confidence in sentencing practice and to involve the public in that process by inviting them to comment on sentencing guidelines and increasing Parliamentary control of sentencing.

The Government also commissioned a major review of the criminal courts published in September 2001. The stated aim of the Auld Review was to ensure that the courts 'deliver justice fairly, by streamlining all their processes, increasing their efficiency and strengthening the effectiveness of their relationships with others across the whole of the criminal justice system, and having regard to the interests of all parties including victims and witnesses, thereby promoting public confidence in the rule of law' (Auld LJ 2001). This clearly embodies a particular view of what promotes justice. Although most of the recommendations relate to the law of evidence, the Report also made recommendations on sentencing, including advance indication of sentencing for defendants pleading guilty (para 114). It also advocated codification of the law of sentencing which, it argued, should be the responsibility of a standing body under the general oversight of the Criminal Justice Council (para 198). It emphasised the need for honesty and simplicity in sentencing (para 199) and practical measures, such as the use of information technology to support judicial sentencing, providing an information service for all judges (para 210).

A further proposal in the Review (2001: Summary, para 4)—that of moving from a two-tier court system to a unified Criminal Court, with three divisions comprising Magistrates', District, and Crown (on the lines of the Family Justice System)—met with considerable criticism, particularly from the magistracy and the supporters of jury trial.

Research on 'consumer' views of the work of the magistrates' courts fed into this review. In particular, Morgan's research for the Home Office revealed the extent of public ignorance of the lower courts and a resulting lack of public confidence, finding that only 29 per cent of the population think magistrates are doing a good job (Morgan 2000: 61 and 72). Sanders found that 61 per cent of the population think magistrates are 'out of touch' (Sanders 2001: 1; also Morgan 2000: vii). Morgan estimated that in the magistrates' courts 91 per cent of cases are currently dealt with by lay magistrates and the rest by district judges (formerly stipendiaries) although the public is not aware of that fact (ibid: 2) and the lawyers and clerks who use the courts on a regular basis appear to prefer district judges (ibid: 65). These research studies highlighted the issue of the role, status, and qualifications of the sentencer: whether that person should be legally trained or whether there are other branches of expertise or knowledge (such as penology, social work or criminology) which are more relevant to the exercise. The existence of the lay magistracy is justified by their lack of expert knowledge: that they bring 'common sense' and a knowledge of 'ordinary' everyday life to the question of deciding guilt or innocence and selecting the 'right' punishment, a knowledge possible because they are not full-time judges. The staffing of the courts raises questions about the nature of the sentencing exercise as well as matters of cost and efficiency.

The Government issued a White Paper in July 2002, *Justice for All*, its response to the Halliday and Auld Reports. It stressed the need to 'rebalance the system in favour of victims, witnesses and communities', to give paramount importance to protecting the public, to restore public confidence in the criminal justice system, and to improve the coherence of the system by closer integration of the police, prosecution, courts and Probation Service (Home Office 2002a). To achieve this it proposed legislation on administrative matters as well as sentencing law. In relation to sentencing it proposed to set out the principles of sentencing in legislation and proposed a Sentencing Guidelines Council to formulate consistent guidelines. The White Paper also put forward plans for new sentences: customised community sentences to allow courts to choose between a range of options for individual offenders; custody minus, a new suspended sentence, which would include the same options as the customised community sentence; custody plus, a sentence of up to 12 months which would comprise a maximum of three months' custody, followed by compulsory supervision in the community; and intermittent custody, which allows offenders to serve their sentence on a part-time basis. A new special sentence for violent/sexual offenders to ensure they remain in custody until their risks are manageable within the community was proposed and also a national strategy for restorative justice.

Justice for All accepted the Auld Report's proposals for a new national Criminal Justice Board responsible for overall delivery of the criminal justice system and made specific proposals regarding the lower courts, including an increase in magistrates' sentencing powers to 12 months and the abolition of magistrates' powers to commit cases for sentencing to the Crown Court. It aimed to encourage early guilty pleas with a formalisation of plea bargaining, by means of a clearer tariff of sentence discounts and it expressed concern at failures to bring offenders to justice, delays in trial, and the problem of wrongful acquittals (although no evidence was offered in support of the last point). It promised more support for victims, including a Code of Practice and a new Commissioner for victims and witnesses, and said that victims of mentally disordered offenders would be entitled to information about their release.

It further proposed to introduce several controversial reforms to pre-trial procedures and rules of evidence. It accepted some of Lord Justice Auld's recommendations but dropped others and rejected multi-ethnic juries in race cases and the proposed middle tier court. It also favoured relaxing the double jeopardy rule in serious cases and proposed changes in the rules of evidence, including a relaxation of the hearsay rule, but it did not favour routine admission of previous misconduct, arguing that it should be up to the judge to reveal it to the jury if it has clear probative value, even if previous allegations led to acquittal.

1.5.3 The Criminal Justice Act 2003

In the Queen's Speech in November 2002 the Government announced six criminal justice bills, including bills to modernise sexual offences law and to increase penalties for sex offenders, and to provide more protection of the public from dangerous offenders. The CJA 2003 is a major piece of legislation with 339 sections and 38 schedules, which embodies many of the proposals in *Criminal Justice: The Way Ahead* and *Justice for All* and reforms criminal procedure, evidence and sentencing. Because it is so massive there is concern that there was insufficient time to consider it fully, and that only the most controversial clauses were subjected to full scrutiny.

The aim of the Act, in line with *Justice for All*, is to rebalance the criminal justice system, by which the government means to increase rights of victims, even if this means fewer rights for defendants. The way this is constructed using a 'zero-sum' view of power, where one side must lose if the other gains, is misleading: increasing the rights of victims does not of itself necessarily mean reducing the rights of defendants. For example, the Youth Justice and Criminal Evidence Act 1999— which seeks to provide greater protection for vulnerable witnesses—also contains complementary provisions to avoid any prejudice to the defendant.

The CJA 2003 incorporates wide-ranging provisions on evidence, procedure and sentencing, including making the defendant's previous convictions admissible, amending the law on double jeopardy, increasing the time limits for detention under PACE, removing the right to jury trial in complex fraud cases, and reforming the rules on the disclosure of evidence and on hearsay evidence. It aimed to introduce the custody plus scheme, and increased magistrates' sentencing powers to 12 months. The custody plus penalty involves intensive supervision at the end of the sentence and requires more probation officers to undertake the supervision. The Government is providing extra funding to the Probation Service for community penalties, which include a new generic sentence with a wide range of components (see Chapter 12, section 12.1.1). However, custody plus has not yet been implemented and intermittent custody, which was intended to be phased in gradually because of resource implications, has been shelved indefinitely.

1.5.4 Policy documents 2004–2008

The Government's plans to reduce reoffending are set out in its National Reducing Reoffending Action Plan published in July 2004. We have also seen a continued focus on 'rebalancing the criminal justice in favour of the law-abiding majority', and on protecting the public from dangerous offenders and from a range of anti-social behaviours, and particularly from unruly young offenders. The policy paper *Rebalancing the Criminal Justice System in Favour of the Law-abiding Majority* (Home Office 2006a) emphasises the need to enhance public confidence in the fairness of the system to law-abiding people and communities. It refers to the fact that 80 per cent of the public believe the criminal justice system is fair to the offender but only 36 per cent think it meets the needs of victims (ibid: para 1.20). It recommends a range of measures to assist victims and witnesses and stresses that this rebalancing programme will be supported by stronger enforcement.

At the same time it is pursuing the use of restorative justice methods and outcomes for juvenile and adult offenders, although most of the initiatives are being introduced on an experimental basis (see Chapter 6).

A further key policy initiative was the government's 'Respect Agenda' aimed at combating anti-social behaviour which it has defined as the most visible sign of disrespect. A Respect Task Force was set up in 2005. The Respect Agenda has a number of dimensions including supporting families and communities, developing parenting services, improving school attendance, intervening in families, homes and schools to promote respect, and extending powers to the community to deal with anti-social behaviour and using civil measures. It has implications for penal policy, and particularly for youth justice policy, as one element of it is improving the way the criminal justice system deals with anti-social behaviour, providing visible and constructive punishment for offenders and improving enforcement (see Chapters 8 and 13).

The consultation paper *Making Sentencing Clearer* (Home Secretary *et al.* 2006) is intended to be part of the rebalancing process. Its aim is to make sentencing clearer for all parties involved, victims, witnesses and defendants, it wants to give judges more discretion and flexibility in reducing the sentence discounts for a guilty plea. It also proposes greater use of fines, stronger community sentences as an alternative to custody, and better protection from dangerous offenders through the use of indeterminate sentences.

1.5.5 Organisational changes

In addition to the sentencing initiatives discussed above, there have been a number of organisational changes, including the establishment of the National Offender Management Service (NOMS) which was set up in June 2004, following the recommendations of the Carter Report (Carter 2003). Although the Government accepted most of the Carter recommendations, including contestability in public service provision, not all of these recommendations have yet been implemented (Home Office 2004b).

NOMS takes over responsibility for the overall management of offenders. It aims to reduce reoffending by 10 per cent by 2010 through improving the way offenders are managed. Strategies used will include improving family links, education and skills in both custody and the community. However, its top priority is public protection, which has implications for the sharing of information between agencies, regular risk assessments and reassessments, and effective supervision and closer cooperation between the prisons and probation service in the process of offender management. It also plays a key role in commissioning services from the private, voluntary and community sectors in relation to the punishment, support and reform of offenders. It will also be working on ways of improving fine enforcement. The Government is also changing the arrangements for the provision of probation services. The new organisational framework is set out in the Offender Management Act 2007 (see Chapter 12, section 12.3.5).

A further major organisational change was the creation of the Ministry of Justice in 2007. The National Offender Management Service and the Prison and Probation Services are now the responsibility of the Secretary of State for Justice and the Ministry of Justice.

So the last few years have seen major shifts, with the Home Office losing responsibility for prisons, probation and sentencing to the new Ministry of Justice. These changes followed a protracted period of criticism of the Home Office during 2006 and 2007, including the revelation that during the period 1999–2006 over 1,000 foreign national prisoners had been released without being considered for deportation. New procedures were introduced to address this issue but when it was revealed that the problem had persisted, the Home Secretary Charles Clarke was sacked in May 2006. Further criticism of the failings over deportation of foreign prisoners led the new Home Secretary, John Reid, to denounce it as 'not fit for purpose' and it was subsequently subject to major reorganisation with several of its key areas of responsibility, including sentencing, moving to the Ministry of Justice. However, these changes did not silence criticism. The burgeoning prison population led to further pressures on the system and public concern over threats to the public from released sex offenders led to demands for John Reid to resign, which he resisted until he retired when Gordon Brown took over from Tony Blair in June 2007.

1.5.6 Current policy criticisms

The Government's reforms have been criticised by criminal lawyers for a variety of reasons. It has been argued that the Government should have waited until the Sentencing Guidelines Council was fully operational and the new sentencing framework in place before superimposing further changes. LAG, Liberty, the Bar Council, and the Criminal Bar Association issued a joint statement criticising the politicisation of the criminal justice debate, and the way the Government has made political capital out of issues in the debate. But this seems to overlook the fact that debates on crime have dominated British politics since the 1970s. Moreover, in a deeper sense the crime question is inherently political in that questions of crime, law, and order raise fundamental questions about the relationship between the state and the citizen, and the problem of how society can be held together, in the face of internal social divisions and the fragmentation of individuals' self-interest,[6] as well as issues regarding how far the state may intervene to protect citizens from each other and from external threats.

There are also concerns over the potential injustice of the increased risk of convicting the innocent by allowing evidence of previous convictions for the same offences. The 2003 Criminal Justice Act was also criticised by the Home Affairs Committee for shifting the balance too far in favour of the state. The increasing range of controls over individuals' movements, in control orders and other civil orders, particularly if based on the prospect of future rather than past offences, has also led to extensive criticisms of the Government (see Liberty 2006, 2007).

---

[6] This problem is at the heart of social contract theory: see T. Hobbes' *Leviathan* (1651) and J.-J. Rousseau's *The Social Contract* (1743).

1.6 **The governance of sex offenders: a case study**

Some of these issues which we have discussed in relation to the formulation of penal policy will now be considered by focusing on the governance of sex offenders in England and Wales, because it raises concerns about the protection of the public, the impact of populist punitiveness, just deserts, human rights, and the influence of risk management and actuarial justice.

A number of measures aimed at improving the control, detention, and arrest of sex offenders were introduced in the UK in the late 1990s. They include the registration scheme established by the Sex Offenders Act 1997 and sex offender orders created by the CDA 1998, a life sentence for a second serious sexual offence in the Crime (Sentences) Act 1997, and legislation dealing with stalkers in the Protection from Harassment Act 1997. New measures to deal with sex tourism were introduced in Part II of the Sex Offenders Act 1997, as amended by Schedule 5, paragraph 4 of the Criminal Justice and Court Services Act 2000, and to prevent the improper use of evidence relating to sexual offences in the Sexual Offences (Protected Material) Act 1997. Special measures to assist complainants of sexual offences were introduced by the Youth Justice and Criminal Evidence Act 1999.

Monitoring of persons working with children was strengthened by the Protection of Children Act 1999 and the Criminal Justice and Court Services Act 2000 and by the establishment of the Criminal Records Bureau. In addition, penalties for possession of indecent photographs of children were increased and the regime for inspecting residential homes was improved. Cooperation between agencies to manage the risk posed by sexual and serious offenders in the community was formalised and given a statutory basis in the Criminal Justice and Court Services Act 2000, re-enacted by the CJA 2003. The government also initiated a review of sexual offences, which aimed to strengthen further the protection of children and vulnerable adults from abuse, and a raft of new measures in the Sexual Offences Act 2003, which changed the law relating to the issue of consent in rape cases. The Act includes provisions on child sex offences, abuse of a position of trust, abuse of children through prostitution and pornography, and introduces new civil preventative orders designed to protect children. A new offence of possession of extreme pornography is also introduced by s 63 of the 2008 Criminal Justice and Immigration Act.

The new measures to control the movements of sex offenders in the Sex Offenders Act 1997 and the Crime and Disorder Act 1998 can be seen as reflecting the New Penology. The Sex Offenders Act 1997 provided for the creation of a register recording all persons convicted of or cautioned for a sexual offence. Although popularly referred to as the 'Paedophile Register', it also included those who committed sexual offences against adults. Part I imposed a requirement for convicted and cautioned sex offenders to notify the police of their name and address and inform them of any changes of residence, including holidays. How long the individual stayed subject to the notification requirements depended on the length of the sentence imposed for the offence. In 2005/6 there were 29,973 sex offenders on the Register. A further new development was the sex offender order which the Government introduced in s 2 of the Crime and Disorder Act 1998. These were civil orders which prohibited the offender from engaging in conduct such as loitering near a school. The Chief Officer of Police could apply for an order if a person who is a convicted or cautioned sex offender had acted, since his conviction or caution, in such a way as to give reasonable cause to believe that an order under the section was necessary to protect the public from serious harm. It was not necessary for a particular victim to be identified nor to prove intent. The test of serious harm was death or serious physical or psychological injury, drawn from the CJA 1991. Once in place the order had effect for a minimum of five years. Once an order was made under s 2 of the CDA 1998, the individual to whom the order applied was also subject to the registration requirements of the Sex Offenders Act 1997. While the orders were civil restraining orders, if breached they incurred penalties of fines and/or imprisonment. The sex offender order was granted on the basis of risk calculations generated by present conduct, so its application was selective in contrast to the Sex Offenders Act 1997. Past convictions were a necessary but not a sufficient condition for granting an order and there had to be an evidential basis for granting an order.

The 2003 Sexual Offences Act repealed the 1997 Sex Offenders Act and also repealed ss 2, 2A, 2B and 3 of the Crime and Disorder Act. It replaced the sex offender order with the new sexual offences prevention order (SOPO). This also is a civil order whose aim is to protect the public from serious sexual harm, although, as before, its breach constitutes a criminal offence, punishable on conviction by a maximum of five years' imprisonment. The order applies to a wide range of sexual offences defined in Schedule 3 of the Act. An application may be made by a Chief Officer of Police and the court must be persuaded that the defendant's behaviour subsequent to the first relevant conviction makes the order necessary 'for the purpose of protecting the public or any particular members of the public from serious sexual harm from the defendant' (s 104(1)(a)). It may prohibit the offender from carrying out any activities described in the order. It will last for a minimum of five years. Once an order is granted the offender becomes subject to the notification requirements of the 1997 Sex Offenders Act, which are now included in the 2003 Act. The order also brings the offender within the remit of the Multi Agency Public Protection Panel arrangements. There is a legal requirement on the police, and the probation and prison services, to organise arrangements to assess and manage the risks presented by violent and sexual offenders, to monitor these arrangements and to furnish annual reports.

The 2003 Act also introduced foreign travel orders which enable the magistrates' court to restrict the travel of those convicted in the UK or abroad of sexual offences against a child under 16, if the court is satisfied that the defendant's behaviour since the relevant conviction makes it necessary in order to protect children from serious sexual harm from the defendant. The orders may prevent travel to a specified country or from travelling to anywhere in the world for a maximum period of six months. Although these are also civil orders, their breach constitutes a criminal offence punishable by a maximum of five years' imprisonment. The Act also introduces a new risk of sexual harm order. This is more extensive, in so far as it is not necessary for the defendant to have been convicted of an offence, but only that on at least two previous occasions, the defendant has engaged in sexually explicit conduct or communication with a child, for example, sending pornographic material to a child over the internet. The order may prohibit the offender from doing anything described in the order which is necessary to protect the child or children from harm from the defendant. The order will be for a minimum of two years but subject to procedures to renew or discharge the order and with a right of appeal. Breaches can be punished by a maximum of five years' imprisonment. Each of the orders in the Act is essentially based on an assessment of the risk of future offending and, as such, raises problems of prediction and justification, which will be discussed further in Chapter 5.

Simon (1998) sees a shift away from the traditional perception of the sex offender as mentally ill, which suggests the potential for diagnostic treatment and understanding in order to change the offender, towards the perception of an evil monster, with the implication that science is of limited value in understanding, or changing the offender. Although Simon is primarily concerned with the American penal system, we find a similar convergence between the New Penology and populist punitiveness in the UK, reflected in the demonisation of the sex offender in government policy and popular campaigns to remove sex offenders from the community. Sex offenders have now been absorbed into the discourse of risk management, and surveillance has extended beyond the prison into ordinary life. Risk assessment is part of this process of transcarceration and the move towards ever greater surveillance and acquisition of knowledge, charted by Foucault (1977), has found expression in the new legislation. There is now less public tolerance of sex offenders in the UK, less sympathy for medical models of individual pathology, and greater willingness to see sex offenders as bad rather than mad, to be removed from the community rather than being changed or cured through treatment. The dominant model in therapeutic programmes is the cognitive–behavioural model which accepts that it is more productive to focus on the development of reasoning skills and new ways of thinking, than to search for the underlying causes of deviant behaviour, which may be too time-consuming and ultimately unattainable.

However, for some sections of the public the measures to control sex offenders currently available are insufficiently punitive and should be supplemented by full disclosure and preventive detention. Attempts to categorise levels of risk of sex offenders for the purposes of the registration scheme may be problematic as the criteria for registration are unwieldy and do not distinguish between them in terms of individual risk but only impose a period of registration as defined formally by sentence length. The penalties imposed for breaches of sexual offender orders have also been variable (see Shute 2004a). The UK government's focus on risk management in response to the public's punitiveness, has also raised problems as it has come into conflict with the protection of human rights.

The move towards restricting the movement of sex offenders reflects a wider use of civil orders to reinforce the criminal law, while avoiding Convention challenges under Articles 6 and 7. As well as the range of measures directed against sex offenders, we have seen in recent years increased use of anti-social behaviour orders, and we now have a new order, similar in some respects to the SOPO and ASBO, the serious crime prevention order introduced by s 1 of the Serious Crime Act 2007, which aims to exert control over the movements and assets of those involved in serious crime. Although creating civil orders, these provisions create new criminal offences of failing to comply with these orders, which attract criminal penalties. The aim is to protect the public by preventing, restricting and disrupting involvement in serious crime. In addition, the courts have powers to impose extensive controls on individuals' movements through control orders under s 1 of the Prevention of Terrorism Act 2005. There are also provisions to create youth rehabilitation orders (s 1) and violent offender orders (s 98) in the Criminal Justice and Immigration Act 2008. The aim of the violent offender order is to protect the public from serious harm by imposing further restrictions on violent offenders. However, it is likely that if the terms imposed are too restrictive the move towards increasing controls may raise future Convention challenges and arguments over whether they constitute retrospective punishments. Collectively we can see a shift towards controls within the community intended to protect the public by preventing possible future offending which, as we shall see in Chapters 2 and 3, raises problems for retributivism.

1.7 Conclusion

1.7.1 Key themes

As we have seen in the preceding discussion the state's response to crime formulated in specific penal policies reflects a number of key influences, the relative importance of which may change over time. We have identified the principal developments since 1990, including the changes in the Criminal Justice Act 2003, and we have noted some of the provisions of the new Criminal Justice and Immigration Act 2008. We have also highlighted issues of equality, fairness, and justice which we will discuss in greater detail in subsequent chapters. But here we offer a case study which invites you to think about these influences in relation to a specific penal policy.

1.7.2 Case study: Damian Cronus

Damian Cronus, aged 40, has a history of sexual offences against young children over the past 15 years, for which he has served custodial sentences. His favoured methods of gaining access to children include watching them in the school playground, following them home, approaching children in amusement arcades and befriending children playing on the seafront.

His last conviction was in 1998 and he is shortly to be released. On his release he plans to move back to his former home town of Brighton where he has many friends and hopes to find employment in the area. The police are concerned that he remains a threat to young children.

1.7.3 Questions

1. Consider what can be done to protect young children living in the area from this person.

   In answering this question select from the range of measures now available to monitor the movements of offenders released into the community and ways of restricting their movements.

2. Consider the influence of the following factors on the introduction of the raft of new measures to deal with sex offenders in and since the 1990s.

   (a) Political factors.

   (b) Economic factors.

   (c) Public opinion.

   (d) Penological theories.

3. Consider the impact of these new measures on the sex offender released into the community. Do the measures you identify treat the sex offender with humanity and justice? Do they respect the ex-offender's human rights? Do they treat sex offenders as a special category and if so, is this special treatment justified?

4. Are you satisfied that the measures you have discussed are adequate to protect children in the local area? If not, what further measures might be introduced and what problems might they raise?

Guidance on approaching these questions is given in the Online Resource Centre, and the following references might also be useful:

online
resource
centre

Cobley, C. (1997) 'Keeping Track of Sex Offenders—Part 1 of the Sex Offenders Act 1997' *Modern Law Review* 60–69.

Knock, K. (2002) 'The Police Perspective on Sex Offender Orders: A Preliminary Review of Policy and Practice', Police Research Series Paper 155, London, Home Office.

McAlinden, A.-M. (2007) *The Shaming of Sex Offenders: Risk, Retribution and Reintegration*, Oxford, Hart.

Shute, S. (2004) 'The Sexual Offences Act 2003 (4) New Civil Preventative Orders: Sexual Offences Prevention Orders, Foreign Travel Orders, Risk of Sexual Harm Orders' *Criminal Law Review* 419.

Thomas, D. (2006a) 'Sexual Offences Prevention Orders: Grounds for Making an Order', *Criminal Law Review* 364–7.

Thomas, D. (2006b) 'The Sex Offenders Act 1997: Notification Requirements' *Criminal Law Review* 553–58.

Thomas, D. (2006c) 'The Sexual Offences Act 2003: Notification Requirements' *Criminal Law Review* 1085–87.

Ibbotson v UK [1999] 1 EHRLR 218.

Jones v Greater Manchester Police Authority [2001] EWHC Admin 189.

2

Just constraints? Sentencing discretion and retributivist principles

SUMMARY

In a principled sentencing system the exercise of discretion by the sentencer must be controlled. This chapter examines the ways in which this is done, not only through law and guidance but also through the use of a justificatory principle as a constraint. It discusses the retributivist rationale in detail with a particular focus on the theories of Kant and Hegel, as well as the approach of modern retributivists such as von Hirsch. Finally it addresses the policy implications of this justification of punishment.

2.1 Introduction

2.1.1 Justice and discretion

The choice of principles or laws most likely to lead to the 'best' justice is a matter for continual debate because, as we saw in the previous chapter, what is construed as fair or just depends on changing ideas of social justice and on the theoretical approach which is taken to understanding the notion of punishment itself. However, there is a consensus that it would be unjust if an agency or individual could use its power to impose and implement whatever punishment it wished to impose. Justice in sentencing, then, requires at the very least that those individuals who undertake the sentencing of convicted criminals are constrained by a set of principles—be they moral, legal, or religious—and by a framework of rules. Further, in a democracy, sentencing may not be perceived as just if those rules and principles are not acceptable to the electorate.

The proper control and exercise of discretion is, consequently, crucial in the quest for justice in sentencing and punishment:

Discretion is one of the most contentious concepts in criminal justice and related circles because it is so important and yet so difficult to define...Indeed it is the day-to-day discretionary action of police officers, prosecutors, defence lawyers, judges, psychiatrists, prison, probation and immigration officers, among others, which are the 'stuff of justice' and which make for justice or injustice.

(Gelsthorpe and Padfield 2003: 1)

That is why we are focusing on this issue first: the second half of this chapter will concentrate on fundamental principles and how they can be, and are, used to constrain discretion. We will examine in detail the classical retributivist justifications for punishment because those justifications have been, and still are, very important in structuring sentencing discretion. They determine what should be the first, and so most influential, questions that the judge or magistrate addresses in the process leading to a sentencing decision. The notion of 'just deserts', that the punishment is what the offender deserves and that it is proportional to the offence, is the term currently used to sum up a retributivist approach to sentencing and so we will also analyse contemporary thinking on just deserts. In Chapter 3 we will examine in detail the ways, and the extent to which, this approach has been incorporated in English sentencing law.

If we consider discretion to be operating on a continuum from complete to no discretion available to those who must make sentencing decisions in individual cases, it can be argued that outcomes at both ends are unjust. At one extreme, sentencing is unjust because there are no constraints whatsoever on the sentencer who can then make decisions, if he so wishes, based on personal prejudices and whims. Since K. C. Davis published *Discretionary Justice* in 1969 a strand of academic thinking has regarded discretion, as he did, as the major source of injustice and something to be confined, structured, and checked (see Hawkins 1992: 16–17). At the other end of the spectrum is the sentencer who has no discretion whatsoever because the rules and principles are so tightly drawn, with all potential factors accounted for, that the sentencer is simply the technician who feeds in the data and reads off the answer, in this case the sentence. This too might be viewed as potentially unjust in that it could not take account of any individual circumstances that had not been foreseen. The logical conclusion is that justice is to be found between the two ends of this discretion spectrum.

One reason why constraints are placed on the sentencer by the state is, then, to respond to the notion that totally unconstrained discretion is inherently unjust: 'In a liberal state, law is to be applied consistently, openly, and dispassionately; rules are regarded as the most appropriate means to these ends. Discretion represents the opposite; it is subjective justice where rules are formal justice' (Hawkins 1992: 150). The expectation is that the rule of law will be upheld because the citizen must have confidence in the law and institutions of the state. Without that confidence, the criminal justice system will lack legitimacy and will not attract the 'moral' allegiance of the citizen, putting the system, and the government, at risk.

In democratic states, then, neither the professional nor the lay judge can do just what they might want to do when sentencing. There are rules that, to a greater or lesser extent, guide them in the exercise of their discretion. Having said that, the discretion of the sentencing judge, established in the course of the eighteenth century, has been described as 'the central principle of the English sentencing system' (Thomas 2002: 473) and the constraint of that discretion is still a live issue. Indeed, the former Lord Chief Justice, Lord Woolf, criticised the new system of sentencing guidelines as contributing to higher rates of custody 'because it reduces the discretion of the individual judge'.[1] How far rules should constrain the sentencer is, then, a matter of debate. There are constitutional issues about the independence of the judiciary on the one hand and the implementation of democratically decided policy on the other. As we shall see in section 2.2 below, in the UK we have

---

[1] BBC News, 'Too many people in jail, says top judge', 30 May 2006: http://news.bbc.co.uk/2/hi/uk_news/5028782.stm.

the paradoxical situation where judges and magistrates have, historically, been provided with an increasingly wide choice of available penalties, whilst, at the same time, the trend has been to circumscribe their discretion.[2]

2.1.2 Discretion as 'bad'

[L]iberalism insists that governance should consistently exemplify standards of legality, defined as strictly rule-governed modes of decision-making in which the decision-maker refrains from allowing anything other than the legal implications of the rules themselves, self-regulated by meta-rules, to determine the outcome. Discretionary decision-making is condemned as a cavalier disregard for this imperative involving the substitution of prohibited determinants for those which judges and officials should draw exclusively upon.

(Salter and Twist 2007)

This idea that discretion is the opposite of formal justice, arising from debates around the concept of 'the rule of law' (Dicey 1885), 'has spawned a series of by now familiar criticisms' (Hawkins 1992: 15). Foremost among these criticisms, representing a long-standing political concern, is the argument that a wide sentencing discretion leads to inconsistency of sentencing in which similar cases may not be treated similarly.

Parliamentary anxiety about the differential treatment of persistent but minor offenders was one of the factors leading to the creation of the Court of Criminal Appeal in 1907 (see Thomas 2002: 474, 484–5). More recently, concern about sentencing disparity has led to research on possible geographical differences, notably in relation to custody rates. In 1988 research showed a custody rate of 23 per cent in Manchester courts but 14 per cent in nearby Liverpool, for example (Cavadino 1988); in 2000 the custody rate in magistrates' courts in England and Wales varied from 0.8 per cent in Elbes (Lincolnshire) to 23.4 per cent in Luton and South Bedfordshire; in 2005 the region with the highest custody rate across all courts was Merseyside with 9 per cent and the lowest Wiltshire with 3 per cent (Home Office 2007c: Table 5.1, Figure 5.1).[3] Research on environmental prosecutions in 1999–2003 (primarily on offences relating to pollution and wildlife) also found that the average length of a custodial sentence varied considerably—from 2 months in Wales to nearly 18 months in the eastern region, with the highest average fine of nearly £5,000 to be found in the London region and the lowest, at under £2,000, in the eastern region and Wales (Dupont and Zakkour 2003: 12, 17).

The concern is that discretion is not being limited to the 'relevant idiosyncrasies' of a case (Feldman 1992: 172–5). Whilst it is not necessarily easy to establish what counts as relevant this must be done or, as Ashworth put it some time ago, the notion of disparity 'might be used as a basis for criticising our sentencing system for not treating all red-haired offenders in the same way' (Ashworth 1987: 24). The problematic nature of this exercise also contributes to the difficulty of undertaking research in this area. One solution has been to analyse cases in terms of particular

online
resource
centre

[2] Arguably, the provisions of the Criminal Justice Act 2003 aimed at more 'flexible' sentencing indicate some increased discretion: see Chapter 12, section 12.2.2. The Criminal Justice and Immigration Act 2008 also reintroduces some discretion in relation to dangerous offenders.

[3] The annually published *Criminal Statistics* web link provides a variety of supplementary tables as well as the national statistics. See the Online Resource Centre.

factors accepted as important in sentencing to see whether courts (internally and across courts) are imposing similar sentences on similar kinds of offender.

If apparent disparities are found, research results have been countered with the argument that no two cases are the same, and that research cannot 'pick up' the crucial differences. On the other hand, as Hood noted, 'magistrates and judges…place particular value upon their experience in sentencing. Now, if this experience is to be of value, then all cases cannot be unique, they must be comparable in some respects' (1962: 16). Whatever the result of such exercises and whether they focus on geography, race, gender or class, whether disparity is proved to 'actually' happen or whether there is only a perception that it does, the policy concern is the same—that the legitimacy of the sentencing process may be undermined in the eyes of the public.

Implicit in the above concern with disparity is the criticism that it allows 'space' for discrimination—whether it be personal or institutional—to occur. Again the focus of research has often been the custodial sentence and, notably, the fact that particular ethnic minorities are over-represented in prison (see Chapter 11). Criminologists have focused on disentangling whether or not this discrepancy is the result of direct or indirect racial discrimination (see Bowling and Phillips 2002: Chapter 7; also Chapter 10, section 10.4 below). Research has also investigated whether personal, class or gender aspects of the defendant's behaviour influence the sentencer. For example, Hedderman's research suggested that 'the interactions between all the participants in the court hearing…contribute significantly to sentencing decisions' and 'women may receive more lenient sentences than men because they are more nervous and act more respectfully and deferentially to the Bench' (1990: 36).

A further argument against the availability of wide discretion is that discretion diminishes the possibility of accurately predicting sentence outcome: sanctions cannot give a clear deterrent message to past or potential offenders, and solicitors and barristers are unable to advise their clients effectively. Further, if judges or magistrates tend to sentence at the top end of what is legally permissible, 'over-sentencing' occurs. This can lead to a crisis of resources for the government. Too wide a sentencing discretion could also make it difficult for a democratically elected government to impose its desired sentencing policy.

Not all academic analysis has concurred with the idea that discretion is inherently 'bad', that inconsistency is caused by individual behaviour, or that discretion needs to be rule-guided. Writing in the context of prosecutorial discretion in the Health and Safety Inspectorate, Hawkins has argued:

Discretion arising from a number of sources suffuses the processes of law enforcement and regulation. Discretion is plastic, shaped and given form to some extent by the institutions of law and legal arrangements and more substantially by decision-makers' framing behaviour. Systems of formal rules, for all their appearance of precision and specificity, work in only imprecise ways. Indeed, precision and consistent practice are not necessarily assisted by the drafting of ever more elaborate schemes of rules.

(Hawkins 2002: 424)

Researchers have, consequently, been concerned with empirically discovering the non-legal norms which influence behaviour (Hawkins 1992, 2002) and also with issues of social justice raised by sentencing behaviour (see Chapter 10 below).

In practice, sentencing discretion and resulting sentencing outcomes must be a government concern: the policy imperatives and conflicts outlined in Chapter 1 come into play. The constraints—the techniques and tools by which sentencing discretion is 'structured'—can take many forms. The more obvious ones are the rules relating to the availability and choice of punishments, and to the maximum and minimum amounts of punishment allowed in a particular jurisdiction. They might also be financial or administrative constraints. What has become increasingly important, as we noted above (in Chapter 1, section 1.4.4) is the constraint of an imposed justificatory principle, a new rationale, and sections 2.5–2.7 below will, therefore, examine retributivism in some detail.

2.1.3 Historical policy trends in structuring sentencing discretion

We saw in Chapter 1 that there are a variety of complex influences accounting for the changes in penal policy in the 1990s and the early years of the twenty-first century. At this point we want to go further back to look at the policy background in relation to long-term trends to widen choice of penalties for courts while narrowing the discretion to choose. The expansion of available penalties and the implementation of constraints on discretion did not occur as an evenly spaced incremental process but, rather, as a result of several periods of more intensive legislative change passed to respond to particular sets of problems perceived at that time.

1895–1914

Garland argues that this was the crucial period in the history of modern penality, with the number of sanctions almost doubling in this period (1985: 19). Legislation, including the Prison Act 1898, the Probation of Offenders Act 1907, and the Prevention of Crime Act 1908, added probation orders, Borstal training, preventive detention, and detention of those we would now call mentally disordered offenders. The impetus was a general social, economic and political anxiety about the 'underclass' and a belief that a mixture of penal and social welfare reforms could 'solve' the problems (Garland 1985: 244–52)[4] with the aid of the newly emerging sciences in psychology, biology, and social work to classify and treat criminals (ibid: 26–31).

1945–73

This period saw two 'bursts' of sentencing legislation taking place immediately after the Second World War and then in the late 1960s and early 1970s. They are similar in that both evidenced a renewed focus on the offender and the development of rehabilitative and community-based penalties. The Criminal Justice Act of 1948 made the use of fines more widely available and introduced new sentences with a focus on the offender. In 1965 another spate of legislation saw the abolition (for most purposes) of the death penalty, and the addition of suspended prison sentences (Criminal Justice Act 1967), absolute and conditional discharges (Powers of Criminal Courts Act 1973), community service orders, and compensation orders (Criminal Justice Act 1972). The social and political contexts for both these periods were ones of social and economic optimism, coming either immediately after

---

[4] For a full list of official reports and legislative responses, see Garland (1985: Appendices 1 and 2).

victory in 1945 or in the 1960s, when there was a strong belief in the power of science, including social work, to solve the problem of crime.

1982–91

These years experienced a less favourable economic climate and the development of the thinking and policies of the New Right to respond to the new situation. The collectivist and welfarist solutions favoured since the 1940s were increasingly seen as unacceptable and gave way to a focus on legal justice, individual responsibility, and the encouragement of the 'privatisation' of penal provision. For sentencers it meant a greater focus on offender culpability, evidenced in the establishment of 'just deserts' as the main sentencing rationale. It also entailed more punishment for those who were not behaving as responsible citizens, evidenced in increases in maximum terms of imprisonment, the prison building programme, and the greater availability of restrictive conditions for supervision and probation orders. On the other hand, the desire to reduce expenditure on prisons influenced the passing of statutory criteria for the use of custodial penalties, first for minors in the Criminal Justice Acts of 1982 and 1988 and then for all offenders in the Criminal Justice Act 1991.

During this period the growing sense of social insecurity and the perception that communities were disintegrating, paradoxically, also led to a greater policy interest in punishment in and by the community (see Chapter 12). The Criminal Justice Act 1991 introduced new combinations of sentences and gave them the new name of 'community penalties'. Further, the emphasis on individual responsibility and economic success, together with the specific problems arising from the enormous profits of crime in relation to drugs, led to new provisions to make it easier for the courts to confiscate the proceeds of crime (see Chapter 6, section 6.2).

1993–2008

This most recent period has evidence of new, but sometimes conflicting, strands of policy affecting sentencing discretion. On the one hand, the new penological thinking and the development of the public's punitiveness encouraged 'tougher' sentencing with a reduced discretion in relation to offenders perceived to be dangerous (see Chapters 1 and 5);[5] on the other hand, there has been a greater focus on community sentences and restorative justice with a corresponding wider range of options for the courts. These different concerns have led to a series of Acts of Parliament which have undermined the coherence of the sentencing approach set up by the 1991 Act. The Criminal Justice Act 1993 apparently allowed more weight to be given to previous offending and the Criminal Justice Act (CJA) 2003 has consolidated this approach. Several Acts have increased the statutory maxima for custodial sentences for various offences; the Crime (Sentences) Act 1997 introduced automatic life (repealed in 2003) and mandatory minimum custodial sentences and the Crime and Disorder Act (CDA) 1998 introduced, inter alia, new youth court orders, extended post-custody supervision, and provided new exclusionary penalties.

A positive and long-awaited development was the consolidation of sentencing legislation in the Powers of Criminal Courts (Sentencing) Act (PCCSA) 2000,

---

[5] Although the Criminal Justice and Immigration Act 2008 will restore some discretion to the courts (see Chapter 5, section 5.4).

although legislation already amends or supersedes it. For example, the Criminal Justice and Courts Services Act 2000 changed the terminology for community penalties, whilst the CJA 2003 introduced new custodial and community sentences and a revised sentencing framework for their use. The CJA 2003 also established the Sentencing Guidelines Council. The Domestic Violence, Crime and Victims Act 2004 signified the increasing policy emphasis on victims whilst the Criminal Justice and Immigration (CJ&I) Act 2008, inter alia, includes a raft of amendments to provisions for existing orders and offences and introduces youth rehabilitation orders and violent offender orders.

This period of legislative provisions to structure sentencing, therefore, evidences 'traditional' constraints, such as the availability of penalties and restrictions on their use, but also new ways of constraining sentencing discretion, notably statutory 'hurdles' to the imposition of certain penalties and also new bodies to provide detailed guidance to sentencers. These will be considered in sections 2.2 to 2.4 below.

2.2 'Traditional' constraints

2.2.1 Penalties available to sentencers

Perhaps the most obvious point to make is that judges and magistrates can only impose a penalty which is legally available in the jurisdiction. As the above review makes clear, the range of penalties has widened considerably over the years. 'In early English criminal law sentencing was a simple matter. The penalty for **felony** was death; the penalty for a **misdemeanour** was unlimited imprisonment or an unlimited fine' (Thomas 2002: 473). Even in 1905 the only available penalties for use in England and Wales (for offenders aged 17+) were death, imprisonment, penal servitude, fines, and common law binding-over powers (including supervision by the Police Court Mission after the Probation of Offenders Act 1887). In contrast, at the very beginning of the twenty-first century, the PCCSA 2000 and the Criminal Justice and Court Services Act 2000 together made the following penalties available to the court:[6]

- imprisonment/detention, suspended sentence
- community rehabilitation (probation) order, community punishment (community service) order, community punishment and rehabilitation (combination) order
- attendance centre order, drug treatment and testing order, drug abstention order
- curfew order, exclusion order
- compensation order, restitution order, forfeiture order
- fine
- discharge.

[6] Where relevant the previous names are given in brackets. The implementation of the Criminal Justice Act 2003 has substituted a community order for some of these community-based penalties: see Chapter 12, section 12.1. There are additional orders for young offenders (for example, referral orders: see Chapter 8) and also orders under the Mental Health Act 1983 (as amended: see Chapter 7, section 7.4).

Judges and magistrates are also constrained with respect to the amount of punishment they can impose in relation to available penalties. There are restrictions on the upper 'amount' of sentence that can be legally imposed—the maximum laid down in legislation—whether it be in terms of sentence length for custodial and community penalties or for the amount of a financial penalty. For example, many of the more serious offences, such as domestic burglary, supplying a Class B drug, and racially aggravated criminal damage, carry a statutory maximum of 14 years' imprisonment. These maxima are changed by Parliament in response to public perceptions of seriousness. For example, Schedule 28 of the CJA 2003 raised to 14 years the maximum for other specified drug-related offences whilst Schedule 26 raised the maxima for certain **summary offences**, including intimidating witnesses and publishing material harmful to children.

Taken as a whole, maximum penalties do not necessarily constitute a well-thought-out and coherent system, despite the efforts of the Criminal Law Revision Committee and the Law Commission. As a report of the Advisory Council on the Penal System stated 30 years ago, 'on looking into the history of maximum penalties of imprisonment in this country, we discovered that they have grown up largely as a result of historical accident. The structure of the present penalty system was first formulated in the five criminal statutes of 1861...' (1978: para 14). Neither should the maximum penalty be seen as the 'normal' top end of the sentencing options: the statutory maximum must be used only for the gravest instance of the offence that could occur (*Smith* 1975). Courts have therefore established their own normal range of penalties to which, in practice, sentencers refer (see Chapter 3). The proposal of the 1978 report to set—for the 'ordinary' case—a new maximum 'fixed at the point below which 90 per cent of prison sentences have fallen for each individual offence in the last three years' was never taken further (Advisory Council on the Penal System 1978: para 23).

2.2.2 Rules governing the use of available sentences

Not all the above penalties are available for all sentencers or for all offenders. There are several different sorts of limit which apply, in addition to the statutory maxima.

Limits on sentencing powers of magistrates' courts

Cases are allocated for trial and sentencing to one or other of the two levels of courts—the magistrates' court and the Crown Court—in England and Wales (see, generally, Sanders and Young 2006: Chapters 9 and 10). For most offences minors must be allocated to the youth court. This has implications for sentencing because the lower courts often cannot use penalties up to the statutory maximum. So, to use domestic burglary as an example, the magistrates' court cannot impose the maximum sentence of 14 years because the statutory maximum custodial sentence available to the magistrates' court by the CJA 2003, s 154(1) is 12 months (previously 6 months).[7] Magistrates are also subject to a minimum term of five days when imposing a custodial sentence (Magistrates' Courts Act 1980, s 132).

---

[7] The proposal in an early version of the Bill (cl 148) to give the Secretary of State powers to raise this limit to 18 months was removed. Consecutive terms of imprisonment are allowed by the Magistrates' Courts Act 1980, s 133.

Age categories

Certain penalties may not be available for children and young people or for adults. For example, reparation orders are currently available only for those under 18 years of age (PCCSA 2000, s 73) although reparation may be part of an activity requirement in a community order for any offender (CJA 2003, s 201(2)). There are also extra restrictions on using custodial penalties for minors (see Chapter 13).

2.2.3 **Financial and organisational factors**

There are also extra-legal factors which influence either the amount of discretion the sentencing courts can exercise or the outcome post-sentencing.

Allocation of resources

In relation to both community and custodial sentences, funding is a major influence on practice. The setting and **ring-fencing** of budgets for the National Probation Service (NPS) and the **out-sourcing** of prison management and services affect the content and availability of community penalties and the custodial experience. This could lead to gender differences in sentencing if, for example, resources did not permit the establishment of community punishment schemes suitable for women, particularly those with young children. It can also lead to a different range of options for sentencers if, for example, a particular NPS had not commissioned specific rehabilitation programmes.

Administrative and executive powers

Traditionally the Home Secretary and also bodies such as the Parole Board have had powers which can affect the length of custodial sentences served. In recent years the influence of the European Convention on Human Rights has affected the operation of these powers and proved to be a constraint on their use (see, for example, Chapter 9 in regard to prison procedures and conditions and Chapter 13 for issues relating to minors).

Government guidance

We will deal below with the guidance from the Sentencing Guidelines Council but here we note that the Home Office, in particular, has been involved for some time in developing and circulating guidance generally on policy and professional practice. For example, 30 years ago the Home Office sent a copy of an interim report, *The Length of Prison Sentences,* to every judge and bench of magistrates. The message of that report was that prison should be used as little as possible: 'the general rule which we advocate . . . is to stop at the point where a sentence has been decided upon and consider whether a shorter one would do just as well' (Advisory Council on the Penal System 1977). More recent examples are the National Standards in regard to the aims and best practice of the Probation Service and Youth Justice Services, and Youth Justice Board (YJB) guidance in relation to, inter alia, restorative justice initiatives and new sentences for public protection.

Training

As Ashworth has noted, the implementation of legislation may not achieve the desired restructuring of sentencing: 'it will only be worthwhile if it operates in practice in the way intended. It is abundantly clear that compulsion may not bring this about: the experience of courts circumventing mandatory minimum sentences is sufficient to substantiate this' (Ashworth 1998a: 217). In other words it has been accepted since at least the report of the Streatfeild Committee in 1961 that judges require training in the principles and approaches desired by Parliament and laid down in guidance. The Final Report of the Bridges Committee in 1978 had, however, been forced to replace the word 'training' used in the Interim Report with 'studies' because of judicial hostility to what was seen as a threat to judicial independence (see Ashworth 1983). The function of judicial training, therefore, is currently undertaken in England and Wales by the Judicial Studies Board[8] which since 1985 has also had responsibilities for training stipendiary magistrates, now district judges, and has an advisory role in the training of lay magistrates.

Other factors

The background to many of the constraints reviewed above is the contentious issue of the relationship between public opinion, the media, and sentencing policy. As Chapter 1 pointed out, the nature of the relationship is problematic, given the public's misconceptions about sentencing and the difficulty of researching either public opinion or its influence on those who decide policy or who sentence (see, further, Richards 1998: Chapter 3). Equally problematic is the potentially influential new constraint, that of the victim's assessment of the seriousness of the offending against him. (For details of the new procedures for gaining the views of victims see Chapter 6, section 6.4.2 below.)

2.3 New constraints

2.3.1 The policy context

As we saw in Chapter 1, the policy imperative to reduce the use of custodial sentencing on the grounds of cost was strengthened by the argument in the 1980s that custody does not 'work' in rehabilitating offenders: research suggested that it did not deter or reform, particularly in relation to young offenders (see Chapters 8 and 12). The development of new ideas for what was believed to be more 'effective' punishment in the community provided an opportunity to place restrictions on the use of custody and so force sentencers to divert offenders to other penalties. However, increasingly in the 1990s, the concern of government was to enhance the legitimacy of the sentencing system, if necessary in ways that conflicted with the need to save money. The Halliday Report made this important statement—echoing our discussion about justice and discretion—on the first page of its report:

At its roots, sentencing contributes to good order in society. It does so by visibly upholding society's norms and standards; dealing appropriately with those who breach them; and enabling the public to have confidence in its outcomes. The public, as a result, can legitimately be expected to uphold and observe the law, and not to take it into their own hands.

---

[8] See http://www.jsboard.co.uk/.

To achieve this there must be confidence in the justice of the outcomes, as well as in their effectiveness.

(2001: para 1.3)

Policy based on these concerns encouraged a reduction in the use of custody for the 'normal' offender whilst allowing its continued or greater use for particular classes of offender where other policy imperatives, notably the need to restore confidence in the criminal justice system, were deemed politically expedient. Again, this is a bifurcationary, or two-pronged, policy to achieve conflicting policy aims by allocating each aim to different sets of offenders. *Justice for All* refers to these divergent policy aims: 'we have an absolute determination to create a system that meets the needs of society and wins the trust of citizens...' (Home Office 2002a: 4); 'sentences must be consistent across the country and prison must be reserved for serious, dangerous and seriously persistent offenders and those who have failed to respond to community punishment' (ibid: 8). Lord Falconer explained the policy rationale in a press release:

We have been accused by some of sending out mixed messages on sentencing but the government has a very clear sentencing policy. Protecting the public is our over-riding concern. For violent and sex offenders this is best done with a prison sentence...Custody is also necessary for seriously persistent offenders and those who consistently breach community sentences. But in other cases, public protection can best be achieved effectively through rigorous community sentences.

(Home Office 2002b)

Such a statement may make policy clearer but there is no discussion of the principles or criteria which have led to the decisions as to what is 'best' for each of these groups. Given, however, these significant changes in the emphasis of sentencing policy, the government faced the question of how to ensure that judges and magistrates are encouraged into 'appropriate behaviour' in exercising their discretion, given that informal socialisation and organisational routines may be equally or more influential than formal training (Feldman 1992: 176–83).

Government concern with public confidence in the criminal justice system has also led to a policy concern with those key questions at the heart of sentencing and, particularly, the principles and theories which might be used to justify current practice and proposed changes. The 1970s and 1980s witnessed a reaction against rehabilitative approaches and a renewed focus on seriousness; the 1990s saw the priority given to seriousness diminishing and new ideas about restorative sentencing becoming more influential (see Chapter 6), with discredited ideas about rehabilitation themselves being rehabilitated under a 'what works?' policy focus (see Chapter 12), and concern with risk and public protection (see Chapter 5).

All these ideas gloss over the issue of what enables a judge to decide that a particular instance of offending is 'serious', or that the offender is 'dangerous', or that a particular level and type of punishment is 'right'. The problem of structuring discretion to achieve these policy aims could be seen as one of 'goal ambiguity' (Feldman 1992: 174–6), where the sentencer finds it difficult to decide what should be the starting point for deliberation and which factors of a case should be deemed most relevant and carry most weight in making the sentencing decision. Four 'new' techniques used in the 1990s to structure sentencing discretion in line with policy aims were the incorporation in legislation of new 'hurdles' for the imposition of custodial and community sentences, the introduction of new mandatory sentences, the prioritisation of a sentencing rationale and the establishment of new bodies to produce guidance on sentencing policy.

2.3.2 Imposing hurdles

The imposition of statutory hurdles, criteria to limit the use by sentencers of a particular penalty, is not strictly an invention of the 1990s. A provision in the PCCA 1973 in relation to the imposition of a custodial sentence on a first-time offender is an earlier example. The provisions introduced in 1991 were also preceded by similar provisions concerned only with juveniles and young adults, an age group where experimentation and control are often seen as more politically acceptable. The Criminal Justice Act 1982 had stated that custody could be imposed on juveniles only if at least one of the following criteria applied: an unwillingness (shown by past behaviour) on the part of the offender to respond to non-custodial penalties, that custody was necessary to protect the public, and that the offence was so serious that only custody could be justified. Their policy import was not immediately understood by the judiciary or magistracy (Burney 1985; Reynolds 1985) but Court of Appeal judgments and pressure from the Parliamentary All-Party Penal Affairs Group led to amendments made by the Criminal Justice Act 1988 to strengthen the constraint (Dunbar and Langton 1998: 73–8).

At least partly because of those provisions, the custodial rate for minors had decreased in the 1980s and that fact was a major influence on the genesis of the CJA 1991 (see Dunbar and Langton 1998: Chapter 8). Section 1 borrowed the 'so serious that only' custody could be justified, and the 'only such a sentence would be adequate to protect the public' criteria from the 1982 Act to apply to the imposition of custody for all offenders. Similarly community penalties could only be imposed if they were 'serious enough' for such punishments and a fine had to reflect the seriousness of the offence. These were re-enacted in the PCCSA 2000 (ss 35, 79–80 and 128) and, with minor amendments, in the CJA 2003 (ss 148, 152 and 164; see Table 3.1 in Chapter 3). They will be dealt with in more detail in Chapters 3, 7, and 12.

2.3.3 Using mandatory sentences

Parliamentary 'encouragement' of the use of particular penalties by sentencers was not unique to the 1990s (see Tonry 1996: 142–59). In addition to the mandatory sentence of life imprisonment for murder there were already presumptive sentences which sentencers have to impose unless the facts of the case fall within defined exceptions. An example is mandatory disqualification for drunken driving unless 'special reasons' prevail, and mandatory activation of a suspended sentence unless it would be 'unjust to do so'.

However, the passing of ss 1–4 of the Crime (Sentences) Act 1997, re-enacted—with the omission of the original s 1—as ss 109–111 of the PCCSA 2000, signalled the introduction into English sentencing law of a more intrusive tool being used in other jurisdictions, notably the 'Three strikes and you're out' legislation of several of the states in the USA. Sections 110–111, in force from 1997 and 1999 respectively, severely limit judicial discretion, operating when there is repeat offending in regard to specified offences. Section 110 relates to Class A drugs offences (see Drug Trafficking Act 1994) and imposes a minimum sentence of seven years on conviction for a third offence. Section 111 similarly imposes a minimum sentence of three years for a third domestic burglary. Until repealed, s 109 mandated the imposition of an automatic life sentence on conviction for a second sexual or violent offence as listed in s 109.[9]

The legislation was preceded by a White Paper (Home Office 1996a) and accompanied by ministerial comment, notably Home Secretary Michael Howard's dictum in his speech in October 1993 that 'prison works'. These put forward various policy arguments to support the enacting of these sections, all essentially specific arguments against the existence of a wide sentencing discretion to ensure that those sentencing achieve the desired policy ends of protection of the public through containment, deterrence through certainty of punishment, and protection of the public by incorporating discretionary release on criteria of risk.

How mandatory such provisions are in practice, and so how far sentencing discretion is curtailed, depends on how widely drafted is what Ashworth refers to as the 'escape clause'. He argues that in relation to the drug and burglary provisions the escape clause, allowing the courts not to impose the mandatory sentence if 'unjust in all the circumstances', is a wide one; not so the 'exceptional circumstances' of the automatic life sentence provision (1998a: 234–5). We shall see, however, that the Human Rights Act 1998 was effective in significantly reducing the constraint imposed on judges by the latter provision (see the case of *Offen*) and the new sentencing framework for 'dangerous offenders' introduced by CJA 2003 replaced this provision with new criteria for life sentences and a new indeterminate sentence for public protection (IPP) (see Chapter 5, section 5.4.1). The IPP caused even more difficulties for the courts, and has led to widespread concern amongst sentencers, campaigning groups and academics that reduced discretion was causing more injustice to offenders than the provision it replaced.

2.3.4 **Criticism: discretion is 'good'**

The use of the tool of mandatory sentences to achieve policy outcomes has been criticised, as noted above, on the basis that constraints on the exercise of judicial discretion have gone too far towards the other end of the spectrum. The main arguments are the following:

(a) Reduced discretion results in a decreased possibility that justice can be tailored to the specific circumstances of a case or individual. This might itself lead to injustice.

(b) Research on practice in jurisdictions which have had mandatory sentencing for some time would suggest that its stated utilitarian aims cannot be delivered. Tonry, in a chapter summarising what is known about the effectiveness of mandatory sentences, begins with, 'the greatest gap between knowledge and policy in American sentencing concerns mandatory penalties' (Tonry, 1996: 134). The conclusion is that selective incapacitation has little deterrent or protective function in practice (see the discussion in Chapters 4 and 5).

---

[9] The Firearms Act 1968, s 51A(2) also imposes minimum sentences for some firearms offences.

(c) Judges and other legal professionals may seek ways to circumvent mandatory provisions. Discretion elsewhere in the criminal justice process could
become the site for increased professional activity to 'negotiate justice' for
clients in order that the mandatory sentence might be avoided (Tonry 1996:
148–54). The image used to illustrate this is that of a hose-pipe in which the
pressure of water must burst out somewhere if all the 'holes' of discretion
are blocked. An example given of this 'hydraulic effect' is plea bargaining:
lawyers would negotiate a lower charge in return for a guilty plea to avoid a
charge which could lead to a severe mandatory sentence. Judges too might
engage in adaptive behaviour and attempt to circumvent sentencing guidelines to avoid doing what they believed would amount to an injustice (Tonry
1996: 150–1, 169–73; see also Ashworth 1998a: 235).

(d) The lack of discretion at the sentencing stage could encourage more 'not guilty'
pleas. The accused might consider that more is at stake if the likely penalty is
severe and so choose to risk a trial. This would increase the work load of courts
and add to the financial cost. Research by the US Sentencing Commission,
Mandatory Minimum Penalties in the Federal Criminal Justice System, did find significantly higher than normal trial rates where the offence concerned mandatory sentences (Tonry 1996: 150; see also, Henham 1997: 273).

(e) The insertion of specific sentences into an otherwise discretion-based sentencing system will skew the 'tariff' which in practice determines a scale of
severity-related punishments.

(f) The lack of discretion may lead to constitutional or human rights violations.

Yet such arguments may have little policy force: 'Officials who support mandatory
penalties often do not care much about problems of implementation, foreseeable patterns of circumvention, or the certainty of excessively and unjustly severe
penalties for some offenders. Their interests are different as recent policy debates
demonstrate' (Tonry 1996: 159). There are, as we have seen, political imperatives
and symbolic goals which may outweigh the money 'wasted'. The second new
constraint that we have discussed—the mandatory sentence—gave a very clear
message to the electorate that Parliament would ensure that sentencers were
sufficiently tough to protect them. The third and fourth new techniques are
rather different.

2.4 New forms of guidance

Discretion is also constrained by various forms of guidance to help sentencers
apply the sentencing framework as consistently as possible. Traditionally this
guidance has been purely judicial, through Court of Appeal decisions, but more
recently guidance has been issued by the Sentencing Guidelines Council (SGC).

2.4.1 Guideline judgments

Guideline judgments were pioneered in the Court of Appeal by Lawton LJ
in the 1970s and taken up by Lord Lane as Lord Chief Justice in the 1980s (see

Ashworth 1984). They consider sentences for a whole category of offences or particular sentencing factors, rather than one individual and individualised case, and give indications of the 'proper range' of sentences, the interpretation of sentencing legislation, and endorse or establish particular factors as legitimately aggravating or mitigating the seriousness of the offending and the level of the punishment. They have also been used to endorse a particular principle (possibly with a limited life) such as the 'clang of the prison gates' principle in the early 1980s to justify short prison sentences on first offenders, particularly if of good character, 'who it was thought would be severely affected by any experience of imprisonment, however short' (Henham 1995: 219; see *Upton* 1980).

An important principle formulated by the Court of Appeal at the beginning of the 1980s but not reiterated with authority until recently, is that prison overcrowding should be a relevant sentencing factor in specified situations. In *Bibi* (1980) Lord Lane CJ responded to the prison crisis by arguing that 'many offenders can be dealt with equally justly and effectively by a sentence of six or nine months' imprisonment as by one of eighteen months or three years' whilst, in the more recent case of *Kefford* (2002), Lord Justice Taylor said that 'the courts must accept the realities of the situation' and, where appropriate, they should use community penalties or fines instead of (short) prison sentences. This, he said, would be better because the prison service cannot reform someone during a short sentence and cannot reform anyone if resources are overstretched.[10]

A principle established by Court of Appeal guidance in the 1980s is now enshrined in legislation. Enacted as the CJA 1991, s 28(2)(b), now CJA 2003 s 166(3)(b), is the 'totality principle': that the aggregate of consecutive sentences should not be out of proportion to the overall seriousness of the offending and so the court can legitimately mitigate the sentence of a multiple offender (see Henham 1995: 220; Ashworth 2000: 226–32).

The Court of Appeal guidance to sentencers clearly has limitations in that, until 1988, only a convicted offender could appeal against his sentence. This did not guarantee that all offences and punishments were systematically reassessed by the Court of Appeal and, in particular, an offender is unlikely to appeal if his penalty is at the lower end of the sentencing portfolio. This situation was somewhat ameliorated by the introduction of the **Attorney General's** reference procedure by the Criminal Justice Act 1988. This empowers the Attorney General,[11] after hearing arguments from the prosecution, to refer a case to the Court of Appeal for leave for them to reconsider it, '[i]f it appears to the Attorney General—(a) that the sentencing of a person in a proceeding in the Crown Court has been *unduly lenient*' (s 36(1), emphasis added). If leave is given, the Court of Appeal can quash the sentence or substitute another (whether higher or lower).

The role of the Attorney General in this process is, therefore, to act as a filter for prosecution appeals to allow appellate discussion of cases where the decision might raise rather than lower the sentence. This widened the range of issues and penalties on which the Court has commented but the result was still very patchy guidance, given 'the apparent failure of the Court of Appeal to consistently advert

---

[10] See Chapter 3 for examples of offence-based and custody threshold guidance.
[11] See, for information on the role and holders of this post, http://www.nationmaster.com/encyclopedia/Attorney-General-for-England-and-Wales.

to other sentencing decisions in the course of developing sentencing principles' (Henham 1995: 218). Ashworth, analysing in detail one early important guideline judgment about sentencing Class A drugs offences, *Aramah* (1983), made the same point (1984: 522–3), arguing that the result was a 'needlessly incomplete framework' (ibid: 523).

It was further argued specifically in relation to the lower courts that 'there is scant authority to assist magistrates in their sentencing jurisdiction', appellate guidance from the Crown Court being 'generally cursory' and the Divisional Court interfering with outcome only exceptionally (Wasik and Turner 1992: 345). The production of guidance by the Magistrates' Association was, therefore, welcomed as a counterweight to the often 'tenacious adherence' to the belief in the uniqueness of each case (ibid: 346). It gives the statutory maxima, and poses questions in relation to seriousness, indicating a guideline starting point, with examples of potentially relevant mitigating and aggravating factors. This Guidance has recently been updated and the new 6th Edition was implemented, subject to training, from January 2004.[12] Further, the Sentencing Advisory Panel (see below) published recommendations for an extensive revision of the Magistrates' Sentencing Guidelines in December 2007 and a definitive version was published in May 2008. Research would suggest, however, that further guidance to magistrates may not be sufficient to reduce the continuing variations in sentencing practice and that a mechanism to ensure adherence to guidelines may be required (Tarling 2006).

2.4.2 The Sentencing Advisory Panel

Given the above criticisms of the scope and usefulness of guidance from the Court of Appeal, but also aware that the judiciary was not favourable to further limits on their sentencing discretion, the new Labour government introduced a compromise solution in ss 80–81 of the CDA 1998. These provisions established a Sentencing Advisory Panel (SAP) to assist and advise the Court of Appeal by making proposals for new guidelines which the Court could issue when a suitable case came up. The SAP started work in July 1999, with Professor Martin Wasik as Chair, and including, among its 14 members, Professors of Law (Andrew Ashworth), Ethnic Health (Lord Chan), and Social Policy (Frances Heidensohn), and members of the judiciary, Crown Prosecution Service, Department for Education and Skills, Parole Board, and Probation Service.

In the relatively short of period of time that the SAP had this particular role, the Panel issued a number of very useful documents which led to guideline cases. Within the first two years the Panel's advice on the importation of drugs, sentencing racially aggravated offences, and handling stolen goods—backed up by consultation and research—were accepted and incorporated in appellate guidelines. In 2002–3 its advice to the Court of Appeal covered offences involving child pornography, alcohol and tobacco smuggling, rape and the offence of causing death by dangerous driving (Sentencing Advisory Panel 2003a: 1).

The obvious value of the reasoned and researched advice given by the SAP, together with an acknowledgement that not all advice could easily and quickly be

---

[12] Obtainable at www.jsboard.co.uk/downloads/acbb/section2a.pdf; see also www.magistrates-association.org.uk/.

incorporated in guidelines, led to the establishment of another statutory body—the SGC (see below)—to take further the process of providing systematic guidance to the courts. The role of the SAP is now to produce advice for the SGC: its first proposal to the SGC in May 2004 was that the Council should issue guidance on street robbery or mugging, robberies of small businesses, and less sophisticated commercial robberies.[13] In that first year, the SAP also published consultation papers on domestic violence and sexual offences, and conducted seminars before issuing advice on the new sentencing framework introduced by the CJA 2003.[14] More recently, the following advice has been issued by the Sentencing Advisory Panel 2006–8: Causing Death by Driving, Magistrates' Court Sentencing Guidelines, Sentencing for Assault and other Offences Against the Person, Sentencing for Bail Act Offences, Review of Guideline: Reduction in Sentence for a Guilty Plea, and Domestic Violence. The Panel has also published consultation papers on sentencing for corporate manslaughter, fraud, breach of an anti-social behaviour order, offences of theft and dishonesty, and theft from a shop.[15]

2.4.3 The Sentencing Guidelines Council

Section 167 of the CJA 2003 established the Sentencing Guidelines Council (SGC) with judicial and lay members and chaired by the Lord Chief Justice. This in effect takes over the Court of Appeal's responsibility for issuing guidelines. Section 169 of the CJA 2003 empowers the SAP to propose to the SGC that specific sentencing guidelines matters should be reviewed, and imposes a duty to collect and assess views on proposals notified to them by the SGC. For its part, the SGC has the duty to publish guidelines and consult with the government. Importantly, the Secretary of State can order the Council to review or produce particular guidelines (s 170(2) and (3)). The SGC, in so doing, must, inter alia, have regard to 'the need to promote consistency in sentencing' (s 170(5)), an aim prioritised by the White Paper preceding the CJA 2003 'to end the unacceptable variations in sentencing' (Home Office 2002a: Executive Summary: 8). Ashworth queried in 2003 whether comprehensive guidance could be produced by the new bodies 'with a part-time panel, an SGC that meets once every few months, and only a modest administrative support' (2003: 9), but the output since then has proved to be such that it has led the judiciary, as noted above, to criticise the SGS for unduly restricting its discretion, notably in relation to the discount for a guilty plea, setting the minimum term in a life sentence and in imposing the indeterminate sentences introduced by the CJA 2003. The well-publicised case of Craig Sweeney, a convicted paedophile who had reoffended shortly after his period of release on licence had expired, highlighted these issues (see Piper 2006a). An independent review of this case found several failings which meant that the risk of harm was not accurately assessed or acted upon (see HM Inspectorate of Probation 2006a).

The SGC produces consultation papers as well as guidelines, often on the same day as the SAP publishes its advice on the subject. The most recent consultations include assault and other offences against the person and causing death by

---

[13] See: http://www.sentencing-guidelines.gov.uk/docs/robbery.pdf.

[14] For a full list see: http://www.sentencing-guidelines.gov.uk/advice/guidelines/index.html#top.

[15] See (for closed consultations): http://www.sentencing-guidelines.gov.uk/consultations/closed/index.html.

driving. Its first guideline at the end of 2004 was *Overarching Principles: Seriousness* (Sentencing Guidelines Council 2004a), followed by *New Sentences: Criminal Justice Act 2003* (2004c), whilst those published more recently include its definitive guidelines on the reduction in sentence for a guilty plea (2007a), the Sexual Offences Act 2003 (2007c), and assault on adults and children (2008a, 2008b).[16]

Section 172 of the CJA 2003 imposes a duty on judges and magistrates to 'have regard' to the guidance issued. In *R v Oosthuizen* (2005) Rose LJ emphasised this duty but quoted the statement of Lord Woolf CJ in *Last* (2005) that 'have regard to' did not mean a guideline had to be followed and also the statement of Judge LJ in *Peters* (2005) that they 'are guidelines: no more, no less': 'it does not necessarily follow that in every case a guideline will be followed'.

2.4.4 A Sentencing Commission?

It would appear that the Government may intend to take further the process of structuring sentencing discretion. In December 2007 the Government published Lord Carter's Review of Prisons: *Securing the Future: Proposals for the Efficient and Sustainable Use of Custody in England and Wales* (Carter 2007). Lord Carter's proposals in relation to sentencing are that 'a structured sentencing framework and permanent Sentencing Commission should be developed, with judicial leadership, to improve the transparency, predictability and consistency of sentencing and the criminal justice system' (ibid: Preface). The report advises that a working group be set up to report to the Government by the summer of 2008 (ibid: 3).

Whether the above constraints and guidance yet amount to a principled structuring of sentencing such that there is consistency of sentencing in the UK is debatable. In 1992 the Council of Ministers of the Council of Europe issued Recommendation No. R (92) 17 on 'Consistency of Sentencing' which declared approved principles and suggested techniques for enhancing consistency (see Ashworth 1998a: 237). The more recent innovations and proposals could enhance such consistency, if properly implemented, but only if they are not undermined by other changes which might produce the opposite effects. This uncertainty of policy outcome—because of the diverse and sometimes divergent policies being introduced—is an issue which will run through many chapters in this book.

2.5 Retributivist rationales

2.5.1 The concept of the individual and the state

In Chapter 1 we noted the importance of sentencing principles and the importance, in particular, of retributivist principles in English sentencing frameworks, notably since the implementation of the CJA 1991 (see Chapter 1, section 1.4.4). It is this imposition of a particular sentencing rationale which is the fourth constraint on sentencing discretion.

[16] For further information and updates see the Online Resource Centre. See also Dingwall (2006/7) for a good discussion of current sentencing guidance.

online resource centre

On the retributivist theory a wrong action should be met by a sanction appropriate to the action and deserved by the offender, so it is argued that: (i) punishment should be given in response to its being deserved; (ii) the penalty should be appropriate to the wrong action; and (iii) the consequences of punishment are irrelevant. The quest for justice is the underlying rationale of retributivism: justice is satisfied if the guilty are punished according to desert and in proportion to the gravity of the offence. An unjust punishment would include an excessive or inappropriate punishment, one which fails to respect the dignity of the offender, and one imposed for external reasons unrelated to desert. Although the rehabilitative model has been seen as an enlightened approach to punishment, retributivist or desert theory is arguably more protective of individuals' rights.

Retributivist philosophy depends on a particular view of human beings. For Kant the model of the individual is of a rational agent on whom law functions as an imperative, not coercively but because the individual recognises that law imposes duties and obligations. Reason is a fundamental dimension of the moral law. Kant sees autonomy and rationality as fundamental characteristics of all human beings. The inherent autonomy of each person requires that he be treated as having dignity and as worthy of respect. All individuals, including offenders, should be accorded dignity and treated with respect. A moral law is one which holds for all persons in similar contexts.

Kant argues that we should not use people as a means to an end, even to serve noble goals: '*so act as to treat humanity, whether in thine own person or in that of any other, in every case as an end withal, never as means only*' (Kant 1785: 56—italics in the original). When we act, says Kant, we do so on the principle of duty, not on our feelings and impulses: we consider the relation between rational beings and the implications of actions for others as ends in themselves. Respecting the dignity of rational beings is more important than possible future advantages. '*Autonomy* then is the basis of the dignity of human and of every rational nature' (ibid: 65—emphasis in the original).

An act which reduces the capacity to act rationally and autonomously would violate human dignity for Kant. Any act which shortens or ends the lives of others is morally wrong, because life has an intrinsic value. Modern examples would be using prisoners, without their consent, to test drugs in order to provide benefits for the population as a whole. For utilitarians such experiments might be justified if they maximise utility; an individual's welfare could be sacrificed if by doing so it maximises the welfare of others. But on a Kantian view, human life is valuable because humans are the bearers of rational life, able to make plans and choices. This capacity to choose is valuable and should not be sacrificed for something of less value. No rational or autonomous creature should be treated as a mere means for the enjoyment or happiness of others. On Kant's theory we may choose to sacrifice our lives for others, but others should not use our lives or bodies as a means to pursue their goals.

Similarly Hegel, who was well versed in the philosophical foundations of utilitarianism through the writings of Hume and others, rejected the utilitarian view of man as seeking the satisfaction of desires, the pursuit of pleasure and happiness (see Walton 1983; Hinchman 1991). Hegel distinguishes men from animals, who are governed by impulses, desires, and inclinations in contrast to the utilitarian model which construes men in precisely this way (Hegel 1832: addition 10). He is critical of those who base their theories of punishment on threats and coercion, because, he says, this 'is to treat a man like a dog instead of with the respect and freedom due to him as a man' (ibid: addition 62). He also rejected the utilitarians' focus on psychological explanations of human behaviour and their methodological individualism, which reduces social processes to the behaviour of individuals. Instead, Hegel argues strongly for an understanding of the individual through his social relations, and paved the way for a new approach to be further developed by Marx and later Marxist sociologists.

Hegelian and Kantian ethics contrast sharply with utilitarian ethics. The utilitarian notion of drawing up a balance sheet when deciding on moral choices was absurd and self-defeating for Hegel. Both Kantian and Hegelian ethics see a good action being undertaken for its own sake, because it is morally right (see Hinchman 1991), instead of it being in pursuit of extrinsic rewards through assessing its consequences in achieving pleasure rather than pain. In performing a moral duty, this confirms our freedom from natural impulses. Like Kant, Hegel focuses on freedom but his notion of autonomy is much more wide-ranging, because it encompasses the political, the aesthetic, and the cognitive as well as the ethical dimension.

Retributivist philosophy also depends on a particular view of the state. In contrast to the social contract theorists, Kant does not see the well-being of a state as lying in the welfare of its citizens or their happiness, but rather '[b]y the well-being of a state is understood, instead, that condition in which its constitution conforms most fully to principles of Right; it is that condition which reason, *by a categorical imperative*, makes it obligatory for us to strive after' (Kant 1796–7: 129). Kant's conception of the relationship between the state and its citizens allows no right to rebellion or revolution; indeed he thinks this would constitute high treason which should be punishable by the death penalty (ibid: 131). He is strongly opposed to the execution of the sovereign even in a defective state; instead, reform should come from the sovereign. Hegel also rejects the conception of the state as a contract. The social contract model does not reach the level of the state as ethical life but construes it as an instrument for individual pursuits and self-protection. His own conception of the state is of a higher entity than merely guaranteeing the life and property of its citizens.

These ideas about the nature of the state and the individual are very important in the theories of punishment developed by Kant and Hegel which will now be examined.

2.5.2 **Kantian retributivism**

Kant's analysis of punishment may be found in his *The Metaphysics of Morals* published in 1796–7, following his *Fundamental Principles of the Metaphysic of Ethics* (1785), and applies the philosophical theory enunciated in his earlier work on practical ethics. Kant is trying to elucidate the fundamental principle of morality, to show how it binds individuals, and to apply it within a system of human duties. Punishment is considered in the context of his analysis of right. 'The *right to punish* is the right a ruler has against a subject to inflict pain upon him because of his having committed a crime,' (Kant 1796–7: 140) so the head of state cannot be punished. '*Punishment by a court*...can never be inflicted merely as a means to promote some other good for the criminal himself or for civil society. It must always be inflicted upon him only *because he has committed a crime*. For a man can never be treated merely as a means to the purposes of another' (ibid: 140).

As we have noted, Kant's theory of punishment rests on coherent ethical principles, which recognise the autonomy and rationality of individuals, their capacity to make choices and take responsibility for their actions, and to act on the basis of reason and principles rather than 'passions' and, for Kant, these principles should also be reflected in specific punishments for specific offenders. If justice is sacrificed, for example, by withholding punishment, the quality of life of the community has been undermined. He considers the example of a prisoner sentenced to death whose execution is waived if he agrees to dangerous medical experiments being conducted upon him which might generate knowledge of benefit to the community as a whole. While such a strategy would be justifiable on utilitarian theory, it would be rejected by retributivists, including Kant, as incompatible with the principle of justice.

The form of punishment and **quantum** of punishment, argues Kant, must be based on the principle of equality, so the 'undeserved evil' the criminal inflicts on the victim is matched by a similar amount on himself. He argues that 'only the *law of retribution (ius talionis)* . . . can specify definitely the quality and the quantity of punishment; all other principles are fluctuating and unsuited for a sentence of pure and strict justice because extraneous considerations are mixed into them' (ibid: 141). To base a decision on whether to punish, how to punish and how much to punish on extraneous considerations, such as which measures are most effective in eliminating crime, cannot generate a just sentence and for Kant is a misjudgment (ibid: 168).

Kant's focus is on the moral foundation of punishment rather than what is useful for society or the criminal justice system and he contrasts his approach—which offers punitive justice grounded in ethics—with mere punitive prudence. Central to punitive justice is the principle of proportionality. The term Kant uses in his discussion of proportionality is *Gleiches mit Gleichem*, usually translated as 'like for like', or measure for measure, which suggests both quantitative and qualitative matching in terms of the amount of pain and type of punishment. He accepts that different types of crime may be difficult to match with the appropriate punishment, but some cases, such as death for murder and castration for rape, may be more clear-cut. Someone who steals should be reduced to the status of a slave through convict or prison labour, he argues, while the person convicted of bestiality should be expelled from civil society because he has shown himself unworthy of membership of it. But the murderer must be executed, says Kant, no other sentence is sufficient to satisfy the demands of justice and a life sentence is inadequate: '[t]here is no *similarity* between life, however wretched it may be, and death, hence no likeness between the crime and the retribution unless death is judicially carried out upon the wrongdoer, although it must still be freed from any mistreatment that could make the humanity in the person suffering it into something abominable' (ibid: 142).

He gives the example of a civil society, of a people inhabiting an island who decide to disperse and go their separate ways. In such circumstances, he says, 'the last murderer remaining in prison would first have to be executed, so that each has done to him what his deeds deserve . . .'. If the crimes go unpunished, he argues, the community that withholds punishment will be collaborating in the public violation of justice. Similarly, the right of the sovereign to grant clemency to the criminal by granting lesser punishment or no punishment at all is criticised by Kant, for failure to punish is the greatest wrong against his subjects and should be used only if the wrong is done to himself and to use it would not endanger the security of the people.

Kant sees the death penalty as appropriate for murder, accomplices to murder, and crimes against the state. However, he notes that, if there are so many accomplices that the state would be left without subjects, then deportation would be appropriate. He gives the example of the Scottish rebellion where rebels acted out of a sense of duty. If a court gave sentenced prisoners a choice between death or convict labour, the man of honour, he says, would choose death while the scoundrel would choose convict labour.

He considers Beccaria's argument against capital punishment, that it is not contained in the social contract, and that people would not have consented to lose their own lives, as mere sophistry. 'No one suffers punishment because he has willed *it* but because he has willed a *punishable action*,' (ibid: 143) says Kant, '... it is not the people (each individual in it) that dictates capital punishment but rather the court (public justice), and so another than the criminal...' (ibid: 144).

For Kant the consequences of punishment are irrelevant: the sole issue is the guilt of the individual. It follows that the innocent person should never be punished, even if it could be shown that to do so would have social benefits. Where punishment is deserved, then the level of punishment should be appropriate to the seriousness of the offence. In focusing solely upon desert Kant is trying to offer a rational and objective standard of punishment which recognises the autonomy of individuals and prevents arbitrariness and bias from influencing outcomes. In this sense his approach may be seen as countering the subjectivity of discretion discussed earlier. It also means that retribution must be imposed by a properly constituted court rather than through private acts of vengeance.

2.5.3 Hegel: the 'right' to punishment

Hegel's theory of punishment is found in Part One of *The Philosophy of Right* (Hegel 1832) in his discussion of abstract right, written in 1820 as part of his analysis of the development of the ethical life of the state. Hegel argues that abstract right is the first stage in the development of the concept of freedom and stresses that right is restored by annulling the crime (ibid: para 99). He is critical of the positivist science of law, which sees punishment merely as 'a preventive, a deterrent, a threat, as reformative'.

Hegel is attacking E. F. Klein's *Grundsätze des peinlichen Rechts*, but the views expressed in that text are essentially those associated with the utilitarian approach to punishment. He criticises it for its superficial attitude to punishment when it should be focusing on the 'righting of wrong'. He accepts that deterrence and reformation have their place and are worthy of examination particularly when considering modes of punishment, but the key element for Hegel is that those who deserve punishment should receive appropriate punishment. 'The injury [the penalty] which falls on the criminal is not merely *implicitly* just, it is an embodiment of his freedom, his right, ... it is also a right *established* within the criminal himself, i.e. in his objectively embodied will, in his action' (ibid: para 100). The reason, says

Hegel, is that his action is that of a rational being, the crime is of the 'individual's volition'. In that sense, 'punishment is regarded as containing the criminal's right and hence by being punished he is honoured as a rational being' (ibid: para 100). It follows that '[h]e does not receive this due of honour unless the concept and measure of his punishment are derived from his own act. Still less does he receive it if he is treated either as a harmful animal who has to be made harmless, or with a view to deterring and reforming him' (ibid: para 100).

In Hegel's remarks we find the essence of the retributivist theory of punishment: the presumed rationality of the criminal, the imposition of punishment only if the individual is guilty, the exclusion of social consequences from the prime purpose of punishment and the view that punishment annuls the crime. By punishing the criminal we acknowledge him as a rational individual, rather than treating him like a mad dog, as dangerous and requiring constraint. The criminal, he says, 'gives his consent already by his very act' (ibid: addition 63).

2.5.4 Punishment as the annulment of crime

'The annulment of the crime is retribution,' says Hegel, and its negation. 'Crime... contains its negation in itself and this negation is manifested as punishment' (ibid: para 101). This might also include an element of reparation, or restoration, as the community is being returned to how it was before crime occurred. Of course, for Hegel, crime is not simply an offence against the individual, but against the law itself, and hence infringement requires a social response in the form of state punishment. Even without an individual victim, crime deserves punishment.

There is a 'necessary connexion between crime and punishment,' argues Hegel (ibid: para 101). He acknowledges the absurdity of a literal notion of equality of punishment, of an eye for an eye or a tooth for a tooth, and the problem of what happens if the perpetrator has no teeth, or only one eye, but stresses that the concept of retribution 'has nothing to do with this absurdity' (ibid: para 101). Rather he says, the notion of equality means focusing on the deserts of the criminal. It is hard to see a theft as equal to a fine, but as injuries they are comparable in their value. 'Injustice is done at once if there is one lash too many, or one dollar or one cent, one week in prison or one day, too many or too few' (ibid: para 214).

'The annulling of crime... is principally revenge, which is just in its content in so far as it is retributive' (ibid: para 102). But Hegel's concept of justice is of justice 'freed from subjective interest' (ibid: para 103). Justice demands equal respect for all, including the offender. Hegel, like Kant, argues that punishment must be administered through a proper criminal justice system rather than informally, and applied only to blameworthy individuals in contrast to the arbitrariness of vigilantism. Hegel's concept of punishment applies to a rational ethical state where obedience is based on duty and reason rather than crude coercion. He also notes that harsh punishments are not necessarily unjust. This will depend on the prevailing conditions, and criminal codes will change through time to reflect this. In Hegel's model the individual is implicitly rational, his concept of the state is a form of ethical life.

Desert is the primary justification of punishment for Hegel. However, this does not mean that reformation, reparation and deterrence have no place in a system of punishment. By applying retributivist punishment we may find that a side-effect is reform and education of the criminal. But deterrence from committing future crimes for Hegel is a result of punishment, rather than operating as a threat, or as its prime purpose (see Harvey 1984). The threat of punishment and the sanctions of criminal law do not coerce men into obeying the law; rather criminal law and institutions are a framework within which men become morally good (Nicholson 1982). This would also be consistent with his dynamic model of the development of ethical life, to the point where the state develops sufficiently that individuals understand fully the rational foundation of laws. Moreover, while punishment may have elements of reparation and restitution it cannot be reduced to them, so we cannot conceptualise crimes in the same way as civil offences.

Hegel is concerned to elucidate the philosophical principles justifying punishment *per se* and the conceptual links between crime and punishment, rather than offering a tariff of particular punishments. So his discussion of the death penalty, for example, is incidental to his theory of punishment rather than offering a specific analysis of its legitimacy and he is not at pains to support or attack it. However, Hegel does accept that the death penalty is appropriate for murder when the only punishment can be the taking away of a second life, but acknowledges that in other types of crime it will be hard to find an equivalent requital (Hegel 1832: addition 64; see also Hetherington 1996; Heyman 1996). The executioner has both a right and a duty to apply the punishment. At the same time he is critical of Draco's recommendation to meet every crime with the death penalty (Hegel 1832: para 96). By the time Hegel was writing, capital punishment had become rarer which, he argues, is appropriate for such an extreme punishment. While also critical of Beccaria's rejection of the death penalty, Hegel argued that Beccaria's campaign for its abolition was useful because, although it did not succeed, it did force a reconsideration of which crimes should receive this punishment (ibid: addition 63).

2.6 Questions raised by the classical retributivist model

2.6.1 Just punishment or injustice?

The merit of the classical retributivist model is that, at the level of theory, it removes arbitrariness and bias from punishment. However, the idea that punishment should and must be imposed regardless of any positive outcomes, simply for the sake of it, could be seen as cruel, pointless, and unjust. Harming others as an end in itself does not restore the balance of justice. If the retributivist tries to modify this by saying that we may sometimes take account of consequences such as deterrence, but desert is the primary justification, then this weakens the basis of the theory. Tonry (1993) argues that proportionality conflicts with parsimony, and the reduction of suffering, because theorists of proportionality will always favour imposing what the offender deserves and treating similar offenders equally, rather than using the most economical means of punishment, imposing the least severe punishment to meet social goals and minimising suffering. Rubin (2003) argues that there is a danger in focusing on retribution as retribution may be achieved by any means and this opens the door to inhumanity in punishment, in terms of the amount of punishment and the modes of punishment. He argues that in the current climate a focus on rehabilitation rather than retribution is better able to raise standards of decency and humanity in the modern prison and protect the prisoner from abuse as retributivism gives no guidance on how the offender should be treated within prison.

However, as we shall see, modern retributivists such as von Hirsch argue that proportionality provides a restraint on unlimited punishment and may in practice mean a less severe sentence than demanded by rival theories.

There is also the problem of to whom the debt is paid, whether it is the victim or society as a whole. But how does society as a whole benefit from the suffering of a criminal unless it is through the deterrent effect or the ultimate rehabilitation of the offender? It is therefore hard to avoid referring to consequences and thereby lapsing into a utilitarian approach.

The assumption of individual responsibility and autonomy is also disputed by those moral philosophers and social scientists who see social, psychological, or socio-biological constraints on action as more important than free will. As the human sciences have progressed since the early nineteenth century, it is now recognised that human behaviour is more complex and the development of the individual may be shaped by a range of environmental factors, family dynamics, and other influences.

2.6.2 **Equivalence and proportionality**

The notion of equivalence, that the punishment should equate with the severity of the crime, is also problematic. Kant advocates a catalogue of qualitative and quantitative punishments, but it may not be so clear-cut and such a system would be difficult to administer in practice. The death penalty for murder might be straightforward but it will be harder with lesser crimes and there may be problems with different types of murder. When we look at sentencing practice, we find a range of mitigating and aggravating factors to consider when deciding the appropriate punishment (see Chapter 3). This is already a very complex process and, if a Kantian model were superimposed, this would mean that there would be insufficient punishments to fit all cases. Feinberg (1994) is critical of those retributivists who try to match the pain exactly to the crime. Apart from the problems of measurement, there are the possible effects on the defendant's innocent family, the problems of comparing blameworthiness, and of dealing with these issues rationally. He argues that it is social disapproval and its expression which should fit the crime rather than the quantity of pain. A severe punishment may well affect innocent third parties vicariously as the international human rights law has recognised, for example in Article 6(5) of the International Covenant on Civil and Political Rights (ICCPR) which states that sentence of death shall not be carried out upon pregnant women.

Classical retributivism does seem to fit our moral intuitions, that it is intrinsically right that the wrongdoer should suffer, but there may be dangers in relying on intuitions, particularly in the theory and practice of punishment. Human feelings can be capricious and inconsistent as we do forgive some acts but not others. Moreover, the fact that the majority intuitively feel that punishment is appropriate in a particular case would not of itself justify it, as Bagaric (2001) points out.

Walker (1991) is critical of what he sees as fundamental weaknesses of retributivism. He argues that Hegel does not establish why annulment should take the form of a sentence rather than another response and it is not clear why Kant's 'last murderer' should be dealt with punitively rather than in some other way, such as persuading the individual to repent. It is difficult to explain desert, argues Walker, without resorting to metaphors, intuitions or superstition. The weakness of retributivism, he argues, is that it does not explain why there should be a moral obligation to inflict the just desert on the offender. Nor can we be sure that the penalty is neither too severe nor too lenient. Commensurability is unattainable so the best the retributivist can offer is proportionality but this, he says, 'is a ladder with rungs that are both sliding and elastic' (ibid: 138). He also highlights the problems for retributivists in dealing with repentance, remorse, and mercy: it is unclear whether they play a mitigating role in retributivism. Most retributivists exclude them from consideration, but where they do take account of them, this would seem to conflict with the principle of proportionality. (For further discussion of mitigation and mercy see Chapters 7 and 10.)

2.7 Modern retributivism

2.7.1 The revival of desert theory

Given the very serious criticisms of classical retributivism that have been advanced and considered above, one might reasonably have expected it to be of historical significance only, rather than the justification for punishment being promoted in the 1991 CJA. For many years, as we shall see in Chapter 4, the other main philosophy of punishment—utilitarianism—was seen as more 'modern' and 'humane'. However, that approach was heavily criticised from the 1970s in several jurisdictions. In particular, criticism focused in the USA on the increased use of indeterminate and extended sentences for dangerous offenders, selective incapacitation, and the apparently unrestrained use of state punishment. In the UK and the USA criticism also focused on the 'inequities' and ineffectiveness of rehabilitation, and on wide judicial discretion. Whilst retributivist thinking has always been present in English sentencing, the proponents of such an approach came to believe that a rejigged version was essential if 'justice' as a specific aim of punishment—rather than as the yardstick for judging any penal aim—was to become more influential in practice.

The leading voice for modern retributivist theory in the 1970s was von Hirsch who argued that fairness and justice should be the key elements of a coherent penal theory. In *Doing Justice* (1976), he maintained that the aim of the penal system should, then, be to 'do justice' rather than to maximise utility. In other words he construed justice—in line with classical retributivism—as giving offenders punishments in proportion to their crimes and, in doing so, recognising them as moral agents possessing autonomy. However, he proposed that penalties should be anchored at a lower level to counter the belief that retributivism leads to harsh sentencing. So, in contrast to the equivalences in proportional punishment favoured by Kant, von Hirsch argued for a maximum incarceration of three years for serious offences and five years for some homicides.

However, theorists have since alerted us to the fact that, depending on the political climate, the adoption of retributivist principles can lead to unintended outcomes. Tonry, for example, has pointed out that 'just deserts' principles do not automatically guarantee the sort of penal system many theorists were hoping for. The pressure for more structuring of what retributivist theorists saw as too wide a judicial discretion, and the focusing only on the offending, can still justify the increased use of higher levels of determinate sentencing. Further, the imposition of rigid guideline systems in the USA are, for Tonry, evidence that 'just deserts has backfired' (Tonry 1996: 13). Yet the 'politicisation' of sentencing and punishment that we discussed in Chapter 1, means, in policy terms, that 'sentencing matters…more than ever before' (ibid: 1) and proponents of retributivist justifications have been continually prompted to rethink and refine their theories. For example, Morris and Tonry have re-conceptualised proportionality and parsimony, and von Hirsch has focused on censure. The next sections will look in more detail at some of these principles.

2.7.2 **The 'why' of punishment: censure**

In *Censure and Sanctions* (1993), von Hirsch describes punishment as the expression of blame—the censure which the criminal deserves. For von Hirsch censure is the prime aim of punishment: 'public reproof' is intended to ensure that the individual recognises his own blameworthiness. If punishment is to achieve this, the degree of censure should be reflected in the severity of punishment and so proportionality is still crucial. A censure-based justification makes sense to most people as in everyday life we make moral judgements about others and blame each other for transgressions. If a person behaves badly—in morally reprehensible ways—others judge him adversely. Censure consists of the expression of that judgement combined with the accompanying sentiment of disapproval. In censuring the individual, we again recognise him as a moral agent, rather than a mere animal, a person capable of choices and worthy of respect, whose dignity is respected. If he were a mere animal, he would not be affected by censure. A dog about to steal another dog's bowl of food will be unmoved by appeals to the moral wrongness of such an act, although he may retreat if met by a growl.

In von Hirsch's reworking of retributivism, censure is addressed not just to the offender but also to the victim and others in society:

1. *The victim*: it acknowledges that the victim's hurt occurred through the fault of the perpetrator.

2. *The perpetrator of the act*: it gives the message that he has harmed someone, he is responsible and society disapproves of what he has done, and that a moral response is expected of him, namely some acknowledgement of his wrong-doing. Even if he is indifferent, he should be made to feel that others do not treat his actions so lightly. If he shows remorse, the negative view of himself is confirmed by censure. However, it is still up to him as a moral agent how he responds.

3. *Third parties*: it gives them a good reason to avoid such conduct, not to avoid the pains of punishment as a utilitarian would argue, but, rather, because they recognise the action as morally wrong.

Censure is given formal expression in the criminal law. Blaming is the central feature of criminal law in contrast to civil law which offers recovery and compensation for losses (see Chapter 6, section 6.2.1). The censure embodied in the sanctions of criminal law conveys that certain types of conduct are wrong and variations in consequences reflect the degree of censure. The moral agent is thus given grounds for avoiding proscribed actions but this appeal to the individual's moral sense of the wrongfulness of the criminal act is backed up by a '**prudential disincentive**'. Censure relies on the individual's sense of moral culpability but, because people are fallible and may be tempted to act badly, they need a further reason to resist that temptation, says von Hirsch, namely a criminal sanction. But this supplements rather than replaces the moral basis of obedience to law. A person who accepts that he should not offend and recognises that he may be tempted can see the sanction as an aid to carry out what he sees as the proper course of conduct. The 'blaming' function has primacy, the prudential disincentive function has only a secondary role, and the level of punishment should not be set too high or fear will displace the moral response. In a recent work, von Hirsch and Ashworth emphasise that the justification of punishment needs to rest primarily on a normative non-consequential retributive theory, namely penal censure, but there is a complementary, albeit secondary, 'preventive' role for punishment, in preventing crime (von Hirsch and Ashworth 2005).

2.7.3 The 'how' of punishment: respect

For von Hirsch a degrading or humiliating or intrusive punishment would be unacceptable because the offender must still be recognised as a human being and treated with respect (von Hirsch 1993). So his theory would preclude torture, routine solitary confinement, verbal abuse such as used in boot camps, and degrading rituals. It would also preclude compulsory 'attitudinising', such as forcing the offender to accept views he does not freely choose, for example on the use of drugs, or wearing self-accusing labels which identify him to others as an offender. So modern retributivists have been very critical of harsh penal policies.

Tonry, for example, has castigated politicians for not giving sufficient policy weight to the harmful effects of punishment on people's lives. He refers to the comment made by Trotsky in relation to the suffering that the 1917 Russian Revolution imposed—that omelettes cannot be made without breaking eggs—and argues that 'many of the more cynical recent proponents of harsh crime control policies have apparently decided that elections cannot be won without breaking people' (1996: 194).

For modern retributivists, then, punishment must be administered in ways consistent with human dignity, so compulsory searches of the offender or constant surveillance at home would be inconsistent, although mere tagging is acceptable. Solitary confinement should be used only if there is an immediate threat to the offender or others. Third parties such as the offender's family should not be affected by a penal sanction any more than is necessary.

2.7.4 The amount of punishment: ordinal proportionality

Von Hirsch is also hostile to individualised or personalised sentences because of the dangers of caprice and inconsistency. The aim should be to standardise punishment by focusing on objective criteria of the degree of blameworthiness and harm caused by the perpetrator. Looking at how much to punish, we need to focus again on proportionality as von Hirsch's censure-based justification for punishment is necessarily linked to that principle. If punishment conveys blame then it is logical that the quantum of punishment should bear a reasonable relation to the degree of blameworthiness of the individual's conduct. He argues that the proportionality principle fits our intuitions: a child would express a sense of injustice if punished excessively for a minor misdemeanour. So the case for proportionality for von Hirsch rests on three arguments:

1. The severity of the sanction expresses the degree of censure: the harshness of treatment reflects the disapprobation.
2. The state's sanctions against the proscribed conduct should take a punitive form, and impose deprivations in a way that expresses blame or censure.
3. The punitive sanction should reflect the seriousness of the conduct and this is important for fairness and consistency.

The appropriate penalty will be determined by the seriousness of the crime, in terms of the harm caused and the extent of the offender's culpability (see also the discussion in Chapter 3, section 3.2.1). By harmfulness he means how it affects the victim's quality of life and standard of living including economic and non-economic interests. Similarly, the severity of the sanction will be measured by how far it affects the material interests and living standards of the offender.

Von Hirsch discusses the distinction between two types of proportionality, **ordinal** and **cardinal proportionality**. Ordinal or relative proportionality consists of three elements: the first element is parity, which means that persons convicted of crimes of similar gravity should receive punishments of comparable severity. This does not mean that there must be identical punishments for all people who commit particular offences, because of course there may be degrees of culpability, but once they are established, offences of comparable seriousness should receive punishments of the same degree of onerousness. Desert theories encompass some modifications to sentencing for aggravated harms and mitigation to allow for degrees in culpability (von Hirsch 1986, Tonry 1996, von Hirsch and Ashworth 2005) but of course these are still linked to, and proportional to, what the individual deserves for the current offence, rather than reflecting external factors.

The second element is rank-ordering which means that, when people are convicted of crimes of differing gravity, then punishments should be graded. Punishments should be ordered on a penalty scale, so their relative severity reflects the seriousness-ranking of the offence. The third element is spacing. If we imagine three crimes, A, B and C, and A is considerably more serious than B, but B is only slightly more serious than C, then, says von Hirsch, there should be a larger space between the penalties for A and B, than between B and C. However, as he points out, we could theoretically have a system which satisfies all the requirements of ordinal proportionality, parity, rank-ordering, and spacing, yet is very unfair because it starts with a prison sentence, say of ten years for a minor offence and progresses to torture and death. We need then to look separately at the important issues of cardinal or non-relative proportionality and **parsimony**.

2.7.5 **Cardinal proportionality and reductionist penal policies**

Before we can determine the relative punishments for different crimes we need an appropriate **anchoring point** for penalty scales. Von Hirsch seeks to challenge the popular common-sense view of retributivists as 'bloodthirsty' by arguing that desert theory is capable of finding an anchoring point which may be set relatively low. A huge increase in punishment for a relatively minor offence could be justified on utilitarian grounds if it was effective in eliminating a particular crime. It cannot be justified on retributivist grounds because the degree of punishment exceeds the blameworthiness. Proportionality, then, can constitute a restraint on excessive punishment. Furthermore, some other non-condemnatory measures, for example, a form of civil quarantine for dangerous offenders which could also be justified on utilitarian arguments, would conflict with desert-based retributivist principles. This is because it would be based on future rather than past crimes and would fail to recognise individuals as moral agents with the capacity to choose to avoid future criminal actions.

Consequently, von Hirsch rules out the use of the death penalty as an inhumane and degrading punishment and favours relatively low levels of incarceration, with a longer prison sentence for the most serious and a fine for lesser offences. But von Hirsch argues that a sentence of three years would still constitute a prudential disincentive so that we could reduce levels of punishment without displacing the censuring message. What his theory does not justify is using the state's resources—its penal capacity—as a starting point: this is unprincipled and would lead to differences between states with different capacities.

Von Hirsch favours using the least severe penalty while seeking to impose the appropriate degree of censure. At first sight this might seem akin to the utilitarian notion of parsimony advocated by Bentham and others, which entails using the least severe penalty necessary to deter the criminal, thereby minimising the public costs of punishment. However, the issue for desert theorists is whether desert can be satisfied by setting a lower anchoring point (von Hirsch 1986).

Morris (1974) incorporated this idea into a theory of 'limiting retributivism', a hybrid theory, incorporating elements of retributivism and preventing crime. The argument is that desert can be applied in a parsimonious way because the aims of retributivist theory can be met with a lower anchoring point (von Hirsch 1986). At higher levels of seriousness proportionality prevails, which prevents harsh, excessive, or aggravated punishments which might otherwise be justified on predictive or rehabilitative grounds. But within the parameters set by proportionality the sentencer should be able to impose the least severe sentence consistent with the aims of sentencing. At lower levels there is more scope for flexible parsimonious sentencing.

Against these arguments, utilitarians would say that, if penalties are set too low, the fear of punishment will be undermined. However, as the available research suggests that changing levels of punishment have little effect on crime rates (Cohen 1978; Tarling 1979), then, argues von Hirsch, the arguments against reducing penalty levels are unconvincing and a reductionist policy is at least worth considering. Moreover, the criterion of success for desert theory, he argues, is not whether it reduces crime, but whether the penal response is scaled to the gravity of the crime. It should therefore be able to resist pressures to increase sentences when crime rises or to selectively incapacitate offenders of particular public concern. To help ensure that this occurs in the USA, Tonry has argued that sentencing law and guidance should 'establish a presumption that, within the range of sanctions set out in applicable guidelines, judges should incorporate the least punitive and intrusive appropriate penalties' (1996: 194).

As Ashworth (2000) points out, however, the overall sentencing structure—the question of both ordinal proportionality and general sentence levels—has in the past rarely been the focus of inquiry in the UK. He noted the Advisory Council on the Penal System's Review in 1978, the discussion of Lawton LJ in the *Turner* (1975) case (ibid: 103) and the sentence levels being operated by the Court of Appeal for various selected crimes (ibid: 104–22). The new Sentencing Guidelines Council, with assistance from the Sentencing Advisory Panel has begun to address the general structure as well as specific offences and issues (see section 2.4.3 above and also Chapter 3, sections 3.2 and 3.3).

The exercise of scaling a penal response to seriousness raises another difficult issue: should the punishment, or the impact of the punishment on the offender in question, be proportionate to the seriousness of the offending? In this chapter we will assume the first approach—where a fixed amount of punishment proportionate to a particular amount of seriousness is imposed. In Chapter 7, we will examine the second approach where just deserts theory operates in relation to the impact of punishment.

2.7.6 Policy implications

Von Hirsch acknowledges that his reasoning—that the best way to resist expansionism is to provide a rational way of anchoring penalties and that desert theory is better able to do this than the alternatives of deterrence and incapacitation—may not be politically acceptable for governments. If there are public pressures for law and order, policy will include increased penalties, and penal theory on its own will be unable to prevent it. As we have seen, in this chapter and in Chapter 1, this is precisely what has happened in both the UK and the USA in the past decade when populist punitiveness has prevailed. 'A jurisdiction's traditions in punishment, its politics, and its public's degree of fear of crime and criminals probably will affect leniency or severity more than any choice of sentencing theory' (von Hirsch 1986: 169). However, as Chapter 1 also noted, the financial cost of the growing prison population is also a political issue. Modern retributivism, with its arguments in favour of parsimony and just deserts, may justify fewer and shorter prison sentences and a less expensive penal policy. But it may also improve the conditions of those held in custody. It has been argued by Lippke, for example, that a modern retributivist approach can provide the basis for minimally restrictive and humane imprisonment rather than extreme or harsh conditions of confinement, by providing constraints on punishment. Retributivism, he argues 'sets exacting requirements for liability to punishment and entails substantial constraints on how it is carried out' (Lippke 2007: 265). On this approach the prisoner clearly remains a citizen during his period of incarceration, retaining the fundamental rights of the citizen enshrined in human rights law (see Chapter 9, section 9.6).

The merit of von Hirsch's principled approach is that it does set limits to punishment in a coherent way. The principle of proportionality can be applied to a range of punishments, offering a way of assessing the burdens of sanctions, and stressing the need for equivalence of penal bite. So, a government with an economic imperative to solve the prison crisis can endorse the application of desert theory to justify increasingly restrictive community penalties as a legitimate punishment which affects the material interests and lifestyle of the offender. Further, a retributivist focus on individual moral culpability buttresses a political ideology stressing the responsibility of the citizen.

Modern retributivism, therefore, seemed to provide a solution to a range of legal, moral, political and economic issues. The response was in the form of the CJA 1991. To an extent, that Act has been modified and superseded by recent legislation, notably the CJA 2003. However, the just deserts legacy of that Act is still vitally important in English sentencing, and current law and practice cannot be properly understood without an understanding of the sentencing framework it introduced. In the next chapter (section 3.1.1) we will, therefore, examine the provisions of the CJA 1991.

The modifications to the CJA 1991—re-enacted in the Powers of Criminal Courts (Sentencing) Act 2000 (PCCSA)—provoked two very different sets of criticism:

- that modern retributivist principles are no longer central to the English sentencing system—and that is a bad thing;
- that retributivist principles are still dominant in sentencing decisions—and that is a bad thing.

Chapter 3, therefore, will also examine sentencing practice in the period 1991–2003 to evaluate the validity of these criticisms which have led to major reviews and to the CJA 2003.

2.8 Conclusions

2.8.1 Do constraints 'work'?

This chapter has examined the traditional and the more recent tools for structuring the discretion of those who sentence. In England and Wales the judges have at times resisted the new constraints, on the basis that a wider discretion gives them the power to do justice in individual cases. On the other hand, public and policy pressure has more usually been in favour of constraining judicial independence on the assumption that this would reduce the injustice of inconsistency and achieve particular policy objectives. Most of these statements and assumptions cannot be tested empirically in any way that will give closure to the debate about sentencing discretion.

One apparently easier question is to ask whether, specifically, the provisions of the CJA 1991 to reduce the use of custodial penalties by sentencers 'worked'. There was a decrease in custodial sentencing in 1992 but an increase from 1993 onwards. So why did the Act not lead to a fall in the prison population? Was it because sentencing discretion was not controlled adequately? Several possible explanations have been suggested: that the amendments made to the Act in 1993 reintroduced discretion in relation to previous offending and associated offences (see Chapter 3), that community penalties lacked legitimacy and were under-resourced, that later legislation provided too many exceptions to the restriction on the use of custody, and that popular and government punitiveness influenced judicial thinking. Some of these factors involve judicial discretion, others do not.

However, the Halliday Report (2001) argued that the system of sentencing and punishment was not 'working' in line with policy objectives, that seriousness is not measured 'properly', and that there should be a 'limited' retributivism. As we have shown in this chapter the amount and the form of sentencing guidance have changed considerably over the last few years. However, there is as yet no standard format for the various SGC guidelines and they are still a matter of considerable controversy. We are not sufficiently clear from empirical research as to the practical effect on sentencing of the guidelines, or whether proposed legislative changes will again restore more discretion to the judiciary.

In the next chapter we look in more detail, however, at how the various components of retributivist sentencing have been placed into legislation, guidance and practice.

2.8.2 Discussion questions

Sentencing exercise

You are a law student who set off on a round-the-world balloon race in the summer vacation. However, you lost all radio contact with the rest of the world and your balloon came down in a remote area (whose inhabitants speak a language you can understand). The local population ask you to act as their sentencing judge because judges in that area must be foreigners but they do not have any written guidelines, sentencing precedents, or any list of available penalties or maximum penalties. You have complete discretion.

The following are the agreed facts of your first 'case':

Max, a 24-year-old, and his friend, Perry, aged 19, came back to Max's family home one evening feeling upset and angry because their twin-sister girlfriends had just ditched them. Max took his grandad's radio—of great sentimental significance to grandad because he had been given it by a dying friend—couldn't find the right wavelength and smashed the radio. Perry insulted and swore at the grandfather.

Perry and Max then decided to take the bicycle from the neighbour's yard (without asking him) and, taking turns, drove the bicycle round the town. (Max had apparently done this twice before.) They then abandoned the bicycle. While they were gone grandad had a stroke and died two hours later.

The 'court' decided that both Max and Perry had committed a crime by using the bicycle. Perry was also guilty of 'insulting behaviour' and Max of damaging the radio.

Task:

You should justify a sentence separately for Max and Perry in relation to each of the following approaches:

1. You decide you will impose a sentence on Max and Perry which provides the amount of punishment that they deserve for what they have done.
   - State what factors of the case you took into account.
   - Would your answer be any different if you had been aware that insulting or harming grandparents is viewed as a very serious matter in that community?

2. You decide on a sentence which you think will be the most effective outcome for either or both of the 'criminal' and the family/community.
   - State the purpose of your decision.
   - State what factors you took into account.

This exercise raises important questions about fundamental issues in sentencing. Your answers under the first and second approaches might be very different from each other simply because you apply a different reason—a principle or rationale—for doing it. The first approach asks you to sentence on retributivist principles; the second allows you to choose a utilitarian or even restorative principle and objective. In relation to Approach 1 you may wish to alter your proposed sentence when asked to reconsider your ideas about seriousness.

Devising a seriousness scale

Select 20 acts of 'wrong-doing' and devise your own seriousness severity scale for those items, listing them from the least to the most serious in your opinion. How would you justify your choice?

online resource centre

See the Online Resource Centre for further reading around the issues raised by these questions.

3

'Just deserts': developments in retributivist sentencing

SUMMARY

This chapter examines the ways in which the 'just deserts' approach to sentencing was endorsed in the Criminal Justice Act 1991 and analyses the extent to which retributivist principles have been undermined by subsequent changes in legislation and guidance. It then reviews the new sentencing framework in the Criminal Justice Act 2003 and examines, in particular, law and guidance on constructing seriousness and the choice of a commensurate sentence. Finally it discusses criticisms of modern retributivism and assesses the role of human rights in limiting excessive punishment.

3.1 A retributivist sentencing framework?

Chapter 2 reviewed the principles of classical retributivism and outlined the ways in which modern retributivism has developed, to address some of the criticisms made of previous versions of retributivism. Imposing on judges and magistrates a sentencing framework based on the principles of modern retributivism—a just deserts approach—is, we suggested, a 'new' constraint on sentencing discretion. However, as Quirk has noted, 'despite its impeccably New Labour-sounding moniker, "just deserts" sentencing has been influential in many jurisdictions and in scholarship over the last 30 years' (Quirk 2006: 955). For England and Wales, it is the Criminal Justice Act (CJA) 1991, passed by a Conservative government, which has been viewed as the piece of legislation most infused with a just deserts approach. Nevertheless, it is not entirely clear whether and to what extent retributivist principles have indeed permeated law and guidance since the passage of that Act. This chapter will start, then, by examining relevant aspects of legislation passed in, and since, 1991 to assess the extent to which such principles have underpinned sentencing frameworks since the implementation of the 1991 Act.

3.1.1 The Criminal Justice Act 1991

The thinking behind the CJA 1991 can be found in the White Paper, *Crime, Justice and Protecting the Public* (see Chapter 1, section 1.4.4). This proposed a bifurcatory policy whereby the bulk of offenders are sentenced on principles of just deserts and parsimony whilst a minority receive sentences for public protection longer than justified on retributivist principles. The proposed primary criteria for sentencing were just deserts and proportional sentences (Home Office 1990a: para 1.6), whilst elements of the utilitarian concern with social consequences were reflected in the proposed aim of crime reduction (ibid: para 1.7). However, the White Paper explicitly demoted deterrence as a sentencing aim: '[d]eterrence is a principle with much immediate appeal...But...it is unrealistic to construct sentencing arrangements on the assumption that most offenders will weigh up the possibilities in advance' (ibid: para 2.8; see also Chapter 4).

The same criticism was made of the CJA 1991 (Ashworth 2000: 84) as is now being made of the Criminal Justice Act (CJA) 2003: that it set up an unworkable hybrid sentencing framework (see section 3.1.5 below; see, also, Ashworth and Player 2005; Koffman 2006). However, the provisions of the CJA 1991 made clear that the main sentencing decision was to calculate offence seriousness and a proportionate (commensurate) sentence. Only if the seriousness calculation pointed to a community sentence could other considerations, such as rehabilitation, determine choice of sentence. Further, the utilitarian provisions empowering courts to impose longer-than-commensurate determinate prison sentences for the protection of the public, were aimed at only a minority of offenders and statistics would suggest that they have been so used in practice (see Chapter 5). The other exceptions within this sentencing framework, notably the role of compensation orders and the options for dealing with mentally disordered offenders, are not necessarily incompatible with the basic retributivist rationale (see Chapters 6 and 7).

Not that the 1991 Act made that rationale explicit: as Ashworth noted, '[t]he 1991 Act proceeds towards its objective by means of allusion and implication' (Ashworth 2000: 85). Nevertheless, the sections which impose 'seriousness' thresholds for custodial and community penalties and also a commensurability principle are clearly based on the principles of modern retributivism outlined in Chapter 2. The 'hurdle' for imposing custody (in s 1(2)(a)) stated that a custodial sentence should not be given unless the offence is 'so serious that only' such a sentence can be justified. If it is justified, s 2 provided that the custodial sentence must be for such term as 'in the opinion of the court is commensurate with the seriousness of the offence'. Section 6 set up a similar approach for community penalties but with the test that the offending must be 'serious enough' to warrant such a sentence. More contentiously, those provisions which downgraded the effect of previous convictions and reformed the process of deciding on the amount of a fine could also be viewed as reflecting retributivist principles.

The re-enactment of the amended CJA 1991 provisions in the PCCSA 2000 gave students and practitioners alike—albeit briefly—a much needed consolidation of the decision-making framework for sentencing set up by the 1991 Act. To make this framework clearer it might be helpful to view it as one which asks the sentencer a series of crucial questions. In the charts below (Tables 3.1 and 3.2) the italics draw attention to the desert-based hurdles to the use of a category of punishment and the underlined words refer to amendments by the Criminal Justice Act 1993. Bold type is used to indicate the three main levels of punishment (custody, community, and financial). The section numbers are given for both the CJA 1991 and their re-enactment in the PCCSA 2000. Where there is a directly comparable provision the section number in the CJA 2003 is also given for later reference.

Table 3.1

Decision Stage	CJA 91 Ss	PCCSA Ss	CJA 2003 ss	Question	Outcome
1.	1	79	152(1)	Is the offence one that is punishable by custody?	If NO go to 4. If YES go to 2.
2.	**1(2)(a)**	79(2)(a)	152(2)	**Is the offence (+ one—_or more_—other/s)** _so serious that only_ **custody is justified?** (But see s 3(1) & (2).)	If NO go to 3. If Yes:
	3(3)(a)	81	156	What information is there about the circumstances of the offence—and the offence or offences associated with it?	and
	2(2)(a)	80(2)(a)	153(2)	What sentence length is 'commensurate with the seriousness of the offence' (or the combination of that offence + one or more associated offences)? (But consider also 5.)	SENTENCE.
3.	1(2)(b)	79(2)(b)	224	Is the offence of a violent or sexual nature? (But see s 3(1) & (6).)	If NO go to 4. If YES:
	3(3)(a) & (b)	81	229 156(2)(3)	What information is there about the circumstances of the offence, and shall we take into account any information about the offender?	and
	1(2)(b)	79(2)(b)	[225–8*]	Would only a custodial sentence be adequate to protect the public from serious harm?	If NO go to 4. If Yes:
	2(2)(b)	80(2)(b		What longer term than one commensurate with the offence seriousness is necessary?	SENTENCE.
4.	**6(1)**	35(1)	148(1)	**Is the offence (+ one _or more_ others)** _serious enough_ **to warrant a community sentence?**	If NO go to 5. If Yes:
	6(2)(a)	35(3)(a)	148(2)(a)	What orders are most suitable for the offender?	and
	7(2)	36(1)	156(2)	What information is there about the offender and shall we take it into account?	and
	7(1)	36(2)	156(1)	What information is there about the circumstances of the offence?	and
	6(2)(b)	35(3)(b)	148(2)(b)	What amount of restriction on liberty in the orders are commensurate with the seriousness of the offence (and any others)?	SENTENCE.
5. Fines	**18(2)**	See below		**What number of units is commensurate with the seriousness of the offending?** What is the offender's disposable weekly income? Calculate the value of the fine.	SENTENCE.

* These provisions are not strictly comparable: see Chapter 5 for a review of dangerous offender provisions in the CJA 2003. Also see the Online Resource Centre for information or updates on amendments made by the Criminal Justice and Immigration Act 2008.

Note: the original s 18 was totally replaced with:

s 18(1) [128(1)] What are the financial circumstances of the offender?

s 18(3) [128(3)] What information is there about the circumstances of the case, including the financial circumstances of the offender?

s 18(2) [128(2)] What fine 'reflects the seriousness of the offence'? And

s 18(5) [128(4)] Should the financial circumstances of the offender increase or reduce the fine?

See Chapter 7, section 7.3 for a discussion of the fines sentencing framework in the CJA 2003.

Table 3.2 If YES or NO are the answers to any of questions 1–5 in the table above, then:

CJA 1991	PCCSA	CJA 2003	Question
28(1) & (2)	158	166(1)	Do we want to take into account other 'relevant' mitigation?
29(1)–(4)	151	143(2),(3)	Has aggravation of offence seriousness been done where 'allowed'/'suitable'? (*previous convictions, failure to respond to previous sentences*, whether offence committed on bail*).
N/A	152	144	Can there be a reduction in sentence for a guilty plea? How much?
N/A	153	145	*Was there racial or religious aggravation*? (Must add to sentence.)
N/A	N/A	146	Was there aggravation related to disability or sexual orientation? (Must add to sentence.)

* This particular aggravating factor is not in the CJA 2003.

As enacted, then, the CJA 1991:

- had a presumptive rationale—just deserts—with a focus on a sentence proportionate to the seriousness of the offence in question (not offending history), unless the sentencer used the exceptions noted above
- treated all sentences as punishments which could be theorised in terms of deprivation of liberty (probation previously had not been so theorised)
- imposed hurdles for passing custodial and community sentences so that parsimony in sentencing could be encouraged. In effect it meant the sentencer 'must justify each upward step in the "sentencing pyramid" in accordance with the seriousness of the offence' (Wasik and von Hirsch 1994: 409)
- specified when the circumstances of the offender can or should be taken into account.

Even so, Table 3.1 presents a complicated system. If viewed as a board game with an aim of avoiding the use of a 'go to gaol' card, it is clear the player could never be certain what would happen next. The lack of clearly spelt-out aims meant that the CJA 1991 'left room for spoiling tactics by those charged with interpreting and applying the Act' (Ashworth 2000: 84). We will evaluate these criticisms levelled at the judiciary in section 3.3.1 but governments and Parliament were also responsible for 'spoiling tactics' and we will deal with those first.

3.1.2 Statutory changes 1991–2003

Three aspects of the CJA 1991 as passed particularly 'upset' influential sections of public and professional opinion (see Worrall 1997: Chapter 3): the new system of unit fines, the sentencing focus on the offence in question and only 'one other' associated offence, and the assumed prohibition on sentencers taking past convictions into account when assessing seriousness. All three were crucial to the aim of reducing the use of custody. The focus on only one or two offences before the court when the statutory hurdle is considered, together with the restrictions on taking

previous offending into account, reduced—for all but first-time offenders convicted of a single offence with no others to take into consideration—the potential
total amount of seriousness to be considered. The commensurate sentence would
then be less likely to be a custodial one. Further, unit fines—successfully piloted
as a fairer system—and the increased punitive bite of community penalties (see
Chapter 12) would, it was anticipated, make non-custodial sentences more attractive to judges and magistrates.

The adverse reactions of sentencers to the reduction of their discretion might have
been anticipated; the hostility of the tabloid press and the Magistrates' Association
to unit fines was more surprising (see Chapter 7, section 7.3). Because of the potentially adverse political effects of the hostility generated, the Government hast-
ily amended these provisions by ss 65–66 of the Criminal Justice Act (CJA) 1993.
Section 18 of the CJA 1991 was replaced by provisions returning the sentencing law
for fines to something akin to the pre-1991 situation (see Chapter 7, section 7.3).
Nevertheless, a just deserts approach was retained by the new subsection 18(2). 'The
amount of the fine fixed by the court shall be such as...reflects the seriousness of
the offence.' Sections 1 and 2 of the CJA 1991 (relating to custody) and s 6 (relating
to community penalties) were also amended, in response to concerns about restrictions on sentencing discretion,[1] to allow the courts to consider 'one or more' associated offences. Where offenders had several associated offences, this inevitably
made it easier to reach the custody threshold or to justify a long prison sentence.

The third problem provision, s 29, dealt with those factors which could aggravate
the seriousness of the offence in question. The message of the original section was
apparently to prohibit sentencers from taking account of previous convictions in
assessing seriousness: '[a]n offence shall not be regarded as more serious' (s 29(1))
because of the persistence of offending. Similarly 'failure to respond' to previous
(community) penalties should not increase seriousness. The amendments made
to this section by the CJA 1993 made clear the court could take these two factors
into account when calculating the seriousness of the offending.[2] The 1993 amendments to s 29—re-enacted as PCCSA, s 151(2)—also added 'offending on bail' as
a factor that courts *must* take into account (see Table 3.2 above). Since then, further mandated aggravating factors have been added: offending that is motivated
by religion or race, and where the offender was motivated by or showed hostility
based on the sexual orientation or the disability of the victim.[3]

When passed, the criteria for the imposition of community and custodial sentences were intended to be rigid barriers to over-sentencing. The provisions in the
PCCSA 2000 for extending the availability of curfew orders and community punishment orders to 'petty persistent offenders' introduced a degree of flexibility.
For persons over 16, if the court is minded to impose a fine but the offender has
failed to pay one or more previous fines *and* his means would not enable the court
to impose a fine commensurate with seriousness, then one or other of these orders

---

[1] The definition was in the CJA 1991, s 31, then PCCSA, s 161(1), as affirmed in s 305 of the CJA
2003.

[2] Because this issue of persistence has been so important a policy issue in relation to both the CJA
2003 and the CJA 1991, we will discuss it in more detail in section 3.2.4.

[3] By the Crime and Disorder Act 1998, the Anti-Terrorism, Crime and Security Act 2001, and the CJA
2003 respectively, the first two provisions having been re-enacted in the PCCSA 2000, s 153 before all
these provisions were consolidated in the CJA 2003. See section 3.2.3 below.

can be imposed even though the offender does not meet the 'serious enough' criterion for a community penalty.[4]

In the decade after 1993 other provisions also altered the balance of the sentencing framework. The Crime (Sentences) Act 1997, as we saw in Chapter 2, added a new constraint on sentencing discretion by legislating for automatic life and mandatory minimum sentences for specified offences. Its operation impinged on a desert-based system of commensurability in those cases where proportionality would have justified a lower penalty than the mandatory or minimum specified. The result, it was argued, was that, by 2000, the provisions of the CJA 1991 represented 'in practical terms, little more than an empty shell. Much that appears in subsequent statutes . . . is incompatible with the 1991 scheme' (Ashworth 2000: 89).

Equally crucial to the just deserts approach was the interpretation of seriousness by sentencers. Despite pressure for a definition to be included in the CJA 1991 this was not done and interpretation was consequently left to the Court of Appeal's Criminal Division and, later, the Sentencing Guidelines Council (SGC).[5]

3.1.3 The Criminal Justice Act 2003

It is debatable whether this most recent Act should be included in a discussion of 'just deserts'. The Halliday Report, when proposing the new framework which was incorporated in the CJA 2003, referred to the three 'tiers' of seriousness established by the CJA 1991 (fines, community punishment and custody) as 'unnecessary rigidities' (2001: para 1.31) and claimed that the just deserts approach had 'failed to take root' in sentencing courts (ibid: para 1.34).

Nevertheless, the calculation of seriousness is still very important. Section 143(1) of the CJA 2003 gives guidance on determining the seriousness of an offence, summarising the approach of the courts before the 2003 Act: that the offender's culpability in committing the offence and any harm caused by the offence must both be considered as part of the assessment of seriousness. Further, s 153(2) retains the principle that the sentence should be commensurate with seriousness whilst adding a principle that has been a feature of modern retributivism and, from time to time, has been restated in case law: the custodial sentence 'must be for the shortest term' that is commensurate with seriousness. Further, the SGC published early guidance on the process of calculating seriousness (Sentencing Guidelines Council 2004a).

There are still hurdles for the imposition of custodial and community penalties though the CJA 2003 amended them somewhat. Section 152(2) replaced the 'so serious that only' custody hurdle though, arguably, the effect is the same: '[t]he court must not pass a custodial sentence unless it is of the opinion that the offence, or the combination of the offence and one or more offences associated with it, was so serious that neither a fine nor a community sentence can be justified for the offence'. However, s 166(2) states that s 152(2) 'does not prevent a court . . . from passing a community sentence even though it is of the opinion that the offence, or one or more offences associated with it, was so serious that a community sentence could not normally be justified for the offence'. Sentencers have been given more

---

[4] Section 59(1)–(4): this provision is in force until s 151 of the CJA 2003 is implemented.
[5] See, in particular, sections 3.2.1 and 3.3.1 below.

discretion and, if they so wish, need not feel legally or morally obliged to impose custody. In practice, how high this hurdle is construed may depend on how low guidance sets the 'anchoring points' (see Chapter 2, section 2.7.5 above).

On the other hand, the CJA 2003, whilst re-enacting the 'serious enough' criterion for a community penalty, provides that, if on three or more previous occasions when convicted of an offence, the offender has received (only) a fine as a penalty, the court on a subsequent conviction can make a community order if it 'would be in the interests of justice' to do so, notwithstanding the failure to meet the seriousness criterion (s 151).[6] However, when implemented, the Criminal Justice and Immigration (CJI) Act 2008 10 will confine the use of community orders to imprisonable offences.

Instead of a range of community penalties as set out in the PCCSA 2000, the CJA 2003 introduced the generic community order with specified components (see Chapter 12, section 12.2.1). As before, the choice of content for community punishment depends on the court's assessment of what is most 'suitable' for the offender and the restrictions on liberty that the order imposes are again to be commensurate with seriousness (s 148(2)). Similarly, the fine must still reflect the seriousness of the offending (s 164(2)) and the financial circumstances of the offender can reduce or increase the amount of the fine (s 164(4)). The Crown Court is specifically empowered by s 163 to fine an offender convicted on indictment instead of, or in addition to, any other penalty.

The Act includes changes to the courts' powers to impose prison sentences of less than 12 months. If implemented, there would be only three such sentences with a maximum of 51 weeks for each offence: custody plus, intermittent custody, and a suspended sentence (see Chapter 12, section 12.1.1). The first two have no equivalents in options available before the 2003 Act whilst the third is designed 'to re-launch the suspended sentence, with the difference that during the period of suspension the offender will be subject to requirements of the kind that can be included in a community sentence' (Ashworth 2003: 9). The custody plus sentence must be for at least 28 weeks, the custodial period being for at least 2 weeks with the licence period being at least 26 weeks in length (s 181). The order will also include requirements, such as unpaid work, a curfew, or supervision, to be complied with during the licence period (s 182). An order for intermittent custody, sometimes referred to as 'weekend' or 'part-time prison', will include a specified period of days to be served in prison, with specified periods of temporary release until that total has been served, and the rest of the period will be under licence (s 183). However, neither custody plus nor intermittent custody has been implemented although the latter order was piloted in specified courts and prisons in the period January 2004 to November 2006.[7]

Suspended sentences can be used for any term of imprisonment from 28–51 weeks and must specify a supervision period (for which community requirements are again imposed) and an operational period, each of which must be for a term of six months to two years (s 189). If an offender fails to comply with the requirements, or commits an offence during the operational period, the court is empowered to

---

[6] Section 151 will replace PCCSA 2000 s59 but is not yet in force.
[7] See National Probation Service Bulletin (2006) Issue 41, 084/06: *Intermittent Custody: Withdrawal of Authority to Supervise Offenders*. The implementation of custody plus was originally planned for the end of 2006 but there are no longer plans to use these orders.

order the original sentence of imprisonment to take effect. There are also new custodial sentences for public protection: see Chapter 5.

3.1.4 Explaining policy change

It should go without saying that criminal justice legislation, much of which is administered by non-lawyers, ought to be as clear, rational and non-technical as possible. No one who has to work with the legislation would ever accuse the current sentencing statutes, for example, of possessing any of these qualities.

(Editorial (2000) *Criminal Law Review*)

The attempt to consolidate sentencing provisions into a more coherent whole in the PCCSA 2000 was quickly overtaken by various pieces of relevant legislation, notably Part 12 of the CJA 2003. That Act was preceded by two White Papers, *Criminal Justice: The Way Ahead* (Home Office 2001a) and *Justice for All* (Home Office 2002a), as well as the Halliday Report (2001) which had argued that the present sentencing framework was a 'muddle' (para 1.36) and called for it to be radically remodelled. What is still debated is whether the reasons given for remodelling in the way eventually enshrined in the CJA 2003 are valid, the solutions workable, and the resulting framework any less of a muddle than before.

The case for change put forward by the Halliday Report (2001) in relation to what was then the current framework was as follows:

(1) The 1991 (as amended) sentencing framework has 'a narrow sense of purpose' and is a 'less than complete guide to the selection of the most suitable sentence in an individual case' (para 1.9). Sentencers are not encouraged to consider reparation or crime reduction.

(2) The framework has too much discretion which has led to inconsistency of sentencing. Indeed sentencers had told the Review that they were not 'inhibited from taking a wide view' by the current legislation (para 1.10). Sentencers have insufficient guidance on the measurement of seriousness (para 1.9) and the framework 'is relatively inaccessible' (para 1.38). It therefore needs greater clarity to aid sentencers and to reduce inconsistency (para 1.44).

(3) The framework has 'a muddled approach to persistent offenders' (para 1.11). Sentencers can take account of previous convictions and 'failure to respond' but this is leading to inconsistency between the two levels of court. The research showed that Crown Courts appear to acknowledge the existence in case law of the doctrine of 'progressive loss of mitigation' whilst magistrates' courts are more likely to 'sentence on record' (paras 1.12 and 1.13). The framework needs to be spelt out more clearly in regard to sentencing persistent offenders because they commit a disproportionate number of crimes.

(4) Magistrates are frustrated by the lack of suitable sentences to tackle the causes of persistent offending, particularly in a short prison sentence. Around half of the prisoners sentenced to a custodial sentence of less than 12 months have been to prison before and/or have offended before. Therefore a short prison sentence is not a deterrent and, because it is too short for rehabilitation programmes and does not have supervised release, it is not useful for tackling the causes of offending (paras 1.17 and 1.18).

One of the most important issues examined in the Halliday Report and incorporated in the CJA 2003 is persistence of offending—the issue of criminal history and recidivism as a factor in the process of determining sentence.[8] It is one of the Halliday Report's main reasons for advocating change and, as we shall see in section 3.2.4 below, the resulting change in the law affects the calculation of seriousness and the choice of sentence which may well then be a custodial one. As *Justice for All* noted, prison must be 'reserved for the serious, dangerous and seriously persistent offenders' (Home Office 2002a: Executive summary: 8).

3.1.5 Critiques of current government policy

The Halliday Report argued for a clearer but also more flexible framework for sentencing so that rehabilitation and reparation could play a larger role. In effect, it saw just deserts as too constraining a principle. The opposite view is that the Report offered 'a pick and mix of almost every criminal justice idea of the last few years—public protection through incapacitative incarceration; reparation and restoration; curfews and electronic monitoring; treatments and controls' (Hudson 2001/2: 17), and that this variety of justification and outcome would undermine the retributive, proportionality principle at the heart of just deserts. For such critics the constraints of retributivism constitute a good to be retained, a prerequisite for justice.

An early critique by Baker and Clarkson, for example, made the following arguments:

(a) The proposals 'would lead to the ultimate demise of the proportionality principle as that principle is widely understood' because the band of deserved punishment 'is so broad and so dominated by non-desert factors as to erode any meaningful proportionality in sentencing' (2002: 82). Once non-desert criteria are admitted, those criteria are likely, especially in the current political climate, to displace desert-based considerations.

(b) The higher importance attached to risk assessment and rehabilitation in deciding on a sentence can increase disparity. The risk-based approach is thus extended from dangerous offenders to all offenders which, they argue, could potentially lead to the absurd situation where a person receives a longer sentence for failure to learn from previous mistakes than from the crime itself.

After the passage of the Act further critical comment appeared. Ashworth, for example, accused the government of neglecting human rights and the proportionality principle. He argues that 'it would be difficult to suggest that there is any form of "human rights culture" in the Home Office when so many provisions of the Criminal Justice Act 2003 raise the possibility of challenge on the ground of infringing on Convention rights' (2004: section 5(I); see also Koffman 2006). The following sections of this chapter will focus on the crucial retributivist elements of the current sentencing framework in order to assess the validity of these criticisms.

---

[8] For a discussion of the effectiveness of longer prison sentences in relation to deterrence and incapacitative policies see Chapters 4 and 5. See also the articles in Volume 43(4) of the *Howard Journal* (2004) which focus on desistance from offending.

3.2 Calculating seriousness

3.2.1 Culpability and harm

Implementing a 'just deserts' approach to sentencing raises several crucial questions which are very difficult to answer. The most contentious are the following:

(a) How should you calculate seriousness? What factors can legitimately make something more or less serious? Should previous offending be considered in this process?

(b) How do you decide what sentence is proportionate to any amount of seriousness? In particular where should the anchoring point be and so where, for example, should the custody level be set? How do you decide what is the shortest custodial or community punishment or smallest financial penalty which can be justified as proportionate to the offending?

(c) To what extent should the personal circumstances of the offender or his family affect the level of the commensurate punishment imposed?

(d) Should the state's desire to avoid trial costs or to reduce the trauma of a trial for the victim affect the amount of punishment imposed?

These are the legal and practical issues on which we will now focus. First, however, we will examine the question of seriousness itself because the discussion of retributivist theory in Chapter 2 made clear how important the concept of seriousness is in that theory. Why we might consider one action (of deviance and/or evil) to be more 'serious' than another—and how we might rank them—become crucial to sentencing.

Sentencing principles based on retributivist theory stress that the total amount of seriousness is constructed from both the harm caused and the offender's responsibility, his state of mind, and motivation. Indeed, s 143(1) of the CJA 2003 enacts this approach: '[i]n considering the seriousness of any offence, the court must consider the offender's culpability in committing the offence and any harm which the offence caused, was intended to cause or might foreseeably have caused'. Yet both these elements of 'gravity'—seriousness—are problematic and, in practice and theory, the calculation of seriousness is far from easy. Decisions about seriousness may be made by reference to one or both of two sets of very different types of judgement.

First, there is a normative judgement about wrongfulness. With the exception of murder, different individuals, communities, and nations may have very different ideas about what counts as most or least serious. In the sentencing exercise provided at the end of Chapter 2, for example, our law student might or might not think that the harm done (theft of a bicycle and radio, and verbal insults) was serious, depending on the importance of such in his peer group or country; he might or might not take into account the feelings of and effect on the victim of the offences, and he might or might not feel culpability had been affected by an incident in the offenders' love lives. Further, 'like the Recording Angel's, most peoples' judgements of others' blameworthiness depend on knowledge of their circumstances' (Tonry 1996: 18).

Cross, drawing on earlier judicial comments and practice, suggested that four factors affect judicial constructions of seriousness as well as the factor of harm done: wickedness, social disapproval, social danger, and social alarm (1981: 178–82).

(a) *The 'evilness' of the perpetrator.* This focus on degrees of wickedness is perhaps the most difficult, depending as it does on normative judgements and underlying moral codes. In the fragmented modern society there may be little consensus as to what actions are most blameworthy and, further, its focus on the mental state of the offender raises difficult questions as to intention, provocation, malice, and excuses.

(b) *Social disapproval.* This is an equally slippery concept, again depending on society's values. The strength of public denunciation of an offence (within its offence category) is often strongly influenced by the age or sex of the victim: babies or children as victims generally attract more social disapproval and so the offending is construed as more serious. There might also be more social disapproval of an offender if he has committed the offence before.

(c) *Social danger or social alarm.* The clearest example of this factor might now be terrorist-related offences: the degree of extreme social anxiety about global terrorism feeds into a heightening of perceptions of the severity of offences such as possession of a firearm or counterfeiting documents. Handling of stolen goods is also seen as very serious because of the danger that the incidence of theft will escalate if those willing to handle stolen goods are inadequately punished. Cross's example of social alarm upgrading seriousness is that of the person illegally entering a residential property—as opposed to commercial property—where the same amount of damage or theft causes a greater alarm.

In providing early guidance on 'seriousness' the SGC approached the issue of culpability by focusing on the 'amount' of intention and identifying four 'levels' for sentencing purposes:

Where the offender:

(iv) has the *intention* to cause harm, with the highest culpability when an offence is planned. The worse the harm intended, the greater the seriousness.

(v) is *reckless* as to whether harm is caused, that is, where the offender appreciates at least some harm would be caused but proceeds giving no thought to the consequences even though the extent of the risk would be obvious to most people.

(vi) has *knowledge* of the specific risks entailed by his actions even though he does not intend to cause the harm that results.

(vii) is guilty of *negligence*.

(Sentencing Guidelines Council 2004a: para 1.7)

The second element of gravity is the factual judgement on the amount of harm caused by the offending. On the face of it, this is a much easier judgement because 'harm' appears as an objective, value-free concept. Arguably this is so if we are talking about theft, where the offence is the deprivation of an amount of money or property whose value is easy to calculate. But, as we saw with our sentencing problem, the value to the victim may be 'sentimental' because, say, of the giver of the gift stolen, or the offence might be assault where the monetary value to be placed on the injury depends not only on the permanence or otherwise of the harm but also on the context of the victim's life. A scar on the face is, arguably, much more serious if the victim is a model whose living depends on facial perfection, and a jaw injury might take away the pleasure of playing in a brass band, but this raises further questions. Should the loss to a particular individual be part of the calculation of harm or should the offender be punished proportionately to the harm an 'average' victim would have suffered from his offending? How do you put a price, not only on potential loss of earnings, but on the more difficult issue of loss of pleasure, whether caused by the loss of a hobby or of one of the five senses?

One can take a broad interpretation, as does the SGC when referring to the statutory provision as 'widely drafted', so that harm 'encompasses those offences where harm is caused but also those where neither individuals nor the community suffer harm but a risk of harm is present' (Sentencing Guidelines Council 2004a: para 1.8). The SGC also provides a list of 'factors indicating a more than usually serious degree of harm' which includes 'multiple victims', 'an especially serious physical or psychological effect on the victim, even if unintended', 'a sustained assault or repeated assaults on the same victim' and offending committed in the presence of friends or relatives (ibid: para 1.23).

Furthermore, the relationship between these two levels of judgement—the normative and the 'factual'—is also problematic: how do you reconcile different amounts of 'wrongfulness' and damage? As the above guidance notes,

Assessing seriousness is a difficult task, particularly where there is an imbalance between culpability and harm:

- sometimes the harm that actually results is greater than the harm intended by the offender;
- in other circumstances, the offender's culpability may be at a higher level than the harm resulting from the offence.

(ibid: para 1.16).

Some time ago, a survey of residents in Dallas, USA, showed that respondents saw the two dimensions as distinct and that where crimes are perceived as more 'wrong' than harmful, the calculation of seriousness mirrors wrongfulness. Conversely, where crimes are perceived to be more harmful than wrong, harmfulness predominates (Warr 1989). This distinction could be critical as 'many crimes are likely to be evaluated quite differently on the two dimensions' (ibid: 797) and reflect, perhaps, different moral or religious codes (ibid: 819).

Yet these difficult issues are unavoidable in the calculation of proportionality. As noted in Chapter 2's examination of retributivist principles, ordinal proportionality concerns the question of how offences should be punished, relative to each other, on the basis of the seriousness of the offending; cardinal proportionality concerns the choice of the level of severity to anchor the ranked penalties. Empirical research suggests there is some consensus on the seriousness ranking of the most serious crimes, such as murder and rape, but that even in this element of ordinal ranking there was not complete consistency, with, for example, social workers and prison staff ranking actual bodily harm higher than other groups (Cavadino and Wiles 1994: 490–3; see also Rossi *et al.* 1974). There appears to be less agreement about where to 'anchor' the penalty scale: responses to hypothetical cases by practitioners produced statistically significant differences between criminal justice agencies as to the level of seriousness deemed necessary to justify custody (Cavadino and Wiles 1994: 493–8; see, also, for references to other surveys, Ashworth 2005: 104–6).

3.2.2 The process towards a proportionate sentence

This chapter is focusing on the retributivist concepts of seriousness and proportionality but, whilst a book may proceed chapter by chapter and deal with separate points in turn, sentencing in practice is not like that. The different issues are intertwined and, when faced with a real case, or a problem question, an overall view of

---

Checklist

In light of the facts of the case in question:

1. Is the offender mentally disordered? Consider the provisions of the Mental Health Act 1983 and any other relevant legislation.
2. Are any of the mandatory (minimum) sentences relevant? (particularly CCSA 2000, ss 110–111). Is the sentence fixed by law (murder)? Are the sentences for public protection applicable (particularly CJA 2003, ss 225–227)?
3. Are there any other powers that should be exercised for the purpose of protecting the public from harm from the offender?
4. Is the case to be dealt with in terms of proportionality/seriousness/just deserts? What statutory provisions are (most) relevant?
5. What is the statutory maximum penalty? If being dealt with in the magistrates' court, what is the maximum that can be imposed?
6. What is the 'normal range' for this offence and what guidelines are there (Court of Appeal and SGC)? If relevant, what do the *Magistrates' Guidelines* say?
7. Which statutory factors must be taken into account to aggravate (or mitigate) severity?
8. Which of the factors from case law or SGC guidance on mitigation or aggravation are relevant?
9. Is any recent guidance relevant for deciding whether the facts of the case justify the required seriousness hurdles for imposing custodial or community penalties?
10. (a) For a fine: should the offender's sentencing record be taken into account?
    (b) For a community sentence: do any facts of the case suggest particular requirements/penalties are appropriate?
    (c) For a custodial sentence: is the sentence length as short as is necessary for the penal purpose?
11. Are there any personal mitigating factors? Should they be taken into account?
12. Is there a sentence discount for a guilty plea? If so, how much?
13. What compensation order should be imposed? If not, why not?[9]
14. What sentence?

---

[9] Compensation orders will be dealt with in Chapter 6, as will confiscation orders and the role of victim impact statements, neither of which are referred to in the list.

the process and possibilities is necessary before decisions can be made about what law and issues are going to be relevant. For this reason, to set the material in this chapter in context, we have provided below a basic checklist. Some of the elements on this list will be dealt with in subsequent chapters and so you are not expected to understand their import at this stage. So, whilst—to a greater or lesser extent—the just deserts approach to sentencing is the 'normal' sentencing framework, steps 1–3 in the checklist above relate to the exceptions to that approach and are triggered when the selective incapacitation or extended supervision provisions apply and when the offender is mentally disordered. They will be dealt with elsewhere (see Chapters 5 and 7).

If we relate the above checklist to the discussion in Chapter 2 about ordinal proportionality, we can see that it reminds us to go through the following elements to calculate a proportionate sentence:

(a) Establish the seriousness of the offence *category* on which the offender has admitted guilt or been found guilty. This requires knowledge of the statutory maximum penalty and guidance about the 'normal' range of penalties for that offence.

(b) Establish the seriousness of the offence *in question*. This requires looking at those factors relating to the specific instance of offending under review which make the offence more or less serious than the 'average' instance of offending within this offence category. It entails examining the facts of the case to see if there are aggravating or mitigating factors which, respectively, increase or decrease the seriousness of the offence. Aggravating factors, such as breach of trust, the age of the victim, the amount of harm, the social position of the offender, the extent of planning and meditation, and the offender's criminal record, reflect the ideas discussed above which account for sentencers considering some aspects of offending as more 'evil' or 'harmful' than others and so legitimately increasing the offender's culpability. Mitigating factors relating to the offence, such as provocation or minimal harm caused, similarly decrease culpability and seriousness.

Then, having ascertained or constructed a ranking of punishments in order of severity, the sentencer must choose the punishment which is commensurate to the amount of seriousness calculated for the offence in question. This exercise clearly raises all the problems we have already discussed in relation to applying retributivist principles in sentencing. Finally, the sentencer should consider mitigation relating to the offender. This may be seen as an 'optional extra' but the sentencer, statutory provisions permitting, may take into account those personal circumstances of the offender which are not strictly relevant to offence seriousness but which the court feels justified in taking into account to mitigate the severity of the sentence (see Chapter 7, section 7.1). The discount for a guilty plea might be seen as personal mitigation—if so, this is the exception in that it *must* be given where it applies. It is a pity the same word—'mitigation'—is used at two very different parts in the sentencing model because the potential impact at each part is different.[10]

---

[10] We will not be discussing the statutory rules regarding sentencing procedures in this book but see Ashworth (2000: 307–15) and Thomas (2002).

3.2.3 **Aggravating factors in statute**

Stages 7 and 8 of the above checklist relate to aggravating and mitigating factors established either by statute or by guidance and the courts should consider such: s 156(1) of the CJA 2003, replicating previous provisions (see Table 3.1), requires courts, when deciding whether the seriousness of the offence in question merits a community or custodial sentence, to 'take into account all such information as is available to it about the circumstances of the offence...including any aggravating or mitigating factors'. However, Ashworth questions whether all the aggravating factors allowed by legislation and guidance can be theorised in relation to culpability or harm and so fitted into proportionality theory because 'courts have often adopted the terminology of deterrence' (2005: 159).

The selection and legitimation of factors which may mitigate or aggravate seriousness is, then, a crucial issue in sentencing. As Lord Bingham CJ said in a burglary guideline judgment, 'the seriousness of the offence can vary almost infinitely from case to case', and so 'whether a custodial sentence is required, and if so the length of such sentence, is heavily dependent on the aggravating and mitigating features' (*Brewster*, 1998 at 225–6). A similar approach was taken in *Howells* (1998).

Statutory aggravations have become increasingly important in the last decade or so. Of supreme importance is s 143(2) of the CJA 2003 which replaces the provision enacted in 1993 and mandates aggravation for relevant previous convictions: this will be dealt with separately in the next section. Linked to this is the practice of asking the sentencer to 'take into consideration' offences with which the offender has not been charged ('TICs'). This practice benefits both the offender and the criminal justice system and '[m]any petty offenders voluntarily aggravate their sentences in this way', although there are circumstances when this is not appropriate (see guidance issued by the Crown Prosecution Service).[11]

Offences committed on bail and 'failure to respond'

The amendments made by the 1993 CJA increased seriousness if the offender had failed to respond to previous penalties and if the offence was committed while the offender was on bail (whether or not that bail related to an offence for which the offender was ultimately convicted and imprisoned). 'Failure to respond' was one of the three justifications for imposing custody on young offenders in the Criminal Justice Act 1982. It was not incorporated in the criteria extended to all offenders by the CJA 1991, s 1 and was prohibited as an aggravating factor in the original s 29, but the PCCSA 2000 re-enacted the failure to respond aggravation. In a further twist, the CJA 2003 has repealed this provision (Schedule 37, Part 7) but re-enacted aggravation for offences on bail (see Table 3.2 above).

Racially motivated offences

In 1998 the Crime and Disorder Act (CDA) added motivation by racial hostility as a new statutory aggravation. This had already been established by case law, notably *Craney and Corbett* (1996), and ss 29–32 of the CDA 1998 mandated an increase in offence seriousness for specified offences by increasing the statutory maximum, as

---

[11] See http://www.cps.gov.uk.

well as imposing a duty to increase seriousness in relation to any other offence in s 82. The rationale for this provision would appear to be increased denunciation 'reflected back in the powerful sense of stigma said to be felt by the defendants', with any deterrent effect of the longer sentences being very much open to question (Burney 2003a: 35). The Sentencing Advisory Panel (SAP) (2000) issued guidance on the amount of sentence enhancement to be imposed and suggested 40–70 per cent for fines, community, and custodial sentences unless this pushed the sentence over a threshold. In *Kelly and Donnelly* (2001) the Court of Appeal adopted the SAP's list of factors to be used to scale gravity, but rejected formal percentage enhancements (see Ashworth 2005: 153–5).

Religion, disability and sexual orientation

The Anti-Terrorism and Security Act 2001 amended the above legislation to add 'religiously aggravated offences', all now to be found in the CJA 2003, s 145, whilst s 146 of that Act added similar provisions to mandate an increase in sentences for aggravation related to disability or sexual orientation (see Table 3.2).

All these statutory aggravations can be found on the list of 'factors indicating higher culpability' in the guidance on seriousness (Sentencing Guidelines Council 2004a: para 1.22). Note also that the guidance in the CJA 2003 about minimum terms to be served by those convicted of murder gives a starting point of 30 years for murders motivated by race, religion or sexual orientation (Schedule 21 para 5).

3.2.4 Persistence as the problem

Whether or not to punish someone more for continuing to offend has always been a difficult sentencing problem (see Flaherty 2006/7). Of the three possible responses—flat-rate sentencing, 'progressive loss of mitigation', and cumulative sentencing—only the first takes no notice of previous record and all raise difficult issues (see Ashworth 2000: 162–9). The second and third responses do consider previous offending but conceptualise the importance—and therefore the potential 'add-on' sentence—differently.

These different responses reflect the fact that modern retributivists have been divided in their approach to persistence—the relevance of past offending and good character—as a sentencing factor. In utilitarian theory the focus on past offending would be relevant to the calculation of future risks, but in retributivism its role is different. Von Hirsch allows previous convictions as the only exception to the principle that offences of comparable seriousness should receive a punishment with the same degree of severity (von Hirsch 1986, 1993). If an offence is committed for the first time it might be successfully argued in mitigation that the action is out of character and so there is, in effect, a penalty discount for first offenders, but with each repeated offence this argument will be less plausible. The offender is still being censured for the current act, but censure may be reduced because we acknowledge that it was the first time the person had succumbed to the temptation to act badly and had resisted it before. But while a 'discount' may be appropriate here, von Hirsch emphasises that there must not be a large differential between punishments for first offenders and recidivists: 'a first offender should receive less punishment than a recidivist, but...this punishment differential should only be a modest one' (1986: 90).

For von Hirsch there would be a limit on how far previous convictions would increase the severity of the sentence and the upper limit would very likely be lower than permitted on utilitarian models (von Hirsch 1986). He acknowledges that past criminal record has implications for desert for the current offence, so he argues for 'primary but not exclusive emphasis on the current offence' (ibid: 78). Other desert theorists, such as Fletcher (1982), would see a focus on previous offending as incompatible with just deserts principles. He argues that previous convictions do not affect desert for the current offence, and should not influence the sentence, as the offender has already been punished for past convictions.

If the offender persists, he would lose what von Hirsch calls his first offender discount and this would be done progressively. However, once that discount had been used up, he would receive the full amount of punishment but no more than this. The alternative of continually increasing punishment for recidivism would lead to the situation where relatively minor offences could incur harsh punishments. The primary concern on von Hirsch's approach is still with the current offence and the size of the differential between the two punishments should be kept 'within proper bounds' (1986: 91).

However, the efforts of retributivist theory to provide a rational basis for dealing with multiple offences through a 'ceiling' on punishment are criticised by Ryberg (2005) who argues that this approach both is theoretically flawed and also cannot provide a practical basis for sentencing.

In cumulative sentencing the sentence increases on each subsequent conviction. If represented graphically, cumulative sentencing is seen as a straight upward line to the 'normal' penalty and beyond to the statutory maximum; progressive loss of mitigation is a line with an upward slope but it then reaches a plateau at the normal ceiling for the offence (Wasik and von Hirsch 1994: 410). Flat-rate sentencing would take no account of previous convictions whatsoever. Figure 3.1 illustrates this in graph form.

The graph assumes:

- the maximum penalty for this offence is ten years
- the normal range is five–seven years and the court uses six years as the norm every time
- previous convictions are all for offences of a similar gravity
- the court starts with a three-year sentence for this offence if there are no previous convictions
- where progressive loss of mitigation operates, the loss for the first offence is greater than for subsequent offences.

Arguably, the progressive loss of mitigation approach was endorsed by the Court of Appeal prior to the CJA 1991 (Wasik and von Hirsch 1994: 411) and *Queen* (1981) was referred to in the White Paper (Home Office 1990a) to justify s 29. As passed, s 29 stated, inter alia, that an offence was not to be regarded as more serious 'by reason of any previous convictions of the offender'. There was some debate as to whether that wording did incorporate the loss of mitigation approach or simply made clear that sentencers could not use previous convictions

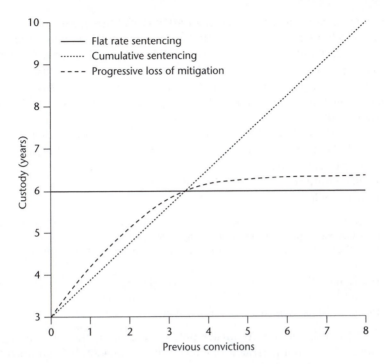

Figure 3.1 Persistence

to aggravate the seriousness in specific cases unless special culpability was dis-closed by the record. Wasik and von Hirsch argued for the former, that ss 28(1) and 29(1) together provided the upward 'slope' (by allowable mitigation in s 28) and then the 'plateau' of the progressive loss of mitigation approach (1994: 411). Be that as it may, the Government repealed the whole of s 29 and substituted a new section by the CJA 1993.

The amended subs 29(1) stated: '[i]n considering the seriousness of any offence, the court may take into account any previous convictions of the offender or any failure of his to respond to previous sentences'. Henham warned that this could 'lead to an increase in cases where individuals are sentenced "on their record" and inevitably a rise in the prison population' (1995: 223). However, Wasik and von Hirsch (1994) argued that this did not give the sentencer 'unfettered discre-tion' in dealing with previous convictions and, further, that recidivism *per se* does not constitute a 'failure to respond' and so cannot satisfy the second limb for aggravation of offence seriousness. They refer to Hansard, which seems to suggest that the Government wanted only to return to (or make clearer) the pre-1991 approach, not to allow a system of cumulative sentencing (1994: 412–13).

Their arguments do of course raise the question as to whether sentencing prac-tice pre- or post-1991 was the same as the case law suggests. Roberts (2002) cites statistics given in the Halliday Report (2001: Appendix 3 Table 1) which show that the probability of being given a custodial sentence increases in direct relationship to the number of previous convictions. He argues that this suggests there is already 'a robust recidivist premium' in practice and that 'cumulative sentencing is alive and well in England and Wales' (Roberts 2002: 430).[12] Others have argued that these changes in 1993 to the 1991 CJA, taken together, were a 'remarkable *volte face*' in sentencing policy (Henham 1995: 223), and were at least partly responsible for the resumed upward trend in custodial sentencing (Home Office 1994a: 1, see also paras 6–10).

The CJA 2003, in line with the Halliday proposals, enhances the role of past record. Halliday had argued that 'clarification needs to be based on a clear presumption that sentencing severity should increase as a consequence of sufficiently recent and relevant convictions' (2002: para 2.7).[13] The CJA 2003 incorporates this intention in s 143(2):

In considering the seriousness of an offence…committed by an offender who has one or more previous convictions, the court must treat each previous conviction as an aggravating factor if…the court considers that it can reasonably be so treated having regard, in particular to—

(a) the nature of the offence to which the conviction relates and its relevance to the current offence, and

(b) the time that has elapsed since the conviction.

Section 151 is also relevant. As already noted, it empowers the court to impose a community order on a persistent offender who has previously been fined three or more times but would not otherwise satisfy the criterion for a community sentence.

The effect of s 143 on sentencing practice depends, notwithstanding its mandatory force, on how the courts exercise the discretion not to consider each previous conviction as an aggravating factor. As in case law on this issue, the discretion focuses on the reasonableness of so doing where the nature of the offence may be very different from the current offence, may be relatively trivial, and may have taken place many years previously. There is scope here for sentencers to interpret it in a way which is not significantly different from the progressive loss of mitigation doctrine, and the Halliday Report argued that there should be a 'ceiling' on the effect of previous convictions (2000: para 2.20). However, detailed guidance would be needed to structure this discretion (ibid: 2.13) as the CJA 2003 does not provide for upper limits (see von Hirsch and Roberts 2004) and the SGC had not yet issued specific guidance. On the face it, however, this is cumulative sentencing and there is no doubt that government policy is to increase the effect of previous convictions on the sentencing decision as well as to promote consistency.

3.2.5 Guidance on aggravation

Much more difficult to establish and summarise is the appellate and SGC guidance about other factors which should or should not legitimately aggravate seriousness

---

[12] On a related point, Wasik (2001) pointed to the 'vital importance' of particular previous convictions in relation to the mandatory (minimum) sentences imposed under ss 109–111 of the PCCSA 2000, noting the practical problems caused for practitioners and his concerns that too high a premium is being placed on the accuracy of criminal records.

[13] The Report also considers in some detail various ways of buttressing this presumption, opting for a preferred approach of 'entry points' (2001: paras 2.12–2.20).

and the extent to which that should be done. In the guidance on seriousness there is a long list—without detail—at para 1.22 of a range of factors which can aggravate (Sentencing Guidelines Council 2004a). For particular offences and offence categories there is now the very useful *Guideline Judgments Case Compendium*, first issued by the SGC in 2005 to summarise appellate guidance and updated several times since. Under the heading 'Generic sentencing principles: Overview of cases' is provided an index to all the cases summarised. This is an easy way to acquire a general idea of the most relevant factors in assessing seriousness within particular offences. However, there is an enormous literature on this issue and an ever-increasing quantity of guidance and this book cannot seek to address the issue comprehensively or in detail. We will simply discuss selected topics which have consistently been upheld as influential, or have been of recent interest.

Breach of trust

Over the years the Court of Appeal has consistently condemned as seriously wrong offending which involves a breach of trust, and research suggests that abuse of trust, together with premeditation, are the two factors most likely to tip the balance in favour of a custodial sentence (Flood-Page and Mackie 1998: 11). In 1999 Walker noted that '[a]lmost any sort of dishonesty in breach of trust is regarded as serious enough to justify a custodial sentence' (1999: 53) although this may no longer apply to less serious offending. *Kefford* (2002) reduced the starting point for 'economic crimes' (in that case false accounting) and Flood-Page and Mackie found that in the Crown Court over half of breach of trust theft cases did not result in a custodial sentence because of balancing mitigating factors (1998: 85). However, the Court of Appeal in *Cook* (2003) (see also *Carmichael* (2003)) confirmed that *Kefford* had not altered the guidance given in *Barrick* (1985) and *Clarke* (1998) in relation to breach of trust cases involving substantial sums of money gained through theft and fraud by professional people. However, *Clarke* laid down longer sentences for 'white-collar' crimes involving breach of trust than had *Barrick* because of the increasing scale of dishonesty.

The consequences to the victim

The effect of the crime on the victim is gaining a higher profile as an aggravating factor. In the context of the burglary guidelines given in *R v McInerney, R v Keating* (2002), Lord Woolf CJ, at the beginning of his *Statement in response to inaccurate comments on the guidelines issued by the Court of Appeal as to the sentencing of domestic burglars* (14 January 2003), noted that the Court had endorsed the principle that 'the consequences to the victim should always be of the greatest significance in determining the appropriate punishment' (para 3, see also Chapter 1, section 1.3.1).[14] SGC guidelines endorse old age or youth, disability, and the nature of a victim's job as potential forms of vulnerability (Sentencing Guidelines Council 2004a: para 1.17) and the vulnerability of the victim is also one that may be linked to abuse of trust in relation to sexual offences with minors.[15] An example is the

---

[14] See also the *Case Compendium* (SGC 2005: 72).

[15] In *Hubbard* (2002) the Court of Appeal heard the first case under the Sexual Offences (Amendment) Act 2000, s 3, where abuse of trust is an integral part of the offence, with a five-year maximum penalty, and upheld concurrent two-year sentences with an extension period of supervision (see Chapter 5) on a plea of guilty by the offender, a teacher, to sexual intercourse with a 15-year-old.

Attorney General's Reference No 46 (2004) where a sentence of five years for inde-cent assault and rape on a 12–13-year-old was held to be unduly lenient largely on account of these two aggravating factors, and a very late guilty plea.

The SGC has also upgraded the focus on the victim in its definitive guideline for sentencing when the offence involves domestic violence. The guideline states that '[a]s a starting point for sentence, offences committed in a domestic context should be regarded as being no less serious than offences committed in a non-domestic context' and then lists various factors arising from the nature of the offender–victim relationship which make the victim more vulnerable and so the offending more serious (Sentencing Guidelines Council 2006: 3–4).

Other forms of vulnerability in the victim have been taken to aggravate. In another reference by the Attorney General (*No 45 of 2000*) reported in 2001, the vic-tim of robbery and false imprisonment was a doctor, seen by the court as a highly vulnerable member of the community when making a house call late at night in unfamiliar surroundings. The judgment stated that courts had a duty to deter the commission of offences against such victims. Where the victim is an elderly person that also normally aggravates seriousness as in *Simpson* (2002), where an 89-year-old woman was the victim of manslaughter and robbery. Walker also notes cases where the severity was aggravated because the victim was a police officer (1999: 52–3).

Other factors

There are a number of other factors in addition to the above which are taken as aggravating in relation to a range of offences. Those generally noted[16] are the fol-lowing: premeditation and planning, a professional or group operation, unneces-sary violence, and the seriousness of the harm done. Prevalence might also be added as *Cunningham* (1993) did not rule this out after the implementation of the CJA 1991 and, regrettably, neither has the SGC: 'There may be exceptional local circumstances that arise which may lead a court to decide that prevalence should influence sentencing levels. The pivotal issue in such cases will be the harm being caused to the community' (Sentencing Guidelines Council 2004a: para 1.39).

Below we focus on two offence categories which raise particular issues about aggravation.

Causing death by dangerous driving

Causing death by dangerous driving is a particularly difficult offence on which to sentence because the two ingredients of seriousness—the culpability of the offender and the harm done (CJA 2003, s 143(1))—may not point in the same direction. The death—the most serious of harms—was not intended and so the calculation of culpability is relatively low in relation to the total of harm caused. 'Unintended consequences' have in effect downgraded the factor of harm done in relation to this offence and the calculation of seriousness is, rather, made in relation to the danger-ousness of, and risk posed by, the offender's driving.

Cooksley and others (2003) incorporated advice from the SAP on sentencing for the offence of causing death by dangerous driving (and also careless driving while under the influence of drink or drugs). As Wasik pointed out in the Preface to the SAP's advice, and as quoted by Lord Woolf CJ in his judgment, '[u]nderstandably,

---

[16] Two sources, apart from appellate guidance, SAP advice and SGC guidance, are Practice notes by the Lord Chief Justice and the latest version of the Magistrates' Association's *Sentencing Guidelines*.

this often leads to calls from the victims' families, and from the wider community, for tough sentencing' (*Cooksley and others* (2003) at para 1). The Court endorsed the view of the SAP that 'briefly dozing at the wheel' should no longer be viewed as indicating a less serious offence (ibid), and that dangerous driving resulting in death should attract a higher sentence than one that does not, the impact on the family being a matter the courts can legitimately take into account (ibid: para 11). The Court endorsed the 16 aggravating factors suggested by the SAP and listed them (ibid: para 15), before discussing sentence length in four bands: no aggravating circumstances, intermediate culpability, higher culpability, most serious culpability. The lowest starting point would be 12–18 months even on a plea of guilty, the highest 6 years or more. The aggravating factors likely to place the case in the 8–10 year category might be a combination of multiple deaths, excessive speed, excessive alcohol, and seeking to avoid responsibility (ibid: para 31).

This tougher approach was upheld in *Emery* (2003) where the driver had fallen asleep at the wheel. He had subsequently been diagnosed as suffering from obstructive sleep apnoea, a diagnosis which he contended he had not been told of seven years earlier when he had undergone nose surgery after falling asleep at the wheel of his vehicle on two occasions. Nevertheless, the Court of Appeal endorsed the comments of the trial judge that he had been 'grossly inattentive' of his sleep problems[17] and upheld the sentence of two years' imprisonment.

A Guideline is now being prepared: in January 2008 the SGC issued a Consultation Guideline, *Causing Death by Driving*. That document lists five factors 'that may be regarded as determinants of offence seriousness': 'awareness of risk, effect of alcohol or drugs, inappropriate speed of vehicle, seriously culpable behaviour of [the] offender and failing to have proper regard to vulnerable road users' (Sentencing Guidelines Council 2008c: 4; see also the advice of the Sentencing Advisory Panel 2008: paras 47–69). The draft guideline recommends, for example, that the starting points for the offence of causing death by careless or inconsiderate driving should be 15 months' imprisonment, 36 weeks' imprisonment or a community sentence depending on the level of seriousness, and lists appropriate aggravating factors such as 'serious injury to one or more persons in addition to the death(s)' and 'irresponsible behaviour, such as failing to stop or falsely claiming that one of the victims was responsible for the collision' (Sentencing Guidelines Council 2008c: 16).

Smuggling

The SAP issued advice on the fraudulent evasion of duty on importing tobacco and alcohol in July 2003.[18] The same month, in *Czyzewski* (2003), the Court of Appeal stated that such an offence is aggravated if a defendant (i) played an organisational role; (ii) made repeated imports particularly after receiving warnings; (iii) was a professional smuggler; (iv) used a legitimate business as a front; (v) abused a position of privilege; (vi) used children or vulnerable adults; (vii) threatened violence; (viii) dealt in goods with an additional health risk because of possible contamination; or (ix) disposed of goods to under-age purchasers. These factors are in line with the SAP's recommendations.

---

[17] Note that an aggravating factor (g) in *Cooksley* is 'driving while knowingly suffering from a medical condition which significantly impairs the offender's driving skills' (at para 15).

[18] See http://www.sentencing-guidelines.gov.uk/saphome.htm. See also Sentencing Advisory Panel (2007b) at pp 43–5 and 60.

It is worth noting that the aggravating factors of abuse of trust, the vulnerability and suffering of the victim, and premeditation, together with concealment of the body and the use of threats, are now listed in paragraph 10 of Schedule 21 of the CJA 2003 to assist the court in its determination of the minimum term of a mandatory life sentence for murder.

3.2.6 **Mitigation of seriousness**

The court must also consider mitigating factors relating to the offence when assessing seriousness but has discretion to assign a weight to such factors and to balance them against the weight of aggravating factors. Again, *Overarching Principles; Seriousness* (Sentencing Guidelines Council 2004a) lists appropriate general mitigating factors and offence-based guidelines provide examples of relevant mitigation. As Ashworth points out, however, mitigating factors comprise a 'much more heterogeneous collection' (2005: 160). Some factors amount to the absence of aggravation: less offender culpability, lack of premeditation/impulsiveness, a lone/amateur operation, lack of violence or intimidation, and no previous criminal record. Others focus on the relative lack of harm done. There are also mitigating factors relating to culpability which are in effect criminal defences, not used or not successful in the pre-conviction process but which have a long history as 'excuses' at the sentencing stage. These are necessity, duress, mistake of law, and provocation,[19] to which can be added entrapment,[20] all justified on the grounds that offending with these motivations or in these contexts entails less wickedness (Wasik 1983). More generally, exceptional stress or emotional pressure are potential mitigations of seriousness, as, for example, when someone steals to provide for a dying relative (Ashworth 2000: 140).

Court of Appeal cases and SGC guidelines lay down a wide range of mitigating factors relating to particular offences. For example, the two mitigating factors discussed in the domestic violence guideline are 'positive good character' and provocation (Sentencing Guidelines Council 2006: 5–6), whilst, in relation to the minimum period for murder, Schedule 21 (para 11) of the CJA 2003 lists the following mitigating factors:

(a) an intention to cause serious bodily harm rather than to kill

(b) lack of premeditation

(c) the fact that the offender suffered from any mental disorder or mental disability which (although not falling within s 2(1) of the Homicide Act 1957 (c. 11)), lowered his degree of culpability

(d) the fact that the offender was provoked (for example, by prolonged stress) in a way not amounting to a defence of provocation

(e) the fact that the offender acted to any extent in self-defence

(f) a belief by the offender that the murder was an act of mercy, and

(g) the age of the offender (see *Sullivan, Gibbs, Elener and another* (2004)[21] for a Court of Appeal case incorporating these factors).

---

[19] The correlative 'excuse' to the insanity defence will not be dealt with here: the treatment of mentally disordered offenders will be examined in Chapter 7 (section 7.4).

[20] Case law has established this is not a defence in English law: see Ashworth (2000: 140) for cases.

[21] A new Practice Direction was issued after this case: see Chapter 5, section 5.4.4.

There is little guidance on how to balance mitigating and aggravating factors and so it would be easy for disparity to occur. Further, where the offence is very serious or where the courts wish to give a particular message, notably a deterrent one, mitigating factors relating to the offence or the offender may have little or no effect (Piper 2007). An example could be taken from *Cooksley* (2002), discussed above, where Lord Woolf CJ said that 'it is important for the courts to drive home the message as to the dangers that can result from dangerous driving on the road...drivers must know that...no matter what the mitigating circumstances, normally only a custodial sentence will be imposed' (para 11).

3.3 Establishing proportionality

3.3.1 The seriousness thresholds

The CJA 2003 re-enacts the 'so serious that' and 'serious enough' criteria for imposing custodial and community sentences respectively, though there are some differences in application (see section 3.1.3 above). In December 2004, the SGC started publishing guidance on the new sentencing framework (see the Online Resource Centre for updates on the work of the SGC and SAP). However, how the appellate courts construed key concepts in the CJA 1991 continues to have an influence on interpretation of the CJA 2003 as did case law prior to the CJA 1991 on the interpretation of that Act. The cases discussed below are not, then, simply of historical interest: their influence is apparent, for example, in the SGC (2004a) guidance on seriousness.

online
resource
centre

In 1997 Ashworth and von Hirsch wrote an important article entitled 'Recognising Elephants: The Problem of the Custody Threshold'. This intriguing title referred to a test set out by Lawton LJ before the CJA 1991 in relation to the very similar 'so serious that only' hurdle for custody of young offenders in the Criminal Justice Act 1982. The conclusions of the article were based on over 50 reported Court of Appeal cases ruling on the CJA 1991 s 1(2)(a) criterion, the first of which was *Cox* (1993). In that case, Lord Taylor CJ retained Lord Justice Lawton's test of the 'right thinking members of the public' laid down in *Bradbourne* (1985 at 183) whereby a custodial sentence was justified if such right-thinking people, 'knowing all the facts', would 'feel that justice had not been done by the passing of any sentence other than a custodial one'. Lawton, 'having formulated this test with some reluctance' (Ashworth and von Hirsch 1997: 187), said that he was confident that 'courts can recognise an elephant when they see one, but may not find it necessary to define it'. How the courts were to ascertain the views of these members of the public is a moot point.

They conclude that this purportedly 'common-sense' test of the 'right-thinking' person was 'conceptually flawed and empirically unsupported' and generally unsatisfactory (Ashworth and von Hirsch 1997: 189). It is encouraging to find that Lord Bingham CJ endorsed these criticisms in *Howells and related appeals* (1999 at 53):

There is no bright line which separates offences which are so serious that only a custodial sentence can be justified from offences which are not so serious as to require the passing of a custodial sentence. But it cannot be said that the 'right-thinking' members of the public test is very helpful, since the sentencing court has no means of ascertaining the views of right-thinking members of the public and inevitably attributes to such right-thinking members its own views. So, when applying this test, the sentencing court is doing little more than reflecting its own opinion whether justice would or would not be done and be seen to be done by the passing of a non-custodial sentence.

The Court of Appeal found itself, however, unable to substitute a new test: they decided it would be 'dangerous and wrong for us to lay down prescriptive rules' (ibid). Its approach, and that of the SGC (2004a), was to focus on the custody/community penalty dividing line, and to specify the mitigating and aggravating factors which would or would not contribute towards tipping the case over the custody seriousness threshold. Lord Bingham CJ first listed five factors for courts 'ordinarily' to take into account: an admission of guilt, self-motivated and proven determination to address the causes of offending if 'fuelled by addiction', youth and immaturity, whether the offender was of previous good character, and whether the offender had previously been sentenced to custody (at 53–4). The Court then dealt separately with *Howells* and each of the other related appeals, discussing these factors and others such as premeditation, the use or threat of violence, the time of day, provocation, and the harm caused. SGC guidance includes these factors in more accessible, simplified lists (2004a).

The case of *Mills* (2002), dealing with offences of dishonesty, also discussed factors that should be considered when the offence is one that often receives a custodial sentence but the circumstances of the particular case reveal mitigating factors. Significantly it stated that, as well as asking whether prison is necessary, 'the sentencing judge also had to take into account the reality of sentencing policy' and, in particular three factors: the inability of the prison service to achieve anything positive in the way of rehabilitation during a short sentence (at 331), the effect on children if a single mother is imprisoned, and, specifically in relation to female prisoners, the fact that she might be allocated to a prison far from her home and children (at 332; also see Chapter 7, section 7.2.5 and Chapter 10, section 10.1.2).

Shortly after the implementation of the 1991 Act the Court of Appeal dealt with another principle in applying the seriousness criteria. In *Cunningham* (1993) the Court was asked to rule on whether deterrence could form part of the calculation of seriousness.

Section 2(2) of the Act provided that a custodial sentence should be commensurate with the seriousness of the offence or offences for which it is passed. That provision did allow the sentencer to take into account the need for deterrence. The purposes of a custodial sentence were to punish and deter. The phrase "commensurate with the seriousness of the offence" must mean commensurate with the punishment and deterrence which the offence required... The prevalence of an offence was a legitimate factor in determining the length of a custodial sentence. The seriousness of an offence was clearly affected by how many people it harmed and to what extent.

(*Criminal Law Review* at 150)

This extraordinary decision, whereby prevalence affected the construction of seriousness in an individual case, reached its goal by eliding a valid general statement about the purposes of punishment with a specific statutory provision designed to ensure that, in individual cases, the commensurate sentence was calculated only in relation to the level of seriousness of the instance of offending in question. Further, it 'proves' its conclusion by the unjustified use of words such as 'must' and 'clearly affected'.[22]

---

[22] For a discussion of judicial thinking about prevalence generally in sentencing, see Ashworth (2000: 91); for comments regarding prevalence by the SGC, see *Overarching Principles: Seriousness* (2004a: Section F; also note the reference on page 92 above).

The above cases would suggest that the custody test established by the CJA 1991 was 'easily satisfied' because of its 'broad interpretation' (Thomas 1995: 146–7) by a Court of Appeal not always eager to uphold the constraints on judicial discretion imposed by Parliament. Certainly the Halliday Report thought that the Act had been 'interpreted by the courts in ways that had not been predicted or expected' (2001: para 1.34).

The *Seriousness* guideline deals with the sentencing thresholds in section E and specifically notes that 'the clear intention of the threshold test is to reserve prison as a punishment for the most serious offences' (Sentencing Guidelines Council 2004a: 8) but it includes the statement that 'it is impossible to determine definitively which features of a particular offence make it serious enough to merit a custodial sentence' and that 'it would not be feasible to provide a form of words or to devise any formula that would provide a general solution to the problem of where the custody threshold lies. Factors vary too widely between offences for this to be done' (ibid: 8, 9). Considerable discretion is left to the sentencer.

3.3.2 Mitigation relating to the offender

There is also mitigation relating to the circumstances and character of the offender rather than to the seriousness of the offending. In effect they mitigate sentence once seriousness has been established and s 166(1) of the CJA 2003, reflecting previous practice, states that nothing in the crucial sentencing sections about the criteria for imposing the three levels of sentence 'prevents a court from mitigating an offender's sentence by taking into account any such matters as, in the opinion of the court, are relevant in the mitigation of sentence'. Further, s 166(2) states that the court is not prevented from imposing a community rather than custodial sentence in the light of mitigating circumstances and s 156(2) specifically gives the court discretion to take into account any information about the offender which is before it in deciding the type of community or youth community order to impose. The CJI Act 2008 s 10 similarly imports discretion in relation to imposing community orders (see Online Resource Centre).

online
resource
centre

Personal mitigation can be placed into three categories, relating to:

1. the good qualities of the offender
2. the efficient and fair operation of the criminal justice system
3. the impact of the sentence on the offender.

The last category of personal mitigation—the adverse or abnormal impact of the sentence on the offender—will not be dealt with here: see Chapter 7. Below we will focus briefly on the first and second categories before dealing in some detail with the guilty plea, a form of personal mitigation justified as a 'reward' for those who help the system.

A 'good' offender

The first category—where the personal characteristics and circumstances of the offender are considered—may not, as we have seen, be given effect in sentencing where the offending is of a very serious nature. The offender or his lawyer has complete discretion to introduce whichever factors appear relevant; the sentencer has complete discretion to accept or reject that they should reduce the sentence.

Where the court does reduce the sentence it can be justified on the basis that the criminal justice system should be administered as mercifully as possible.

The factors which may be considered by sentencers include the following: stress in life at the time of committing the offence (for example, extreme poverty or imminent childbirth), meritorious conduct (for example, making reparation for harm done), leading a law-abiding and stable life since the offence was committed (for example, finding employment or getting married), and the age of the offender (for example, if below 21 or of an advanced age). Moral credit has also sometimes been given for something unconnected with the offence, such as a 'good' war record, donation of a kidney, or starting a youth club (see Walker 1985: 50) and the effects of the sentence on others, notably children, has sometimes been influential (ibid: 52).[23]

Fair operation of the system

There are other circumstances which can mitigate sentence severity. They can be rationalised either as allowing the criminal justice system to be seen to be administered with as little injustice as possible, or as encouraging cost-efficient and effective criminal justice processes. The discount for a guilty plea is the obvious example of the latter and will be dealt with below. The factor of assisting law enforcement clearly also falls into the latter, with the position of informers being a good example. Mitigation—or not—on this basis has a long and varied history. In *Sherman* (1913) two co-burglars received sentences of seven and ten years; the one who had informed on the other successfully appealed and had his sentence reduced from seven to three years. The judge explained that, '[i]t is expedient that they should be persuaded not to trust one another, that there should not be honour among thieves'. The unfavourable publicity given to the effects of such mitigation in the 'supergrass' cases of the 1970s led to smaller sentence reductions but *Sivan and others* (1988) and, more recently, *A and B* (1999) have confirmed a reduction in sentence where assistance to the police is given before sentence.

Mitigation relating to 'fairness' includes the approach taken to sentencing co-defendants and to multiple sentences. In relation to the former the sentence may be reduced in order that like cases may be seen to be treated alike. For the latter the court can impose concurrent sentences if the total punishment appears unjust and disproportionate. This 'totality principle' is now enshrined in legislation (see Chapter 2, section 2.4.1). There is no statutory guidance on the use of concurrent sentences but practice tends to be that consecutive sentences are imposed where the sentences are for unconnected offences,[24] but concurrent sentences where the offences are all part of the same offending incident (Walker 1999: 98–100). The issue of how to charge and sentence multiple offenders, whether they be offenders whose offending incident gives rise to a variety of charges or whether a prolonged period of offending behaviour produces a long list of similar offences, is, however, much more complicated than this, and the justifications are varied. Ashworth devotes a whole chapter to these issues (2005: Chapter 8) and we would refer readers to this.

---

[23] The influence of the impact of sentence on the offender and his or her family will be examined further in Chapter 7.

[24] See CJA 2003, s 155 for powers of magistrates' courts.

3.3.3 **Discount for a guilty plea**

Justified as giving credit to the offender for his contribution to the efficiency of the system, the discount for a guilty plea can have a substantial effect on the level of sentence and is potentially available for all offenders. The discount should be applied after all the matters noted above have been dealt with. As stated in recent guidance:

When deciding the most appropriate length of sentence, the sentencer should address separately the issue of remorse, together with any other mitigating features, before calculating the reduction for the guilty plea. Similarly, assistance to the prosecuting or enforcement authorities is a separate issue which may attract a reduction in sentence under other procedures; care will need to be taken to ensure that there is no 'double counting'.

(Sentencing Guidelines Council 2007a: para 2.4).

In the past, the discount for a guilty plea was theorised either as mitigation based on the good personal quality of contrition or as a reward for the offender's part in reducing the need for a trial with its cost implications and its burdens on witnesses. In *Hussain* (2002) the Court of Appeal said that a guilty plea might be indicative of some remorse but, given that the discount is almost automatic, SGC (2004b) guidance places it more logically into the second category. The CJA 2003, s 144 replaces the PCCSA 2000, s 152[25] but the law is the same: where the offender has pleaded guilty the court must take into account the stage in the proceedings at which he indicated his plea of guilt and the circumstances in which it was given.

A particular difficulty has arisen in relation to those who are caught 'red-handed'. *Hussain* (2002) upheld the previous position in case law whereby particular circumstances, such as being caught red-handed, might justify the non-implementation of a discount but stated that some credit by way of discount must always be given if a trial is avoided, especially if there is a vulnerable victim as witness. SGC guidance stated that it is in everyone's interest that those who are guilty of an offence indicate willingness to plead guilty at the earliest opportunity (2004b: Preface) and said that the normal sliding scale applied to those caught red-handed but that '[i]f the not guilty plea was entered and maintained for tactical reasons (such as to retain privileges whilst on remand), a late guilty plea should attract very little, if any, discount' (ibid: 5).

However, the 2004 guideline received criticism in relation to this issue amongst others and a consultation exercise was undertaken by the Sentencing Advisory Panel, at the request of the SGC, in 2006. The key issues were:

- Does a maximum reduction of one-third properly balance the interests of justice and the encouragement of guilty pleas?
- Should there be an upper limit on the amount of the reduction?
- What further clarification of the 'first reasonable opportunity' for entering a guilty plea is necessary?
- To what degree, if any, should the fact that the prosecution case is overwhelming influence the level of reduction?

---

[25] First enacted as s 48 of the Criminal Justice and Public Order Act 1994 and repealed 4 April 2005.

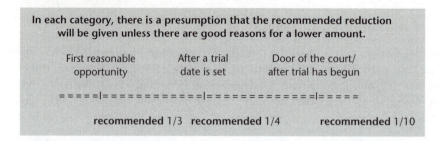

Figure 3.2 A sliding scale
Source: Sentencing Guidelines Council (2007a).

New guidance was issued in July 2007 (Sentencing Guidelines Council 2007a). It confirmed that the level of reduction 'should be a proportion of the total sentence imposed, with the proportion calculated by reference to the circumstances in which the guilty plea was indicated, in particular the stage in the proceedings' and that 'the greatest reduction will be given where the plea was indicated at the "first reasonable opportunity"' (ibid: para 4.1; but note the exception in relation to mandatory minimum sentences for domestic burglary and class A drugs offences: see CJA 2003 s 142(2)). The maximum discount remains at one-third with recommended reductions of one-quarter and one-tenth for pleas given at later stages of the process (see Figure 3.2).

The Council has agreed with the SAP that some discretion should be introduced where the prosecution case is 'overwhelming' (ibid: para 5.3) and suggested, as an example, that instead of the usual one-third discount where the guilty plea was indicated at the first reasonable opportunity, 20 per cent might be appropriate (ibid: para 5.4). The SGC did not accept the recommendation of the SAP to cap the effect of a reduction on very large fines. The guideline specifically noted that where the maximum penalty for the offence is thought to be too low a sentencer cannot remedy perceived defects by refusal of the appropriate discount (ibid: para 5.6).

Annex 1 to the guidance provides further clarification of 'first reasonable opportunity' by listing examples which would count as such depending on the circumstances. So, 'the first reasonable opportunity may be the first time that a defendant appears before the court and has the opportunity to plead guilty' but the court 'may consider that it would be reasonable to have expected an indication of willingness even earlier, perhaps whilst under interview' (ibid: 10).[26]

The general approach of the guideline follows the Magistrates' Association Guidelines before 2003 which suggested a discount of about one-third. However, various research projects and criminal statistics had indicated that reductions in practice varied between 22 per cent and 40 per cent (see Ashworth 2000: 145–7 for references and discussion). Research would also suggest that—at least in the mid-1990s—35 per cent of judges did not consider the stage at which the plea was entered to be of any importance (Henham 1999: 527). Further, whilst discounts appear to be given for custodial and financial penalties, there seemed to be no significant difference in length of a community service order or a probation order (Flood-Page and Mackie 1998: 92).

online
resource
centre

[26] SGC guidance specifically in regard to sentencing for murder sets a maximum discount of one-sixth: see the Online Resource Centre.

3.3.4 **Not a mathematical exercise?**

We have dealt in turn with the most important aspects of the process of determining a proportionate sentence under retributivist principles. At one level this might be seen as a logical process which can be worked through in an entirely objective way. The following guidance from the SGC might appear as such. In dealing with the custody threshold, *Overarching Principles: Seriousness* provides the following decision-making approach as a series of questions for the sentencer:

- Has the statutory threshold been passed?
- Is custody unavoidable?
- Can the sentence be suspended, (or be served intermittently)?
- What is the commensurate sentence?

(Sentencing Guidelines Council 2004a: para 1.33).

However, the third update to the *Case Compendium* produced by the SGC in 2007 sounds a cautionary note when providing the following summary of the *Martin* case in the 'Generic Sentencing Principles' section.

R v Martin [2006] EWCA Crim 1035

- The sentencing decision does not represent a mathematical exercise, nor does it result from an arithmetical calculation.
- It is not the case that each element relevant to the sentencing decision has or should have ascribed to it some notional length of sentence so that, depending on whether the individual ingredient constitutes aggravating or mitigating material, the actual sentence should increase or reduce in accordance with that figure. The reality is that a sentencer must balance all the circumstances of the case in order to reach an appropriate sentence.
- Although consistency of approach is to be encouraged, guidelines (whether provided by the Court of Appeal or the Sentencing Guidelines Council) remain guidelines. Section 174 of the Criminal Justice Act 2003, which imposes a duty on the court to give reasons for and explain the effect of its sentence, recognizes a significant difference between sentences which are within or outside the normal range indicated by guidelines. The use of the word 'range' should be emphasized.

We are well aware that just deserts sentencing leaves many difficult decisions about seriousness and proportionality to the judges and magistrates and that guidance on sentencing levels does not yet appear to constitute a consistent set. That the effect of mitigation—both of seriousness and the offender's circumstances—and aggravation can be so crucial in relation to the choice or length of a custodial sentence is an issue we will return to in Chapter 7. The question of whether the difficulties still lie with retributivism itself will be examined next.

3.4 **Theoretical critiques of modern retributivism**

We have reviewed current sentencing practice within a predominantly just deserts framework and summarised the recent changes to that framework and criticisms of them. What the next section aims to do is to examine more fundamental criticisms of just deserts as a primary rationale.

Criticism of retributivism has come from all shades of the political and theoretical spectrum and so we will, in this section, consider the current penological debates and also the critiques from Marxist perspectives, before looking at Rights Theory in section 3.5.1.

3.4.1 The limits of just deserts

The approach of modern retributivism, based substantially on the work of von Hirsch, does not satisfy all critics of retributivism or resolve all the problems with the retributivist approach. In particular, there remains the issue of the extent to which proportionality as the primary purpose of sentencing should take priority over other factors in 'exceptional' cases. For example, should effectiveness and efficiency, or public safety, take priority over individual rights as in the case of dangerous offenders who need to be quarantined, or, with certain 'abhorrent' crimes, is it sufficient simply to apportion blame, when it appears difficult to find a commensurate sentence? Perhaps the greatest difficulty in practice is how to find a mechanism and a consensus to calculate seriousness, to rank offences, mitigations, and aggravations, and to rank penalties in such a way that the key element of proportionality is clear and justly operationalised. However, the attempt to achieve clarity by producing accurate theoretical models of ordinal and cardinal proportionality could result in as many types of punishment as there are offenders, with different degrees of culpability, which would be impossible to administer.

As we have seen, the present system has been criticised for its complexity and incoherence. The problem that emerges is that, even if we take full account of desert and proportionality, we can still end up with some cases of lesser offences receiving much harsher sentences than serious offenders with mitigation, and such instances have implications for the legitimacy of the system and public support. So it may be better, as Bagaric (2001) argues, to have fixed penalties (see Chapter 7, section 7.3.4), but this raises the sort of questions about the inflexibility of grid-type sentencing that prompted Tonry to rethink retributivism.

These difficulties with the key issue of proportionality in desert theory have prompted new thinking. Braithwaite and Pettit (1990) have developed an alternative theory, grounded in restorative justice (see Chapter 6, section 6.1.2). They distinguish their own model, which advocates instrumental shaming, from the penal censure of retributivism, because they seek to separate shaming from the degree of severity of sanctions. They also advocate reducing the level of punishment until the point at which crime starts to increase. Censure for them is essentially stigmatising and may be achieved by a variety of means, including adverse publicity.

Another major issue is whether it is ever possible to make the justification for a retributivist approach sufficiently clear and logical for both popular understanding and political legitimacy. For example, it has been argued that von Hirsch's modified form of retributivism may be hard to justify without lapsing into consequentialism, which is a utilitarian rather than retributivist notion. Von Hirsch, Bagaric (2001) argues, never establishes why his censuring account of punishment is morally justifiable. Yet there are good consequentialist reasons to support his theory, such as von Hirsch's recognition of the role of deterrence and the positive functions of blaming, and the beneficial social consequences of the acknowledgement of harm done to the victim which satisfies the victim and may prevent vigilantism. As Bagaric observes, there is no point in blaming the offender if there are no beneficial effects. Showing the third party that an action is wrong may ultimately prevent offending, that is, another good consequence.

Retributivism has also been criticised more generally as a conservative and repressive theory which can too easily lend legitimacy to punitive penal policies. The main elements of that critique are that the theory, by focusing only on desert, fails to acknowledge the implications of poverty and social inequality for offending behaviour, and that it is most strongly associated with reactionary regimes around the world—whether based on religious or secular principles—and is repressive in the sense of generating an escalation of punishment. Rubin (2003), for example, argues that embedding retribution within the Model Penal Code of the American Law Institute would have an adverse effect, leading to longer sentences. But each of these assumptions is problematic and is not a valid basis for jettisoning just deserts.

First, there is no automatic association between right-wing regimes and retributivism. As von Hirsch (1986) emphasises, if we look around the world we find the most progressive regimes in Scandinavia have used proportionality and desert as principles of punishment rather than incapacitation or rehabilitation. One might also point to the Stalinist penal regime, as one of the most repressive in history, a regime based on an extreme form of 'social efficiency' rather than desert.

Second, a concern with desert and proportionality may limit excessive punishment in its rejection of exemplary sentences and selective incapacitation. Although it is true, as von Hirsch acknowledges, that incarceration increased in some states in the USA, such as California, which adopted a just deserts model, closer examination shows that the prison population was already increasing before the model was adopted in the mid-1970s. Further, proportionality was not used in making the decision to impose custody, but only in determining the length of the sentence. On the other hand, argues von Hirsch (1986), the Minnesota sentencing guidelines of the late 1970s and early 1980s, which were based on a modified desert principle, did lead to consistent sentencing. At the time they prevented the expansion of the prison population because they imprisoned those convicted of the most serious crimes, but imprisoned fewer convicted of lesser crimes, and were subject to safeguards to limit the size of the prison population. Moreover, as he points out, the Sentencing Commission in Minnesota did take account of prison capacity when drawing up the sentencing guidelines. It has also been argued by Lippke (2007) that retributivism, by limiting punishment to those who have committed serious harms to others, and not sentencing simply to satisfy public opinion, can be an effective constraint on increased punitiveness. Furthermore, he argues, a penal system which recognises and does not crush offenders' capacities to lead autonomous lives will result in a more humane form of imprisonment.

A major critique of retributivism has been that it is no longer the most effective way of limiting excessive punishment, given the possibility of appeals to human rights (see, for example, Walker, 1991, 1999). A humanitarian approach can impose a limit regardless of desert or crime reduction. We will return to this in section 3.5.

3.4.2 Radical critiques of retributivism

A longer-standing source of criticism has come from those radical approaches which have criticised retributivism for not addressing the underlying social problems of inequality, poverty, and injustice, which may be linked to offending.[27] Marxist critiques of retributivist theory, for example, have used social scientific

---

[27] Some of these problems in relation to social exclusion will be considered in Chapters 7, 10 and 11.

research to show the problems with individualist models and the links between marginalisation and criminality. This is a valid criticism but it raises the question whether it is the task of any penal theory to undertake the gargantuan task of solving problems of social inequality: certainly rival theories of punishment from utilitarian traditions or from restorative justice do not do so. But at the least one can say that desert theory is not antithetical to progressive social policies, as evidenced by those European jurisdictions—such as Sweden and Finland—which have both the clearest desert-based sentencing systems and the most progressive welfare and social programmes.

Radical critiques also raise the issue of whether we should focus on the social disadvantage of offenders when imposing punishments, and treat disadvantage as a mitigating factor. On desert theory the individual is still culpable even if this culpability is reduced by extreme poverty or economic distress. In any case most crime falls far short of necessity in the sense used in the criminal law[28] and recent studies of wealth and poverty in the UK have focused on inequality and relative deprivation rather than absolute poverty (see Dorling *et al.* 2007). Even if deprivation is a factor in the circumstances surrounding the offence, this does not mean proportionality is no longer relevant, although reducing a sentence for a particular offender on social grounds would be unfair on the retributivist model. Moreover, if social and economic factors are given precedence over issues of desert, this may work to the disadvantage of economically and socially deprived offenders; for example, social and economic factors are already included in the OASys Assessment System to predict the risks posed by offenders and to make decisions on their release and management.

Furthermore, one could argue that poor or disadvantaged offenders may be more strongly protected by desert theory than by rival theories. Von Hirsch (1993), for example, argues that there is more scope for raising such issues in desert theory and that poorer offenders would be better protected by lowering the anchoring points for penalties than by looking at individual disadvantage, which might encourage the disadvantaged offender to be seen as a higher risk, although this argument is unlikely to satisfy those who want compensation for disadvantage.

The problems which arise in taking account of the impact of punishment in an unequal society are further considered in Chapters 7 and 10, whilst the issues of inequality and discrimination will be considered in Chapter 12 in relation to the experience of imprisonment.

Marx himself says little on punishment and does not offer a theory or justification of punishment but, rather, is concerned to contextualise punishment in its social, economic, and historical context. He did write a short article on 'Capital Punishment' (Marx 1853) where he argued that it would be 'very difficult, if not altogether impossible, to establish any principle upon which the justice or expediency of capital punishment could be founded' while Engels says that how to punish criminals is a topic he leaves to his readers (Engels 1843).

However, Marx is more sympathetic to retributivism than to **utilitarian theories of punishment**. Although critical of the view that punishment may be

---

[28] *Dudley & Stephens* (1884) 14 QBD 273. While Kant accepts the non-criminality of homicide from necessity and gives the example of the person who, in order to save his own life in a shipwreck, pushes another person, whose life is equally in danger, off a plank on which he has saved himself, this is far removed from the kinds of choice relevant to discussions of 'everyday' crime (Kant 1796–7). See also von Hirsch and Ashworth (2005).

ameliorating or intimidating, because of the absence of proof of the effectiveness of punishment in preventing crime, he does praise Kant's and Hegel's theory of punishment because it recognises human dignity and the rights of the person punished, treats the individual as 'a free and self-determined being', and focuses on rights and autonomy. But he argues that the retributivists' reification of free will fails to take account of the impact of social and economic pressures on the individual (Marx 1853)[29] and that German idealism abstracts the individual from society. What the idealists see as universal features of all societies are products of a specific mode of production and limited to specific strata. Given the incidence and recurrence of crime in nineteenth-century society, effort should be addressed to dealing with the underlying social system which generates crime, rather than focusing attention on refining systems of punishment.

Marx's relationship to retributivism is considered by Murphy (1973) who argues that, while Marx sees retributivism as the most defensible theory of punishment, the conditions in modern society render the theory inapplicable in most modern societies and rob those societies of their moral right to punish. The picture of individuals exercising free will and of autonomy and rationality fits uneasily with the reality of the alienation of modern capitalist society which is crime-ridden, where individuals act out of greed and self-interest, and society is marked by an absence of reciprocity, in contrast to the Hegelian State where there is a genuine community and where the rules are internalised. In our society, says Murphy, it is hard to see how the socially deprived benefit from membership or to construe individuals as acting freely when responding to severe social deprivation, but these issues are overlooked by the classical retributivists. Murphy cites the work of the Marxist criminologist Willem Bonger (1916) who links crime and deprivation.

Murphy argues that, if society were reconstructed to meet the Marxian ideal of a society where all individuals participate in relations of mutuality, then it would fit the retributivist model because there would be genuine autonomy of all individuals and in that case retributivist punishment would be justifiable, although, in any case, in such a society crime would be likely to decrease.[30]

The implications of social deprivation for retributivism will also be considered in the context of a discussion of equality of impact and impact mitigation in Chapter 10.

3.4.3 Modern Marxian critiques

Modern Marxists have been more concerned with processes of criminalisation than with punishment, although humanist Marxist social historians, including Thompson (1977) and Hay *et al.* (1975) have considered the historical development of modes of punishment, the legitimacy of punishment, the significance of the notion of the rule of law as an ideal and ideology, and the role of law in maintaining the hegemony of the ruling class. Critical legal scholars have subjected key concepts of liberal legalism, including rights and equality, to a rigorous critique. An

---

[29] A similar argument is advanced by Marx and Engels in their critique of the Young Hegelians in *The Holy Family* (1845).

[30] The relationship between justice and the mode of production may itself be problematic within Marxian theory. See Wood (1972, 2004), McBride (1975) and Easton (2008a). But Marx argues in *The Holy Family* that in communism, 'under *humane* conditions punishment will *really* be nothing but the sentence passed by the culprit on himself' (1845: 179) which is closer to the Hegelian ethical idea.

historical materialist approach to punishment means understanding punishment historically, changing through time and varying with each mode of production. On classical Marxist theory the specific form which punishment takes will reflect underlying economic conditions, and the needs of the dominant class. In early capitalism, as the demand for labour increased in the new factory mode of production, imprisonment displaced capital punishment.

Punishment does not simply reflect desert as on a retributivist model but punishment is a means of social control. Punishment is also used to discipline the working class, in so far as conditions in prison are made worse than the poorest conditions in the labour market outside, to inculcate work discipline through the experience of imprisonment and, historically, to provide a source of labour through transportation to the United States, replacing slave labour after the abolition of slavery (see Rusche and Kirchheimer 1939). Rusche and Kirchheimer see the declining use of imprisonment in the early twentieth century as reflecting the shift towards disciplining the work force within the production process, as new processes such as the assembly line developed.

Structuralist Marxists such as Althussser (1971) consider the role of the penal system as part of the repressive state apparatus but also emphasise the ideological functions of law. Using historical materialist methods, we can see that the levels and forms of punishment vary according to economic conditions in the sense that when labour is scarce, punishment is less severe and when labour is oversupplied, punishment is harsher. So in times of full employment, such as the 1960s, we see a liberalisation of punishment, concern with reform and rehabilitation, and loss of support for capital punishment here and in the United States. But in times of recession punishment becomes harsher and incarceration rates increase and at the level of consciousness fear of crime supplants fears of economic decline. Recent economic analysis, for example the work of Loic Wacquant (2001a, 2001b, 2007), has focused on the role of the prison as a way of absorbing surplus labour as changes in the forces of production have reduced demand for unskilled labour, while the marginalisation and demoralisation of the 'lumpenproletariat' has contributed to rising crime.

How useful are Marxian and critical approaches to punishment? Classical Marxism has been criticised for its economic reductionism and failure to offer concrete proposals for penal reform. Modern critical approaches have been criticised for their failure to generate radical changes in the penal system or criminal justice system generally. Even those modern theorists sympathetic to sociological models of punishment, such as Garland and Murphy, find Marxian theory of limited value in giving guidance to modern penal institutions and policies and, as we have argued, this was not a project of interest to Marx himself. But the value of the model is to highlight the inherent problems facing crime reductionist policies which fail to take account of underlying social and economic conditions which are criminogenic. It also offers an alternative to liberal conceptions of state punishment. Although Hudson dismisses Marxism as a form of modernism whose time has gone, many of Marx's concepts, such as alienation, are still relevant to postmodern debates on crime and social exclusion (see Easton 2008b).

Placing punishment in its social, historical, and political context is part of Marx's legacy and is reflected in modern sociological perspectives on punishment. For example, Garland (1991) has considered the impact of economic and social factors on contemporary sentencing and, while cautious regarding monolithic explanations of complex behaviour, he appreciates that Marxian analyses transcend a narrow approach to penal theory and practice. There has also been interest in developing communitarian approaches to punishment and to criminal justice which recognise the primacy of social relations. For example, Lacey (1988) has challenged the traditional liberal framework of the justifications of punishment from a communitarian standpoint.

3.5 Conclusions

3.5.1 Rights theory

In the above section we examined critiques of modern retributivism from penological and criminological perspectives. However, the recent developments in rights theory provide justifications for limiting excessive punishment which are independent of such thinking. While rights theory has developed within the retributivist traditions of Kantian and Hegelian philosophy, and retributivists are usually strongly committed to rights, one may find appeals to rights without a commitment to retributivism, notably in civil libertarian critiques of capital punishment. For example, Amnesty International's critique of the death penalty construes the use of the death penalty as ultimately a rights issue.

From a rights perspective, abolitionists argue that the inalienable right to life is violated by the death penalty, the manner in which the punishment is carried out is inhuman and degrading and shows no respect for human dignity, and the punishment cannot be justified on the grounds of self-defence because it is not undertaken in response to an immediate threat to life.

In the Universal Declaration of Human Rights in 1948 each person has the right to life (Article 3) and no person shall be subject to torture or to cruel, inhuman or degrading treatment or punishment (Article 5). Capital punishment is premeditated killing when other means are available. It is cruel treatment because it is a physical and mental attack on a helpless person. It raises the question whether there is a meaningful difference between, for example, hanging as a form of torture and hanging as a form of execution. Shooting or electrocuting a helpless person would also be seen as torture, so critics argue: it does not make any difference that the state is carrying out that punishment.

UN policy now favours abolition, reflected in Article 6 of the International Covenant on Civil and Political Rights (ICCPR) which protects the right to life. It states that in countries which have not abolished the death penalty, the sentence may be imposed only for the most serious crimes and then not on persons below the age of 18 or on pregnant women, but stresses that nothing in Article 6 shall be invoked to delay or to prevent the abolition of capital punishment, by any state parties to the Covenant. International human rights law is becoming more important in the debate, as shown, for example, in *Lagrand* (*Germany v United States*) (2001). On the rights-based argument the death penalty is wrong even if we can show that it meets a social need such as crime control, prevention of homicides, or assists efforts to combat drug trafficking. The whole point of the right is that it should not be jettisoned whenever the public interest or welfare seem threatened.

Similarly, torture may conceivably be very useful in matters of crime control but this could not justify its use. On the Dworkinian model rights always trump utility and rights have a privileged position, usurping the principles of desert and proportionality (Dworkin 1977). Rights apply to all and even the worst offenders who have committed terrible crimes retain these rights.

Under the European Convention on Human Rights, Article 2 protects the right to life, but Article 2(1) explicitly states that '[n]o one shall be deprived of his life intentionally save in execution of a sentence of the court, following his conviction from a crime for which the penalty is provided by law'. So here the Convention is not as progressive as the ICCPR. However, in practice European states comply with the spirit of Article 6 of the ICCPR. The Sixth Protocol to the European Convention expresses commitment to abolition and not allowing any executions in the interim period. It has been ratified by all member states of the Council of Europe except Russia. Protocol 13 to the Convention adopted by the Committee of Ministers of the Council of Europe in February 2002 abolishes the death penalty in all circumstances including times of war or public emergency. It has now been ratified by most member states and came into force on 1 July 2003. The last execution within the Council of Europe was over ten years ago, although some of the Convention issues were considered in the case of *Ocalan v Turkey* in 2003. In this case, the leader of the Kurdish Workers Party (PKK) was given a death sentence, later commuted to imprisonment. Here the European Court found that there was a breach of Article 5(4) because Ocalan had been unable to challenge the legality of his detention pre-trial and a breach of Article 6 because he had not been tried by an impartial tribunal. Article 3 was also breached because the death penalty had been imposed following an unfair trial, wrongfully subjecting Ocalan to the fear that he would be executed. The courts also took account of the fact that member states had now rejected the death penalty, in deciding that in this particular case the death sentence amounted to inhuman treatment.

However, the status of the death penalty has arisen in relation to extradition cases to the USA and raises the issue of whether the penalty is a cruel, inhuman, and degrading punishment and therefore prohibited by Article 3. In *Soering v UK* (1989), a case concerning the extradition of a prisoner to the USA to face the death penalty, the Strasbourg Court said the circumstances in which the death penalty was administered could amount to inhuman and degrading treatment, although the death penalty *per se* was not inhuman and degrading. Here the circumstances were that the applicant was likely to be on death row for years and there were also mitigating circumstances in that case. There is now an understanding that defendants will not be extradited to the USA if they will receive the death penalty but will be dealt with by other means.

This 'gentleman's agreement' has been criticised for leading to inconsistency and may be challenged in future if there are applications to extradite those suspected of committing terrorist crimes in the United States. The informal arrangements between the US and Europe were formalised in 2003 with a new UK–US Extradition Treaty and a separate EU–US Extradition Treaty. Article 7 of the UK–US Treaty states that the executive authority may refuse extradition unless the Requesting State provides an assurance that the death penalty will not be imposed, or if imposed, will not be carried out. However, the EU–US Treaty is weaker as it does not make assurances regarding the non-use of the death penalty mandatory.

Moreover, within the US domestic law, there have been constitutional rights-based challenges to the penalty under the Eighth Amendment prohibition on cruel and unusual punishment. These led to a temporary moratorium on its use in the 1970s in *Furman v Georgia* (1972), and a narrowing of the application of the penalty to offenders with learning difficulties in *Atkins v Virginia* (2002) and offenders under 18 in *Roper v Simmonds* (2005). The methods of execution are also currently being challenged: the United State Supreme Court recently heard oral arguments challenging the use of lethal injection in *Baze v Rees* (2008) and the State of Nebraska Supreme Court heard a challenge on the use of the electric chair in *State v Mata* (2008).

Rights-based critiques also extend to corporal and custodial forms of punishment. Article 3 of the European Convention, based on Article 5 of the UN Declaration of Human Rights, states that no one should be subjected to torture or to cruel, inhuman or degrading treatment or punishment. Moreover the right is absolute, allowing no derogations in time of war or public emergency. Even when a punishment is deserved and even if a deterrent effect could be established, an extreme punishment would be precluded if it constituted inhuman or degrading treatment. For example, corporal punishment in the Isle of Man was seen as degrading in *Tyrer v UK* (1979–80). Article 3 is relevant to extreme punishments although in practice conditions in prison have to be quite severe to constitute a breach (see Chapter 9). While UK lawyers traditionally have been wary of rights, a rights culture is now being established. A rights-based system of punishment will achieve legitimacy for a system of punishment and the use of international standards will be a key restraint on punishment systems and an antidote to discretion.

However, this distinction between retributive and rights-based systems should not be exaggerated as the right not to be subjected to a disproportionate punishment is being given more weight in international human rights instruments (see van Zyl Smit and Ashworth 2004).

3.5.2 **Case study**

This sentencing exercise is about Jemma who was arrested, charged, and pleaded guilty to obtaining property by deception, pursuant to s 15 of the Theft Act 1968, for which the maximum penalty is 10 years' imprisonment. The facts of the case, on which the Crown Court Judge must pass sentence, are as follows:

Jemma, a 21-year-old undergraduate, has been working part-time for the last two years as a care assistant at a Care Home for the Elderly. In this capacity she persuaded six elderly residents to hand over £50 each to her, ostensibly to pay into a Christmas fund. This they all did one morning as arranged and she told them she would collect another instalment the following month. Jemma used the money to pay her rent as she was no longer eligible for a student loan, she had debts, and she could not rely on her father because his business had just collapsed. She was seriously depressed and was attending counselling sessions.[31]

Jemma's deception was discovered before the next instalment was due because one of the residents from whom she had obtained money asked the Matron about

---

[31] You are not expected to use the provisions of the Mental Health Act 1983 in this exercise: these possibilities will not be dealt with until Chapter 7, section 7.4.

the Christmas fund. Jemma did not at first plead guilty, fearful that she would never obtain employment on graduating and believing the elderly residents were too ill and mentally confused to give evidence. In the event, a change of medication dramatically improved the physical and mental health of one of them. Jemma, therefore, changed her plea to guilty before the trial.

In between the offending and trial, Jemma graduated and was left a legacy of £3,000 by an aunt. After paying her debts she has £150 left. She was given a reprimand[32] at the age of 14 for shoplifting and had one previous conviction, at the age of 16, under s 18 of the Offences against the Person Act 1861, for which she received a probation order. (She was not given detention in a young offender institution because of mitigation in relation to the death of her mother and a subsequent depressive illness.)

1. Sentence Jemma, explaining and justifying your chosen sentencing framework and particular sentence.

2. Decide whether your sentence would be different if:

    (a) Jemma had no previous convictions.

    (b) Jemma defrauded the residents because they were all South Asians.

    (c) The current offence was committed whilst Jemma was on bail awaiting trial for a drug offence—a charge of which she was subsequently acquitted.

    (d) Jemma worked in a children's home, had obtained property by deception from her fellow care workers and also had previously been convicted of possession of indecent photographs of a child under the CJA 1988, s 160. What if Jemma had incited a fellow care worker to commit an offence under the Protection of Children Act 1978, instead of obtaining property from them by deception?

**online
resource
centre**

You will need the checklist provided in section 3.2.2. The Online Resource Centre will provide further guidance.

---

[32] Reprimands and warnings replaced police cautions for minors: see Chapter 8, section 8.5.3. The court might view this as a previous conviction.

4

Utility and deterrence

SUMMARY

In this chapter we examine an approach which focuses on the consequences or outcomes of sentencing and punishment. We examine the origins of this approach in the work of Beccaria and Bentham, and its modern expression in the work of writers such as Wilson. We will focus here on the specific outcome of deterrence, considering whether deterrence is effective in reducing offending, reviewing the available research and the problems which arise in establishing a deterrent effect. We will also consider some of the difficulties with this justification for punishment.

4.1 A focus on outcome

4.1.1 Policy trends

We will focus on some of the ways in which sentencing and punishment have been justified in terms of the outcome, the desired end product of imposing a particular penalty on an offender. This is in contrast to the retributivist, 'just deserts', sentencing framework, discussed in Chapters 2 and 3, which is not primarily concerned with outcome or the consequences of the sentencing decision other than that of ensuring that justice has been done. Only when we discussed the *Cunningham* (1993) case could outcome be said to have had any relevance in our discussion of just deserts. In that case, the Court of Appeal, considering whether the custodial penalty was 'commensurate with the seriousness' of the offending, as required by the newly implemented Criminal Justice Act (CJA) 1991, argued that the prevalence of the offence in question increased its severity and so justified a sentence which was, in effect, a deterrent one.

In the Introduction to the White Paper, *Criminal Justice: The Way Ahead* the Government argued the case for an effective, well-run criminal justice system, stating that such a system:

must be:

- effective at preventing offending and reoffending;
- efficient in the way it deals with cases;
- responsive at every stage to the needs of the victims and the law abiding community; and
- accountable for the decisions it takes.

(Home Office 2001a: para 4)[1]

---

[1] These characteristics relate to the criminal justice system as a whole but Part 2 of the document makes it clear they also relate specifically to the sentencing stage.

On the face of it this is a disparate set of ideals: the first is a very specific intended outcome, the second and fourth can be seen as managerialist concerns, reflective also of economic and political needs, the third focuses on relatively new 'clients' of the criminal justice system, but the list as a whole is important. It focuses on factors, notably sentence effectiveness, victim satisfaction, and good management, which have not been part of our previous discussion of retributivist sentencing, but are extremely influential in current policy. More specifically, *Criminal Justice: The Way Ahead* gave priority to the aims of reduction of offending and reparation to the victim: sentencing will be 'based on the offender not just the offence', and will pay 'more attention to sentence outcomes such as crime reduction and reparation' (Home Office 2001a: para 2.66). The courts will correspondingly be provided with a 'menu of options' to provide 'elements of punishment, crime reduction and reparation' (ibid: para 2.70).[2]

Since that document was published, other policy proposals have focused on outcome. For example, the Halliday Report made clear that, of the sentencing goals identified, 'reform and rehabilitation' (rather than incapacitation or deterrence: see 2001: paras 1.58–1.68) were their favoured methods of achieving crime reduction, the evidence of effectiveness being sufficient to justify a sentencing framework 'that would be more supportive of the attempts being made to reduce re-offending' (ibid: para 1.69). 'The [sentencing] framework can, and should, do more to support recent and foreseeable developments in work with convicted offenders to reduce their re-offending through "What works"' (ibid: para 1.73), for example, through the introduction of reformed short-term prison sentences 'to make them more effective in reducing crime and protecting the public' (ibid: para 0.10, recommendation 15). One result of these proposals was the inclusion in the Criminal Justice Act (CJA) 2003 of new, but not yet implemented, prison sentences of custody plus and intermittent custody with community supervision components to put the released or 'intermittent' prisoner through offending reduction programmes (see Chapter 3, section 3.1.3). The CJA 2003 also rejigged suspended custodial sentences and increased the supervision component of longer custodial sentences, both with provision for offending reduction programmes. Further, the community punishment order can include very specific crime reduction measures. These will all be examined further in Chapter 12.

More recently, in the Foreword to *Making Sentencing Clearer* (Home Secretary *et al.* 2006), the Government again made very clear that its sentencing aims are outcome focused: '[t]he proposals in this document are ... designed to ensure that the public are better protected from dangerous offenders and that resources are targeted at the offenders who pose the most significant risks'. This policy focus on outcome, notably the reduction of the likelihood of reoffending, sits alongside a continuing endorsement, albeit in a modified form by the increased attention to offending history, of just deserts as the primary sentencing principle for 'ordinary' offenders. The Halliday Report (2001) acknowledged but side-stepped the philosophical confusion this causes. It noted that, in addition to the aim of ensuring the public has confidence in the criminal justice system, the review had found 'widespread

---

[2] Reparation and responding to the needs of victims constitute an approach that is already being implemented with young offenders but which cannot easily be 'pigeon-holed', and so we will examine separately its implications in Chapter 6 when we focus on restorative justice.

agreement' that sentencing has three other purposes: 'punishment, crime reduction and reparation', but simply stated that '[o]pinions differ as to whether punishment is a goal in its own right or is, rather, a means of achieving the other two goals' (2001: paras 1.4 and 1.5).

What this means, in terms of our concerns, is whether sentencers are to determine punishment retributively (where a proportionate—and so 'just'—punishment is a sufficient end product) or whether they decide on a punishment because they desire a particular outcome of punishment. The latter approach would constitute a penalty justifiable on utilitarian (or possibly restorative) principles, but not retributivist ones. If the justification is utilitarian, the issue of proportionality is either downgraded or ignored; if the justification is retributivist, the sentence is calculated solely on the basis of proportionality. However, in a retributively justified system this does not mean that—either after the primary sentencing decision or at the punishment stage—the specified amount of retributively imposed punishment cannot be used by penal institutions to achieve outcomes other than that of a sense of justice achieved through the application of retributivist principles. This 'secondary' focus on outcome is in effect the approach set up by the CJA 1991: the CJA 2003 has simply increased the focus on this second set of aims and so reinforced the utilitarian aspect of sentencing and punishment.[3]

4.1.2 Deterrence as a sentencing aim

Aiming to reduce offending by deterring offenders or others from committing crimes in the future is only one outcome-based sentencing aim and it is not one to which recent sentencing policy documents have given any priority. However, there is a widespread assumption that the resulting punishment *will* deter the convicted offender from reoffending, or potential offenders from offending and, as was clear from the determination of the Court of Appeal in *Cunningham* (1993) to retain notions of deterrence in sentencing, deterrence as an aim of punishment is still in the forefront of sentencers' minds. The 'exemplary sentence', where the penalty is arguably higher than a strictly proportionate sentence, is justified in terms of general deterrence and, Ashworth points out, there are several offences, notably robbery or 'mugging', for which this rationale has been a long-standing sentencing feature (2000: 67). Whilst *Cunningham* did not endorse exemplary sentences in individual cases, it did uphold 'prevalence' of offending—albeit only if it creates a climate of fear—as a valid factor in sentencing (at 448), a factor 'clearly linked to general deterrent reasoning' (Ashworth 2000: 92). Guidance from the Sentencing Guidelines Council (SGC) also allows prevalence in exceptional circumstances if justified in terms of greater harm caused (2004a: para 1.39). However, in *R v Oosthuizen* (2005), where the judge at first instance had decided to impose a deterrent sentence owing to the prevalence of robbery of handbags in the area because '[w]omen in Guildford were entitled to feel safe on the streets in broad daylight' (at para 9), the Court of Appeal stated that the deterrent element in a sentence must be supported by statistics about prevalence: 'even a judge with experience of that area should not assume that prevalence was more

---

[3] The Criminal Justice and Immigration Act 2008 makes some relevant changes: see the Online Resource Centre for updates.

online resource centre

marked in that area than nationally' (at para 16). In *R v Hussain (Mohammed)* (2005), a custodial sentence of three years and seven months was given to Hussain for stealing postal votes: the aim of the sentence was to deter electoral fraud.

So we see deterrence linked with punishment and even with proportionality in a retributivist system of sentencing. This is evident in the phrase 'retribution and deterrence' or 'punishment and deterrence' used, commonly, by official guidance and by the courts in relation to the 'tariff' or minimum period of a mandatory or discretionary life sentence (see Chapter 5) or of detention during Her Majesty's pleasure for minors (see Chapter 13). For example, the Prison Service, on its web site providing information for prisoners, explains the tariff as being 'the part of your life sentence which you must serve in prison as punishment for the offence you committed and as a general deterrent to others'.[4] So, in the House of Lords, in *R v Lichniak, R v Pyrah* (2001), Lord Hutton similarly noted that the young person is not detained indefinitely 'but rather is only detained for the tariff period sufficient to satisfy the requirements of retribution and deterrence in the circumstances of the particular case' (at para 29).[5] More recently, Mr Justice Silber used the same phrase—'retribution and general deterrence'—in relation to the minimum term to be served in *Gareth Wealleans* (2008 at para 10).

The inclusion of 'deterrence' in this phrase is rarely explained. In advice from the Sentencing Advisory Panel (SAP 2002) on minimum terms[6] in murder cases, for example, 'retribution and deterrence' is used only in the introductory pages. The detailed justification for the proposed minimum terms is (only) in terms of gradations of seriousness and the mitigating and aggravating factors that would contribute to a decision in an individual case (ibid: para 15 (*et seq*)).[7] There is no discussion as to what would deter others: the 'public' are mentioned only in terms of risk to the public and of public confidence that the murderer is sufficiently punished.

Deterrence is then the taken-for-granted outcome of punishment and one which causes concern only if it is believed that a sentence would not be sufficiently tough to deter. So whilst it is currently neither a priority aim in sentencing law and policy, nor—at the level of individual deterrence—a current factor in the delivery of punishment, deterrence is an outcome which is still of significance in judicial and policy thinking and one to which the public has great attachment. As we shall see below, the theory and the delivery of deterrence are much more complicated than political and media pronouncements would suggest. Deterrence is also only one form of punishment outcome which can be justified on utilitarian grounds.

Other beneficial consequences of punishment would include incapacitation of the offender to protect the public and rehabilitation of the offender and we will deal with these desired outcomes in Chapters 5 and 12 respectively. First, we will examine utilitarian theory before returning to a focus on deterrence.

---

[4] See http://www.hmprisonservice.gov.uk/life/.

[5] Unless there are 'elements of dangerousness and risk' to justify longer detention (*Stafford v United Kingdom*, Application No 46295/99, 28 May 2002 at para 87): see Chapter 5.

[6] The SAP suggested that 'tariff' should be replaced with 'minimum term' for the sake of clarity (2002: para 2).

[7] See http://www.sentencing-advisory-panel.gov.uk/c_and_a/advice/minimum_terms/minimum_terms.pdf.

4.1.3 **Utilitarianism: good or bad?**

Utilitarian philosophies of punishment have received a mixed press. On the one hand, an apparent advantage over retributivist justifications is that they justify punishments which are more clearly *not* pointless ones. They are consequentialist in orientation: they aim to reform or deter or prevent reoffending in some way, and by focusing on costs and benefits, may appear to offer the prospect of a more efficient use of punitive resources. Further, a utilitarian theory of punishment has for long been associated with reform of punishment, for example, in the work of its earliest 'modern' proponents, Beccaria and Bentham, in the eighteenth and early nineteenth centuries. Bentham was concerned to assess institutions of punishment against the yardstick of utility: if an institution fails to meet its stated purpose, then reforms are necessary. In the nineteenth and early twentieth centuries, utility was a major theoretical tool used to implement and defend reforms in the USA, UK, and Europe. It focused public policy on the concrete effects of the penal system and considered the implications for human suffering and the broader social aims of deterrence, rehabilitation, and social protection.

On the other hand, utilitarian philosophies, or reductivist philosophies as they are sometimes called because they aim to reduce offending, can justify harsher sentences than retributivist theory. For example, from a utilitarian point of view, it may be seen as in the public good to give some offenders very harsh punishments to deter others, or long prison sentences to incapacitate them and so severely restrict their capacity to reoffend. Such sentences may undermine individual rights and appear unjust, in that the needs of the state or the community are given more importance than the severity of the offending in question, when the sentencing decision is made. These summaries of the perceived strengths and weaknesses of the major competitor to retributivist philosophy do not, however, give a full picture of how the utilitarian approaches sentencing and punishment. The next section qualifies and elaborates on these statements.

4.2 **Utilitarian justifications**

4.2.1 **Classical principles**

Utilitarian theories have their origins in the classic criminology of Beccaria and Bentham. Beccaria's *On Crimes and Punishments*, first published in English in 1767, was one of the first utilitarian theories of punishment and a key influence on Bentham. Like Bentham, Beccaria sees individuals as motivated by the pursuit of pleasure and avoidance of pain and uses utility as a basis of social criticism. Laws should be assessed, he argues, 'from the point of view of whether they conduce to the greatest happiness shared among the greater number' (1767: 7). He saw the retributivism of his time as pointless, arbitrary and excessively harsh. For Beccaria the aim of punishment is to prevent offenders from committing new harms and to deter others from doing so, rather than to punish just for the sake of it:

the purpose of punishment is not that of tormenting or afflicting any sentient creature, nor of undoing a crime already committed...Can the wailings of a wretch, perhaps, undo what has been done and turn back the clock? The purpose, therefore, is nothing other than to prevent the offender from doing fresh harm to his fellows and to deter others from doing likewise...[P]unishments and the means adopted for inflicting them should, consistent with proportionality, be so selected as to make the most efficacious and lasting impression on the minds of men with the least torment to the body of the condemned.

(ibid: 31)

So he includes the key utilitarian notions of deterrence and the optimal level of punishment, the minimum pain necessary to achieve the aims, but also refers to proportionality. Punishment should be enacted as swiftly as possible, and fit the nature of the crime, so non-violent thefts, for example, should be met with fines, violent thefts with a combination of corporal punishment and penal servitude, and social parasites should be banished.

He was also one of the first to focus on the importance of certainty rather than severity: '[o]ne of the most effectives brakes on crime is not the harshness of punishment, but the unerringness of punishment...The certainty of even a mild punishment will make a bigger impression than the fear of a more awful one which is united to a hope of not being punished at all' (ibid: 63). If punishment is too severe, the offender may seek to evade it by committing further crimes: 'the harm of punishment should outweigh the good which the criminal can derive from the crime, and into the calculation of this balance, we must add the unerringness of punishment and the loss of the good produced by the crime. Anything more than this is superfluous and, therefore, tyrannous' (ibid: 64). It is essential, he argues, that punishment 'should be public, speedy, necessary, the minimum possible in the given circumstances, proportionate to the crime, and determined by the law' (ibid: 113), rather than imposed through acts of vigilantism. It is better to prevent crimes, for example, through public education, he argued, than to punish them.

The level of punishment should be as much as is necessary to prevent harm to society, to protect the public from the offences committed by individuals. Beccaria thought that, as society progressed, the severity of punishment would diminish. He was also very critical of the death penalty, and saw it as wasteful, of questionable deterrent value, and denying the community the person's future potential contributions.

It is, however, Bentham, whose work has become synonymous with utilitarianism. Although the principle of utility had already been used by Beccaria, Hutcheson, and Priestley, Bentham is seen as the source of modern utilitarianism and a key voice of the English enlightenment. His work on *The Rationale of Punishment*, published in English in 1830, is seen as a major contribution to nineteenth-century debates on penal reform, but in fact was written much earlier, in the 1770s.

4.2.2 Bentham's approach

Bentham's *Introduction to the Principles of Morals and Legislation*, first published in 1789, aimed to promote the public interest and happiness through the use of reason. It contains a discussion of the principles of utilitarianism and develops his analysis of human psychology. He offers a critique of judge-made law and advocates a scientific approach to law, crime and punishment. His philosophical approach is quite distinct from retributivism. Bentham's approach to punishment expresses his concern to introduce rationality into the criminal justice system at all stages of the process from prosecution to trial process, in the law of evidence and following the verdict, in the application of punishment.

For Bentham utility is the arbiter of law and morals. The principle of utility is 'that principle which approves or disapproves of every action whatsoever, according to the tendency which it appears to have to augment or diminish the happiness of the party whose interest is in question' (Bentham 1789: 12). Utility means the minimisation of pain and suffering and the maximisation of pleasure. 'Nature has placed mankind under the governance of two sovereign masters, *pain and pleasure*' (ibid: 11—emphasis in the original).

Utility is maximised when the result adds up to the greatest happiness of the greatest number. Bentham devised a felicific calculus, and argued that how we assess acts, choices, and ways of behaving is to calculate whether the sum of pleasures exceeds the pain. In calculating the costs and benefits we measure a number of factors: the intensity of pain and pleasure; its duration; the certainty or uncertainty of benefits accruing; the propinquity or nearness of the ensuing pleasure, that is, how quickly the pleasure will be generated; its fecundity, whether it will generate further pleasures or pain; its purity, whether or not it is likely to be followed by its opposite, pain or pleasure, whether it is unmixed with painful consequences; and its extent, that is, the number of people affected by it.

By using these criteria, we can see if the sum total of pleasures outweighs the costs. Bentham says that the quest for pleasure and the avoidance of pain is the key to understanding human behaviour. We can build social policies on this assumption and use rewards and punishment to channel behaviour to maximise the greatest happiness of the greatest number.

Like all utilitarianism, Bentham's theory is consequentialist: the only matter for the evaluation of laws and policies is consequences in terms of the pain and pleasure resulting from the event, policy or state of affairs. A good policy maximises the happiness of the majority, and utilitarianism is essentially a majoritarian approach.

When this theory is applied to punishment, then punishment is justified only by the good consequences which will result from it, so suffering should never be imposed unless it will prevent greater suffering, because all suffering is intrinsically bad as it causes pain: '[b]ut all punishment is mischief: all punishment in itself is evil. Upon the principle of utility, if it ought at all to be admitted, it ought only to be admitted in as far as it promises to exclude some greater evil' (ibid: 158). Punishment should not be inflicted just because someone has done something wrong because that, considered on its own, will only increase the total amount of human suffering. But if by inflicting it we can prevent greater suffering, either by preventing the offender from doing further harm, or by deterring others from doing the same thing, it is not only morally justified but morally necessary. So Bentham's view of punishment follows from the general principles of his moral theory.

Punishment for Bentham cannot be justified merely as an act of retribution but only by the fact that the harm done by punishing the offender is outweighed by the benefits. Given that punishment is a 'cost-expense' in terms of the suffering of the incarcerated and the cost to society of keeping them in prison, the aim should be to maximise income, that is the deterrent effect, at the least possible expense, using a cost–benefit model. Punishment should not be inflicted if it is groundless, inefficacious, unprofitable, or needless, argues Bentham. The aim should be to prevent future offences as cheaply as possible.

Examples of groundlessness would be where a person has freely consented to the act in question, or where the act was necessary to produce a greater benefit outweighed by the mischief, or to prevent an imminent calamity, or 'where there is a certainty of an adequate compensation' (ibid: 160). Cases where punishment would be inefficacious would include *ex post facto* laws, or where the punishment cannot be carried out because the person is not within the reach of the law, or where the punishment would have no effect in preventing them from engaging in a future act (because of the offender's extreme infancy or insanity, or intoxication by drink or drugs), or where the individual is subjected to an immediate superior force, such as physical danger, or is acting involuntarily.

Some cases may turn out to be too unprofitable to punish at all because costs outweigh benefits, for example, trivial offences or victimless crimes, where the evil of punishment outweighs that of the original offence. Even when the evil of the offence does appear to outweigh the evil of punishment, there may be particular circumstances which redress the balance, such as losing the services the offender could give the community, or incurring the displeasure of the people if they think that the offender should not be punished. Cases where punishment is needless would be 'where the purpose of putting an end to the practice may be attained as effectually at a cheaper rate: by instruction, for instance, as well as by terror: by informing the understanding, as well as by exercising an immediate influence on the will' (ibid: 164).

Bentham says relatively little in the *Introduction to the Principles of Morals and Legislation* on the justifications of punishment or on the means of punishment, but he confines his remarks to a footnote:

The immediate principal end of punishment is to control action. This action is either that of the offender, or of others: that of the offender it controls by its influence, either on his will, in which case it is said to operate in the way of *reformation;* or on his physical power, in which case it is said to operate by *disablement:* that of others it can influence no otherwise than by its influence over their wills; in which case it is said to operate in the way of *example.*

(Bentham 1789: 158n)

The aim of punishment is to prevent offences, to prevent worse offences, to minimise the 'mischief', and to prevent the mischief as cheaply as possible, to achieve the object with least possible expense (ibid: 165). He also refers to the collateral ends of satisfaction to the injured party, and to other members of the public concerned about the offence.

4.2.3 'The Bloody Code' and 'frugality'

Bentham argues that we should calculate the optimum level of punishment and, if effective deterrence could be achieved by a lesser sentence than on utilitarian principles, it is a useless and needless expense to impose a higher sentence. Of course when Bentham was writing judges had greater discretion in passing sentence, and there was concern about the partiality and bias of judges hostile to workers combining into unions, and the fact that some judges allowed subjective feelings to enter into decisions. There was also a strong demand for proportionality between crime and punishment in England in the eighteenth century and a concern with excessive punishment, particularly the 'Bloody Code', the expanded use of the death penalty for lesser offences.[8] Bentham was critical of the death penalty and the excessive and arbitrary punishments of his time. He wanted an external standard against which sentencing decisions might be judged, so ideally two sentencers armed with the same knowledge of the facts of a particular case would reach the same decision on the type and level of punishment.

For Bentham, punishment is not justified on the ground of being good for the individual as the individual can have no interest in being punished at all. Instead, what justifies punishment is what is good for society, sacrificing a few individuals for the greater good of others. Punishment deters others from engaging in certain acts, promotes the public good, and promotes greater happiness. The 'happiness' of the person punished is considered alongside that of others but if it is necessary to ensure the happiness of the majority, his happiness may be sacrificed.

Bentham is committed to the principle of frugality, or what we would now call parsimony, to use the most economical means of punishment, to impose the least severe punishment to meet the social objective. Frugality is achieved where no superfluous pain is imposed on the person punished. The amount of punishment should not be less than needed to outweigh the profit of the offence. If it is too little it will be inefficacious, if too much it will be needless. The optimal level of punishment will depend on the circumstances. The type of punishment should 'bear an *analogy* to the offence' (ibid: 179). Generally the greater the mischief of the offence, says Bentham, then the greater is the expense which it may be worth incurring in the administration of punishment and punishment should be adjusted so that a person would favour a lesser rather than a greater offence.

So there should normally be gradations in severity of punishment to match the seriousness of the offence. While punishment should be no more than is necessary to meet the criteria above, the offender should be punished for each part of the offence, and the amount of punishment should increase with the profit of the offence. Bentham says that there should be upper and lower limits on punishment to guide judges. So, notwithstanding Bentham's critique of retributivism, there is room for proportionality in his theory of punishment because penalties will normally be linked to the gravity of the crime. However, proportionality is deployed on a basis quite different to retributivism, as it is determined by the need to deter the offender, rather than being based on desert, and is linked to crime prevention. Bentham argues that greater deterrence will be achieved by increasing the penalty as much as is necessary to prevent future crimes, rather than reflecting the degree of censure or blame. But deviations from the principle of proportionality, such as exemplary sentences, for example, may be justified in the public interest. As von Hirsch says: '[w]hen the proportionality principle is thus defended—when its basis is said to be crime-preventive efficacy and nothing more—then it loses its status as an independent ethical requirement and can be subject to whatever dilutions seem needed in the name of crime control' (von Hirsch 1986: 32).

---

[8] See E. P. Thompson (1977) for a discussion of the Black Act. For a historical overview of changes in punishment between the seventeenth and twentieth centuries, see Rawlings (1999).

Bentham argues that we should consider the intensity, duration, and magnitude of the punishment, the responsibility of the offender and the inclinations of the public for or against any quantity or type of punishment. If the quantum is insufficient to outweigh the profit of the offence it will be inefficacious, argues Bentham (1789: 175). We should consider whether a less expensive means of punishment could achieve the same purpose and whether it is profitable to punish at all. In deciding on a mode of punishment we should take account of the aims, the principal ones being example, reformation, disablement, or what we would now call incapacitation, and compensation. However, Bentham acknowledges that achieving disablement may run counter to frugality, for example, when a disabled offender could still benefit others through future actions.

Bentham favours imprisonment because it is able to achieve fine gradations and in the 1780s he designed a model prison completely based on utilitarian principles. Capital punishment is the most unfrugal method of punishment, apart from the problem of irreversibility in cases of error. He acknowledges that the legislator should take account of the absence of popularity of a punishment or popular support for the law will be undermined.

For Bentham, the system of law and punishment should be designed so that when people seem to follow their interests, they are led to do those things which result in the greatest happiness of the greatest number. Prolonged punishment of an infirm individual who is unlikely to reoffend, or to threaten society, would be hard to justify, while on a retributivist model, the offender's advancing years or state of health at the time of sentencing would be irrelevant; what is important is his culpability at the time of committing the offence. Bentham is usually seen as an act-utilitarian, in so far as he focuses on the immediate consequences of a particular course of action, and this is contrasted with rule-utilitarianism, in which one considers the effect of generalising that particular course of action as a general rule and then considering the consequences of such a rule.[9]

Utilitarians may favour leniency in applying the principle of parsimony, accepting in some cases a punishment which is less severe than retributivists favour, depending on the particular circumstances. Retributivists, on the other hand, favour punishment that is appropriate, so severe punishment is justifiable if appropriate. But for the utilitarian it depends on the consequences and empirical facts of the particular case. There may be situations where the utilitarian might demand a harsher punishment than a retributivist would contemplate, punishing disproportionately to the offence to achieve a positive outcome, for example, dealing severely with a minor player in a joint crime. Utilitarians might also recommend punishment where a retributivist would say there should be none at all, as in the extreme case of punishing the innocent. It is for this reason that many find the utilitarian approach unacceptable.

4.2.4 **Contemporary utilitarianism**

Bentham's work has been a major influence on modern utilitarianism. Modern writers in this approach would include J. Q. Wilson (1985), J. Andenaes (1974), and

---

[9] For further discussion of rule and act utilitarianism, see Mill (1861) and Smart and Williams (1973).

E. van den Haag (1981). These theorists are primarily concerned with incapacitation and deterrence rather than rehabilitation. In contemporary utilitarianism the consequences which justify punishment are:

1. General deterrence, that is deterring the general public from doing the act punished.
2. Special deterrence, that is, deterring the person being punished.
3. Incapacitation, that is, protecting the public by removing a dangerous person from society so he or she is unable to reoffend. This has been an important part of penal policy in recent years. It recognises that prison may not work in deterring offenders but it does at least succeed in protecting society, by giving the public a temporary break from a persistent offender, or by removing dangerous offenders from society until they are no longer a threat, if necessary, by incarcerating them permanently.
4. Rehabilitation, where a period in custody, or of supervision within the community, is used to rehabilitate an offender, so that in the future the person can contribute to society.

Although each of these consequences may be construed as utilitarian, they may conflict with each other. For example, as Simon (1995) observes, indeterminate sentencing, which is usually associated with a rehabilitative model, makes it harder for an individual to make rational calculations of the costs and benefits of criminal activities, while determinate sentences have been criticised for undermining both rehabilitation and incapacitation, because sentences cannot be individualised. So rehabilitation has been criticised by those who favour incapacitation and deterrence as well as from the retributivist standpoint.

Utilitarianism is also associated with the use of predictive sentencing to control crime in contrast to retributivism which focuses on punishment for past crimes. In modern sentencing practice utilitarianism is reflected in sentencing tailored to the individual while retributivists favour sentencing according to a tariff. Utilitarians use scientific knowledge to target resources effectively and counter limitless penal expansion whilst retributivists argue that a desert-based theory which reserves prison for the most serious crimes, limits expansionism more effectively (see von Hirsch 1986). Moreover, utilitarianism may generate penal expansion through exemplary and predictive sentences, the most expensive penal option, although a strict application of the principle of parsimony should in some cases provide a brake on expansionism.

Utilitarianism has survived and flourished in modern penal policy and practice. Because utilitarians are concerned with future effects, utilitarian approaches to punishment have found favour because they seem appropriate to the rational planning essential to a complex modern society. Although the particular justifications of punishment, drawn from utilitarianism, have been subjected to criticism, utilitarianism has survived these specific challenges. As we noted above, utilitarianism, in effect if not name, is found in the Halliday Report (2001) and in the White Paper, *Criminal Justice: The Way Ahead* (Home Office 2001a). Similarly in *Rebalancing the Criminal Justice System in Favour of the Law-Abiding Majority* (Home Office 2006a) the utilitarian approach is paramount; the key aims are cutting crime, reducing reoffending and protecting the public. The stress is on meeting the needs of whole communities and giving more weight to the needs of the majority and less to the offender, to protect the public from crime and to make the criminal justice system more efficient. Utilitarian considerations also underpin the current focus on the anti-social behaviour of deviant individuals and families which threatens the peaceful habitation of the majority. (See also Chapter 8, section 8.4.3 for a discussion of the use of anti-social behaviour orders.) In *Penal Policy: A Background Paper* it is emphasised that 'an effective penal policy will protect the public and reduce re-offending' and will be a policy in which the public have confidence that they are being protected from harm and that prisoners are being effectively rehabilitated and are addressing their offending behaviour (Ministry of Justice 2007c: 2–3).

Although the quantum of punishment is still to be limited by just deserts, that limit could be expanded by persistent criminal conduct and, within the limit, more attention could be given to the risks of reoffending and measures to reduce reoffending. *Criminal Justice: The Way Ahead* (Home Office 2001a) further argued that sentencing should take more account of crime reduction, by considering the outcomes of sentences and what works for particular groups of offenders. It also argued that prisons need to focus more on preventing reoffending, such as preparing for work outside, as well as 'punishing'. The Government considers that the CJA 2003 has started to put more 'effective' sentencing and punishment in place but the 2006 White Paper makes clear that further development towards outcome-based sentencing is required: '[w]e must also do more to tackle prolific offenders, including drug users to try to prevent their re-offending' (Home Secretary *et al.* 2006: para 1.19). Similarly, in the United States the financial costs of prison expansion have led to greater attention on the effectiveness and efficiency of punishment, instead of focusing simply on retribution which has been seen as contributing to that expansion. As Steen and Bandy argue (2007) these costs issues have encouraged increasing attention to the need to be 'smart on crime' and to target resources effectively and this stimulates penal reform.

4.2.5 **Collateral issues**

Particular outcomes as specific aims of sentencing and punishment raise a complex set of issues which we cannot discuss within the confines of one chapter. Because of its underlying importance in criminal justice policy and in public thinking about punishment, we will concentrate, for the rest of this chapter, on the particular issues raised by deterrence. However, in current sentencing and penal policy, it is incapacitation and rehabilitation which are given prominence and, as noted above, we will focus on incapacitation in Chapter 5 when we also focus on the discourse of risk and danger in penal policy because incapacitation—either in terms of custody or using electronic means to control the activities of offenders in the community—has been the main tool for responding to the new concerns. Rehabilitation will be discussed in Chapter 12 when we focus on punishment in the community, as it is the Probation Service which will be at the forefront of offence-and drug-focused programmes to reduce reoffending. Offending behaviour programmes in custodial establishments will be considered in Chapter 9.

4.3 **Deterrence**

4.3.1 **Key concepts**

The aim of utilitarian theory is to maximise the happiness of the greatest number and punishment is one tool in this strategy. So penal institutions may combine individual and general deterrence: if conditions are harsh in prison it will deter the individual offender from reoffending and also warn those outside prison of the costs of committing a crime. For general deterrence to work, then, the public need to be aware of the probability of punishment, so perceptual deterrence must be enhanced. Bentham advocated using the principle of **less eligibility**, whereby the conditions in prison must be worse than outside for the deterrent effect to operate on the individual or the general public.

Whether punishment does have a deterrent effect has been subject to debate and raises questions about how a deterrent effect may be measured or ascertained (see sections 4.3.4a 16). Even if we accept the desirability in principle of using a particular mode of punishment or level of punishment to reduce crime rates, in practice we may have insufficient knowledge to ensure the success of a policy designed to deter. We also need to distinguish between primary deterrence, when a deterrent effect results from a punishment imposed on conduct previously unpunished, and marginal deterrence, changes in deterrence which result from an alteration in the level of punishment for actions already punishable. Most modern policy debates have been centred on increasing levels of punishment rather than creating new criminal offences. Although the research so far has been most promising in linking effective deterrence to the certainty of punishment rather than the severity of punishment (see section 4.3.2), policy debates in the UK and the USA, as we saw in Chapter 1, have tended to focus on increasing the severity of punishment as a significant element of the populist punitiveness of the 1990s. So, even when there is a lack of evidence of a deterrent effect for a particular punishment, it may be retained for political reasons, to satisfy public demands. For example, the Three Strikes laws in California have imposed significant financial burdens, yet there is no strong evidence of a deterrent effect. But it has not been possible politically to amend or repeal these laws (see Domanick 2004.)

Deterrence theory was popular in the late 1970s and early 1980s in the work of writers such as J. Q. Wilson (1985) and E. van den Haag (1981) who argue that crime may be reduced through sentencing. On this approach, sentencing should be used to either deter or incapacitate and issues of desert are displaced to the outer limits of setting punishment scales. The emphasis in modern utilitarianism has been primarily on special deterrence rather than general deterrence, although the latter is still important.

Wilson is committed to the use of punishment to deter as well as to selectively incapacitate, and to using preventive detention when appropriate, strategies which would normally be prohibited on a retributivist model. In *Thinking about Crime*, he argued that deterrence does work in reducing crime and that it does so not simply by removing offenders from society (Wilson 1985). Wilson claims that there is sufficient evidence to justify the claim that the crime rate is influenced by the costs of crime and that we could reduce the crime rate by increasing the certainty of criminal sanctions. In terms of criminal justice policy, then, we should try to enhance the benefits of compliance while increasing the costs of crime. In assessing deterrence, argues Wilson, we need to calculate the amount of crime which can be prevented by increasing the certainty, or the severity of punishments. He gives the example of Ehrlich's work on the death penalty, which calculated that for every murderer executed, eight murders were prevented (Ehrlich 1975).

For Wilson, crime is a rational enterprise and like other activities, shaped by rewards and penalties and, he argues, criminals make similar calculations to ordinary citizens: 'People are governed in their daily lives by rewards and penalties of every sort... To assert that "deterrence doesn't work" is tantamount to either denying the plainest facts of everyday life or claiming that would-be criminals are utterly different from the rest of us' (1985: 121). Even if criminals have a weaker conscience than others, they still take account of the costs and gains of crime and make rational choices. Deterrence theory is useful because it seems to fit our intuitions and because we act in ways consistent with it in everyday life, that is, we do engage in cost–benefit calculations. Research suggests that the certainty of sanctions is a major influence on this calculation.

4.3.2 The certainty of punishment

Despite methodological problems in devising appropriate experiments, there are some indications that the crime rate is influenced by the costs of crime, if detection, imprisonment, and punishment are certain. Wilson cites the work of Wolpin (1978), who examined changes in crime rates and changes in the chances of being arrested, convicted, and punished in the period 1894–1967 and found that 'changes in the probability of being punished seemed to cause changes in the crime rate' (Wilson 1985: 123).[10] Another example often cited is Sherman and Berk's (1983) experiment in Minneapolis with different police strategies to deal with domestic violence. Those who were arrested were less likely to be reported to the police for subsequent assault than those receiving counselling or sent out of the house to calm down. However, this policy was more effective with employed, married perpetrators than with unmarried and unemployed perpetrators.

There is evidence to suggest that, when certainty is removed, the crime rate increases.[11] An example often cited is the Melbourne police strike in 1923 when mobs poured into the city and looting lasted for two days before order was restored. In Britain, when the breathalyser was first introduced, there was a decline in road accident casualties (Ross 1973). If fear of detection does reduce crime, then an increased police presence may be more useful than increasing the severity of sentencing.

Wilson argues that evidence suggests that 'changes in the probability of being punished can lead to changes in behaviour' (Wilson 1985: 137). Even in crimes undertaken under the sway of emotions, rational calculations occur. He gives the example of the fact that the arrival of a police officer will often end a fight and that

[10] However, Wilson acknowledges that it may be difficult to draw a sharp distinction between rehabilitation and special deterrence, as both involve inducements and negative sanctions for non-compliance with therapy and both involve restrictions and coercion.

[11] For further discussion of the significance of certainty, see Blumstein *et al.* (1978), Beyleveld (1980), and Ross (1992).

costs are still calculated at times of heightened emotions, so in a pub brawl one is likely to avoid hitting the toughest opponent, while arguing couples will avoid throwing the best china.

Wilson argues that we need to see people's deterrability as lying on a continuum. Some people have strong internal restraints on their behaviour and may also think how much they have to lose by being caught, but others may have few internal controls yet fear external constraints of imprisonment. Some have little fear and few internal constraints, others may wish to commit crimes because of their status within a criminal subculture. Some individuals, he argues, mostly young males, will lack strong internalised restraints on misconduct and greatly value a quick reward. 'People differ by degrees in the extent to which they are governed by internal restraints on criminal behaviour and in the stake they have in conformity...' (Wilson 1985: 142). Some may conform not simply because of the fear of sanctions, but because of the belief that crime is morally wrong, while others will commit crime regardless of the risk, and others are 'only dimly aware that there are any risks' (ibid: 252).

The results of recent surveys reflect this complexity. A *Youth Lifestyles Survey* conducted in the UK in 1998–9 asked 12–30 year olds what would stop them committing a number of crimes. Almost half (45–47 per cent) of respondents said they would not commit any of the specified offences because 'it was wrong' (2004).[12] On the other hand, in a MORI *Youth Survey* in 2000, 45 per cent said that the main deterrent would be 'worry about how parents react', 45 per cent also said that 'fear of being caught' would have the biggest effect. Clearly the options open to respondents in their replies is crucial here but, just as important, we need to know more about the social context in which offending occurs and the impact of other influences on decision making before we can adequately assess research findings.

The issue of certainty of detection has been considered in the context of the use of Closed-Circuit TV Cameras (CCTV) to deter crime, but the results have been variable. Gill and Spriggs (2005) conducted a study of the impact of cameras across 13 sites but found a decline in crime in only one case, which could be attributed to their presence, namely vehicle crime in a car park. A review of the impact of CCTV by Welsh and Farrington also found that CCTV reduced crime only to a small degree, but was most effective in car parks (Welsh and Farrington 2002). However, cameras may, of course, still have value in providing evidence of crime and technological tools are being increasingly used to deter car and other crime (see Lyon 2006). For example, the DVLA has developed a set of initiatives to deter car crime including a range of vehicle identity checks.[13] Research on offenders suggests that they are unconcerned about cameras, but those who have been caught through cameras see them as more of a threat.

Deterrence theory has been criticised by those who reject the underlying rational choice approach to crime, while others question the empirical findings, arguing that empirical research is not encouraging, that crime rates and recidivism have increased despite deterrent sentencing, while some question the methodology used to 'prove' a deterrent effect.[14] Critics of deterrent penalties usually point to the high rate of recidivism as evidence of their failure to deter.

---

[12] See http://www.crimereduction.gov.uk/toolkits/.

[13] See http://www.dvla.gov.uk/vehicles/vcrat/htm.

[14] See, for example, Robinson and Darley's critical review (Robinson and Darley 2004).

Walker (1991) argues that scepticism over deterrence is due to exaggerated interpretations of the empirical evidence. Instead of saying 'nothing works', we can say that deterrence may be intermittent and that some people may be temporarily undeterrable. Certainly the association of crime rates with the length of imprisonment is weak. Much of the research on deterrence is on the deterrent effect of the death penalty on homicides, but less is known on other offences, although homicide may be comparable to serious assaults. A person who is minded to consider the consequences before committing violence, is more likely to focus on *whether* he is likely to go to prison rather than how long.

Von Hirsch *et al.* (1999) reviewed research on deterrence from the 1970s to the late 1990s and found that the research shows that deterrence does work and that recent studies continue to support the thesis that the certainty of punishment can affect decisions to offend. Increasing certainty of punishment, they conclude, can increase marginal deterrence. Changes in sentencing policies may also affect how a crime is committed rather than whether to commit it; for example, the decision to expedite a burglary to avoid staying at the crime scene. In the research drawn from England, the USA and Western Europe, we do find a negative correlation between certainty of punishment and crime rates. The National Academy of Sciences Research Study (Blumstein *et al.* 1978) drew attention to the methodological problems of proving the effects of either incapacitation or deterrence on crime rates, but did find that deterrent sanctions influenced some individuals.

4.3.3 The severity and celerity of punishment

However, the evidence is much less convincing for a link between the *severity* of punishment, that is, how stringently the person is punished once caught, whether a custodial sentence is imposed and its duration, and crime rates (von Hirsch *et al.* 1999). Although perceptions of severity are important, changes in severity levels will be less visible and immediate than a stronger police presence. What evidence there is suggests that the imprisonment rate is more important than the length of imprisonment.

The celerity of punishment also needs to be considered, that is, how quickly the punishment is delivered. Beccaria in 1767 argued that punishment should be enacted as swiftly as possible to strengthen the association between the ideas of crime and punishment and that delay would weaken the link between the two ideas. Bentham also argued that in calculating the consequences of an action the proximity of the punishment to the offence would be considered and weighed against the immediacy of the profit of the offence (Bentham 1789: 169). So, if the individual receives immediate gratification from the offence, this may well be more significant than the prospect of a distant punishment.

However, the celerity of punishment has been under-researched, compared to certainty, although it has been discussed in relation to capital punishment and in relation to penalties for drink-driving (see Ross 1992). The delays in delivering the punishment have been seen by supporters of the death penalty as weakening its deterrent value. Jeffrey (1965) argues that it should be enacted immediately to be an effective deterrent. However, Bailey (1980) found no evidence that the speed of executions was significant.

4.3.4 **The type of punishment**

The role played by the actual nature of the penalty is less clear: although there are some positive examples. Replacing parking fines with wheel clamps in central London did lead to a substantial decline in illegal parking (see Walker 1991). We also know that disqualifications are more feared by drivers than fines. So the nature of the penalty may be a consideration (see also section 4.4.1).

Reconviction rates have been used as a measure of the effectiveness of different types of punishment in deterring and/or rehabilitating offenders and research on reoffending is regularly conducted by the Home Office.

A study of England and Wales in 1972 referred to by Walker (1991) found that reconviction rates for imprisoned offenders were better than for those with suspended sentences, which suggests that the experience of prison deters more than a mere threat. However, some more recent studies have found little difference between prison and community punishments.

Kershaw *et al.* studied the reconviction rates of offenders sentenced or discharged from prison in 1995. They found that 58 per cent of all sentenced prisoners discharged in 1995 were reconvicted of a standard list offence within two years (Kershaw *et al.* 1999). Standard list means all **indictable offences** and some of the more serious summary offences, such as indecent assault, child neglect and assault on police officers, but it excludes most summary motoring offences. For offenders commencing community penalties, that is, the then community service orders, probation orders and combination orders in 1995, the reconviction rate was 56 per cent. So after taking into account all possible relevant factors, in this study there was no significant discernible difference between custodial and community penalties. The results of similar comparisons suggest little real difference in reconviction rates for earlier years. 44 per cent of offenders given a conditional discharge and 43 per cent of offenders fined for a standard list offence in 1995 were reconvicted for another such offence within two years, and there were lower rates for fines and discharges than for community penalties.

A study published by the Home Office in December 2005 supplied information on reoffending by adults, defined as over 18 (Cuppleditch and Evans 2005). The reoffending rate of adults rose from 57.6 per cent in 2000 to 58.5 per cent in 2002. For the purposes of this research reoffending means that the offender committed an offence within the two-year follow-up period and was convicted in court. The figures relate to those released from prison and those who commenced community penalties in the first quarter of 2002. A follow-up study was conducted in March 2007 for the Home Office by Cunliffe and Shepherd (2007). This showed that for 2004 the reoffending rate was 55.5 per cent.

As not all of those who reoffend may be caught or convicted and some may reoffend beyond the two-year period, then these figures may be under-estimates of the true reoffending rate.

4.3.5 **The type of offender**

A number of factors affect the propensity to reoffend including age, sex and previous criminal history. Some studies of recidivism have found that men are more likely to be reconvicted than women, teenagers are more likely to be reconvicted than older offenders (although in the longer term recidivism does decline with age), those with the greatest number of previous convictions are more likely to be reconvicted in future, and the unemployed are also more likely to be reconvicted than the employed (see Kershaw *et al.* 1999). Reoffending rates also vary with the type of offences.

In Kershaw's study for the Home Office, burglars had much higher reconviction rates than sex offenders. Prisoners serving sentences for burglary, theft and handling were most likely to be reconvicted within two years (Kershaw *et al.* 1999). The rates were 77 per cent for burglary and 69 per cent for theft and handling. The lowest rates, calculated as the percentage reconvicted within two years, were 18 per cent for sexual offences, 29 per cent for fraud and forgery, and 33 per cent for drug offences. Most of the prisoners were not reconvicted for the same offence, although they were more likely to be convicted if originally convicted for burglary or theft. The reconviction rate was higher for young male offenders than for adult males. Those originally convicted for homicide and released on licence have lower reconviction rates than other offenders, which has implications for the debate concerning the alleged uniquely deterrent effect of the death penalty. Although reconviction rates for women were lower than those for men in the 1990s, in 2002 reconviction rates for women in England and Wales reached the same level as those for men (Home Office 2003f). Older offenders tend to have lower reconviction rates than younger offenders; reconviction rates are lower for those serving longer sentences. The greater the number of previous convictions the higher were the reconviction rates. So past criminal history is the most influential variable for prediction of any future offending, although controlling samples to take account of prior probabilities of reconviction may be difficult.

Of course we cannot know for sure whether some individuals did not reoffend or reoffended but simply did not get caught. We also cannot infer a causal connection from a correlation without further analysis of the intervening variables. However, given the contemporary concern with risk management, an actuarial approach to criminal justice could take these statistics at face value, without a full understanding of the underlying factors, and could concentrate resources on those offenders perceived to be most at risk of reoffending (see Chapter 5).

Witte's (1980) work on ex-convicts, cited by Wilson, shows that deterrence works but that it works differently for different types of offenders: for property offenders the certainty of imprisonment was most significant, while the severity of the sentence was most significant for violent or drug offenders. Gender is also an issue to consider although gender differences in relation to deterrence have been under-researched. However, Corbett and Caramlau (2006) studied the deterrent effect of speed cameras and found significant differences between men and women on issues of driver safety: women drove more safely than men, were more safety-conscious and more positive regarding the value of speed cameras than men. Male drivers in the study were more likely to have been 'flashed' by cameras at least twice and were more likely to view them as a money-raising exercise than as a genuine contribution to road safety. Differences were also found between older and younger drivers with the former being more safety-aware.

Deterrence theorists assume that people's attitude to lawbreaking is rational and calculating, that we obey the law to avoid the pain of punishment, but there may be a moral obligation independent of the fear of consequences, as retributivists would argue. Many of us think it is wrong to steal irrespective of the penalty and this element has received little attention within deterrence theory. Moreover, rationality may not be universal and the development of reasoning skills is an important feature of offending behaviour programmes which use cognitive-behavioural models. We also do not know if offenders will favour short-term benefits against longer-term costs.

4.3.6 Methodological problems in proving deterrence: interpreting the evidence

The difficulty is how to test the deterrent effects of punishment. Even if they do not reoffend, it may not be clear whether individuals were deterred by the unpleasant experience of a penalty, reformed because they now believe it is wrong to offend, or were rehabilitated by being given useful employment. It is also unclear whether we should measure the deterrent effect of imprisonment simply by looking at those who have already been punished and returned to society, or the population as a whole who may be tempted to commit a crime, that is, general deterrence. Those who have already committed a crime have shown themselves to be less deterrable than the rest of the population, because they have already risked punishment by committing the crime.

When considering deterrence in relation to any offence, we need to be aware of possible methodological problems. For example, as Walker notes (1991) many studies measure the objective probability of conviction, when it is the subjective probability which is the most important influence on behaviour and this will depend on the individual's skills, circumstances, and access to a lawyer; so potential offenders may consider whether they are likely to get caught, and if so, whether they would receive a custodial sentence and of what duration, as a low estimate of risk is usually associated with high frequency of offending and vice versa.

The methodology is also crucial in determining the correct time scale if we try to ascertain the likelihood of future offending, or view offending retrospectively. If there is a long delay then the initial response to a change in sentencing levels may no longer operate and if there is a short delay, then it may be too early to consider whether the individual has been fully deterred. The deterrent effect of a change in punishment may also decline over time, a process known as deterrence decay, as perceptions of apprehension change, for example if individuals think they might have miscalculated the chances of being caught or over-estimated the rigour of enforcement.

If we consider general deterrence, we find that some societies with harsh systems of punishment, such as the USA, also have high crime rates which are used to justify the high incarceration rates (see Garland 2001c). When crime rates do fall it may be hard to link this with the degree of severity of punishment but the fact of being punished may be more important than the precise level of punishment. Moreover, when we look at these statistics, we face the problem of isolating the precise causal effect of punishment from the numerous intervening variables and of distinguishing deterrent and incapacitating effects.

If we find an increase in punishment severity and a fall in crime rates we could not immediately infer a causal relationship. We need to know whether the changes actually led potential offenders to refrain from crime and clearly many factors may influence the final crime figures.

Official statistics are notoriously inaccurate as a true measure of crime; for example, figures on prison populations may be an inaccurate measure of criminal activity if not all offenders are caught and punished. Prison numbers may decline through sentencing policies, which themselves are influenced by prison overcrowding; for example, the recent guidelines for custodial sentences for burglars may affect numbers to some extent, as well as the other factors considered in Chapter 1.

Even if the crime rate fell following an increase in punishment we cannot be sure that this resulted from the punishment rather than from the numerous other factors which affect crime. If we find a group for whom a particular punishment does have a deterrent effect, it may be hard to generalise. Moreover, sanctions may affect behaviour without necessarily deterring; for example, sanctions against drugs use or arms dealing may lead users and arms dealers to become more secretive rather than giving up their habit, or curtailing their trade.

Statistics do not take account of local variations in law enforcement and local applications of sentencing policies. This is a problem in the USA, where there may be variations between states obscured by aggregated statistics, but there have also been concerns in the UK regarding inconsistency between courts. Moreover studies of deterrence do not always distinguish sufficiently clearly between the issues of certainty and severity.

Most of the comparative work has been undertaken on England and the United States but we also need to know more about other similar European societies. What we do know of other European countries, such as the Netherlands, suggests that a reductionist policy does not necessarily lead to a sudden increase in crime rates. We also need to control for other significant variables which might affect crime rates. If crime rates fall as the quantum of punishment increases, we cannot infer a causal effect, we need to know whether the increase affected the behaviour of offenders or whether other factors were operating. To ascertain this, it would be useful to compare the effects of two similar laws in two jurisdictions, one with sanctions attached to it which are strongly enforced, and one without such sanctions or enforcement, to measure the effect. It might be difficult to find a government willing to suspend sanctions. But even if we find a difference, this might be attributed to other factors, such as cultural factors or strong religious sanctions.

The problem for utilitarian theory is to calculate the optimum level of punishment. If punishment is increased over time it may have diminishing returns, if individuals do not believe it will apply to them, or think that they will not be caught. If an increase in punishment produces an immediate response in terms of crime reduction, this may not be sustained in the long term. So a punitive policy may prove uneconomic on the principle of parsimony, regardless of the issues of unfairness which would trouble retributivists. An increase in sentencing levels across the whole range of crimes may also weaken the gap between serious and less serious offences. An increase in punishment at the lower end of the scale may be unnecessary if it is excessive for those who would have been deterred by a lesser punishment and are unlikely to commit offences in any case. On the other hand, an increase at the higher end may have little effect on those strongly committed to criminal activity or with long criminal careers. Some of these issues have been addressed in relation to the death penalty.

4.3.7 **The death penalty**

In the UK the death penalty has not been available as a sentence since 1965. However, we are including a brief discussion here because research on whether the death penalty for murder has a unique deterrent effect has been an important element of the debate on deterrence. Empirical research in the 1950s and 1960s in the UK and other jurisdictions challenged its unique deterrent effect and brought into question the underlying assumptions of deterrence theory. However, deterrence theory revived in the late 1970s and Ehrlich's work on the deterrent effect of capital punishment contributed to this revival (Ehrlich 1975). While it might be argued that the offence of homicide raises specific issues which make it hard to generalise research findings to many other offences, murder is not dissimilar to other serious offences against the person.

While evidence of the unique deterrent effect of the death penalty is inconclusive, nonetheless many defenders of the death penalty still argue that it has a uniquely deterrent effect in preventing future crime, particularly homicides and drug trafficking offences, thereby promoting public welfare. Public support for the penalty is often based on the belief that it does deter, as well as retributivist grounds. However, Sarat (1976) argues that, if the public were fully informed about the absence of a unique deterrent effect, their attitudes would change.

The debate on deterrence has produced much empirical work, often conflicting in its findings, and which is beset by difficult methodological problems, some of which are discussed above. The body of work has been reviewed periodically and the empirical research suggests that the death penalty does not have a unique capacity to deter.

The Royal Commission on Capital Punishment's Report (1953) found that the evidence available at that time did not support the claim that abolition of capital punishment would lead to an increase in homicide rates, or that its reintroduction after abolition would lead to a fall in homicide rates. Reviews of research in the 1980s (Zimring and Hawkins 1986) and the 1990s (Bailey and Peterson 1997) also found no conclusive proof to support the claim that it had a greater deterrent effect than life imprisonment. There was no clear link established between the penalty and changes in crime rates. We can find abolitionist societies, such as Canada, where the homicide rate fell after the death penalty was abolished in contrast to the UK where the homicide rate increased in the 1960s following abolition. However, the increase in the homicide rate was smaller than the increase for other violent offences which were not affected by abolition.

In the United States we can find variations in crime rates in states with and without the death penalty, which suggest that other variables may influence crime and homicide rates. Murder rates are lower in non-death penalty states than in states with the penalty and this gap has increased over the past ten years. In societies which have used the death penalty to control drug trafficking, such as Malaysia, drug trafficking has continued despite these penalties, which has led some to argue that measures such as surveillance, crop elimination in supplier states, and building up local economies may have more success in controlling the supply of drugs. Hood (2002) also concludes from his review of the evidence that it has not provided scientific proof that executions have a greater deterrent effect than life imprisonment and any future proof is unlikely to be forthcoming.

There are several reasons why it is difficult to sustain the argument for the unique deterrent effect. First, the causes of crime are complex and punishment is only one factor in crime control and may be swamped by other factors which affect offending. It is difficult to draw any meaningful inferences from the figures from longitudinal studies before and after abolition, because of the difficulties of isolating the causal effect of abolition. But even if a correlation were found between the death penalty and high or low crime rates, this would not of itself establish a causal link. Donohue and Wolfers reviewed the available statistical evidence on the United States and found that 'the death penalty... is applied so rarely that the number of homicides it can plausibly have caused or deterred cannot be reliably disentangled from the large year to year changes in the homicide rate caused by other factors' (Donohue and Wolfers 2006: 791).

Societies moving towards abolition may use the penalty less frequently in the years leading up to abolition because of changing attitudes, which may make it difficult to accurately test the deterrence thesis. There is also the problem of determining the appropriate time span for comparison. The Royal Commission found some examples where societies experienced an increase in crime rates for a short period following abolition, but there was no long-term increase in crime. Cross-cultural comparative studies are difficult as one may be comparing societies with quite different cultures, legal systems, criminal procedures, and social problems.

Second, if many homicides are committed under the sway of emotions, or psychological disturbances, or in a state of panic, or under the influence of alcohol or drugs, it is unlikely that offenders weigh up the consequences of their action and consider the outcome in a rational way. It may well be that many murderers do not make a meaningful decision to kill at all, initially, let alone weigh up the penalties if caught. Of course some homicides are premeditated but even those who do calculate rationally may find the prospect of a long prison sentence as frightening as a quick death. Project criminals, that is, professional robbers who commit well-planned and organised crimes purely for financial gain, may be more calculating, but may still think the risk worth taking as they are unlikely to get caught precisely because the crime is highly planned. Examples of project crimes would be the Great Train Robbery in 1963 and the Heathrow Brinks-Mat Robbery in 1983.

The RCCP did find an American case where a man drove his wife across the state line to kill her because there was no death penalty there, but not all homicides will be so calculating. In the case of premeditated terrorist or political crimes, the perpetrators may not be deterred if their motives are altruistic rather than individualistic. Thirdly, murderers as a group have relatively low rates of reoffending compared to other offenders, and good parole records. This might be used to support the claim that prison has a sufficient deterrent effect, or simply indicate that the nature of the crime is such that it is unlikely to be repeated. A study in New York of the period 1930–61 found that of 63 first-degree murderers released on parole, only 1 committed another crime (see Stanton 1969). Similar results have been found for other states and in later studies (see Marquart *et al.* 1989; Bedau 1997). In the UK murderers released on parole have lower recidivism rates than many other offenders, so prison may achieve the necessary deterrent effect.

What we can say is that the death penalty may have a stronger deterrent effect than other methods of punishment on *some* people, but a negligible effect on others. Imprisonment may be sufficient to deter some potential murderers, but not others. Walker argues that 'if a person is minded to commit a murder then either the thought of an indeterminate prison sentence will dissuade him or nothing will' (1991: 16).

Given that it is difficult to establish the uniquely deterrent effect, and in the absence of conclusive evidence, the utilitarian principle of parsimony would suggest that it would be better to use more humane methods of punishment if they can achieve the desired deterrent effect in a less painful way. However, the fact that the deterrent effects are inconclusive may not defeat the case for the death penalty. For example, van den Haag (1985) argues that, even if the deterrent effects of the penalty are uncertain and inconclusive, it is still better to risk the lives of convicted murderers than to risk the lives of innocent people who might be possible future victims. When outcomes are uncertain he argues, future victims should be given more weight in our calculations than convicted murderers.

4.4 Problems with the theory and practice of utilitarianism

4.4.1 Does deterrence work?[15]

In the light of the above problems and the empirical research available, we cannot say that deterrence never works, but we can say that punishment may deter fewer offenders and potential offenders than we would like. Prison deters some offenders, provided that they are in deterrable states of mind. At the other end of the penalty scale, there is also some limited evidence that deterrence operates. Research in the 1980s on 'regulatory offences'—where there is a breach of a regulation, generally an omission rather than a deliberate act of commission—such as road fund licence evasion or not declaring excess duty-free goods, suggested that people were deterred by having to go to court and receiving adverse publicity rather than by the size of the fine (Orton and Vennard 1988: 168). The exception was TV licence evasion where 40 per cent of respondents regarded the size of the fine as a deterrent (ibid). However, the researchers pointed out that respondents gave their answers within the context of 'mostly mistaken' ideas about the likelihood of being caught and the maximum level of fine (ibid: 175–6). In the context of custody, the 'pains' of imprisonment may affect different offenders differently. In a study of the subjective experiences of adolescent male offenders in Germany sent to prison for the first time, Windzio found that there was a deterrent effect from the deprivation of contact with people outside the prison, but this did not affect those without strong bonds, so prisoners will experience prison in different ways. He also found no deterrent effect from the fear of other prisoners, but rather he found that 'the higher the fear of other inmates, the higher the rate of recidivism' (Windzio 2006: 341).

For deterrence to work, it is not essential that all individuals conform to Bentham's model of economic rationality, calmly calculating costs and benefits using the felicific calculus. The question is whether deterrence operates to a sufficient extent, to influence enough people to make a difference, so even though some individuals may be unaffected by the prospect of punishment, if *enough*

---

[15] Problems specific to incapacitation and rehabilitation will be dealt with in Chapters 5 and 12 respectively.

individuals are affected it may influence crime levels and make a deterrence-based policy justifiable. Some individuals may be acting under the impulse of emotions or mind-changing substances or may simply have so little to lose that an increase in certainty or severity of punishment would have little effect. Von Hirsch (1999: 36) cites Farrington's (1997) work to show that impulsivity is a key characteristic of persistent offenders which raises problems when using deterrent strategies in such cases.

One problem is that increasing levels of punishment and drawing more individuals into the punitive net, may have the effect of normalising punishment so it is less stigmatising. Within criminal subcultures the experience of surviving harsh punishment may itself be a source of status within the group and imprisonment may become more tolerable over time as the individual develops adaptive strategies. This is discussed, for example, in Clemmer's work on the process of '**prisonisation**' which examines how different groups adapt to imprisonment (Clemmer 1940) and also in more recent studies by Toch (1976) and Gravett (2003).

Explaining why punishment fails to deter in some cases, may mean we need to look at the social context of offending, drawing on the symbolic interactionist approach in criminology, focus on the effects of labelling and the nature of the changing self-image. Moreover, incarceration may itself provide increased illegitimate opportunities to commit crimes, both inside prison and on release, in enabling offenders to make contact with each other. Punishment is only one factor in reoffending. Recent research using data from OASys, the Offender Assessment System, shows that offenders have on average four problems or 'criminogenic needs' which may contribute to their offending: for example, accommodation, unemployment, substance misuse and education (see Harper and Chitty 2005). Moreover, many offenders have poor basic skills which contribute to their poor employment histories and these are the issues which need to be addressed in rehabilitation programmes in custody and in the community.

In testing the effects of specific policies we need to know whether potential offenders were aware of those changes, whether the changes affected their behaviour and if so, what they perceived as possible outcomes and the significance of being punished within their social groups. Perceptual deterrence is under-researched but what we do know is people's awareness of sentencing may be misinformed and unrealistic, as we saw in the discussion of the British Crime Survey research in Chapter 1, section 1.3.3. If the public underestimate levels of punishment or the certainty of punishment, then the deterrent effect of a change in policy will be weakened. Improving their understanding of sentencing policy and practice is an important feature of current penal policy and this not only may reduce the fear of crime, but communicate the risks of committing crime to potential offenders. Most research on perceptions so far has been on whether fear of punishment will affect the decision to offend, rather than on whether a specific change in severity, certainty, or celerity of punishment will affect decision making.

4.4.2 **Theoretical difficulties**

Criticism has been levelled at the underlying principles governing utilitarianism as well as the specific problems raised by the utilitarian theory of punishment.

The problem with a deterrence-based approach is that increasing severity of punishment imposes substantial economic costs, but also social costs, increasing the social exclusion of offenders. Moreover, an indiscriminate increase in levels of punishment may weaken the gap between less and more serious crimes and undermine the incentive to commit less serious crimes. A deterrence policy may itself be a high-risk policy if it imposes social costs without the benefits of crime reduction. Using the utilitarian calculus, we need to consider whether to focus attention on crimes which affect large numbers of people such as property crimes; or crimes which affect fewer people but cause more damage, such as crimes of violence; or whether to focus on crimes where risks are widely distributed; or where they are concentrated. We also need to decide who to include in the calculation: just victims of crime or also those who may be affected by fear of crime. So refining sentencing policy will require these calculations and the problem, as we have seen, is that we may not have the necessary information to formulate an effective policy, on utilitarian criteria, regardless of the issues it raises for retributivism.

Punishing the innocent

A strong objection to this theory is that it potentially allows for punishment of the innocent if circumstances warrant it. As a majoritarian approach, utilitarianism accepts that the individual may be sacrificed for the benefit of others, in sharp contrast to the Kantian view that people should be treated as ends in themselves. For example, it is possible that punishing innocent third parties, such as relatives of the offender, could achieve greater deterrence than punishing the specific offender. Some regimes have done this: in Stalinist Russia the Criminal Code created the offence of being a relative of the enemy of the people, and a principle of collective family responsibility for the transgressions of individual family members is in operation now in North Korea. It has also been reported that a utility company in Vladivostok is planning to confiscate the family pets of those who do not pay their fuel bills. Yet our moral intuitions tell us that the punishment of the innocent is morally wrong and inappropriate to a legal system which tries to do justice.

According to Bagaric (2001), a modern supporter of utilitarianism, the reason utilitarianism lost favour was because it seems unable to confine punishment to wrongdoers and punishment of the innocent is inconsistent with the concern for individual rights. But Bagaric argues that punishment of the innocent is no worse than many other measures we condone in extreme situations. If society is faced with desperate circumstances then it may have to sacrifice individuals for the good of the whole. In any case retributivists have to accept that punishment of the innocent is a possibility, as any system of punishment is open to error. The risk of error could be substantially reduced by improvements in criminal procedure, for example, by a corroboration requirement for confessions, but not necessarily eliminated.

Punishing the guilty: the problem of proportionality

Utilitarianism also raises problems even if punishment is confined to the guilty because it does not take sufficient account of proportionality, yet this is a fundamental principle of systems of law in France and Germany, European Union law, and the European Convention on Human Rights: the punishment should be proportionate to the crime and the remedy should be proportionate to the mischief.

In the United States the Supreme Court will hold grossly disproportionate sanctions invalid under the Eighth Amendment, the constitutional prohibition on cruel and unusual punishment.

But while there is room within utilitarian theory for proportionality, it may be jettisoned when the public interest demands. Bagaric (2001) argues that proportionality is the best way of dealing with the issue of severity of punishment and sanctions should be commensurate to the offence. A disproportionate sentence undermines the criminal justice system and leads to social disorder, while proportionality improves the consistency and fairness of the sentencing process. But unlike retributivism, the proportionality principle is not absolute. However, Bagaric argues, we should retreat from proportionality only when necessary to pursue the more pressing utilitarian objective of punishment.

Ethical problems

Once proportionality is rejected in favour of utility, there may be consequences which are ethically unacceptable. Nothing is ruled out *a priori* on a strong utilitarian approach if it maximises happiness and public welfare. If we find that those with longer criminal histories are more likely to commit future offences, then a risk-based strategy might allow this to determine the length of sentence. For most retributivists, however, the sentence should be based on the current offence and the risk of reoffending is irrelevant to the sentence given. Even those, such as von Hirsch, who accept that first offenders should be treated less severely than recidivists, would still argue that primary emphasis should be given to the current offence and that any differential between first offenders and recidivists should be kept as low as possible. In practice most modern sentencing systems have far too wide disparities. For retributivism, as we have seen, desert is always the prime determinant of the severity of punishment for different offences. Once any minor deviation is allowed, it opens the door to larger deviations. As von Hirsch says 'in practice, it may be quite difficult to permit only small deviations from desert parity, while holding the line at larger deviations. The operation is like inviting the hungry Doberman to share in the family picnic, but only one bite' (1986: 163). However some modern utilitarians, such as Bagaric, would also reject additional weighting of past convictions, because it violates the principle of proportionality and effectively punishes the offender twice for the same offence. Instead he favours fixed penalties. Bagaric (2001) also argues that suspended sentences should be abolished because they involve no pain for the offender. He favours using sanctions such as the denial of work and education, even if this incurs welfare costs, as they will still be cheaper than imprisonment.

A further difficulty is that it is not clear whose interests policy makers should be concerned with, those living now or in the future, whether short-term or long-term effects should take priority and how conflicts between them should be resolved. This is important for penal policy in deciding whether to pursue an expansionist prison policy or to focus on the underlying causes of crime where the benefits may take longer to reap.

The concept of the individual

Difficulties also arise with utilitarianism as a theory of human behaviour. No coherent account is given of the disinterested individual, although Bentham does accept that they exist; indeed he sees himself as one, trying to make social life better for others, but altruistic individuals are still seen as deriving pleasure from helping others. The assumption that people are governed by self-interest is clearly a crude generalisation. To dismiss altruistic individuals as pleasure seeking does not do justice to them. Bentham's model seems to reduce humans to 'cheerful robots', or to what Marcuse would describe as a 'one-dimensional man', when other motivations may supersede the pursuit of pleasure and it is hard to find a place for perfectionist aspirations within this model (Marcuse 2002). His assertion that pushpin, a precursor of bingo, is equal to poetry in his *Rationale of Reward* (1825) would be seen as philistine by perfectionists who would distinguish higher and lower pleasures, particularly when formulating public policy and funding allocations. It is also difficult to apply his felicific calculus if there is a 'subjective' element and one man's pleasure is another's pain, or to talk meaningfully of calculations in the moral sphere. However, one might defend Bentham's model of the self-interested individual governed by the quest for pleasure and avoidance of pain, by saying it fits *enough* people to make policies based on it workable, even if there are some exceptional individuals who cannot be accounted for within the theory.

4.4.3 Rights versus utility

The role of rights in the utilitarian model is also problematic. Bentham (1843) himself dismisses rights as mischievous nonsense and there is no room in his approach for non-legal rights. On the contrary he is extremely sceptical regarding their value as is clear in his discussion of the French Revolution (see Schofield 2007). Bentham is sceptical of the value of rights in resolving difficult ethical, social and political problems because, he argues, rights cannot be construed apart from positive law. Even if we could identify fundamental rights, sooner or later rights conflict, and when that happens we have to weigh up conflicting interests and fall back on utility. It is this potential for rights violations which underpins the liberal critique of utilitarianism. But for Dworkin (1977) and others, rights will always trump utility.

Utilitarianism, Bagaric (2001) argues, is not necessarily antagonistic to rights. There is room for rights within utilitarian ethics as the recognition of rights promotes utility. An example here would be Mill's argument in *On Liberty* (1859) that the right to free speech leads to the truth, and may add to the happiness of the community. But for the utilitarians rights have no independent life of their own. Utilitarianism can also resolve clashes between rights, by considering the consequences when rights conflict, thereby providing a rational way of deciding between competing rights claims in such cases.

4.5 Conclusions

4.5.1 Alternative approaches

Utilitarianism, as we have seen, offers more scope for individualised sentencing while retributivism favours a tariff approach. But are these the only possibilities?

Given the inherent problems with both retributivism and utility, several writers have tried to combine the two.

Braithwaite and Pettit (1990) have formulated a consequentialist theory of justice which seeks to retain the future-oriented approach of utility and the use of calculations, but which treats individuals as persons rather than means to ends and focuses on autonomy and choice. But they are critical of proportionality, the linking of the sentence to the gravity of the offence. They focus on dominion rather than utility, by which they mean the individual's ability to exercise choice over how he or she lives. This would act as a restraint on sentencing because a very severe sentence would not enhance an individual's sense of control over his life. In sentencing, calculations could be made considering how much loss of dominion was caused by crime and fear of crime and how much a particular level of punishment would reduce the dominion of the person punished. The aim would be to find an optimum level which gives least loss of dominion. They also argue for a decremental strategy which reduces the levels of punishment until the point crime starts to increase.

Von Hirsch is critical of their approach and says that it would be even harder to devise a scale of punishments on this approach than on traditional utilitarianism. Moreover, on their theory preventive detention could be justified because the extended sentence would protect the dominion of potential victims. But this may open the door to the intensification of punishment if the protection of victims' dominion warrants it, especially if fear of crime is also taken into account.

These are issues to which we will return in Chapters 5 and 6.

4.5.2 **Problem scenario**

online
resource
centre

To clarify the differences of approach between the utilitarian approach considered in this chapter and the retributivist approach discussed in Chapters 2 and 3, you may wish to reflect on the following scenario. Guidance on approaching this question is given in the Online Resource Centre.

Consider the following problem:

In 2001 a request was made by the Lithuanian government for the extradition of Anton Gecas to face trial for participating in war crimes and genocide in Lithuania. Gecas was believed to have been the leader of a platoon of the notorious 12th Lithuanian Police Auxiliary Battalion. The Battalion was responsible for the murder of partisans, Jewish citizens, and Communist Party members in Lithuania and Belarus during the Second World War. Documents in the Lithuanian and Belarusian archives show that the platoon's principal function was to carry out executions and hangings, often in village streets and city squares. Commanders were under orders to maximise the deterrent value of terror by advertising these atrocities.

Gecas fled to the West at the end of the war, escaping prosecution in the Soviet Union. He never faced a criminal trial for his alleged participation in these crimes. He settled in Scotland in 1947, changed his name and ran a bed and breakfast business there for many years. He lost a civil action for defamation against Scottish TV in 1992 which had referred to his role in the atrocities in Lithuania and Belarus. When the Lithuanian government submitted a request for his extradition in 2001, he was a frail and infirm octogenarian, receiving treatment in an Edinburgh hospital, having suffered two strokes. He insisted that he was too ill to travel and he died before the matter could be resolved.

On the facts of this case, do you think Gecas should have been extradited to Lithuania to stand trial for the crimes of which he was accused? Why or why not? Give reasons for your answer.

5

Risk and danger

SUMMARY

This chapter reviews the current policy focus on protecting the public from the risk posed by an offender's reoffending, and the changes in sentencing law which have resulted from this. It locates the changes in a culture of control and examines the utilitarian justifications for selective incapacitation of offenders, or groups of offenders, believed to be dangerous. The chapter focuses on particular types of penalty and order, and the provisions for control of dangerous prisoners through discretionary release procedures.

5.1 Managing criminality

Around the turn of the 19th century, Vincent van Gogh painted...his famous picture *The Round of Prisoners*. It presents a well-known image: a circle of prisoners that completely embraces the perimeter of a prison courtyard....One century later, we can think about another circular view...according to the most rigorous and official data (from the UN) there are at present about 8,700,000 prisoners all over the world. Nowadays, this human contingent can form another 'round', another circular view: such a number could go twice round the world.

(Rivera Beiras 2005: 167)

5.1.1 A culture of control

The cover of this book reproduces the van Gogh painting to which Rivera Beiras refers in his vision of a world encircled by prisoners. His aim is to illuminate and explain worldwide trends towards new punitive rationalities which have resulted in a greater use of incapacitation through imprisonment as part of an overarching strategy to minimise risks (2005: 174–5). In this chapter we focus on incapacitation as another utilitarian tool, one which uses the temporary removal or, in those jurisdictions with the death penalty, the permanent removal of an offender from public life for purposes other than just deserts. Chapter 4 examined custodial penalties in terms of their deterrent aim whereas this chapter examines the use of (longer) terms of imprisonment as a means of managing risk—of preventing an offender from reoffending, or at least of confining his offending behaviour within the walls of the prison. In particular, it examines the increasing use for 'dangerous' offenders of indeterminate sentences which require evidence of rehabilitation before release. In Chapter 4 we reviewed current policy trends to introduce more purpose, more useful outcomes, into punishments and concentrated on the issue of deterrence. We will leave until Chapter 12 an examination of the policy aim to lower reoffending rates of convicted offenders by tailoring community punishments to individual offenders, and by forms of legislating for custody which will best incorporate rehabilitation in the community.

Many would see incapacitation as a key aim of punishment at the present time, at least for certain categories of offender. For them, even if there is no prospect of reforming or deterring offender, at least they can be contained. If this is the only justification, prison becomes simply warehousing. Recent penal policies have included provisions for 'selective incapacitation', whereby selected offenders or categories of offence can be given custodial terms which could not be justified on retributivist principles. The development of such policies is rooted in new ideas about crime control, about who counts as a 'dangerous' offender, and new techniques for the management of risk. Garland (2001b) has referred to these ideas collectively as a 'culture of control', a culture which is underpinned by new criminologies, that is, by new perspectives on crime and criminality.

Garland places these criminologies into two categories: criminologies of 'everyday life' and criminologies of 'the other' (2001b: 182–5). Whilst both view crime as 'a normal, routine, commonplace aspect of modern society' they have very different conceptions of 'the criminal' and of responses to criminality (ibid: 15). From the perspective of the criminology of everyday life criminals are normal and rational, and can be deterred or diverted by systematic and pragmatic techniques. These might include situational crime prevention, that is, the reduction of opportunities for crime by removing security weaknesses or coordinating transport and housing systems. Garland characterises this approach as 'amoral and technological' (ibid: 183). It does not deal in values so it 'sits easily' with policies on the one hand that would exclude certain groups of people—if that would reduce crime—or, on the other hand, that would transfer increased crime prevention resources to the most vulnerable—if they are the targets for criminality (ibid).

The criminology of the other, by contrast, focuses on values and seeks to assert absolute moral standards. The very 'normality' of crime is a catastrophe and one to be combated by the imposition of order and authority. Furthermore, from this perspective, some criminals are decidedly not 'normal' but are, rather, evil or wicked. They are, then, dangerous, different from us and, being 'other', can be dealt with in ways, such as very long or indeterminate prison sentences or community exclusion orders, which we might not otherwise endorse (ibid: 184).

Crucially, both these criminologies view the offender in ways which are very different from the 'social criminologies' dominant in the mid-twentieth century (see Garland 2001b: Chapter 2). In the context of enhanced notions of risk, 'the resulting sense of insecurity has led us to embrace habits and policies that would have seemed unthinkably repressive thirty years ago' (Owen 2007: 4) and which are 'completely at odds with the politics of solidarity that underpinned the welfare state and the sociological criminology that dominated at mid-[twentieth] century' (Garland 2001b: 185). They also differ from the perspectives of classical utilitarianism which underpinned the more 'welfare'-orientated approach of non-custodial sentencing at that time. Certainly, the rise of incapacitation in the USA and UK has been paralleled by a loss of support for welfare. Beckett and Western (2001) argue that states with social welfare are negatively associated with incarceration, and penal institutions have replaced the modernist strategy based on rehabilitation

and welfare. Rivera Beiras also documents the trend towards 'the punitive management of poverty, the thoroughgoing flexibilization of markets, more and more
criminalization for dissenters and the "rolling back" of state-provided welfare'
(2005: 180). This represents an alternative mode of governance which reflects
a shift towards a more exclusionary and punitive approach to the regulation of
social marginality. Incapacitation in the current climate reflects the view that it is
pointless to expect to find the underlying causes of crime, or to search for social or
political explanations of crime, if the individual is responsible for crime. So, in the
USA, states with large minority populations, particularly those with larger black
populations, spend less on welfare and have higher rates of incarceration.[1]

Because the new criminologies conceptualise the offender differently from
previous perspectives, they justify different responses. In what is referred to as a
'post-modern penality', the individual is, it is argued, increasingly invisible. He is
submerged in the actuarial, group-based approach of the New Penology to which
we referred in Chapter 1.[2] Further, it is argued that, in the new penality, a 'super-
ordinate goal' for punishment—a specified consequence—is absent (Feeley and
Simon 1992: 459). This is not to say that outcomes are unimportant, but that the
search for, and adherence to, general justifying aims and consequences are no
longer of great importance in postmodern thinking. On the other hand, the new
criminologies have refocused thinking on the particular outcome of deterrence,
and also buttress the new incapacitative policies which this chapter will explore.

The movement from the more 'social' style of reasoning of most of the twentieth
century to a more 'economic' one is evidenced by the increasing importance of a
managerial discourse in the criminal justice system (see Chapter 1). Criminal justice, including penal policy and practice, is infused with managerial concepts and
aims such as effectiveness, monitoring, key performance targets, quality audit and
control, league tables, systems management, out-sourcing, and value for money.

Managerialism—with its portable, multi-purpose techniques for accountability and evaluation and its 'can-do' private sector values—has flowed into the vacuum created when the
more substantive, more positive content of the old social approach lost credibility. The
crime control field—from crime prevention work and policing to the prison regimes and the
practice of parole—has become saturated with technologies of audit, fiscal control, measured performance, and cost–benefit evaluation. The old language of social causation has
been displaced by a new lexicon (of 'risk factors', 'incentive structures', 'supply and demand',
'stocks and flows', 'crime costing' and 'penalty pricing') that translates economic forms of
calculation into the criminological field.

(Garland 2001b: 188–9)

How did this happen? Garland suggests that thinking about crime in this way
probably occurred first in the private sector in, for example, private security firms
and businesses wishing to reduce losses through crime (ibid: 189–200). However, if
we focus on one element of the managerial discourse—that of risk management—
we can contextualise it more widely within 'the risk society'. This is the term

---

[1] However, as we shall see in Chapter 12, rehabilitationism has survived the challenges of the past
thirty years to emerge in a new form.
[2] Mauer has argued that this is also due to the increase in determinate, retributively based sentencing: 'the most significant change within the criminal justice system is the loss of the individual in the
sentencing process, as determinate sentencing and other "reforms" have taken us from an offender-
based to an offense-based system' (2001: 12).

which some theorists have coined to symbolise the apparent increasing preoccupation with risk—at the level not only of the economic but also of the personal and political—by the end of the twentieth century.

5.1.2 Notions of risk

In Chapters 2 and 3 on retributivism and just deserts sentencing there was little reference to risk assessments or sentencing influenced by calculations of risk to public safety. It is true that sentencers must work within statutory maxima and offence categories that Parliament has imposed in response to particular perceptions of risk and danger: the sex offender legislation is one example of this, the Dangerous Dogs Act 1991 another. Just deserts sentencing, however, should not include an assessment of risk because it looks to the past rather than the future. So those provisions which entail an assessment of the offender's potential to reoffend and to harm members of the public, inevitably sit uneasily alongside the sort of sentencing we have examined in Chapter 3, where the focus is (only) the seriousness of the offences already committed.

The 'risk society' is seen as one where the management of insecurity—of potential and unknown harms—has become the dominant theme (see, for example, Beck 1992; Giddens 1990; Vail *et al.* 1999). 'The idea of a "risk society" might suggest a world which has become more hazardous, but this is not necessarily so. Rather it is a society increasingly preoccupied with the future (and also with safety) which generates the notion of risk' (Giddens 1999: 3). In criminal and youth justice, and also in child protection and mental health, scientific and expert knowledge cannot ensure certain and predictable outcomes when applied to individual children, offenders, or patients. Instead, generalised prescriptions regarding risk of harm have been developed so that decisions which reduce societal anxiety can still be made. In relation to children and young people, their 'scarcity' and irreplaceability have put a much higher premium on risk management (see Farrington 2007; James and James 2008; Piper 2008). In relation to offenders, the high political and economic costs of failing to protect the public from dangerous people (see Chapter 1) have similarly imposed such a premium.

There are three implications of these trends to which we wish to draw attention. First, the attempts to manage crime and risk of crime are not confined to sentencing. Indeed, the criminal justice system itself is only one part of the government's crime reduction and risk management strategy. Paradoxically, sentencing has gained a greater political importance at a time when its practical effect is diminishing. Statistics which show how marginal sentencing is in terms of the ability to punish all those who commit offences underline the importance for governments of spreading crime prevention much more widely across policy areas. Much crime is neither reported nor recorded: only 3 per cent of crimes are proceeded with and a third of these are cautioned rather than prosecuted.[3]

Consequently, 'a whole new infrastructure has been assembled at the local level that addresses crime and disorder in a different manner' (Garland 2001b: 16)

---

[3] For a discussion of the difficulties of gaining information about crime including from official statistics, see Maguire (2002); for a discussion of the decline in the numbers of cases proceeding to prosecution, see Ashworth (2004: section 3).

with programmes and initiatives such as Safer Cities, Neighbourhood Watch, the Neighbourhood Renewal Fund, and New Deal for Communities. These are all geared towards strengthening communities and are oriented towards a new set of objectives, 'prevention, security, harm-reduction, loss-reduction, fear-reduction', that are very different from traditional criminal justice goals (ibid: 17). What we have then is a network of community 'empowering', crime-prevention partnerships which utilise managerial techniques to produce the most cost-effective ways of managing risk and of targeting resources (ibid: 19). For example, each of the 42 Strategic Management Boards responsible for reviewing Multi-Agency Public Protection Arrangements for managing high-risk sexual and violent offenders in the local community now has two lay members.

The second implication of the trend towards the cultural pre-eminence of a managerialist and technological culture is that the risk-management culture exerts control in new ways and in new contexts. It justifies a selective response to offending and its emphasis on cost effectiveness can cut across 'justice' issues. The use of risk-management tools has also, it is argued, reduced professional discretion to decide suitable and individualised responses (see Chapter 12).

Third, these developments led to the evolution in the 1990s in the UK of a sentencing policy which treats what was until recently a very small minority of offenders as dangerous, Garland's 'other', and from which the public needs protection. Such offenders are so 'risky' that a quite different sentencing framework is legitimate for dealing with them. How important is this new focus on risk and preventive sentencing? We have made frequent reference to Garland's influential book, *The Culture of Control*. He began that text with the following statement:

We quickly grow used to the way things are...On both sides of the Atlantic, mandatory sentences, victims' rights, community notification laws, private policing, 'law and order' politics, and an emphatic belief that 'prison works', have become common place points in the crime control landscape...

(Garland 2001b: 1)

Not only have we grown used to the increase in crime but we have also, he argues, accepted harsher punishments for those so selected. 'A show of punitive force against individuals is used to repress any acknowledgement of the state's inability to control crime to acceptable levels' (Garland 1996: 460). He argues that 'the most prominent measures of crime control policy are increasingly orientated towards punitive segregation and expressive justice' (2001b: 17) with components of exclusion such as the curfew and exclusion requirements in community orders and on early release which stipulate times and places which are 'out of bounds'. As we saw at the end of Chapter 1, the Sexual Offences Act 2003 has also introduced a range of civil orders, including the foreign travel orders, which aim to control the dangerous with the threat of a penal sanction for non-compliance and in section 5.4.3 below we review other prevention orders.

Other analysts have also argued for this crucial shift in the penal culture of Western punishment in the 1990s from the focus on seriousness that had characterised two centuries of penal policy. Pratt explains this as the move from an era of the 'civilising' of punishment to penal developments which are 'beyond the cultural limits of modern penality' and to which the public would have been hostile in the past (1998: 506; 2000: 42). With new cultural notions of risk, such developments are not only acceptable but, at least in the tabloid press at the beginning of the twenty-first century, are welcomed and encouraged. This has been described as 'a new culture of intolerance' (Pratt 2000: 47).

On the other hand, some commentators contend that these developments are not as novel as they are portrayed and even Garland makes the point that nothing in the penal system has actually been replaced. His argument is, rather, that their repositioning has been crucial in changing the penal culture. Brown similarly argues, in the context of nineteenth-century colonial history, that current more punitive policies can be 'interpreted within a framework of *recursions* within penal modernity, rather than signalling an end or fundamental transformation of the modern state' (2002: 403). Further, the focus on the dangerous offender is not a totally new development although those who are perceived as dangerous change over time (Dingwall 1998; Pratt 1996; see section 5.1.3 below).

However, the Criminal Justice Act (CJA) 2003 not only introduced changes to the **protective sentencing** framework, 'strengthening further the arrangements to manage dangerous offenders' (Home Office 2001a: para 2.96), but also used for the first time the heading 'Dangerous Offenders' and the term 'dangerousness'. Those terms were found in commentary and reports in the past, but not in sentencing legislation until 2003. Further, the numbers of those sentenced as 'dangerous' increased significantly after the implementation of that legislation.

5.1.3 **The dangerous offender**

Like the poor the dangerous have always been with us.

(Freiberg 2000: 51)

Risk, and the designation of individuals as dangerous because they pose an unacceptably high risk to the public, are not inventions of the twentieth or twenty-first centuries. Many examples of groups being designated as risks to the social order can be found in the nineteenth century (Pratt 2000: 36) and legislation was part of a mix of protective measures being taken by the state at the end of the nineteenth century against various 'evils' such as unemployment, crime, and poverty—a form of early state risk management (ibid: 38). At one level, then, 'the dangerous' are those groups which represent social dangers which are historically contingent, shaped by the result of ideas and events from a specific time and place. Such groups are not confined to the population of (convicted) offenders.

Even in relation to the offending population, it is by no means self-evident what we mean by dangerous offenders. The fact that different ideas, different constructions of dangerousness, have developed historically and internationally would suggest that the concept of dangerousness is constructed for political, professional and judicial purposes. The Floud Committee, which focused in detail on dangerousness, noted, '[d]angerousness is not an objective concept. Dangers are unacceptable risks' (see Floud 1982). This transfers the quest for a definition of dangerousness to the risk discourse and rephrases the analysis into a designation of those people and crimes seen as unacceptable risks.

These two levels are linked. The development of policy has been from a concentration in the early nineteenth century on 'dangerous classes' to the current emphasis on dangerous offenders, or groups of offenders such as sex offenders

(Pratt 2000: 36–8). Nevertheless, current dangerousness laws 'have the potential to remove an increasingly broad range of the socially undesirable' (ibid: 47) in that they target those who are often already socially excluded.

However, the focus on the individual offender reveals another development—the pathologisation of the dangerous offender. Mason and Mercer (1999) draw on Foucault's analysis of six serious cases during the period 1799–1835 to examine the medicalisation of the offender. That development construed dangerous offenders as mentally ill and brought into question the border between sanity and insanity. This can lead to problematic responses in regard to both the dangerous offender and the mentally ill (see section 5.4.2 below and Chapter 7, section 7.4). As Greig notes, in relation to her analysis of a high-profile Australian case, 'when the fluidity of madness is superimposed onto the notion of badness, it elicits an intuitive sense of fear among observers' (Greig 2002: 11). Further, most preventive sentencing measures are aimed at the offender who is mentally 'normal': there are clear and separate provisions for those who fit within the legally defined category of the mentally disordered. Yet the normal offender is affected by those social ideas which fuse mental abnormality and offending because all offenders can then be seen as in some way irrational and a threat. Consequently, the social fear they engender can be reduced by the imposition of indefinite and disproportionate custodial sentences. So, as we saw in relation to sex offenders in Chapter 1, when perceptions of such offenders as ill have become less powerful, they have been replaced by perceptions of them as evil (Simon 1998). Both constructions of the dangerous are, then, of the 'abnormal' and legitimise the continuous surveillance of offenders even when they are released on licence.

5.2 Incapacitation and public protection

5.2.1 Assessing the utilitarian justification

Incapacitation as a means of crime reduction is a strong strand in current penal policy in the UK and the USA. It gathered support in the early 1980s and was a key element of the penal policy of the Reagan administrations in the USA. It has also been used in the UK since the early 1990s and is apparent in the tendency towards longer sentences and also in other types of penalty. For example, the disqualification of drivers for motoring offences is a form of precautionary, incapacitative sentencing.

Unlike deterrence theory or rehabilitationism, incapacitation does not rest on a particular theory of human nature, but it is still justifiable on utilitarian grounds, the aim being to maximise happiness and restrain dangerous offenders, to protect the majority of society by removing harmful individuals. For persistent offenders who are not dangerous, prison removes offenders from the community for a temporary period even if it does not succeed in deterring them.

Incapacitation as a form of justification is not necessarily incompatible with rehabilitation, as incapacitation could be combined with programmes intended to reform the individual. In the UK we find a strong commitment to offending behaviour programmes designed to rehabilitate, as well as acceptance of protective sentencing. But one could incapacitate while recognising that there is no prospect of reform.

On the utilitarian model, society should be protected for as long as possible from persistent and dangerous offenders, so the individual is sacrificed for the greater good of society. While the most effective form of incapacitation is the death penalty, imprisonment is seen as the best method in abolitionist jurisdictions. However, there is still the risk of escape and there may be opportunities to commit crimes in prison. Offending may be resumed upon release so incapacitation will not solve long-term problems of crime. Because incapacitation is an expensive penal policy, a shift towards the use of prisons as warehouses may mean that reduced funding will be available for costly treatment programmes within the prison. The incapacitative strategy also seems to assume a finite pool of offenders, yet there is no reason why, when offenders are incarcerated, others will not fill the vacuum, particularly in drug turf wars.

There is also the question of whether prison does incapacitate effectively if it ultimately leads to higher offending rates than non-custodial sentences because of factors such as the stigmatising effects of prison, the difficulty in obtaining employment on release, the effects of prison dehumanisation on the offender, and the opportunities to learn from other offenders. Obviously this is a vexed question and difficult to establish, not least because of the problems of isolating the effects of prison from other criminogenic forces. But even if we could establish that imprisoning more offenders and increasing sentence length leads to a reduction in crime, we would need to assess the economic burdens because we know that the Three Strikes laws in the United States, for example, are very expensive and that the new indeterminate sentence for public protection (see below) has increased the prison overcrowding problem in England and Wales (Piper and Easton 2006/7).

If one could ensure that crime rates would fall by expanding the use of imprisonment, there would be political advantages for governments in implementing such a policy, despite the economic costs. For the high costs of incapacitation to be justified, the effect on the crime rate of removing offenders from society would need to be substantial and proven. But the available research suggests that even a substantial increase in the use of custody would achieve only a small cut in the crime rate, the reason being that punishment is only one factor linked to criminality (see Tarling, 1979, 1993; Brody, 1976). Tarling (1993: 154) estimated that we would need a 25 per cent increase in the prison population to obtain a 1 per cent fall in the crime rate in England, and the Carter Report (Carter 2003) calculated that only a 5 per cent reduction in crime in the period from 1997 to 2003 resulted from the higher custodial rates in that period. Conversely, Brody and Tarling (1980) calculated that if the prison population were cut by 40 per cent in the UK this would lead to an increase in crime of just 1.6 per cent. Using incapacitation as a crime reduction strategy is therefore an extremely expensive option. It is also difficult to isolate the causal significance of changes in the size of the prison population. When the prison population increased in the United States in the period 1991–98, the crime rate was falling, but when the prison population increased in the period 1984–89, the crime rate also increased.

Incapacitation may not be cost effective if we have to incarcerate large numbers to produce a small effect on crime rates. There are a number of reasons for the relative ineffectiveness of incapacitation. First, punishment is only one factor which may influence crime rates and it may be swamped by other factors. Second, the impact of punishment on crime will be limited if only a small number of offenders come before the court and receive custodial sentences, which raises the question of whether it is better to invest resources in policing than in punishment. Third, as with deterrence, there is the problem of isolating the effects of incapacitation on the overall crime rate.

Moreover there is an inherent tendency for incapacitation to be an expansionist policy, for if mistakes are made in predicting high-risk offenders, then the public's response may well be to demand that the range of offenders/offences within the net is broadened. As we saw earlier, governments may be reluctant to resist pressures for more incarceration and so be unable to abandon incapacitation as a strategy (see Chapter 1).

In the light of these problems, the tendency in recent years has been to focus on the incapacitation of particular offenders or groups of offenders who are most at risk of reoffending. From a utilitarian standpoint it is better to reserve prison for those most likely to reoffend which would also reduce the overall costs of imprisonment. As Wilson argues, 'all the evidence we have implies that, for crime-reduction purposes, the most rational way to use the incapacitative powers of our prisons would be to do so selectively. Instead of longer sentences for everyone, or for persons who have prior records, or for persons whose present crime is especially grave, longer sentences would be given primarily to those who, when free, commit the most crimes' (1985: 153–4). So, following the scepticism over deterrence in the late 1970s and 1980s, and particularly in view of the critique of methodological problems, more specific studies were undertaken which sought to identify the offenders most at risk of reoffending. This was seen as necessary to target resources most effectively as the costs of incarceration increased.

5.2.2 Selective and categorial incapacitation

We need to distinguish different forms of incapacitation. Selective incapacitation means incapacitating particular individuals who may be at high risk of reoffending, and here a variety of factors may be identified including employment history and drug use. Categorial incapacitation focuses on incapacitating those who commit specific categories of crime, offences which carry a high risk of reoffending such as burglary. Both selective and categorial incapacitation are forms of predictive sentencing.

Selective incapacitation has become popular as it offers the possibility of reducing crime by incarcerating the most crime-prone offenders, but it may also serve to contain the size of the prison population, allowing precious resources to be used most effectively against those offenders. So it is not surprising that it is popular with governments. To calculate the risks of reoffending various indices have been used, such as data on crimes, the individual's record, his employment or social circumstances.

However, selective incapacitation has been seen as ethically flawed as it may mean that an offender is given a higher sentence than he deserves if he is deemed to be at risk and because it denies autonomy to the individual. It presumes the individual will follow a particular course of action in the future and punishes them accordingly for a choice not yet made: we do not know that the individual would have reoffended, especially if the person was a first-time offender. For both reasons it conflicts with retributivist principles. Such policies also raise the issue of who should shoulder the risk of harm: potential future victims or the offender who may receive a longer sentence.

One problem with selective incapacitation is that we are still a long way from certainty in our predictions of future offending. Research studies usually are based on convicted offenders rather than the wider population of offenders which includes unconvicted and potential offenders. If we over-estimate the risk, there is the danger of incarcerating unnecessarily. However, the public is more concerned that the risk will be under-estimated exposing them to the release of dangerous offenders into the community. If selective incapacitation of dangerous offenders is introduced but the policy fails to detain all dangerous offenders, then there will be an increase in public demands to broaden the categories of risk. While risk-management techniques are becoming more sophisticated, they may still be insufficiently precise to provide a basis for fair and just penal policies.

But is it inherently unfair? As Walker (1996) argues, someone who has committed an offence has a higher probability of committing further offences than someone who has not. A person subjected to a protective sentence, even though he might not have reoffended, is not presumptively innocent but has committed exactly the type of offence for which he is being detained and future detention or control may be justified. Moore argues that predictive sentencing is compatible with desert theory because a dangerous person is more deserving of punishment if the criminal record suggests that he is a bad risk (Moore *et al.* 1985). But while some retributivists would give some weight to past history, the prime focus is on the current offence. In any case, as von Hirsch (1986) points out, a predictive index would include factors such as drug use, age and employment and may also use self-reports of offending behaviour, factors which would be irrelevant to retributivist sentencing.

Because of the above problems, many prefer categorial incapacitation in which an entire class of offenders will be incarcerated to prevent reoffending. This meets the objection of unfairness raised against selective incapacitation. It satisfies the principle of equality, in so far as it treats all burglars alike, but we still cannot know for certain that everyone in the class would have reoffended, or indeed any of them.

However, we do know that recidivism rates vary between offences. For example, murderers have low recidivism rates and robbers higher rates, so we could in theory maximise crime prevention by giving longer sentences to those with the highest potential for reoffending. Von Hirsch (1986) finds categorial incapacitation more compatible with desert theory than selective incapacitation, provided the sentence is linked to blameworthiness and proportionality. But while it satisfies the retributivist demand for parity between offenders committing the same crime, it does not give parity with other serious crimes. Even if we operate within broad desert limits on sentencing, we are still treating offenders as a class differently, on the basis of the offence, compared to other serious offenders, although within the class we are treating all members of that class equally. It is also problematic for rank ordering if one offence is taken out of the ordering and still does not tell us where to anchor the scale, so it does not address the issue of cardinal proportionality.

An attempt to converge past and future crimes in crime prevention strategies will undermine the principles of fairness and proportionality. Von Hirsch is sceptical regarding the attempt of Morris and Miller (1985) to converge prediction and retributivism by using prediction within broad limits governed by desert, so the punishment extended by dangerousness would not go beyond that justified as a deserved punishment independent of the prediction. As he says, this still begs the question of the reliability of evidence underpinning claims of dangerousness as well as the moral objection that it is 'unjust to give unequal punishments— and thereby unequal amounts of condemnation—to offenders whose conduct is equally reprehensible' (von Hirsch 1986: 141).

5.2.3 **Mass imprisonment in the USA**

An extreme example of the use of incapacitation as a penal policy is to be found in the United States where the imprisonment rate, that is the numbers in custody as a proportion of the general population, has increased substantially since 1972 and is much higher than in European and Scandinavian countries. For most of the twentieth century the imprisonment rate in the USA was around 110 per 100,000. In 1972, the rate had decreased to 93 per 100,000 but since then it has increased substantially, reaching 452 per 100,000 by 1999. Indeed, the 1990s saw a doubling of the prison population until there were over 2,000,000 in prison by 2001, a shift Zimring (2001) characterises as being from 'lock them up' to 'throw away the key'.

The expansion of imprisonment in the USA has been marked by the presence of young black males from urban areas. One in three black men aged 20–29 is in penal custody or under penal supervision compared to 4 per cent of white males and 14 per cent of Hispanic males (Mauer and Huling 1995). This has had a number of social effects, including the disenfranchisement of a chunk of the population, an increase in the number of single-parent families headed by women in those communities, and the alienation of those groups affected. The result has been the overlaying of penal exclusion on racial and economic exclusion, so deepening social divisions. The economic costs are also substantial.

This shift towards 'mass imprisonment' has been attributed to a combination of factors, including the rise of determinate sentences and mandatory sentences and the war on drugs. The Three Strikes laws have also narrowed the gap between serious and non-serious offences, so undermining the retributivist sentencing framework.

The 1990s were also marked by increasing inequality stratification in the USA, as the gap between the middle class and black working class widened. Arguably, it is easier to punish those with whom there is little contact outside the courtroom. The prison population is still increasing in the USA and as Mauer points out 'this is seemingly unrelated to crime rates or any rational calculation of its benefits to society' (2001: 10). Yet, despite the social and economic costs of incapacitative policies, they are unlikely to be jettisoned in the USA because of the rise in populist punitiveness and the emergence of crime and punishment as a key political issue. Instead, they may become more central to penal policy. Moreover, the constitutionality of the Three Strikes laws was upheld in *Ewing v California* (2003). In that case a 25-year sentence imposed for a minor theft was held not to infringe the test of gross disproportionality (see the discussion in van Zyl Smit and Ashworth 2004).

5.3 Sentencing on risk of harm

5.3.1 The history of protective sentencing

'The criminal justice system has always been concerned with protecting society from offenders who are perceived to be dangerous' (Dingwall 1998: 177) and defining and dealing separately with the dangerous was given a statutory basis at the beginning of the last century. Those early provisions for preventive detention were aimed at the persistent offender, the 'habitual' or professional criminals seen as a danger because of their propensity not just to reoffend but to engage in criminality as a way of life. Such behaviour not only threatened in particular the propertied classes but was evidence of a continued refusal to conform. So, for example, the Prevention of Crime Act 1908 was passed in England and Wales, the Habitual Criminals Act 1906 in New Zealand, and the Crimes Act in 1914 in Australia. In England and Wales the 1908 Act provided for post-sentence preventive detention of 5–10 years, replaced by a sentence of preventive detention for 5–14 years by the Criminal Justice Act 1948. That in turn was replaced by the extended sentence in the Criminal Justice Act 1967 (Powers of Criminal Courts Act 1973), with a much longer period of rehabilitative probation, aimed at the persistent more serious offender who was a risk to society. This sentence was abolished in the Criminal Justice Act (CJA) 1991 (see Dingwall 1998; Scottish Executive 1999: Chapter 4).

Yet what is clear from research on the operation of these early provisions in England and Wales and other jurisdictions is how little they were used (Dingwall 1998: 179; Freiberg 2000; Walker 1999: 62). Explanations have been in terms of judicial adherence to retributivist principles, suspicion of expert evidence, judicial concern at encroachment on sentencing discretion, or because of more widely held ethical, constitutional or human rights concerns. These reasons have ensured that preventive measures have generally remained as exceptions to a 'normal' sentencing approach. Consequently, the first wave of such legislation in the early twentieth century was, in practice, used by sentencers for only a minority of offenders. Recent developments, as we shall see, may be evidence that the current 'culture of control' is modifying sentencing law and practice.

Which offenders are now perceived as the most 'dangerous' to the public? The new provisions in sentencing policy in the 1990s—selective additional incapacitation, mandatory minimum sentences, and new forms of custodial sentences with extended licence periods—and the new sentencing framework for the dangerous offender in the CJA 2003, reflect the fact that drug traffickers and domestic burglars have been added to a longer-standing legislative concern with sexual and violent offenders. However, the persistent offender is again viewed as a social danger: in the CJA 2003, the repetition of offences is part of the 'proof' of risk in some of the provisions, and is a mandatory aggravation in relation to all provisions (see Chapter 3, section 3.2.4).

5.3.2 Longer than commensurate sentences

Contrary to the government's statement that the CJA 2003 introduced for the first time 'a distinction between dangerous and non-dangerous offenders as a basis of custodial sentencing' (Home Secretary *et al.* 2006: para 1.10; see also Piper and Easton 2006/7), the first protective sentence introduced in the more recent past was the 'longer than commensurate' or LTC sentence, in the CJA 1991 and later consolidated in ss 79(2)(b) and 80(2)(b) of the Powers of Criminal Courts (Sentencing) Act (PCCSA) 2000 (see Table 3.1 in Chapter 3). These provisions enabled sentencers to impose longer determinate custodial sentences on those convicted of sexual or violent offences than were proportionate to seriousness.[4]

The range of offences to which these provisions related (re-enacted as a list in s 161 of the PCCSA 2000) was relatively narrow, reflecting the policy aim to reduce custody for most offenders whilst allowing for (longer) custodial sentences for the small minority of dangerous offenders (see von Hirsch and Ashworth 1996). The presumptive provisions about 'seriousness' in the CJA 1991 and then the PCCSA 2000 could be over-ridden in favour of a protective sentence if 'only such a sentence would be adequate to protect the public from serious harm from him'. In such cases, the court could pass a sentence 'for such longer term (not exceeding that maximum) as in the opinion of the court is necessary to protect the public from serious harm from the offender'. This amounted, in effect, to selective (additional) incapacitation. The Act noted that 'harm' covers 'death or serious personal injury, whether physical or psychological, which would be occasioned by future violent or sexual offences committed by the offender' (PCCSA 2000, s 161(4)) whilst 'serious' harm had already been interpreted by the courts in *Birch* (1989) in relation to s 41 of the Mental Health Act 1983. In that case, Mustill LJ stated that the court 'is required to assess not the seriousness of the risk that the defendant will re-offend, but the risk that if he does so the public will suffer serious harm...the potential harm must be serious, and a high possibility of a recurrence of minor offences will no longer be sufficient'.

However, this left several key issues to be interpreted by the courts, including the definition of a 'violent' offence (see Clarkson 1997: 286) and the question of whether the calculation of risk could be based solely on a history of previous similar convictions or whether a clinical diagnosis of dangerousness was required (ibid: 287). Guidance was not always consistent. For example, *Bowler* (1994) endorsed the taking into consideration of the 'less robust than average' victim in predicting future harm whilst *Fishwick* (1996) appeared not to allow deviations from the 'average' victim in this decision. Further, very little guidance emerged from the courts on the crucial question of the likelihood of reoffending. The most difficult issue for the sentencer, however, was the calculation of the 'additional element' to be added to a commensurate sentence, providing the total did not exceed the statutory maximum. Until *Chapman* (2000), cases often, but by no means always, supported the statement in *Crow and Pennington* (1994) that there should be a 'reasonable relationship with the seriousness level'. In those cases, buggery and arson respectively, where a sentence of seven years was reduced to four and the sentence of eight years upheld, the Court of Appeal said the enhancement could be up to 50 per cent (see also *M (James Samuel)* (2003)), whilst the average of 31 decisions made by the Court of Appeal 1993–97 was a 73.5 per cent enhancement (see Clarkson 1997: 289). In *Chapman* (2000), however, where an LTC determinate sentence was substituted for a life sentence, the Court argued that there was no necessary ratio between the

---

[4] These provisions are repealed by the CJA 2003 Schedule 37 Part 7. However, some of the case law remains relevant.

punishment—justified on retributivist principles—and the protective parts of the sentence.[5]

In some respects this latter reasoning was logical: if an offender is a serious risk, but does not meet the criteria for a life sentence, a few more years of public protection (see *Szczerba* 2002) may appear ineffective in relation to a life time of offending. With relatively short periods of extra incapacitation, especially when early release is taken into account (see below), LTC sentencing in practice was not, perhaps, based on the rationale—protection of the public—which justified the sentence (Clarkson 1997: 285). Indeed, Walker (1999) argued that the Court of Appeal had shown a lack of 'sense' by upholding sentences which were too short for utilitarian purposes and Freiberg (2000) makes the same comments on the approach of Australian judges. Further, *R (Giles) v Parole Board* (2004) tested the legality under Article 5(4)[6] of the ECHR of implementing the extra period of custody without an independent review once the punitive element had been served. The Court of Appeal and then the House of Lords refused to treat such a sentence as similar to a discretionary life sentence (see sections 5.3.4 and 5.4.4) and followed *Chapman* (2000) in stating that the whole sentence was pervaded by a punitive element and a protective determinate sentence was not to be treated as having two parts.

Not surprisingly, therefore, it was argued that the 1991 provisions had been interpreted narrowly, so that Parliament and the Court of Appeal were at cross purposes (Dingwall 1998), and that rights issues had not been given adequate appellate consideration. Further, it appeared that, as in the past, the preventive LTC sentences had been used sparingly by the judiciary. Flood-Page and Mackie (1998) found in 1995–6 that only 3 per cent of custodial sentences for violence and 6 per cent for sexual offences were given LTC sentences and Henham's research confirmed this paucity though revealing a judicial preference for the newer form of extended sentence provided in s 85 of the PCCSA 2000 (Henham 2001: 707). The precursor of this latter provision was in s 44 of the CJA 1991, which empowered the courts to make an order extending the period of release on licence in regard to sexual offences (then, for sexual and violent offences, ss 58–62 of the Crime and Disorder Act (CDA) 1998). As consolidated, s 85 of the PCCSA 2000 allowed an extension to be added to commensurate or LTC sentences if the normal period of licence was inadequate for the purpose of rehabilitation and crime prevention. The CJA 2003 provides a new extended sentence with similar effects but discontinues the LTC sentence (see section 5.4.1).

5.3.3 Mandatory (minimum) sentences

The second set of new sentences introduced in the 1990s were also problematic because they were mandatory and because one of them imposed a life sentence. These factors raise rights issues. Until 1997, only one mandatory penalty was in existence for use by English courts—that of life imprisonment for murder, deemed

---

[5] In *Attorney General's Reference No. 7 of 1996 (R v Hodgeon)* (1997), for example, where the offender had previous convictions for rape and ABH and the 'normal range' was 5–8 years, the Court gave 7+5 = 12 years.

[6] 'Everyone who is deprived of his liberty by arrest or detention shall be entitled to take proceedings by which the lawfulness of his detention shall be decided speedily by a court and his release ordered if the detention is not lawful.'

in *Lichniak* (2001) not to contravene either Article 3 or 5 of the ECHR.[7] The House of Lords said it was justifiable to postpone to the end of the tariff period the judgment about future risk of harm to the public. However, the judiciary, in this and other jurisdictions,[8] have resisted the imposition of mandatory provisions on the grounds that they restrict judicial discretion (see Chapter 2). The new sentences added by ss 1–4 of the Crime (Sentences) Act 1997 and re-enacted in ss 109–11 of the PCCSA 2000 were mandatory in relation to specified forms of reoffending. The first of these provisions provided what became known as an 'automatic' life sentence on conviction for a second offence when both offences were in the list provided specifically for the purpose of s 109. The second and third provisions mandate a minimum sentence for a third specified offence. The choice of offences highlighted the crimes seen as currently dangerous, and the use of a form of cumulative sentencing reflected the increasingly held view that persistent offending is itself a danger. Parliament specified those offences where custody had to be imposed, possibly where it would not otherwise have been imposed or where a shorter term might have been imposed. Where these provisions apply, they take precedence over the just deserts sentencing framework. The difficulties with such legislation arise from the 'get-out' clauses: the 'exceptional circumstances' of s 109 and the 'unjust to do so' of ss 110–111.

The automatic life sentence was repealed by the CJA 2003 but its use had already been severely curtailed by *Offen No 2* (2001). Early appeals (notably *Kelly* (1999); *Offen No 1* (2001)) had confirmed the interpretation of 'exceptional circumstances' to cover only circumstances that were unusual, special and uncommon. If regularly encountered before the courts they would not be. After the implementation of the Human Rights Act (HRA) 1998, Offen's further appeal, *Offen No 2* (2001), was successful: the lack of any unacceptable risk of future harm from the offender was taken to constitute 'exceptional circumstances'. The importance of rights jurisprudence in these cases cannot be over-estimated. In Matthew Offen's case, a history of psychiatric illness in childhood, and the fact that he had committed the 'amateurish' robbery in carpet slippers, that he admitted the offence to his friends immediately afterwards, and that the money was quickly recovered, had not been construed as exceptional circumstances in *Offen No 1* (2000). Similarly in Ian Turner's case, a gap of 30 years between the commission of the two relevant offences had not amounted to exceptional circumstances but, when the Criminal Cases Review Commission brought the case back to the Appeal Court after *Offen No 2*, the imposition of the automatic life sentence was overturned because Turner presented no risk to the public (*Turner* (2001)).[9] *Offen* meant that the justifying focus had to be on risk of future harm to the public: see *Baff* (2003), and *Wallace* (2001). In 2002, 44 offenders were given automatic life sentences under s 109 (Home Office 2003h: Table 4G).

The sentences in ss 110–11 of the PCCSA 2000 remain in force: the court must impose a minimum sentence of seven years on the third conviction for a Class A

---

[7] The judgment in *Offen No. 2* (2001) (see below) was distinguishable because that dealt with cases less serious than murder. Note however that the (English) Privy Council has jurisdiction over territories where the death penalty still pertains. See, for example, Bailin (2002) for rulings on death penalty cases in the Eastern Carribean.

[8] See, for example, van Zyl Smit (2000) in relation to similar sentences introduced in South Africa in 1997.

[9] See also *Stark* (2002), *Watkins* (2002).

drug trafficking offence and three years on a third domestic burglary conviction.[10] Ashworth argued for the relative unimportance of these provisions, given that most third-time offenders would receive seven years in relation to drug trafficking, and that few burglars had been sentenced under s 111 (Ashworth 2002b: 1096). However, whilst the number of third-time burglars sentenced under this provision was only 6 in 2001, the number rose to 13 in 2003, 46 in 2004 and 89 in 2005 (Home Office 2007c: Table 2.6).

Since January 2004 there has also been a further mandatory sentence which courts must use. Sections 287 and 292 of the CJA 2003 amended the Firearms Act 1968 and the Firearms (Northern Ireland) Order 1981, respectively, to provide for a mandatory minimum sentence of five years' imprisonment for those aged 18 or over in England and Wales (21 or over in Scotland and N. Ireland) convicted of possessing a prohibited firearm.[11] For those aged 16–17 in England and Wales (16–20 in Scotland and Northern Ireland) the mandatory minimum is three years. These minimum sentences, according to the government, represent a significant increase in sentencing levels from a previous average of 18 months.[12]

5.3.4 Discretionary life sentences

This sentence is available where the statutory maximum (not mandatory) penalty for an offence is life imprisonment: it cannot be used unless a life sentence is legally available (*Hodgson* 1996). Further, this sentence is 'not to be treated as a sentence to be passed for the most serious manifestation of each offence' (Ashworth 2000: 189–90). Until the implementation of s 225 of the CJA 2003, its use for all offences was governed by the criteria laid down some time ago in *Hodgson* (1967). In relation to offences listed as eligible for the imposition of LTC sentences the Court of Appeal stated that those provisions also had to be complied with when imposing a discretionary life sentence.

Since the implementation of the CJA 2003, however, s 225 provides the statutory criteria for all life sentences imposed in relation to the long lists of sexual and violent offences to be found in Schedule 15 of the Act (see section 5.4.1 below). As the Bar Council notes, only the relatively few offences not on that list but which carry the life sentence as their maximum penalty, for example Class A drugs trafficking, are subject solely to the *Hodgson* criteria (Bar Council 2006; section 3B). For that minority of cases, to impose a discretionary life sentence the court must first find the crime to have been grave and the offender to be suffering from mental instability. It must then assess the risk posed by the offender and decide that he will probably reoffend and be a danger to the public for some (unforeseeable) time.[13] In *Wilkinson* (1983) Lord Lane CJ noted that it must be used only in 'the most exceptional circumstances' and generally with offenders who cannot be

---

[10] For examples of cases where the mandatory custodial sentence was not imposed because 'unjust in all the circumstances' see *Hoare* (2004) and *Gibson* (2004); see also guidance on this matter in *McInerney and Keating* (2002).

[11] Firearms Act 1968 s 51A as amended by the Criminal Justice Act 2003. The Firearms (Sentencing) (Transitory Provisions) Order 2007 (SI 2007 No. 1324) was introduced as a response to an appellate decision about the illegality under the Act of the sentence for those aged 16 and 17.

[12] See http://www.connected.gov.uk/facts/legislation/index.html.

[13] Note that here mental instability is not a medical term and is not the same as 'mentally disordered' which is the term used and legally defined in the Mental Health Act 1983.

dealt with under the Mental Health Act 1983. Smith's research, which examined 50 Appeal Court judgments over a 10-year period, found that discretionary life sentences were most commonly imposed in respect of rape convictions (23 cases) and manslaughter (12) (Smith 1998). In *Chapman* (2000) the Court stated that it might place less weight on the seriousness of the current offence, meaning that the Court might not require an offence whose seriousness was proportionate to at least five years' imprisonment, if the prediction was of very serious future harm.

Case law had established that decisions on whether there was mental instability indicating dangerousness should normally be based on medical evidence, although inference from the facts of the offending had been allowed, as for instance in *Virgo* (1989), a child destruction case. Research by Smith (1998) suggested that the quality of psychiatric reports varies. *Spear* (1994) had confirmed that ongoing mental instability was a requirement for the imposition of a life sentence but in *Whittaker* (1996) the Court approved its use for an offender who was not 'unstable' (there being no psychiatric evidence to that effect) but was considered to be very seriously dangerous and likely to remain so. Walker introduces discussion of this case with 'eventually the court yielded to realism' (1999: 68).

The court must specify the part of the sentence—the relevant part—which is imposed for the purposes of punishment and deterrence. This should equate to one-half to two-thirds of what would have been the appropriate determinate sentence. As we shall see in section 5.4.4 below, the determination and the consequences of this period—the minimum term—are very important.

The new criteria introduced by the CJA 2003 for the life sentence and for the new sentence of imprisonment for public protection (IPP), whose effect is almost identical to life imprisonment, have prompted a current focus on the 'discretionary' life sentence. As we shall see below (section 5.4.1), the apparent lack of sentencing discretion has increased the numbers in custody on an indeterminate sentence. Official estimates suggest that—without changes in law and guidance (see below)—the number of offenders on the IPP sentence by 2012 would have amounted to a third of the current prison population (see, for example, Carter Report 2007: 7; The Howard League for Penal Reform, 2007). However, for some time England and Wales has had the highest lifer population out of all the 45 countries of the Council of Europe and it is argued that the protective sentences introduced in the 1990s, together with the fact that nearly 70 offences provide a life sentence option, have produced this position (Prison Reform Trust 2004a).

5.4 Recent legislation

5.4.1 The Criminal Justice Act 2003

The sentencing provisions of the CJA 2003 (Part 12) include a separate chapter dedicated to 'Dangerous Offenders' which sets up a new sentencing framework for sentencing those from whom the public is deemed to need protection, although for offences committed before 4 April 2005 the old provisions apply. Schedule 15 of the Act provides a total of 153 specified offences for the purposes of these provisions, including 65 specified violent offences in Part I of the Schedule. This makes the applicability of the provisions on 'violent' offences much clearer but, as we shall see, the criteria for the new sentences include problematic concepts and ideas very similar to those in previous legislation. This means that cases arising from the protective provisions in the PCCSA 2000 may still be relevant and similar problems persist.

Sections 225–228 (in force since April 2005) provide sentences of 'life imprisonment', 'imprisonment for public protection' (with comparable forms of detention for offences committed by those under 18 years of age: see Chapter 13), and a new extended sentence (for under-and over-18-year-olds). They can be imposed only in relation to the 'specified' offences listed in the Schedule but there is an important sub-group of specified offences called, confusingly, 'serious offences'. These are defined as specified offences punishable by imprisonment for life or by a determinate sentence of at least ten years. All specified offences count as a 'relevant' offence for these provisions (s 229(4)).

These provisions, until they are amended by the Criminal Justice and Immigration (CJI) Act 2008, in effect provide mandatory sentences. If the criteria are met, the court 'must' impose the relevant sentence of imprisonment or an extended sentence. The choice of sentence depends on whether or not the 'specified' offence is also a 'serious' offence. The new life sentences and also the new (IPP) sentences are applicable only to those offenders who have been convicted of offences defined as 'serious offences' (see above); the extended sentences are also applicable only to specified offences and, until s 15 of the CJI Act 2008 is implemented, only to specified offences which are not also serious offences as defined in the CJA 2003.

The extended sentence is a determinate sentence made up of the 'appropriate' (commensurate) custodial period and an extension period which must not exceed five years for a specified violent offence or eight years for a specified sexual offence. The whole must not exceed the maximum allowed for the offence (ss 227 and 228 for adults and minors respectively).

The life sentences and IPP sentences are both indeterminate sentences, the Act specifically stating that the court should specify a tariff period when imposing the new IPP sentence (s 225(4)). Schedule 18 of the Act also amends s 31 of the Crime (Sentences) Act (CSA) 1997 to include reference to the new sentence (see section 5.4.4 below).

Both life sentences and IPP sentences apply to persons over 18 and only where 'the court is of the opinion that there is a significant risk to members of the public of serious harm occasioned by the commission by him of further specified offences' (s 225(1)(b)). The choice of a life sentence or an IPP sentence then depends on two factors: whether the life sentence is legally available for the offence in question and whether the court considers the seriousness of the offence (and one or more associated offences) justifies a life sentence. If both criteria are met—and there are clear echoes here of the 'grave' crime requirement of *Hodgson* (1967)—the court must currently impose a life sentence. If a life sentence is not available and/or the circumstances of the offence are not sufficiently serious, the court must impose an IPP sentence. For extended sentences the role of the risk criterion is very similar: if met, it again mandates the court, until amendments to s 277(2) are brought into force, to impose an extended sentence.

In assessing whether any of the sentences provided by ss 225–228 of the CJA 2003 are to be imposed, what becomes crucial is the assessment of the offenders'

dangerousness. If they are considered 'a significant risk' to the public, what Ashworth
has referred to as 'swingeing new sentencing powers' (2004: n 10) must be invoked.
Section 229, headed 'the assessment of dangerousness', gives guidance in relation
to the assessment of risk. It does not provide a definition but, as passed in 2003,
is, in effect, a presumption which is reversed for different offenders. So, if the
offender has no previous 'relevant' conviction or is under 18 years of age, the court
must take account of all information about the offence and may consider information about the offender, and any pattern of behaviour of which the offences form
a part, in making a judgment. For adult offenders, however, if the current conviction has been preceded by a previous conviction for a relevant, that is specified,
offence then 'the court must assume there is such a risk', unless the court considers
it 'unreasonable' to so conclude (s 229(3)). This is clearly akin to the automatic life
sentence (imposed under s 109 of the PCCSA 2000) which it replaced although
these provisions were drafted specifically to avoid the human rights issue to which
Offen No 2 (2001) drew attention although, as Ashworth noted, the provisions
appear to have been based 'on a policy of going as far as possible to minimize or
otherwise avoid these rights' (2004: section 5(i)).

What these dangerousness provisions provide is not only a replacement for the
'two strikes' automatic life penalty but also an indeterminate sentence replacement for the LTC sentence. This means that, when 'significant risk' is determined
in relation to a 'serious' (as defined) offence which is not serious enough for (commensurate to) a life sentence to be imposed, the court no longer has to decide on
the extra 'protective' period. This is left, as in discretionary life sentences, to the
early release system but with special provisions relating to IPP sentences.

In relation to offenders with no previous relevant convictions where the current
presumption of significant risk does not apply, difficulties of application and interpretation, noted above in relation to provisions to be replaced, continue. Where
the presumption operates, the difficulties relating to 'exceptional circumstances'
became apparent in relation to the 'unreasonableness' of imposing a s 225 sentence. Such considerations also apply to the extended sentence. With the removal
of the presumption by s 17 of the CJI Act 2008, the difficulties in assessing risk will
increase, not decrease (see below).

IPP sentences

It is these sentences which have caused the most difficulties, not just in relation to
the crucial assessment of risk but also in terms of resources: as noted, the very constraining statutory provisions have had a significant impact on prison overcrowding
as a result of the increased numbers of indeterminate sentences passed since the
implementation of the CJA 2003. The first case to give guidance on the new provisions was *Lang* (2005) which focused (inter alia) on the issue of what is 'serious' such
as to justify life imprisonment. In his judgment the Vice-President, Rose LJ, argued—
'on the basis that that Parliament is presumed to know the law'—that Parliament did
not intend to introduce 'a new, more restive, criterion for seriousness' and that previous case law such as *Chapman* (2000) still applied. Likewise, for the interpretation of
'serious harm' he stated that previous case law such as *Bowler* applied (ibid: para 11).

Lang (2005) also dealt with extended sentences, emphasising that they were
available only for specified offences that are not subject to a maximum custodial term of more than ten years but that for such offences the sentence is

mandatory if the criteria are met. The Court stressed that the custodial term must be a proportionate one and that the parsimony principle applies (ibid: para 12).

Paragraphs 15–19 are, however, the crucial paragraphs in the *Lang* judgment, dealing as they do with the assessment of dangerousness. Referring to these sections as 'labyrinthine', Rose LJ stated that, '[i]n our judgement, when sections 229 and 224 are read together, unless the information about offences, pattern of behaviour and the offender...show a significant risk of serious harm...from further offences, it will usually be unreasonable to conclude that the assumption exists' (ibid: para 15). Extensive guidance was then given on the factors to be borne in mind in assessing whether there is a significant risk, including the statement that '[i]f the foreseen specified offence is not serious, there will be comparatively few cases in which a risk of serious harm will properly be regarded as serious' (ibid: para 17). The Court also noted that '[i]t cannot have been Parliament's intention, in a statute dealing with the liberty of the subject, to require the imposition of indeterminate sentences for the commission of relatively minor offences' (ibid). It could be argued, then, that the tenor of *Lang* was towards a restrictive interpretation of the new provisions.

However, *Lang* left considerable discretion in the application of statutory criteria and the somewhat divergent judgments in the cases of *Folkes*, *McGrady* and *Thomas* in 2006 led to the following comment:

> The source of the problem is the ill-conceived legislation which deprives courts of discretion in deciding when to use the dangerous offender sentences and when not to do so—it is unlikely in the extreme that any of the offenders in these three cases would have received a sentence of life imprisonment or a longer than commensurate sentence under the earlier legislation.
>
> (Thomas 2007: 172)

In its third update to the *Case Compendium* (April 2007), the Sentencing Guidelines Council (SGC) used *Reynolds* (2007) as its leading case on dangerousness. *Reynolds* referred to *Lang* (2005) and *Johnson* (2006) as providing the guidelines but also gave guidance on 'how any mistakes made in their application may be rectified'. Clearly courts were having difficulties in applying the 2003 provisions.

In September 2007 the SGC issued guidance which deals with the assessment of dangerousness in Part 6. It makes clear, citing *Lang*, that there are two parts to the 'serious risk' test:

- there must be a significant risk of the offender committing further specified offences (whether serious or not), and
- there must be a significant risk of serious harm to members of the public being caused by such offences.

(Sentencing Guidelines Council 2007b: para 6.1.2)

It further notes that '[t]he court is guided, but not bound, by the assessment of dangerousness in a pre-sentence report' (ibid: para 6.1.4). Again citing *Lang*, it states '[u]sually it would be unreasonable to assume that the offender is a dangerous offender if, but for the assumption of dangerousness, the offender would not be found to be a dangerous offender' (ibid: 6.2.4).

In relation to assessing future risk the guideline gives the following:

There are three groups of factors that are relevant in the assessment of whether there is a significant risk of the offender committing further specified offences:

- the nature and circumstances of the current offence and the offender's 'offending' history…including whether the offending demonstrates any pattern,
- the offender's social and economic circumstances including accommodation, employ-ability, education, associations, relationships and drug or alcohol abuse,

  and

- the offender's thinking, emotional state and attitude towards offending and Supervision.

(ibid: para 6.4.1)

Citing *Johnson* (2006 at 21), the guideline specifically states that '[t]he existence (or non-existence) of previous convictions does not determine whether an offender is a dangerous offender: an offender with no previous convictions may be a dan-gerous offender, whilst an offender with previous convictions may not' (ibid: para 6.4.3.1). It goes on to discuss further how to assess the significance of offend-ing history and also refers the court to consideration of '[a]ny information which formed the basis for the imposition of an Anti-Social Behaviour Order' (ibid: para 6.4.3.5, citing *Hillman* (2006)).

There is a heavy reliance on the pre-sentence report prepared by the Probation Service which will have used the OASys (Offender Assessment System) actuarially based tool for assessing the offender's level of risk of reoffending (see NPS 2003; Home Office 2005a). That will be given as low, medium, high or very high. The guideline notes that '[t]he principles which determine the level of risk are whether the foreseen behaviour meets the pre-sentence report definition of serious harm, the likelihood of the behaviour occurring and the impact of such behaviour' and defines the levels of risk as follows:

- Low: current evidence does not indicate any likelihood of causing serious harm.
- Medium: some risk has been identified but the offender is unlikely to cause serious harm unless circumstances change.
- High: a risk of harm has been identified. The potential event could occur at any time and the impact would be serious.
- Very high: there is an imminent risk of serious harm. The potential event is more likely than not to happen imminently and the impact would be serious.

(Sentencing Guidelines Council 2007b: para 6.5.5)

It also provides the caveat that 'a pre-sentence report may assess only the risk of the offender causing serious harm, not whether such harm will be caused by the commission of further specified offences' (ibid: para 6.5.6). There is still much discretion for the sentencer.

The Criminal Justice and Immigration Act 2008

It is, however, the lack of discretion which has caused the difficulties and has led to a use of the IPP in relation to less serious trigger offences. As the Carter Report noted:

The fact that an IPP must be given, no matter how serious or otherwise the trigger offence, has led to substantial numbers of IPPs with short tariffs. This has led some stakeholders to question whether IPPs can be appropriate in these cases, and additionally creates a serious management problem for the system.

The Review and NOMS have jointly developed proposals that will mean that the trigger offence must reach a reasonable seriousness threshold. They will allow sentencers much greater discretion about when to give an IPP; those who do merit an IPP will continue to get one.

(Carter Report 2007: Annex E)

The CJI Act 2008, when in force, will reintroduce such discretion. Section 13 will substitute 'may' for 'must' in s 225 of the CJA 2003 in relation to the imposition of an IPP: the court is given a power rather than a duty. Further, this power could be employed only if the offender has met one of the following conditions in a new subsection 3:

(3A) The condition in this subsection is that, at the time when the offence was committed, the offender had been convicted of an offence specified in Schedule 15A [this is a new schedule in the CJA 2003 listing 'very serious' offences].

(3B) The condition in this subsection is that the notional minimum term is at least two years.

The Explanatory Notes to the Bill (as published in January 2008) explained that the new criteria impose 'a seriousness threshold on both indeterminate and extended sentences for public protection, set at 2 years minimum custodial time' but aim at 'removing the rebuttable presumption of risk (requirement for judges to conclude that the offender is dangerous) where there is a previous conviction for violent or sexual crime'. The Notes further explained that the greater discretion means that 'where all the conditions for a sentence of imprisonment for public protection are met (sexual/violent offence which carries a penalty of 10 years or more; risk test; seriousness threshold met) the court may impose a sentence of imprisonment for public protection, extended sentence or other sentence as it finds most appropriate in the case'.

Section 15 similarly gives the court a power rather than a duty to impose an extended sentence, again to be exercised only where either of two conditions is met: the immediate offence must attract an 'appropriate custodial period' of at least four years; or the offender has on a previous occasion been convicted of one of the 23 offences listed in Schedule 15A for England and Wales, with separate lists for Scotland and Northern Ireland.

5.4.2 Controlling the dangerous mentally disordered offender

Policy in mental health as well as crime is now 'permeated by perceptions and attributions of risk': mentally disordered offenders who also fall into the current constructions of 'dangerous for sentencing purposes' are then particularly likely to be perceived as 'an unquantifiable danger' (Peay 2002: 747). This is despite the fact that 'most mentally disordered offenders are neither seriously ill nor dangerous' (Burney and Pearson, 1995: 292) and evidence from the USA suggests that major mental disorder accounts for up to 3 per cent of violence (see Bowden, 1996, Peay 2002: 772–3). Indeed, research suggests that a diagnosis of schizophrenia is associated with lower rates of violence than a diagnosis of depression (see Peay 2007: 513). What is true is that more prisoners are mentally ill than the rest of the population (see Chapter 9, section 9.2.1) and we will consider the implications of this in Chapter 7 (section 7.4; see also Chapter 10 in relation to women prisoners).

Those offenders who can be categorised as 'mentally disordered' under s 1 of the Mental Health Act (MHA) 1983, to be amended by the Mental Health Act (MHA)

2007 when s 1 of that Act is in force, and who meet the necessary criteria' can be given various therapeutic disposals. Those provisions allow, when the conviction is for an offence punishable by imprisonment, for the imposition of a hospital order with restriction order under s 41 of the MHA 1983 (as amended by s 40 of the MHA 2007), if a Crown Court considers such an order necessary 'for the protection of the public from serious harm'. Section 41(1) lists the factors the court must consider in assessing dangerousness and the effect of adding a restriction order is that the offender cannot be released without the consent of the Secretary of State or a Mental Health Review Tribunal.[14] A person serving a custodial sentence may be transferred to a hospital under s 47 of the Act and a restriction direction can be added (see Peay 2007: 510–11; see also ss 294–297 of the CJA 2003 for revised details about transfers to hospital). Arguably, such an open-ended order may appear more punitive than a determinate prison sentence. The court which imposes a prison sentence on a mentally disordered offender may also add a direction for immediate admission to hospital, subject to restrictions (a hospital and limitation direction under s 45A of the MHA 1983).

The hospital order leads to compulsory admission to a psychiatric institution or unit in a general hospital. These treatment sites are categorised in terms of degrees of security. The highest security hospitals, previously called special hospitals, are at Ashworth, Broadmoor and Rampton, although patients subject to a restriction order, and others, may also be treated in regional secure units, NHS psychiatric in-patient acute units or independent hospitals. The number of restricted patients at the end of 2006 was 3,601 (the highest figure for the last decade), of which 650 males and 56 females were detained in high security hospitals (Ministry of Justice 2007d; for an analysis of earlier statistics see Howard and Christophersen 2003). In 2005, in addition to the 2,344 detained under a hospital order with restriction, 561 were transferred from a prison service establishment after sentence and 11 detained on a hospital and limitation direction (Home Office 2006e: Table 2).

The focus on danger and security has led, it is argued, to inappropriate 'custodial' measures in secure units and hospitals. For example, the proposals of the Tilt Report (Tilt *et al.* 2000), which examined the issue of security, have been criticised by psychiatrists. 'The emphasis throughout the report on the more tangible aspects of security such as high walls and better locks, and the virtual absence of consideration of the less overt contribution of relational security, fits in with the official preoccupation with "dangerousness" in recent years' (Exworthy and Gunn 2003). Again, the tension between the focus on risk and on treatment is apparent.[15]

If, on the other hand, the use of non-punitive therapeutic disposals is to be promoted for the dangerous but mentally ill offender, then there are clear difficulties with the current sentencing framework. Section 158(3) of the PCCSA 2000, and now s 166 of the CJA 2003, make clear that courts are not required to pass custodial sentences (where they would otherwise have done) on offenders who are mentally disordered. It does not say they cannot pass custodial sentences and

---

[14] Section 40 of the MHA 2007 removes the power of the Crown Court to make restriction orders under MHA 1983 s 41 for a limited period.

[15] See Prins (2005): this is an update of a text first published in 1980, providing a useful interdisciplinary approach to the issues raised in this section.

Mustill LJ in *Birch* (1989) made clear that, whilst a judge might be forced to impose a custodial sentence if there was no hospital bed available, otherwise the judge had a choice between prison and hospital. Where there was an element of culpability which merited punishment, or where there was no connection between the disorder and the offence, the imposition of custody might be a proper exercise of discretion. However, for the 'dangerous and disordered', hospital and restriction orders were the right approach.

The discretionary life sentence (see above) is also seen as an option (where available as a sentence on conviction) for the dangerous and mentally ill offender who cannot be fitted into the criteria of the MHA 1983. One particular group of the mentally disordered, for whom the provisions of the MHA 1983 have been seen as inadequate by legislators, are offenders suffering from a 'psychopathic disorder' as defined in the MHA 1983, s (12) (to be amended by the MHA 2007). For a hospital order to be made in relation to that disorder there is currently a further requirement in s 37 (to be removed by s 4(5) of the MHA 2007) that the disorder is amenable to treatment 'likely to alleviate or prevent a deterioration' of the offender's condition. However, as Peay points out, there 'is likely to be some association between disorders of personality and criminality, since the legal definition of psychopathic disorder under the 1983 Act includes the element that the disorder has resulted in "abnormally aggressive or seriously impossible conduct"' (2002: 778–9). The new requirement that 'appropriate medical treatment is available for him' may still be problematic in that such disorders are generally believed to be resistant to treatment and the psychiatric report may not offer the court the reassurance it legally needs. This difficulty fed into government initiatives for other means to deal with dangerous people with severe personality disorder, notably the DSPD Programme (see Department of Health/Home Office 2000; Impalox Group 2007) which has become 'a prime focus for service development and legislative provision' (see Peay 2007: 518), notwithstanding the fact that 'the programme and all its associated publicity have the potential to further demonise this group' (ibid: 519).

There have been proposals for such persons to be detained indefinitely, until they are no longer a risk to the public, even if they have not committed a crime and regardless of whether there is any effective treatment. Following the Richardson Report and a Green Paper in 1999, and the White Paper of 2000, a Draft Mental Health Bill was published in June 2002.[16] It proposed a new compulsory treatment order which would be available for those considered a risk to the public but who could not currently be sectioned under the MHA 1983' but the Draft Bill was strongly criticised by a range of professionals on the grounds, inter alia, that the proposed reforms would divert resources from other mentally ill people, that the treatment proposed is unclear, that civil liberties might be infringed and innocent people detained compulsorily, and that such provisions would increase the stigma of mental illness. In the event s 32 of the MHA 2007 introduces a community treatment order (CTO) available for a person who had previously been detained in hospital, provided that—inter alia—it 'is necessary for his health or safety or for the protection of other persons that he should receive such treatment' (new s 17A inserted in the MHA 1983).[17]

---

[16] See http://www.dh.gov.uk/PolicyAndGuidance/HealthAndSocialCareTopics/mentalhealth/fs/en.

[17] The Mental Health (Care and Treatment) (Scotland) Act 2003 Part 7 introduced new compulsory treatment orders for Scotland, in force since October 2005.

The justice of new forms of civil detention for the dangerous offender has also been considered by penologists. For example, von Hirsch (1986) acknowledges that in the case of a dangerous physical illness we might accept medical quarantine to protect others but this would be very exceptional and used only if such a strategy proved to be effective in containing disease and provided that the person is not stigmatised. But incapacitation of dangerous or persistent offenders is far removed from this situation. While it might be acceptable if it were an effective strategy, it is difficult to justify if it does not work. In connection with its use in criminal justice, distinguishing between offenders who have committed the same offences is also problematic, as it shifts the focus away from the blameworthiness of the present conduct.

Finally, whilst in place, the automatic life sentence under s 109 of the PCCSA 2000 (see above) was, until the implementation of the HRA 1998, an exception to the general rule that courts are not required by statutory provisions to impose custody in relation to the mentally disordered. The Government and then the Court of Appeal (reluctantly) made clear that an offender's mental state did not constitute 'exceptional circumstances' (see *Drew* (2001) and *Newman* (2000)). Whether mentally disordered or not, offenders became subject to the risk criterion. This is not so with the new provisions. Amendments to s 37 of the MHA 1983 (in force since April 2005) inserted a new subsection 1A so that, in the case of an offence coming under the otherwise mandatory provisions of s 51A(2) of the Firearms Act 1968, ss 110(2) or 111(2) of the PCCSA 2000, or ss 225–228 of the CJA 2003, 'nothing in those provisions shall prevent a court from making an order...for the admission of the offender to a hospital'.

5.4.3 Prevention orders

As we noted in Chapter 1 (see, in particular, section 1.6), various additional and free-standing orders have contributed to the control of the dangerous offender.

Sexual offences prevention orders

Most recently in the Sexual Offences Act (SOA) 2003 sexual offences prevention orders have been introduced to replace the order in s 5 of the SOA 1997. Section 104(1)(b) of the SOA 2003 empowers the court to make such an order if it is 'satisfied' that it is necessary to do so for the purpose of protecting the public from serious sexual harm' whilst s 106 notes that the harm can be physical or psychological. In *Richards* (2006) the court noted that the order was not dependent on a conviction or any particular sentence so that it could be imposed even if an extended sentence under the CJA 2003 (s 227) was not required.

Violent offender orders

The CJI Act 2008 makes provision for violent offender orders (Part 9) whereby magistrates' courts are empowered to make orders, on application from a Chief Officer of Police (s 100), of at least two years' duration (s 98). The orders will impose restrictions on the offender for the purpose of protecting the public from the risk of serious violent physical or psychological harm caused by the offender committing one or more 'specified offences' (s 98(1) and (2)).[18] For the purpose of these new orders, a specified offence is (only) one of the following:

(a) manslaughter;
(b) an offence under section 4 of the Offences against the Person Act 1861 (c. 100) (soliciting murder);
(c) an offence under section 18 of that Act (wounding with intent to cause grievous bodily harm);
(d) an offence under section 20 of that Act (malicious wounding);
(e) attempting to commit murder or conspiracy to commit murder; or
(f) a relevant service offence.

(s 98(3)).

The order may be imposed on an offender aged 18 or over who has been convicted of a specified offence (as defined above) and been given a prison sentence of at least 12 months. It can also be imposed on an offender found not guilty by reason of insanity, or who has been 'found to be under a disability and to have done the act charged in respect of a specified offence', and been given a hospital or supervision order (s 99). The Act also contains provisions for imposing violent offender orders on offenders found guilty in countries other than England and Wales of relevant offences.

When considering an application to impose an order on the offender (P) the magistrates' court must consider whether the following conditions have been met:

(a) that P is a qualifying offender,
(b) that P has, since the appropriate date, acted in such a way as to make it necessary to make a violent offender order for the purpose of protecting the public from the risk of serious violent harm caused by P (s 101(3)).

If, whilst the proposed order is in force, there are other enactments which provide measures to protect the public from P, then an order would not be 'necessary'. The order could not come into force until a custodial sentence or its licence period (or that of a hospital order or a supervision order) had come to an end (s 101(4) and (5)).

5.4.4 Early release

We have chosen to introduce the legal framework for early release here because it has become an important policy tool in protective sentencing and risk management, and because the most difficult rights issues have been raised by the law and procedures for those dangerous offenders given indeterminate sentences. However, we shall be examining aspects of early release in Chapter 12 in relation to the post-custody community supervision. Release from custody before the period of custody specified has been fully served provides, then, another example of the co-existence in English law, albeit uneasy, of retributivist and utilitarian principles and also of the co-existence of more than one utilitarian objective. The earliest form of early release was the 'ticket of leave' system, awarded for good

online
resource
centre

---

[18] See the Online Resource Centre for updates on implementation of, and guidance on, this new order.

behaviour to offenders subject to transportation. This was later replaced by forms of remission—in which time is remitted or taken off (for good behaviour in prison or automatically because of legal rules)—and parole—for early release on licence. The terms of the release determine whether the non-custodial period operates as a continuation of punishment in any meaningful sense in the community.

However, Lord Carter's Review of Prisons: *Securing the Future: Proposals for the Efficient and Sustainable Use of Custody in England and Wales* (2007) stated that one of the drivers of the current increase in prisoner numbers is the 'greater awareness of risk, and greater political prominence of public protection' (2007: 5), of which one consequence is that the Parole Board release rate has reduced from a peak of 52 per cent of 7,297 cases considered in 2004/5 to 36 per cent of 6,923 cases considered in 2006/7 (ibid: 12). On the other hand, as the next section shows, there are policy imperatives which encourage early release.

The history of early release

Early release from a custodial sentence has always been viewed as problematic. With a just deserts-based system of sentencing, early release, especially where discretionary, can be seen as a process which upsets all the fine-tuning of calculations of proportionality. It was quite possible, as Ashworth points out, for two offenders, given sentences of 12 and 18 months respectively, to each serve 6 months (2000: 255). Further, there are problems in relation to the legitimacy of the criminal justice system, given the frequently expressed view of the public that prisoners do not 'really' serve their sentences and that, therefore, the system is both too lenient and dishonest. In response to this latter criticism, the Conservative Government in a White Paper (Home Office 1996a) said it wished to establish 'honesty in sentencing' and enacted, in the Crime (Sentences) Act 1997 Chapter 1 of Part II, a new approach. This would have entailed no automatic early release and a subsequent change in sentencing practice to take this into account. The new Labour Government repealed Chapter 1 and criticism has continued with further proposals for change. The provisions for custodial sentences in the CJA 2003 (see below), whilst aiming at more effective intervention to reduce the risk of reoffending, also address the issue of dishonesty by introducing a clear scheme of custodial penalties with specified supervision post-release.

Given publicly expressed concerns, there would appear to be a clear policy imperative to restrict the possibilities for early release but early release is subject to conflicting aims, one of which has already been mentioned—that of providing an opportunity to control and/or rehabilitate offenders on their release from prison. Custodial time is traded in for the opportunity to either re-integrate the offender more successfully back into the community or put conditions on the offender and allow the possibility of recall to prison for the purpose of public protection.

Another major rationale for early release has been the issue of prison discipline: offenders are given a specified period of remission of their sentence for good behaviour. This is a response to the difficulty of operating suitable sanctions for what might be termed anti-social behaviour in a custodial setting. The approach has been to specify a period which will automatically be taken off the sentence for good behaviour and then to reinstate units of that period for bad behaviour. Lastly, significant changes in early release provisions have, on two occasions, been the result of a need to reduce the prison population quickly. In 1940, when manpower was needed for the armed forces at a critical stage in the Second World War, the standard period of remission was increased from one-sixth to one-third; in 1987, at the height of a prison overcrowding crisis, the period was increased from one-third to one-half for offenders serving sentences of less than 12 months. The introduction of the Home Detention Curfew (HDC) Scheme in 1999 for earlier release[19] of prisoners, with the use of electronic tagging, can also be seen in the same context as can the 'end of custody licence' introduced in June 2007, which allows release up to a maximum of 18 days early for prisoners serving terms of 4 weeks to 4 years.

Before the implementation of the CJA 1991 the system of early release was based on a specified element of remission for purposes of prison discipline, together with a system of discretionary release through the Parole Board established by the Criminal Justice Act 1967. The latter allowed for earlier release under licence to the Probation Service but was essentially granted to 'good' prisoners and required a prisoner to acknowledge their guilt. Before this system ended about 80 per cent of those serving sentences of less than two years received earlier release under licence whilst the possibly more dangerous or criminally minded had to serve their sentence until the period at which their remission began. They were therefore released directly into the community without supervision, making the practice difficult to justify because it meant that the 'worst' offenders were not controlled, supervised or reformed on release. Further, it was seen by offenders as an unfair system and one that led to prisoner stress, given the time the process took, the lack of transparency about decision making, and the difficulty for prisoners of dealing with an unfavourable decision within a custodial setting.

Finally, an increasingly important rights discourse meant that the discretionary elements of decision making, and the fact the decision-making body was not subject to the sentencing system or clear rules of due process, would come under greater criticism. Because of these problems, the government set up the Carlisle Committee whose Report (1988) led to proposals in the 1990 White Paper (Home Office 1990a) for 'a coherent new scheme' (ibid: para 6.6). Short sentences would no longer be subject to discretionary release but 'dangerous and uncooperative prisoners who might need the full sentence to protect the public' would continue to be subject to discretionary early release (ibid: para 6.10).

Fixed-term prisoners

The law is now to be found in the CJA 2003 but the scheme set up by the 1991 CJA for determinate sentences had three principles which are still relevant: that all parts of the sentence should have some punitive meaning, that supervision post-release should be for the purpose of public protection, and that decisions on release should be based solely on an assessment of risk factors (Ashworth 2000: 255–7). The 1991 Act therefore abolished remission as such so that all release became conditional in the sense that the offender is liable to be returned to custody on reoffending. Automatic release could be delayed if the offender were awarded additional days for prison offences.

---

[19] The average length of an HDC in 2002–3 was 52 days: see http://www.publications.parliament. uk/pa/cm200304/cmhansrd/vo040126/text/40126w50.htm.

The previous framework was also more complex in that s 33 of the 1991 Act set up different frameworks for 'long-term' (four + years) and 'short-term' (under four years) prisoners. For short-term prisoners half the sentence was served. For those on sentences of more than a year early release was made subject to supervision and recall but those on sentences of less than a year were not subject to supervision by the Probation Service on release. For 'long-term' prisoners release was on licence and set at two-thirds of the sentence. Discretionary release was not entirely abolished: s 35 gave the Parole Board the power to recommend the release of a long-term prisoner after half of the sentence has been served; s 32(6) stated that the Board must have regard to the protection of the public and the prevention of reoffending in doing so. (For recent changes in relation to long-term prisoners sentenced before April 2005 see the Online Resource Centre.)

online resource centre

Changes in the CJA 2003

The CJA 1991 scheme remained essentially the same until replaced by Chapter 6 of Part 12 of the CJA 2003 (Gullick 2004). This is not to say that the new scheme is wonderfully simple. Further, there are currently prisoners subject to old, new and transitional release regimes. As Padfield begins a recent case commentary:

> English rules on early release from prison are a nightmare to understand. Not only have the rules been dramatically and regularly changed...but under each regime different rules apply to different 'categories' of offenders: short-term, long-term, indeterminate, determinate, and so on. In addition, there are difficulties in calculating release dates due to the complex and changing rules on consecutive sentences and the effects of pre-trial remands.
>
> (Padfield 2007: 255)

There is also the difficulty that one proposed change—for offenders receiving sentences of 51 weeks or less—has not been implemented because 'custody plus' sentences have not yet been implemented. (For the new 'intermittent' or 'suspended' custody rules regarding release and supervision, see Chapter 12, section 12.1.1). If such sentences are implemented no offender receiving one will be released without moving on to probation supervision, which is not currently the case.

What is less complex is the scheme for *all* sentences of 12 months or more (except for the extended sentences introduced by ss 227–228 of the CJA 2003) by which there is a duty to release on licence at the half way stage of the sentence (s 244). This first half of the sentence is the 'requisite custodial period' which has to be served (with different periods for intermittent and consecutive sentences).

Another major change in the CJA 2003 is that the court is empowered to recommend conditions which should be included in the licence granted to the offender on release (s 238; see also Sentencing Guidelines Council 2004c: 18–19). This is not a duty and does not mean the recommendations will necessarily form part of the punishment: the Secretary of State must simply 'have regard to' the recommendations. Section 239 continues the role of the Parole Board in decision making not only in regard to these new provisions for fixed-term prisoners but also in relation to life prisoners under Chapter 2 Part 2 of the Crime (Sentences) Act (CSA) 1997.

There remains the power to release on licence any fixed-term prisoner (except on an extended sentence) before the mandatory release date. Section 246 allows this to occur up to 135 days before that date, providing the requisite custodial period is at least 6 weeks, that the offender has served at least 4 weeks of his sentence and at least one half of the custodial period.[20] The possibility of release on an HDC, before the date of automatic release, available previously only for prisoners serving less than four years, is now a possible outcome for all prisoners (CJA 2003, s 246). Those serving less than four years might also be eligible for the end-of-custody licence scheme which could mean release 18 days early. Particular rules for extended-sentence prisoners are to be found in s 247.[21]

Indeterminate sentences

Indeterminate sentences have long raised issues about the use of executive, as opposed to judicial, authority to determine the release date. More recently they have raised rights issues, and several of the more recent changes in case law and statute have been the result of cases brought in relation to rights in the ECHR, particularly Articles 3, 5, 7 and 14.

The law on release from discretionary life sentences, and (as amended by Schedule 18 of the CJA 2003) sentences of imprisonment (or detention for minors) for public protection (IPP sentences), remains that established in the CSA 1997 and Practice Directions from the Lord Chief Justice. For all life sentences, the judge must now set, and explain in court, what used to be called the 'tariff' part of the sentence. Since the *Practice Statement* (*Crime, Life Sentences*) (2002) Lord Woolf CJ, following advice from the Sentencing Advisory Panel, mandated the use of 'minimum term' to specify the part of the custodial sentence which must be served before discretionary release can be considered. For discretionary life sentences this is normally calculated as half of the determinate sentence that would have been passed 'for punishment and deterrence', commensurate with seriousness (PCCSA 2000, s 82A(3)).

Discretionary release for murderers

For life imprisonment for murder (a sentence 'fixed by law') previous practice was for the trial judge to decide on the minimum term to be recommended to the Lord Chief Justice after the trial. He in turn conferred with the Home Secretary who made the final decision. In *R (Anderson) v Secretary of State for the Home Department* (2002) the House of Lords ruled that this procedure contravened Article 6 of the ECHR and the CJA 2003 introduced provisions to rectify this. Section 269 of the CJA 2003 requires the trial judge to specify the minimum term in open court (see also Home Office Circular 62/2003).

The Supreme Court and Lord Woolf CJ have been greatly exercised with the question of the minimum term for murder, the starting point for decision making about release. The *Practice Statement* (*Crime, Life Sentences*) (2002) gave extensive guidance, a major influence being the Practice Statement on the minimum term for juveniles convicted of murder issued after the European Court of Human Rights upheld the Article 6 claims of *Venables and Thompson* (2000) (see also Valier 2003 and Padfield 2002). A new Practice Direction (*Practice Direction* (*Crime: Mandatory Life Sentences*)) was issued in May 2004 to give guidance in relation to the statutory provisions on setting the minimum term contained in Schedule 21 of the

---

[20] For other exceptions see s 246(4).
[21] For the likely impact of these changes on time in custody, see Gullick (2004).

CJA 2003. The 2002 Practice Statement set the minimum term at two levels for murder: a 'normal' starting point of 12 years and a 'higher' starting point of 15–16 (comparable to 24- and 32-year sentences respectively); the CJA 2003 gives starting points (and indicative criteria) of 'whole life', 30 years or 12 years, and the Practice Direction of May 2004 gives guidance on these categories. This direction also gives guidance on transitional provisions, which have since been amended in the *Practice Direction* (*Crime: Mandatory Life Sentences*) *No 2* (2004), following the guidance from the Court of Appeal in *Sullivan* (2004).

Successful applications to the European Court of Human Rights (see *Thynne, Gunnell and Wilson* (1991); *Hussain v United Kingdom* (1996)) established that all life sentence prisoners have the right to challenge the grounds for continued detention after the minimum period has expired (Article 5(4)). A panel of the Parole Board meets at the prison where the offender is located and the prisoner is entitled to Legal Aid at the hearing. The prisoner must be released if he no longer needs to be detained for the protection of the public.

It is now established that continued detention contravenes Article 5 of the ECHR if it is not justifiable on the grounds of public protection. The case of *Stafford* (2002) concerned an offender who had been released on life licence in 1979, after spending 12 years in prison for murder. He was detained again in 1989–90 following a breach in his licence conditions but was again released on licence. In 1994, when convicted of fraud the Home Secretary revoked his life licence for the murder conviction and so, when he became eligible for release from his custodial sentence for fraud the Home Secretary refused to order his release, on the grounds of risk of future non-violent offending. The House of Lords in 1999 decided that the Home Secretary had properly used his discretion and Stafford appealed to the European Court of Human Rights. That Court held that, once the punishment for fraud was completed, no medical or other evidence of risk of future violent offending had been put forward to justify continued detention for murder. Article 5(1) requires a sufficient causal connection between the original offence and the risk of reoffending; Article 5(4) requires that detention after the expiry of the minimum period in custody can be justified only on the grounds of risk of reoffending associated with the original sentence.[22]

For life-sentence prisoners the licence remains in force until the offender's death and many contain specified conditions (CSA 1997, s 31). A new s 31A is inserted by the CJA 2003 such that, for prisoners serving IPP sentences, the Parole Board may order the licence shall cease to have effect at the end of the 'qualifying period' provided the offender is no longer deemed a risk to the public. The qualifying period in this instance is ten years (of release on licence).

All these provisions have resource implications. The protective sentences potentially provide longer sentences for more offenders. The early-release provisions reduce the time spent in custody for many offenders, but the new provisions for licence and conditions in licences increase the cost of community supervision. They also enhance the role of the Probation Service in protective sentencing (see Chapter 12). As we have seen, there are also several important rights issues raised by discretionary life, extended and other indeterminate protective sentences. Many cases are currently before the courts and they may effect a change in law

---

[22] For further discussion on these issues see Amos (2004); Shute (2004b).

and practice. Further, this section has been able to review only some of the issues: see the Online Resource Centre for recent developments.

5.5 **Conclusions**

5.5.1 **Critique of current policy**

We have already examined the criticisms of incapacitative policies from the per- spective of retributivist theory (see section 5.2). There are also specific critiques of the provisions in the CJA 2003, notably that 'the concept of risk is becoming more and more woolly for sentencing purposes' (Carlen 2002), that there are gender dimensions to risk (Hannah-Moffat and O'Malley 2007) and that incapacitation is now part of a 'smorgasbord' of sentencing aims to which the CJA 2003 returns the sentencing framework (von Hirsch and Roberts 2004). At one level these are con- tradictory critiques—that sentencing on risk is increasing or that it is now simply one of several approaches, including the increasingly important aim of rehabili- tation. However, we have noted the use of a new form of rehabilitation (see also Chapter 12) aimed at increasing desistance from reoffending and we have also referred to the increased use of controlled periods of supervision on release from prison for the same purpose. Public protection—whether via incapacitation or risk management in the community—is the common thread and the public justifica- tion for these and a wider range of policies and legislative provisions. What is also apparent is that, whilst the new dangerousness provisions in the CJA 2003 are confined to specific sexual and violent offences, the list in Schedule 15 is very long. Further, 'three strikes' provisions in relation to domestic burglary, drug trafficking and firearms offences remain, and the enhanced role of previous convictions in the calculation of seriousness will increase the sentences imposed on all but first- time offenders. All these changes suggest that the scope of the class of potential 'risky' offenders is now very wide indeed.

Ashworth, referring to a raft of recent legislation as well as the CJA 2003, points out that all have been put forward by the Government in the name of public pro- tection and the building of safe and strong communities (2004). Such a goal seems difficult to contest, but this focus 'tends to underplay the problems of identifying and dealing with risk' and to 'neglect discussion of values and principles' (ibid). He is especially concerned that, while the apparent focus is objective risk, protec- tive policies are also linked to subjective feelings of danger and insecurity. They can justify a dangerous conversion of punitiveness into public protection (ibid: section 4) and a legitimation of provisions that pay little more than lip service to rights considerations. Further, even if such policies increase public confidence and decrease feelings of social insecurity, they are not justified on that basis because the power of politicians and the media could, instead, 'be used to highlight the declining crime rate, the role of alcohol and drugs, the importance of prevention and detection rather than harsh sentences, and other realities' (ibid: conclusions).

Not only from a retributivist but also from a human rights perspective, dispro- portionate sentences of the kind that will emerge from the new protective provi- sions raise serious moral, constitutional and practical problems which are under academic discussion (see van Zyl Smit and Ashworth 2004) but which have yet hardly surfaced in public discussion and media comment. Even if we accept that a measure of (extra) detention for purposes of public protection is justifiable, the crucial question is, given our knowledge of the difficulties of accurate prediction of risk and of the limited effectiveness of extra incapacitation, 'how much inaccuracy and individual injustice can be justified in the public good?'

5.5.2 **Case study**

- Review the ethical and moral issues raised in this chapter by the practice of sentencing for public protection.
- Review the justifications from penal theory for a policy of selective or categorial incapacitation.
- Read the summary below of the results of a recent Home Office Research Study.

Then answer the following question:

How much inaccuracy of prediction of risk can be justified on the grounds of public good?

A recent study of reconviction rates years after their release from long determinate prison sentences among serious sex offenders who were classified as high risk by the Parole Board, found the proportion reconvicted of another sexual offence during both follow-up periods was under 10 per cent, but those who were reconvicted had committed very serious offences (Hood *et al.* 2002). The figures varied according to the type of victim. None of those imprisoned for an offence against a child in their own family unit was reconvicted of a sexual or serious violent crime. Just over one-quarter of those imprisoned for a sexual offence against a child outside the family were reconvicted of another sexual offence and nearly one-third were imprisoned for a sexual or violent crime. Of those imprisoned for an offence against an adult, one in 13 was reconvicted of an offence against an adult and one in 7 was imprisoned for a sexual or violent offence within six years of release from prison. All the offenders who were reconvicted of a further sexual offence within the four-year follow-up period, and all but one followed up for six years, had been identified as high risk or dangerous by at least one member of the Parole Board. Where no member of the Parole Board panel had identified a sex offender as high risk, only one was reconvicted of a sexual offence after six years.

You may also wish to look now at the sentencing exercise at the end of Chapter 7. This also raises issues around sentencing on risk of future harm.

6

....

Making amends

SUMMARY

This chapter reviews the various ways in which the sentencing system is able to mandate or encourage offenders to make amends for the harm they have caused by offending. Some of these developments have aimed to ensure the offender does not profit from crime and pays financial compensation to the victim. More recent developments focus on restorative justice approaches. This chapter will, therefore, examine these very different strands of policy and the penal justifications which underpin them, as well as locating them within the current policy emphasis on victims and their rights.

6.1 Towards a restorative justice policy[1]

6.1.1 A different focus

Over the past four decades, words and phrases—such as making good or making amends, compensation, community, reconciliation, restoration, reintegration, and reparation—have gradually appeared in the literature of sentencing and punishment; words which have not always been associated with punishment.[2] Since 1997 in the UK some of these words have become very important in criminal justice policy proposals. Further, 'the victim' has increasingly been the focus of policy and practice.

These words have been absent from, or peripheral to, our discussions of sentencing and of justifications for punishment in Chapters 2–5. In those chapters we examined two main ways of calculating punishment: on the basis of the offender's past culpability, or on the basis of what will be most effective in reducing offending. Whilst all potentially benefit from successful utilitarian strategies, the victim and the community are largely bystanders in these accounts. In this chapter the victim and community take centre stage with the offender in the context of new ideas about responding to offending. These ideas constitute a third paradigm—that of restorative justice.

However, this chapter is not solely concerned with new ways of encouraging a just response to offending but also with longer-standing means of making amends. Confiscation and compensation are becoming increasingly important in sentencing but their origins are earlier, and their development was not part of an

---

[1] We have entitled this chapter 'Making amends' but are aware that this term has been used to describe one particular model of restorative justice (see von Hirsch *et al.* 2003). However, we use it in its most general sense.

[2] You may wish at this stage to complete the first exercise in section 6.5.2 below.

articulated restorative justice agenda. This chapter, therefore, has sections which are united under the aim of making amends but which are not necessarily conceptually and theoretically coherent. We have decided to deal with the 'old' and 'new' forms of reparation and restoration here because there are links and issues of 'fit' which the courts and professionals are being forced to address.

Nevertheless, it is reparation and restorative justice which have been 'receiving more concentrated attention than ever before from both criminologists and policy makers' (McEvoy *et al.* 2002: 469). This particular statement is taken from an article in an issue of the *British Journal of Criminology* which was concerned solely with aspects of restorative justice. The European Forum for Victim–Offender Mediation and Restorative Justice was established in 2000,[3] the Restorative Justice Consortium in the UK published its *General Principles for Restorative Justice* in 2002,[4] the UK Government published a Consultation Paper on its restorative justice strategy in 2003 (Home Office 2003a; see section 6.3.3 below), the Domestic Violence, Crime and Victims Act was passed in 2004 and, also in 2004 the Government published *Compensation and Support for Victims of Crime* (2004a).

In the few years before and since the publication of our first edition there has been an increased academic interest in restorative justice, evidenced by a plethora of books on restorative justice (see, for example, Aertsen *et al.* 2006; Braithwaite 2003; Christie 2007; McEvoy *et al.* 2002; Miers 2004; Morris and Maxwell 2001; Murphy and Harris 2007; Roche 2003; Sherman *et al.* 2007b; Strang 2003, 2007; von Hirsch *et al.* 2005; Weitekamp and Kerner 2002; Woolford and Ratner 2007). However, it is difficult to find as much evidence of practical changes, as Strang notes when reviewing recent developments in several jurisdictions:

There is no shortage of writings on restorative justice. Indeed, it seems sometimes that there is more energy put into writing about it than actually doing it. While restorative justice as a justice practice attracts oodles of advocates and scholars and much commentary about its supposed unstoppable spread, there has not actually been very much extensively institutionalized in its most recent manifestation.

(Strang 2007: 204)

The same impression is given by Baroness Miller's comment in a Parliamentary debate on restorative justice in November 2007: 'There was a moment when the Government seemed very keen on restorative justice. Back in 2003, the then Home Secretary, David Blunkett spent some time talking about it'.[5] A written answer given to Parliament earlier in 2007 suggests one reason why, except in relation to children and young people, despite the continuing high policy profile and academic interest, there is less activity 'on the ground':

The Government's strategy is to encourage, but not require, the use of adult restorative justice whilst building the evidence base to establish the impact of its use, particularly in relation to reoffending. It has [commissioned independent research to evaluate] the crime reduction programme restorative justice pilots [which] is expected to be completed and published this year and this will inform future strategy.

(*Official Report*, 14 June 2007; col. WA277)

---

[3] See http://www.euroforumrj.org.uk.
[4] See the RJC web site at http://www.restorativejustice.org.uk for information on the organisation and its publications.
[5] Hansard HL 26 November 2007, Col 1101.

The Government is clearly concerned not to spend any more money until there are proven cost benefits in terms of reduction of reoffending rates. However, as we shall see in the next section, reparative and restorative measures are still important in sentencing and punishment because of the coming together of a number of influences and motivations, not all of them consistent with each other.

6.1.2 **Restorative justice**

Restorative justice has many routes that cannot be easily separated. It emerged as a 'movement' espoused by a relatively small but energetic group of activists, academics, non-governmental organisations and policy entrepreneurs.

(McLaughlin *et al.* 2003: 2)

One important strand in the early movement was that which originated in religious communities who gave priority to the reduction of conflict and the promotion of harmony. This is not surprising as many of the world religions promote restorative justice as an implicit part of their ideas. More specifically, the Mennonite sect in the USA and the Quakers in the UK for example, were influential in bringing restorative justice ideas to the forefront of debate. Because the principles of restorative justice are more intangible perhaps than those of, say, utilitarianism, proponents may reveal a sort of missionary zeal. The following comment was made by a restorative justice coordinator in a youth offending team about a training session: 'Quakers' Meeting House in Euston was a good choice of venue. Despite being a committed atheist myself, I recognise you do need a certain amount of evangelical fervour to promote the use of Restorative Justice not only to the public, but also to colleagues and managers in the agencies that make up the criminal justice system' (Jones 2003: 9).

Such fervour is required because the proponents of restorative justice in its wider forms must persuade others into a quite different way of thinking about crime, conflict, and justice. What is being encouraged is not a new form of punishment but something to replace punishment, a form of penal intervention which does not carry the same connotations as punishment. One of the most influential early writers on restorative justice, Howard Zehr, wrote,

[w]e define crime as an offence against the State. We define justice as the establishment of blame and the imposition of pain under the guidance of right rules.

I think it is essential to remember that this definition of crime and justice, as commonsensical as it may seem, is only one paradigm, only one possible way of looking at crime and at justice. We have been so dominated by our assumptions that we often assume it is the only way, or at least the only right way, to approach the issue.

It is not. It is not the only possible model or paradigm of justice—not logically not historically.

(Zehr 1985: 4)

In this article Zehr used words associated with 'restorative justice' such as restitution, atonement, community, victim, accountability, victim involvement in outcome, reintegrative shaming, repairing damage, and problem solving—words which signify concepts underpinning a different paradigm (see Table 6.1).

Restorative justice as a new paradigm not only looks for different responses to crime but locates crime in a different context altogether; not the criminal

Old Paradigm: Retributive Justice	New Paradigm: Restorative Justice
1. Crime defined as violation of the state	1. Crime defined as violation of one person by another
2. Focus on establishing blame, on guilt, on past (did he/she do it?)	2. Focus on problem solving, on liabilities and obligations, on future (what should be done?)
3. Adversarial relationships and process normative	3. Dialogue and negotiation normative
4. Imposition of pain to punish and deter/prevent	4. Restitution as a means of restoring both parties; reconciliation/restoration as goal
5. Justice defined by intent and by process: right rules	5. Justice defined as right relationships: judged by the outcome
6. Interpersonal, conflictual nature of crime obscured, repressed; conflict seen as individual vs. state	6. Crime recognised as interpersonal conflict; value of conflict recognised
7. One social injury replaced by another	7. Focus on repair of social injury
8. Community on sideline, represented abstractly by state	8. Community as facilitator in restorative process
9. Encouragement of competitive, individualistic values	9. Encouragement of mutuality
10. Action directed from state to offender: – victim ignored – offender passive	10. Victim and offender's roles recognised in both problem and solution: – victim rights/needs recognised – offender encouraged to take responsibility
11. Offender accountability defined as taking punishment	11. Offender accountability defined as understanding impact of action and helping decide how to make things right
12. Offence defined in purely legal terms, devoid of moral, social, economic, political dimensions	12. Offence understood in whole context—moral, social, economic, political
13. 'Debt' owed to state and society in the abstract	13. Debt/liability to victim recognised
14. Response focused on offender's past behaviour	14. Response focused on harmful consequences of offender's behavior
15. Stigma of crime unremovable	15. Stigma of crime removable through restorative action
16. No encouragement for repentance and forgiveness	16. Possibilities for repentance and forgiveness
17. Dependence upon proxy professionals	17. Direct involvement by participant

Table 6.1 Paradigms of justice old and new
Source: Zehr (1985).

justice system but the whole range of social and interpersonal conflicts and disputes. That wider approach to conflict management not only renders problematic current notions of crime and criminology but also means that restorative justice proponents have encouraged the use of those alternative dispute resolution (ADR) techniques that have been pioneered by the ADR and mediation movements. Restorative justice shares values of community and individual responsibility and empowerment with the ADR movement (see Mulcahy 2000). Conversely, there-fore, some sections of the new 'dispute—processing industry' which has developed in the last thirty years have incorporated and promoted restorative justice prin-ciples and techniques in their professional practice (see Kennedy 1990; Olson and Dzur 2004).

An influence on both 'movements' was evidence from historical and anthropo-logical studies to show that the distinction between the civil and the criminal is not universal, and that disputes (including those which might otherwise be categorised as crimes) have been settled in various ways at different times and in different places.[6] For example, in Imperial China law was exclusively penal (Stein 1984: 56), whereas in Anglo-Saxon England (before the increased power and re-conceptualisation of monarchy) justice was largely compensation-based and kinship-based.[7]

Given that restorative justice is primarily concerned with repairing damage done and restoring harmony, the role of the victim is very important in theory and practice, whether the victim be perceived as an individual or a community. Braithwaite, a leading criminologist and influential exponent of restorative justice, notes that it has two important dimensions.[8] The first is the issue of process—how decisions should be made by all those involved in the harm or offending done, and the second dimension is that of values—values signified by those concepts such as reintegration and respect that we have already noted (Braithwaite 2003: 7–14).

So, in relation to process, restorative justice advocates that the victim and/or community as well as the offender should be involved in decision making, so that techniques such as mediation become very important in this process. In relation to values this means that, in the mediation of outcome, the values of reintegration and forgiveness take precedence over notions such as punishment and retribution. For this to happen, the victim or a representative of the community must be involved in the process and also, as relevant, in the outcomes. An outcome may include an apology to the victim or it may include some form of practical reparation to the victim or to the community. This emphasis on values sits easily with Third Way or communitarian ideologies of governance which have underpinned New Labour policies. Le Grand (1998), for example, outlined four core values underpinning the Third Way: community, opportunity, responsibility and accountability (CORA) and the policy discourse in the social inclusion and also the 'Every child matters' agendas is one of opportunities, increased choice, positive activities, respect and support. The emphasis in relation to restorative justice is particularly on encour-aging the offender to own a sense of responsibility for what he has done and to be motivated, therefore, to put things right.

This does not mean that the objectives of restorative justice are in practice necessarily different from those of the traditional criminal justice system. The restorative aim of reintegrating the offender into the community entails prevent-ing the offender from reoffending, a traditional aim of the criminal justice sys-tem. Nor is a desire to be cost-effective and to 'do justice' excluded from thinking in restorative justice. However, the concept of justice is different and the criteria

[6] See, for example, Roberts (1979); Stein (1984: Chapter 5).
[7] For example, see Sayles (1950: Chapters 11 and 14).
[8] For a good review of two of Braithwaite's books (2002, 2000) see Sanders (2003).

for cost-effectiveness will relate not only to the narrow objectives of the criminal justice system, but may well relate to community 'health' as well as to victim satisfaction and offender reformation.

Although restorative justice is concerned with reparation and reconciliation it still involves denunciation. Censure within a restorative context can record a wrong done but is thought to be less damaging than harsh retribution. 'Reintegrative' shaming of the offender may be effective in deterring him from future criminality and allow for the offender's reintegration into society (Braithwaite 1989; Richards 1998). Braithwaite (1989) argues that if the offender is simply stigmatised he will be alienated and less likely to change his behaviour, whereas if he is allowed to express his regret and to be re-accepted by the community this may be more effective in preventing reoffending.[9] So, crime prevention and deterrence may be achieved in ways other than harsh punishment, as, for example through continuous reparation, and victims may want redress for harms suffered rather than punishment. Restorative justice recognises the autonomy of the offender and victim and some proponents argue that there should be a right for victims to meet offenders and a right for offenders to offer reparation and contribute something back to victims and society (see Wright 1996).[10]

Supporters of restorative justice, in common with the ADR movement, subscribe to one or other of two fundamentally different aims: that of establishing a totally new system of justice/dispute settlement to replace the traditional systems of justice, and that of establishing new techniques and principles to graft onto the old. The remainder of this chapter will examine developments in the UK to see which of these objectives is being pursued.

6.1.3 Current policy in the UK

The web site of the Home Office, the lead agency for the formulation of criminal justice policy in the UK,[11] is instructive. One of the small number of links from the opening page is to victim matters.[12] This page now gives links to a range of criminal justice pages including 'victims of crime' which then has various links, including victims' rights, victim support and restorative justice. Victims therefore have a very high priority in the message that the Home Office wishes to convey.

The same high priority is to be found in many policy documents and speeches which also provide reasons for this priority. In 2003 Lord Falconer[13] said that 'restorative justice offers victims in particular things which traditional justice can't', such as speaking directly to the offender, having a chance to receive an apology and also answers to questions like 'why me, why did this happen to me?' For

---

online
resource
centre

[9] However, this is based on research on white-collar offenders and, as Walker says, it is more likely to work for young first offenders from law-abiding regimes than with sophisticated criminals in large cities (1991: 48).

[10] For further reading on restorative justice see the Online Resource Centre.

[11] Although the Department for Constitutional Affairs, which incorporates the Lord Chancellor's Department as it was, and the Attorney General's Office also have responsibility, as do several agencies such as the Crown Prosecution Service.

[12] In 2004–5 the link was to 'justice and victims', in 2008 it is 'crime and victims': see http://www.homeoffice.gov.uk/crime-victims.

[13] Then Secretary of State for Constitutional Affairs and Lord Chancellor, speaking to magistrates at Newcastle University, 25 July 2003.

offenders, 'meeting the victim can be a turning point—an experience which puts them back on the straight and narrow'. In 2004 a government web site, billed as 'the number one online information resource for the crime reduction community' gave the following message:

The government aims to maximise the use of restorative justice in the criminal justice system (CJS) as it works well at both addressing the needs of the victim and in reducing offending.

Evidence suggests that restorative justice can help to deliver key objectives across the CJS: improving victim satisfaction, reducing crime and re-offending, delivering justice effectively and building public confidence.[14]

That web site also now has a 'Victims' Virtual Walkthrough' which

aims to guide any victim of crime through the processes that they will encounter, from the time a crime is reported, through the police investigation, prosecution decision making, court processes, and sentencing. It also provides information on the personal support that is available at all stages, including, when relevant, after the court case. The virtual tour aims to make the process that bit more easier to understand and provides a victim with some idea of what they can realistically expect to happen.

(CJS online)[15]

Another Home Office document, *A New Deal for Victims and Witnesses: A National Strategy to Deliver Improved Services*, shows how policy often links the roles of victim and witness:

[M]any people, often victims themselves, are witnesses to a crime, or have evidence that can help to convict an offender. Too few come forward with that evidence; and when they do, for too many the experience is an unhappy one...the government...wants to do everything it can to make sure victims and witnesses are treated with respect...supporting victims and witnesses is a worthwhile end in itself. It is also fundamental if justice is to be achieved.

(Home Office 2003d: Foreword)

Key Elements of Effective Practice (KEEP): Restorative Justice, guidance issued by the Youth Justice Board, states that 'actively involving victims of crime by young offenders in the youth justice process, helping them to get over any harm done, are key elements of the Youth Justice Board's aims and objectives' (para 1), and explains that 'actions to achieve these aims are usually called restorative justice or restorative practices...they have been shown to be effective in reducing reoffending by young people...and to provide greater satisfaction for victims...' (para 2[16]).[17]

The instrumentalist thinking behind these policy priorities was made evident in *Justice for All* which proposed to put victims and witnesses at the 'heart' of the criminal justice system (Home Office 2002a: para 0.22) and is in the statement on the Home Office web site that 'by putting victims and witnesses at the heart of the justice system we believe justice will be done more often and more quickly'.[18] As Jackson notes, the strand of policy now given the most emphasis is the apparent need to 'rebalance the criminal justice system in favour of the victim and the

---

[14] http://www.crimereduction.gov.uk: in a section entitled 'Working with Offenders' on the web site early 2004.

[15] http://www.cjsonline.gov.uk/victim/walkthrough/index.html.

[16] Undated, accessed via the Youth Justice Board web site throughout 2004.

[17] Taken from the penultimate version; see, for most recent 'KEEP' for restorative justice within the youth justice system, Sherman *et al.* (2007a).

[18] http://www.homeoffice.gov.uk/crime-victims/victims/?view=Standard.

community so as to reduce crime and bring more offenders to justice' (Jackson 2003: 311; Home Office 2002a: para 0.3).

Similarly, the *Restorative Justice* Consultation Paper stated:

The government is committed to placing victims' needs at the centre of the criminal justice system (CJS). We also want a system that encourages responsibility, so that offenders face up to what they've done, and make amends. And we want the wider community to be involved in finding positive solutions to crime and anti-social behaviour. I believe restorative justice can help us deliver a CJS like this.

(Home Office 2003a).

In Northern Ireland, restorative justice options have also been extensively reviewed (Dignan and Lowey 2000). The first section of *Restorative Justice Options for Northern Ireland* focuses, as do Home Office policy documents, on 'Restorative Justice as a Response to Offending Behaviour' (ibid: 4–9). A number of the recommendations of the review group have been put into effect under the Justice (Northern Ireland) Act 2002, notably family group conferencing (O'Mahoney 2004). O'Mahoney and Doak (2004) cautioned, however, that their research showed evidence of net-widening and a need for resource-intensive processes to secure the attendance of victims. The Northern Ireland Office has now published a *Protocol for Community-based Restorative Justice Schemes*[19] and in Scotland, too, criminal justice policy has given a high priority to victims. A *Scottish Strategy for Victims* was published in 2001 with an accompanying *Action Plan* (Scottish Executive 2001). The strategy has three 'pillars', echoing English policy objectives: provision of practical and emotional support, information to victims and greater participation in the criminal justice system. However, the Scottish Executive also published a Paper (2002a) specifically to explain how the Scottish criminal justice system complies with the Articles in the EU Framework Decision on the Standing of Victims in Criminal Proceedings.

This European Framework, adopted by the European Council in 2001 and implemented 2002–6,[20] was the result of an initiative by the Portuguese Republic. Article 2, for example, states that '[e]ach Member State shall ensure that victims have a real and appropriate role in its criminal legal system. It shall continue to make every effort to ensure that victims are treated with due respect for the dignity of the individual during proceedings and shall recognise the rights and legitimate interests of victims with particular reference to criminal proceedings.' Victim Support published its response, *New Rights for Victims of Crime,* in 2002, including information about 'addressing unequal treatment across Europe'.

Against this backdrop of the Council of Europe's concern to ensure a minimum standards for treatment of victims across the EU, the above set of inter-related policy objectives raises several questions. Clearly a link is being made between victims and the effectiveness of witnesses but another explanation Jackson notes is that the concern for victims is linked 'to the logic of Labour's philosophy that tackling crime effectively' also depends upon 'reviving the spirit of the community and empowering individuals' (Jackson 2003: 311–12). Jackson's argument is that the 'outcome-related' measures designed to bring confidence to victims, if necessary

---

[19] See Hansard HL 5 February 2008, Col WS32; for details of current projects in Northern Ireland and the Republic of Ireland see http://www.extern.org/restorative/RJ_in_Ireland.htm.
[20] L 082; for details, see: http://europa.eu.int.

against the interests of defendants, are more important in policy than the 'process related' measures designed to improve the experiences of victims by offering them various support services (ibid: 312). These tensions raise the very real concern that victims are being 'used' by the Government for policy purposes.

Jackson's analysis is of proposals for criminal justice reform generally but the issue is similar in relation to sentencing: is victim involvement a means to an end of restorative measures to impact on reoffending, a means to improve the victim's health and happiness, or a means to increase public confidence in the criminal justice system? According to Sanders,

> This is often framed in terms of a zero-sum game: what's good for suspects and defendants (less punitiveness, more welfare) is bad for victims and vice versa. Thus increasingly authoritarian penal measures, in the UK for example over the last 10 years, are often justified by government claims to be putting victims 'at the centre' of penal policy...Advocates of Restorative Justice (RJ) describe this apparently win–lose situation as actually a lose–lose situation.
>
> (Sanders 2003: 161)

On the other hand, McEvoy and colleagues have suggested that restorative justice appeals to governments 'because it offers the possibility of taking crime seriously without ever-increasing repression and exclusion. Above all, it appeals because it offers the prospect of escaping the "zero-sum", whereby what benefits victims must be painful for offenders' (McEvoy *et al.* 2002: 469). It appears as a solution at last to the perceived need, underpinning the proposals of the Royal Commission on Criminal Justice (1993), to 'balance' the interests of offenders, state and victims when formulating criminal justice policy (see Ashworth 1998b: 30–40).

The crucial question is whether the possibilities and prospects offered by restorative justice can be delivered in practice. To an extent, the answers can be only speculative, given that restorative justice initiatives in quantitative terms 'remain at the margins of criminal justice' in systems across Europe, North America and Australasia (Crawford 2000: 29) and the body of research is only now becoming useful in terms of quantity and quality.

This chapter is also concerned with earlier measures that encouraged or mandated reparation by offenders without necessarily referring to, or being based in, restorative justice. They were, rather, added to the traditional range of disposals justifiable on retributive or utilitarian principles and their presence raised conceptual difficulties. Because, chronologically, they were developed first and reveal other origins for reparative sentencing, we will deal with them first.

6.2 Confiscation and compensation

6.2.1 The historical context: 'traditional' remedies for loss and harm

As we have noted, it would be wrong to think of reparation and restorative justice as totally new concepts. Within modern times, in the English legal system generally— as opposed to the criminal justice system in particular—the place of reparation has been in the civil courts. There have always been substantive laws and procedures by which civil liability can, potentially, be established and a remedy awarded to the 'victim'. Those remedies are contained within particular branches of law such as contract and tort and the remedies take the form of damages—financial restitution—or injunctions, ordered by the court or negotiated in the shadow of the law. However, the norms—the jurisprudence—and the aims of civil and criminal law have traditionally been very different. Whereas the civil law gives remedies, the criminal law aims to punish (whether for retributivist reasons or utilitarian ends) the person who commits one of those 'wrongs' which have been specifically designated as a criminal offence, an offence which is against the public good. So criminal law is activated by the state, the civil law can be activated only by an individual wronged.

In Chapter 1 (section 1.2.1) we focused on this question why certain actions are designated as ones for which the response must or could be punitive, contrasting that response with possible social welfare, medical, or even military, responses to deviant action. In this chapter, we are not focusing on these particular alternative responses to deviancy but on alternative outcomes for those who have committed offences and for the person wronged. In a country with a traditional criminal justice system, such as the UK, if an action is specified as an offence and dealt with accordingly, the victim's remedy is to see the offender punished by the state. This may be exactly what the 'victim' wants, money not being able, in the victim's mind, to compensate for the wrong done. If so, the fact that the resources of the state are available to apprehend and punish the wrongdoer is a considerable advantage. On the other hand this may not be what the victim wants.

Certainly, increasing evidence of the ineffectiveness and unfairness of the system of civil remedies for harm was one factor feeding into the pressure for change. The attractiveness for the wronged individual of using the civil justice system to achieve compensation or reparation decreased as evidence of the 'roulette' character of civil justice accumulated through the work of radical lawyers and socio-legal researchers in the 1960s and 1970s. To use that system the individual must successfully pass through a series of hoops: the circumstances of the wrong done must fit the legal criteria and it must be possible to pinpoint a named individual as causing the wrong; the claim against the perpetrator must be accompanied by evidence and proof which may be hard for the wronged individual to obtain; the perpetrator must be available but may be in prison, dead, or untraceable; the perpetrator must have enough money to pay the damages and must not avoid attempts to make him pay; the person wronged must have the psychological or financial resources to take court action (see, for example, Genn 1988, 1999).

6.2.2 New influences on policy

As well as these internal, and increasingly visible, deficiencies in the civil system, external factors contributed to the pressure for alternatives. A new factor coming into play was the focus on victims.

The victim

In the 1980s, Stockdale and Devlin, both Crown Court judges, quoted the following comment from a Canadian writer, J. W. Mohr, in 1980, noting it now applied to England: '[t]here has been a development, even if ever so slow, to shift from principles of punishment, deterrence and rehabilitation to the principle of undoing the harm done by means such as restitution, compensation and community service'.[21] They write of a 'growing concern about the victim' which has 'coincided with increasing disenchantment with the traditional theories of punishment' and their ability to ensure the volume of crime decreases (Stockdale and Devlin 1987: 36). Further, they argue, '[w]hatever doubts one may entertain about other aims of punishment, nobody doubts the justice of aiding the victim' (ibid: 37).

The above passage points to some of the new measures being introduced in the criminal justice system at that time by which a person wronged by offending behaviour could gain a remedy for loss. The passage also points to the importance of the victim focus in the legitimation of new approaches in sentencing policy. Such a focus appears as a self-evident 'good': to argue against helping victims is akin to arguing against peace. This raises the question why victim-based policies became so important at that particular time.

The contexts are the changes in governance to which we referred in Chapter 5 when rising crime rates and changing economic climates led to a view that the crime problem could not be solved but only managed (Walklate 2004: 29; see also Garland 2001b). In that transformation, not only have the public voice and interest groups become more influential, but the victim has been 'politicised' (Walklate 2004: 30–2). Consequently, the powerful idea that the state had 'stolen' the 'wrong' (offence) from the victim (Christie 1977), allowing the victim to feel excluded, powerless, neglected, and uncompensated was, paradoxically, a politically useful one. It prompted self-evident and positive remedies: helping victims to 'cope' with the effects of crime is a welcome policy initiative to a 'less than confident State', tackling rising crime rates which appear impervious to policy initiatives (Rock 2002: 9).

By 1997 the authors of a book on victims of crime could begin by stating, 'in less than 20 years, there has been a revolution in the criminal justice system. Each criminal case involves more than the government versus the defendant. There is another party with a burning interest' (Davis *et al.* 1997: vii). The interests and feelings of victims 'are now routinely invoked in support of measures of punitive segregation' and the 'symbolic figure of the victim has taken on a life of its own', argues Garland (2001b: 11; see also section 6.4 below).

Yet the development of the academic study of victims—victimology—within criminology was problematic, the early victimology being regarded as the 'lunatic fringe' of criminology (Rock 2002: 3), and even a recent review has referred to 'this dismal science' (Burney 2003b: 405).[22] 'Until the late 1970s, victims were almost wholly neglected in criminology and criminal justice' (Rock 2002: 1), all the four main theoretical approaches to crime and deviance that Rock outlines having no 'place' for victims (ibid). Even in interactionist studies, 'they were barely visible, often not much more than rhetorical artefacts' (ibid: 2). A positivist victimology, the earliest strand, does date back to the middle of the twentieth century with the work of criminologists such as von Hentig and Mendelsohn but this early strand

---

[21] Stockdale and Devlin (1987) citing Grosman, B. (ed.), *New Directions in Sentencing* (1980: 26).

[22] Burney, reviewing Davis *et al.* (2003) argues, 'whoever coined the term "victimology" did the English language a grave disservice because the spectrum of perspectives in this branch of criminology is so broad that its validity becomes questionable' (2003: 405).

focused upon the responsibility of the victim for a criminal event occurring, a 'blame the victim' approach which hardly improved the plight of victims.[23]

Sanders argues that it was the growing interest in the effects of crime on victims and in victim involvement in the criminal justice system which re-invigorated victimology in the 1980s (2002: 198, n 2) rather than the other way round. Particular concern focused on victims of rape, domestic violence, race hate crimes and, consequently, the campaigning of the feminist movement, as well as anti-racist campaigns, was particularly influential in the development of a new strand of victimology in the 1980s. However, it is fair to argue, as do Maguire and Shapland, that the reasons for the recent growth of interest in victims of crime across the world 'are not totally clear' (1997: 212).

Additional factors

The focus on victims did not, of itself, challenge retributivist-based sentencing. On the contrary, the focus on 'just deserts' in sentencing also encouraged a focus on restitution for victims. If the punishment must be proportionate to culpability then any profit from offending must be taken into account and, in that process, returned to the offender as goods or compensation. Linked to this development was a very specific influence which stemmed from the increasingly large scale of drug trafficking in the 1980s. Because of the vast sums of money such trafficking involved, with extremely high profits for the criminal, the previously neglected issues of 'the profits of crime' became more important. Confiscation and compensation were prioritised in the Drug Trafficking Offences Act (DTOA) 1986 which specifically targeted drug-related crimes and profits and which became the forerunner of more general provisions, in particular Part VI of the Criminal Justice Act (CJA) 1993. More recently the concern with terrorist activities and the 'laundering' of money for such purposes has given a further impetus to confiscation provisions. Similar legislative developments have happened in other European jurisdictions and in the USA in relation to organised crime generally. They were driven by a sense of justice and of proportionality but were supported, and given examples of implementation, by those campaigning for a new and restorative approach more generally (Richards 1998: Chapter 5).

The consolidation of retributivist sentencing was a factor that encouraged those critical of that development to look to other penal philosophies. As we saw in Chapters 2 and 3, in the 1980s in many jurisdictions, and after 1991 in the UK, there was a clear trend in sentencing based more consistently and comprehensively on just deserts principles. This trend did not attract universal approval and was opposed by a body of thinking which desired an outcome-focused approach. Utilitarian theories of rehabilitation and reform were relatively unpersuasive in the 1980s, and proponents of restorative justice consequently tailored their arguments to appeal to this philosophical 'gap'. For example, Richards specifically reviewed the arguments made against classical justifications for punishment and argued instead for restorative justice (1998: Chapter 4). Restorative justice was also an impetus for ADR more generally (see Table 6.2).

---

[23] See Davis *et al.* (2003: 2–5) for a review of the strengths and weaknesses of the three perspectives in victimology which developed in the second half of the twentieth century.

Source	Objective
1 Access to justice	Involvement of citizens more directly in crime resolution; bring legal institutions closer to the people
2 Victim movement	Satisfaction of victims' needs, both material and emotional
3 Abolitionism	Liberation from state domination and bureaucracy, and specifically the eradication of prisons
4 Decentralisation and local community control	Create community fora and institutions for dealing with own conflicts and misdemeanours
5 Participatory justice	Involvement of citizens in crime resolution in order to make use of community resources
6 Social work professions	Reduction in misbehaviour by (a) encouraging social responsibility in offenders, (b) involving their families and other community supports, and (c) reducing the stigma of prosecution
7 Some legal professionals and various 'liberal' pressure groups	Find more effective means of dealing with crime which are also more humanitarian and less reliant on punishment
8 Caseload and resource crisis in criminal justice	Find less costly and de-escalatory methods of dealing with crime
9 Privatisation	Reduction in state responsibility in favour of market forces
10 Conflict resolution movement	Apply constructive conflict resolution techniques and problem-solving approach in favour of more lasting resolutions
11 Restorative justice	Synthesis of several of the above, notably 2–7 and 10

Table 6.2 Sources of the mediation movement and their objectives
Source: Marshall (1997).

This range of separate developments since the 1960s has encouraged the development of the current policies we reviewed in section 6.1.3. The result appears to be three new sets of policy aims:

- to ensure the return to the victim, or seizure by the state, of the 'fruits of crime'
- to make greater use of techniques of mediation and reparation in sentencing and in punishment and to encourage restorative justice principles
- to focus on the needs of the victim.

This latter aim is both an independent strand and one which feeds into the previous two strands. Nevertheless the development of new forms of confiscation and compensation to victims 'should not be seen as being associated with a broader victims' movement and was not informed by victims' experiences' (Davies *et al.* 2003: 20). Some of the developments to be discussed in the following section were not, then, essentially the result of restorative justifications for punishment. They were, rather, changes in response to some of the above pressures within a largely retributivist framework. It is not surprising that these provisions were introduced before some of the other sentencing changes in relation to victims of offending because they can more easily fit into traditional sentencing frameworks. Nevertheless Stockdale and Devlin pointed to a 'dilemma facing the courts' even in regard to these provisions. They noted the reluctance of the police and the courts to be involved in processes that have the appearance of allowing defendants to 'buy their way out of trouble' by offering or being able to make restitution or pay compensation (1987: 37).

6.2.3 The 'fruits of crime': restitution, forfeiture and confiscation

Section 28 of the Theft Act 1968 gave the court the power to order the restitution, the handing back, of stolen goods (or their equivalent) to the victim. The Powers of Criminal Courts Act (PCCA) 1973 originally gave the courts very limited powers of forfeiture of property connected with the offence (s 43) but the amendments made by the Criminal Justice Act (CJA) 1988 extended the courts' powers to any offence, whether indictable or summary, and whether punishable or not by custody (by s 69). It also allowed a court to order the sale of forfeited property and the proceeds to be paid to the victim (by s 107). Sections 13(5) and (6) of the Proceeds of Crime Act (PCA) 2002 also impose a duty on the court to order that monies obtained from the sale of confiscated property should be used to pay part or all of a compensation order if the defendant would not otherwise have sufficient means.

Courts already had a duty to confiscate any proceeds. The DTOA 1986 first imposed this requirement specifically in relation to the growing drug trafficking problem. As noted above, the CJA 1988, Part VI extended it to the benefits of property obtained in relation to (that is, as a result of or in connection with the commission of) any indictable offence.[24] In 1993 the DTOA 1986 was amended introducing detailed practical provisions to make confiscation easier for the courts to impose (CJA 1993, ss 7–13). The civil standard of proof is to be used to address the practical difficulty for the court of finding and proving what was gained in the commission of the offence. The CJA 1988 was also amended to give more compensation order situations (CJA 1993, ss 27–8) and the Terrorism Act 2002 increased powers in relation to forfeiture orders. Cases have tested the rights compliance of these provisions, *Welch* (1995) finding that confiscation orders are to be considered as a penalty, and so retrospective implementation is in breach of Article 7 of the European Convention on Human Rights.[25] The court commented that the order, following conviction, caused a detriment to the offender, and the aims of crime prevention and reparation are consistent with a punitive purpose.

The Proceeds of Crime Act (PCA) 2002,[26] 'designed to make the recovery of unlawfully held assets more effective' (Home Office 2002g), consolidated some existing powers and added new powers to ascertain the whereabouts of proceeds of crime.[27] It came into force early in 2003, requiring the Crown Court—providing the second condition is also met—to make a confiscation order against the offender in relation to any offence if (first condition) the offender was convicted, or committed

---

[24] This provision also relates to a summary offence if it is joined with an indictable offence and with a high-value benefit.

[25] The House of Lords has since considered the potential impact of ECHR Article 6 and Article 1 of the First Schedule on the confiscation provisions in s 72AA of the CJA 1988 in *Rezvi* (2002), finding them to be reasonable and proportionate responses to a public interest.

[26] Schedule 12 of the PCA 2002 has repealed Part VI of the CJA 1988.

[27] The Halliday Report (2001) dealt only briefly with compensation orders: see para 6.18. For an interesting article on the tax evasion provisions see Alldridge and Mumford (2005).

for sentence, at the Crown Court (s 6(1) and (2)) or if the prosecutor asked the magistrates' court to commit the convicted offender to the Crown Court with a view to a confiscation order being considered (s 70). The second condition is that the prosecutor or the Director of Public Prosecutions asks the court to proceed under s 6 or the court believes it is appropriate to do so (s 6(3)). The court is then instructed to decide 'whether the defendant has a criminal lifestyle' (s 6(4)(a)). If he has, the court must decide whether he has benefited from his 'general criminal conduct'; if not it must decide 'whether he has benefited from his particular criminal conduct' (s 6(4)(b) and (c)).[28] If the court decides that the offender has benefited from either, it must decide the recoverable amount and make a confiscation order (s 6(5)). Only if the victim is engaged in civil proceedings against the offender does this duty become a power (s 6(6)).

The property which may be confiscated is defined as 'all property wherever situated' and includes money, all forms of real or personal property, and 'things in action and other intangible or incorporeal property' (s 84). Confiscation orders can take precedence over fines, forfeiture, and deprivation orders (s 13), but otherwise do not influence sentencing so can be combined with other penalties. There are no limits on the sum to be confiscated provided it does not exceed 'the defendant's benefit from the conduct concerned' (s 7(1)).

The context for the PCA 2002 is wider than sentencing alone: the concern is with the use of proceeds of crime and illegal laundering of money for terrorist and other organised international crime. Part VII of the Act (which deals with money laundering) imposes much wider—and potentially draconian—duties on the 'regulated sector', which includes practising solicitors: professional advisers must disclose information to help detect money launderers and so ultimately assist the criminal justice system and further the possibility of making confiscation orders.[29] Failure to disclose information obtained in situations not covered by the narrowly defined 'privileged circumstances' (s 330(10)) can amount to an offence (s 331), punishable by a maximum penalty of five years (s 334(2)). If any person is involved in dealings in relation to 'criminal property' (see ss 327–329) the maximum penalty is 14 years (s 334(1)). The thinking is that, 'if you find the hoard you can catch the criminal. That, put simply, is the purpose of Part VII of the Proceeds of Crime Act 2002' (Brasse 2003: 492).

The Serious Organised Crime and Police Act 2005 introduces further relevant measures. Section 97 extends the above powers in Part 2 of the 2002 Act to magistrates' courts, with a limit of £10,000 on any confiscation order, whilst s 98 inserts a new s 245A in the 2002 Act such that the enforcement authority can apply to the court for freezing orders as well as recovery orders. Further, ss 95–96 deal with international obligations in respect of forfeiture and freezing of property. In particular the provisions respond to the Council Framework Decision 2003/577/JHA of 22 July 2003 on the execution in the European Union of orders freezing property or evidence.

---

[28] 'Criminal lifestyle' is defined at s 75 and 'criminal conduct' at s 76.

[29] An implication of the confiscation order for family lawyers is to be found in *CPS v Grimes* (2003) (see *Family Law* 2003: 635). A spouse of an offender needs to be an equitable owner or have a divorce pending; otherwise the matrimonial home could be included in the proceeds that the offender has confiscated. See also *X v X* (2005) (re confiscation order against husband—case note in *Family Law* 2005: 543–4).

Nevertheless, there will be benefits to victims where compensation results from confiscation, and where s 72 of the PCA 2002 is used. This provision empowers a court to award compensation without a conviction in two circumstances providing there has been 'serious default' by members of specified bodies such as the police force or the Crown Prosecution Service (s 72). The circumstances are that either a criminal investigation was initiated but did not result in criminal proceedings, or criminal proceedings did not result in a conviction.

6.2.4 **Compensation to the victim**

The attempts to find a direct remedy for the victim's loss and powerlessness in the face of offending took two forms in relation to compensation: first to develop state compensation and, second, to develop a means by which the offender could be made to pay the victim as a convicted offender in a criminal court.

Compensation by the state

Compensation paid to the victim by the state was set up in the 1960s—earlier than the statutory scheme for criminal compensation orders. The Criminal Injuries Compensation Board (CICB), established in 1964, technically as a voluntary scheme created by administrative fiat, was the first of such schemes to be set up in Europe. This scheme is separate from sentencing and does not require an offender to be successfully prosecuted and sentenced, although a sentencing court will take into account any compensation paid by the CICB and vice versa so that a victim cannot be compensated twice. Not until 1988 was the scheme given a statutory basis by ss 108–117 of the CJA 1988, with the relevant definitions in ss 109–112 (replaced in 1995: see below).

Nevertheless, the scheme set up in 1964 was highly significant because it meant that the state had accepted responsibility for harm done to citizens through offending. The state very rarely accepts such responsibility and, as Harris notes, 'it is testimony to the political power of the victim lobby that the 1980s should have seen such unquestioning support for this position when the emphasis in other areas of social life was on self-help and personal responsibility' (1992: 60). Such schemes may be seen as a symbolic act by governments to show concern for victims and to allow some responsibility for upholding law and order.[30] The European Convention on the Compensation of Victims of Violent Crime was enacted in 1983 to recognise the duty of states to compensate victims if other sources were not available.

However, such state compensation schemes have significant disadvantages for governments because of their high initial cost and the relative inability of governments to control take-up (Maguire and Shapland 1997: 217). In the UK, as in some other jurisdictions where schemes are relatively long-standing, there has been a policy of restricting access to such compensation. In England and Wales and Scotland, for example, the 1964 scheme was originally a very wide-ranging scheme 'providing compensation to any victim of violent crime (or person assaulted in the course of preventing crime) of any nationality who was victimised or injured in Britain' (ibid). The increasing cost of the scheme led the government to pass

---

[30] For a detailed discussion see Miers (1990).

the Criminal Injuries Compensation Act in 1995 to introduce an 'enhanced tariff' approach based on types of injury rather than individualised consideration of harm and damage. There has also been a tendency in such schemes to define the kinds of victims that are seen as deserving by states and so, for example, awards may be reduced or refused if victims are not believed to be truly blameless. Maguire and Shapland argue that 'victims see it (quite correctly) as a judgement by the State on the worth of their claim and their status as victim' (1997: 218). In Northern Ireland the compensation scheme has been revised by the Criminal Injuries Compensation (Northern Ireland) Order 2002 (SI 2002 No 796) in the light of the particular problems presented by victims of terrorist violence.

Victims' surcharge

In 2004 the UK Government announced its proposal to establish a Victim's Fund in England and Wales, with money coming 'principally from imposing a surcharge on offenders . . . and from resources released from changes to the Criminal Injuries Compensation Scheme' (Home Office 2004a: 4). Publication of these proposals provoked adverse media comment, but largely on the ground that the surcharge would apply to all offences, including traffic offences dealt with by fixed-penalty notices (ibid: 16, paras 40 and 44). The reason given for establishing the Fund was that existing schemes do not deliver a good enough deal to victims whose offender is not convicted so the resulting monies will be ring-fenced to fund victim support organisations and schemes. In this connection there is also debate as to whether pay rates for prisoners should be increased so that they are better able to compensate victims. The Domestic Violence, Crime and Victims Act 2004 inserted a new s 161A in the CJA 2003 requiring a court to impose a surcharge when dealing with an offender for one or more offences although, if the court wishes to impose a compensation order and the offender has insufficient means to pay both, the court may reduce the surcharge accordingly, 'if necessary to nil'. The CJA (Surcharge) Order 2007[31] fixed the amount of the surcharge at £15. The amount to be charged depends on the offence(s) committed, the age of the offender and how the offender is being dealt with, including whether he is being fined (s 161B(2)). This surcharge came into operation on 1 April 2007 and does not apply to fixed-penalty notices.[32] At December 2007 only a fraction of the anticipated income had been collected because the computer system could not yet cope with all offenders: only those being fined were charged.

Compensation orders

The other form of compensation to be developed on a statutory footing was that of compensation orders to be imposed on individual offenders. The Report in 1970 of the Advisory Council on the Penal System: *Reparation by the Offender* led to the Criminal Justice Act 1972 (re-enacted as PCCA 1973, ss 35–38), amended by the CJA 1982, s 67. These provisions gave criminal courts a power and duty to consider making a compensation order at the sentencing stage in relation to a conviction or to offences taken into consideration. The power could only be exercised if the

---

[31] SI 2007 No. 707.
[32] For answers by the Solicitor General to Parliamentary questions on the surcharge see http://www.publications.parliament.uk/pa/cm200607/cmhansrd/cm070426/debtext/70426–0003.htm#07042640000981.

offence had caused personal injury, or loss or damage to a victim, but did not cover compensation to relatives in cases of murder. The Report of the Hodgson Committee (1984), *The Profits of Crime and Their Recovery*, resulted in the CJA 1988 under which compensation could be awarded to relatives for murder (except car death) and details were given about the relationship between such an order and damages in civil proceedings (ss 104–105). The CJA 1982, s 67 amended s 35 of the 1973 Act so that a compensation order could be a 'stand-alone' order, in other words it could count as the punishment. The legislation to make provision for compensation orders in Scotland was somewhat later (Criminal Justice (Scotland) Act 1980 Part IV), coming into force in 1981.

The legislation applicable to England and Wales[33] has now been re-enacted in the PCCSA 2000, ss 130–134,[34] which give the court a discretion to impose a compensation order but, if the court does not impose an order, it must give reasons (s 130(3)). Further provisions are that:

- the maximum award in magistrates' courts is £5,000 but there is no limit in the Crown Court (s 131(1) and (2))
- a compensation order can be instead of any other disposal or punishment: PCCSA 2000, s 130(1), except in relation to those mandatory sentences found in recent legislation: s 130(2).[35] The compensation order can take priority over a fine and be the sole punishment but this is rare: Moxon *et al.* (1992) found that 94 per cent of compensation orders had been accompanied by another penalty.

Compensation orders, which may be ordered for damages such as pain and suffering as well as for material loss, would seem to be an ideal response to the problem of victims' difficulties in gaining damages through the civil courts in relation to offences. Compensation must be considered by sentencers (PCCSA 2000, s 130) who have to give reasons if they do not order compensation where there is an identifiable victim of the offence. Such orders can take priority over other penalties and so if the offender has any means at all they can be diverted to compensation orders rather than to fines.

However, compensation orders raise practical and theoretical difficulties. One problem has been the under-use of legislation. Moxon *et al.* (1992: 6) found that, after the 1988 CJA amendments to encourage their use, the award of compensation orders had risen to 17 per cent of Crown Court cases in 1989 (as compared with 11 per cent before the Act) and to 39 per cent (from 31 per cent) of cases surveyed in magistrates' courts (1992: 10).[36] These figures were still low and figures for indictable offences in 1996 reveal only occasional use for more serious offences: 19 per cent in magistrates' courts (half in relation to offences of violence and criminal damage), with 8 per cent in Crown Courts (Wasik *et al.* 1999: 662). Scottish research, which analysed data from all levels of the Scottish courts in the period 1989–92, also found that the already low use of compensation orders fell

---

[33] See PCCSA 2000, s 167 for the extent of the provisions of the Act.
[34] As amended by the CJA 2003: Schedule 32 para 117. Sections 137–138 of the PCCSA 2000 deal with compensation orders to be paid by a parent or guardian where the offender is under 18 years of age.
[35] See Chapter 5, sections 5.3.3 and 5.4.1.
[36] See Newburn (1988) for earlier Home Office research on the use of compensation orders.

during that time from 5.5 per cent to 4.6 per cent of persons with charges proved (Hamilton and Wisniewski 1996).

It would seem that sentencers have difficulties not only in assessing the amount of a compensation order but also in using an order as part of the 'punishment' repertoire. Perhaps some sentencers continue to be uneasy about mixing 'what they saw as an essentially civil matter with criminal sentencing' (Maguire and Shapland 1997: 220).

The first tier of courts is guided by the *Magistrates' Court Guidelines* (Magistrates' Association 2003). The 1997 version of the *Guidelines* incorporated examples of suitable amounts for various injuries, based on the Home Office Circular of 1993 (see Wasik *et al*. 1999). For example, a fractured little finger was placed at £750, the loss of front tooth at £1,000, and a laparotomy (6–8" stomach scar) at £3,500. The 2003 *Guidelines* increased the first two to £1,000 and £1,500 respectively, whilst the laparotomy stays at £3,500 (Magistrates' Association 2003: 90). However, the average level of the order in 1996 was only £194 in the magistrates' court and £1,072 in the Crown Court. The Criminal Statistics for 2002 show that in magistrates' courts, based on all offences dealt with, excluding summary motoring offences, 49 per cent of orders were for £50 or less, only 5 per cent being over £500 (Table S1.6B). For Crown Courts, reflecting the greater seriousness of the offending, 30 per cent of orders were for sums over £500, yet 6 per cent were £50 or less (ibid: Table S2.8B). One reason for the small amounts is that offenders are often not able to pay the full amount. The amount they can pay is assessed in line with assessment for imposing fines. So, whilst case law allows compensation to be paid in instalments and stresses that there can be some hardship to the offender in paying, there is still a limit to what can be paid and that limit may be less than is due to the victim. (See Chapter 7, section 7.3 for comparable provisions for fines.) If an offender is imprisoned he may have no way of providing—for a long time—the means to pay a compensation order, a fact taken into account in *Sullivan* (2003) where the court stated that '[a] compensation order should not be made if it would subject the offender on release from prison to a financial burden he might not be able to meet without committing further crime'.

A related difficulty, to which we have already referred, clearly concerned Scarman LJ when compensation orders became available: 'compensation orders were not introduced into our law to enable the convicted to buy themselves out of the penalties of crime' (*Inwood* (1974)). So, in line with this thinking, the voluntary repayment to the victim in advance of the trial is normally accepted as a mitigating factor, but the court would require evidence that the offender feels genuine remorse. There have also been instances where the offender misled the court into believing he had the means to pay a compensation order (and so perhaps avoid a stiffer sentence) when he did not. In *Dando* (1996) the court stated that in those circumstances the offender must pay the compensation or serve a period in prison in default.

All these difficulties arise from the uneasy mix of aims arising from the awarding of what is comparable to a civil order for damages in a sentencing court, where punishment is expected and the enforcement procedures are currently limited in scope and effect. The compensation order ought to be a pragmatic compromise which satisfies judge and victim, but so far it has not always proved to be so.

6.3 New forms of reparation

6.3.1 Mediation and reparation in the 1980s

In the 1980s the burgeoning interest in restorative justice and in alternative dispute resolution together provided an impetus for the development of victim–offender mediation schemes. Experimental projects were funded by the state or charitable bodies, and were professionally developed to pilot new ideas. These were 'supply led' and had a different rationale from that of both forms of compensation that we reviewed above. The latter are based on the idea that the state should retain some responsibility for reimbursing the victim of crime, directly or though the agency of the sentencing courts. Victim–offender mediation, on the other hand, depends on an idea that offending is a harm which is primarily a matter between individuals, and that the two main people, the victim and offender, should have responsibility for outcome. The experimental schemes developed in the 1980s therefore took from restorative justice the principle that reparation and apologising to the victim are very important, whereas they took from the ADR movement the idea that the agreement should be voluntarily negotiated and imposed.

The schemes were implemented in the UK at three different points in the criminal justice system: at the pre-prosecution stage as part of diversion of young offenders from prosecution, at the stage between conviction and sentence, and also as part of punishment itself. In the 1980s the pre-prosecution schemes were possibly of the highest profile, given that they were being developed against a background of rapid expansion and official endorsement of cautioning young people (see Chapter 8). Early research was done on the Exeter scheme set up in 1979, in which minors who had previously been cautioned might be offered some form of what became known as '**cautioning plus**', in which reparation and mediation were a part. Davis *et al.* (1988) found that such schemes very rarely gave the victim any practical remedy for harm done, the reparation being in terms of apologies and other symbolic offers of help. Davis concluded that reparation was being used to 'sell' diversion to magistrates and the police (1992: 137), and other researchers reached the same conclusion in relation to the Corby scheme (Blagg 1985). Victims sometimes felt under pressure to take part in these schemes of mediation, and young people were rarely in a position to offer any reparation that victims viewed as adequate. However, evaluation of court-based schemes in South Yorkshire showed that participating victims found it rewarding to help young offenders change their attitudes (Smith *et al.* 1988) although Davis pointed out that 'the mature socially responsible' victims who agreed to take part, were probably the ones who least needed the involvement for their own benefit (1992: 138).

Reparation inserted between conviction and sentence can be seen as reparation which gives the offender the possibility of providing himself with mitigation because a report on the outcome of victim–offender mediation was given to the court before sentencing. In the 1980s four such experimental schemes were funded by the Home Office. However, Young found that this link between mitigation and reparation appeared to be 'unpalatable to both victims and offenders' (R. Young 1989: 464) and he criticised the scheme for allowing the offender little choice as to whether his sentencing would be deferred, which meant victims doubted the voluntariness of the offender's involvement. The inducements to attend mediation were generally seen as counter-productive because 'altruism and contrition is called into question' (Davis 1992: 140) and so two-thirds of the offenders felt that even if they were genuine in their desire to mediate, the victim would still think that they were lying.

The third stage in which reparation was inserted into sentencing and punishment in the 1980s was as part of punishment itself. Such schemes for use with offenders in custody were developed in North America and were referred to as victim offender reconciliation programmes (VORPs). They were 'intended to make offenders personally accountable for their behaviour, instil in the offenders a sense of the human impact of crime, present offenders with the chance to face their victim and repay the damage done to the victim, enhance victim participation in the justice system, and improve the... justice rendered to both victims and offenders' (Umbreit 1994 in Smith and Hillenbrand 1997: 250). In the UK these schemes were pioneered within the youth justice estate, the first of such groups being run at Rochester Youth Custody Centre in the 1980s, with later projects at the Mount Prison in Hertfordshire and at HMP Long Lartin (Liebmann 2000: 1). These usually entail a series of group meetings of victims and offenders, so that it is not the offender meeting his particular victim but a group interaction aiming to educate young people into changing their attitudes.

Researcher results were mixed or critical. 'The current attempts to promote reparation in this country are half-baked' wrote Davis and colleagues (1988: 128) and, by the 1990s, the schemes were described as 'bit players' (Shapland 2003: 211), a survey of all known victim–offender projects in 1996 finding only nine major projects where such activity was 'substantial' (Stewart 1998; Table 6.1). So by the early 1990s, one commentator wrote, 'it is rare for a set of ideas to catch on as quickly as did the enthusiasm for victim–offender mediation and reparation in the UK in the mid 1980s... It is now fair to say that, within government circles, mediation and reparation schemes constitute something of a "dead" subject' (Davis 1992: vii).

Yet those professionals involved in the 1980s in the three kinds of scheme summarised above communicated a 'broad consensus that room should be found within the criminal justice process for some kind of reparation or reconciliation' (Smith *et al.* 1988: 378). This view was also evident in the 1980s in the speeches of the Home Secretary, the Labour Campaign for Criminal Justice, Home Office surveys and the Home Office funding of experimental projects (ibid: 378–9). Why then were these schemes generally seen as unsuccessful?

One possible reason is that the words 'restorative justice' or 'restorative principles' were rarely used in relation to these schemes. The terminology was more often in terms of mediation, reparation and, sometimes, reconciliation, and those proponents of restorative justice at the time who saw mediation and reparation simply as process tools for different end products were concerned that the focus was too narrowly on crime and the reduction of reoffending. So, for example, Marshall (1992) argued that restorative justice principles would locate such experiments differently: 'crime is unimportant... it is just part of a wider problem'. The experiments were also relatively small, time-limited under threat of withdrawal of funding, and scattered across the country.

Dignan and Lowey (2000: 45)[37] refer to the 1980s schemes as representing a 'stand-alone' model for implementing restorative justice. They stood alone in the sense that there was no specific statutory provision authorising their development and they could have only a limited impact on mainstream practice. All these developments were accomplished within the existing legal frameworks for sentencing and punishment and developed through professional discretion to decide on forms of treatment and reparation.

Surprisingly, one very critical researcher nevertheless stated: 'despite what might appear a disappointing outcome, it will be the contention of this book that these experiments were important, that the vision that they largely failed to realise will endure, and that the shortcomings of our criminal justice system are so profound that further attempts will be made' (Davis 1992: 1). These predictions have apparently been fulfilled. The politicisation of law and order in the 1990s which we reviewed in Chapter 1 led to a higher priority for criminal justice policy and so a greater willingness on the part of the government to look seriously at any alternatives, including restorative justice. Nevertheless, as we shall see, some of the conclusions of the above research have reappeared in more recent studies.

6.3.2 Restorative justice for young offenders

A further reason why restorative justice, mediation, and reparation have now been given greater priority and more resources is because of the increased salience of the youth justice 'problem'. Traditionally, 'the UK system, though not devoid of restitutive creativity, has expended much of it on juvenile work' (Harris 1992: 62); politically it is less risky. Restorative justice projects include victim–offender mediation (between the offender and the victim or a representative of the community), victim awareness programmes, reparation (symbolic in the form of an apology or as a practical piece of work), and family group conferences (FGCs).[38]

The Crime and Disorder Act (CDA) 1998 had a substantial component directed at children and young people (see Piper 1999), and the Youth Justice and Criminal Evidence Act 1999 gave statutory backing for the first time to restorative justice processes in youth justice. The Government presented this reform package as moving the system 'away from exclusionary punitive justice and towards an inclusionary restorative justice capable of recognising the social context in which crime occurs and should be dealt with' (Muncie 2000: 14).

Court orders

The scheme of reprimands and warnings for first- and second-time offenders (see Chapter 8), introduced by the CDA 1998, includes referral to a Youth Offending Team (YOT) on a 'final' warning. Victim–offender mediation and an apology or reparation to the victim or community can be part of the programme devised to reduce the likelihood of the young person reoffending. Reparative components have also been added to court orders for young offenders. The PCCSA 2000 (ss 73–75)[39] provides for reparation orders and action plan orders, the former being

---

[37] See http://www.nio.gov.uk for this report to the Northern Ireland Office.

[38] For a discussion of FGCs in relation to youth justice, see Jackson (1999); for details of some projects see http://www.nch.org.uk/ourservices/index.php?i=79.

[39] Originally enacted in the CDA 1998, ss 61–64 and 69–79.

for a maximum of 24 hours within a 3-month period and the latter for 3 months. In the first year of operation 2,261 reparation orders and 2,873 action plan orders were imposed on 10–17-year-olds.

The reparation order can stand alone and the reparation can be directed at the community or the victim. Supervision orders as well as action plan orders and the new youth rehabilitation orders to be introduced by the Criminal Justice and Immigration Act 2008 can include a requirement that the young offender engage in reparation. The CJA 2003 continues the status of the reparation order as a penalty that is not a youth community order or community order (see Chapters 8 and 13). The restrictions on liberty imposed by community orders and reparation orders must be commensurate with offence seriousness (CJA 2003, s 148(3)(b)). This is in line with Recommendation No R (99) 19 of the United Nations Congress on Crime Prevention and the Treatment of Offenders which was adopted by the Committee of Ministers of the Council of Europe on Mediation in Penal Matters: '[t]he proportionality requirement means that there should be correspondence between the burden on the offender and the seriousness of the offence'. This contrasts with a purely utilitarian approach where a desired outcome could justify a burden heavier than that determined by seriousness.

The Youth Justice and Criminal Evidence Act 1999 Part I introduced the referral order as the presumptive sentence for first-time offenders in the youth court. Referral is to a young offender panel where a 'programme of behaviour' is agreed which can include reparation (see Chapter 8; also Ball 2000: 211–22). YOTs are encouraged to use restorative processes in the delivery of all intervention programmes (Home Office/Youth Justice Board 2002: para 10.15) which are part of the warning scheme and must use the YJB's Asset assessment tool to determine the young offender's risk profile 'and thereby the intensity and duration of the programme' (ibid: paras 10.11–10.14; see Chapter 13). Similarly referral orders should lead to some reparative component and, in the eleven areas in which referral orders were piloted and researched, the most common compulsory element (in 40 per cent of all contracts) was some form of reparative activity. The most common form of reparation was community reparation (42 per cent), followed by a written apology (38 per cent) with direct reparation to the victim or payment of compensation counting for 7 per cent (Newburn *et al.* 2002: viii–ix).

Conferencing

Mediation and reparation have had a high profile in policy documents but more recently the model of family group conferencing has been promoted in consultation documents—*Respect and Responsibility* (Home Office 2003b), *Every Child Matters* (DfES 2003) and *Youth Justice—The Next Steps* (Home Office 2003c)—as well as in Parliament when the Secretary of State noted in 2008 that, '[w]hile the use of FGCs is for local authorities or other agencies to determine in individual cases, the Government have taken steps to encourage their use where appropriate'.[40] An extensive literature on FGCs has also been built up over the last decade or so. It is argued that the process of using referral orders 'draws elements from family group conferences and children's hearings in Scotland' (Ball 2000: 217),[41] whilst the meetings at

---

[40] Hansard HC 26 February 2008, Col 1540W.
[41] For children's hearings see Chapter 8, section 8.2; for a wider discussion see Young (1997).

which the new warnings (and sometimes reprimands) are given should if possible be organised as restorative group conferences.

Different versions of family group conferencing were pioneered in New Zealand and Australia, where there are now statutory bases for their use. In New Zealand the first scheme was set up in 1989 and involves those most directly involved—the victim, offender and family members—in meetings aiming to negotiate outcomes which take into account the victim's interests but also make the offender account-able. The impetus for their development was concern expressed by a working party in 1987 about the 'cultural appropriateness' for the Maori people of the principles of family law derived from a colonial system of justice (King 1997a: 134–5). This concern about the loss of indigenous systems of justice with restorative principles was also expressed in Canada and Australia: see Tauri and Morris (2003: 45).

In the UK the early schemes were ad hoc initiatives (Gelsthorpe and Morris 2002: 245) which 'encountered a familiar litany of problems' (Dignan and Marsh 2001) but the context is now different. Their use[42] as part of statutory orders and processes is now encouraged by extensive guidance from the Youth Justice Board and the Home Office.[43] Restorative cautioning or conferencing, developed as local initiatives by police forces in the 1990s (Hoyle *et al.* 2002: 7), has been endorsed and formalised in Home Office Guidance about the process of giving (final) warn-ings. The Guidance states that '[t]he impact of a final warning on a young offender can be significantly enhanced by delivering it as part of a restorative conference. If the victim does not want to take part, similar principles can be applied by giving a restorative warning' (Home Office/Youth Justice Board 2002: para 9.25). In the Thames Valley Police, the model developed before the schemes were nationally encouraged is one based on the police-led model of conferencing developed in Australia though they reserve the term 'restorative conference' for meetings with a victim present. However, most cases in the sample resulted in 'restorative cautions' where the attendance of significant others in the life of the offender—rather than a victim—was designed to produce positive shaming (Hoyle *et al.* 2002).

Restorative approaches are being encouraged to bring home to young offend-ers what they have done and so help reduce the likelihood of reoffending. The guidance to the police and YOTs on the final warning scheme specifically dis-cusses restorative processes on pages 19–20, beginning with, '[a] restorative approach can make final warnings more meaningful and effective...Research into the delivery of final warnings shows that the use of restorative processes reduces offending...and can be of benefit to victims' (Home Office/Youth Justice Board 2002: para 9.22).[44]

Restorative justice is also seen as a way of promoting both the welfare and the rights of children and young people. Allen (1996), for example, suggests that tak-ing part in restorative justice initiatives helps restore personal respect and encour-ages the taking of responsibility, avoids stigmatisation, promotes reintegration in the community, and individualises the process, so avoiding the 'contamination' of young offenders being punished together (as in custodial institutions).

---

[42] For details of the four distinct stages of a family group conference model see NACRO (2003f: 4–5).

[43] See, for example, *Key Elements of Effective Practice: Restorative Justice, Guidance* (Youth Justice Board 2004), soon to be updated.

[44] Holdaway and Desborough found that 31 per cent of their sample reoffended within a year (2004: 5).

No More Excuses (Home Office 1997a: 31–2) summed up the principles, as had other proponents of restorative approaches,[45] as the '3Rs' of restoration, reintegration, and responsibility. However, NACRO has questioned the commitment of the providers of restorative justice projects to the third 'R' of 'reintegration' (NACRO 2003f) a sign that it is still proving easier to incorporate individual responsibility or restoration—the making of amends—into the criminal justice system than the much wider aim of providing support and guidance to reintegrate a young person into social and economic structures that will decrease exclusion and offending.

The stated benefits of restorative approaches, in helping offenders to understand and regret the effects of their offending, are benefits, research would suggest, that can be delivered only if restorative procedures are done well (Hoyle *et al.* 2002; Holdaway *et al.* 2001: 39). Professional assumptions and biases can undermine the tenets of restorative justice as can any abuse of process such as the administering of final warnings without a clear admission of guilt. The use of a 'script'—'doing' the techniques—is not effective without a proper understanding of the underlying principles. Dignan makes a similar point that experience has shown that it is 'the dialogue which accompanies the face-to-face meeting with victims and offenders which provides the transformative experience for both parties' (1999: 54). This is one of the 'key differences' between 'a more conventional retributive response' and a restorative approach, and so Dignan notes with approval that attention to this issue has entered guidance about the reparation order (ibid: 55). There are also 'indications that the basis for a receptive professional culture is there' (Dignan and Marsh 2001: 95).

However, not all research is uniformly encouraging. Wilcox *et al.* (2004) compared the reconviction rates of offenders experiencing traditional cautions with those experiencing restorative cautioning in their Thames Valley Police study but were unable to establish whether restorative cautioning made an impact on 'resanctioning' rates or the seriousness and frequency of subsequent offending. (The study used the word 'resanction' to cover cautions, final warnings and reprimands, and convictions.)

Evaluation of 30 funded projects including final warnings in 18 police forces also found that, whilst the majority of parents and young offenders[46] expressed positive views about the projects, over half the projects did not target young people on final warnings (Holdaway and Desborough 2004: 6). The mean age of participants was 14.3 years (ibid: 5) and the summary of the research findings on delivering final warnings suggest that—at least a few years ago—it was still difficult to ensure well-conducted meetings with a victim present:

A clear, measured and realistic tone should set the scene for a Final Warning.

Mothers attended warnings more frequently than fathers. Just 6 of our 21 case studies included a father attending.

Despite their benefits, very few Final Warnings were restorative conferences. The overwhelming majority of warnings, 80%, were of the standard type. 16% were restorative warnings and just 4% were restorative conferences.

Very few victims were present when a Final Warning was delivered.

(ibid: 7)

---

[45] See, for example, NACRO (1997) 'A New 3Rs for Young Offenders'.
[46] See, also, Hine (2007) for the findings of research to assess young people's perspectives on final warnings.

This reflects research on schemes in the 1980s in the UK which revealed that victim participation can be very difficult to secure (King and Piper 1989). Research on the new referral order panels also concluded that 'the involvement of victims and in particular their attendance at panel meetings across the pilot areas has been both lower than was originally anticipated and significantly lower than comparative experiences from restorative justice around the world' (Newburn *et al.* 2002: viii).

There are other obstacles to the success of more recent initiatives. Research conducted in 2002–3 in the juvenile secure estate found that, whilst staff were 'broadly sympathetic' to the idea of restorative justice, 'there is little restorative justice intervention of any kind taking place in the secure estate' (Youth Justice Board 2004: summary). The main reason given was the high numbers of young people in custody placed away from their home area where their victims and families live. Government policy is still to encourage such initiatives. In January 2008, in explaining what responses had been made to the Carlile Report (2006), the Government reported that 'the YJB is also in the process of developing more sophisticated conflict resolution techniques. Pilots in restorative justice and therapeutic crisis intervention techniques are both under way.'[47] However, the Howard League for Penal Reform (London) submitted a statement on restorative justice (RJ) in England and Wales to the 11th UN Congress on Crime Prevention and Criminal Justice (Bangkok, April 2005) reviewing and praising the increasing use of RJ processes in youth justice but criticising the UK Government's failure to use the same processes in relation to anti-social behaviour.

Miers reviewed research on both process and product outcomes from restorative justice interventions (2004: 29–37), noting that 'there is no shortage of evaluations of the many forms assumed by restorative justice interventions' (ibid: 29). He concentrated in particular on the evaluation of seven schemes conducted for the Home Office in 1999–2000, five dealing with young offenders (see Miers *et al.* 2001) but pointed out that it was difficult to make generalisations because of the differing conceptions of restorative justice and methods of delivery (Miers 2004: 30). As when earlier schemes were researched (King and Piper 1989), there were substantial differences in the volume of work of different schemes, some having relatively few cases (Miers 2004).

6.3.3 **Criminal Justice Act 2003**

There are now further restorative justice possibilities for adult offenders. The *Restorative Justice* Consultation Paper (Home Office 2003a)[48] outlined the Government's intention to produce Codes of Practice to accompany the new conditional caution for adults, introduced by s 22 of the CJA 2003,[49] and to set up a diversion pilot and a restorative justice network for the correctional services. The aims are 'more

---

[47] Hansard HC 28 January 2008, Col 153W. For an article on restorative justice in prisons see the article by Daniel Ness in the July 2005 issue of *RJ Online* (also at http://www.restorativejustice.org.uk/?RJ_in_Prisons:Prison_Publications).

[48] For responses to this consultation document, see http://www.homeoffice.gov.uk/docs3/rjconsultreplies.pdf.

[49] This is in effect a development of the reprimands and warnings system which has already been in operation for minors.

high quality reparation post-conviction', with Probation and Prison Service joint initiatives, and an increase in the satisfaction rate for victims participating in restorative justice in the youth justice service (ibid: Annex A). In addition the Government planned to appoint a Commissioner for Victims and Witnesses (ibid: Work Strand 7) although recruitment in 2006 failed to find a suitable candidate. The Government also aims to develop work with agencies in the voluntary sector to raise understanding of restorative justice amongst the public and professionals, to hold meetings with key stakeholders to develop training and accreditation policies, to integrate restorative justice more fully into the criminal justice system, and, at Work Strand 11, to ensure that restorative justice approaches within and outside the criminal justice system are 'consistent and mutually supportive'.

One outcome of the new policy is that the mediation and reparation 'as mitigation' schemes piloted in the 1980s have, in effect, been resurrected (see section 6.5.1). The Halliday Report proposed that there be an interim review order: which would be, in effect, a deferment of sentencing for a period of no more than six months (as is currently possible) but with the power for the court to ask for an undertaking from the offender to enable the offender 'to tap into reparation and restorative justice schemes, where they exist, at the pre-sentence stage' (2001: para 6.20). 'The activities carried out and the progress shown would act as a mitigating factor in any subsequent sentence passed' (ibid: 44). The CJA 2003 (s 278 and Schedule 23) introduced this procedure so that ss 1 and 2 of the PCCSA 2000 now read:

(1) The Crown Court or a magistrates' court may defer passing sentence on an offender for the purpose of enabling the court, or any other court to which it falls to deal with him, to have regard in dealing with him to—

(a) his conduct after conviction (including, where appropriate, the making by him of reparation for his offence); or

(b) any change in his circumstances;

One might question the potential effectiveness of this proposal, however, given the criticisms of the earlier schemes.[50]

The CJA 2003 also puts into legislation the Halliday proposals on non-custodial sentences. In deciding on the various requirements of the community sentence the court would 'be required to consider the aims of punishment, reparation and prevention of re-offending' (Halliday 2001: Chapter 6). The possibility of imposing a reparative penalty is to be found in the CJA 2003, s 201(2) which gives details of the 'activity requirement'. Under that section the specified activities 'may consist of or include activities whose purpose is that of reparation, such as activities involving contact between offenders and persons affected by their offences'. The aggregate number of days for any activity cannot exceed 60. Similar requirements can be specified in a licence for prisoners serving the community part of a custodial sentence or for the requirements that can be specified in a suspended sentence order (s 182). The unpaid work component is another vehicle. (See *Working to Make Amends* which is the report of an inspection of a scheme of enhanced

---

[50] Edwards (2006) examined two cases where the Court of Appeal had taken into account—as mitigation—the offender's engagement in a restorative justice programme in prison but these appear to be isolated reported cases.

community punishment and unpaid work under the previous sentencing options (HM Inspectorate of Probation 2006b)).

Appendix 5 of the Halliday Report summarises research regarding, inter alia, practitioner support for restorative justice, with support ranging from 34 per cent (judges) to 73 per cent (probation officers).[51] It would be interesting to know whether support is now greater.

6.4 Victim involvement and victims' rights

6.4.1 What role for victims?

To examine the changing role of victims in criminal justice policy in England and Wales, Newburn (1995) focused on three periods: 1960–75, which is the period associated with the development of compensation, 1975–80, the period associated with the development of specific schemes to support victims, such as Victim Support, and the period from the 1980s onwards when victim support was institutionalised and the greater involvement of victims in the criminal justice process was demanded. The focus on victims in the last two decades has had two very different aspects: one could be called a victims' welfare approach, as evidenced by the Victim Support movement, whilst the other approach is to give victims a status to influence outcome.

The needs of victims were strongly emphasised in *Criminal Justice: The Way Ahead* (Home Office 2001a). Since October 2001 victims have been able to submit a personal statement to the court setting out the effects of the crime on them and their lives. Already victims of violent and sexual offences are informed and consulted about 'their' offender's early release conditions. A new Code of Practice for the Victims of Crime became law in April 2006[52], whilst a 21-page document issued under s 32 of the Domestic Violence, Crime and Victims Act 2004, it gives the victim of crime the 'right' ('is entitled') to a minimum standard of service; the Parliamentary Ombudsman is the final arbiter of complaints from victims who believe they have not received the service to which they are entitled.

Apart from the victim's interests in any reparative components of sentencing and punishment, current criminal justice policy, to summarise, covers the following disparate elements:

- victim support initiatives
- facilities for, and communication with, victims during the criminal process
- the Victim's Charter 1996 (reviewed 2001–2) and replaced by a Code of Practice in 2006
- victim personal statements.

This list could be seen as one that progresses from the least problematic to the most problematic aspects of victim-focused policies. The victim supportive initiatives are essentially those where a victim is contacted after they have reported an

---

[51] See Figure 11 and paras 86–89.
[52] See http://www.cjsonline.gov.uk/downloads/application/pdf/Victims%20Code%20of%20Practice.pdf.

offence to the police and are given counselling and any practical help which is acquired in order to cope with the aftermath of the offending. Secondly, facilities being provided for victims and communication with them in the course of the progress of the case may also be seen as relatively unproblematic, although not when it overlaps with the issue of support to victims in order to give evidence. That raises issues as to whether the support and possible coaching of victims is unfair on the accused and, more generally, raises the possibility of a conflict between the rights of victims and of defendants and offenders (Fenwick 1997). JUSTICE also noted that 'integrity' should be shown to both victim and offender (1998: 5).

Whether or not the Victim's Charter/Code of Practice is a rights-based document has been queried, notwithstanding the original subtitle, 'A statement of the rights of victims of crime'. Fenwick noted that 'the Charter appears to provide a response to certain international declarations on victims' rights, including the UN Declaration of the Basic Principles of Justice for the Victim of Crime and Abuse of Power', adopted by the General Assembly of the UN in 1985 (Fenwick 1997: 317). The Charter appeared to give victims a certain number of rights, some of which were 'placed on a quasi-legislative footing in Home Office Circulars' (1997: 323). However, when the Charter was relaunched in 1996 the subtitle was changed 'to the much less ambitious, but more accurate "A statement of service standards for victims of crime"' (Williams 1999: 387) and the web site confirmed that approach.[53] The Ombudsman is a 'complaint handling service for victims of crime who have a complaint about the way in which any of the criminal justice agencies has carried out its obligations under the Code':[54] remedies for upheld complaints are not specified.

It would appear that the Code can be located within a managerialist discourse where objectives are formulated and standards are set for citizens to be able to complain if necessary. The Charter, by framing rights in terms of consumerist principles, 'thus provides a mechanism for putting added pressure on the public agencies to be more cost efficient and productive' (Williams 1999: 388) and the Code would appear to have a similar function. Further, it is argued, the prioritising in policy documents and funding of the Victim Support organisation marginalises the more radical, anti-racist, and pro-feminist victim support groups (ibid: 388–9).

6.4.2 **The Victim Personal Statement Scheme (VPSS)**

In some jurisdictions the victim has an influential say in sentencing, either by giving a victim impact statement or by being able to decide the penalty. Such schemes, variously called in the past and in other jurisdictions victim impact statements (VIS), victim opinion statements (VOS), or, as now in England and Wales, victim personal statements (VPS), are of great importance because they give victims a limited opportunity to give their views to the court about the impact of the offending on them. This is seen as problematic if it potentially unduly influences the sentencing decision or is a procedural right to be involved in sentencing in a

[53] Accessed 5 January 2005. See the Online Resource Centre for links to information on current policy developments.
[54] From the leaflet for complainants: see http://www.ombudsman.org.uk/pdfs/victims_code.pdf.

online resource centre

way which undermines established notions of justice. Unfavourable reference is made to those states where the victim's family can decide whether the death penalty should be imposed in the case of the murder of a relative. The victim personal statement is a far cry from that situation and is seen by its supporters as a desirable form of victim participation in criminal justice.

When such proposals were first mooted for the UK, it was argued that 'the right to submit a VIS may be high in profile but low in improving genuine respect for victims. We should hesitate and reconsider before going further in this direction' (Ashworth 1993: 509). The issues raised were the question of sentencing for unseen results of offending behaviour on the victim, the preservation of defendants' rights, and the difficulty of raising expectations in the minds of victims which cannot be met (ibid: 505–7). To focus too narrowly on the victim has drawbacks: 'the victim's interest is part of the public interest but only part' (ibid: 503). Sanders *et al.* also argued that their research supported Ashworth's view that victim impact statements are 'misconceived in principle and unsatisfactory in practice'. They further noted that 'a firm theoretical basis for victim participation in adversarial systems has yet to be mapped out' (2001: 448).[55]

In England and Wales the VPS is now produced by the police in consultation with the victim/witness and can be updated at particular stages of the process. The guidance issued in respect of the current scheme, introduced experimentally in 1996, stresses that the scheme is optional for victims and that the VPS 'is not primarily a sentencing tool' (Home Office 2001b). 'Victims can say as much or as little as they wish' (ibid). In a Practice Statement the Lord Chief Justice also made clear that it is only information about the consequences to the victim of offending which will be added to all the factors taken into account in sentencing; the opinions of the victim about sentence are not relevant.[56] However, one of the two exceptions to this is '[w]here the victim's forgiveness or unwillingness to press charges provide evidence that his or her psychological or mental suffering must be very much less than would normally be the case'.[57] The sentencer can exercise his or her discretion as to whether it should influence evaluations of seriousness and the VPS gives the victim no right to give a statement in person (as it does in the USA). However, oral family impact statements are currently being piloted (see Department for Constitutional Affairs 2006). The scheme applies only to offences of murder or manslaughter charged on or after 24 April 2006.[58]

What is not clear, however, is why victims are given this role in sentencing. Edwards reviews four possible justifications, arguing that none has achieved prominence in the UK (2001: 44–5). One rationale is that the making of a VIS is therapeutic but this is not universal in practice; nor can the VPSS ensure that the criminal justice system operates more efficiently, nor that sentencing outcomes are improved, nor that it will contribute towards establishing a more participatory and rights-based system. 'It is perhaps unrealistic though to expect sentencing

---

[55] This article also reviews the arguments of Erez (1999).
[56] *R v Perks* (2001).
[57] See also the SGC *Case Compendium*, section on 'Victim's Wishes' and also Edwards (2002).
[58] See *A Protocol Issued by the President of the Queen's Bench Division Setting Out the Procedure to Be Followed in The Victims' Advocate Pilot Areas*: accessed at http://www.judiciary.gov.uk/docs/victims_advocate_protocol_030506.pdf.

procedures themselves to do too much, such as delivering real psychological benefits to victims' (Edwards 2001: 51).

6.4.3 The role of the Probation Service

The Probation Service has a major role to play in many of the restorative justice initiatives. Probation officers may be the responsible officers for young people aged 16–17 who are given reparation orders, they have to liaise with victims of serious sexual or violent offences in those cases where the offender is sentenced to more than 12 months' imprisonment, and must in those cases distribute the 'Release of Prisoners leaflet for victims'. They are responsible for the reparative components of the community punishment order and also for any reparative elements of the new cautioning system for adults introduced by the CJA 2003. Traditionally, however, the focus of the work of the Probation Service has been with offenders and there is some evidence that the Service finds the focus on both the victim and the offender difficult (Wargent 2002; see also Chapter 12, section 12.3). It has been argued that 'little thought appears to have been given as to how this obligation [to work directly with victims] should be translated into practice' (Crawford and Enterkin 2001: 708): guidance was not issued until the Home Office Circular of 1995 (HO 61/95), since revised in 2001 (HO 62/2001).

A thematic inspection report by HM Inspectorate of Probation focused on the victim perspective in 2000 (Home Office 2000b). In the Foreword to this document the Chief Inspector of Probation noted,

I was encouraged by the finding that the service has taken a constructive approach implementing the contact service to victims, placing their concerns and safety first...the public can be reassured by many of the findings which demonstrate that the service has taken seriously its key role in responding to victim concerns. There is ample evidence of cooperation with other agencies which is essential in some cases to secure the protection of victims.

A subsequent inspection found that most of the nine areas inspected had improved their performance on victim contact work but that not all areas offered a firm appointment in the initial contact letter with each victim (Home Office 2003e). This led to a variable take-up rate with three areas only achieving a face-to-face meeting in 50 per cent of cases. All areas were found to have adopted the national complaints scheme for victims and good working relations were found to exist between the Probation Service, the police and the victim support scheme (ibid).

There is also potential conflict for the Probation Service between the aims of punishment and reparation. In 1997, responding to a series of articles in the *Howard Journal*, Masters had argued that 'the Probation Service would be best to adopt a relational ethos in all their current work' (1997: 243), suggesting also an inter-agency 'restoration team' (ibid). Anthony Duff (2003) has more recently applied to probation work his ideas on sentencing and punishment as 'communicative penance' within a restorative framework. He suggests that probation should now be conceptualised as 'constructive reparative punishment' which would side-step the 'punishment versus welfare' conceptions of Probation Service practice. For him and, he would argue, for the Probation Service, the 'supposed opposition' between restorative and retributive punishment, which he notes 'has become a commonplace amongst theorists', is not a problem (ibid: 195, n 3).[59]

6.5 Tensions in policy, theory, and practice

6.5.1 Critiques

This chapter has reviewed the diverse developments in policy, sentencing law, and practice which in some way try to 'make amends' to the victim, or to society more generally, for harm done or loss suffered through criminal behaviour. In most of these initiatives, and particularly more recently, the victim and restorative justice principles have played key roles. This has raised questions as to the policy imperatives behind these developments and their likely consequences. The difficulties in drawing conclusions arise because of the lack of clear and coherent links between the different aspects of policies to make amends. They also stem from similar deficiencies in linking the different victim roles. As we have seen, and as Miers summarises it, the victim is cast as supplier of information, beneficiary of compensation and other benefits, and partner in crime prevention (2004: 23). Victims are consumers on the one hand and, given the values of restorative justice, are also participants (ibid: 24). Victims will not automatically benefit from the initiatives promoted on their behalf. Strang drew lessons from research on failed conferences to list the conditions which must be right if restorative practice is to be beneficial (Strang 2003; see also Tickell and Akester 2004: 24–7) and more recent research (Sherman *et al.* 2007b) also focuses on the detail of delivery and targeting.

It is not yet clear that restorative justice principles have infused all projects and the approaches of the professionals involved or that the specified outcomes can be delivered for most offenders and victims. Miers concluded that research for the Home Office undertaken in 1999–2000 (Miers *et al.* 2001) offered 'no conclusive support' for the view that restorative justice is more likely to lead to mutually satisfactory outcomes than standard criminal justice responses (2004: 32). He also noted that the study could reach no reliable conclusions concerning reoffending among young offenders (ibid: 34) but that the mixed findings confirm a 'generally held view among both victims and offenders that such interventions are, at least at the time, "better" than the conventional alternatives' (ibid). What is not known is how durable these benefits are or whether they produce behavioural change in the longer term. Further, they highlight the problematic nature of any 'what works' analysis in this area (ibid: 34–7).

The review by Sherman, Strang and colleagues of research on schemes in the UK and elsewhere has been more positive although they argue for more research and less generalised measures: 'The most important conclusion is that *RJ works differently on different kinds of people*. It can work very well as a general policy, if a growing body of evidence on "what works for whom" can become the basis for specifying when and when not to use it' (2007b: 8) and, surprisingly perhaps, '*RJ seems to reduce crime more effectively with more, rather than less, serious crimes*' (ibid; italics in

---

[59] See also the contributions to the volume by von Hirsch *et al.* (2003).

the original).[60] Shapland *et al.* also concluded that 'overall, the findings suggest that victims and offenders participating in the three restorative justice schemes were very happy with how the schemes operated and with their experiences of restorative justice' and that, although victims had different expectations, most of their expectations were met (2007a: 46). However, they note that 'particularly if [the scheme] is set within a framework provided by criminal justice, participants need to know whether the offender has tried to complete elements of the outcome agreement and what happened at sentence (if the meeting was pre-sentence). The continuing failures of criminal justice personnel to notify victims of the outcome of cases do not help in this' (ibid: 48).

What is often overlooked in policy discussion, though now well documented, is that in practice the categories of victim and offender are often not separate ones. Many people are both victims and offenders.[61] Indeed, official statistics make clear that high crime areas are also areas with high rates of victimisation. Further, the criminal justice system, and particularly its custodial establishments, has its own potential to victimise the offender (see Chapters 9 and 11). Developing policy through separate categories is unhelpful. As with young offenders (see Chapters 8 and 13), it can lead to distorted images of victims and offenders, and may not provide the best basis for policy development.

Not surprisingly, then, the material covered in this chapter reveals more tensions, ambiguities, and complexities than any other chapter in this volume. Restorative justice also generates more vivid prose than most topics:

So restorative justice at the moment is an adventure of research and development, where the research is proving tremendously encouraging in some ways, discouraging in others. As we use empirical experience to repair this leaky ship at sea, we should be careful about being too sure about a plan for the voyage.

(Braithwaite 2003: 4)

A critique has been developed on two levels, the practical and the theoretical: does restorative justice 'work', and are policy and practice conceptually coherent? The two levels are linked in the sense that a focus on practice and 'effectiveness' necessitates establishing the criteria for evaluation: those depend on aims, and they in turn depend on the theoretical frame and the conceptual values that underpin practice. Morris and Maxwell rephrase the research questions into 'are the values underpinning the particular model chosen...restorative?' and 'what are the consequences of adopting restorative justice processes compared with those associated with the continued existence of retributive or conventional criminal justice processes?' (2001: 267). Even this approach assumes a consensus that may not exist on the core, inalienable values of restorative justice (Harris 1998).

There are now good detailed reviews of the research on restorative justice programmes which summarise findings about different outcome measures and different models of victim–offender meetings or FGCs, which compare the results of using or not using statutory frameworks and mandatory referrals, and which focus on the influence of factors specific to particular jurisdictions and cultural contexts. All emphasise that it is not possible to generalise, but that there are examples of

---

[60] For further analysis see Christie (2007); Murphy and Harris (2007); Woolford and Ratner (2007).

[61] For a review of research and theory about the inter-relationship, and also recent research about the 'victimisation' of offenders on probation, see Farrall and Maltby (2003).

well-run projects with clear principles which achieve restorative outcomes. Within the confines of this chapter it is impossible to do justice to these reviews where the detail and the caveats are so crucial. What is clear is that 'restorative justice, which was virtually unheard of as a movement ten years ago, has now become embraced by the countries of the United Nations as a preferred option for the future resolution of disputes' (Morris and Maxwell 2001: 277).

What is less clear is how far such preferences are influenced by evocations of a, perhaps fictional, past time when communities could resolve disputes in such ways (ibid), or are grasped as a desperate attempt to address what is perceived as an ever-escalating crime problem. Consequently, the restorative justice movement now faces the same problems as those faced by the family mediation movement over a decade ago. Is it better for the restorative justice movement to keep control of their principles—such as voluntary participation and of outcomes which are not necessarily those of the formal justice system—at the expense of expansion or even survival, or to accept government money and monitoring, and work within a system with different values in order to prove the worth of restorative justice used more widely?

There is also the danger that expansion will be at the expense of adequate training in restorative principles and mediation management. Reviewing the literature, Tickell and Akester note that 'examples have shown that a space for creativity may also prove a forum for more destructive purposes. Anger, resentment and hostility will not automatically wither away in the face of good intentions' (2004: 25). Roche (2003) provides an example of the subversion in practice of the restorative justice notion of reintegrative shaming (see Braithwaite 1989). The aim is that the offender should be encouraged to feel shame but that the restorative encounter should also provide expressions of support and validation for the offender. In Roche's example a 12-year-old boy caught shoplifting agreed in a restorative conference to the proposal of his mother and the store manager that he wear outside the shop a T-shirt announcing 'I am a thief' (2003: 1). It is difficult to distinguish this from the increasing use of degrading and punitive 'shaming penalties' which can provoke vigilantism (ibid: 18).

Over twenty years ago von Hirsch wrote: 'it is unfair, once the institution of punishment is in place, to shift in an eclectic fashion between condemnatory and non-condemnatory responses: to mediate when the parties are prepared to talk to one another, but punish otherwise' (1986: 36). Restorative justice raises some of the same questions prompted by the development of informal justice and negotiated justice in the 1980s, notably in relation to both procedural and substantive rights. Those issues have again surfaced (Ashworth 2002b; see also Chapter 14).

Recent discussion has also focused on the viability of restorative justice and victim-focused policies within a traditional criminal justice system (Shapland *et al.* 2007b) and many aspects of the wider debate are discussed in a collection of papers (von Hirsch *et al.* 2003) with their relevance to youth justice being addressed in the volume edited by Weijers and Duff (2002) specifically in relation to youth justice. Some commentators are concerned, on the other hand, not with the difference between restorative justice and the traditional criminal justice system, but that restorative justice has a 'correctional ethos' embedded within it (Hutchinson 2006: 450). It is not therefore seen as inconsistent with penal developments focusing on preventative and retributivist aims but the concern is that it can have marginalising and repressive tendencies (Hine 2007; Hutchinson 2006). There is also potential gender discrimination in relation to restorative justice programmes which has so far received little attention. For example, case studies of victim–offender conferences in the *Restorative Justice* Consultation Paper (Home Office 2003a) suggest that such meetings might have a disparate impact on boys and girls: the reference by a participant in one case study to a 'a broken little girl' is of concern (see Piper 2006b: 178–9).

Whether all these fears materialise, and whether the tensions prove easy or difficult to resolve still remains to be seen.

6.5.2 Discussion exercises

Reparation

Do the following colour association test:

- *without* taking time to think in any conscious or considered way
- decide what colour you think of when focusing on the word 'reparation'.

If you completed this exercise when you first started reading this chapter you may wish to note whether your ideas have changed. If you are doing this for the first time you might wish to consider what parts of the chapter most influenced your response.

This may seem to be a rather odd way of reflecting on the issues dealt with in this chapter. Our intention is to help you appreciate the complexity of the concept of reparation within criminal justice and the ambiguities inherent in the different ways of encouraging or mandating the offender to make amends. At the Online Resource Centre you will find some comments on responses to this exercise.

online
resource
centre

Most of the associations suggested by the chosen colours are part of the complex mix of motivations and concepts that underpins the range of reparative and restorative options currently available in the criminal justice process. Understandings of reparation do indeed range from an account-balancing process, akin to a financial 'eye-for-an-eye' approach, to a visionary and, possibly, idealistic paradigm about social harmony and personal reintegration. Not surprisingly, questions such as 'what is reparation?' or 'what does restorative justice mean?' have no easy answer. As we have seen, it is difficult to isolate one perspective or one influence which has been the major determinant on the development of options to 'make amends' for the harm done to property, people, and relationships. For further reading on these issues see the Online Resource Centre.

online
resource
centre

Sentencing exercise

Decide which outcome is appropriate for Ade. You might refer to the sentencing checklist in Chapter 3 (section 3.2.2) and consider, in particular, any restorative options. The Online Resource Centre discusses possible approaches.

online
resource
centre

Ade, a student aged 20, worked on Saturdays in the local newsagents until the proprietor—Mr B—cut down on part-time staff. Because she knew about a dodgy

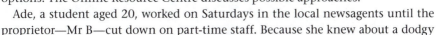

window catch she broke into the shop one night and took several boxes of crisps and chocolate. She sold these to a local youth club for £50 (having been asked to get new supplies), saying that she had lost the till receipt. She was found guilty of burglary at the local magistrates' court. She has no previous convictions.

Would your answer be different if Ade had worked in an electronics factory and had stolen goods worth £5,000?

7

Mitigating the sentence?

SUMMARY

This chapter examines the issue of the impact of a sentence on the offender and whether personal and structure factors should be taken into account in deciding on the appropriate sentence. It considers the role of mitigation in retributivist and utilitarian sentencing, and reviews arguments on reduced culpability where there are social, economic, and medical factors which might make (commensurate) penal outcomes unjust. To illustrate the points raised, financial penalties and policy towards mentally disordered offenders are used as case studies.

7.1 Justifying impact as a sentencing factor

7.1.1 Personal mitigation

In Chapter 3 we examined the factors that could mitigate the seriousness of the offending and also those personal factors about the offender which might be taken into account in order to mitigate the severity of a proportionate sentence (see Chapter 3, section 3.3.2). Such mitigation has always been highly contentious but is an increasingly important issue now because recent research indicates that it plays a crucial role in the sentencing decision (Jacobson and Hough 2007: vii). Earlier research by Hough *et al.* (2003) in England and Wales had also indicated how important mitigation is on the 'in/out' line: in those 'cusp cases' where the seriousness of the offending lies on the community/custodial sentence boundary. In line with this finding, research in Scotland has suggested that the criminal history of the offender is much more influential in justifying the imposition of custody, rather than a community penalty (Tombs 2004). Particularly in the lower courts, sentencers 'claimed to know when "enough was enough", when "the time had just come" for a prison sentence' (Tombs and Jagger 2006) with the result that a relatively minor offence could lead to custody as a 'last resort'. These findings have important implications: 'to move more "cusp cases" down the penalty ladder would require a challenge to these assumptions of the "need" for custody and also a greater awareness of personal mitigation' (Piper 2007: 153). That is why we have incorporated in this second edition more material on this issue than we did in the first edition.

Jacobson and Hough (2007: vii) summarise their key findings as follows:

- personal mitigation takes many forms, relating to: the offender's past; the offender's circumstances at the time of the offence; the offender's response to the offence and prosecution; and the offender's present and future

- personal mitigation plays an important part in the sentencing decision; it can be the decisive factor in choosing a community penalty in preference to imprisonment
- judges cited at least some factor of personal mitigation as relevant to sentencing in almost half of the 162 cases observed in the study
- in just under a third of the 127 cases where the judge made the role of mitigation explicit, personal mitigation was a major—usually the major—factor which pulled the sentence back from immediate custody
- in a just over a quarter of the 127 cases, mitigation including personal factors resulted in a shorter custodial sentence

As we noted in Chapter 3, however, there is very little guidance on personal mitigation although, as Jacobson and Hough point out, 'personal mitigation casts into sharp focus some fundamental issues about sentencing principles and judicial discretion' (2007: 1) and yet they note that 'few of our respondents made explicit the connection between particular sentencing rationales and particular forms of mitigation' (ibid: 39). Indeed one of their respondents, a judge, who described sentencing as 'terrifying because it's a very subjective exercise', commented that 'when the offender comes into court, and you have that first long, hard look at him, you can see so much in that first split second' (ibid: 48). As Jacobson and Hough conclude, 'a descriptive account of the role of mitigation then poses a set of normative questions about the acceptability of current sentencing practice' which necessitate guidance on principles of mitigation from the Sentencing Guidelines Council (ibid: 61, 63).

Considerations of space preclude a more detailed discussion of all forms of personal mitigation but, instead, we will focus on a particular form, that relating to the impact of punishment on the offender, because this ties in with our discussions of the prison experience and of sentencing rationales. In this chapter we will review arguments in favour of placing more emphasis on impact mitigation and will be focusing in some detail on cases relating to the illness, age, employment and parent status of an offender, as well as using financial penalties and the court's approach to mentally disordered offenders to illuminate some of the issues. However, the approach of the courts to other personal mitigation is very similar to their response in the impact cases on which we will focus below. *Robinson* (1993), for example, was a case where the personal circumstances of the postmistress included bankruptcy (because of a large loan and subsequent drop in property values), the loss of employment by her husband and his being in hospital. Nevertheless, the court imposed a custodial sentence because the mitigation did not amount to sufficiently 'exceptional circumstances' to outbalance the seriousness of the offending which involved breach of trust.

We will take up the theme of mitigation and personal circumstances in Chapter 10 where we review socio-economic factors associated with offending as well as related personal factors, such as family issues, which are more difficult to theorise as coming within penal, rather than social, policy. Chapter 11 will then examine the difficulties posed for the Prison Service by the fact that particular types of prisoner and categories of problem are over-represented in the prison population.

7.1.2 **Equal impact**

So far in our analysis of sentencing and punishment, we have looked only tangentially at the question of the impact of a particular punishment on an individual offender. We have reviewed research on the impact on offenders generally of deterrent and incapacitative sentencing (in Chapters 4 and 5) and we will deal with the general effect of rehabilitative penalties in Chapter 12. In Chapter 6 we also focused on the increasing use of confiscation orders so that the punishment is not negated by the offender benefiting from offending (section 6.2.2).

This low priority for the issue of sentence impact is reflective of the fact that, whilst current policy now focuses on the offender and what will deter or reform him most effectively, 'just deserts' is still the dominant sentencing principle. The seriousness of the offence deserves a proportionate amount of punishment which the offender can both anticipate and feel is deserved (see Chapters 2 and 3) and so what Shapland (1981: 55) categorised as 'future personal circumstances' present particular difficulties for retributivist theory precisely because they are future-oriented. Not only that, this is also an issue where public opinion is a policy factor.[1] The public apparently needs to 'see' equality of treatment for similarly serious offences: an outcome that 'looks' too lenient or too severe in comparison to known cases generates a sense of injustice and undermines the legitimacy of the sentencing system. This approach to equality in sentencing appears to assume that the offender is not a variable in this calculation: the impact of the punishment is the same for all offenders, or any differential impact is irrelevant.

Yet it is possible to argue that a retributivist approach to sentencing does not depend on an end product of a fixed amount of punishment for a particular amount of seriousness. It can also operate in terms of a proportionate amount of punishment impact where, in effect, the 'quality' of the experience is taken into account, rather than simply the quantity. This form of equal treatment means that punishments for the same offence may look different and so, whilst the offender and the sentencer may believe that a fairer proportionality has been achieved by a focus on impact, the process may lack legitimacy, particularly to those without knowledge of the individual offender concerned.

If it were accepted that the aim of retributivist sentencing was a just amount of impact for a particular offender, or class of offenders, then the focus of attention would shift to the selection and justification of factors in the life and health of an offender that should be allowed to influence the sentencer in determining impact. These factors could be personal or they could be structural, that is, relating to general social and economic factors. In sentencing policy (but only to a certain extent in the eyes of the public, as we will see in relation to unit fines), the financial means of the offender has been a legitimate factor to take into account—and the courts routinely do so—in the calculation of financial penalties.[2] Apart from fines, the exercise of sentencing discretion has usually focused on the impact of custodial rather than community penalties. Even here, the courts only reluctantly take into account the health and family circumstances of the offender (see section 7.2).

---

[1] For a general discussion of the importance of public opinion see Chapter 1, section 1.3.3.
[2] With the exception of fixed penalties: see section 7.3.4.

There are also utilitarian arguments for taking impact into account. For the utilitarian, the assessment of what Bentham referred to as 'the several circum-stances influencing sensibility' (Bentham 1789: 169) and the calculation of the 'pain' of punishment, are aimed at assessing the likely effectiveness of punish-ment. So Bentham was concerned with the issue of impact in relation to sentence outcome: 'a punishment which is the same in name will not always either really produce, or even so much as appear to others to produce, in two different persons the same degree of pain' (ibid). Therefore, in determining the quantity of punish-ment, he argues, we should take account of 'the several circumstances influenc-ing sensibility' (ibid). Bentham specifies 32 circumstances influencing sensibility, including health and strength, firmness of mind, strength of intellectual powers, moral biases, sympathetic biases, insanity, sex, age, rank, education and social sta-tus (ibid: 52).

Whilst such an extensive list could not be put into operation, more recent com-mentators have focused on the issue of 'sentence feasibility', the likelihood that an offender will be able to undertake the proposed sentence effectively. The utilitar-ian is also frugal: the amount of punishment should be the least possible and the most cost effective for the purpose. Therefore, if an effective outcome is unlikely, this would justify reducing the use and amount of imprisonment, or not impos-ing particular community penalties, if it were the case that, for example, the very old or very ill, were not capable of responding to rehabilitation programmes or were not in a position to reoffend. So Carlen, noting that many offenders have disadvantaged backgrounds in relation to housing, employment and income, com-ments that 'their probation officers might rightly calculate that, given the tensions and frustration already existing in their homes, the clients would be unlikely to complete any [community] order involving home calls, curfews or house arrest' (1989: 22). Further, lack of substitute carers for their children might preclude par-ents from being offered a community service programme, as might lack of public transport to some community schemes (ibid). Carlen also comments that 'it might be unrealistic to expect emotionally and mentally damaged recidivist clients to complete a punitive...order' (ibid).

This chapter will focus on the issue of equality of impact by examining finan-cial penalties, the treatment of mentally disordered offenders and the approach of the courts to (physical) disability, employment, old age, illness, vulnerability in prison, and family circumstances. This is clearly a selective discussion of the many aspects of justice and fairness raised by the question of sentence impact. Limitations of space necessitated the choice of issues on which to focus; personal interest and current policy concerns combined, importantly, with the availability of research and analysis, influenced our selection. Further, other issues, notably race and gender, are addressed in Chapters 9–11. Where we may have neglected issues, this is not to say they are of any lesser importance.

There is an issue regarding the distribution and impact of punishment which is beyond the scope of this book, a problem which Lacey has called 'the prob-lem of uniformity of application': 'should each and every dispositionally respon-sible offender be detected, convicted and punished?' (1998: 404). Like cases are not treated alike if only a small proportion of offenders are detected, arrested, prosecuted and sentenced. There is no punishment impact on the 97 per cent of offenders who do not proceed to sentence. Pettit and Braithwaite have used this as a justification for the differential treatment of offenders on conviction under their republican theory of criminal justice: 'a concern with the material differences between how we punish convicted offenders is not as well motivated as it might be if we were able to identify and indict most offenders' (1998: 330).

The fact that so few offenders proceed to the sentencing court raises political issues concerning the allocation of resources and the minimum levels of policing, prosecutions, and punishment necessary to accord the system legitimacy. It also leads to questions about priorities in crime detection, processing, and punishment: it is not just a matter of the level of resources but the targeting, say, of crimes more or less likely to be committed by the socially disadvantaged. It may also be linked to our focus on ethnic minorities, in section 10.4 below, if **racism** plays a part in any of these decisions.

7.1.3 Disproportionate punishment?

Given the above arguments in favour of taking impact into account in order to construct an 'equal' sentence or an effective one, it is possible to isolate instances where punishment could be seen as disproportionate and so the sentencing for such punishment as unjust. In particular, 'full-time' deprivation of liberty can exacerbate or impose suffering stemming from personal circumstances or characteristics, whilst the Prison Service has a limited capacity to treat inmates differentially (see Chapter 11). Those who are very young, ill, old or disabled, and those who have family members who have depended on them, may suffer greater physical and psychological harm from a lack of freedom than do other inmates. In addition, those whose offending attracts the most social denunciation, notably those who sexually assault or murder children, also face a high risk of ostracism or harm from their fellow prisoners.

For all these types of offender, their vulnerability is likely to make the punishment disproportionately worse for them. As Tonry has observed:

> In subjective terms...two years' imprisonment in a single setting will have very different meanings to different offenders who have committed the same crime. Two years' imprisonment in a maximum security prison may be a rite of passage for a Los Angeles gang member. For an attractive, effeminate twenty-year old, it may mean the terror of repeated sexual victimization. For a forty-year-old head of household, it may mean the loss of a job and a home and a family. For an unhealthy seventy-five-year old, it may mean a death sentence.
>
> (Tonry 1996: 19)

One particularly problematic category of offenders is mentally disordered offenders.

Mentally disordered offenders

The offender who has been deemed sufficiently mentally 'well' to plead guilty or to be found guilty may, nevertheless, be sufficiently mentally ill to come within the relevant provisions of the Mental Health Act 1983. Those provisions allow the sentencing court to treat the offender as one whom Parliament has decided need not be punished after conviction. The rationale for this exception is not entirely clear. Those offenders deemed to be mentally disordered have also been held to be criminally liable, and so a penal response which is proportionate to culpability is theoretically justifiable and is still open to the courts. We return to the choice of therapeutic or punitive disposals—and the impact issues that choice raises—in section 7.4.

One possible justification for special provisions is that the offender may be treated unfairly if the sentencing outcome is equal to that of a mentally 'normal' offender: the impact of a particular punishment may be greater for the mentally disordered offender. Further, the offender may be less receptive, because of mental illness, to the intended utilitarian effect of punishment, whether that be deterrence or rehabilitation. Peay (2002: 746) has referred to the need for a 'capacity-based intervention' (for all offenders) so that therapeutic, crime reduction and reparative measures can be tailored to the individual capacity—abilities and vulnerabilities—of the offender. Without taking into account mental illness, the retributivist punishment may be too severe—the quantum may be unjustifiable—and the utilitarian or restorative purposes may be frustrated and pointless.

There are, of course, valid arguments against admitting impact as a mitigating factor (Easton 2008c) and we shall examine them in more detail in Chapter 10. To summarise, such mitigation may not satisfy the requirements of retribution and denunciation and may entail a loss of deterrent effect as some classes of offender might feel they can offend with impunity because they would not have to pay much or would not be sent to prison for long. It can also be argued that it is not unjust to ignore mitigating factors: the offender whose particular circumstances are dire should know that his punishment will have more serious impact. This equates to a 'you should have thought of this before you offended' approach to offenders for whom punishment will impact particularly harshly on family, health, or social and employment status.

7.2 Impact as mitigation in practice

7.2.1 The approach of the Court of Appeal

In practice it is possible for the defence to argue successfully that the particular impact of the sentence on the offender should be treated as a mitigating factor. However, whilst sentencers, from magistrates up to the Court of Appeal, have accepted such arguments from time to time,[3] there is no duty on the sentencer to take impact into account, or for mitigation to have any precedence over factors relating to the gravity of the offence (see Chapter 3, section 3.3.2). Further, if impact operates as a mitigating factor it can only lead to a reduction in sentence, it cannot operate to increase a sentence to allow for greater equality of impact across the board. Given the retributivist approach to mitigation, 'character', including the propensity—or not—to offend, cannot be taken into account as mitigation although it could be considered in assessing dangerousness (Hudson 2003: 30–1).

---

[3] See, for example, Shapland (1981) for research on the process of, and speeches in, mitigation; Walker (1999: 100–3) on the 'exceptional circumstances' justifications for suspending a prison sentence; Jacobson and Hough for their recent research in relation to the influence of physical illness and employment issues on sentencing in the Crown Court (2007: 36–7).

Whilst there is, as yet, no detailed guidance from the Sentencing Guidelines Council (SGC), the Court of Appeal has tried 'to bring some order to an area of law which may appear as chaotic as some of the lives under review' but, in doing so, has tended to treat mitigating factors as 'of little significance' (Piper 2007: 142). The first concern of judges is not to downgrade a message about seriousness. So, if the court is dealing with what it considers to be serious offending, the court is anxious not to reduce the potential deterrent effects or the amount of censure by reducing a sentence. Therefore, if the circumstances of the offending are relatively less serious then the courts are more likely to take into account mitigation based on impact.

If, when impact factors are taken into account, the courts explicitly justify their approach then the reduction in sentence is generally explained as an exceptional act of mercy. For example, the following statement made by Lord Lane CJ almost two decades ago in *Attorney-General's Reference (No. 4 of 1989)* (1989) was recently endorsed by Sir Igor Judge when declining to increase the sentence on an 81-year-old sex offender: 'Leniency is not in itself a vice. That mercy should season justice is a proposition as soundly based in law as it is in literature' (*Attorney-General's Reference No. 73 of 2006* (2006)) and one could argue that the courts are 'mean with mercy' (Piper 2007: 142). This approach has led to two unhelpful outcomes: there is no clear or clearly articulated justification for taking impact mitigation into account and, in the current sentencing climate with higher levels of seriousness accorded to particular offences and factors, it is now less likely that mitigation based on impact will influence sentencing.

7.2.2 **The offender: vulnerability and age**

The Court of Appeal has been faced with the issue of added impact of punishment stemming from the personal vulnerability of a prisoner, whether stemming from old age, youth or the expected 'dangers' of prison life. When being of an advanced age is allowed as mitigation, the justification is on grounds of physical infirmity and also of shorter life expectancy. Personal mitigation in *Varden* (1981) rested on old age but also the issue was how far the circumstances in which a sentence would be served should be taken into account.[4] Varden was a man of 71, who had unlawful sex with a 13-year-old child with severe learning difficulties. He would inevitably be spending his sentence under Rule 45 (of Prison Rules 1999, formerly R.43) in a vulnerable prisoner unit where a prisoner is segregated for his own protection. The statutory maximum for that offence was two years and the normal sentence for his particular offence would be quite near the maximum. His age and likely segregation were taken into account as mitigating factors and he was given an eight-month prison sentence.

However, other cases at that time held that the impact of Rule 45 was not relevant and, more recently, *Parker* (1996) took the same approach. The appellant had been given a sentence of 18 months for a robbery in which he had shaken a 16-year-old girl in the street, she had fallen down and he had tried to pull off her rucksack. He appealed because he was a socially isolated person who was bullied and assaulted in prison and so was put on Rule 45 for his protection. But the Court of Appeal said that it was not relevant to sentencing that an offender found it exceptionally hard

---

[4] See Ashworth (1995: 144) for further discussion of 'collateral consequences'.

to adjust to prison life, an approach also taken in *Nall-Cain* where a sentence of five years imposed on Lord Brocket was upheld because 'a defendant's treatment by other inmates is not generally a factor to which this court can have proper regard' (1998 at 150, *per* Rose LJ).

The overriding importance of offence gravity is also evident in a decision on the minimum term to be served by an elderly prisoner on an indeterminate sentence. *Bata* (2006) was an application for a reduction in his 10-year minimum term (previously notified by the Secretary of State) by an 80-year-old prisoner who had been sentenced to life for murder imposed for shooting a person on his neighbouring allotment at close range. The judge believed that the 10-year minimum already incorporated a considerable reduction for old age and illness, given the seriousness of the circumstances of the offending.

The effect of the increasing number of long determinate and indeterminate sentences, together with this cautious approach to reducing the sentence of a serious offender on account of old age, has had an effect on the composition of the prison population which ought, perhaps, to be further taken into account by sentencers. There are now more prisoners serving life sentences than in the early 1990s and more prisoners serving indeterminate sentences for public protection. Older prisoners are also more likely than younger prisoners to be serving longer sentences because of the type of offences committed. They may experience particular problems if they are held far from home as this will make it hard for them to maintain family ties if their visitors are also older. They may also be more likely to suffer health problems associated with longevity.

Older prisoners, that is prisoners aged 50 or more, constituted 9 per cent of sentenced male prisoners and 6 per cent of sentenced female prisoners in 2006 (Ministry of Justice 2007a: 77). In 2006 there were 972 receptions into prison of persons under an immediate custodial sentence aged over 60, compared to 538 in 1996 (ibid: 87). Prisoners in the 60+ years old category also had the largest percentage increase (149 per cent) in the decade 1996–2006, the 40–49-year-old age group increased by 97 per cent and the 50–59 group by 74 per cent (ibid: 96). This contrasted with an increase of 27 per cent for the 21–24 age group. The number of older women prisoners has also increased (see Wahidin 2004). These numbers may well increase further as the impact of the guidelines for the minimum term for murder takes effect. The Lord Chief Justice, Lord Phillips, has warned that in 30 years' time the prisons will be full of geriatric lifers (Phillips 2007). Steiner (2003) has drawn attention to the formal system for dealing with the early release of seriously ill and elderly prisoners introduced in France in 2003 and asks whether a similar reform should not also be considered for England and Wales.

Of course there are also issues around age and vulnerability in relation to younger offenders. In Chapter 8 we examine the justifications for treating children who offend differently and in Chapter 13 we examine the use of custodial penalties for children and young people, where it is acknowledged that youth is a factor to be taken into account. We noted above that old age may be accepted as mitigation: the offender has not much time left and there is a common notion that time 'goes more quickly' the older a person is. When youth is taken into consideration it rests on the notions of reduced culpability and also loss of precious 'developmental time'. There is also research based on offenders 'doing time' which examines perceptions of time itself. This has shown that for young prisoners time does pass slowly, and examines the various techniques and strategies that may be used to make time go more quickly (Cope 2003).[5]

Recent cases would also suggest that the courts consider 'youth', as with other impact mitigation, of little significance if the offending is very serious. In *Attorney-General's Reference (Nos 21 and 22 of 2004)* (2004), for example, where the offenders were aged 17 and 19, the court stated that, for such types of offending (robbery late at night on public transport as part of group), a custodial sentence must be imposed 'save in the most exceptional cases, such exceptions arising, for example, by reasons of extreme youth'. No distinction was made between the two offenders on grounds of age and no reduction was given for age. Similarly, the fact that an 18-year-old had a mental age of 10-and-a-half had little influence on the decision in a case involving a series of offences with very serious aggravating factors: '[the] youth and low intelligence of the second offender, provide no explanation and only modest mitigation' (*Attorney General's Reference (Nos 39, 40 and 41 of 2005)* [2005] at 26, *per* Holland J).

For reasons of space, we have neglected the age category of 18–20-year-old offenders in this book. They were ignored by the reforms of the Crime and Disorder Act (CDA) 1998 which apply to those under 18, and Government intentions to improve the standard of custodial accommodation and offending programmes have not led to significant improvements. 'Improved regimes for the under 18s have thrown into sharp relief the poor treatment of 18–20-year-olds', as revealed in reports of the Chief Inspector of Prisons (Lyon 2003: 28) and in a recent briefing by the Prison Reform Trust (2007a). This is an important issue and one which deserves a much higher profile than is possible within the constraints of this book.

7.2.3 Illness and disability as mitigation

There are also issues for sentencers raised by the resource difficulties in relation to the ill and disabled in prison. The increase in the size of the prison population and the increase in older prisoners have also entailed a growth in the number of prisoners with disabilities and serious illnesses. The Disability Discrimination Act 2005 applies to prisons so the issue of accessibility of resources and treatment is becoming more important. More research is now being undertaken on this particular group (see Crawley and Sparks 2005, 2008) and the new Commission for Equality and Human Rights has taken over the role of the Disability Rights Commission and will enforce duties under the Act. In the latest report by the Chief Inspector of Prisons, women with disabilities were particularly critical of a range of services, including healthcare (HM Chief Inspector of Prisons 2008: 28).

However, the guideline judgment given in *Bernard* (1997) makes clear that a medical condition that might in the future affect life expectancy does not preclude a prison sentence (see Ashworth and Player 1998: 256–61). Cases before and after *Bernard* suggest, however, that a high risk of (earlier) death because of prison conditions and facilities may be accepted by the court as excessive impact of punishment which merits a reduction in sentence. In *Moore* (1990) and *Stark* (1992)

---

[5] See also Chapter 4 and the texts by Clemmer (1940) and Toch (1976) on 'survival' techniques used by prisoners generally.

the Appeal Court decided that the fact that Moore was HIV positive and Stark was suffering from AIDS was not relevant to sentence—it was a matter for the exercise of the Royal Prerogative. In *Green and Leatherbarrow* (1992) Green had sickle cell anaemia and Leatherbarrow had chronic emphysema. Green's sentence had been fixed at 18 months (and would have been 5 years if the illness had not been taken into account).[6] The Court of Appeal suspended 14 months of the 18-month sentence so he could be released immediately because of the risk of sudden death if there were no immediate access to suitable medical facilities.[7] Leatherbarrow's 15-month sentence had not taken the illness into account; on appeal, 8 months of the sentence were suspended to allow immediate release.

Furthermore, in *Avis, Thomas, Torrington, Marques and Goldsmith* (1997), for example, the Court's approach was a common one. This was a guideline judgment for firearms offences where, in relation to some of the appellants, old age and illness were submitted as mitigating factors, but the Court argued that the aggravating factors outweighed the mitigation. It is, therefore, relatively rare for the Court of Appeal to find it appropriate to downgrade a message about seriousness by taking into account factors impacting on the prison experience.

A case involving a disabled prisoner makes clear that the courts will only apply 'mercy' when, as in equity, the claimant has clean hands. Where the court believes that the offender has 'traded' on his disability then it is unlikely any reduction in sentence will be given. Indeed, the facts might aggravate seriousness as in *Kesler* (2005) where Ouseley J, having noted that '[h]e used to give the impression of innocent behaviour by going out with his dog to collect the drugs, and because of his disability had a stick, but it was hollowed out so that he could keep his drugs in it' (at 8), concluded as follows, '[i]t is plain that he has been using his health as a means of obtaining sympathy and of deception and he has already gained from his previous sentences such benefit as could possibly be accorded to him for those matters' (at 14).

7.2.4 Loss of employment

The same balancing approach has been taken in relation to expected loss of employment resulting from conviction or imprisonment. As we saw in Chapter 3 (section 3.2.5), in *Hubbard* (2002), a case concerning abuse of trust in relation to a sexual offence, the Court of Appeal upheld a two-year sentence, apparently not taking into account the devastating personal consequences for the teacher. Generally, where the offence is serious the loss of employment is not given any weight. Where the offence is less serious and where job loss is accompanied by other mitigation (*Dockerill* (1988), *O'Hara* (2004)), it may be taken into account. Loss of employment is also more likely to be taken into account if it impacts on third parties, whether they are family members or employees of the offender's business.

However, recent research provides 'some evidence that a defendant's steady job, or involvement in studies or vocational training, can be a mitigating factor', including evidence from one case where the 23-year-old offender was in the process of completing entry to the Marines and 'the judge stressed that the offence

---

[6] For further discussion on these issues, see Ashworth (2000: 153–5).
[7] See Dyson and Boswell (2006) for information about the medical context for *Green*.

deserved custody but passed a community sentence—stating that a custodial sentence would prevent him "taking a course in your life that could do all of us some good"' (Jacobson and Hough 2007: 37).

There is, however, an ambivalence here which is reflected in public opinion. As Tonry has pointed out,

[t]he relevance of employment to sentencing varies with circumstances. Most people believe it is irrelevant that a wealthy securities law violator will, if imprisoned, lose his or her job...People have widely divergent views on whether a lower-middle-class head of household's job loss, if imprisoned, is relevant...From the perspective that employed defendants are often middle-class, and more likely than unemployed defendants to be white, concern about racial and class disparities may make job loss appear irrelevant.

(1996: 22–3)

There is also the point made earlier: 'although it seems reasonable to view the loss of a job as a quasi-fine, taking prospective job loss into account unintentionally discriminates against the unemployed who are unfortunate enough to have no job to lose!' (Levi 1989: 432).

Even if loss of employment is not a mitigation issue, employment status may well affect the choice of sentence. Research some time ago by Crow and Simon (1987), based on six magistrates' courts, examined unemployment rates and sentencing statistics in 1974–84, controlling for courts with above- and below-average custody rates and with un/employment categories. Of the six courts, all imposed fines more often on the employed, four courts used community service orders more for the unemployed and two courts used immediate custody more for the unemployed. Therefore, for the unemployed, the movement could be up or down the scale of penalties. Further, Crow and Simon concluded that the effect of employment status on sentence was statistically small and interviews with magistrates confirmed that they gave more weight to the seriousness of the offending and to criminal record.

However, the small differences stemming from employment status could have a 'ratchet' effect in relation to sentencing on a subsequent conviction whilst further research in the early 1990s concluded that 'the sentencing of unemployed offenders differs considerably from the sentencing of those in employment' (Home Office 1994a: para 17). It found that 69 per cent of all adult male offenders sentenced to indictable offences in one study period were unemployed at the time they were sentenced and noted that some offenders lost their jobs following arrest (ibid: para 15).

Unemployment is another dimension of the financial circumstances of the offender which are considered in relation to the issue of compensation orders (see Chapter 6). But the clearest impact of wealth and poverty is in relation to fines, which we will deal with in section 7.3 below.

7.2.5 Separation from children

The case of *Mills* (2002), also discussed in Chapter 3, does seem to allow as mitigation the particular impact, if the offender is a mother, of being allocated to a prison far from her home and children.[8] This can be theorised as causing a

---

[8] For a review of judicial thinking in the 1960s on the social consequences of conviction and the use of mitigation, see Martin and Webster (1971).

disproportionate impact of punishment because the sorrow at loss of contact with your child is greater for the main care-giver, usually the mother, and because a female prisoner is likely to be further away from home than a male prisoner and so the visits will be less frequent (see Chapter 11, section 11.3.2). There is, also, a growing concern about the separation of fathers from their children, perhaps as a spin-off from the high profile given to fathers' groups campaigning for more contact with their children on separation and divorce (see Watson and Rice 2004). Both these circumstances, to a greater or lesser extent, could be included in the calculation of proportionate impact because the extra suffering, particularly for mothers, is now well documented.

Although we note in Chapter 11 (section 11.5.3) that there might be some draw-backs for women in the use of the intermittent custody order (see Chapter 3, section 3.1.3), it would, if ever implemented, provide a means of imposing custody which does not totally disrupt care-giving relationships. When such an order was suggested in a Green Paper issued as long ago as 1984,[9] the explicit aim was to reduce the disruption of family ties and loss of employment which may result from continuous custody. The intention of the new provision in the Criminal Justice Act (CJA) 2003 was also to 'maintain jobs, family ties or education, all of which have been shown to play a part in reducing reoffending' (Explanatory Notes to the Act). In line with this, SGC guidance notes '[t]he circumstances of the offender are likely to be the determining factor in deciding whether an intermittent custody order is appropriate' (Sentencing Guidelines Council 2004c: para 2.3.10).

7.3 Equality of impact: a focus on fines

7.3.1 Fines as punishment

Fines might appear to be the easiest punishment to fix proportionately, there being available a very detailed tariff of pounds and pence. On the other hand, it has been argued that financial penalties constitute a particular difficulty in operationalising proportionality. The argument is that the issue of equality of impact is much more significant and much more 'compensatable' in relation to fines than for other penalties. The problematic categories of offender are also more clearly defined: the very poor, particularly those dependent on state benefits and the unemployed, and the very rich. There is also the policy imperative to encourage the use of non-custodial sentences, including fines, to reduce the use of custodial penalties.

A fine is a presumptive sentence in the sense that it can be imposed without passing a seriousness hurdle as is the case with custodial and community penalties (see Chapter 3). A fine can be used when the statutory criteria do not apply, so it is suitable for offences which are not at the top end of the seriousness scale. However, a fine can be added to other penalties (CJA 2003, s 163) and can be imposed in magistrates' and Crown Courts (though there is a maximum limit—set at £5,000 in 2002—in magistrates' courts). It should, then, be a very useful penalty and in numerical terms it has been: in 1995, 75 per cent of all those dealt with by the

---

[9] *Intermittent Custody*, Cmnd 9281, London, HMSO.

courts were fined (Brownlee 1998b: 137) though this had dropped to 69 per cent in the official statistics for 2002.

The fine has been the most commonly used penalty for a long time but its use is declining (Brownlee 1998b: 137) whilst the use of prison and probation has increased by a quarter since 1996 (Carter 2003: 3). In magistrates' courts, whilst the number of male offenders over 21-years-old found guilty for indictable offences was around 14,000 in 1975 and in 2000, the proportion being given a fine decreased from 63.2 per cent to 33.5 per cent in that time whilst the numbers being given immediate custody or transferred to the Crown Court for sentencing increased (see Tarling 2006: 29–31). Furthermore, the use of financial penalties in the Crown Court has decreased by 46 per cent over the period 1995–2006 (Carter 2007: 7). For the latest statistics see Figures 7.1 and 7.2 below, which are taken from *Sentencing Statistics 2006* (Ministry of Justice 2007e).

Given that the policy aim is to reduce the use of custody for all but the most ser-ious offences, why should this decline in the use of fines occur? Young (1989: 46) argued that earlier fluctuations were due to changes in ideas about whether a fine is a suitable means of punishing an offender and, therefore, whether it is perceived as 'really' a punishment or not. It is certainly the case that one of the causes of this ambivalence over fines is that it is the designated penalty for those categories of offence which some sections of the population do not regard as 'really' criminal. Parking offences and regulatory offences like those in relation to TV licences might come into this category. More controversially, other motoring offences—such as speeding—and health and safety infractions might also be included (see Corbett 2000; Carter 2003). Where citizens do not regard an offence as really criminal, they do not perceive the outcome as a punishment but rationalise it instead as a tax—a morally neutral nuisance which is the occasional result of choosing not to obey what are deemed as non-criminal regulations. The problem is that such thinking then influences the conceptualisation of financial penalties for 'real' crimes.

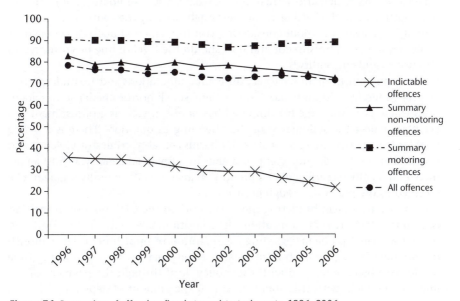

Figure 7.1 Proportion of offenders fined at magistrates' courts, 1996–2006.

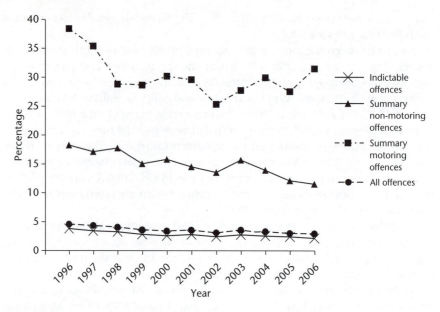

Figure 7.2 Proportion of offenders fined at the Crown Court, 1996–2006.

In relation to property offences there is the added difficulty that 'the value of the punishment must not be less in any case than what is sufficient to outweigh that of the profit of the crime' (Bentham 1789: 166). From a utilitarian perspective, the fine or other punishment, taken together with any compensation and confiscation orders, must be sufficient to make committing the crime unprofitable, otherwise there is no deterrent effect. From a retributivist perspective, as we have seen, commensurability would also be undermined by disregarding the profits of crime.

The difficulty which arises, then, is this: what amount of financial punishment is proportionate to the level of seriousness established by the court? This question cannot be answered without considering two fundamental questions: how does a fine operate as a punishment and how should the level of fine be correlated to seriousness and culpability?

Money and punishment have very different connotations and are underpinned by very different cultural values. So there are 'shock horror' media stories about cases where even the large fine imposed has not been seen as a punishment sufficient to reflect the seriousness of the offending in question. There is a strong popular feeling that there are particular harms, notably crimes of violence and sexual offences, that are not 'compensatable' by a financial penalty. Whilst a fine, then, may legally be sufficient and proportionate to gravity, morally it may not be accepted by the public as enough punishment.

So, a major problem hindering the use of fines in the UK, and also in the USA (see Tonry 1996: 124–7), is its ambivalent position as a punishment. However, there is a related problem regarding the quantum of punishment. Fines punish the offender by depriving him of whatever consumables or non-working time would have been purchased with the money 'lost' through the payment of the fine. The problem with this approach is that the amount of deprivation or loss is affected by how much disposable income the individual retains, or how much impact the fine has on the person's financial circumstances. It could be theorised as the deprivation of the amount of time, 'liberty', required to earn enough to replenish personal savings. As Tonry points out, this is possible: some European states and some states in the USA have a more positive attitude to fines as punishment. For example, in the Netherlands a fine is legally presumed to be the preferred penalty for every crime and reasons need to be given for rebutting this presumption (Tonry 1996: 124).

7.3.2 Units of financial deprivation

Two approaches are possible for correlating seriousness with an amount of money:

- to have a fixed fine for each amount of seriousness (for example, by fixing a certain sum of money as the fine for each offence and with specified factors to take the amount above or below the starting point)
- to have a unit of financial deprivation correlated with each unit of seriousness (that is, the penalty is fixed at a particular percentage of the offender's financial resources for a specified level of seriousness).

The outcome in terms of an amount of money will often be very different. Let us take the scenario of a £2,000 fine which is considered adequate punishment for a specified serious offence. The sentencer and the public may be happy with that amount and justice may be perceived to have been done. But students with an income of £6,000 are left below the breadline, whereas those on £60,000 may not be unduly concerned. If, instead of 'visible' equality of justice, we decide to aim at equality of impact then either the fine imposed on the student need be only £200 or, instead, £20,000 on the high earner, so that both 'suffer' an equal impact on their lives in terms of deprivation of goods that can no longer be purchased. However, the £200 fine might appear to the media as proof that the student had 'got away with it'. On the other hand, a £2,000 or £20,000 fine would seem to be a very large amount of money to a person who is not used to the state depriving him of resources, and who feels the fine is disproportionate and unjust in comparison with the student's fine.

These ambivalences are illustrated by some of the earlier reported cases. In *Markwick* (1953) a wealthy man was fined £500 for stealing—in breach of trust— what would now be 25p from a golf club changing room where he was a member. The original court believed that amount reflected the gravity of the offence and the offender could afford to pay it. On appeal the Court increased the sentence to two months' imprisonment, justified on the ground that imposing a high fine instead of custody 'would give prisoners of means an opportunity of buying themselves out of being sent to prison'. On the other hand, in *Fairbairn* (1980), where a fine of £7,500 and a custodial sentence were imposed to reflect both the gravity of the offence and the offender's ability to pay, the fine was reduced on appeal to £1,000 on the grounds that any higher sum was disproportionate because only £700 had been stolen. Yet the offender owned two houses and, in terms of financial impact, £1,000 was relatively lenient.

The approach of English sentencing law and practice until 1991 was to use a fixed amount of fine which could be reduced by the court if the offender was unable to pay. At the end of the 1980s, however, the government pursued the idea of 'day fines' which were already being used in parts of the USA and in Scandinavia. These were called day fines because what the offender earns in a day became the basis for assessments of the total fine. In England such a scheme was successfully piloted (see Gibson 1990), though referred to as 'unit fines', and was implemented across the country for magistrates' courts by means of s 18 of the CJA 1991.

In the original s 18, seriousness was designated by a number of units from 1–50. The fine was then determined by multiplying the number of units by an amount of money calculated on the basis of the offender's income. This figure was one-third of the offender's disposable income after deductions as specified in the regulations. 'Determining the number of units of "blameworthiness" was, in essence, the total extent of the judicial function' (Brownlee 1998b: 144). Problems arose where the offender refused to submit details of his financial circumstances to the court for assessing this sum. The legislation provided for this by allowing the courts to take the highest figure where no information was forthcoming. The instances where this happened were highly publicised in sections of the media and brought disrepute on the system.

Nevertheless, this does not explain why the original s 18 was replaced so quickly in 1993 by what has been referred to as 'perhaps the most astonishing and unjustified *volte-face* in the history of the English Criminal Justice System' (Cavadino and Dignan 2002: 128). It is true that the scheme rolled out was more draconian than the scheme piloted but the assessment problems could have been overcome, and the education of the public on the principle of equal impact could have been attempted. At the time, Brian Block, a lay magistrate, suggested that the sense of outrage was fuelled by better-off members of society: 'Whereas previously a well-heeled driver exceeding the speed limit by about 20 m.p.h. would have been fined around £60, he is now likely to be fined £500. Failing to comply with a traffic sign, going through a light on red or parking on a zig-zag was previously worth the price of a meal out for two; now it can cost as much as taking the family to Florida' (1993: 308). The Magistrates' Association, although concerned at their loss of discretion, apparently did not push for the abolition of unit fines (Brownlee 1998b: 146) but the Conservative government, having suffered significant losses in by-elections in 1993,[10] did not wish to alienate public opinion further.

Whatever the political imperatives, a new s 18 was inserted by s 65 of the CJA 1993 and largely re-enacted in the PCCSA 2000 (s 128). These provisions in effect returned the situation to what it had been before 1991 with one difference: the court could raise as well as lower the amount of the fine in taking the offender's means into account. Research would suggest that magistrates returned to imposing lower than proportionate-to-impact fines on the employed (Brownlee 1998b: 147). Since 1993, therefore, the legal framework for imposing fines has been largely as before the CJA 1991 and ss 162–165 of the CJA 2003 largely re-enact ss 126–129 of the PCCSA 2000.

However, the wheel is again turning: a new system of unit fines was proposed in the Carter Report (2003). Under the heading 'Fines rebuilt as a creditable punishment', the proposal was that fines should replace the 30 per cent of current community orders imposed on low-risk offenders (2003: 27). The Report then

---

[10] See http://www.election.demon.co.uk/.

explained that 'day fines' are used successfully in much of Europe and should be introduced in England and Wales. There is no mention of the ill-fated unit fines system although the report did propose, perhaps with the English experience in mind, that fixed penalty and minor offences should be excluded to 'avoid excessive fines for very low level crimes' (ibid). Given also that the Report proposed that the maximum deduction from benefit for fine payment should be increased, equality of impact would seem to be ruled out for the least serious offences and for the poorest, despite the argument that day fines would 'offer a transparent link with ability to pay' (ibid).

The Government's response to the proposed day fines was that it was 'something we will explore further' (Home Office 2004b: Annex para 35)[11] and to endorse the greater use of 'revitalised fines' for low-risk offenders (ibid: para 34). A study of two large city-centre magistrates' courts, which included interviews with magistrates, civilian enforcement officers, and defendants, also supports the establishment of a new system akin to unit fines (Moore 2003a). Examining fine default, Moore found that magistrates were not paying sufficient attention to the financial circumstances of offenders (ibid: 19) and that in some cases it might not be possible to implement the principle that a fine should have detrimental impact but not cause significant financial hardship (ibid: 23–5). This finding might militate against the Carter Report's proposal to move more offenders onto fines.

The Management of Offenders and Sentencing Bill, introduced in January 2005, consequently proposed to amend s 164 of the CJA 2003 so that fines would be fixed by reference to daily disposable income. The Bill was not passed before Parliament was prorogued for the General Election and, although the Queen's Speech of 17 May 2005 stated that the Bill would be reintroduced it was not, either in 2005–6 or 2006–7, and the Criminal Justice and Immigration (CJI) Act 2008 does not include such provision.

The Sentencing Commission for Scotland has recently published its own report on day fines. The Chairman's Foreword, however, includes the following statement:

We do not consider that there is at present a compelling case to change the existing system governing the imposition of fines in this country. While a number of other European jurisdictions operate a system of unit or day fines, we do not consider that a simple, reliable and cost-effective method of obtaining information on offenders' income currently exists in Scotland. The availability of such a method is vital to the success of any such system (Rt Hon Lord Macfadyen).[12]

This failure to proceed with the proposed reform is disappointing as a more impact-based system of fines would be both justifiable and more just. There is also no reason, given good management, why the problems of unit fines in 1992–3 should be repeated. There are, nevertheless, some difficulties with such a system. Greene argues that the unit fine 'is best suited for defendants with regular, measurable (and legal) income flow' (1998: 269) and this will clearly not apply to all offenders. Its success also depends on an efficient collection and enforcement administrative system—an issue which we will now examine.

---

[11] See http://www.homeoffice.gov.uk/docs2/changinglives.pdf and also the Online Resource Centre.

[12] See http://www.scottishsentencingcommission.gov.uk/docs/fines/basis%20-%20fines.pdf.

online
resource
centre

7.3.3 Default and enforcement

Fines become payable as soon as imposed but guidance has established that payment can be by instalments. These are not normally spread over more than 12 months, concern being that a long repayment period allows the poorer offender to be fined to an amount that has more impact than the same amount imposed on an offender who can afford to pay it immediately. *Olliver* (1989) allowed the period to be, exceptionally, 24 months. Despite these provisions many offenders do not pay any or all of their fine. The full payment rate for fines was only 62 per cent in 1999–2000, dropping to 55 per cent in 2002–3.[13]

The Government, reflecting public concerns, considers the problem of fine default to be a major reason why fines are not used more extensively. According to their website, 'the National Criminal Justice Board's vision for 2008 is that, "rigorous enforcement will revolutionise compliance with sentences and orders of the court"'[14] and the Courts Act 2003, amending parts of previous legislation, is said to provide a new framework for fine enforcement. A Unified Courts Agency was created, operating formally from April 2005, and heightened policy priority has been given to enforcement performance. The phased implementation of a new National Enforcement Service began in April 2007.[15]

Section 82 of the Magistrates' Courts Act 1980 provides the criteria for imposing custody on fine default. Sections 79–118 provide other process options and powers for reviewing and enforcing fines. Home Office research in the mid-1990s found that, despite Best Practice Guidelines issued in 1992 and 1996, there was no one standard practice—attachment of earnings or deduction from benefit, distress warrants,[16] reviews, warrants for arrest—by which fines were enforced (Whittacker and Mackie 1997: 5). Half of the defaulters in the sample had more than one outstanding fine. The average amount outstanding was £358 and four out of five defaulters owed less than £500 (ibid: 15). The main reasons defaulters gave for their fine arrears were that there had been a (detrimental) change in their financial circumstances since the fine was imposed and/or that they had other financial commitments and debts. Women defaulters were typically in very restricted financial circumstances with 81 per cent having dependent children and only 11 per cent were in employment, whilst 22 per cent of male defaulters were unemployed (ibid: 13–14).

The Report of the Select Committee on Public Accounts found that, of a total of £397 million of fines imposed in 2001–2, around 59 per cent were collected, but £58 million were written off (largely because the offender could not be traced), and £90 million of fines were cancelled because of successful appeals or a significant change of circumstances (2002: para 2). There were wide variations in the collection rate with, for example, 34 per cent in Merseyside and 89 per cent in Dorset. The Report commented, very critically, that 'payment of fines appears to

---

[13] But standing at 91 per cent in the period April 2006–January 2007 (Harriet Harman, Minister of State, Department for Constitutional Affairs, Hansard HC 16 April 2007, Column 9W).

[14] See http://lcjb.cjsonline.gov.uk/ncjb/42.html.

[15] See Einat (2004) for a review of empirical research on the Israeli enforcement system introduced in 1995 and also other research on enforcement in Europe and the USA.

[16] For a discussion of the use of distress warrants, see Moore (2003b).

be almost voluntary over much of the country' (ibid: para 4), explaining the situation by reference to ineffective administration and the (former) Lord Chancellor's Department's failure to prioritise the issue. They suggested improving the use of IT systems and more feedback to magistrates.

Until the early 1990s immediate or suspended prison sentences were the main response to fine default. Statistics suggest that reliance on this sanction decreased and that there was a different climate in the courts towards the end of the 1990s (see Brownlee 1998b: 148–9 for references). More recently, Mackie *et al.* found that, whilst magistrates were concerned at the 'increasing sophistication and determination' of offenders to escape paying financial penalties, it was acknowledged that fines were likely to impact disproportionately on offenders with limited means and that fines now often 'seemed like the imposition of "debt" rather than punishment' (2003: 28; see also Raine *et al.* 2004).

The Crime (Sentences) Act 1997 extended the availability of non-custodial penalties for fine default. The CJA 2003 consolidates and augments the possible sanctions. Section 300 empowers magistrates to impose a 'default order' whereby the offender must comply with an unpaid work or curfew requirement. This latter requirement may include electronic monitoring, as can community orders (s 177(3) and (4)).[17] Section 301 allows the magistrates' court to disqualify the defaulter from driving for a period of up to 12 months.

Under the Fines Collection (Amendment) Regulations 2004[18] the Department for Constitutional Affairs is piloting a range of new fine-collection measures including a new type of attachment of earnings order.[19] The Criminal Justice and Immigration (CJI) Act 2008 also includes a provision to improve the procedures for disclosure of information in order to enforce fines by amending Part 3 of Schedule 5 to the Courts Act 2003 in relation to attachment of earnings orders and applications for benefit deductions.[20]

The difficulty is that, while some offenders are in the 'won't pay' category which appears to be the focus of the Select Committee's concern, others 'can't pay': their non-payment is not necessarily wilful. Even research evidence that people pay fines at the last minute—when threatened with an imminent custodial order—does not prove they could have paid all along. It is also explained by the generosity of friends who offer financial help only when that threat is likely to be implemented (Morris and Gelsthorpe 1990: 842). Where offenders have genuine difficulties in paying even small fines, for example many of the single mothers fined for non-payment of their TV licence, 'enforcement, be it deductions from benefits that are already inadequate, seizure and sale of family possessions, or especially imprisonment, that is not mitigated by positive intervention and assistance in other areas of life can only serve to reinforce existing patterns of social inequality in the criminal justice system' (Brownlee 1998b: 151).

---

[17] The CJI Act 2008 amends s 300 of the Criminal Justice Act 2003 to give the courts the power to impose an attendance centre requirement on a fine defaulter aged 16–24.

[18] Attachment of earnings: SI 2004 No. 1407

[19] See http://www.hmso.gov.uk/si/si2004/20041407.htm; http://www.paypershop.com/news-cat/courtak.html.

[20] Section 41 of the Act inserts new paragraphs 9A–9C.

7.3.4 **Fixed and regulatory penalties**

There are fixed penalties for some offences, notably many motoring offences. These have been described as a compromise between the principle of equal impact and administrative efficiency (Ashworth 2000: 211); the level of fine does not vary according to the offender's means and the assumption is that the level is set sufficiently low for it not to cause injustice. There are also so-called 'regulatory offences', often 'newer' offences regulated by bodies other than the police, which deal with issues of, for example, fair trading, consumer protection, vehicle licensing, and health and safety. We looked briefly at the deterrent effect of such fines in Chapter 4 (section 4.4.1) in relation to regulatory offences generally, and particularly TV or road fund licence evasion. There are also now PNDs (penalty notices for disorder)—the so-called 'on the spot' fines issued by the police—currently set at £50 or £80, which were introduced by ss 1–11 of the Criminal Justice and Police Act 2001 and implemented across England and Wales by April 2004.

Recent official statistics also show that the number of crimes handled directly by the police through cautions and fixed-penalty fines has now exceeded those dealt with by convictions in courts. There was a 37 per cent increase in the number of fixed-penalty notices (FPNs) issued in 2006 compared with 2005 (Ministry of Justice 2007e: para 5.14 and Tables 5.4 and 5.5). The largest percentage increases in 2005–6 were for the offences of theft (retail) under £200 and criminal damage under £500 (para 5.15). There has also been a gradual increase in full payment of FPNs in England and Wales from 77 per cent in 1997 to 87 per cent in 2003[21] and 104,546 out of the 201,197 fixed-penalty notices issued between 2004 and 2006 were paid in full (ibid).

These exceptions to the range of variable fines for standard criminal offences, which were the focus of the discussion in section 7.3.2 above, raise two rather different issues. In relation to fixed penalties the difficulty is again the setting of the financial amount. If it is too high it may be unfair on offenders of limited means and it might also increase evasion of payment. If it is too low it might not act as a deterrent and be treated simply as a (small) tax to be paid for the advantage gained by the illegal action. In relation to regulatory penalties, and in relation to **white collar crime** generally, the issue has been whether those subject to such sentencing are treated too leniently: that the level of fines for such offenders is then unfair to other criminals treated more harshly.

Croall found that few offenders were imprisoned for business regulatory offences and that fines were most commonly used but were relatively low for offences under safety and public health legislation (1992: 111). Offences of fraud and tax evasion were given a broader range of punishments including custody. Croall concluded that 'the broad distinction between crimes against and crimes in the course of capitalism appears to have some substance' (ibid: 112; see also Sanders 1985). Cook came to similar conclusions in relation to the differential treatment of those defrauding the Inland Revenue by evading tax, and those defrauding the Department of Social Security by claiming benefits to which they are not entitled. However, her research revealed a complex set of factors accounting for the apparent leniency towards the tax evaders (1989; see also Levi and Pithouse 2000).

---

[21] Hansard HC 16 April 2007, Column 9W.

7.4 **The treatment of mentally disordered offenders**

7.4.1 **Sentencing policy**

In Chapter 5 (section 5.4.2) we briefly examined the sentencing provisions in relation to those offenders who are deemed to be both dangerous and mentally disordered.[22] Here our concern is with the issue of impact and just punishment in relation to all offenders who are, or could be, categorised as mentally disordered.

Our starting point is the fact that there are higher rates of mental illness in the prison population than in the wider population, with higher rates of neuroses, psychoses, personality disorders, drug dependency and abuse (see, for example, Burney and Pearson 1995: 292–4). 7 per cent of male sentenced prisoners and 14 per cent of female sentenced prisoners in a major study of over 1,000 prisoners had a psychotic disorder (Singleton *et al.* 1998). One in twelve of male sentenced prisoners and 15 per cent of female sentenced prisoners in this survey had previously received treatment in psychiatric hospitals. In addition, the number of prisoners transferred to hospital because they suffer from mental illnesses which are too serious to be treated within prison has increased since 2002 (HM Prison Service 2007b: 33).

A report on the treatment of mentally ill male prisoners, *Troubled Inside: Responding to the Mental Health Needs of Men in Prison* (Rickford and Edgar 2005), published by the Prison Reform Trust, reviews the treatment of mentally ill offenders and highlights the problems prisons face in managing mental illness and the damaging effects of imprisonment on those suffering mental illness prior to entering prison. It was highly critical of the use of prisons to warehouse the mentally ill instead of diverting them from prison and recommended improvements in policy and practice to improve their treatment (see also Seddon 2006; Peay 2007). A review by HM Inspectorate of Prisons, *The Mental Health of Prisoners: A Thematic Review of the Care and Support of Prisoners with Mental Health Needs* (2007), was also critical of the use of drugs rather than counselling etc. in dealing with prisoners' mental health problems.

The above statistics and research findings have fuelled demands for improvements in healthcare provision not only to meet the mental health care needs of prisoners, but also to divert offenders from prosecution to voluntary mental health services where appropriate, or, at the sentencing stage, to treatment under the Mental Health Act (MHA) 1983 (as amended by the MHA 2007). As the Report *Snakes and Ladders: Mental Health and Criminal Justice* (O'Shea *et al.* 2003), published by the 'Revolving Door' charity, points out, many mentally ill people are caught in a cycle of crisis, crime and mental illness, in which they are repeatedly in contact with the police and often detained in prison.[23] The prevalence of mental health problems within the prison population also has implications for the experience of imprisonment and can add to the demands made on the Prison Service when

---

[22] For further discussion of these issues, see Baker (1993).
[23] See, for a review of this report, Bui (2004).

it is already overstretched by the numbers entering prison. This issue will be considered in chapter 11 (section 11.4.4) in relation to women prisoners and their health needs.

The treatment of mental health problems in prison was also an issue considered by Lord Keith in his inquiry into the death of Zahid Mubarek who was murdered by a prisoner with a personality disorder (Keith 2006). The Mubarek Report noted that, because of insufficient appropriate resources, these prisoners could be shuttled between healthcare centres and the segregation unit or left with other prisoners.

Given the high incidence of mental illness in the prison population and the problem of the lack of resources to deal with mentally ill prisoners, the prisoners' mental health problems may be exacerbated. Although some prisoners find their health improves in prison, with a more settled routine, proper meals and denial of access to drugs and alcohol, those with pre-existing mental health problems may find them exacerbated by imprisonment which could have severe consequences for their fellow prisoners as well as themselves. Until recently a prisoner with personality disorder could be transferred to a secure hospital only if his or her condition was treatable. This has now been replaced with a new 'appropriate medical treatment' test by s 4 of the MHA 2007 (see section 7.4.2 below).

The Mubarek Report recommended a comprehensive review of the quality of care given to prisoners with mental health problems. The National Institute for Mental Health in England (NIMHE) has been commissioned to implement a comprehensive national prison mental health programme to improve the quality of mental health services for offenders. Since the death of Zahid Mubarek there has been more training in mental health awareness for officers: this should be reviewed and expanded and advice on dealing with prisoners with mental disorders should be published and made freely available to officers. The commissioning of healthcare services has now been transferred to Primary Care Trusts.

Mentally disordered offenders were considered by the Reed Report which proposed a clear policy that mentally disordered offenders should, 'wherever appropriate, receive care and treatment from health and personal social services' (Department of Health and Home Office 1992: para 2.1). This policy had been affirmed in Home Office Circular 66/1990 (*Provision for Mentally Disordered Offenders*), giving guidance that there should not be a prosecution unless it was required by the public interest. Health service options should be used, rather than penal options with a focus on diversion of mentally disordered offenders from the penal system (see Laing 1999).

However, this policy has not been implemented unproblematically. As we have already noted in Chapter 5, there is a common perception of the mentally disordered as prone to act in dangerous and anti-social ways, with a corresponding reluctance to promote therapeutic disposals which are not under the control of the penal system.[24] From time to time such concerns are fuelled by publicity about murder cases where the defendant has been involved with mental health services. These concerns reflect an underlying ambivalence in policy and practice, a tension

---

[24] See Prins (2005)—an update of a text first published in 1980—which provides a useful inter-disciplinary approach to the issues.

between treatment and public protection aims. Further, a policy of diversion requires resources to identify and provide services and treatment for the mentally ill criminal but this is not a use of scarce resources which attracts widespread public support.

The result, according to Peay, is that 'the impact of Circular 66/90 and its underlying themes have been leavened by a series of risk-infused policy developments' (2002: 748). The proposals contained in three documents published at the end of the 1990s reveal these often conflicting underlying principles of public protection, treatment, non-discrimination and equal human rights (see Ashworth 2000: 342–3; Peay 2002: 748). The Richardson Report (Department of Health 1999) focused on civil powers, upheld principles of patient autonomy and equal treatment for the physically and mentally ill, and gave priority to treatment over punishment for mentally disordered offenders. The Consultation Paper (Department of Health 1999), on the other hand, was concerned with public protection and risk assessment, whilst the Home Office (1999a) paper on dangerous people with severe personality disorder presaged a concern with finding ways to detain such people without their having committed an offence. The subsequent White Paper on high-risk patients (Department of Health/Home Office 2000) and the draft Mental Health Bills of 2002 and 2004 (see Chapter 5, section 5.2) reflected, together with other developments, 'a growing desire to maintain penal control over mentally disordered offenders' (Peay 2002: 749).

This policy trend persists despite the evidence as to the (small) size of the 'dangerous' section of the mentally disordered offender population and the prevalence of non-dangerous mental illness in the total offending population. Research studies in the 1990s found that 37 per cent of male and 56 per cent of female sentenced prisoners had psychiatric disorders, with an incidence in the remand population of 63 per cent, and 5–10 per cent suffering from psychosis (see Peay 2002: 761, 772–5).

The studies noted above which are evidence of the higher level of 'non-dangerous' mental illness and disorder amongst the prison population than in the population as a whole, prompt the question as to why this should be so. Possible explanations are that the mentally disordered are more inept and visible offenders, that they are repeat petty offenders, or that the 'gatekeepers' who make the decisions in the criminal justice system have stereotypical views. For example, Cummins (2006) examines the role—in this outcome—of police powers and the appropriate adult at the questioning stage of police investigation. However, it may be that there is simply a lack of adequate mental health services to diagnose offenders early in the process.[25]

7.4.2 **Treatment under the Mental Health Act 1983**

Statutory definitions are very important in sentencing (possibly) mentally disordered offenders: they will determine the 'label' and the options for the defendant. The legislative history of current provisions can be found in the criticisms of the Mental Health Act 1959 by the Butler Committee and a DHSS Review in the 1970s. The legislative framework set up by the resulting MHA 1983 remains

---

[25] For a systematic review of the international literature on the *Epidemiology of Mentally Disordered Offenders* see the Centre for Reviews and Dissemination (1999).

largely unchanged. Until the amendments made by the MHA 2007 are in force, s 1(2) defines mental disorder as 'mental illness, arrested or incomplete development of mind, psychopathic disorder and any disorder or disability of mind', although no definition of 'mental illness' is given. 'Psychopathic disorder' is defined as 'persistent disorder or disability of mind...which results in abnormally aggressive or seriously irresponsible behaviour': a definition which did not 'absolve itself of a tautological association with behaviour likely to be criminalized' (Peay 2002: 753). For the purposes of sentencing the mentally disordered, there is also a further categorisation into, in effect, major and minor forms of mental disorder and several powers could be used only for the first category (see Peay 2002: 753). To use the powers under s 37 of the MHA 1983, there is also the extra criterion of 'treatability' for the second category. As we saw in Chapter 5, however, an offender with a personality disorder is often assessed as unlikely to respond to any available medical treatment.

The MHA 2007 amends both these sections of the MHA 1983. The following are the main changes relevant to sentencing as summarised in the Government's Explanatory Notes:

> *Definition of mental disorder*: The Act changes the way the 1983 Act defines mental disorder, so that a single definition applies throughout the Act, and abolishes references to categories of disorder. These amendments complement the changes to the criteria for detention. Section 1, therefore, amends the wording of the definition of mental disorder in the 1983 Act from 'mental illness, arrested or incomplete development of mind, psychopathic disorder and any other disorder or disability of mind' to 'any disorder or disability of the mind'.
>
> *Criteria for detention*: It introduces a new 'appropriate medical treatment' test which will apply to all the longer-term powers of detention. As a result, it will not be possible for patients to be compulsorily detained or their detention continued unless medical treatment which is appropriate to the patient's mental disorder and all other circumstances of the case is available to that patient. At the same time, the so-called 'treatability test' will be abolished. Because of the removal of categories of disorder by s 1, the appropriate medical treatment test applies equally to all mental disorders.[26]

The relevant orders for the sentencing court are to be found in Part III of the MHA 1983. Section 37 allows the court to order that the offender be admitted to hospital, provided the receiving hospital agrees—s 37(4), or be placed under the guardianship of the local social services department.[27] The conditions include that the offence of which the offender has been convicted is an imprisonable offence and the court believes an order under s 37 is the most suitable method of dealing with the offender. Evidence from two doctors is necessary to establish that the offender is suffering from one of the forms of mental disorder and that detention for treatment in hospital is appropriate. Transfer from prison to hospital by order of the

---

[26] See, for further details, http://www.opsi.gov.uk/acts/en2007/ukpgaen_20070012_en.pdf. This gives, at page 9, a useful chart summarising changes in relation to the treatability test and the relevant court orders. At the time of writing no date has been announced for commencement of these new provisions.

[27] Guardianship orders are rarely used.

Home Secretary is possible under s 47, and Crown Courts may impose a s 45A order (see 7.4.3 below), both on similar criteria to those in s 37.

The effect of a hospital order is as outlined in the following information provided by the charity MIND:

The order is initially for six months. At the end of that period, you have the right to apply to the Mental Health Review Tribunal. Your Responsible Medical Officer (RMO) has the right to discharge you at any time, but can also renew the section [the s 37 order] at the end of the first six months, again at the end of a second period of six months, and at yearly intervals thereafter. If your section is renewed, you can apply to the Mental Health Review Tribunal for discharge.[28]

The Mental Health Review Tribunal (MHRT) gives the following information to patients and family about its role:

The MHRT (Medical Health Review Tribunal) is the statutory, independent body responsible for hearing appeals against detention. It operates like a mobile court and sits in the hospital where the patient is detained....An MHRT will consist of a lawyer, a doctor and a lay member. The patient, their hospital doctor and social worker will also be at the hearing together with the patient's nearest relative, unless the patient objects. The legal member will chair the proceedings.[29]

A patient can reapply for release once a year after the first 12 months and there is automatic referral to the MHRT every three years.

If the Crown Court believes that further restrictions should be placed on release from hospital it may also make a restriction order 'where necessary for the protection of the public from serious harm' (MHA 1983, s 41; see Chapter 5). A magistrates' court may refer a case to the Crown Court for consideration of this order. MHA 2007 s 40 also amends s 41 of the 1983 Act, removing the power of the Crown Court to make restriction orders for a limited period. As a consequence such orders imposed by a court will remain in force until they are discharged by the Secretary of State for Justice or the MHRT. The court cannot make such an order unless at least one of the two doctors recommending a hospital order gave evidence orally. The effect is to remove the hospital doctor's power to release the prisoner, giving the power only to the MHRT and the Home Secretary. During a prison sentence only the Home Secretary can order release though the MHRT can make recommendations. At the end of the custodial term (now the 'release' date under s 294 of the CJA 2003) the restriction order ceases to have effect and provisions similar to those of the hospital order apply.[30]

7.4.3 **Penal disposals**

The above section briefly outlined the main possibilities for treating an offender as mentally disordered rather than as requiring punishment. There are in addition two 'mixed' orders where a penal disposal is given but it includes treatment. First, a probation or supervision order with a psychiatric treatment condition had been available since the Criminal Justice Act 1948. The PCCSA 2000, Schedules 2, 3 and 6,

[28] See http://www.mind.org.uk/Information/Booklets/Rights+guide/Mind+rights+guide+5.htm.
[29] See http://www.mhrt.org.uk/.
[30] See, further, http://www.mind.org.uk/Information/Legal/OGMHA.htm.

re-enacted the criteria and requirements in relation to community rehabilitation orders and s 207 of the CJA 2003 provided, instead, for the imposition of a similar mental health treatment requirement in the new community order (and also a suspended sentence order). Such a requirement under s 207 is 'with a view to the improvement of the offender's mental condition', and the treatment can be as a resident or non-resident patient in a care home or hospital, or under the direction of a medical practitioner or psychologist. A doctor must certify that the offender's condition 'may be susceptible to treatment' but does not warrant a hospital or guardianship order.

Second, the Crime (Sentences) Act 1997 inserted a new s 45A into the MHA 1983 to provide the courts with hospital and limitation directions. If the offender is suffering from a psychopathic disorder and the court, having considered a hospital order, decides to impose a custodial sentence, it can, nevertheless, direct that the offender be admitted immediately to hospital (with similar further criteria as for hospital orders). If the offender does not respond to treatment (or, possibly, recovers), he is then transferred to prison. This new order is, arguably, an unjustifiable compromise between treatment and punishment. It is a clear example of the response by government and the courts to public fears that a mentally disordered offender will 'escape' punishment and control.

Such sentences do, however, provide treatment. As Peay notes, while 'some restriction orders are imposed unnecessarily ... most disordered offenders do not receive a therapeutic "hospital order" disposal, even though their culpability may be mitigated, if not absolved, by their mental state' (2002: 755). One possible reason why the mentally ill are not treated as such at the sentencing stage is that they are not diagnosed early enough to be diverted from the penal system; another is that not all such offenders may 'fit' the MHA 1983 criteria, notably the treatability and availability of hospital care issues (see Genders 2003). A third explanation lies in the widespread ambivalence over the offender's culpability and just deserts, reflecting much deeper concerns as to the origins of 'evil' in the 'normal' offender.

As a result of these conflicting imperatives and ideas, the sentencing framework allows the sentencer to choose or reject the penal options even when the MHA 1983 criteria are met. Section 166(5) of the CJA 2003 empowers the court to disregard provisions which would otherwise mandate the passing of particular sentences when the offender is mentally disordered. Section 157(1) mandates the court to obtain a medical report before passing a custodial sentence on an offender who 'is or appears to be mentally disordered', although that requirement does not apply if, 'in the circumstances of the case', the court feels that it is unnecessary. Further, before passing such a sentence the court must consider any information about the offender's mental condition and assess 'the likely effect of such a sentence on that condition and on any treatment which may be available for it' (s 157(3)).

If the court decides that it cannot or will not use MHA 1983 options, it could choose penal disposals ranging from 'non-punitive' discharges and bind-overs, through fines, community penalties and imprisonment. In the case of the latter, a determinate and proportionate sentence may be passed or, where available, a discretionary life sentence. Where a relatively long sentence is passed there may be time and opportunity for therapeutic treatment to be given in prison, but there can be no guarantee of this and, paradoxically, the encouragement of shorter sentences may preclude the possibility of such treatment.[31]

This area of sentencing law and practice is complex and difficult and we have been able only to outline the possibilities and problems. What is clear is that, despite advances in diversion schemes and the standard of mental health care in prisons, our treatment of the mentally disordered offender is still a prime example of unprincipled compromise in relation to issues of sentence impact and effectiveness, as well as offender culpability. It is also an area where a propensity to label as a homogeneous category what is in practice a diverse group of people with diverse needs makes any assessment of sentence impact in individual cases very difficult.

7.5 **Review**

7.5.1 **Conclusions**

This chapter has covered a very wide range of issues in relation to the impact of punishment. It has inevitably revealed competing claims for what should count as justice. As we saw in Chapter 6, one of the strengths of restorative justice is that it allows for 'tailor-made' agreed outcomes: 'Diversity and flexibility are crucial in dealing with individual circumstances. There is no definitive model and "one size" is never likely to fit all' (Tickell and Akester 2002: 102). A similar comment could be made about punishment imposed on utilitarian or retributivist principles, if no account whatsoever is taken of structural disadvantage, institutionalised discrimination, or severe personal difficulties. On the other hand, individualised sentencing, as we have seen, can also lead to inequalities of treatment which may be unjust, in the same way as restorative conference outcomes may be punitive and heedless of rights.

In the remaining chapters of this book we will revisit some of these themes in relation to the punishment of minors in Chapter 8, and when focusing on community penalties in Chapter 12. The issue of the differential impact of custodial penalties on adults will be examined in more detail in Chapter 11. There we will focus specifically on the experiences of ethnic minorities and women, asking whether justice requires difference or equality in the treatment of prisoners with different needs and backgrounds.

7.5.2 **Case study**

We have seen that there is no clear approach to taking account of the impact of the financial, medical and social factors that we have examined above. That is not surprising, given that the questions raised by the issue of impact relate to the fundamental principles and assumptions underlying the criminal justice system and what justice might mean.

---

[31] There is a similar concern in relation to the amount of time required for rehabilitation programmes to be effective: see Chapter 12.

Below is a sentencing exercise which draws on the material in Chapter 5 as well as on the themes discussed in this chapter. It brings together difficult questions relating to proportionality, dangerousness and personal mitigation. Further help is available in approaching this exercise at the Online Resource Centre.

online
resource
centre

Facts of the case:

Zack is 38 years old and has suffered from mild schizophrenia for almost 20 years. Three years ago he spent a month in hospital for psychiatric treatment to establish a new medication regime. His condition has since been stable and he works as a labourer. He has always lived with his mother who is now elderly and infirm and depends on him for her shopping and laundry.

When doing building work over a period of time in a family home Zack made friends with Yasmin, the 7 year old daughter of the family, and persuaded her to let him take several photos of her, in particular poses, when she was undressing. He told her to keep the 'photo shoot' as their little secret but Yasmin was excited, thinking she could become a model when she grew up, so she told her parents about the photos. They contacted the police and the photos were found on the computer in Zack's house. The computer provided evidence that he had copied the photos to three friends.

Zack pleaded guilty at the Magistrates' Court to a charge of taking and distributing indecent photographs of a child (section 1 of the Protection of Children Act 1978). The maximum penalty for this offence on indictment is 10 years and it is a specified offence listed in Schedule 15 of the Criminal Justice Act 2003. The Magistrates transferred his case to the Crown Court for sentencing. The photos were referred to COPINE (Combating Paedophile Information Networks in Europe) which graded the images as being of the lowest category of obscenity. Zack has two previous convictions (for being drunk and disorderly and for theft in breach of trust) for which he received a fine and a short custodial sentence respectively.

You are Zack's solicitor. Explain to him what options are open to the Crown Court judge at the sentencing hearing and what the judge is most likely to decide.

8

Treating children differently

SUMMARY

This chapter focuses on the ways in which, and the extent to which, the state deals differently with children and young people under 18 years of age who commit criminal offences. It examines the policies developed in the last century to divert minors from prosecution, notably cautioning, now reprimands and warnings, and reviews the ways in which the treatment of minors who offend have been theorised. It also analyses the changes in policy in the 1990s, reviews key elements of the youth justice system set up by the Crime and Disorder Act 1998 and summarises current sentencing options.

8.1 Introduction

8.1.1 A separate system

Part A of this book has examined sentencing principles and policies, mainly with reference to adult offenders. Much of the discussion in previous chapters is also relevant to those under 18 years of age.[1] For example, the focus on rights in Chapter 3 (section 3.5.1) raises issues about the treatment and punishment of young people who are the potential beneficiaries of rights conventions. Their sentence and punishment should also be governed by the proportionality principle. Chapter 6, when focusing on restorative justice, referred mainly to schemes for young offenders (section 6.3.2) because the youth justice system is where restorative policies are currently most important. Further, whilst the justifications for the punishment of minors have often been located within different theoretical frameworks, retributivism and utilitarianism have underpinned those frameworks.

However, in the UK, as in many other jurisdictions, the system for dealing with children and young people who offend is separate from the system which processes adult offenders. The nature of the systems for adults and minors may or may not be different, and the degree of 'separateness' may vary, but the distance, conceptually and spatially, from the adult criminal justice system, has been the essential attribute of the juvenile, now youth, justice system from its inception over a century ago. The policy aim to keep young and adult offenders separate stems from our ideas about children and their development, and our fears for their 'contamination' by adult offenders.[2]

---

[1] In the criminal justice system for England and Wales, 'children' are those under 14 years of age and 'young person' is used for the 14–17 age group, the 18th birthday normally being the date of entry to the adult system.

[2] For a historical review of developments in juvenile justice in the USA see Zimring (2005).

The legislation which set up the first courts specifically for juveniles in the UK endorsed the idea that young offenders are 'children in trouble'. In the terminology of the nineteenth century, they could be 'saved' from a life of crime because 'kindness could nip crime in the bud' (Harris and Webb 1987: 15). Statutory provisions to set up the earlier industrial and reformatory schools[3] were also based on those ideas, although we might dispute whether treatment was kind by later standards. By the early twentieth century, new branches of knowledge of why children offend led to the belief that the 'deprived', those we would now refer to as 'children in need', and the 'depraved', now children and young people who offend, are not necessarily separate categories.

Recently, commentators have expressed fears that the separateness of the juvenile justice system, and the ideas underpinning it, may disappear. According to Weijers and Duff, 'the last few decades ... have witnessed remarkable changes in views both of juvenile offenders and of the proper role of the state ... A century after its foundation, the future of the juvenile system is very much in doubt' (2002: 1). This might seem a surprising conclusion given that the United Nations Convention on the Rights of the Child (CRC), which in effect lays down principles of separate treatment, was adopted by the UN as recently as 1989, came into force in 1990 and was ratified by the UK in 1991.[4] Article 40 is of particular importance in this respect because it states that:

States Parties shall seek to promote the establishment of laws, procedures, authorities and institutions *specifically applicable* to children alleged as, accused of, or recognised as having infringed the penal law, and, in particular:...

(b) Wherever appropriate and desirable, measures for dealing with such children without resorting to judicial proceedings, providing that human rights and legal safeguards are respected.

(para 3: emphasis added)

The policy aim, then, should be to ensure that all formal processes are child-friendly and that, where possible, formal criminal proceedings should be avoided. Separate and different processes would appear to be encouraged. This chapter will review past and present developments to assess how far this is happening in England and Wales, and we examine the youth justice system's compliance with rights conventions in Chapter 13 (section 13.4.1).

The difficulty is, however, that we are writing at a time when, in the UK and elsewhere, the response to offending and anti-social behaviour by minors is being rethought, with a mix of policy aims—often divergent and sometimes incompatible—and with projects being piloted, which makes prophecy about the future difficult. Even to try and establish whether the future of a separate and different system is 'very much in doubt', we need to look further than the substance of sentencing principles and policies covered in earlier chapters. We need also to appreciate how important are ideas and fears about children, families, morality and social stability in understanding developments in juvenile justice: how we 'visualise' children has implications for how we decide what counts as justice for

---

[3] For a discussion of the Industrial School Acts 1857–1880, and the Youthful Offenders Act 1854 which set up reformatory schools, see Pinchbeck and Hewitt (1973: Chapter 16).

[4] Although with reservations (not yet withdrawn) about the care of young offenders. For the CRC generally, see Fortin (2003: 36–49). For a recent critique see Williams (2007).

them when they offend. Further, it involves an acknowledgement of the relevance of policy areas other than youth justice: the concerns of government and public opinion about wider social issues have also led to a policy focus on the child who offends (see Koffman 2008; Piper 2008: chapter 3; Welshman 2007).

For all these reasons, this chapter has a wider focus than sentencing law and policies although it briefly summarises sentencing options available to the youth court, leaving a more detailed review of the use and impact of punishments to Chapter 13. Prosecution and sentencing are not necessarily the next stages after offending has been admitted by minors, as they are for most adult offenders. This chapter examines why that is so, and what alternatives have developed. However, it also focuses on the other options that have been developed for young people whose behaviour is seen as problematic, notably the civil orders to deal with anti-social behaviour.

8.1.2 **Offending by minors**

Another difficulty when seeking to understand developments in this area of law and policy is that media and political debate is not always conducted in the context of what we know about the extent of offending by minors. Often the assumption that offending is on the increase is used to promote particular responses. This is understandable in that different sets of data suggest conflicting trends. Even the House of Commons Home Affairs Select Committee's 1992 Inquiry into juvenile offending was sceptical that the official statistics reflected the real situation (Graham and Bowling 1995: 1). There is some consensus that there were large increases in recorded crime for adults and juveniles from the 1930s to the 1970s, but that the rate of increase of recorded crime in England and Wales slowed down in the 1980s and fell after 1992 (Gelsthorpe 2002: 47). For example, based on official statistics, the number of 10–17 year olds convicted or cautioned for indictable offences fell by 17 per cent in the period 1988 to 1998 (NACRO[5] 2000c: 1). In Scotland, too, in 2000–1 only 0.4 per cent of young people aged 8–16 were referred to a Children's Hearing because of their offending and such referrals have decreased over the period 1974–2001 (Scottish Executive 2002b). There is particular concern about young people who commit the most serious of offences and it is true that the number of 10–17-year-olds sentenced to some form of detention for life increased from 11 in 1996 to 28 in 2005. However, these figures hide the fact that a total of 29 was reached in 1999 and in 2001 whereas the figure was again 11 in 2003 (Home Office 2007a: Table 2.7): there is no clear trend.

On the other hand, Farrington argues that any apparent decrease 'is almost certainly an illusion' (Farrington 2002b: 425). Life history interviews, self-report studies, and victimisation surveys in various jurisdictions do confirm that 'actual' offending rates are higher than official statistics would suggest. The 1998 MORI survey of 11–16-year-olds reported in the 1999 Annual Report of the new Youth Justice Board found that only 70 per cent of children could say with certainty that they had not committed an offence in the previous 15 months (see NACRO 2000c: 1).

---

[5] The crime reduction charity, formerly the National Association for the Care and Resettlement of Offenders.

The Audit Commission noted that 'between 1999 and 2003, the rate of self-reported offending by young people remained constant at one in four' (2004: 3)[6] although self-report methods also have their limitations (Graham and Bowling 1995: 8–10). Further, there are different messages from official statistics and self-report studies about the issue of 'growing out' of crime: the reduction in offending after the age of 20 may be due to engagement in less visible offending as well as reduced frequency of offending (Graham and Bowling 1995: 30). The higher visibility of offending by young people may also account for public perceptions of the danger from young criminals. The Audit Commission, using Home Office statistics, gives a figure of 5 per cent of the 10–17 age group as having been arrested for a notifiable offence in 2002–3 (2004: 8).

It was estimated that 11 per cent of all known offenders were between 10 and 17 years of age in 1997 (Mattinson and Mirrlees-Black 2000: 11; but see Goldson 1999: 6 for higher estimates) and 12 per cent in 2005 (NACRO 2007f: 2), statistics seen as contributing to the view that juvenile crime is disproportionate. However, the significance of the 11–12 per cent figure is dependent, not only on whether the unrecorded crime figure is itself disproportionately higher or lower for juveniles, but on whether you believe children 'grow out of crime' or 'learn the habits of a lifetime' during their minority. Further, as NACRO has pointed out, it is adults aged 21 and above who are responsible for more than three-quarters of offences (2007f: 2). Nevertheless there is now some consensus that the long-term trend up until 2003 of a decline in recorded crime committed by those aged 17 and under has not continued (see below).

The 'peak' ages for offending are thought to be in the age group 15–20, with different peaks for males and females, and for different offences (Farrington 2002b: 426; Graham and Bowling 1995: Chapters 2 and 3; Flood-Page *et al.* 2000: 10): in 2005 statistics for recorded indictable offences suggested a peak age of 17 for males and 15 for females (see NACRO 2007f: 2). The majority of youth crime is not serious offending but is property-based: theft and handling stolen goods alone account for almost half of the crimes committed by the under-18-year-olds, whilst less than one in five of recorded indictable offences by children and young people relate to violence against the person (NACRO 2008: 4). This is clearly not a figure to be discounted, particularly as police detection rates, in one study, fell from 29 per cent to 23 per cent in the period 1999–2001 (Audit Commission 2004: 9). The number of minors cautioned or convicted for drug offences and robbery together with violence has risen but 'accounts for only around one-third of indictable juvenile crime (Audit Commission 2004: 8, based on 2001 official statistics)' (NACRO 2007f).

However, the latest statistics appear to show that the decline in detected youth crime from the 1990s up to 2003 may have been reversed: the number of children receiving a reprimand, final warning or conviction for an indictable offence increased by 19 per cent in the period 2003–6, although the number is still lower than the equivalent figure for 1992 (NACRO 2008: 2). In response, NACRO and the Howard League for Penal Reform have provided a range of very detailed reasons why these statistics are more reflective of target-led police practices and court responses

---

[6] Based on an annual school survey by MORI of children aged 11–16 (Audit Commission 2004: 8–9); self-reported offending by excluded pupils was also constant but at almost two in three pupils (ibid).

than actual increases in offending (NACRO 2008; see the Online Resource Centre for further discussion).

What we know about the incidence of offending by children and young people is, then, contested and does not prove that offending is on the increase, either in total or in severity,[7] despite the fact that the public continues to believe that it is. Recent research found that almost two-thirds of respondents (63 per cent) thought that crime had increased over the previous 12 months, with 30 per cent believing that it had risen a lot (Patterson and Thorpe 2006: 34; see also NACRO 2007f: 1). However, it is still a valid cause for concern. The factors associated with offending suggest that young offenders are marginalised young people, often with a range of problems which require medical, social work, or educational responses (see section 8.2.1). Furthermore, it cannot be in the longer-term interests of young people to allow them to persist in offending without providing support and appropriate help: only a few people pursue a 'successful' career in crime.

8.1.3 Sentencing powers

Strictly speaking this subheading is inaccurate: juveniles are not 'sentenced' after 'conviction'. Instead, since the implementation of the Children and Young Persons' Act 1933, the youth court 'makes an order upon a finding of guilt' (s 59) in relation to those minors who have been successfully prosecuted. However, ss 65–66 of the Crime and Disorder Act (CDA) 1998 in effect introduced the presumption that children and young people under 18 will not normally be prosecuted for the first two known offences. Provided the young offender admits the offence and there would be sufficient evidence for the police to prosecute, he will receive a reprimand and then, for a subsequent offence, a warning. The Criminal Justice and Immigration (CJI) Act 2008 will introduce a third option (see section 8.5.3 below). If the minor is prosecuted the case is normally heard in the youth court, the name having been changed from juvenile court when the upper age was raised from 17 and non-criminal cases were moved to the newly created Family Proceedings Court.[8]

On a first appearance at a youth court a minor is normally given a referral order (but see Chapter 13, section 13.1.2). This order was introduced by the Youth Justice and Criminal Evidence Act 1999, re-enacted in Part III of the Powers of Criminal Courts (Sentencing) Act (PCCSA) 2000 and since amended, and entails referral to a multi-disciplinary Youth Offender Panel (YOP). This includes lay members who agree a contract of activities with the young offender (ss 18, 21–27). On subsequent appearances the full range of disposals from fines, through youth community orders[9] (or community orders for young people aged 16 and above, but see Chapter 13, section 13.2.2 below)[10] to a detention and training order (DTO), is available to the magistrates.

---

[7] The Home Office web site gives the following: 'statistics from public agencies such as the police suggest that changes to the youth justice system in 1998 and 1999 have steadied the crime rate' (accessed 19 March 2008).

[8] Criminal Justice Act 1991, s 68 and Schedule 8, Children (Allocation of Proceedings) Order 1991, SI 1991 No. 1677.

[9] But s 177 which introduces these community sentences has not been implemented for those under 18 and so the orders in the PCCSA 2000 are still law.

[10] Both these orders are defined in the CJA 2003, s 149 (see Chapter 13) but note that the CJI Act 2008 will replace existing community orders for minors with youth rehabilitation orders.

It is worth noting that the situation in Northern Ireland is very similar, although different legislation and terminology apply to many aspects of youth justice. In 1999, Northern Ireland also changed the name of the juvenile court to the youth court (Criminal Justice (Children) Order 1998 Article 27) and s 63 of the Justice (Northern Ireland) Act 2002 raised the upper limit from 17 to 18 years old. Sections 57–61 of the 2002 Act provide youth courts with powers to refer offenders to a 'youth conference' where an agreed plan is negotiated, somewhat similar to the referral order in England and Wales. Scotland, as we shall see, is different.

In England and Wales, community and custodial orders for minors, as for adults, have been subject to statutory seriousness hurdles since the Criminal Justice Act (CJA) 1991 (see Chapter 3). The criteria for the imposition of a DTO, which is an option if the offence is one for which an adult could be imprisoned, are to be found in s 100 of the PCCSA 2000 (see Chapter 13, section 13.3.1). Section 298 of the Criminal Justice Act (CJA) 2003, if implemented, will amend the PCCSA 2000, s 101(2), so that 6 months would be the maximum term magistrates could impose on a young offender for a summary offence if the maximum for an adult is 51 weeks. It appears to have left in force s 101(4) which allows a maximum of 24 months for the detention and training order for other offences (**triable either way** or indictable).[11] Before 2000, the youth court could, after trying a case, commit a 15–17-year-old to the Crown Court for sentence if it believed that its powers were insufficient.[12] Given that this power could lead to the imposition of longer custodial sentences, its repeal is to be welcomed. For murder and for certain serious offences (for example, where the adult maximum penalty would be 14 years' imprisonment), the Crown Court has powers to make orders for detention at Her Majesty's Pleasure or detention for a specific period (PCCSA 2000, ss 90 and 91), and also orders for detention for life or for public protection for specified serious offences (CJA 2003 s 226; see Chapter 5 and also Chapter 13, section 13.3.1). Such cases will be transferred to the Crown Court. This mandates the court, where the conditions are met, to make an order for detention for life or for public protection for specified serious offences committed by those under 18 (see Chapter 13, section 13.3.1).

The Audit Commission (2004) reported on the use of the sentencing options available before the CJA 2003. In the period 1996–2001, it found a decrease in the use of lower-tariff sentencing options, such as fines, but an increase in the use of community sentences (2004: 34). The number of young people sentenced to custody rose by about 40 per cent between 1992 and 1997 but levelled off and then fell in the period 2001–3 (ibid: 35; see also Figure 8.1 which shows trends up to 2002).

However, whilst the number of DTOs imposed remained stable in 2000–3, there was a slight increase in sentence length (ibid) and an increasing number of 10–14-year olds have been given custody (ibid: 36). The percentage of sentenced young offenders given custody in 2001 ranges from approximately 6 per cent of the 10–14-year olds to 14 per cent of the 15–17-year-olds. Further, the use of ss 90–92 sentences (for the more serious offences: see above) rose during 2002, and the greater differential use of custody for certain ethnic minorities also increased (ibid: 36–7).

The sentencing trends for young people aged 15–17, evident in Figure 8.1, illustrate the immediate effect of the introduction of the referral, reparation and action

---

[11] The CJA 2003 Schedule 37 Part 7 repeals s 100(4). We hoped this might be a misprint for s 101(4).
[12] The CDA 1998 repealed s 27 of the Magistrates' Courts Act 1980.

England and Wales

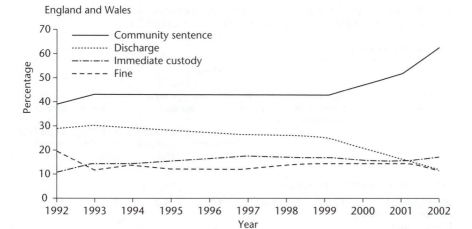

Community sentences broken down by type of sentence

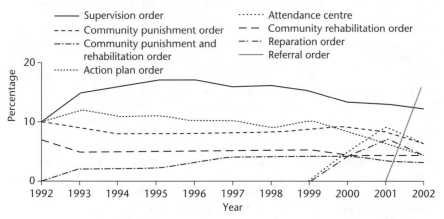

Figure 8.1 Percentage of male offenders aged 15 to 17 sentenced for indictable offences who received various sentences or orders[1] 1992–2002

(1) Community sentences include curfew orders from 1998 and drug treatment and testing orders from 2000, both of which are excluded from lower graph due to small numbers involved.

Source: Home Office (2003h: Figure 4.9).

plan orders as being an increase in community sentences and decrease in the use of discharges. The use and length of custodial orders is again rising: *Sentencing Statistics 2005* (Ministry of Justice 2007a: Table 2.4) shows that the numbers of 10–17-year-old males sentenced to immediate custody rose slightly from 5,284 in 1995 to 5,512 in 2005 but the average sentence length—excluding the new IPP and life sentences—rose from 7.7 months to 10.5 months (see Table 8.1).

The number of community sentences given to males aged 10–17 remained stable between 2002 and 2005 (ibid: para 3.11) but the use of fines continues to fall (ibid: Table 4.4). Earlier figures showed that parents were ordered to pay the fine in only 11 per cent of cases where 10–17-year-olds were fined for indictable offences (Audit Commission 2004).

These sentencing patterns—which reveal no decrease in the use of custody for children and young people—are of concern and reveal a more punitive approach

Table 8.1 Average time served in prison by prisoners discharged from determinate sentences on completion of sentence or on licence—young offenders

England and Wales 2006

Length of sentence[1]	Number of persons discharged[2,3]	Average length of sentence	Months			
			Average time served		Percentage of sentence served	
			Including remand time	Excluding remand time	Including remand time	Excluding remand time
MALE AND FEMALE YOUNG OFFENDERS						
All lengths of sentence less than indeterminate	**12,500**	**9.8**	**4.9**	**4.2**	**51**	**43**
Up to and including 3 months	2,800	1.9	1.0	0.9	55	49
Over 3 months up to and including 6 months	4,700	4.8	2.5	2.1	52	45
Over 6 months less than 12 months	1,900	8.6	4.2	3.5	49	41
12 months	700	12.0	6.1	5.3	50	44
Over 12 months up to and including 18 months	700	17.0	8.3	7.2	49	43
Over 18 months up to and including 3 years	1,000	28.4	13.6	11.7	48	41
Over 3 years less than 4 years	300	42.4	20.5	17.5	48	41
4 years	100	48.0	28.0	24.8	58	52
Over 4 years less than indeterminate	100	59.7	34.4	31.0	58	52
MALE YOUNG OFFENDERS						
All lengths of sentence less than indeterminate	**11,700**	**9.9**	**5.0**	**4.3**	**51**	**43**
Up to and including 3 months	2,600	1.9	1.0	0.9	55	49
Over 3 months up to and including 6 months	4,400	4.8	2.5	2.1	52	45
Over 6 months less than 12 months	1,800	8.6	4.2	3.6	49	41
12 months	700	12.0	6.1	5.3	51	44
Over 12 months up to and including 18 months	700	17.0	8.4	7.3	49	43
Over 18 months up to and including 3 years	1,000	28.5	13.7	11.7	48	41
Over 3 years less than 4 years	300	42.4	20.5	17.5	48	41

Table 8.1 *Continued*

| Length of sentence[(1)] | Number of persons dis- charged[(2,3)] | Months | | | | | |
| | | Average length of sentence | Average time served | | Percentage of sentence served | |
			Including remand time	Excluding remand time	Including remand time	Excluding remand time
4 years	100	48.0	28.2	25.1	59	92
Over 4 years less than indeterminate	100	59.6	34.4	31.0	50	52
FEMALE YOUNG OFFENDERS						
All lengths of sentence less than indeterminate	**800**	**8.0**	**3.8**	**3.2**	**47**	**40**
Up to and including 3 months	300	2.0	1.0	0.9	50	45
Over 3 months up to and including 6 months	300	4.8	2.4	2.1	50	43
Over 6 month less than 12 months	100	8.5	3.7	3.2	43	38
12 months	30	12.0	6.0	5.2	50	43
Over 12 months up to and including 18 months	20	16.9	7.2	6.2	42	37
Over 18 months less than indeterminate	70	33.6	15.7	13.5	47	40

(1) On discharge: the sentence may change after reception if there are further charges or an appeal.

(2) Excludes discharges following recall after release on licence, non-criminals, persons committed to custody for non-payment of a fine and persons reclassified as adult prisoners.

(3) Rounded to the nearest 100 or to the nearest 10 for number less than 100.

Source: Ministry of Justice (2007a: 117)

to young offenders than is to be found elsewhere in Europe. The 1996 Council of Europe Survey showed that 18 per cent of the prison population in England and Wales is under 21 years of age, compared with France 10 per cent, the Netherlands 8 per cent, Portugal 6 per cent, Sweden 4 per cent and Switzerland 4 per cent.[13] There are now 2,742 boys and girls in prison (minors on remand or sentenced) in England and Wales, up on the 2,500 when we wrote the first edition and double the number in 1993.[14] These are figures which sit uneasily with the precepts of rights conventions (see Chapter 13, section 13.4).

The above overview, however, can give very little idea of what happens in practice and why. Arguably, the system is 'a strange blend of authoritarianism and liberalism—indeed it is permeated with contradictions and tensions' (Fortin 2003:

[13] See House of Commons Home Affairs Select Committee Session 1997–8, Minutes of Evidence, Annex A, 5 May 1998.

[14] See http://www.howardleague.org.uk.: figures are for December 2007.

547), ideas and tensions that go back a long way but which still influence how young offenders are sentenced and punished. The next section will examine some of these ideas concerning the ways in which young people who offend should be treated. It is entitled 'welfare versus justice' because theorising about juvenile justice has used this polarised framework to analyse developments. We will concentrate on the period since the 1950s, simply noting that in the first half of the twentieth century the separateness of the juvenile court had been consolidated[15] and social work approaches developed.

8.2 Welfare versus justice

8.2.1 A theoretical framework

The terms 'welfare' and 'justice' need some explanation in the juvenile justice context. Section 44 of the Children and Young Persons Act 1933 established that courts must 'have regard to' the welfare of the child, as did the Prosecution of Offences Act 1985 in relation to the Crown Prosecution Service (CPS). This has been an important mandatory requirement to ensure that children have been given at least a modicum of 'special' treatment when appearing in a court and, particularly, when appearing in a youth or Crown Court.

However, it is a weak welfare principle in comparison with the **paramountcy principle** in the Children Act 1989 which is applied by courts in the family justice system dealing with the upbringing of children and which means that the child's welfare must be the determining factor in the court's decision. However, this remit does not cover decisions about guilt or sentence in the criminal jurisdiction. The duty to 'have regard to' means that, providing consideration has been given to the interests of the child or young person, the youth, magistrates' and Crown Courts can legally give precedence to other interests such as the need to protect the public and to prevent reoffending. There is, admittedly, some overlap between the family and youth justice jurisdictions. Offending may be a factor in care proceedings which are governed by the paramountcy principle, but such offending is relevant only in so far as it is evidence that the child is at risk of suffering significant harm (Children Act 1989, s 31). Further, the case of *R (on the application of the Howard League for Penal Reform) v the Secretary of State for the Home Department* (2002) established that the duties of the local authority to children in need or at risk (Children Act 1989, ss 17 and 47) do not end at the door of a prison service establishment (para 136 *per* Munby J). However, the paramountcy principle is not thereby incorporated into decision making in the youth justice system or the Prison Service, whilst s 37(1) of the CDA 1998 established a potentially conflicting aim by declaring the prevention of offending as the 'principal aim' of the youth justice system in England and Wales.

In 2003 NACRO produced a Youth Crime Briefing,[16] which discussed the tensions inherent in the co-existence of the two principles, together with the further

---

[15] For example, the Children and Young Persons Act 1933 made it a requirement that there should be an hour's interval between sittings of the adult and juvenile courts. The CDA 1998 ss 47–48 repealed this requirement and also amended Schedule 2 para 15 of the 1933 Act to allow a stipendiary magistrate (now District Judge) to sit alone in a youth court.

[16] *The Sentencing Framework for Children and Young People*, which is currently reproduced on the Home Office 'Crime Reduction' web site (at http://www.crimereduction.homeoffice.gov.uk/youth/youth59.htm).

need to set sentences proportionate to seriousness. The update concludes as follows: 'While there is potential for these elements to clash, a sensitive balance can be achieved which gives an appropriate weighting to each. In general terms, the principle of proportionality establishes the appropriate programme to be imposed on a young offender. Providing that the prevention of youth crime is treated as a longer-term aim, welfare, proportionality and the reduction of offending will be the likely outcome'. However, the CJI Act 2008 amends s 44 of the Children and Young Persons Act 1933 to make very clear that the 'principal aim' of the youth justice system must take precedence: '[t]he court must have regard primarily to the principal aim of the youth justice system, that is, to prevent offending by children and other persons aged under 18'.[17] The use of the word 'primarily' might well upset the 'sensitive balance' hoped for by NACRO.

We can see the same dual aims evident in the recent Justice (Northern Ireland) Act 2002. The principal aim of the youth justice system 'is to protect the public by preventing offending by children' but the relevant persons 'must also have regard to the welfare of children affected by the exercise of their functions... with a view to furthering their personal, social and educational development' (ss 53(1) and (3)).

These shorthand terms of welfare and justice have, then, been used to indicate whether the *main* focus of policy and practice is the child's needs or the child's offending, and whether the constraining principle is the child's best interests— widely interpreted—or the young offender's rights to due process and an outcome which accords with his or her 'just deserts'. Consequently, the justice approach is characterised as involving 'informed and transparent decisions' in courts, and with an end product of punishment 'portrayed as rational, consistent and determinate' (Scraton and Haydon 2002: 311). The welfare approach is, instead, associated with interventionist measures of care, protection and rehabilitation, which have drawn on knowledge from medicine and criminology since the early twentieth century. To quote Shaw, Lord Advocate in 1908, 'many high-minded men and women, and many philanthropic societies, have been working upon this subject, and of recent years one is glad to note a large development of scientific knowledge. All these facts...made out a case for this Bill' (speaking in the debate on the Children Act 1908).[18]

The welfare approach is, consequently, associated with decision making by professionals trained in social work or the 'psy-sciences', exercising their discretion to determine what is in the child's best interests. From the justice perspective, this approach is criticised for 'leaving children to the discretionary, permissive powers of professionals' (Scraton and Haydon 2002: 311) and for being based on philosophically unsound principles. According to Asquith, 'it is not possible to identify criteria which can either be employed to explain delinquent behaviour or to inform the measures to which children are subjected in their "best interests"' (2002: 276). Some proponents of children's rights would argue that 'only in a system in which children are punished for what they have done can their rights be best protected' (ibid), an echo of the debate referred to in Chapters 1 (section 1.2.3)

---

[17] Clause 9 of the CJI Bill at 4 December 2007.
[18] Hansard, 1908, Vol 186, cols 1 251–2.

and 4 (section 4.4.3) on whether rights are more protected under a retributivist system than a utilitarian one.

On the other hand, the justice approach is criticised on the same ground as modern retributivism: it is unable to deliver substantive justice because it cannot take sufficient account of social mitigation (Scraton and Haydon 2002: 315; see also Chapter 10 below). 'Critics, therefore, posit the notion of a ' "just" criminal justice system within an unjust society' as a contradiction in terms' (Morris and Giller 1987: 246, referring to Bottoms 1985: 110) and this is one of the 'five main areas of attack' on the justice model which Morris and Giller summarise (1987: 246). It is also implied by Goldson when he states 'it is well established that the social circumstances of children in trouble, "young offenders", are invariably scarred by complex configurations and multiple interrelated forms of disadvantage' (Goldson 1999: 3, also 2000b; see also Fortin 2003: 548–9 and references therein; see also Barry 2005). For example, there is research evidence of the abusive background of a large proportion of 12–14-year-olds eligible for what are now detention and training orders (Crowley 1998), of those sentenced for murder and very 'grave crimes' (Boswell 1991) and of persistent young offenders (Hagell and Newburn 1994). The vast literature on the childhood risk factors which correlate with offending by young people tell the same story (see, for example, Beinart *et al.* 2002; Farrington 2007; Youth Justice Board 2001).

These correlations between harm done to children in childhood and their offending persist into adulthood, so it might be argued that children are not a special case. Logically, the sentencer should take these correlations into account for both adults and children or disregard them for both. However, the idea that responsibility and culpability should be mitigated has more force in its application to minors. Offenders who are minors do not have the capability and independence to rise above their circumstances and, further, propensities to offend can more easily be 'treated' when the offender is young. Deciding outcomes on retributivist or restorative principles requires, then, a better understanding of the stages by which children acquire the ability to be given, and benefit from, an appropriate level of responsibility (see Weijers 2002: 139–42).

What the above review suggests is that perceptions of justice for minors who offend are in large part determined by a choice of one of two overarching principles to determine outcome: the welfare of the child or due process rights. But it is more complex than this. What counts as justice also depends on changing ideas about the most important issues for promoting the welfare of the child, and changing conceptions of the child as a rights holder. Ideas about children and childhood are relevant as are the debates charted so far on justifications for the punishment of adults.

The justice approach—to a greater or lesser extent in different decades for different age groups—has incorporated a retributivist ethos of personal culpability (see Morris and Giller 1987: 247–8). The 'welfare' approach is more clearly a utilitarian approach as its justification lies in the intended outcome of improvements in the minor's development and well-being. So, in the Scottish Children's Hearings system for young offenders, established as a welfare approach, 'the anticipated consequences of the different available disposals are the overriding criteria in all decisions made on behalf of children' (Adler 1985: 77).

In practice, of course, even if it is possible to delineate theoretically 'welfare' and 'justice' approaches in the history of juvenile justice in England and Wales, there has always been an uneasy integration of both elements. Sections 102–103 of the Children Act 1908 established that, to protect the child, there should be separate places of detention for the under-17s but these were still penal establishments. Further, as noted above, the long-standing duty to have regard to the child's welfare contrasts with the just deserts-based criterion of seriousness for imposing sentences of detention on young offenders (now CJA 2003, s 148) and may conflict with the narrower aim of preventing offending. The next sections therefore will briefly review the history of juvenile justice in the UK, noting a different development in Scotland, and summarising the policies of **bifurcation** and diversion which emerged.

However, there are also important new discourses around offending by children and young people, notably the 'respect' and inclusion policy agendas, which cut across concepts of welfare and justice and which make problematic the boundaries, not only between the juvenile and adult justice systems but also between social and penal policy relevant to children and young people. We will deal with these later in this chapter.

8.2.2 Diverging policies in the UK

The 1960s have generally been seen as a watershed in the way young offenders were dealt with in different parts of the UK. Commentators present the debates in that decade as 'the heyday of youth justice welfarism' (Muncie and Hughes 2002: 7) when 'the welfare ideology reached its apotheosis in the Children and Young Persons Act 1969' (Ashworth 2000: 323). It is clear that the postwar 'broad consensus' (Gelsthorpe 2002: 48–9) had fallen apart by 1970, although the significance of these changes is contested (see Clarke 2002).

It is argued that the two strands of welfare and justice became more distinct and juvenile justice became 'politicised' when the different approaches tended to become aligned with political groupings (Pitts 1988). Broadly speaking, the Left aligned with the 'welfare' approach to juvenile justice and the Right with the 'justice' approach but this is an over-simplification (Harris and Webb 1987: 24, 26). Two White Papers for England and Wales (*The Child, the Family and the Young Offender* 1965 and *Children in Trouble* 1968) and for Scotland (the Kilbrandon Report 1964) set out the agenda for change, receiving polarised responses in the different jurisdictions of the UK but with a more concerted opposition in England and Wales (Harris and Webb 1987: 26–9). The result was that policy in England and Wales diverged from that in Scotland.

For England and Wales, the Labour Government introduced the Children and Young Persons Act (CYPA) 1969. It was a compromise scheme in that juvenile courts remained but Social Services Departments had a bigger role, detention in the criminal system was ended, the age of criminal responsibility was lowered and 'intermediate treatment' (referring to new preventative programmes) was introduced. However, a change of government meant that several key sections were not implemented and the juvenile justice system, it was argued, 'retained its traditional commitment to imprisonment as the ultimate disciplinary back-stop' (Pitts 1992a: 173–4). In effect, there occurred, as in the USA, a 'back to justice' swing (Asquith 2002: 276) despite the increased role for social workers. In comparison, for Scotland, the Social Work (Scotland) Act 1968 produced a clearer change. Issues of guilt (determined if necessary by the courts) were separated from issues of child welfare, with a network of Children's Panels to oversee assessment, treatment and reappraisal by social workers with outcomes such as care, supervision and residential orders. Scotland, then, developed a decision-making forum with a 'welfare' approach whilst England, Wales and Northern Ireland retained a 'justice'-based juvenile court, albeit one able to draw on, if it so wished, a wider range of 'welfare' intermediate treatment options.

There were, however, some differences in relation to Northern Ireland. The institution of a juvenile court by the Children Act 1908 applied to Northern Ireland and the Children and Young Persons Act (Northern Ireland) 1968 continued the mixed care and crime jurisdiction of the juvenile court as in England and Wales, with a similar range of options. However, in practice, until 1995 the most common form of custodial sentence was the training school order, and the four training schools were used for 10–16-year-olds who needed care and protection, as well as for those convicted by the courts. It was a semi-determinate sentence, on average lasting 12 months and implemented with a welfare ethos. The result was that juvenile offenders spent 'longer in custody than their counterparts in England and Wales and indeed longer than young adult offenders in Northern Ireland' (O'Mahoney and Deazley 2000: 56). The criticisms made of the 1960s version of welfare in England and Wales have, consequently, been made of more recent 'justice' practice in Northern Ireland (ibid: 57–8).

This does not mean there are agreed ways to incorporate 'welfare' into practice. In France, for example, a study found the juvenile court judge, the *juge des enfants*, most commonly interviewed the juvenile in his or her office on court premises, usually with the minor's parents (Hackler and Garapon 1986: 7), and focused on the child and family functioning rather than on the facts of crimes as indicative of 'the appropriate action' to be taken (King and Piper 1995: 113). In this process there is little distinction made between the delinquent and the child in need, although the French system also includes the option for minors who commit more serious offences to be referred to the appropriate criminal courts. Courts are, however, only part of the story of juvenile justice.

8.2.3 'Bifurcation' and diversion: 1970–90

'Bifurcation' has been a useful tool in English criminal justice policy: we have examined in previous chapters the different sentencing approaches of 'just deserts' and 'public protection' for use with 'normal' and 'dangerous' offenders (see Chapters 3 and 5). In the case of juvenile justice, bifurcation refers to the policy of diverting most young offenders from prosecution, whilst a smaller number of serious offenders are processed through the criminal justice system and punished (Bottoms 1985). This policy means that, as with adult sentencing, the higher-profile serious cases can be seen to be treated in a 'tough justice' fashion whilst the rest can be diverted, either *from* the system or, increasingly, *to* preventative measures. The practice of diversion is not part of sentencing as such but the starting point is the same—a 'finding' that an offence has been committed—and records of reprimands and warnings (see below) are made available to the courts on subsequent convictions. For these reasons we are examining diversion in some detail.

In the UK the main policy tool for diverting young offenders from the criminal justice system in the second half of the twentieth century was cautioning, first tried with young offenders after the First World War but discouraged by the Moloney Report (1927). Policy initiatives after the Second World War (see Home Office 1951) led to the establishment of 17 juvenile liaison schemes in England and Wales by 1969, when an official policy of encouraging diversion began to develop. A Home Office Circular in 1978 stated that first offenders should be cautioned for all but serious offences and that subsequent offences could also result in a caution if the offences were trivial or there had been some time since the previous offence had been committed. Subsequent circulars did not have an overt aim to increase cautioning, but that was probably the aim implicit in the 1985 and 1990 circulars urging more uniformity of police practice (Wilkinson and Evans 1990: 166).[19] The first and second editions of the *Code for Crown Prosecutors* (CPS 1988, 1991)[20] gave a similar message by stating that the factor of 'youth' could 'properly lead' to a caution instead of prosecution and that prosecution might actually increase the likelihood of reoffending:

The stigma of conviction can cause irreparable harm to the future prospects of a young adult, and careful consideration should be given to the possibility of dealing with him or her by means of a caution.

(CPS 1988: Code, para 8(iii))

It is a long standing statutory requirement that the Courts shall have regard to the welfare of the juvenile...There may be positive advantages for the individual and for society, in using prosecution as a last resort and in general there is in the case of juvenile offenders a much stronger presumption in favour of methods of disposal which fall short of prosecution unless the seriousness of the offence or other exceptional circumstances dictate otherwise. The objective should be to divert juveniles from court wherever possible. Prosecution should always be regarded as a severe step.

(CPS 1991: Code, paras 20–21)

The Government endorsed this approach: 'Minimum intervention is a key concept in work with juvenile offenders....Most juveniles commit offences during their adolescence...and most grow out of it. It is of central importance that our response to delinquent acts does not serve to drive a wayward youngster into becoming a career criminal' (in Britton *et al.* 1988: 26).

The resulting growth in the out-of-court decision making necessary to implement this policy led to the establishment of various inter-agency bodies to make the 'diversion' decisions (see Rutter and Giller 1983: 20; see also Chapter 6, section 6.3.1). Such bodies could be consultative or have permanent staff who administered projects. Local authorities cooperated in or managed these inter-agency panels and sometimes set up their own juvenile justice teams. The source of their authority to make cautioning decisions was the police power to caution.[21] As a result, fewer children and young people were prosecuted: between 1980 and 1988

[19] Similarly in Northern Ireland, from 1975 the police operated a specialist Juvenile Justice Liaison Scheme for 10–16-year-olds (O'Mahoney and Deazley 2000: 36–7).

[20] The Code gives guidance to the Crown Prosecution Service (CPS) in making a decision whether or not to prosecute any suspect above the age of criminal responsibility. It is issued by the Director of Public Prosecutions under s 10 of the Prosecution of Offences Act 1985.

[21] See *Chief Constable of Kent and Another ex p L* (1991).

the numbers of children sentenced by the courts for indictable offences fell by over 58 per cent (NACRO 1989: 50), at a time when the demographic drop in that age group was around 11 per cent, and the use of cautioning vastly increased for juvenile offenders in the 1970s and 1980s (Ball 1995; Goldson 1999, 2000a).[22] The use of cautioning for 17–20-year-olds had also risen after Circular 14/1985 (Evans and Wilkinson 1990).

Cautioning proved to be a useful peg on which to hang preventative initiatives in the form of cautioning plus under which a caution was accompanied by the minor's voluntary involvement in some other activity set up by local authority Social Services Departments and the police (see Marshall 1985). The additional element included offence counselling, mediation, reparation, making an apology, being referred to other agencies for particular problems like drugs, or attending a scheme intended to reduce the likelihood of reoffending.

The other 'half' of the bifurcated policy for responding to offending by minors is the use of sentencing and punishment through the courts (see Chapter 13) and there is some evidence that diversion encourages the belief that minors who are prosecuted are the 'hardened criminals' towards whom the courts can justifiably be tough. For example, in the period 1965–77 more minors were given 'custodial' orders (Pitts 1992a: 174). The policy of bifurcation has continued in a modified form (see section 8.5 below) and this concern remains.

8.3 Diversion in a changing climate

8.3.1 'Systemic' management

The increased use of cautioning in the 1980s reflected the economic, political and criminological developments discussed in Chapter 1. The (then) juvenile justice system was not immune to the reaction against rehabilitation generally, to the need for cost cutting and to the increasing influence of a managerialist discourse and techniques. By the end of the 1980s 'corporatism' and 'systems management' became important in private and public enterprises: 'if we are to succeed in effectively managing the problem of juvenile offending, then it must be effectively organised' (Locke 1988: 1). Better management—with an aim of limiting the use of punishment and promoting the diversion of young people who offended from the courts—became an end in itself. The most influential pioneers were a group of researchers and consultants associated with Lancaster University who analysed, monitored and locally managed the different agencies in the juvenile justice system.[23] The aim of diversion might be welfarist but the decision-making was often offence-focused and within a justice frame (King and Piper 1995: 122–5)[24] and

---

[22] The proportion of juveniles cautioned rather than prosecuted rose from a quarter to nearly a half in the period 1968–73 and to nearly 60 per cent by 1983 (NACRO 1985: 6). By 1994 figures for 10–16-year-old males showed a national rate of 78 per cent with police force area rates ranging from 93 per cent in Suffolk to 63 per cent in Durham.

[23] See, also, Cavadino and Dignan (2002: 292–8) for a useful discussion of systems management.

[24] For details of projects and decision-making bodies, see King and Piper (1995: 120–5).

economic considerations helped drive social work cooperation with the police (Pitts 1992a).

Until the 1990s diversion was, then, supported as a policy aim for a complex variety of professional and policy reasons. Inter-agency initiatives, increasingly favoured in government policy, and including social workers whose 'expert' status had at that time increased, were used to oversee preventative programmes.

There was another specific 'scientific' impetus for diversion—the development of labelling theory (see Lemert 1967) which endorsed the idea that most children will 'grow out of' offending if they do not receive and internalise the label of 'criminal'. The 1968 White Paper *Children in Trouble* had endorsed this view: 'It is probably a minority of children who grow up without ever behaving in ways which may be contrary to the law. Frequently such behaviour is no more than an incident in the pattern of a child's normal development' (Home Office 1968: 3–4). Similarly, in Northern Ireland the Black Committee (1979) argued that a court experience 'is often a significant step in their delinquent career' and as late as 1988 a Consultation Paper argued that 'even a short period of custody is quite likely to confirm them as criminals…They see themselves labelled as criminals and behave accordingly' (Home Office 1988a: paras 2.17–2.19). Further, statistical monitoring consistently showed that cautioning of 10–17-year-olds was at least as successful as other outcomes in reducing reoffending.

Diversion also 'benefited' by becoming more closely linked to the legal system: it took on some of the legitimacy of that system. The CYPA 1969 prescribed pre-court consultation and liaison, and the 1978 Home Office Circular established that cautions could be cited in juvenile courts. Perhaps most crucially, cautioning, even if accompanied by preventative intervention, was much cheaper than prosecution followed by either detention in the penal system or care in the child protection system—an increasingly important factor at a time of recession (Pitts 1992a: 175–6). Partnerships of children's charities, Social Services Departments, and the Probation Service developed innovative schemes, such as car theft, assault, and social and life skills projects and, whilst not numerically important, these projects allowed experimentation in ways of reducing offending (see NACRO 1986).

Arguably, these professional ideas and policy advantages allowed the focus to shift from the causes of offending to the managerialist agenda. Juvenile justice could then be reconceptualised as a 'delinquency management service' which was 'subjugating professional skills and autonomy to management ideals' by the 1990s (Muncie 1999: 149–50; see also McLaughlin *et al.* 2001: 308). Associated with managerialism is the New Penology and actuarially based decision making (see Chapter 1) and fears that it is 'colonising' juvenile justice began to be expressed (Kempf-Leonard and Peterson 2000: 88).

Yet the 1970s and 1980s also revealed very clearly the complexities and pitfalls in both formulating and analysing juvenile justice policy. The CYPA 1969, designed to create a less 'penal' system for dealing with young offenders, 'led paradoxically to a massive increase in the incarceration of young people in the 1970s', whilst the 1980s was 'the decade of what was called "the successful revolution"…in juvenile justice' despite the increasing law and order rhetoric (Cavadino and Dignan 2002: 284, 292). On the one hand the 1980 White Paper (Home Office *et al.* 1980) called for a tougher approach in dealing with young offenders, and the 1982 Criminal Justice Act 'restored to the magistracy some of the powers taken away by the 1969

Act' (Ashworth 2002: 324). On the other hand, the amendments to the 1982 Act, to introduce restrictions on custodial sentencing by imposing criteria for custody (see Dunbar and Langton 1998: 75–6), were used to curb the apparent predilection of sentencers for 'imprisoning' minors[25] and there was a decrease in the use of custody for minors in the 1980s, at least partly the result of these legislative changes.

Cautioning and cautioning plus continued into the 1990s to be replaced by reprimands and warnings. But policy attitudes to diversion and to the use of custody changed in the 1990s.

8.3.2 Prosecution and diversion in the 1990s

The Home Office Circular and National Standards issued in 1994 (Home Office 1994b) and the revised *Code* for the CPS (CPS 1994) provided evidence that the policy of diversion was 'threatened with reversal' by the new guidance on cautioning (Evans 1994: 566). The Circular no longer referred to young offenders as those who should normally be diverted from prosecution (Home Office 1994b: Note 3A) and it appeared to amend the policy of multiple cautioning (ibid: para 8; see also NACRO 1993). Similarly, the revised CPS *Code*, issued two months later,[26] indicated a tougher approach. According to the Home Secretary when he introduced the new Code, 'from now on your first chance is your last chance. Criminals should know that they will be punished' (Michael Howard, quoted in Ball 1995: 198). The 1994 CPS *Code* amalgamated and amended sections from previous Codes to dilute the message about diversion to be found in earlier versions:

Crown Prosecutors must consider the interests of a youth when deciding whether it is in the public interest to prosecute. The stigma of a conviction can cause very serious harm to the prospects of a youth offender or a young adult. Young offenders can sometimes be dealt with without going to court. But Crown Prosecutors should not avoid prosecuting simply because of the defendant's age. The seriousness of the offence or the offender's past behaviour may make prosecution necessary.

(CPS 1994: para 6.8)

In the further revised CPS *Code* issued six years later the removal of the second and third sentences of the above paragraph weakened the presumption further. Instead, 'Crown Prosecutors should not avoid prosecuting simply because of the defendant's age. The seriousness of the offence or the youth's past behaviour is very important' (CPS 2000: para 6.9). What we have here is a much starker focus, and one which by 2000 related to the replacement for cautions. However, the trend was apparent before the 1998 Crime and Disorder Act (CDA) was implemented: the percentage of those cautioned (out of the total of those cautioned or convicted) fell from 70 per cent in 1992 to 58 per cent in 1999 (NACRO 2001b), a trend which

---

[25] Research suggested that not all magistrates and judges initially complied with the spirit of the Criminal Justice Act 1982 (Barker 1985; Burney 1985; Reynolds 1985) but appellate decisions in the 1980s (NACRO 2001d: 2; Dunbar and Langton 1998: 77) and amendments made by the Criminal Justice Act 1988 tightened up the criteria.

[26] The Attorney General's policy intention was 'that the public interest factors *in favour of* prosecution [are] brought out more clearly': see Hansard HC, 14 December 1993, Vol 234 col 1049, italics added: see Piper (2001: 34).

continued at least until 2001 (Audit Commission 2004: 33–4). The next section will review possible explanations for this apparent change of direction.

8.3.3 New factors

What happened later in the 1990s was an unpleasant and unexpected shock to youth justice professionals after a period—from the 1970s to the early 1990s— when it seemed as if some stability had been reached in juvenile justice policy. There had been a downward trend in the use of custody (see Harding 1994: 104) accompanied by an upward trend in the use of community punishments and one study found a reoffending rate after one year of around only 20 per cent for cautioning, 50 per cent for fines and supervision orders, but nearly 90 per cent for custody (Audit Commission 1996: 42–3).

In policy terms there are two main sets of 'needs' which help to explain the changes that occurred in the 1990s: an economic imperative to reduce government expenditure and a political need for the government to be seen to be 'doing something'. Governments needed to restore confidence in, and boost the legitimacy of, the criminal justice system generally and the youth justice system in particular. The economic case for reform was put forward by the Audit Commission (1996, 1998) in its reports entitled *Misspent Youth*, based on statistics up to 1995 and 1997 respectively, and was immensely influential. It produced a clear and damning account of the cost of wasted processing time and the cost of court processing in relation to outcome, focusing on the following findings:

- two out of five young offenders apprehended by the police were proceeded against, but a quarter of these had their cases withdrawn, discontinued, or dismissed: the numbers pleading guilty declined from 65 per cent in 1989 to 55 per cent in 1994 (Audit Commission 1996: 24–5, 33)
- prosecution through the courts was not value for money in terms of preventing reoffending: the cost was around £2,500 per person and about a quarter received a conditional or absolute discharge (ibid: 26, 35–6, 45)
- custodial sentences were ineffective: 90 per cent of young males aged 14–16 sentenced to custody for up to one year were reconvicted within two years (ibid: 42; see also Audit Commission 1998: 31–6)
- long delays were documented—these were presented as costly and as reducing the deterrent effect of the use of a prosecution (Audit Commission 1998: 11–20 and Appendix 2)
- the probability of reoffending after prosecution was greater than that after the first and second cautions but there was an almost equal probability after the third caution. On the fourth caution the probability of reoffending was greater than after prosecution (Audit Commission 1996: 23).

The Audit Commission found that only 2 per cent of young offenders nationally participated in a caution plus scheme although with wide regional variations (1996: 20). The 1996 and 1998 Reports both emphasised that money saved by reducing the processing of offenders through the courts could be used to fund programmes aimed at challenging offending behaviour. Further, their findings seemed to show that a more interventionist approach might be cost effective in relation to repeat offenders.

Despite their considerable influence on policy, the Audit Commission's reports have not escaped criticism. Arguably, they reveal an inadequate understanding of youth crime and the criminal justice process and lend support to the endorsement of cheaper, but more controlling, options for change (Jones 2001; Downes 2001/2: 9; Gelsthorpe 2002: 55).

The second set of factors, the political issues, was perhaps even more influential. The political climate which emerged by the mid-1990s reflected social anxiety and political instability. Before the general elections in the 1990s, both main parties wanted to be seen to be more effective in reducing youth crime and the fear of crime. By 1996 there was, in effect, 'a Dutch auction of who could seem to be most tough in relation to young people' (Littlechild 1997: 80), epitomised by oft-quoted sound bites from, respectively, a Conservative and a Labour leader, to 'punish more, understand a little less' (John Major) and be 'tough on crime, tough on the causes of crime' (Tony Blair).

There was also one particular crime which played a major part in refocusing law and order rhetoric about young offenders. This was the murder of James Bulger by the two 10-year-old children, Robert Thompson and Jon Venables. As Haydon and Scraton note, 'the James Bulger case took the debate over childhood indiscipline and lawlessness to a different level', but they argue that it was 'an exceptional tragedy conveniently exploited' to construct a 'crisis' (2002: 314). This crisis used the rhetoric of a moral panic, a theoretical concept developed in the 1960s and 1970s with the pioneering studies of Jock Young and Stan Cohen into drug taking and the 'mods and rockers' episode. They analysed the role and influence of agents of social control, notably the police, as well as media coverage, in the 'amplification' of deviance (McRobbie and Thornton 2002: 69). Similar analyses have been done in relation to the Bulger episode (see, for example, Diduck 1999; Hay 1995; King 1997b).

The developing policy focus on increasing control of young offenders was not confined to youth justice concerns. The Youth Service, the umbrella organisation for youth and community services set up by the Education Act 1944, became increasingly underfunded during the 1980s. It consequently became more reliant on sources of funding other than the local authority and looked, for example, to 'Safer Cities' and 'City Challenge' initiatives as well as the Prince's Trust and large corporations. These led to new priorities, which included crime prevention and a focus on young people 'at risk' of offending (Piper 2001: 32–3). The influential discourse around anti-social behaviour and community safety has also influenced thinking about young offenders and has reflected a sense of social insecurity which has been utilised by politicians to legitimise the introduction of new statutory responses to the behaviour of children and young people, notably the new civil orders—anti-social behaviour, child safety, and parenting orders. Their introduction by the CDA 1998 led Muncie to conclude that 'now it is not so much neglect and delinquency that are conflated, but misbehaviour and crime' (1999: 170). They are not strictly within the remit of this criminal justice text[27] but they do appear on the Youth Justice Board's web site under the

---

[27] Though, Brown has asked, in relation to the separate anti-social behaviour sessions at criminology conferences: 'is this because anti-social behaviour is a distinct category of behaviour, or a sub-set of criminal behaviour?' (2004: 203).

heading 'Sentences, Orders and Agreements' and they will be discussed further in section 13.1.1 below.

Gelsthorpe and Morris (1999: 211) isolate eight inter-related strands which influenced thinking about criminal justice generally in the 1990s: just deserts, managerialism, actuarial justice, 'community', restorative justice, 'public voice', active citizenship and populist punitiveness. These influences are discussed elsewhere in this volume but, in relation to minors, the result of all these new factors was, according to Tim Newburn, that the 1990s saw 'a return of unbridled "authoritarian populism" in juvenile justice' (Newburn 1996: 69). Section 8.5 below will consider the new administrative system set up to implement policies of early intervention, offender responsibility, and restorative justice for young offenders, which were outlined in the White Paper of 1997 and introduced in the CDA 1998. First, however, we want to examine the ideas about children and their parents which underpin more recent policies.

8.4 Discipline and responsibility

8.4.1 Constructions of childhood and adolescence

There is now clear evidence of a policy rhetoric which is more punitive and more controlling and it is reflected in images of children which currently underpin youth justice and even family policy. In contrast to the ideas about childhood that helped ensure the establishment of juvenile courts a century ago, we now hold, it is argued, 'extraordinarily narrow views' about children and offending (Fortin 2003: 556) which are reflected in changing nomenclature. The juvenile court is now the youth court and, as we saw above, the *CPS Code* reveals, in successive versions, minors being transformed from 'juveniles' and 'young offenders' through 'youth offenders' to, simply, 'youths' (Piper 2001). There is a valid case for changing from 'juveniles'—it had acquired pejorative overtones—but 'youth' as a replacement is problematic. As Garland has noted, 'penal laws and institutions...are framed in language and sign systems which embody specific cultural meanings, distinctions and sentiments and which must be interpreted and understood (1990: 198). At present, the cultural meanings constructed around 'youth' are negative, with its image of an older (male) person and, arguably, 'youths hanging about' have become 'the universal symbol of disorder and, increasingly, menace' (Burney 2002: 473).

Such changes in thinking are important because how we conceptualise 'a child' (Jenks 1996: 51) and what we believe distinguishes a child from an adult (Archard 1993: 20) help determine what is appropriate treatment of children. Referring to minors as youths, we would argue, has facilitated the introduction of criminal justice policies for minors which are at odds with former ideas about the offending child as one who is 'in trouble' and in need of help (Vaughan 2000; Piper 2001). If 'youth' draws on disparate ideas ranging from the 'dangerous' to the 'nearly adult', it conveys the connotation of a person who can legitimately be disciplined, be accorded culpability from a young age and be held to account. He (or she) can then be expected to take part in the processes of mediation and reparation which assume responsibility in the participants (see Chapter 6). He or she can also be expected to participate in intensive community programmes designed to prevent reoffending which have potentially severe penalties for non-compliance (see Chapters 12 and 13), and can legitimately be punished more harshly for persistence. Scraton and Haydon have criticised this development: 'it imposes surveillance disguised as prevention, subservience disguised as discipline and punishment disguised as correction' (Scraton and Haydon 2002: 315).

This development has been linked to another policy element, that of the 're-moralisation' agenda, which further legitimises a focus on discipline and responsibility.

8.4.2 'Re-moralisation'

In the 1990s an influential moral discourse explained the perceived increased lawlessness of the young as being the result of their not having been taught right from wrong. The approach, grounded in influential ideas about children's need for discipline (Fortin 2003: 556), was part of a wider project to 're-moralise' the family and so strengthen the moral basis for an ordered society. There is another perspective, from psychology, to explain this policy focus on minors who offend, which arises from an acknowledgement of 'profound changes in the economic, technological and social make up of western societies' that have combined to undermine social cohesion and stability (Junger-Tas 2002: 40). What has resulted are feelings of social and personal insecurity which have been projected on to the deviant and the criminal (ibid).

The strength of these ideas stems from the relative fragility of social order in democracies: a liberal state is dangerously dependent on its members internalising norms of self-control and citizenship, given that, by definition, it cannot routinely maintain order by physical force. Analysts who use the theoretical framework developed by Michel Foucault (see, for example, Foucault 1977; Donzelot 1980; Rose 1987, 1990) have focused on this issue of social discipline and have examined ways in which techniques of control have been deployed historically through the workhouse, the factory and the prison, for example. Most importantly they have focused on the family as a site for forms of 'gentle' social control. What is now seen as problematic is whether the family, this traditional main 'tool' for the inculcation of morality, still has the ability and the authority to act as 'a place of socialisation of the young' (Junger-Tas 1994: 18).

The current Government thinks the family does have the ability—with support and 'encouragement'—and so policy now focuses very strongly on the role and responsibilities of parents. *Building on Progress: Families* stated that the family is a 'fundamental building block of society' and, consequently that 'the role that families play within society requires a legal framework to function effectively' (PMSU 2007: 10). The clear message of policy documents is, however, that the help offered to parents to improve their parenting *should* be accepted. Reece argues that meanings of parental responsibility and autonomy are changing as parents are being made more and more accountable: 'It is interesting that "responsibility" is able to mean its opposite. "Authority" is the reverse of "accountability". While authority embodies independence and freedom, answerability implies dependence and loss of control' (Reece 2005: 467–8). Hollingsworth's recent review of new mechanisms used to encourage parental responsibility in the youth justice context focuses on a 'matrix of powers' to 'instil' parental responsibility: the liability of parents in relation to fines and the new parental compensation orders, the power of the courts to bind parents over,[28] the introduction and increasing scope of parenting orders, and the sanctions for non-compliance (Hollingsworth 2007b). These civil orders for parents can also accompany civil orders imposed on their children and can be imposed where children have been playing truant from school. Further, Baroness Butler-Sloss has recently urged that Parliament has 'to get the message across to the entire country about the long-term adverse effect on children of bad or inadequate parenting. It will also affect people's ability to parent the next generation after the current one, so...we need to recognise that bad parenting will continue if we do not get at the generation who are not yet parents.'[29] So parents and children are both part of the re-moralisation project to prevent offending now and in the future.

This is not a new concern. Institutions such as schools, reformatories and the armed forces have in the past been used as norm-imposing substitutes for family or religion, and since the nineteenth century, voluntary organisations and the state have experimented with new sources of socialisation. However, in the 1920s, the 'psy-sciences' took over from religion in imposing on families the responsibility and blame for the offending conduct of their children (Gelsthorpe 1999), and it would appear that research on young offenders 'habitually produces results that point to the adverse effects of certain features of family life' (Day Sclater and Piper 2000: 138).[30] Not surprisingly, then, the 'parenting theme' has always been dominant in policy debates about criminality.

Consequently, current policy arises from a long-standing concern in social policy to strengthen the family when it is perceived to be in danger (ibid: 136). This anxiety has bred extreme statements such as the following: 'We have a historically unprecedented crisis in human relations on our hands...But it is not just marriage that is under threat—it is the family...These amount to the loss of the framework of society itself...Civilisation is at stake' (Morgan 1996: 1–2). Debate focuses on the correlation between offending and family disruption, and includes a particular concern that boys are not receiving discipline and support from (non-residential) fathers. Recent research which found, for example, that boys not living with their mothers were most likely to become persistent offenders, would suggest the situation is more complex (Haas *et al.* 2004).

The 'solution' to these contemporary concerns, although they stem from a complex set of structural and demographic changes, has been presented as a simple one: a 'normative project' to re-impose 'traditional' duties on families. Witness the following statements from Michael Howard and Tony Blair respectively:

My approach is based on some simple principles. That children—at home and at school—must be taught the difference between right and wrong.

---

[28] CJA 1991 ss 57–58 and Criminal Justice and Public Order Act 1994 Schedule 9 para 50. In 1994 the Law Commission had recommended abolition of binding-over (Law Comm No 222) but in a 1998 consultation paper (*Bind Overs: A Power for the 21st Century*, Cm 3908) the Home Office instead proposed changes to allow binding-over to be used with more effectiveness and clarity.

[29] Hansard HL 29 March 2007, col 1831.

[30] For a summary of such research, see Audit Commission (1996: 60–6); see also Farrington (2002b).

Families are the core of our society. They should teach right from wrong. They should be the first defence against anti-social behaviour.[31]

None of this proves that there is a decline in moral authority or parental discipline but these attitudes have 'seductive appeal': they feed into a belief 'that the process of change and modernity has gone too far' (Pearson 2002: 45–6) and they have legitimised those provisions noted above relating to the parents of offenders to be found in the CJA 1991, the CDA 1998 (see Gelsthorpe 1999), and the CJA 2003. They reflect the belief that the family is crucial in teaching children to act responsibly and refrain from offending and so, if parents do not act responsibly in this way, they themselves must be 'trained' (see Koffman 2008). A policy concern to involve fathers is evident here, given that research on the pilots for parenting orders revealed that over 80 per cent of the parents involved were female, whilst 80 per cent of the children and young people involved were male.[32] *Youth Justice—The Next Steps* the Government urged youth justice agencies to make more use of parenting orders and contracts, 'more actively *engaging fathers*, making sure *both parents* generally come to court' [emphasis in the original] (Home Office 2003c: 5, para 9) and the YJB web site now notes that encouraging the involvement of both parents is good practice.

The focus on the family to ensure the young are adequately socialised has another implication if it is believed that the task of moralisation cannot safely be left to the family alone. 'The only norm enforcing system that remains in force and has the pretension to fill the void is the criminal and juvenile justice system' (Junger-Tas 2002: 40). From this perspective, an increase in the scope of, and sanctions available to, the youth justice system is both necessary and legitimate. Further, it has legitimised the range of civil orders to control both parents and children which focus on anti-social behaviour rather than offending but are increasingly being seen as part of the repertoire of youth justice. It has also legitimised an extension of these controlling measures as part of the 'Respect' agenda.

8.4.3 **The Respect agenda**

As we noted above, politicians found it politically expedient to play the law and order card in the 1990s and the Audit Commission had flagged up the difficulties for the police in dealing with what they referred to as 'juvenile nuisance', the subject of 10–20 per cent of calls to the police (1996: 13). Jack Straw had written in 1996, for example, in a Labour Party policy document: 'There is a rising tide of disorder which is blighting our streets, parks, town and city centres and neighbourhoods...Disorder...has profound effects on individuals who feel frightened and unsafe: it can help to tip whole areas into decline, economic dislocation and crime; it can undermine the commercial viability of town and city centres' (Straw 1996: 1). As a result of these pressures, anti-social behaviour orders (ASBOs) for children of 10 years old and above (see Cracknell 2000)[33] and child safety orders for the under- 10-year-olds (see Hayes and Williams 1999; Piper 1999) were introduced

---

[31] Respectively, Michael Howard, October 1993 and Tony Blair, April 1997, cited in Goldson (1999: 10).

[32] There are gender issues here and concerns about domestic violence and child abuse: see Piper (2006).

[33] Although the early guidance showed that the original intention was to avoid their use for the under-18s: see Burney (2002: 473). For a Home Office-commissioned review of the use of ASBOs see Campbell (2002).

by the CDA 1998. The same message was given some years later in the White Paper, *Respect and Responsibility—Taking a Stand against Anti-social Behaviour*, which argued that anti-social behaviour 'creates an atmosphere in which more serious crime takes hold…It blights people's lives, undermines the fabric of society and holds back regeneration' (Home Office 2003a). That Paper proposed further civil penalties to be imposed on children and their parents for anti-social behaviour via housing and education law, and located behaviour which may not constitute an offence within a wider policy framework. It urged that 'all organisations in any local area need to follow a consistent principle—that the protection of the local community must come first' (Home Office 2003b: para 2.51).

To implement and promote such changes the Government developed its 'Respect Agenda' and there is a Home Office web site at www.respect.gov.uk which, by the beginning of 2008, is devoted to 'tackling anti-social behaviour and its causes'. This web site has been developed from the government's 'Together' and 'Respect' campaigns run between 2004 and 2008. The Respect campaign was run by the Respect Unit, based in the Home Office, but that has recently been moved to the new Department for Children, Families and Schools (DCFS) where the Respect Task Force has been replaced by a Youth Taskforce.[34] It is hoped that this move—from a department with a clear law and order ambiance—to bring it within a department with responsibility for implementing *The Children's Plan: Building Brighter Futures* (DCFS 2007), reduces the emphasis on using punitive forms of behaviour control with children and young people. The Respect Unit and the Respect agenda—with their responsibility for developing new ways of responding to behaviour which could be classified as criminal but might not be—have, however, been instrumental in endorsing negative images of young people.

Youth Matters (DfES 2005) proposes measures to give all youngsters equal access to opportunities to allow them to be fully 'included' young people. The Green Paper has relevance to the youth justice system because of its funding proposals and because of the following policy statement in the Preface: 'It is wrong that young people who do not respect the opportunities they are given, by committing crimes or behaving anti-socially, should benefit from the same opportunities as the law-abiding majority. So we will put appropriate measures in place to ensure they do not' (ibid: 1).

At the beginning of 2006 a new Respect Action Plan issued by the Home Office included similar messages. This document set out powers to 'promote respect positively; bear down uncompromisingly on anti-social behaviour; tackling its causes; and offer leadership and support to local people and local services' (Respect Task Force 2006: 1). To do so it aimed to 'intervene earlier in families, homes and schools to prevent children and young people who are showing signs of problems from getting any worse' (ibid: 7) and so was presented as part of the early intervention raft of programmes. Chapter 2, headed 'Activities for Children and Young People', argues that 'the future depends on unlocking the positive potential of young people' (ibid: 8). The generation of new money to fund family projects and preventative schemes is to be welcomed but, reflecting the Government's focus on responsibility, the document also states that 'respect cannot be learned, purchased or acquired, it can only be earned' (ibid: 30). Consequently it also focuses on

---

[34] See http://www.dcsf.gov.uk/pns/DisplayPN.cgi?pn_id=2007_0178.

enforcement and changes to ASBOs (see also Home Office 2006f). *Tools and Powers to Tackle Anti-social Behaviour* (Respect Task Force 2007) summarises the results of research by the task force into the use of parenting contracts and acceptable anti-social behaviour contracts and agreements as well as anti-social behaviour and parenting orders (see Chapter 13). This rapid growth in the use of both voluntary contracts and court orders in the last three years is somewhat alarming. McDonald (2006) argues that, by 'demonising the very children that the Government is trying to regulate and control with their strategies and early intervention', the action plan 'would appear to be creating the very problem that it is seeking to tackle' (ibid: 196, 198).

What these developments also illustrate is that non-criminal deviance, anti-social behaviour, is being dealt with in ways which blur the boundaries of the criminal and civil systems and law. This has been viewed as an indicator of a trend noted in other jurisdictions towards the use of 'criminalisation' as a state response where structural factors such as poverty and educational disadvantage ought rather to be addressed (Boyle and Lipman 2002; see also Chapter 10). It is apparent, for example, in the Executive Summary to the Green Paper on children at risk of neglect or harm, *Every Child Matters*, which has a bullet point 'reforms to the youth justice system' that begins with '[t]he government intends to revise the Child Safety Order to make it more effective and build on the success of the Intensive Supervision and Surveillance Programme by using it more widely as an alternative to custody' (DfES 2003: 7). This is an odd elision, given that the child safety order (CSO) is for children who cannot be held criminally liable. What we are seeing, to quote a recent Barnardo's Report, *Children in Trouble*, is 'a tendency to criminalise children unnecessarily and at younger ages, and a corresponding tendency to treat them as adults too soon' (Monaghan *et al.* 2003: 6).

We will return to these civil orders in Chapter 13 (section 13.1) when we review evidence that, although they were—at least in part—intended to help control the behaviour of children and young people so they do not move into the criminal justice system, such orders can also hasten a move into that system.

8.5 The 'new' youth justice system

8.5.1 No more excuses

In 1997 the new Labour government issued a White Paper whose title, *No More Excuses—A New Approach to Tackling Youth Crime in England and Wales* (Home Office 1997a), indicated a more interventionist response to offending which would hold children and young people to account and implement those responsibilising elements of New Labour's 'Third Way' policies to which we have already alluded. The Preface stated that the Government aims to 'nip offending in the bud' because 'today's young offenders can too easily become tomorrow's hardened criminals', whilst the Introduction argued that 'allowing young people to drift into a life of crime undermines their welfare and denies them the opportunity to develop into fully contributing members of society'. It proposed reprimands and warnings to replace cautions and argued for the earlier use of prosecution. It thereby undermined the premises of labelling theory and appeared to presage a more interventionist and less diversionary approach (see Goldson 2000a).

The White Paper of 1997 made clear its intention to remove the presumption that children aged over 10 and under 14 years of age are **doli incapax** so that all children over 10 would be liable to prosecution. It argued that 'presuming that children of this age [10–14] generally do not know the difference between naughtiness and serious wrongdoing...is contrary to common sense' (Home Office 1997a: para 4.4). What such 'common-sense' thinking ignores is that emotional maturity, and the understanding which comes with more experience of life, are prerequisites of understanding not just the 'fact' of wrongdoing but also its impact. The very notions of death as permanent and injury as 'un-mendable' are acquired with age, and the Beijing Rules (see Chapter 13) state that the age of criminal responsibility should 'not be fixed at too low an age level' (rule 4.1).

No More Excuses also extolled the benefits of restorative justice, pointing out that its proposals for reform build on the principles underlying the concepts of restorative justice—restoration, reintegration, and responsibility (Home Office 1997a: para 9.21). It argued that 'reparation can be a valuable way of making young offenders face the consequences of their actions and see the harm they have caused' (ibid: para 4.13) and proposed victim–offender mediation as part of final warnings (ibid: para 5.1.5). In Chapter 6 (section 6.3) we considered experimental restorative schemes in the 1980s and reviewed the current use of restorative justice approaches. As we pointed out then, government enthusiasm for such approaches in the late 1990s was an intriguing development, given that schemes set up in the 1980s had generally not survived as anything other than localised, small-scale projects (Shapland 2003: n 14). It would appear that the high policy profile being given to the victims of crime, the growing strength of the restorative justice lobby, and the political need to be seen to be doing something different about young offenders, gave reparation and mediation a new lease on life.

8.5.2 A national system

The CDA 1998 set up a national and local administrative framework for the youth justice system in England and Wales. It might be seen as a further development of the managerialist approach to youth justice that was developed in the 1980s. Section 38 imposed duties on each local authority, police authority, probation committee, and health authority to provide—or cooperate in providing—youth justice services, and s 38(4) lists ten functions for these services. It required that youth offending teams (YOTs) with a specified inter-agency composition be set up in each local authority (LA) area (s 39), and mandated the formulation and implementation of a youth justice plan (s 40).[35] Further, the Act set up a national Youth Justice Board for England and Wales to monitor the youth justice system and to advise the Secretary of State (s 41).

As presaged by the White Paper (Home Office 1997a: paras 2.3–2.6), s 37(1) of the CDA 1998 introduced for the first time in legislation in the UK an aim for the new youth justice system—to prevent offending. Bottoms (2002) has characterised it as

---

[35] These are similar to the Children's Services plans which are necessary for the proper operation of s 17 of the Children Act 1989. These two plans should now be integrated.

'explicitly correctionalist', suggesting something different from welfare or justice, and we have noted above the amendment by the CJI Act 2008 to give this aim priority over 'having regard' to the young offender's welfare (see section 8.2.1).

The youth offending team (YOT) is now one of the seven partners of the children's services authority listed in s 10(4) of the Children Act 2004. All of these partners 'must co-operate with the authority in the making of arrangements' as specified, 'with a view to improving the well-being of children' in relation to the five outcomes for children which are also specified in s 10. The statutory guidance to the Children Act 2004 notes that YOTs will have 'an important role to play' in the work of Children's Trusts in planning and delivering services relevant to existing statutory duties (HM Government 2005: para 1.16). They can also 'jointly commission and pool budgets with other partners for the benefit of children at risk of offending and those involved in the youth justice system' (ibid: para 2.51).

The responsibility of the youth justice system in England and Wales is for children and young people from the age of ten until their eighteenth birthday. In line with the White Paper proposals, s 34 of the CDA 1998 abolished the presumption that children aged 10–13 are not capable of being held criminally responsible. Consequently, there is now no presumption to rebut in order for children under 14 (but over 10) to be processed through the youth justice system if they offend. This reform has been much criticised (see Ball 2004: 174–5; Bandalli 1998) as the age of criminal responsibility in England and Wales is now one of the lowest in Europe, with the age being set, for example, at 18 in Belgium and Luxembourg, and 16 in Spain and Portugal.[36]

8.5.3 Reprimands and warnings

Sections 65–66 of the CDA 1998 introduced a new pre-court system of reprimands and warnings to replace cautions. Like cautions they are the responsibility of the police but, unlike cautions, they do not require the consent of the minor. They were presented in the White Paper as part of the Government's 'Effective Intervention in the Community' proposals (Home Office 1997a: paras 5.12–5.15), with the aim of earlier intervention in the life of the young offender and a reduction in the use of repeat cautions. The reprimand is, in effect, the first caution although a young offender can be moved directly to a warning if the offence is serious (s 65(4)). Normally, the first warning is the only warning although a second may be given if there has been at least a two-year gap since the first (s 65(3)(b)).[37] A warning can be cited as a conviction (s 66(5)(c)).

Guidance emphasises that seriousness of offending will be a very important factor in the decision whether or not to reprimand, warn or prosecute and that the police should use the Gravity Factor System devised by ACPO (the Association of Chief Police Officers). This gives all offences a score of 1–4 and the guidance states that a score of 4 should always lead to a charge with a 3 leading to a warning

---

[36] The Republic of Ireland raised its minimum age from 7 to 12 in 2006.

[37] Research would suggest that not all those operating the scheme are yet clear about the details of the new legal framework: sometimes several reprimands were given, for example (Audit Commission 2004: 17).

(for a first offence) or a charge (Home Office/Youth Justice Board 2002: paras 4.21–4.25).[38]

The *Durham* (2005) case, which concerned a young person who had not been told that a final warning for indecent assault involved a registration requirement as a sex offender, raised rights issues about the final warning. In that case the House of Lords in a unanimous decision concluded that reprimands and warning do not constitute punishment and that informed consent is not required of children and young people in connection with the use of these provisions. Koffman and Dingwall (2007) have argued that juveniles are in fact being diverted, not from punishment, but to a different form of punishment and, therefore, see the decision in this case as contentious.

The policy of the Youth Justice Board (YJB) is that the warning should, if possible, be given at a restorative conference (see Chapter 6, section 6.3.2; see also Fox *et al.* 2006 for recent research) and guidance on the administration of such meetings states that YOTs should contact the victim within five working days of being notified (Home Office/Youth Justice Board 2002: 16). The warning is then accompanied by referral to a YOT for assessment, and there is a presumption that the young offender will engage in a rehabilitation programme (s 66(2)). The YJB set a target that 80 per cent of warnings should lead to such a programme by the end of 2004, 70 per cent already having been achieved (Audit Commission 2004: 19). The YJB Key Performance Indicator (KPI) is now 95 per cent and various local youth justice boards report meeting that target.[39]

The preventative measures are generally offence-focused. There can be a 'prior assessment', completed by a member of the YOT using the Asset assessment tool,[40] before the police make a decision, to explore whether the offender will engage effectively with a rehabilitation programme as well as to suggest the content of it (Giller 2000). A matrix is provided to help YOTs decide the appropriate levels of intervention. This, for example, equates low Asset assessment scores with a low risk of offending and 1–4 hours of intervention whilst a score of over 20 requires 10 hours of intervention (Home Office/Youth Justice Board 2002: para 10.14). Sanctions are also available: 'unreasonable non-compliance with the intervention programme could be cited in any future criminal proceedings' (ibid: para 10.6).

The principles of early intervention and offender accountability are seen as crucial to the effectiveness of reprimands and warnings in reducing reoffending. The latter principle was also seen as crucial in implementing effective restorative justice initiatives with young people (see Chapter 6). These principles have been consistently evident in Government policy since *No More Excuses* (Home Office 1997a). As *Youth Justice—The Next Steps* noted: 'A key part of the reforms has been the introduction of Reprimands and Final Warnings. Young offenders who admit their offence can be dealt with up to twice without going to court, but in a structured way that ensures that they face up to their behaviour. Most Final Warnings

---

[38] Additional guidance—to supplement and update the Guidance issued in 2002—was published as Home Office Circular 14/2006. It includes guidance on the anti-social behaviour order, discharges, restorative processes and the offender's record.

[39] See for example, Leicester CC's Youth Justice Plan for 2006–7 which reports a figure of 96 per cent: see http://www.leics.gov.uk/index/your_council/council_plans_policies/youth_justice_plan0708_contents/youth_justice_plan0708_summary.htm.

[40] We have concerns about the use of the Asset tool: see Chapter 13, section 13.2.1.

are supported by intervention programmes, and if the young person offends again they go straight to court' (Home Office 2003c: para 4).

The effect of such a policy could be either the prevention of reoffending or more use of prosecutions. The Government believes it is the former: 'The Reprimand and Final Warning Scheme, which diverts juveniles from court, is really proving its worth. It is speedy, efficient, frees up court time, and early intervention through the scheme has been successful in reducing offending. The government considers that diversions from court should be used wherever possible' (ibid: para 5).

The use of pre-court disposals (cautions or their replacements since 2000) fell, however, in the period 1996–2004, with a corresponding rise in the number of 10–17-year-olds prosecuted and sentenced (Audit Commission 2004: Exhibit 4, para 21). The findings of early research, summarised by the Audit Commission, suggested that the interventions accompanying final warnings 'have led to an improvement in [young offenders'] thinking and behaviour and their attitudes to offending' (ibid: 19). This conclusion is based on the period 2001–3 in relation to 13 aspects of the lives of the young offenders: with around 30 per cent and 18 per cent of young people respectively experiencing improvements in 'thinking and behaviour' and 'attitudes to offending'. Less than 10 per cent experienced improvements in relation to family, neighbourhood, employment and training aspects of their lives (ibid: Exhibit 5, para 28). Given that the budget of the YJB rose considerably in this period (ibid: 15), it is not surprising that the Audit Commission suggested the introduction of 'a more tailored approach that uses resources in a more targeted way' (ibid: 19).

The CJI Act 2008 will also introduce a new pre-court disposal—the youth conditional caution (YCC). This was not mooted in *Youth Justice—The Next St*eps and is another example of the treatment of young offenders being brought into line with that of adults because a statutory conditional caution was introduced for adults in the CJA 2003. Sections 48–50 and Schedule 9 of the CJI Act 2008 will introduce this option for 10–17-year-olds. A young person who had previously been given a reprimand and/or warning would still be eligible for a YCC although those existing two options could be bypassed. They would not be available after a YCC had been given. As originally drafted the new caution would have applied only to 16–17-year-olds: it will be piloted on this age group.

8.6 Conclusions

8.6.1 The end of 'welfare versus justice'?

The above review of current developments in youth justice, together with the analyses in Chapters 5 and 6 above, suggests a complex picture of policy concern with the lives, as well as the offending, of young people and their victims. Yet there is also a prevalent rhetoric of, and a narrow practice focus on, intervention to reduce the risk of reoffending within a policy context of responsibility, discipline and control. What this chapter has revealed are the pitfalls in attempting to categorise current policies in terms of the two simple categories of welfare and justice which have been used to analyse juvenile justice policy. Writing in 1985, Clarke argued that it was already 'ill conceived' to see juvenile justice as the site for 'justice v welfare' (Clarke 2002: 284), arguing that social work had contributed to, rather than replaced, punitive juvenile justice (ibid: 287). In addition, developments based on restorative justice principles are proving particularly difficult to fit into the existing theoretical frameworks. Gelsthorpe and Morris have asked whether restorative justice amounts to 'the last vestiges of welfare' (2002: 238) and Vaughan has noted how the new aim of prevention is justified both as a welfare measure and a retributivist focus on offending (2000: 355). Further, crime control perspectives cut across and deconstruct such labels and the distinction between welfare and justice also does not adequately elucidate the place of rights in current youth policy and practice.

One way forward is to abandon the assumptions that welfare and justice are signified by particular places or particular types of professional, or, indeed, that justice and welfare are the most appropriate categories. An approach developed by Teubner and Luhman focuses on systems of communication, law being one such system, and how they 'think' about the people with whom they have to deal. What results are 'semantic artifacts', 'not real flesh and blood people . . . They are mere constructs' (Teubner 1989: 741) and law has a range of such artefacts. Applied to children, this means that law can construct children as victims, offenders, witnesses and so forth, and that these constructs are not necessarily consistent with each other or with constructs from social work or medicine. This approach, based on the theory of **autopoiesis**, sheds light on the difficulties of inter-agency cooperation: failure results not only from the lack of workable and effective means of communication but also because of quite different ways of thinking and of establishing 'truth'.

This has implications for the role of law in relation to youth justice. Law functions with a binary code: it provides decisions on, for example, what is legal or illegal, and what constitutes guilt or innocence in the problems brought to it (King 1997a: 15), and has a particular difficulty if the 'truths' of other systems do not 'fit' law's ways of thinking. That has happened in relation to family disputes and also to juvenile offending in those periods when social and psychological science constructed the courts as 'bad' for children. To cope with this situation, while still retaining its authority as the arbiter of disputes, the juvenile justice system has 'lost' direct authority over those offenders diverted to police-based outcomes but retained authority in dealing with offenders through the traditional criminal court system (King and Piper 1995: 103–12).

One result of applying autopoietic theory is the finding that even the earlier diversionary schemes operated with legal constructs such as 'offence', 'seriousness' and 'culpability', rather than with child welfare science constructs such as 'emotional and physical development' or 'needs' (ibid: 115–25). What we know of current diversion schemes, notably the provision in official guidance of offence-based and gravity-score criteria for reprimand, warning, or prosecution decisions, would suggest this is still so. Whilst more evidence has emerged since the first edition of this book it is still difficult to draw clear conclusions about what is happening in youth justice practice. These developments in out-of-court processing have also legitimised the lack of any substantial change to youth courts: they continue to be used basically as adult sentencing courts. Indeed, arguably, the raising of the upper age limit of the youth court and the changes made by the CDA 1998 have, further aligned the adult and youth courts. The requirement that there be an hour's interval between sittings of the adult and youth court (now repealed) was originally enacted to strengthen the provisions, to ensure that the young offender was never likely to come into contact with the adult criminal who might encourage him in criminality. We might deride the 'medical' analogies behind the earlier provisions, but the issue is a serious one: that one more element of separate and different treatment has disappeared.

8.6.2 Stability and continuity

The 'new' never replaces the old. In the twenty-first century discourse of protection, restoration, punishment, responsibility, rehabilitation, welfare, retribution, diversion, human rights and so on exist alongside each other in some perpetually uneasy and contradictory manner.

(Muncie 2004: 249; see also Muncie 2006; Cobb 2007: 369).

Many of the provisions enshrined in legislation passed in 1994–2003 were developed in the 1980s, often as ad hoc local initiatives, using powers and resources available to the Police and Probation Services and Social Work Departments. The most notable examples were the developments in 'cautioning plus' (see section 8.3 above) and restorative justice initiatives (see Chapter 6, section 6.3.2). *No More Excuses* (Home Office 1997a) echoed a much earlier document in its use of the courts to order preventative programmes: in 1927 an official report had concluded that the practice of cautioning to divert from court was 'objectionable' because it was 'usurping the functions of the tribunal' (Moloney Report 1927: 22). The notion of 'treatment' for children who offended was influential but the court was perceived as the site for assessment (see Pratt 1986: 214–19). The Ingleby Report had also argued that trivial offences are 'often only a symptom of an underlying condition requiring early and specialised treatment that was revealed only when the child came before the court' (1960: 51). To go back further, the split custody and community penalty, introduced in 1994 for the 12–14 age group and then enshrined in the detention and training order, has echoes of the Borstal approach developed at the beginning of the twentieth century.

A policy paper in 2003 again promoted diversion from court, asking for 'views on how pre-court interventions can be developed further' (Home Office 2003c: 4). In section 8.3.1 above we summarised the policy reasons for support for diversion in the 1970s and 1980s and there is clearly continuity between those factors and the policy imperatives in the early twenty-first century, notably the need to legitimise the system by reducing offending, and by locating initiatives within—or in proximity to—the legal process. There are further continuities in the policy desire to reduce expenditure by diversion from custody and also to reduce recidivism through pre-court interventions.

Concern has been expressed, however, that there has been a re-packaging or re-invention of 'old' products without learning lessons from the past. Downes has suggested that the reasons for this apparent downgrading or denial of past developments lie in a desire to be seen as modernising and starting with a clean sheet: 'These pitfalls stem from a combination of false memory syndrome and flawed audit. The "Year Zero" tendency of New Labour and the Youth Justice Board entails defining previous "best policy" and practice as "soft on crime" and bumblingly inefficient' (2001/2: 8).

There is the related concern that there is little acknowledgement of the disadvantages of pre-court processing. Cautioning was not without its critics in the 1970s and 1980s, particularly in relation to the issue of whether there was 'injustice by geography' or whether discriminatory decision making was taking place, which research suggested there might be (Ditchfield 1976; Farrington and Bennet 1981; Landau 1981). Commentators were particularly concerned about 'net widening', the possibility that, because diversionary procedures existed, a greater number of young offenders were being drawn into the juvenile justice system. Pratt talked of an 'inflationary spiral': 'in this grey world of mundane transgression...we find a hive of industry and activity' (1986: 212). He concluded that the result has not been progress towards a more humanitarian form of juvenile justice but simply more regulation of young people (ibid: 227–30).

Where the current diversionary systems differ from those of the 1970s and 1980s is in their apparent lack of acknowledgement of the potential dangers of 'heavier' intervention in lives of young people, and, arguably, in the downgrading of the importance of social work skills in favour of risk-based assessments and narrowly focused preventative programmes. It is a pity that these historical insights into the positive and negative factors to be found in the practice of diversion and pre-court intervention were disregarded in the development of the 'new' youth justice system because commentary on the new system is now making very similar criticisms: see, for example, Field (2007); Hine (2007); Koffman and Dingwall (2007).

History also suggests, however, that we cannot assume that the effective lowering of the age of criminal responsibility, by abolishing the presumption of *doli incapax*, heralds a more punitive policy. Debate as to when and to what extent a minor can distinguish right from wrong is a long-standing one: in 1852–3, a Select Committee of Parliament heard conflicting evidence on the issue with opinions setting the age of capability between 10 and 16 (May 2002: 109). In fact the age of criminal responsibility was not raised to 8 until 1933 and then 10 in 1963. The CYPA 1969 had intended to raise the age from 10 to 14 (s 4) but this was never implemented and was repealed in 1998.[41] There are jurisdictions with a low age of criminal responsibility, but with infrequent use of criminal processes for children as, for example, in Scotland, where the age is still 8. Conversely, a youth justice policy which aims to make young people more accountable does not necessarily require a lower age: the recent Canadian Youth Criminal Justice Act 1999 left the age of criminal responsibility at 12 (Junger-Tas 2002: 33). What matters is how the possibility of prosecution is used. The statistics quoted above in relation to sentences of detention on those under 14 years of age would suggest, regretfully, that, at the very least, there is a punitive strand in current youth justice policy. In Chapter 13 we will look more closely at that policy element.

8.6.3 Discussion questions

This chapter has touched on many related issues: the linked web page gives suggestions for further reading on several topics. You may also wish to consider the following questions before consulting the Online Resource Centre for guidance.

online
resource
centre

[41] In contrast, in Germany the age of criminal responsibility has been 14 since the Youth Court Act of 1923, with the equivalent of a rebuttable presumption for 14–18-year-olds (see Crofts 2002).

1. Do you think that the benefits of the current system of reprimands and warnings, together with the new option of conditional cautions, 'outweigh' the disadvantages?

2. What lessons are to be learnt, if any, from an examination of past policies and practices?

3. How important a part of policy and practice is restorative justice in the youth justice system? [Before you answer this question you may wish to reread Chapter 6, especially section 6.3.]

PART B

Punishing Offenders

9

....

Justice in the modern prison

SUMMARY

In this chapter we will consider the treatment of adult prisoners, examining a number of aspects of prison life as well as considering the aims of imprisonment. The treatment of young offenders given a custodial order will be considered in Chapter 13. This chapter will also focus on key developments since 1990 including the Woolf Report (Woolf and Tumim 1991), managerialism and privatisation, the Human Rights Act 1998, and the 'decency' agenda, to consider whether the just treatment of prisoners has been achieved. We will also consider whether, despite substantial improvements in the prison regime since the early 1990s, it will be possible to sustain these developments with an expanding prison population and whether there are any prospects for limiting prison expansion in the current political climate.

9.1 Introduction

9.1.1 Justice behind prison doors

Throughout the book we have been exploring the notion of a just punishment with reference to a range of theoretical traditions, as well as its implications for sentencing law and policy, and for particular groups of offenders such as young people. However, justice extends beyond the prison door. This has been stressed by the European Court of Human Rights and by the Woolf Inquiry, the findings of which have been a key factor in prison reform in recent years. As the Woolf Report emphasised: 'The system of justice which has put a person in prison cannot end at the prison doors. It must accompany the prisoner into the prison, his cell and to all aspects of his life in prison' (Woolf and Tumim 1991: para 14.19). Lord Woolf argued that this does not mean formal judicial processes operating in all areas of prison life but rather that 'prisoners as well as staff, must feel the system is itself fair and just' (ibid: para 14.20). Justice, he says, is broader than fairness, as specific structures are needed to achieve justice while fairness applies to treatment in the particular case. However, it does mean that there should be minimum standards to protect prisoners. These standards should cover the physical conditions in which the prisoner is kept as well as grievance and disciplinary procedures. 'If the Prison Service contains that prisoner in conditions which are inhuman or degrading, or which are otherwise wholly inappropriate, then a punishment of imprisonment which was justly imposed, will result in injustice' (ibid: para 10.19).

Fairness and justice are crucial because prisoners are especially vulnerable to arbitrary treatment because of their isolation and the fact that they are in prison 24 hours a day, dependent on the prison organisation for every need and also shielded from the wider society. Given that they are 'invisible' and marginalised, then protection for prisoners, whether through a system of formal rights or principles of fairness, is essential. Their rights should be infringed no more than is necessary to safeguard the security of staff, other prisoners, and the public outside the prison. Respecting rights emphasises the common heritage of prisoners and ordinary citizens and contributes to the process of **normalisation**, bringing conditions inside prison closer to those outside, contributing to a sense of justice and recognising that prisoners remain citizens during their period of incarceration.

The treatment of prisoners is linked to the justifications of punishment. On retributivist theory the offender as an autonomous individual should be treated with respect and the punishment consists purely in the deprivation of liberty. The offender should not be subjected to degrading or inhuman treatment during the period of incarceration. On utilitarian theory, the pains of imprisonment should not be imposed without positive outcomes, so the effects of imprisonment in reducing reoffending must be assessed. The New Rehabilitative approach (see Chapter 12, section 12.4.4) argues that prisoners have a right to rehabilitation, the right to services and activities which enable them to address the problems which led to their offending. The state has a duty to provide them with an environment which facilitates their rehabilitation. This may also mean provision of sufficient opportunities to attend relevant courses. This is especially important if release decisions are based on assessments which require information based on completion of offending behaviour courses.

9.1.2 The aims of imprisonment

The aims of imprisonment have been much debated by penologists and philosophers, and this debate flourished in the 1970s and 1980s (see May Committee 1979; King and Morgan 1980). However, in recent years the focus has shifted to the performance of prisons and the detailed day-to-day life of prisons measured on a number of variables. However, the formal and 'official' aims of the prison system in the UK have been set out in statements issued by the Prison Service, embodied in the Prison Rules, and reflect the justifications of punishment discussed in Chapters 2, 3, 4 and 5. However, there is no consensus amongst commentators on which of these aims should be given priority or the extent to which they have been realised in practice. The Woolf Report argued that prisoners should be treated with humanity and justice, by striking a balance between security, control and justice, and that the need for justice should not be swamped by concerns with control and security (Woolf and Tumim 1991: para 1.148). Many critics argue that prisons are now merely warehouses as they struggle to cope with rising numbers. The focus on security has been strengthened following a series of escapes in the mid-1990s and concerns over drug use and assaults in prison. The increase in populist punitiveness, discussed in Chapter 1, has also created a climate in which penal expansion and penal austerity may flourish. However, as we shall see, this has been counterbalanced by an increasing emphasis on rights.

The aims of imprisonment are set out clearly in the Prison Service's Statement of Purpose, namely to look after prisoners 'with humanity and help them to lead law-abiding and useful lives in custody and after release' (HM Prison Service 2007b). The Objectives in the 2006–7 Business Plan reflect the new emphasis on contestability and on working closely with others involved in offender management: namely, 'to protect the public and provide what commissioners want to purchase by: holding prisoners securely; and reducing the risk of prisoners re-offending' and also 'to provide safe and well-ordered establishments in which prisoners are treated humanely, decently, and lawfully'. (HM Prison Service 2007b: 1). The stated principles to secure these objectives include working in close partnership with their commissioners and others in the criminal justice system to achieve common objectives, obtaining 'the best value from the resources available, using research to ensure the best correctional practice' and promoting diversity, equality of opportunity, and combating unlawful discrimination, and ensuring staff have the right leadership, organisation, support and preparation to carry out their work effectively. The priorities were reducing reoffending, decency, maintaining order and control, race and diversity, security, prison health and winning and maintaining business.

Prison Rule (PR) 3 (formerly PR 1) states that the purpose of the training and treatment of convicted prisoners shall be to encourage and assist them to lead a good and useful life. The reference to treatment here suggests that the reports of the death of the rehabilitative ideal are somewhat exaggerated. Preventing reoffending is still a key rationale governing education and training provision in modern prison regimes. The problem has been putting PR 3 into practice in the context of rising numbers, increasing financial costs of imprisonment and in the face of public punitiveness, as we saw in Chapter 1. Moreover, the focus on treatment in the past has been used to justify indeterminate and extended sentences (see Chapter 5). Prison reformers have argued that the prisoners should not be subject to treatment coercively that they should be subject to the minimum levels of security necessary to protect the public and that as far as possible the same standards which apply to ordinary citizens in the wider society should be applied to offenders. Moreover, as far as possible prisoners should also be entitled to protection of the formal rights enshrined in the European Convention (see section 9.6). Although prison reform may be limited by potential conflicts with populist punitiveness and the less eligibility principle, this principle is itself being eroded by the increasing role of external standards, in the form of international human rights instruments, in prison life.

9.1.3 The impact of managerialism

The Prison Service is now subject to performance testing using Key Performance Indicator Targets. These have been criticised as being more concerned with cost cutting than quality of life, but they have included access to purposeful activities, overcrowding, and time unlocked, as well as cost per place and escapes. They now include literacy and numeracy as measured by basic skills awards, and the stress is on quantifiable measures such as escapes, assaults and completions of offending behaviour programmes. The impact of managerialism also means devolved budgets for the Prison Service.

The managerialism of the Prison Service reflects a wider shift towards managerialism in the criminal justice system and public services as a whole, including the police and court services, which originated in New Right theory and the Citizen's Charter of the Thatcher era but which has been retained during the Blair and

Brown administrations. The Prison Service now publishes a Business Plan each year, setting out goals and targets. It measures performance on Key Performance Indicators (KPIs) and also uses league tables to assess relative performance. The Plans of the 1990s focused increasingly on cost effectiveness, limiting spending, improving efficiency, and maintaining security and safety including controlling drug use. In the last few years improving levels of literacy and numeracy have been a key target.

Since 2000 the majority of the targets have been met and the latest Annual Report for 2006/7 shows that 9 out of 12 Key Performance Indicator targets were met, including targets on resettlement, healthcare and completion of drug treatment programmes and offending behaviour programmes (HM Prison Service 2007a), but not the targets on serious assaults, black and minority ethnic staff representation or overcrowding (HM Prison Service 2007a). What counts as a target may change—for example, time unlocked and time in purposeful activity are no longer targets—so some of the key yardsticks for prison conditions are no longer included in the calculations. Moreover, some of these targets, such as those on overcrowding, are arguably pitched too low and are unenforceable, while some targets critical to prison conditions have now been excluded. However, the use of financial penalties to ensure compliance with targets has been proposed by the Carter Review (2007) as a means of raising standards and efficiency in the least effective prisons.

The Prison Service was made an Executive Agency of the Home Office in 1993. This was intended to enhance its autonomy and make it more efficient, but it is questionable whether it had that effect. In 2004 it became part of the National Offender Management Service (NOMS), following the recommendations of the Carter Review of Correctional Services, *Managing Offenders, Reducing Crime* (Carter 2003), and in 2007 NOMS became part of the new Ministry of Justice. NOMS as an organisation is much larger than the Prison Service, and is responsible for offender management in both prison and the community. It is headed by a Chief Executive, but the Director General of the Prison Service still has operational freedom on a day-to-day basis to run the Prison Service, albeit on the basis of operating targets and an annual plan agreed with the Chief Executive.

The current emphasis is also on promoting contestability and a new system of commissioning has been introduced, intended to improve the efficiency and effectiveness of service provision (see also Chapter 12, section 12.3.5). With NOMS taking on a commissioning role as a purchaser of services, the Prison Service is now defined as a provider organisation but one which is in open competition with other providers of services so the emphasis will be on improving standards and cost effectiveness in order to compete successfully. Regional Offender Managers will commission work with offenders both in custody and in the community. The new focus on offender management means that there will be a continuous plan for offenders in the community and in custody to plan and manage their individual sentences.

New provisions relating to prison governance are also found in the Offender Management Act 2007, including new provisions on powers of search and detention in contracted-out prisons (ss 16, 17), offences relating to prison security (ss 21–24) and the removal of the requirement to appoint a medical officer (s 25), a post incorporating managerial and clinical responsibilities. The change reflects the fact that clinical duties are now performed by externally contracted GPs from the NHS and managerial responsibilities are no longer part of the medical officer's role.

The Act reflects some of the proposals in *Improving Prison and Probation Services: Public Value Partnerships* (Home Office 2006d). This document set out the Government's plans to extend contestability, and partnerships with the private and voluntary sectors, and also ways of challenging underperforming prisons and Probation Boards. The Carter Review of Prisons in 2007 also envisages further development of contestability and the need to ensure cost effectiveness in the supply and functioning of prisons (Carter 2007). Moreover, he argues that service level agreements with public-sector prisons should be similar for private prisons with sanctions for missing targets.

9.2 The prison population

9.2.1 The composition of the prison population

Information on prison life and the prison population may be obtained from official statistics, reports from the Prison Department, and reviews and reports from HM Chief Inspector of Prisons. There are relatively few qualitative studies, not least because of the problem of access to prisons and the transience of the population. The need for security and the smooth running of the prison also makes ethnographic research difficult. However, research has been undertaken by the Home Office and for the Chief Inspector of Prisons and by campaigning groups such as NACRO and the Prison Reform Trust (PRT) who have focused on particular problems and particular groups of prisoners, and have highlighted the importance of humane regimes. We also have information from government-sponsored reviews, such as the Wedderburn Report and the Corston Report on Women Prisoners, as well as from the Mubarek Inquiry (see Chapter 11) and from independent researchers. Recently the Howard League for Penal Reform launched an independent commission on prisons, The Commission on English Prisons Today, which will report in 2009. It is intended to promote public and academic debates on prison, looking at the aims and limits of the penal system and the forces influencing change.

Although prisoners may come from a wide range of social groups and classes, a profile of the typical prisoner can be compiled from Home Office data and research studies. These indicate that the typical prisoner is likely to be young, male, economically and socially deprived, or socially excluded, and a persistent property offender, experiencing problems with accommodation, and with finding employment, or if in work in an unskilled occupation, from an inner-city area, of low educational achievement, and with past experience of being in care. Social exclusion is the most striking characteristic of the prison population.[1]

According to the Social Exclusion Unit (2002), prisoners are 13 times more likely to have been in care than the general population, 13 times more likely to have been unemployed and 10 times more likely to have been an habitual truant. It is estimated that one-third of prisoners suffered from housing problems before

---

[1] For further discussion of social exclusion see Young (1999), Byrne (2005), Pantazis *et al.* (2006), Dorling *et al.* (2007) and http://www.socialexclusionunit.gov.uk.

entering prison and a similar number face housing problems on release. Moreover, prisoners may lose their housing as a direct result of imprisonment. A large number of prisoners are unemployed before going into prison and of course many will lose their jobs through imprisonment. This is important as homelessness and unemployment are also significant factors associated with reoffending.

The prison population is also still overwhelmingly male as we can see from Figure 9.1 below. The proportion of female prisoners varied between 3 per cent and 4 per cent of the total prison population during most of the 1990s but by 2004 had reached 6 per cent and in March 2008 was 5.4 per cent.

The demographic structure of the prison population is changing as far as age is concerned. One-quarter of prisoners given immediate custodial sentences and received into prison in 2006 were over 36. Like the population at large, the prison population is ageing and the number of elderly prisoners has increased significantly since 1995 (Howse 2003). As we saw in Chapter 7, this may have implications for sentencing. However, there are still relatively large numbers of prisoners in the 18–20 age group (over 9,000 in 2007) and 25 per cent were aged 21 or less. Members of this group are more likely than adult prisoners to experience mental health problems and are at higher risk of suicide. There were also over 2,000 children aged 15–17 in prison. The problems young offenders face in custody will be considered in Chapter 13.

Although some prisoners have gained degrees while in prison, the majority of prisoners have no formal qualifications on entering prison. Over half of male adult prisoners and over two-thirds of female adult prisoners have no educational qualifications. Over one-half of the prison population have low levels of numeracy and literacy; one-third of prisoners were habitual truants while at school, whilst one-third of female sentenced prisoners and nearly one-half of male sentenced prisoners were excluded from school (Prison Reform Trust 2007a: 18). These figures are

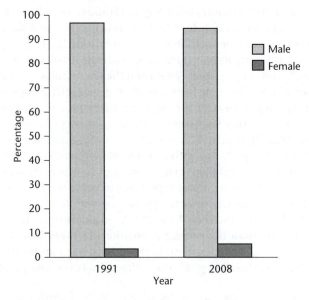

Figure 9.1

much higher than for the general population. For this reason, there is increasing emphasis on acquiring basic work and literacy and numeracy skills while in custody. It is also estimated that as many as 30 per cent of prisoners have learning disabilities which will affect their ability to cope with imprisonment (see Talbot 2007; Talbot and Riley 2007; Loucks 2007). Information on these disabilities will not necessarily be available to staff on arrival at prison and may not always be identified while there.

The rate of homelessness amongst prisoners is also higher than the general population as is the incidence of mental illness, alcohol and drugs problems. A high number of prisoners will have been drug users before admission. The number of prisoners imprisoned for drugs offences and drugs-related crime has increased and drug use will frequently be resumed on release from prison.

About 55 per cent of male prisoners and 33 per cent of female prisoners were living with their spouses or partners before imprisonment. About 59 per cent of male prisoners and 66 per cent of female prisoners have dependent children (Prison Reform Trust 2007a: 16). It is estimated that 160,000 children now have a parent in prison.

Offenders are more likely than non-offenders to be unemployed (Crow *et al.* 1989; Crow 1996). Moreover, if unemployed they may be less likely to receive a fine or suspended sentence and more likely to receive a custodial sentence or community penalty and if they subsequently experience further unemployment, then reoffending may be more likely (see Chapter 10). The link between unemployment and imprisonment is complex but employment status will have implications for bail, as being in regular employment will increase the chances of being given bail, as will having stable accommodation.

There are also disproportionate numbers of ethnic minority prisoners compared to their representation in the population as a whole. The over-representation of ethnic minorities is highest in young adult prisoners (see Chapter 11). In 2006 prisoners from ethnic groups other than white comprised 26 per cent of the prison population (Jones and Singer 2007: 87). At the end of March 2007 the population of public-sector prisons included 19,119 prisoners from minority ethnic groups. The composition of the prison population in 2006/7 was 73 per cent white, 16 per cent black British, 7 per cent Asian or Asian British, 3 per cent of mixed ethnicity and 1 per cent from Chinese or other ethnic groups. The implications of this for issues of discrimination and equality of impact will be considered in Chapter 10. Foreign national prisoners constitute 14 per cent of the total prison population.

In looking at the composition of the prison population, it is also interesting to examine the distribution of offence groups within the prison population and to compare it with a decade earlier. The breakdown of prisoners by offence groups for remand and male and female sentenced prisoners is given in Figures 9.2, 9.3 and 9.4.

As can be seen clearly, offences of violence constitute a large proportion of the male offence groups with theft and handling constituting a larger proportion of the female offence group. The category 'other offences' includes breach offences which are becoming a more important element of the offences triggering a custodial sentence. Drugs offences are also becoming more significant, accounting for 15 per cent of male sentenced prisoners and 30 per cent of female sentenced prisoners and, of course, many property offences may be drug-related.

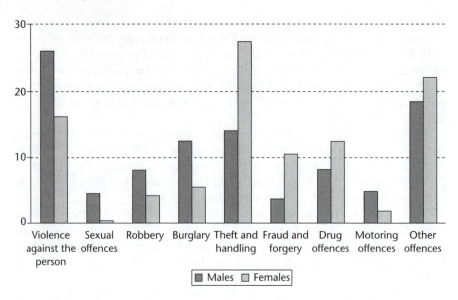

Figure 9.2 Percentage[a] of untried receptions into prison by offence group and sex, 2006
[a] Percentages are calculated excluding offence not recorded.
Source: Ministry of Justice (2007a: 73).

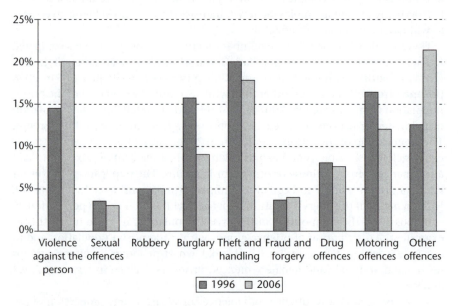

Figure 9.3 Percentage of immediate custodial sentenced males by offence group and year
Source: Ministry of Justice (2007a: 75).

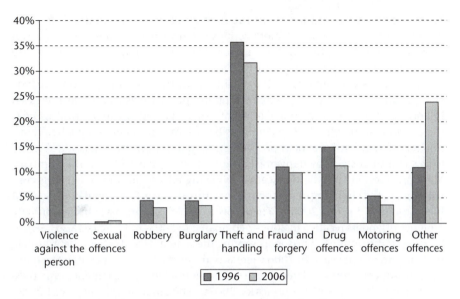

Figure 9.4 Percentage of immediate custodial sentenced females by offence group and year
Source: Ministry of Justice (2007a: 75).

9.2.2 **Prison expansion**

The most significant feature of the prison population is its massive expansion during the postwar period from 15,000 in 1945 to nearly 75,000 in 2004. The population has steadily increased with the most dramatic increases in the 1990s.[2] On 16 November 2007 it reached 81,547. On 14 March 2008 there were 77,418 male prisoners and 4,447 female prisoners plus 49 prisoners held in police cells under Operation Safeguard, making a total of 81,914, as well as 2,490 offenders under Home Detention Curfew Supervision.

Remand prisoners constituted about 17 per cent of the prison population in 2006, there having been an increase of 13 per cent between 1996 and 2006. The average time spent on remand in 2006 was 58 days (Ministry of Justice 2007a). As the majority of remand prisoners are remanded for non-violent offences (see Figure 9.2 above) and only one-half of remand prisoners will receive a non-custodial sentence, then this might be one area where the population could be safely reduced.

The most important causes for the dramatic increase in the prison population since the early 1990s are the increases in both the custody rate and sentence length. The custody rate in the magistrates' court increased from 3.1 per cent in 1995 to 4.0 per cent in 2006 and in the Crown Court from 9 per cent in 1995 to 14 per cent in 2006.[3] Given the large numbers of offenders dealt with in the magistrates' courts, even a slight percentage increase may entail substantial demands on the prison system. The average length of determinate sentences in the Crown Court for indictable offences increased from 22.4 months in 1996 to 25.2 months in 2006.[4]

---

[2] Prison statistics are published annually and updated weekly on the Prison Service web site.
[3] Ministry of Justice statistics.
[4] However, the figures for 2006 do not include indeterminate sentences, Imprisonment for Public Protection (IPP) and life sentences.

There has also been an increase in the number of offenders coming before the courts and in the number of more serious offences being sentenced as we can see from Figure 9.3, although this is more evident in relation to male than female offenders, as we can see from Figure 9.4.

Other factors contributing to the expansion in the prison population include changes in sentencing law, increased public punitiveness, and the increased importance of punishment and of bringing offenders to justice in political agendas (Piper and Easton 2006/7). The emphasis on risk management and public protection reflected in sentences of imprisonment for public protection, has added to the time spent in custody by dangerous offenders which has added to the numbers. More prisoners are also being recalled following release on licence which is contributing to the changing demographic structure of the prison population (see HM Inspectorate of Prisons 2005b). There was a 29 per cent increase in determinate sentence offenders recalled in 2006–7 compared to 2005–6. There has also been an increase in the number of prisoners serving life sentences and other indeterminate sentences in recent years. In 2006 there was an increase of 24 per cent in the number of prisoners serving indeterminate sentences (including life sentences and IPPs) compared to 2005 (Ministry of Justice 2007a). The amount of time served under licence and under supervision has increased under the 2003 Criminal Justice Act.

The reluctance to take risks with public protection is also reflected in a fall in the numbers released by the Parole Board, from 52 per cent in 2004/5 to 36 per cent in 2006/7 (Parole Board 2006, 2007). This followed incidents where prisoners had been released and went on to commit further crimes. There were also fewer offenders released on Home Detention Curfew (Ministry of Justice 2007a: 3). However, the number or prisoners released on parole was still higher in 2006 than a decade earlier. As we saw in Chapter 1, there has also been an increase in the number of civil orders available to and imposed by the courts, the breach of which may incur custodial penalties.

There has also been an increase in the numbers serving short sentences. Some offenders are now being sent to prison when they would not have been ten years ago (see Hough *et al.* 2003; Prison Reform Trust 2004c). Although the use of community penalties since 1995 has also increased, this has not had the effect of reducing the use of custodial sentences but in fact both have increased, while the use of fines has fallen. There has also been a decline in the numbers released on Home Detention Curfew reflecting greater reluctance to take risks and the fact there are more prisoners now classed as higher risk.

At present the prospects for a dramatic reduction in the prison population are unfavourable. The latest prison projections for 2014, based on current sentencing trends, published in July 2007, suggest that the lowest figure will be 88,800 and the highest figure 101,900 (da Silva *et al.* 2007). However, some slight reductions in the prison population may be achieved by early release from detention and training orders and by the use of intensive supervision and surveillance programmes for juveniles (see Chapter 13).

The Government's current policy is ambivalent: on the one hand it acknowledges the need to contain prison expansion, because of cost concerns, and yet since Labour came to power in 1997 an additional 20,000 prison places have been provided. As we saw in Chapter 1, the average cost per prison place in 2006–7 was £28,734 and the average cost per prisoner was £26,737, so at current levels of incarceration this means a cost of over £2.2 billion (HM Prison Service 2007a). The Government also recognises the limits of prison in dealing with certain groups of prisoners. But at the same time it is committing itself to further building to meet the expected demand for places. As we saw in Chapter 1, some of the Government's reductionist measures, such as the expansion of early release, were unpopular with the public, so the Government's policy to increase confidence in the criminal justice system in bringing offenders to justice and punishing them appropriately may inhibit the use of reductionist measures.

It is also notable that the incarceration rates in England and Wales are the highest in Western Europe: at 148 per 100,000 of the population in 2007 (International Centre for Prison Studies 2008). If current projections prove accurate this is likely to increase further. The average incarceration rate within the European Union is 124, with Eastern European states averaging over 150, while most of central Europe averages below 120. Within the EU the prison population is rising by about 2 per cent a year, but the rise over the past 10 years within England and Wales has been steeper (see Tavares and Thomas 2007: 10).

9.2.3 The prison estate

The increased demand for prison places has been met by an expansion of prison building. Since the Second World War several new prisons have opened: Long Lartin in 1972, Durham in 1978, Channings Wood in Devon in 1982. Since the early 1980s there has been a substantial building programme, with 21 new prisons opened between 1980 and 1996. Although additional prisons have been built since then, these have been primarily in the private sector, although a new public sector prison, HMP Kennet, opened on Merseyside in 2007. A prison ship, *HMP Weare*, was also used from 1997 to 2005. By the end of 2007 there were 139 prisons in England and Wales providing 81,500 places, including 11 closed private prisons.[5] A further 8,000 places within the next 5 years were promised by the Government in 2006 in *Rebalancing the Criminal Justice System* (Home Office 2006a) while in June 2007 this figure increased to 9,500 places.

The modern prison system is shaped by the legacy of the past, reflected in the prison infrastructure in the survival of Victorian prison buildings which make up about one-quarter of the prison estate. The prison estate includes conversions of country houses and former military camps, as well as purpose-built prisons. So while some prisoners are still housed in old Victorian buildings, these have been refurbished and now include new modern wings, whilst many prisoners are housed in prisons built since the war. The prison estate is divided into 11 geographical areas with Area Managers, as well as separate divisions for high-security prisoners and contracted-out prisons. There are 17 women's prisons, including open, closed and semi-open prisons and 7 mother and baby units. The treatment of women prisoners will be considered in Chapter 11. A map of the geographical distribution of prisons can be found at http://www.imprisonservice.gov.uk/resourcecentre/.

---

[5] Scotland and Northern Ireland have separate systems and space precludes a focus on their prison estates. However, information on prisons in Scotland and Northern Ireland can be obtained from the Scottish Prison Service on http://www.sps.gov.uk and the Northern Ireland Prison Service on http://www.niprisonservice.gov.uk. The prison population is also rising in both countries.

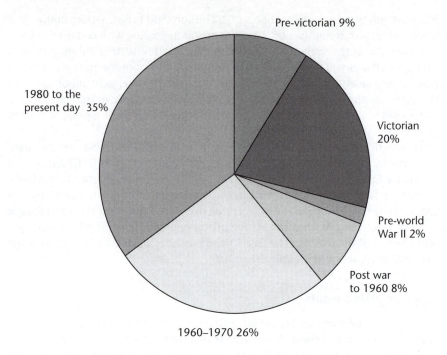

Pre-victorian 9%

1980 to the
present day 35%

Victorian
20%

Pre-world
War II 2%

Post war
to 1960 8%

1960–1970 26%

Figure 9.5 Prison places by age of establishment
Source: Carter (2007: 24)

Local prisons, located in towns and cities, hold remand prisoners pending and during their trials, and convicted prisoners immediately after sentence, for assessment before transferring to training prisons. They may also hold convicted prisoners serving short sentences and those nearing the end of long sentences. They often have the worst overcrowding as well as the worst conditions, and include inner-city dilapidated Victorian prisons as well as modern prisons such as Belmarsh (see Figure 9.5).

Training prisons may be closed or open, and may be located further away from towns and cities. They include specialist prisons, for example, the therapeutic prison, Grendon in Buckinghamshire, and there are also therapeutic units inside prisons at Gartree, Blundeston, Dovegate and Send. Closed training prisons have varying levels of security. Prisoners in open training prisons, such as Leyhill and Ford, clearly enjoy much greater freedom. They may work in the prison or in the local community and are allowed out on shopping visits, but the rules governing prison life will be strongly enforced to compensate for the absence of external boundaries.

Vulnerable prisoners, such as sex offenders, are housed in special Vulnerable Prisoners' Units (VPUs) for their own safety to protect them from assaults by other prisoners. Severely disruptive or violent prisoners may be transferred to Close Supervision Centres. There are also Protected Witness Units for those at risk, entry to which is possible only if the application is supported by a representative of

Table 9.1 Comparisons of cost per place by prison

Prison	Date opened	Category	Certified normal accommodation	Cost per place
HMP Blakenhurst	1993	Male local	827	£23,886
HMP Bullingdon	1985	Male local	759	£27,723
HMP Moorland	1991	Male C	1000	£20,959
HMP Holme House	1992	Male local	857	£23,851
HMP High Down	1993	Male local	588	£28,724

Source: Carter (2007: 23)

the Crown Prosecution Service and a senior police officer at or above the rank of Assistant Chief Constable (Prison Service Instruction (PSI) 71/2000).

The modern prison system is still very expensive to run despite concerted efforts to reduce costs and much more expensive than community punishments (see Table 9.1). Cost effectiveness or value for money has become an increasingly important issue in the past ten years as costs have risen. Spending on prisons increased by more than 25 per cent in real terms between 1997 and 2005 (Home Office 2005b: para 5.2) and constitutes a substantial claim on public spending. Additional costs may also be incurred if it is necessary to use a police cell under Operation Safeguard or, on occasions, court cells.

But these figures refer only to running costs, not to the capital costs of building and maintaining prisons, which pushes the average cost up to nearly £40,000 per year. Costs of maintenance and refurbishment will be substantial in the older prisons which are not purpose-built. Older buildings may also be more expensive to staff, and staffing costs account to about 80 per cent of the prison budget. The location of some of the prisons also means additional costs in transporting prisoners across the country and for visitors and there are currently insufficient places within the London area. If we include other ancillary costs such as prison escort services, then the cost rises substantially. Nor do these figures encompass the total public costs of imprisonment; for example, there may also be additional welfare costs for a prisoner's dependants with the loss of the prisoner's income. As is often observed, it costs more to send an offender to prison than to public school or to university.

9.2.4 The categorisation and allocation of prisoners

Decisions on the categorisation of prisoners are distinct from and precede decisions on allocation. The procedures and criteria for both processes are set out in Prison Service Order (PSO) 0900. Prisoners are divided into four categories, following the recommendations of the Mountbatten Report (Mountbatten 1966).

Decisions on category A prisoners are made by a special Category A Committee of Prison Service officials. Categorisation decisions for other prisoners are a matter for the Governor and are made in accordance with the guidelines in the Prison Service

Order. Prisoners should be placed in the lowest category consistent with the need for security and control. Prisons should have procedures for reviewing the categorisation of prisoners and there is now a duty to give reasons for such decisions. Categorisation should take account of the current offence and sentence, previous convictions, and previous escapes, escape attempts and absconds. Categorisation is reviewed at regular intervals and reconsidered on the basis of risk to the public and the risk of escape. There are also separate procedures for those serving life sentences and other indeterminate sentences.

Category A prisoners are those who would be highly dangerous to the public, police, or the security of the state and for whom escape must be made impossible. Category B prisoners are those who do not require the highest security conditions, but for whom escape must be made very difficult. Category C prisoners are those who cannot be trusted in open conditions, but who lack the will or resources to make a determined escape attempt, while category D prisoners can be reasonably trusted in open conditions. Remand prisoners may be categorised A or are unclassified (U). Similarly, young offenders may be categorised A, but otherwise are unclassified initially, but are then assessed according to similar security criteria as adults. Category U prisoners will usually be sent to category B accommodation. Women prisoners may be classified as category A, or held in closed conditions, where the highest security conditions are not necessary but they cannot be trusted in open conditions or open conditions are not appropriate for them; they may also be categorised as suitable for semi-open conditions, that is, prisoners who present a low risk to the public but who require a level of physical perimeter security to deter absconding, and those who can safely be held in open conditions.

Category A is further divided into three levels of risk: standard, high and exceptional risk. High risk would include, for example, members of criminal gangs with access to sufficient resources to help them escape. Prisoners are classified as exceptional risk when they have the skills, external resources, abilities and determination to overcome the security measures used in relation to category A prisoners, and therefore need to be contained within the most secure units available within the Prison Service.

Regimes for category A prisoners are the most stringent, for example requiring closed visits. These prisoners are more likely to be transferred to other prisons than other categories and the courts are more reluctant to interfere with transfer decisions in such cases. If they are transferred, it is difficult for them to complete educational or offending behaviour courses, which affects their chances of future classification. Prisoners may be placed on the 'escape list', that is, they are deemed to be at risk of trying to escape, for example, because they have done so in the past, and will be placed on a strict security regime and required to wear special clothes.

Prisons are becoming more secure in so far as the number of escapes has declined since the early 1980s. Prison categorisation was reviewed, however, when two category A prisoners escaped from Gartree in 1987 with the help of a helicopter which landed inside the grounds of the prison. Following this incident, exceptional risk categories are held in special security units for high-risk prisoners.

Once sentenced, category A prisoners go to high-security prisons. These prisons will have high levels of security, including dog patrols, electronic surveillance, high walls, searching of visitors, high levels of staffing, and more searches of inmates as they move around the prison. There are currently eight high-security prisons, at

Belmarsh, Frankland, Full Sutton, Long Lartin, Wakefield, Whitemoor, Manchester and Woodhill. Conditions are generally better in higher security prisons for those serving longer sentences, with more educational and work opportunities, and prisoners may be able to cook their own meals and wear their own clothes.

There are also special units for dealing with difficult prisoners called Close Supervision Centres, where prisoners can be closely supervised and encouraged to address their disruptive behaviour. They have a structured regime through which prisoners must progress satisfactorily before leaving the unit. Conditions are harsher in so far as more time is spent locked up, visits are restricted, the furniture is made of cardboard, and prisoners sleep on concrete plinths rather than proper beds. There are also special cells for segregating difficult prisoners within high-security prisons and at local prisons.

The categorisation of prisoners was reviewed in *R (P) v Secretary of State for the Home Department* (2002). Here an elderly and ill prisoner had been placed in category A even though he would be unlikely to be able to escape, but if he did escape, he would be highly dangerous to the public, or to the police or to the security of the state. The court held that the Prison Service was entitled to have a policy to make the escape of highly dangerous prisoners virtually impossible, but should consider prisoners' cases on an individual basis, so that if the escape risk of a particular prisoner could be managed in lower security conditions, then it would be unlawful to preclude consideration of this possibility.

Category B prisoners may stay in local prisons if serving a short sentence, or go to high-security or closed training prisons. Ordinary category B training prisons will have less security than high-security prisons. Category C go to closed training prisons with lower security and a more relaxed regime. Category D go to open training prisons, although some may be held in category C prisons. Within some C and D prisons there are also resettlement prisons to which prisoners may be transferred shortly before release, to arrange work and to increase contact with their families.

Decisions on allocation to particular prisons are made on the basis of the need for security and control, individual prisoner needs, and optimum use of available space, needs which may sometimes conflict. Individual needs would include age, vulnerability, any educational needs and the prisoner's home area. Prisoners do not have a right to be allocated to any particular prison. Similar principles will apply to the allocation of young offenders although maintenance of family ties will be a key consideration, so normally young offenders are allocated to a prison as close to home as possible and when allocating women prisoners, family ties and facilitating visits from children will be a significant allocation issue.

9.3 **Prison conditions**

Bearing in mind the objectives of imprisonment (see section 9.1.2 above) we will consider the conditions in the modern prison and problems which inhibit their realisation. We will consider improvements made in recent years in response to the problems of disorder and the findings of the Woolf Inquiry. If we compare prisons in 1990 and 2008 we find considerable progress, following the Woolf Report, but also room for further improvement. We can also identify a number of changes during the 1990s which occurred independently of Woolf, principally the privatisation of prisons, the rise of the New Managerialism within the Prison Service (see section 9.4.2) and the development of New Penology or actuarial justice (see Chapter 1, section 1.2). The impact of managerialism has increased the time spent on paperwork, while the focus on risk assessment has limited the scope for developing progressive regimes and limited the autonomy and discretion of prison governors.

9.3.1 Overview

Prison conditions have improved considerably since the Woolf Report was published and further improvements have been introduced following the Human Rights Act 1998, to comply with the European Convention on Human Rights (ECHR) which will be considered in section 9.6. However, conditions still remain unsatisfactory in some prisons, particularly for those held on remand. Although they are entitled to wear their own clothes, have better visiting rights and access to correspondence, remand prisoners are often housed in the worst prisons with fewer facilities available for work and training. The day-to-day life inside prison is governed by very detailed Prison Rules[6] issued under s 47 of the Prison Act 1952.[7] The Rules include provisions on a range of issues, including work, education, access to visits, offences against discipline, and the use of constraints, and they generate a substantial number of disciplinary offences each year. In 2006, the latest date for which figures are available, there were 105,960 proven offences against prison discipline. This means that there were 136 proven offences against prison discipline per 100 prisoners (Ministry of Justice 2007a: 106).

A number of performance improvement strategies have been implemented, notably the introduction of prison league tables which rank prisons on their performance against a number of criteria. League tables were first published in July 2003 when Holloway was awarded the lowest ranking (level 1) for failing to meet performance targets or providing secure, ordered, or decent regimes but it subsequently moved up the table. Pentonville was also graded level 1 in 2006–7 and moved up recently. It had been heavily criticised by the Chief Inspector of Prisons in her Report on an Unannounced Inspection of Pentonville in 2006 because of the inadequate physical conditions, including a cockroach infestation in the kitchens, and problems in the supply of bedding and food, as well as poor relations between staff and prisoners (HM Chief Inspector of Prisons 2006b).

The league tables are now published quarterly and the figures published by the Prison Service on 13 December 2007 show there are no public sector prisons at level 1, 17 prisons (13 per cent) at level 2, 88 prisons (70 per cent) at level 3 and 22 prisons at level 4 (17 per cent), the highest level.[8] The highest performing prisons are given High-Performing Prison Status. Performance ratings for contracted out prisons are now compiled separately by NOMS on a regional basis, so it is harder to make a direct comparison between public- and private-sector performance.

---

[6] Prison Rules 1999, as amended in 2000, 2002, 2003 and 2005.

[7] For further discussion of the Prison Act and Rules see Creighton and King (2000) and Livingstone, Owen and Macdonald (2008).

[8] Cookham Wood was unrated in this table because it changed function from a women's prison to a male YOI.

The purpose of the current focus on contestability is also intended to drive up standards and penalise poor performance, through the competition between prisons for contracts.

Prison conditions are crucial to debates in penology as they have implications for human rights but also will have implications for reoffending. Some of the most enlightened and progressive regimes, which are 'humanised', such as the regime at Grendon, have achieved some success in reducing reoffending (see Genders and Player 1995).

9.3.2 Overcrowding

Overcrowding is normally measured by comparing actual numbers with Certified Normal Accommodation (CNA), that is, the uncrowded capacity calculated for each prison. Overcrowding initially declined during the 1990s as the supply of places expanded due to the prison building programme but in some prisons overcrowding remained a problem. For example, a Report on Birmingham in 1998, following a visit by the Chief Inspector of Prisons, found that the prison was 32 per cent overcrowded at the time of inspection. Since the early 1990s, the supply of places has not kept up with demand despite the building programme and, by 2003, prison overcrowding was further increasing with new prisons also experiencing overcrowding. Overcrowding may arise not simply because of a lack of accommodation, but, in part, because of inflexibility of use because prisons may be too specialised to allow transfer of prisoners between them. Increasingly prisons have been broadening their functions with expansion and one reason for the recent proposal for 'Titan' prisons in the Carter Review of Prisons (Carter 2007) is to allow for more flexibility in allocating accommodation.

With the rapid expansion of the prison population inevitably overcrowding has increased. In 1995 the level of overcrowding was 17 per cent. In 2006–7, the number of prisoners held in accommodation units intended for fewer prisoners was 24.1 per cent which exceeded a target of 24 per cent, but these levels, while worrying, are still much lower than the 1980s when the figure was as high as 41 per cent (in 1986). But given the current size of the population this means large numbers of prisoners are being held in cells designed for fewer prisoners.

One measure used in June 2007 to deal with the immediate problem of overcrowding was an End of Custody Licence (ECL). This permitted lower-level offenders imprisoned for no more than four years and nearing the end of their sentence to be released 18 days early. Similar measures were used in 1940 to boost the number of men available for the war effort and to reduce overcrowding in 1987 (see Chapter 5, section 5.4.4).

Moreover, overcrowding will not be evenly distributed throughout the prison system, so there may still be unsatisfactory levels in specific institutions even if the total level of overcrowding is not substantial. Overcrowding is generally worse in local prisons, which house mostly remand prisoners and those serving short sentences or awaiting transfers. Usually training prisons and Young Offender Institutions will be protected from overcrowding at the expense of local prisons.

The Woolf Report (1991, para 1.190) recommended a new prison rule under which prisons could not accommodate more prisoners than provided in its CNA, except in very limited cases, but this recommendation was not implemented.

However, the level of overcrowding is used as a KPI although, as we have noted, the target is not set very high, namely that no more than 24 per cent of the prison population should be held in accommodation designed for fewer prisoners.

The effects of overcrowding are widespread; as well as worsening physical conditions, there may be more frequent transfers, so it is hard to implement proper training and educational programmes accessible to all prisoners and to complete necessary assessments of prisoners. Overcrowding also makes prison life more impersonal, affecting the opportunity to establish good personal relationships, which may also have implications for the prevention of reoffending, moving prisons closer to a warehousing than a rehabilitative role, and for the safety of prisoners. In severe cases overcrowding may amount to inhuman and degrading treatment.

What is surprising is that the increase in numbers in custody in the 1980s and 1990s paralleled a policy that prison should be used as a last resort, and alternatives should be used where possible. In fact, the UK has more alternatives to custody than many other European states. But it would seem the alternatives available during that period, such as community service orders, probation and fines, had the effect of net-widening rather than leading to a reduction in the prison population.

Ultimately of course, it is sentencers who make the decision on whether to give a custodial sentence, but they are constrained by sentencing law and procedure when looking at the individual case. In addition, magistrates and judges will have their own views, philosophies and traditions as well as subscribing to the principles of judicial independence and autonomy (see Chapters 2 and 3).

9.3.3 Constructive regimes: work, training and offending behaviour programmes

In 1991 the Woolf Report recommended that work opportunities should cater for a range of abilities and that prison regimes should try to provide constructive and purposeful employment in factories and workshops for as many prisoners as possible who could usefully be deployed. The choice of work, argued Woolf, should be influenced by the need of prisoners to find work after release. A planned programme 'should bring together work, training and education in a way that provides the most constructive mix for the prisoners who are to be involved in it' (Woolf and Tumim 1991: para 14.134). The Prison Service, he argued, should give the prisoner the opportunity to serve his sentence in a constructive way (ibid: para 14.9) and by making proper use of his or her time, reduce the likelihood of reoffending (ibid: para 14.10).

The need to increase the level of constructive activity in prisons was endorsed by the 1991 White Paper *Custody, Care and Justice* (Home Office 1991). Prison Rule 31(1) states that 'a convicted prisoner shall be required to do useful work for not more than 10 hours per day, and arrangements shall be made to allow prisoners to work, where possible, outside the cells and in association with one another.' Exceptions are made for those who are ill or unable to work for other reasons. Otherwise, prisoners are classified into suitability for heavy, light or medium work. Prison Rule 31 does not stipulate a minimum time spent in work. In the late 1990s the time spent in purposeful activity was used as a KPI and the target was 24 hours a week, although in practice it varied enormously. In the mid 1990s, the average time spent out of a cell in weekdays was 11.2 hours but this fell to 10 hours by 2005/6 (Hansard, House of Commons written answers, 9 January 2007). Time unlocked has not been used as a KPI since 2004.

The quantity of time spent in purposeful activity is also no longer a Key Performance Indicator Target. At the present time, the criteria used to measure the provision of constructive regimes are completion of basic skills and offending behaviour programmes. There is a duty on the Governor to ensure a safe working environment in accordance with health and safety legislation. The prisoner is entitled to be paid and, if he or she is willing to work and none is available, to receive basic pay instead. But rates are very low compared to the labour market outside prisons. At the present time board and lodging may not be deducted from this small income. Remand prisoners are permitted to work but not obliged to do so, but it is usually harder for them to obtain access to work. But most prisoners want to work to relieve the boredom and to earn money. The minimum rate that must be paid is £4 per week but pay schemes are a matter for governors and for directors of contracted-out prisons (see PSO 4460). So each prison sets its own pay rates and the average is about £8 per week but may be as much as £12. Pay may be given not just for employment but for 'constructive participation' in purposeful activities, so this would include work, training, education and participation in offending behaviour programmes (ibid: para 2.3.1). Remand prisoners are paid the same rate as convicted prisoners.

Pay is also linked to the Incentives and Earned Privileges (IEP) scheme, so the level of pay will depend on one's position in the scheme, whether basic, standard or enhanced, and higher rates may be given under the IEP. Prisoners working for outside employers must be paid the National Minimum Wage. Prisoners are obliged to pay tax and National Insurance contributions if their earnings reach the threshold and to make contributions to maintain their dependants if their earnings are sufficient. The Woolf Report recommended that prisoners' pay should be substantially increased, to encourage them to take greater responsibility for their family, to contribute to victim support and to enable them to buy additional goods for themselves (Woolf and Tumim 1991: para 14.172). If levels of pay were more realistic and closer to market rates, then this would be possible.

Since the Woolf Report, there have been improvements in the provision of constructive regimes and access to basic skills education. A new Regime Directorate was established in 1997. Constructive regimes include work, education, physical education, and offending behaviour programmes. Their aim is to reduce reoffending, to challenge offenders' behaviour and attitudes which led to their crimes, and to provide value for money. For prisoners, constructive regimes can also make custody more tolerable (see Gravett 2003). Constructive regimes are important precisely because so many prisoners are unemployed before beginning their sentence and because, as we have seen, there are clear correlations between reoffending and unemployment. Given the links between offending and social exclusion, both work and education programmes can offer a means of integrating prisoners into society.

Prisoners may be employed in prison workshops, in agriculture and horticulture, and in provision of services within the prison. With the expansion of prison numbers there has been an increased demand for labour within the prison in providing cooking, cleaning and other domestic services and most work will be within the internal labour market. But prison work has received less investment than other areas of prison life. Prison industries are expensive to run and it is difficult to find outside work. The prisoners who do work outside the prison are those serving in open prisons near the end of their sentence.

A great deal of work is carried out within the prison for the prison, for example, in gardens, farms, kitchens, and laundries, as well as cleaning, and making furniture. There is also some work for the clothing industry, textile weaving, and unskilled light assembly work for outside employers. But opportunities for industrial training work are limited (Simon 1999). Prison workshops may be under-used because of the costs of staff supervision. However, there have been some successful collaborations with the private sector. What is needed is sufficient good quality work, training and education for all prisoners. The European Prison Rules stipulate that sufficient work of a useful nature or other purposeful activities should be provided to keep prisoners actively employed for a normal working day. But there is no similar provision in the Prison Rules and levels of inactivity are still higher than desirable.

The Purposeful Activity Expansion Scheme (PAES) which began in 1999 was piloted in selected prisons and then extended to other prisons. It aims to provide access to skills and training and improved earnings, increasing purposeful activities to 30 hours a week, including increasing hours of work per week, expanding the number of offending behaviour options, and offering a variety of work, training, education, offending behaviour, and physical education programmes. Preparing for work is important as there is a strong correlation between reoffending and unemployment, and whilst a correlation is not a cause, ex-offenders are more likely to reoffend if they have no legitimate source of income. The problem of providing suitable work and other purposive activities will become harder with continued expansion without corresponding increases in resources.

However, prisoners who are serving short sentences or prisoners serving longer sentences, but subject to transfers, may not remain in the same institution long enough to benefit from interventions, for example, in drug treatment and education programmes. There is also the problem of following up the work when the prisoner is released. As the Carter Review of Correctional Services noted, access to programmes may also depend on where the offender is sent (Carter 2003: 33).

The provision of constructive regimes is an important element of rehabilitation as it gives prisoners the opportunity to change their behaviour. In 2006/7 there were 7,921 offending behaviour programmes completed and 1,160 sex offender treatment programmes completed (HM Prison Service 2007a). However, there may still be insufficient courses to meet demand which raises problems when completion of a rehabilitation programme is a key factor in parole decisions. Some prisoners affected by this problem have brought actions challenging this failure. The issue was considered in *Wells and Walker* in 2007 where the High Court said this was arbitrary, unlawful and unreasonable, while in *James* in 2007 the High Court said that if the prisoner had completed the minimum term of his sentence and he could not access the appropriate course, then he should be released. In fact his release was deferred pending an appeal by the government to the Court of Appeal. In *Secretary of State for Justice v Walker and James* (2008) the Court of Appeal found that the Secretary of State had acted unlawfully in failing to provide appropriate access to courses to allow IPP prisoners to demonstrate to the Parole

Board that their detention was no longer necessary to protect the public. There was a 'systemic' failure to put the appropriate resources in place to allow prisoners to prepare for their Parole Board assessments. The Court also said that if prisoners were detained for this reason for a long time after the minimum term had been completed it *could* breach Article 5(4) of the ECHR although it declined to uphold an order for James's release. Both the Secretary of State and James are now seeking to appeal the Court's decisions.

9.3.4 Education

Prison Rule 32(1) states that '[e]very prisoner able to profit from the educational facilities provided at a prison shall be encouraged to do so.' It also states that educational classes shall be provided at each prison and special needs should be provided for. 'Reasonable facilities shall be afforded to prisoners who wish to do so to improve their education by training by distance learning, private study and recreational classes, in their spare time' (PR 32(2)). Library facilities should be made available at every prison and every prisoner should be allowed to have library books (PR 33). It is estimated that about one-third of prisoners are attending education classes.

In the past decade there has been increased awareness of the value of prison education on the part of policy makers and at the higher levels of the prison management hierarchy, especially in view of the difficulty of finding adequate work for prisoners and the value placed on the constructive use of time as well as the perpetual problem of controlling prisoners. The Woolf Report was critical of the uneven provision of education between prisons, long waiting lists for classes, and cancellations because of staff shortages. Woolf argued that education should be given equal standing to work within the prison's activities (Woolf and Tumim 1991: para 14.102). He also suggested using prisoners to teach other prisoners where appropriate.

The range of educational opportunities has expanded since the 1960s and 1970s with opportunities ranging from basic literacy and numeracy, to Open University degrees by distance learning. Spending on education increased in the 1980s and the number of student hours has increased. Since 1994 National Vocational Qualifications have been offered, but the levels of education and training have varied from establishment to establishment. Problems still persist of ensuring regular access to classes; classes may be disrupted by prison activities and prisoners are not always motivated to attend, because education is unpaid, and many prisoners may have a negative experience of school, often being former truants and under-achievers. Classes need staff cover for security so educational provision may be vulnerable to cuts at times of staff shortages.

Before Competitive Contractual Tendering (CCT), education was provided by local education authorities. Education was contracted out in 1993, under the Further and Higher Education Act 1992. This was meant to give Governors more flexibility to vary contracts, to use more part-timers, to buy direct from suppliers instead of local education authorities, and to cut costs, although critics argued that CCT would lead to instability, loss of morale among staff, and to a narrower range of options. The government accepted that education is an essential part of the opportunities available in prison and must be provided and this is embodied in the Prison Rules (Home Office 1991). However, actual provision is adversely affected by insufficient funding, lack of clear definition of objectives of education programmes, and lack of standardisation of programmes. Although prison education is expected to play a key role as part of a constructive prison regime, in practice it may be marginalised. There are problems of maintaining commitment to education programmes when prisoners are transferred.

We saw earlier that the poor educational background of many prisoners means that the starting point for the acquisition of skills is very low, so remedial work is needed. A priority now in prison education is to improve the basic skills of literacy and numeracy and to include a learning plan as part of the sentencing plan and offender management. Education and training are key elements of the new constructive regimes. Moreover, one of the Government's policies is to increase the vocational and academic qualifications of young people, including prisoners.

The Government's 2001 White Paper, *Criminal Justice: The Way Ahead* (Home Office 2001a) stated that the priorities for prisons are to spend more on educational and vocational training, including literacy and numeracy, as well as drug programmes. The aim is also to provide better preparation for work outside on their return to the community and a Custody to Work initiative was launched in 2000. Developing literacy and numeracy skills are early essential elements in preparing prisoners for release.

The Learning and Skills Council took over responsibility for vocational and education training in prisons in July 2006. The provision of learning and skills is overseen and co-ordinated by the Offenders' Learning and Skills Service, part of the new Department for Innovation, Universities and Skills. The figures for the period from April to July 2006 show that targets were met with 66,368 Work Skills and 15,468 Basic Skills Awards being achieved by prisoners in that period.

9.4 **Prison unrest**

9.4.1 **Prison riots**

The worst riots in British penal history occurred in 1990 in Strangeways in Manchester, and this was followed by serious riots at Glen Parva, a Young Offenders Institution and remand centre, Cardiff and Bristol, both local prisons, Pucklechurch, a remand centre holding mostly young offenders, and Dartmoor, a training prison and elsewhere. These incidents of disorder led to damage to property, assaults and loss of life. In Strangeways, a local prison containing adult and young prisoners, sentenced and remand prisoners, the prison sustained severe damage, staff and inmates were injured, one prisoner later died and another killed himself. Some prisoners were assaulted, one was stabbed and thrown over the wing balcony. In Dartmoor a prisoner died in a fire.

Following the riots in April 1990, an inquiry headed by Lord Justice Woolf was set up which reported in 1991. Its remit was to consider events leading up to the riot at Strangeways, and how the riot was ended, having regard to other serious riots which occurred shortly after the Strangeways riot (Woolf and Tumim 1991: para 2.4). Its findings are considered below.

However, prison riots were not confined to that period but have a long history in the UK. There were riots in the 1970s at Brixton, Hull, Gartree and Parkhurst, and in the 1980s at Wormwood Scrubs, Albany, Haverigg and Risley. Riots have erupted in training prisons, local and remand prisons, Young Offender Institutions and contracted-out prisons, and in prisons with a reputation for relaxed regimes.

Since 1990 there have been some incidents of disorder and riots, but they have been less frequent not on the same scale as the 1990 riots. There were incidents in Portland Young Offenders Institution in 2000, and a serious riot in Lincoln Prison in 2002, resulting in assaults on officers and other prisoners, looting and damage to buildings and property. Several prisoners were convicted of prison mutiny and other charges. There were also riots at Hindley Prison in Wigan, which houses adults and young offenders, in October 2005, and at Stoke Heath Young Offenders Institution in October 2006.

The concern is that with increased overcrowding incidents of disorder will become more frequent and more severe. Moreover, there has been continuing industrial unrest within the Prison Service in recent years which was a significant factor in relation to the unrest of the late 1980s. In the summer of 2006 the Prison Officers Association (POA) threatened to take industrial action over pay rates and collective bargaining rights, despite a no-strike agreement. A statutory prohibition removing the right to strike had been enacted in s 127 of the Criminal Justice and Public Order Act 1994 but subsequently disapplied in 2005 and replaced by a voluntary agreement. The strike was called off in September 2006 but there was a wildcat strike in August 2007 which ended when the High Court granted an injunction prohibiting this action. The POA then threatened to withdraw from the agreement while the Government threatened to reinstate the statutory ban.[9] The Criminal Justice and Immigration Act 2008 has amended the legislation to that effect (s 138).

9.4.2 Explaining prison unrest

Various explanations of the 1990 riots have been advanced as significant causative factors, including the fact that there was substantial overcrowding during the 1980s.[10] The quality of the buildings was also poor in many cases and in prisons where the infrastructure was poor any attack on the building worsened the situation, leading to further deterioration. However, we find dilapidated prisons in other European societies, such as the Netherlands, but we also find good relations between prisoners and staff in those regimes. But the quality of prison life in the UK in the late 1980s and early 1990s was much worse than at the present time in a number of respects. While there had been an expansion of judicial review relating to prisoners' complaints, this primarily concerned procedural problems rather than prison conditions. The Council of Europe's Committee for the Prevention of Torture found that conditions in Wandsworth, Brixton and Leeds prisons in 1990 were inhuman and degrading (Council of Europe 1991). Subsequent reports by HM Chief Inspector of Prisons on individual prisons have revealed continuing problems of poor physical conditions and poor staff relations which indicates that some of the problems have persisted (HM Chief Inspector of Prisons 2006a).

In the 1980s there were no national operating standards for prisons. Today there are National Operating Standards, introduced in 1994, and prisons in England and

---

[9] See Bennett *et al.* (2007) for a discussion of the current issues facing prison staff.
[10] See Boin and Rattray (2004) for a general theory of the causes of prison riots but which includes discussion of the Strangeways riot.

Wales are now subject to KPIs and are performance-tested. The UK has also adopted the European Prison Rules[11] which apply international standards to the context of imprisonment. They set out the requirements of good principle and practice in the treatment of prisoners and the management of penal institutions. These rules are not binding in law and are not legally enforceable but guidelines for best practice and recommendations for states parties who have adopted them, and they allow for exceptions if circumstances dictate.

There were also incidents of brutality and physical mistreatment in the 1980s. The levels of activities and work were lower and were reduced in the 1980s, because of industrial action in 1986. Relations between inmates and staff were generally poor in the 1980s, characterised by a lack of trust. The management of prisons was also criticised in the Woolf Report, particularly the gulf between central management and local staff.

A key complaint by prisoners in the late 1980s related to the unfairness of grievance procedures and to the way disciplinary matters were dealt with at that time. Moreover, decisions over transfers and segregation, for example, were shrouded in secrecy and prisoners were not given reasons for such decisions. This generated an expansion in the use of judicial review to challenge this situation, which has now been improved. While the impact of bad conditions, overcrowding and staffing problems may each have contributed to the tension, the sense of injustice was the crucial factor highlighted by the Woolf Report.

There were also problems of control in the 1980s and an increased focus on security because of fears of escape. It was argued, at the time, that the policy of dispersing high-security prisoners throughout the prison system may have contributed to the problems, because it had an adverse impact on the receiving prisons, increasing the levels of security more than was warranted for other inmates. Volatile political prisoners and disturbed prisoners and lifers were also blamed at the time for contributing to the problems, although, again, some of the riots occurred in prisons without such prisoners.

9.4.3 The Woolf Report

Lord Woolf argued that 'the Prison Service must set security, control and justice in prisons at the right level and it must provide the right balance between them. The stability of the prison system depends on the Prison Service doing so' (Woolf and Tumim 1991: para 1.148). By security he meant preventing prisoners escaping, by control he meant preventing prisoners causing a disturbance, while 'justice encapsulates the obligation on the Prison Service to treat prisoners with humanity and fairness...' (ibid: para 1.149). Lord Woolf concluded that the riots happened because these three elements were out of balance (ibid: para 1.150). Once control is lost, then security is also at risk and 'the ability of the Prison Service to provide conditions which accord with justice will be impaired' (ibid: para 10.41). Conversely, 'the achievement of justice will itself enhance security and control' (ibid: para 14.437).

The Woolf Report was critical of the poor physical conditions in English prisons but stressed that this was not the only or the key factor in the riots. While

---

[11] The full text of the rules can be obtained from http://www.coe.int.

overcrowding may account for some of the unrest in English prisons, riots occurred in prisons where numbers were declining.

But the key issue was that the prisoners felt aggrieved that their complaints were not dealt with properly. Justice, as he points out, does not figure in PR 1 (now PR 3), nor in the Statement of Purpose, although fair treatment is now emphasised in the current Statement of Purpose. At that time Boards of Visitors dealt with discipline and were able to impose punishments including loss of remission, but they were not seen as sufficiently independent. Given that prisoners could be punished by a loss of remission, it was felt that there were insufficient safeguards for prisoners. This led to a sense of injustice and perceptions here are important, for if individuals see the world as unjust, it will influence their actions whether or not that perception accurately reflects reality. Woolf noted that '[i]t is not possible for the Inquiry to form any judgement on whether the specific grievances of these prisoners were or were not well-founded. What is clear is that the Prison Service had failed to persuade these prisoners that it was treating them fairly' (ibid: para 9.25).

If prisons can achieve justice and prisoners feel that they are being treated fairly, then the problems of disorder, control and insecurity will diminish. However, if the problem is approached from the other standpoint by focusing on security, this is likely to increase the prisoners' sense of injustice. Improving standards of justice inside prisons means giving prisoners reasons for decisions which affect them, such as transfers and segregation, as well as a fair grievance and disciplinary procedure: 'Prisoners should know why a decision which materially and adversely affects them is being taken. This is essential to achieving satisfactory relations within prisons. If prisoners consider they have a genuine grievance, they should be able to have resort to a grievance procedure which has at its final stage the necessary degree of independence' (ibid: para 1.207). The grievance procedure should be independent, simple and expeditious. The reason for decisions should be given as soon as is practicable and in writing for matters like transfers (ibid: para 14.308).

Transfers against prisoners' wishes were a source of resentment, and resentment following transfer was a precipitating incident in the riots. Woolf was also critical of the handling of the riots and the fact that warnings were not heeded. If there is also a loss of legitimacy and a sense of unfairness, then relationships between staff and prisoners will be undermined and in that climate it will be easier for specific incidents to trigger disorder.

Woolf made several practical recommendations, including closer cooperation between different parts of the criminal justice system (1991: para 1.167) and argued for improvements in both physical conditions and grievance and disciplinary procedures. Woolf recommended a separate Statement of Purpose for remand prisoners, lower categorisation for them, and better conditions to enable them to prepare for trial, and to deal with work and family affairs. Remand prisoners, he argued, should be held in separate prisons or separate units (ibid: para 11.72) to comply with Rule 3 of the European Prison Rules (Council of Europe 1987).

Prisoners wanted more transparent decision making and openness in procedures, so the goal should be to ensure that the prison regime is seen as fair as well as humane. He advocated housing prisoners as near their homes as possible by building community prisons, with small self-contained units, near large cities, so that prisoners can stay in contact with their families, and visiting will be less onerous for families. This would also make it easier for prisoners to return to the community. Existing prisons need to be broken down into smaller units holding 50–70 prisoners, with no more than 400 prisoners in one prison, which would improve the quality of the regime and would also make it easier to manage. However, many prisoners are still now housed far from their homes. Woolf also advocated improvements in home leave and frequency of visits, extending the use of phone cards to all prisons, and removals of limits on the number of letters that prisoners could post.

Prisoners, Woolf argued, should not have to share a cell (1991: para 11.81), they should have proper access to sanitation (ibid: para 11.97) and the standards of hygiene in prison should be commensurate with those in the community (ibid: para 11.113). The prison system should give all prisoners the opportunity to serve their sentence in a constructive way, making proper use of the time they spend in prison, and making the best use of the money available. This should include a range of work opportunities. The needs of specific groups such as mentally disordered offenders and sex offenders should also be recognised. The regime should encourage the prisoners to take responsibility for themselves, to give them the opportunity to obtain skills, to enable them to keep links with their families and communities, to prepare properly for release, and to reduce the likelihood of reoffending after release. Other recommendations included an additional therapeutic prison and greater integration of sex offenders within the prison community. Lord Woolf also argued for more alternatives to custody, such as bail hostels, and a greater use of community penalties.

The Woolf Report recommended introducing a national system of accredited standards governing the treatment of prisoners, with which all prisons would be expected to comply in order to be accredited. At first this would not be a formal requirement, but an aspiration, and once all prisons reached that level, these standards would become part of the Prison Rules enforceable through judicial review.

The Report also advocated improvements in the training of officers. It stressed the need to improve relations and cooperation between the Home Office, the prison administration, and prisons, and between the Prison and Probation Services. Lord Woolf argued for more visible leadership by the Director General of the Prison Service, as operational head of the service, in charge of day-to-day matters. He advocated the creation of a forum to consider issues affecting the criminal justice system (ibid: para 10.175) and a Criminal Justice Consultative Council was set up in 1994.

A Prison Governor has the power to impose segregation and transfer where this is in the interests of good order and discipline. Woolf recommended that prisoners should be given reasons for decisions which affect them—such as transfer and segregation—and this has now been implemented. The Report also proposed improvements in the way disciplinary offences are dealt with, recommending that the Boards of Visitors should lose their adjudicative role, and this was implemented in 1992. The Boards also have now been renamed Independent Monitoring Boards.

Woolf stressed the need to distinguish disciplinary and criminal proceedings, with serious criminal offences attracting long prison sentences being dealt with by the courts, while disciplinary proceedings, including minor criminal offences, should be the responsibility of the Governor (1991: para 14.405). Prisoners should also have access to an independent Complaints Adjudicator.

The system in place at the time of Lord Woolf's inquiry was seen as unjust because of its inconsistency and arbitrariness: 'by giving Governors the degree of discretion which is at present open to them in deciding what "privileges" to grant and what not to grant, the result has been the creation of a system which many prisoners see, with justification, as arbitrary. The evidence before the Inquiry suggests that this has led to a deep sense of injustice and grievance' (ibid: para 14.36). Woolf argued that access to goods such as books, newspapers and radios should not be privileges, but rather 'normal expectations' (ibid: para 14.32). Woolf proposed that all prisoners should have contracts or compacts with the prison setting out the expectations of both parties (ibid: para 1.183). Further the Report proposed that each prisoner should be allocated a prison officer as his Personal Officer (ibid: para 14.73) and that each prisoner sentenced to 12 months or more should be given a sentence plan in addition to the contract (ibid: para 15.68). Woolf also recommended redrafting the Prison Rules to reflect the changes he recommended.

9.4.4 The impact of the Woolf Report

The Woolf Report was very significant, its proposals were seen as fair and it received support in principle from the Government, in its White Paper *Custody, Care and Justice* (Home Office 1991). The Report was generally welcomed by prison reformers, although some felt that the Report was not critical enough. The immediate response was an improvement in access to phones and visiting arrangements, followed by substantial improvements in prison conditions, including an end to slopping out. However, the Government said at the time that it would take 25 years to implement all the recommended improvements.

National operating standards were introduced in 1994, but they are not legally enforceable and have now been overtaken by KPIs and Key Performance Targets. Changes in the disciplinary system were introduced in 1992. The Prison Rules were subsequently revised in 1999 and amended in 2000, 2002, 2003 and 2005.[12]

Each prisoner is now allocated a Personal Officer. Sentence Planning has also been introduced, the purpose of which is to make the best use of the prisoner's time, to reduce the risk of reoffending, to prepare the prisoner for release, to co-ordinate the custodial and licence elements of the sentence, to inform the parole process, to act as a focal point for staff and prisoner relationships and provide opportunities to review the prisoner's progress, and to assist in targeting resources. It is intended to move beyond humane containment to addressing offending behaviour. There may also be insufficient resources to implement Sentence Plans fully because there may not be an available place on a recommended programme. Sentence planning is time consuming and much of the time is spent completing the necessary paperwork. In addition, transfers may disrupt sentence planning. The emphasis now is on end-to-end management of the offender throughout his time in custody and on supervision with much closer cooperation between the Prison and Probation Service.

Comparing prisons now and before Woolf, we find significant improvements in the complaints and disciplinary systems. A Prisons Ombudsman was appointed in 1994 as a final means of appeal against decisions in disciplinary hearings. The Prisons and Probation Ombudsman can deal with complaints on a wide range

---

[12] Prison Rules (1999) SI 1999 No. 728, Prison (Amendment) Rules 2000, Prison (Amendment) (No. 2) Rules 2000, Prison (Amendment) Rules 2002, Prison (Amendment) Rules 2003, Prison (Amendment) Rules 2005, which came into force on 3 January 2007.

of matters including adjudications, deaths in custody, prison conditions, and the treatment by officers in both state and private prisons. The Ombudsman has the power to make recommendations, but these are not binding, so whether they are accepted is a matter for the Secretary of State. From the complainant's standpoint the Ombudsman is preferable to judicial review because the merits of a decision can be reviewed. However, for a complaint to be eligible the internal complaints procedure of the prison must be exhausted first, so using the Ombudsman is not an effective route for those serving short sentences. Since 1999 the number of complaints received has risen every year and there has also been an increase in the number of complaints deemed eligible. In 2006–7 the Ombudsman received 4,321 complaints about the Prison Service, of which 1,560 were investigated. The most common complaints related to general prison conditions and loss or damage to property but complaints also related to categorisation and discipline (Prisons and Probation Ombudsman 2007). The remit of the Prisons and Probation Ombudsman was extended to complaints in immigration detention on 1 October 2006. The proportion of complaints upheld was 24 per cent.[13]

There are now more safeguards for prisoners compared to the early 1990s. For example, transfer should not be used as a system of punishment, reasons should be given, and inmates should be advised in writing of the reasons for transfer or segregation within 24 hours. Complaints should be made within seven days to the Governor of the prison where the transfer decision was made. The prisoner may be transferred for a month and then returned, or sent to another prison. However, transfers are still used to juggle the demand for places. Decisions on transfer are reviewable, but the court is unlikely to interfere because it is open to the Governor to make the decision, if he believes the prisoner's presence affects the smooth running of prison.[14]

Although many of the Woolf Report's recommendations have been met, some still remain to be implemented. For example, the proposal for a new Prison Rule prohibiting overcrowding was rejected. Woolf also recommended using smaller community prisons to allow prisoners to be held nearer their homes but many are still housed far from home. Moreover, in recent years the government seems to have shifted its provision towards larger prisons. But neither the Carter Report nor the Government response (Home Office 2004b) seems to have acknowledged the need for smaller community prisons and the Carter Review of Prisons (2007) recommended the use of super prisons whilst mergers of smaller prisons have already commenced.

The Woolf changes were introduced in the context of expansion and cuts in prison budgets. There is still insufficient work provision and there are still frequent complaints about food, particularly the timing of meals which are scheduled to fit in with staff shift changes rather than normal routines. Problems of bullying, violence, and assaults persist and may be under-reported, although reducing the number of assaults is a Key Performance Target. In 2006–7 the target for reducing the number of assaults to below 1.53 per cent of the prison population was not met with the actual rate being 1.66 per cent (HM Prison Service 2007a).

---

[13] This figure refers to the overall rate based on all three areas of the Ombudsman's concern.

[14] Procedures governing the process of transfer are set out in the relevant Prison Service Order, PSO 4700.

Apart from minimum statutory visits and phone calls, prisoners do not have basic entitlements or rights, but rather earn privileges which may be withdrawn. All prisons now have an Incentives and Earned Privileges (IEP) Scheme, set up in 1995 under PR 8, in which privileges are earned by good behaviour or by reaching high standards in work or other activities. The schemes apply also to remand prisoners with appropriate adjustments, for example, to allow for the fact that they do not have to work. Each prison can decide on its own scheme although it must conform to national requirements, which stipulate key privileges to be included, such as time out of cell, extra visits, access to cash, higher rates of pay, wearing one's own clothes, and access to television. Governors can then include additional ones, such as cooking facilities. These are over and above basic statutory rights to letters and visits. There are three levels, basic, standard and enhanced, and all prisoners start on the standard level. Challenging a decision to place a prisoner on a lower level may be difficult as the courts are reluctant to interfere in the way schemes are run. From the prisoners' standpoint it may feel more like an informal means of discipline without the proper safeguards of the formal disciplinary system. The contracts intended by Woolf to protect prisoners have been used in practice to control them, as the focus has been on a system of incentives and privileges earned through good behaviour, rather than on prisoners' rights or legitimate expectations. Although the IEP scheme was intended to establish a national framework, the lack of standardisation has led to complaints about the variations in schemes between prisons, which present problems for prisoners who are transferred, who may find themselves on a lower level. Greater standardisation is therefore desirable.

It has also been argued that justice has been subordinated to security and control. The effect of the escapes in the mid-1990s was that all prisons became more security-conscious. Following the escape from Whitemoor in 1994, the Woodcock Report published in 1994 was very critical of security procedures and concern intensified after the escapes from Parkhurst in 1995. The Learmont Report (1995) was also critical of the standards of security, following which the then Director General of the Prison Service, Derek Lewis, was sacked.

The effect of enhanced security measures meant cuts in home leave, restrictions on contact with the community and extra time spent in cells. Prisoners were also handcuffed in hospital and, in one notorious case, while in labour. An increased concern with security usually means a decline in prison conditions as more time is spent locked up. New rules on cell searches were introduced after the Woodcock Report (1994), the key one being that a prisoner is no longer allowed to be present when the cell is searched, which makes prisoners anxious about their possessions being damaged or evidence being planted. There are also privacy issues as their papers, including legal papers, may be examined, and so far the courts have not been very sympathetic to these concerns. These changes have further increased prisoners' sense of injustice as prisoners not involved in escapes or disorder have still been subjected to the enhanced security regime. The modern prison regime is much more security-aware, using technological means of surveillance, such as CCTV as well as greater staff surveillance, but escapes still occasionally occur, often while in transit, although in 2006/7 there were no escapes of category A prisoners and the escape rate expressed as a proportion of the average prison population was 0.01 per cent. There has also been increasing emphasis on drugs control and policing through mandatory drug testing. In 2006–7 the rate of positive tests was 8.6 per cent (HM Prison Service 2007a).

9.4.5 Suicide and self-harm

But rioting is not the only expression of dissatisfaction or the only way prisoners deal with the pains of imprisonment. Problems with the experience of imprisonment may also be expressed through suicide and self-harm. Suicide rates in prisons increased during the 1990s despite improvements in conditions. They did fall briefly from 78 in 2005 to 67 in 2006 but increased in 2007 to 92 (Ministry of Justice 2007a: 123). In 2006–7, 30 per cent of suicides were committed by remand prisoners.

The number of recorded suicides amongst prisoners has increased since 1995 and although these suicides may be attributed to mental health problems, isolation is a contributory factor, so any policies which increase contact with home may reduce the risk. The target on self-inflicted deaths was met in 2006–7, seeing 96.3 SIDs per 100,000 of the prison population with a target of no more than 112.8, but the numbers are obviously still too high (HM Prison Service 2007a). One-fifth of the suicides in 2007 occurred within the first week of imprisonment (HM Chief Inspector of Prisons 2007). The suicide rate in prison is much higher than in society at large. Fazel *et al.* (2005) studied suicide in male prisoners in England and Wales between 1978 and 2003 and found that the suicide rate for males in prisons was five times higher than for males outside prison and for boys aged 15–17 was 18 times higher. Reducing suicide is now part of the 'decency' agenda and proposals have been made to address this problem (see Dear 2006).

9.4.6 Challenging prison conditions

As well as expressing their grievances through riots, prisoners have also challenged the conditions in which they are held through the courts, using private and public law. Actions have been brought in negligence, but the court will consider the context and judge by the standards appropriate to a prison. However, judicial review has been more successful in providing prisoners with an avenue to challenge administrative decisions and as a means of achieving justice. Decisions on disciplinary matters, categorisation, transfer and segregation, and mandatory life sentences have been subjected to judicial scrutiny as the disciplinary regime of the prison has been integrated into public law since the late 1970s. Generally judges have felt more comfortable dealing with quasi-judicial matters, such as disciplinary hearings, rather than intervening in relation to prison conditions. The Prison Rules allow for considerable discretion, but this should not be exercised unreasonably. Before the Human Rights Act 1998 (HRA), the criterion would have been the test in *Associated Provincial Pictures Houses v Wednesbury Corporation* [1948], but now the courts will consider Convention compliance where rights issues are raised, so the test will be that of proportionality (see *Daly* (2001); *Huang* (2007)). Human rights jurisprudence is becoming increasingly important in prisoners' litigation (see section 9.6 below). Prisoners may also use the internal complaints procedure, and also have access to the Prisons and Probation Ombudsman.

9.5 **Prison privatisation**

9.5.1 **The privatisation debate: the case for and against privatisation**

A further significant development in the 1990s was the introduction of prison privatisation. There are now 11 private prisons and it is expected that about a half of the prisons to be built in the next few years will also be private. The Wolds and Doncaster were built and financed by the public sector but are privately managed, while the remainder were built and are also run by the private sector. They are Dovegate, Altcourse, Parc, Lowdham Grange, Forest Bank, Ashfield, Rye Hill, Bronzefield and Peterborough. The proportion of prisoners held in private prisons has been steadily increasing and private prisons now hold about 10 per cent of the prison population compared to 7.2 per cent in the United States (Department of Justice, Bureau of Justice statistics for the 12 months ending 20 June 2006).

The privatisation of prisons is just one aspect of a wider programme of privatisation which took place in Britain in the 1980s and 1990s. A prison previously built and run by the Prison Service may be contracted out to a private company. New prisons may also be privately designed, constructed, managed and financed, following which the Prison Service pays a fee for each place. Privatisation may also mean privatising specific ancillary services within the prison, such as cleaning or catering, and canteens and shops have now been privatised.

Private companies were already involved in running detention centres at airports in the 1980s (see Home Office 1988c) and the provisions for contracting out prisons and also escort duties were introduced in the 1991 Criminal Justice Act (ss 80–88). Sections 96 and 97 of the Criminal Justice and Public Order Act 1994 provide for contracting-out of parts, functions and activities of public sector prisons. A number of services have been contracted out, including education and catering, so there is now a substantial market for private sector involvement.

When prison privatisation was proposed in the 1980s, a number of arguments were raised in favour of it. It was purported to be a more cost-efficient way of running the prison system, as advocates argued that private companies could construct, manage, and run prisons more cheaply than the state and build them more quickly to meet the ever-increasing demand for prison places. It was thought that competition between private companies for contracts would encourage the provision of better standards at lower cost, in contrast to the monopoly position of state prisons at the time. The standards would be specified in the contract and penalties imposed if they were breached, or future contracts would be lost. It was argued that the private prisons would be more innovative in design and management, able to learn from the mistakes of the public sector and, particularly, to avoid the problems of industrial conflict and grievances by recruiting new staff from outside the Prison Officers' Association. Proponents also argued that private prisons would be more open to public scrutiny, unable to hide behind Crown Immunity or the Official Secrets Act.

However, the case for privatisation was vigorously opposed.[15] It was argued that free competition could not be guaranteed as the firm which wins the initial contract is likely to dominate the industry; because of their experience their costs may be lower, which will give the state an interest in renewing the contract which may deter other companies from submitting bids. Once the company is in a strong bargaining position it then may be able to negotiate higher prices for average standards, and in the USA prices increased as the private sector became more established. In the UK the market is dominated by relatively few companies, including at the present time, the Premier Custodial Group, Falck AS, Kalyx and Securicor Justice Services.

The commercial context and in particular the obligations to company shareholders may conflict with the duty to provide the best conditions for inmates, and to achieve these aims, there will be pressures to lower costs and maximise profits (see Genders and Player 2007). As the greatest cost is staffing, there is the danger that private companies will reduce costs by recruiting fewer staff, paying lower wages, or reducing training, which may mean increased risks to staff and prisoners as they may be unable to manage difficult prisoners. If staff are poorly trained, they may be less aware of when or how they can restrain prisoners, using reasonable force. It may be difficult to monitor a decline in the quality of provision as prisoners' lives are largely invisible and hidden from the public.

It could also be argued that punishment should be exclusively the prerogative of the state or the integrity of the criminal justice system will be undermined. The contractual checks on deviant companies are also inadequate because, if the company fails to meet the terms of the contract, fines in the UK are currently limited to only 5 per cent of the contract price, which has been criticised by the House of Commons' Public Accounts Committee. But if the penalty were higher, it is thought this would deter potential contractors as it would eat into profits. Yet the supply and management of prisons is one of the few businesses where demand can be guaranteed, so it is hardly a high-risk venture for shareholders. In any case, problems may persist while the contract runs its course and before a new contract partner is found.

To encourage private companies to invest, the Government is signing long-term contracts. For example, Securicor Justice Services has a 25-year operating contract to manage Parc Prison and Young Offenders' Institution. But this also makes it harder for a new government, if it so wishes, to change the privatisation policy (see Jago and Thompson 2001).

Critics also argue that private companies are not necessarily cheaper providers. Comparing costs accurately may be difficult as private companies are more likely to be given low-risk prisoners and, in the early stages of privatisation, the programme was focused on remand prisoners. Older prisons holding more difficult prisoners are less likely to attract bids from the private sector as happened when Brixton was put out to tender. If higher-risk prisoners are included, costs will inevitably increase. Cost comparisons also do not include the additional high costs of procurement which add to the expense of running a privatised system of

---

[15] For further discussion of the concerns regarding privatisation of prisons, see Matthews (1989), Schichor (1995), Jago and Thompson (2001), Prison Reform Trust (2005) and Genders and Player (2007). See also the July 2002 issue of *Punishment and Society* which was devoted to prison privatisation and considers the problems in both the UK and the USA.

punishment. In any case state prisons in the UK have become more cost effective in recent years. Initially the Prison Service was not permitted to bid for contracts but this has now changed and it has won contracts in competition with the private sector, for example, at Strangeways Prison in Manchester. Some private prisons, for example Buckley Hall and Blakenhurst, have returned to the public sector. It has been suggested that cost per place is actually higher in most categories of prison in the private sector than in the public sector.[16]

There are also issues regarding control and accountability as it is arguably harder to control the private sector. There is a rigorous system of auditing public bodies and Parliamentary controls over Ministers, but private contractors are more removed from democratic controls. In the UK, borrowing from the United States' experience, there are now government monitors or controllers appointed by the Secretary of State working within the system to ensure that contracts are complied with. The overall management of the private prison is in the hands of the Director, an employee of the private company but appointed by the Director General of the Prison Service.

Concerns over accountability may be addressed by appointing controllers and inserting penalties into the contract. There is a range of mechanisms in the state sector, including Parliamentary scrutiny, Independent Monitoring Boards, the National Audit Office, the Prisons and Probation Ombudsman, judicial review, and an inspection process, which also apply to the private sector. If private prisons do not function properly and the prisoner seeks redress for grievances, he or she will have access to the courts and to the Ombudsman. Private prisons are subject to the Prison Act and Prison Rules and prisoners have the same legal rights as in public sector prisons, including the protection of the HRA 1998. The problem of invisibility of prisoners remains, but this applies equally to public sector prisoners. Area Managers are now the direct line managers for private prisons. Prison officers, or custody officers, receive similar training to public sector prison officers. If control of a private prison was lost, during a riot, for example, the state would have the power to take it over. In this sense, the state is still responsible for punishment, even within a contracted-out prison; it has a responsibility to see that the service is provided properly. If there is a conflict between the private company's duty to shareholders and the duty to provide care for inmates, this could be addressed by financial penalties if conditions fall below the stipulated standard, and if current levels of fines are inadequate, then they could be increased. For example, there are already penalties for, inter alia, overcrowding, unless the overcrowding is requested by the Prison Service.

There have been concerns over the want of probity of some of the companies involved in the prison industry. The industrial work programme at Coldingly in the UK was criticised when an internal audit in 1999 discovered false accounting and mismanagement; a large sum was recovered from Wackenhut and the contract returned to the Prison Service. The inadequate monitoring of financial arrangements has also been criticised by the Chief Inspector of Prisons.

Incidents of mistreatment have been reported in private prisons, such as the case of Alton Manning at Blakenhurst in 1995, which was at that time in the private sector but has now been returned to the public sector, but there have been

---

[16] See Hansard, House of Commons, written answer 9 January 2007.

incidents in public sector prisons as well. Manning had been strip-searched, during which, it was argued, he had resisted, and had been held down by officers using a neck-lock on him, following which he died. Although there were several security cameras in operation, an investigation into the death found that videotapes which should have been recording the incident were blank. The inquest found that Manning had been unlawfully killed through choking from the illegal neck-lock (Inquest 1998).

9.5.2 The experience of privatisation

Research has now been conducted to test some of these claims and to assess the relative strengths and weaknesses of public and private prisons in England and Wales. Of course in the past ten years public sector prisons themselves have moved closer to the ethos of the private prison, under the influence of the New Managerialism. Indeed, defenders of privatisation argue that it is precisely the use of KPIs and the New Managerialism which has improved the standards in the public sector. Moreover, with the current focus on contestability in offender management and on financial controls and value for money, private prison management has been endorsed as a model for public sector financial management by the Carter Review of Prisons (Carter 2007).

James *et al.* (1997) conducted fieldwork in the Wolds (a private prison) and Woodhill (a new public sector prison). They were struck by the similarities between the two prisons in terms of their 'business like approach to management'. The Wolds was the first private sector prison and it opened in 1992. James *et al.* found that, despite some initial problems, the regime there was innovative and successful. This lent support to the argument that private prisons would be more adaptable to change and more innovative than traditional public sector prisons. An ethos of treating prisoners with respect prevailed which allowed for a normalisation of the prison environment. At the Wolds there were good staff relations, more time out of cells, better access to facilities although, because of prisoner apathy, they were not always used, a high number of hours in purposeful activities, and good mechanisms for accountability.

However, the researchers also found similar innovations and achievements in some new public sector prisons, including Woodhill, as well as in larger more complex prisons with different functions. Woodhill opened in 1992 at Milton Keynes, and at the time of their research, housed 500 prisoners including both convicted and remand prisoners. It recruited younger staff to avoid using staff from the pre-Woolf era. The aim was to provide a humane regime where as much time was spent out of cells as possible, the regime was relaxed and prisoners wore their own clothes. There were good relations between staff and inmates. With its strong focus on financial planning, careful budgeting and devolution of budgets to units within the prison, Woodhill was similar in many ways to a private prison. Since then, however, the conditions have been criticised by the Chief Inspector of Prisons in 1998 (HMCIP 1998).

James *et al.* also examined the regimes at Blakenhurst, then a contracted-out prison, and three new public sector prisons, Belmarsh, Bullingdon and Highdown. The researchers concluded that there was no necessary connection between innovation in regime delivery and contracted-out management status. They found that prisoners were treated with respect in both types of prison, and some public prisons had a strong value-for-money ethos with effective and high quality senior managers. Physical conditions are usually better in newer prisons than old ones, irrespective of their public or private status. Given the poor state of prisons in the late 1980s, it would have been hard to create private prisons which were worse than the existing ones.

We also find that both types of prison have faced similar problems of disturbance and disorder. Since 1996, there have been disturbances at the Wolds, as well as drugs problems and incidents of assaults, disorder and bullying at Doncaster, where there has also been concern over the physical conditions, and suicides, especially as the prison includes a Young Offender Institution. Parc Prison in Bridgend opened officially in 1998, but took inmates from November 1997. It failed to recruit sufficient staff and suffered disturbances in 1998, with cells damaged and hostages taken. There has been a high turnover of staff and senior managers and custody officers may lack experience in managing such difficult situations. The contractors have been fined for failing to meet minimum standards. There has also been overcrowding at Doncaster, Blakenhurst and the Wolds (Park 2000). UKDS was fined in 1994 after losing control of Blakenhurst and it was later returned to the public sector. Rye Hill prison has also been subjected to criticism by HM Chief Inspector of Prisons for failing to provide a safe regime (HM Chief Inspector of Prisons 2005). The contract was then given to Global Solutions Ltd but a damaging investigation by the BBC and Guardian Films broadcast in April 2007 showed bullying and intimidation of staff by prisoners. The regime at Ashfield prison was also heavily criticised in 2002 although it has since improved. Doncaster has also been criticised by HM Chief Inspector of Prisons (2007).

There is a higher turnover of staff generally in private prisons than public sector prisons which has been attributed to the poorer working conditions in the private sector. The National Audit Office has expressed concern over inexperienced staff working in private prisons and over the number of assaults at Dovegate, Altcourse, Ashfield, Rye Hill and Forest Bank. By 2001 fines imposed on private prisons amounted to almost £1 million and these related to failings including double occupancy, and assaults on staff and prisoners (Jago and Thompson 2001). There is also a lower staff-to-prisoner ratio which may have implications for safety. However, private prisons still suffer from the problems of overcrowding.

Research since the 1990s has shown significant variations in performance and quality of public and private sector prisons with some successes, but also some continuing causes for concern. For example, there is more time spent in purposeful activities in private sector prisons and the physical infrastructure of the prison is usually better because they are new and purpose-built rather than older buildings or conversions. The study in 2005 by the Prison Reform Trust, *Private Punishment: Who Profits?*, which examined ten private prisons, also found mixed results, with variations in performance. Although some private prisons were doing well, others were having problems. The review also raised questions regarding accountability, conflicts of interest and profiteering from the use of private finance (Prison Reform Trust 2005). Pay and conditions for staff were worse in the private than the public sector. They also questioned the long-term impact of privatised justice on the prison system; for example, the pressure for economies of scale in commercial enterprises may have adverse implications for the prison system.

The mere fact that a prison is privately managed does not guarantee high-quality performance any more than it would simply by virtue of being in the public sector. The problems prisons face will not disappear just because they are privatised; there is still overcrowding in both sectors and debates over privatisation are a diversion from the fundamental issue of why we have such a high incarceration rate and whether this can and should be reduced. Although good practice may be found in the private sector, it is hard to link this causally to privatisation *per se*. Bearing in mind the fears expressed at the time and the clash of ideologies in the privatisation debate, we can say that we can find good practice at private prisons, but also progressive regimes in public sector prisons, for example, the homework club for children of prisoners at Wandsworth Prison to encourage prisoners and their families to maintain contact. However, it may be difficult to sustain high standards over time with increasing costs and with increasing pressure on prison places. The issue is now not whether to privatise or not, as privatisation is deeply embedded in current penal policy, but how to facilitate creative innovative regimes, at a time of high numbers and limited resources, and pressures to maintain security, and how to reduce numbers to allow for improvements to be implemented.

While some of the concerns of critics of privatisation may have been allayed, it is clear to see that the ideological debate over the issue of privatisation has now been 'lost' in so far as private prisons are now so well established, with neither of the two main parties opposed to them. Indeed, the continuing focus on contestability has widened the net to other areas of the criminal justice system. Despite the opposition to prison privatisation expressed before coming to power, the Government under Prime Minister Blair said that contracted-out prisons provide value for money although the gap between public and private prison costs is narrowing, and the commitment to contestability has been accepted by the Brown administration and is being extended to community punishment. The Carter Review of Correctional Services (Carter 2003) advocated the expanding use of competition from private and voluntary sectors in the prison and probation services to increase effectiveness and value for money (ibid: 25), while the recent Carter Report on Prisons (Carter 2007) proposes market testing of prisons' administrative functions. So the commitment to privatisation seems likely to continue in the future.

9.6 Human rights and imprisonment

9.6.1 Rights, fairness and justice

The protections afforded prisoners both internally and through the courts have improved the safety of prisoners and raised standards in prison, but there is still some way to go. While procedural justice has improved substantially since the Woolf Report, the day-to-day conditions in which prisoners are held still leave much room for improvement and there is considerable variation between prisons, as illustrated by the league tables. A system of accreditation in which minimum standards actually become part of the Prison Rules advocated by Woolf has not been accepted. A penal tribunal with lay members might also provide greater procedural fairness than judicial review, or the internal complaints system, as it would offer independence. It will be interesting to see the recommendations of the Commission on English Prisons in its forthcoming Report on these questions.

Focusing on rights, fairness, and justice would also provide positive benefits to the Prison Service as reducing dissatisfaction would improve good order within prisons. It would also create a better climate for the rehabilitation of prisoners as it would strengthen adherence to liberal-democratic values within the regime. Respect for rights is also a key means of ensuring the legitimacy of the system. The value of a human rights-based approach is that enforceable rights offer a means of maintaining and ensuring minimum standards inside prison and arguably provide greater protection than the Key Performance Indicator Targets of New Managerialism, particularly at a time of increased pressure on resources and a strong focus on public protection and risk management.

A right to a minimal standard of living would potentially contribute to the improvement of prison conditions, provided that there are adequate enforcement mechanisms in place. An open grievance procedure enhances the legitimacy of the prison authority structure. There should be a right to the maximum autonomy compatible with the rights and freedoms of others and with the fact of imprisonment, but prison reform has not been couched in a rights framework in the UK. The Prison Service has resisted rights talk and a rights culture, preferring to use the currency of privileges and incentives which are not legally enforceable entitlements. They can be withdrawn and used as a disciplinary measure to maintain good order and discipline within the prison. Moreover, guaranteeing legally enforceable rights is much more expensive both in terms of compliance and in defending claims made in relation to alleged breaches.

The development of prison law has met with some resistance from governments and the Prison Service because of a concern with the financial costs if it opened the floodgates to litigation, but this has not happened, in part because there are disincentives for prisoners to complain, a fear of being seen as a troublemaker, and also the need for literacy skills to bring an action. The requirement for leave for judicial review and the continuing scope for discretion have also acted as a brake on litigation. Moreover, even when prisoners have succeeded in their claims, the level of damages awarded has been relatively low.

Prison reformers argue that prisoners should have a legal right to training, work, education and medical treatment. Even though people outside prison may not possess these rights, it could be argued that prisoners are a special case because they are vulnerable and dependent, and are unable to obtain access to these goods through their own efforts. We need a clear delineation of rights and liberties in a legal form as well as positive rights to work, education and association.

9.6.2 Rights Conventions

In English law the approach of the courts has been that prisoners have the same civil rights as non-prisoners except for those taken away expressly or impliedly by imprisonment.[17] But this clearly falls far short of according prisoners special rights by virtue of the fact that they are prisoners. Because of this *lacuna*, international

---

[17] *Raymond v Honey* (1983).

human-rights instruments have particular significance for the prison system in the UK.

Article 5 of the Universal Declaration of Human Rights states that '[n]o one shall be subjected to torture or to cruel, inhuman or degrading treatment or punishment'. The rights in the Declaration are elaborated in rights instruments, including the International Covenant on Civil and Political Rights (ICCPR). The UK has ratified the ICCPR which includes general provisions of relevance to punishment, such as the right to life and the right not to be detained arbitrarily. Article 10 deals specifically with the penal system:

1. All persons deprived of their liberty shall be treated with humanity and with respect for the inherent dignity of the human person.

2. (a) Accused persons shall, save in exceptional circumstances, be segregated from convicted persons and shall be subject to separate treatment appropriate to their status as unconvicted persons;

   (b) Accused juvenile persons shall be separated from adults and brought as speedily as possible for adjudication.

3. The penitentiary system shall comprise the treatment of prisoners the essential aim of which shall be their reformation and rehabilitation. Juvenile offenders shall be segregated from adults and accorded treatment appropriate to their legal status.

However, the most significant rights protection in recent years has come from the European Convention on Human Rights (the Convention), which protects a number of rights relevant to the context of imprisonment and detention. Even before the Human Rights Act 1998, the Convention influenced the English courts, although the recommendations of the European Court of Human Rights were persuasive not binding. Many of the issues raised in the early Convention cases are now covered by the European Prison Rules. In addition prisons have been inspected by the European Committee for the Prevention of Torture. However, in its jurisprudence, the European Court of Human Rights has tended to focus on the Convention rights themselves, rather than the standards in the European Prison Rules.

The Convention has implications for the practice of punishment. It has been extensively used by UK prisoners and has had considerable impact on prisoners' lives. Prisoners retain their rights under the Convention notwithstanding their imprisonment and restrictions on those rights need to be justified within the criteria set out in the Convention. The UK government has responded to decisions in the European Court of Human Rights by issuing Circulars, in some cases amending the relevant legislation. It has also reached a friendly settlement, on some occasions, in anticipation of the Court's decision. Convention compliance will also be considered when introducing regime changes.

The Convention has improved the experience of punishment in a number of areas. For example, Article 2 has been used to challenge the procedures for dealing with deaths in custody, in *Edwards v UK* (2002), and in relation to the failure to prevent suicide in *Keenan v UK* (2001). Article 3 has been used to challenge inhuman and degrading prison conditions. Article 5 has been used to challenge the lawfulness of continued detention by mentally disordered offenders as well as by discretionary life prisoners (see Chapter 5). Article 6 has been used to gain access to the courts, and to challenge the conduct of disciplinary hearings. Article 8, the right to private and family life, has been used to challenge interference with prisoners' correspondence and excessive restrictions on prison visits, and to improve contact with prisoners' families. Article 8 has also been used to successfully challenge denying a prisoner facilities needed to artificially inseminate his wife, in *Dickson v UK* (2007). Article 12 has been used to claim the right to temporary release from prison to marry. Article 3 of Protocol No. 1 has been used to challenge the ban on convicted prisoners' voting in *Hirst v UK* (2005).

From the standpoint of the Strasbourg Court, prisoners possess rights rather than expectations or privileges. However, the potential of the Convention is limited by the fact that several of the rights protected by the Convention may be qualified, to prevent crime, in the interests of national security and to protect the rights and freedom of others, which may be particularly appropriate to the context of imprisonment, and these qualifications have been interpreted liberally by the Court. States have been accorded a wide margin of appreciation in interpreting and applying the Convention and the Strasbourg Court has sometimes been reluctant to substitute its judgment for that of the domestic authorities. It has characterised the Convention as a living instrument to be interpreted in the light of present-day conditions, that is, dynamically, and stressed the need to strike a balance between the demands of the general interests of the community and the protection of individuals' fundamental rights, using the principle of proportionality.

9.6.3 The Human Rights Act 1998

Since the Human Rights Act 1998 (HRA) came into force, reliance on Convention rights has been much enhanced. The HRA 1998 incorporates the ECHR into domestic law. Legislation must be interpreted so as to be compatible with the Convention. If it is not possible to do so, the court should issue a declaration of incompatibility. Section 6 of the HRA makes it unlawful for public authorities to act in ways which are incompatible with the European Convention. The White Paper which preceded the Act, *Rights Brought Home: The Human Rights Bill* (Home Office 1997b), made it clear that it was intended to open the way to challenges to central government, including executive agencies, the police and the Immigration Department, the Prison Service and public and contracted-out prisons. The HRA 1998 applies to private companies if they are responsible for areas of activity which were previously in the public sector, so the Act can be used against private prisons. Companies managing contracted-out prisons perform a statutory-based activity and are constrained by the same statutes as public prisons, namely the Prison Act and Prison Rules. The Act also applies to the Independent Monitoring Boards (formerly Boards of Visitors) and the Parole Board. When the HRA 1998 came into force the Prison Service took the view that its policies operating at the time were compliant with the Convention but since then, the application of some of these policies has been successfully challenged.

Because of the amount of time it has taken in the past for a case to be heard at Strasbourg, the Convention was of value only to those serving longer sentences. With the HRA this problem has been substantially reduced, so that rights cases may now be an option for prisoners serving shorter sentences. If a case does ultimately go to Strasbourg the procedures there have also been streamlined, with the abolition of the Commission in 1999, which came into effect in October 2000.

Before the Act, pursuing a Convention case was a burdensome and lengthy procedure. The original incident in the case of *Campbell and Fell*, for example, occurred in 1976, and the European Court's judgment was published in 1984. Those whose Convention rights are infringed can now bring proceedings and claim remedies, including damages, in the domestic court. A Prison Service policy may be challenged under the HRA, if it raises fundamental rights issues. All officers and inmates are informed of the Act and its implications and a brief Guide to the Human Rights Act, produced jointly by the Prison Service and the Prison Reform Trust, is given to all prisoners and employees. Given the courts' record of protecting prisoners in private law, it might seem over-optimistic to be looking to the judiciary to protect prisoners' rights. Judges in the UK have tended to favour a conservative rather than a broader interpretation of prisoners' rights, in part because the majority have a background in private law, far removed from the types of problem typically experienced by prisoners.

Nonetheless, more recently, the response of the judiciary has been more favourable to prisoners' rights claims because a rights culture is now more embedded in domestic law and prisoners are increasingly using Convention rights to challenge prison regimes. For example, there have been several challenges by life-sentenced prisoners to delays in parole reviews for mandatory lifers following the European Court of Human Rights' decision in *Stafford v UK* (2002). However, the English courts subsequently have stressed in *R (Middleton) v Secretary of State for the Home Department* (2003) that the authorities should be allowed a reasonable time to take account of any changes. Following *Stafford* the arrangements for parole reviews have been amended so that all mandatory life prisoners who are near the end of the tariff will have a review which complies with Article 5(4). The review is conducted first on the papers and a recommendation made; then either party, if unhappy with the recommendation, can request an oral hearing.

Moreover, the House of Lords has also held that the Home Secretary's power to set minimum tariffs for mandatory-life-sentence prisoners under s 29 of the Crime (Sentences) Act 1997 breaches Article 6 of the Convention because the tariff should be set by an independent and impartial tribunal and not by the Home Secretary. The House of Lords issued a declaration of incompatibility in *R (Anderson) v Secretary of the State for the Home Department* (2002) (see Chapter 5, section 5.4.4). The Criminal Justice Act 2003 subsequently set out the principles by which judges fix minimum tariffs and required judges to give reasons in court if they impose a term inconsistent with those principles. Successful challenges to delays in the parole process have been made by prisoners serving determinate sentences: these delays have been held to be unlawful and a breach of Article 5(4) (see *R (Johnson) v Secretary of State for the Home Department and Another* [2007]).

There have also been changes in relation to disciplinary procedures. Until 2002 the power to award additional days was vested in the Governor. However, in *Ezeh and Connors v UK* (2002) the European Court of Human Rights ruled that only independent adjudicators, not Prison Governors, may impose additional days as punishment for disciplinary offences. Ezeh and Connors were charged separately with using threatening language and assault. They were found guilty at hearings before the Governor at which they were not represented. Ezeh received 40 additional days and Connors 7 additional days. The European Court of Human Rights deemed that, given the charges they faced and the extent of the penalty, Article 6 was engaged, and the refusal to allow representation did violate Article 6(3)(c).

Following that decision, the Governor should decide whether a charge is so serious that it could lead to additional days if the prisoner is found guilty (PR 53A(1)). If so, the Governor must refer the case to an independent adjudicator in which case the prisoner must be offered the opportunity to seek legal representation (PR 54(3)). If the charge will not incur additional days' punishment, then the Governor can conduct the adjudication (PR 54A(2)(b)). If the Governor does proceed, but it becomes clear that additional days should be awarded, the Governor can then refer the case to an independent adjudicator, during the hearing or after the hearing, but before imposing punishment (PR 53A(3)). The independent adjudicator can award up to 42 additional days for adult prisoners and 21 additional days for young offenders. The procedures for adjudication were revised and updated in January 2006 when PSO 2000 replaced the *Prison Discipline Manual*.

But while more human rights cases may now be brought, this does not mean that all will succeed, as many cases taken to Strasbourg in the past by prisoners failed. While cases on access to the courts and interference with privileged correspondence have met with success, cases on conditions have been less successful. The Prison Service can defend cases under the HRA 1998 only if it can show that the decision was imposed because of necessity, rather than demonstrating its reasonableness. Prisoners are therefore more likely to succeed if they focus on areas which have previously enjoyed success at Strasbourg, such as correspondence, access to lawyers, family contact, disciplinary procedures, and treatment of life-sentence prisoners, or reviews of their detention, rather than challenging prison conditions. Even if those conditions are harsh, the nature of the prison environment means that considerable weight will be given to issues of security. In *R (G) v Home Secretary* [2005] a prisoner, who had been held in a Protected Witness Unit (PWU), committed further offences after release from prison. When he was returned to prison, he was initially detained in a PWU but was then transferred as a category A prisoner to a self-contained unit at HMP Belmarsh. Through judicial review, G challenged both the regime and the categorisation as a breach of Article 2, but without success.

There are also difficulties with the Convention itself, particularly the fact that it does not include social or economic rights, such as the right to work or rights to welfare and health or housing, which are of particular significance to prisoners, in contrast to more recently drafted rights instruments such as the South African constitution. The absence of social rights reflects the political context in which the Convention was drafted in response to civil rights violations in Europe in the 1930s and 1940s. However, social rights are assuming more importance in international human rights law (see Búrca and de Witte 2005). On the positive side, however, the HRA 1998 has created a rights culture and means that domestic courts are obliged to consider rights issues in all areas of law, and already the Act has had an impact. Moreover, with increasing pressure to improve standards from international rights jurisprudence, the principle of less eligibility becomes less significant in governing prison life.

A further conduit by means of which international standards enter into penal management is through the revised and updated European Prison Rules adopted by the Committee of Ministers of the Council of Europe in January 2006. Although these do not amount to enforceable rights, they do reflect the jurisprudence of the Strasbourg Court. The revised Rules take account of changes in the penal field since the 1980s, the case law and jurisprudence of the European Court of Human Rights on prison conditions, and the Reports of the European Committee for the

Prevention of Torture and Inhuman or Degrading Treatment or Punishment. The changes cover a range of issues, including healthcare in prison, disciplinary measures and conditional release.

9.6.4 **Prisoners' right to vote**

An important area where a Convention challenge has succeeded in the European Court of Human Rights is in relation to prisoner disenfranchisement. In *Hirst v UK* in October 2005, a former prisoner argued that the provisions preventing convicted prisoners from voting in s 3 of the Representation of the People Act 1969, as amended in 1983 and 2000, violated Article 3 of Protocol No. 1 of the Convention, which imposes on states the obligation to hold free elections under conditions which will ensure the 'free expression of the people in the choice of the legislature'.[18] The majority of the Strasbourg Court concluded that a blanket restriction which applies regardless of individual circumstances, or the gravity of the offence, falls outside the margin of appreciation. The UK government had not considered fully whether such a ban was necessary. The impact of the ban excluded thousands of citizens from voting. Voting by convicted prisoners has been permitted in some other jurisdictions for many years, for example, in the South African constitution.

Since *Hirst* was decided the UK government has undertaken a consultation process to consider whether some categories of convicted prisoner should be permitted to vote (Department for Constitutional Affairs 2006). Although the government accepts that the law will need to be amended to comply with the Convention, it does not envisage restoring the vote to all convicted prisoners but only to some categories of prisoner, which have yet to be decided. Options being considered include determining the right by length of sentence or by giving sentencers the discretion to decide whether a disqualification is appropriate. Cases were brought by prisoners challenging the legality of the May 2007 elections in the domestic court on the issue of Convention compliance but were unsuccessful although the amount of time taken to amend the law was criticised by the Courts (see *Traynor and Fisher* [2007], *Smith v Scott* [2007] and *Re Toner and Walsh* [2007]). The government has defended its position on the grounds that disenfranchisement is an appropriate punishment and will encourage civic responsibility and respect for the law but these did not satisfy the Court in *Hirst*, and these arguments are difficult to support as it could be argued that including prisoners in the electoral process will encourage civic responsibility and promote social inclusion (see Easton 2006).

9.7 **Expansionist and reductionist penal policies**

If we review penal policies and particularly the use of custody in recent years, we find a tension between expansionist and reductionist penal policies with a continuing expansion of prison numbers and commitment to prison building, on the

---

[18] Remand prisoners, and prisoners convicted for non-payment of fines and those imprisoned for contempt of court are permitted to vote.

one hand, and attempts to exert controls and limits on this expansion through the use of alternatives to custody and greater controls on sentencers. As governments have tried to negotiate the pressures of public opinion and anxieties over crime and punishment with spiralling costs and political crises of accountability, we find conflicting trends and conflicting messages for sentencers.

Since 1990, the principal response to the problems facing the prisons has been to build more prisons. When the deeper problem of the best way to deal with offending and reoffending has been addressed, there has not been a great deal of consensus on the best way forward. A further sign of expansion is found in the new guidelines issued by the SGC relating to the sentencing discounts which are now in operation. While the maximum discount is still one-third for a guilty plea, if the prosecution's case is overwhelming without an admission from the defendant, then a 20 per cent reduction may be given (see Chapter 3, section 3.3.3), so this will have a potentially inflationary effect on sentence length.

The Government also seems to have accepted the need for super-prisons rather than the smaller community prisons which were recommended by Woolf and are advocated by prison reformers as offering the best hope of humane regimes and ones which reduce the risk of disorder (see the Carter Report 2003; the Government response in Home Office 2004b; and the Carter Review of Prisons 2007). Some of the most promising elements of the 2003 Criminal Justice Act which might have had a reductionist effect, namely custody plus and intermittent custody, have been shelved (see Chapter 3).

However, we can find some evidence of a continuing shift towards reductionism in recent policy developments, as the Government has struggled with the increasing costs of expansionist policies at a time of increased public spending on health and on military campaigns overseas, and recognition that the impact of imprisonment on crime reduction is limited. The Carter Review of Correctional Services (2003) estimated that an increased use of prison since 1997 had reduced crime by about 5 per cent and concluded that 'there is no convincing evidence that further increases in custody would significantly reduce crime' (Carter 2003: 15). The Review recommended a number of reforms which build on the sentencing framework in the Criminal Justice Act 2003 such as income-related fines for low-risk offenders, and more demanding community sentences for medium-risk offenders, with greater use of surveillance and electronic monitoring. However, at the same time, it noted that, if evidence showed that custody was effective in reducing crime, then resources should be provided to build more prisons. It argued that custody should be reserved for the most serious and dangerous and persistent offenders, but greater help should be given to persistent offenders.

Although spending on the work of both the Prison and Probation Service has increased since 1993, it is not clear that this has always been effectively targeted. Carter argued that implementing the measures proposed in the Review would reduce the numbers in custody by the end of the decade to below the projections available at that time. The Carter recommendations were endorsed by the Government (Home Office 2004b) who accepted that more emphasis should be given to reparation, that greater use of fines should be considered, and that persistent offenders should be given tougher but more flexible sentences. In its *Five Year Strategy for Protecting the Public and Reducing Re-offending* (Home Office 2005b) the Government announced an intention to introduce Day Fines, and as we have argued, this would also deal with some of the problems of unequal impact referred to in Chapter 7. The Government also introduced further constraints on sentences to limit sentencing severity to constrain further demand on prisons (see Chapter 2, sections 2.3 and 2.4). It recommended that the Sentencing Guidelines Council formulate guidelines which take account of the need to use prison places in the most cost-effective way. It was announced in December 2007 that the Government was considering setting up a Sentencing Commission which would link the sentencing framework specifically to prison resources. The Government also accepts that alternatives to custody should be considered and developed for particular groups of offenders, namely female offenders, mentally ill offenders and young offenders.

Other strategies to reduce demand for prison places have been deployed, including encouraging foreign-national prisoners to return home by offering financial incentives, and where they are awaiting deportation to speed up the process, particularly in the light of adverse publicity on this issue (see Chapter 1), and an Early Removal System to release foreign-national prisoners early for deportation. It is also transferring more remand prisoners into bail hostels and making greater use of electronic monitoring for remand prisoners, and improving resettlement to reduce reoffending, because remand prisoners constitute a considerable proportion of demand for prison places. In 2006–7, 36,501 prisoners had either an employment, education or training outcome when they were released from prison and 65,733 had accommodation arranged on release (HM Prison Service 2007a: 13). Current policy and practice on resettlement is reviewed by Hucklesby and Hagley-Dickinson (2007).

The policy document, *A Five-Year Strategy for Protecting the Public and Reducing Re-Offending* (Home Office 2005b), contains both expansionist and reductionist elements. It emphasises the primary duty is to protect the public and to reserve prison for the most dangerous offenders, keeping them in for longer and in some cases permanently, through the use of indeterminate sentences for public protection, to develop specialist units for particular types of offender, and to improve the consistency and monitoring of surveillance systems if and when they are released. However, it also stressed the need to provide a regime which prevents reoffending, through using named offender managers for every offender, and introducing 'going straight' contracts between offenders and offender managers. It also reasserts the importance of commissioning and contestability programmes in developing services to reduce reoffending. Interestingly, this document does refer to developing community prisons (at para 4.17), but subsequent developments suggest that this has been shelved along with custody plus and intermittent custody. So the progressive elements of the Government's strategy seem to have been swamped by the expansionist elements.

The Government also asked Lord Carter to conduct a review of prisons which was published in 2007 (Carter 2007). It considered ways of balancing the supply and demand for prison places, including changes in the sentencing framework, and assessed the pace, scale and value for money of the current prison building programme, and the efficiency of public sector prisons, and explored the potential for renewing the prison estate, including replacing expensive and poor quality establishments with new prisons and including the implications for other parts of the criminal justice estate. The Review also included a value-for-money review of two public sector prisons, Blakenhurst, which is now in the public sector, and Stafford.

The Report clearly envisaged a continuing expansion of the prison system. In addition to the extra places already planned, Carter proposed a further 6,500 places by 2012 to meet the expected demand for prison places based on current projections. He also proposed building three large-scale 'Titan' prisons to replace some older decrepit prisons, and recommended speeding up the existing building programme to match increased demand. The emphasis in the Report is on cost effectiveness, running prisons more efficiently and improving financial controls for public sector prisons. Carter also proposed a permanent Sentencing Commission to ensure predictability and consistency in sentencing. He also argued that a structured sentencing framework would make it easier to predict changes in the prison population. The framework would include sentence lengths, types of community sentence, levels of fines, seriousness ranking of offenders and offender characteristics with ranges set by the Sentencing Commission which the government would be unable to change.

Some elements of the Report have been welcomed by prison reformers. On the one hand, it does acknowledge the need to constrain expansion by greater use of community penalties and points to the need for an informed public debate to consider the issue of whether expansion is desirable. Carter acknowledges that temporary measures such as early release may undermine public confidence in the system and he recommends greater flexibility in the use of indeterminate and extended sentences for public protection, and favours reforming the Bail Act, to reduce the numbers remanded in custody. He also supports the findings of the Corston Report that different regimes are appropriate for women and young offenders and custody should be used as a last resort for female offenders (see Chapter 11). So there are a number of proposals in the Report which, if implemented, would have an effect on prison numbers.

But the Report's recommendation for large-scale prisons runs counter to the available research which suggests that smaller-scale units are more effective in providing humane regimes rather than simply 'warehousing'. Large-scale prisons may be more cost effective in the short term but raise problems of containing disorder and disruption which may be managed more easily on a smaller scale. The rationale of the larger prison is to concentrate facilities to achieve economies of scale and better value for money as medical and catering services, for example, could be centralised, so it is primarily cost-driven. Each prison would hold up to 2,500 places in units of 500 for adult male offenders; it is envisaged that juveniles and females could be held in smaller units within the perimeter. They would be built where demand is highest: in London, the North-West and the West Midlands. The Government announced in January 2008 that it was merging three prisons in the West Midlands—Blakenhurst, Brockhill and Hewell Grange—to form one large prison, to be named HMP Hewell and hold 1,428 prisoners.

Carter also recommends increasing the use of former military bases, and providing closed accommodation in some open prisons, buying and converting a vessel into a prison ship, refurbishing cells not already being used, and speeding up existing building projects as well as building further new prisons, all of which suggest acceptance of an expansionist strategy.

9.8 Conclusion

As we have seen there have been substantial improvements in procedural justice and conditions in prisons in the past decade, so there are no public sector prisons now at the lowest level. Although the numbers in prison have continued to rise, there have been some promising developments and considerable progress. The 'decency' agenda introduced in 1999, 'caring for and treating with respect everybody in the Service's care', which has implications for suicide, accommodation, assaults, equal treatment and participation in constructive activities, has focused attention on prisoners' right to be treated fairly and respectfully (HM Prison Service 2007b: 26). The expansion of human rights jurisprudence has had an effect on raising standards in prison and on recognising that prisoners remain citizens while incarcerated. Entrenched human rights provide a counterbalance to both populist punitiveness and the principle of less eligibility.

But the problems discussed in Chapter 1, of reconciling the public to prison improvements, given public punitiveness, have persisted and limited the scope for reductionist policies, and protecting the public and reducing the risk to the public has been reflected in the commitment to expanding prison capacity (see Roberts and Hough 2005). Progressive developments, as we have seen, have coexisted uneasily with the managerialist focus in prisons and the quest for cost effectiveness and the increasing focus on risk management (see Murphy and Whitty 2007). New developments and initiatives have come under threat with the pressure of providing for an ever-expanding population. There are also variations between prisons in terms of opportunities for work and training as well as accommodation. Maintaining constructive regimes during a period of expansion and pressures on accommodation and resources may be difficult. But it certainly seems likely that prison reform will remain on the political agenda.

9.8.1 Discussion questions

In this chapter we have examined life inside modern prisons and changes of regime. In revising this material you may wish to reflect on the following issues:

1. Have prisons improved since the early 1990s? If so, in what specific ways? What further improvements could be made?
2. Does the treatment of prisoners in the UK comply with the European Convention on Human Rights?
3. Why has the prison population expanded in the last 15 years? How significant are changes in sentencing law and policy in this expansion?
4. What effect has this expansion had on prison conditions?
5. What are the aims of imprisonment? What do you consider to be the best means of achieving these aims?

online resource centre

Some guidance on answering these questions is given in the Online Resource Centre.

10

....

Equality and difference in punishment

SUMMARY

This chapter examines in more detail the issues around the impact of punishment on various groups of offenders, depending on differential circumstances, both structural and personal. In particular we focus on the arguments against proposals that more account of should be taken of impact mitigation at the sentencing stage (which we discussed in Chapter 7) and suggest that some disadvantages must be dealt with by social, rather than penal, policy. We then engage in a detailed discussion of gender and race differentials in crime and punishment and analyse the meaning of equality within those contexts.

10.1 Differential treatment

10.1.1 Establishing the limits of personal mitigation

Mitigation, like aggravation, is usually, though not always, based on retributive reasoning, which concludes either that the offender's culpability was not as great as the nature of the offence suggested or that, while he was fully culpable he will suffer more than most offenders from the normal penalty.

(Walker 1999: 95)

In Chapter 7 we focused on mitigation in sentencing, and reviewed the justifications for taking into account the impact of a punishment on an offender. In particular, we examined the approach of the courts to illness, old age, employment, vulnerability in prison and separation from children as factors which might increase the 'pains' of punishment and so justify a reduction in sentence. We then used fines and the law and practice in relation to mentally disordered offenders as examples of quite different ways of taking sentencing impact into account. However, the debate as to whether personal circumstances should be taken into account in sentencing and in punishment is wider than the above. So in this chapter we focus on issues stemming from socio-economic factors, race and gender in order to analyse the appropriate division between social and penal policy and to examine the argument that equality of treatment in relation to gender and race may require differential treatment, particularly in the context of custodial punishment. In doing so, we will introduce arguments against taking punishment impact into account in sentencing.

10.1.2 **Impact of punishment on the offender's family**

Whatever the sex of the prisoners, imprisonment has a disruptive impact on the family. But the effect, particularly on children, is most acute when it is their mother, rather than their father, who is imprisoned.

(Prison Reform Trust 2000)

As noted in Chapter 9 (section 9.2.1) almost three out of five male, and two out of three female prisoners have dependent children but whilst the children of fathers in prison will usually be looked after by the other parent, this is much less likely for the children of mothers in prison.

Whereas the majority of the children of male prisoners are looked after in their home, this is the case for only 5 per cent of the children affected each year by the imprisonment of their mother. The large majority are looked after by friends or family; in most cases this involves leaving home. About 8 per cent are taken into local authority care. It is estimated that the living arrangements of at least 8,000 children are affected each year by the imprisonment of their mother.[1] This is significant, because a predictor of future offending is previous experience of being in care.

Once in prison, many prisoners lose contact with their families, because of imprisonment itself, or because they are held a long way from home. For women, the average distance from home in September 2005 was 58 miles, and for men 50 miles (Prison Reform Trust 2007a: 17), but these figures are averages and for many prisoners the distance may be over 100 miles.

The issue of prisoners' children has come to both public and academic attention in recent years (see Brooks-Gordon and Bainham 2004; Codd 2004, 2008; Salmon 2004: 18–20; for a review of wider legal issues, see also Munro 2002) and the sentencing courts do sometimes take into account the impact on 'innocent others', particularly children.[2] However, whilst retributivist reasoning justifies the punishment only of the offender, not significant others in the offender's life, this rationale causes problems as inevitably there will be some third-party collateral costs for prisoners with families.

But giving more weight to family impact would be problematic as it would infringe the principle of equal punishment if offenders with and without families were treated differently. It might also mean that sentencers would need to judge the parenting skills of an offender to decide whether dependent children would be harmed or benefited by their absence, thereby introducing extrinsic factors into the sentencing process. An alternative approach might therefore be to focus on reducing the impact on third parties by giving more support to maintaining family contact during the period of imprisonment.

We noted in Chapter 7 (section 7.2.5) that the message in *Mills* (2002) was that, where possible, the court should take into account the fact that the offender is a primary carer for a child. Generally, however, the appellate court has taken a

---

[1] http://www.womeninprison.org.uk/index.php?option=com_content&task=view&id=35&Itemid=44.

[2] There is another issue about impact which we cannot deal with here and that is whether prisoners and their partners should have access to artificial insemination facilities: see Jackson (2007). The European Court of Human Rights recently held in *Dickson v UK* (2007) that the refusal of a prisoner's request for AI facilities had breached Article 8.

quite stringent approach which is exemplified by a recent series of cases involving women who took Class A drugs into prison for the person they were visiting (see Piper 2007: 147–8). Jeanne Batte, Sarah Witten and Carmen Mackenzie[3] all had their sentences reduced but their family circumstances were horrendous. Batte, who was 60 and severely depressed, cared for a disabled brother of 69, had suffered the death of one child and cared for two others who were severely ill. Witten had three children aged six, five and three; Mackenzie had two dependants—one child and a husband with a life-threatening illness. However, relatively minor reductions were given so that the detriment to the children was only marginally reduced; the courts made clear these were exceptional cases, and in other cases, for example, that of Angela Babington,[4] no reduction was given.

Currently impact is taken more seriously in relation to the impact of offending on the families of victims, evident, as we saw in Chapter 6, in the piloting of oral family-impact statements to court (see Department for Constitutional Affairs 2006). The focus on the victim may also increase the level of seriousness of the offending which, as we noted in Chapter 7, means the court is less likely to take personal mitigation into account.

Neither the approach of the courts nor the rationales for taking into account impact on innocent others is satisfactory. The sentencing reductions cannot adequately be justified by reference to penal theory, they are applied in an unprincipled and therefore potentially discriminatory fashion, they do not significantly address the problem of children facing trauma and disruption. It might, however, be appropriate as an explicit public policy for the courts to take into account factors which do not directly concern impact on the offender. In other words, 'mercy' could also be routinely and consistently exercised as a policy decision imposed on the courts via legislation or guidance. Whether this would be politically acceptable is another matter.

10.1.3 Arguments against impact mitigation

Impact mitigation raises problems for both retributivism and utilitarianism. For the former, the harm caused to the victim is not lessened by the social origins or personal problems of the offender, even though we might feel compassion or sympathy for their circumstances. Reductions in such cases would seem to strike at the principles of proportionality, equality of treatment of offenders and the presumption of human agency at the heart of retributivist theory (see Easton 2008c). If the punishment varied according to the wider social circumstances and personal problems of the offender this would bring arbitrariness back into the punishment process. While retributivists recognise the existence and effects of social inequality, the answer to the problem of inequality is deemed to lie in social welfare rather than variations in sentencing. For Hegel (1832) the answer to problems of poverty and inequality was to use social welfare to mitigate the effects of the market, rather than to retreat from the key principles of retributivist punishment.

For modern retributivists such as von Hirsch (1993), the best way to deal with this issue is through social policy combined with a limit on overall sentencing levels

---

[3] *Batte* (1999); *Witten* (2002); and *McKenzie* (2004).
[4] *Babington* (2005). The court distinguished *Witten* because Babington's children were older, had all been in care and only one of her children was living with her at the time of sentence.

for all through the setting of appropriate anchoring points. In a recent discussion von Hirsch and Ashworth (2005) consider the use of compassionate mitigation in Sweden and whether it could be extended to social deprivation but conclude that it would raise both practical and political problems. As we have seen, a major barrier to changes in penal policy is public opinion. The only circumstances in which culpability would be reduced would be extreme necessity. The injustice of punishing someone who steals in extreme circumstances, such as the fictional Jean Valjean,[5] would be dealt with under the criminal law of necessity.

The problem, however, is that although poverty does exist in the UK, the levels of deprivation in the modern UK sentencing context are usually far removed from the levels of poverty and deprivation of the nineteenth century France described by Victor Hugo, so that the issue of necessity is less significant than relative deprivation (see Dorling *et al.* 2007). For those whose lives are adversely affected by their social circumstances the solution lies in social rather than penal policy.

For utilitarians, there would be concerns over reducing the deterrent value of penalties if sentences were reduced on the ground of deprivation. Bentham (1789) was opposed to introducing feelings into punishment, so concessions on grounds of sympathy and compassion for the accused would be difficult to justify on his theory. For Bentham, the principle of utility took precedence over principles of sympathy and antipathy which he sees as adverse to utility. Introducing feelings into punishment may lead to disproportionate punishment, both excessive and lenient.

10.2 Socio-economic factors

10.2.1 Justifications

As we saw in Chapter 3, one of the criticisms of retributivism from radical and Marxist viewpoints is that the theory allows little scope for a focus on the social disadvantage of offenders when imposing punishments, or for treating disadvantage as a mitigating factor. The rejoinder from retributivists would be that if social disadvantages are 'factored in' to sentencing decisions, these are most likely to work against offenders. If the criteria for assessment of possible completion of community punishment, or of risks of reoffending, include factors such as homelessness and unemployment, for example, the poor and unemployed will be seen as higher risks.[6] Both these points of view need further discussion.

As noted in Chapter 7 (section 7.1.2), Bentham reviews numerous 'sensibilities' but he discusses his 32 points in the context of factors affecting the experience of pain and pleasure generally, and not specifically in relation to punishment, so it may be that some, for example climate, might not be relevant to punishment (Bentham 1789: 52). Further, even Bentham admitted that it would be impracticable to put fully into operation the aim of producing the same amount of 'pain'

---

[5] A character in *Les Misérables*, a novel by Victor Hugo.
[6] There is some suggestion that this is happening in youth justice: see Chapter 13, section 13.2.1 regarding risk assessments.

in a sentence for offences of equal culpability. To do so would require detailed assessments of the likelihood of greater physical, emotional, mental, economic and social hardship and the very fluidity of the principle has been seen as a compelling reason not to attempt its general application. However, it has also been argued that, even if it is impracticable to take the principle of equal impact to its very detailed logical conclusions, it should still be influential in more *extreme* cases of possible social and economic inequality.

The utilitarian and retributivist justifications for doing so are very different. The statement by H. L. A. Hart that for 'those below a minimum level of economic prosperity... [perhaps] we should incorporate as a further excusing condition the pressure of gross forms of economic necessity' (1968: 51) is founded on a notion that the offender is fully culpable but that non-legal factors could 'excuse' or mitigate responsibility. For the retributivist, then, it may in some cases be unfair to apportion a sentence commensurate to harm and culpability without taking account of the fact that similar offenders may not have equal responsibility because of 'life' factors, but this would apply only in extreme cases of economic necessity, or because of extreme immaturity in the case of juveniles.

For the utilitarian, the issue, as noted in relation to personal mitigation in Chapter 7, is whether the sentence will be effective, and so information about the offender and his or her circumstances is needed in order to choose the sentence most likely to deter or rehabilitate.

Hudson (1998), for example, defends reduced penalties for socially deprived offenders. She recognises the value of the proportionality principle but argues that social circumstances can be considered in assessing desert. For Hudson, social and penal policy cannot be sharply distinguished and punishment has the potential to achieve justice. Individual social and economic circumstances may reduce culpability if the effect is to limit choices, and where the individual is so 'constrained by poverty or other disadvantage or situation that the "reasonable person" would have been unable to refrain from crime in similar circumstances' (ibid: 207–8). An individual's social circumstances are worthy of consideration for the purposes of a pre-sentence report, so there would be no reason to exclude them when assessing culpability.

'Selective leniency' runs the risk, as Hudson acknowledges, that the outcome will depend on how favourably or unfavourably the defendant presents himself as a specially deserving case. 'Categorical leniency' might be preferable: particular crimes which are statistically correlated with unemployment and poverty could be downgraded in terms of seriousness. However, this would not take account of differences in individual freedom of choice which should remain an important factor (ibid: 207).

The issue is again that of 'justice in an unjust society' which runs through several discussions in this book. For example, Duff, having outlined an ideal model of 'constructive punishment' in the community, acknowledges that 'the preconditions of just punishment are not met within our political societies, and are not likely to be met within the near future' (Duff 2003: 192). The issue is not the 'substantive wrongfulness' of the offender's conduct—which is accepted—but whether, given the social and economic differentials to which we have alluded, we have the 'moral standing to call them to answer... for that conduct: if we have collectively failed to treat them as our fellow citizens' (ibid).

Some of these issues are approached in an original way by Renaud (2007), a Canadian judge, who explores the principles through a fictional sentencing conference involving the major characters of *Les Misérables,* Valjean, Fantine, Javert and the Bishop. The problems of their lives are discussed in the context of modern principles of sentencing, policing and punishment and some of the difficulties raised in accommodating these issues within those theories are explored.

There are further critiques of sentencing theory on this issue which are external to classical or 'conventional' punishment theory (see von Hirsch and Ashworth 1998: 361–8). Norrie, for example, argues that Kant and Hegel (see Chapter 2 above) were (just) able to hold together retributivist theory in the light of emerging issues of social injustice but, by the nineteenth century, 'the effects of poverty and pauperism, of idleness and drunkenness, of exploitation and vice upon the criminality of the body politic could not be ignored or represented as a matter of pure individual choice' (1998: 371). He also argues that 'the radical disjuncture between the ideal and the actual is no passing feature'; rather it is 'a constant and fixed quality which necessarily undermines a principled justification of punishment in an unprincipled society' (ibid: 379). For Norrie, therefore, punishment cannot be based on individual desert, and mitigation cannot adequately encompass social and political differentials.

In section 10.4 below we focus on the experience of ethnic groups in relation to compensating for disadvantage because research suggests that ethnic minorities make up a disproportionate number of prisoners, and this in part reflects problems with housing and employment.

This again raises the question whether these factors should have been incorporated at the mitigation stage of sentencing. However, if a black unemployed offender, for example, were compensated for disadvantage by a reduction in sentence, this might appear unfair to those black offenders who are in work, as it seems to conflict with the principle of treating like cases alike. The just response might, instead, take the form of focusing on rehabilitation to deal with drug problems, or on using educational programmes to promote social inclusion.

Strict proportionality would demand punishing only those actions which are genuinely chosen by the actor, so proponents of impact mitigation would argue that taking account of adversity would be compatible with it. The approach might consider how the effects of factors such as unemployment and poor housing may be prevented from affecting outcomes, rather than how to reduce sentences for disadvantaged offenders (von Hirsch and Roberts 1997). Specifically in relation to racial or class issues, how can policies and biases be prevented from exacerbating the situation?

10.2.2 Social exclusion as a criterion

Using neutral criteria like social exclusion might be fairer because it would cover a wider range of offenders. Imprisonment can be seen as both a form of social exclusion and a reflection of it, if crime can be linked to social exclusion, but imprisonment may also exacerbate and perpetuate social exclusion. Although there are debates on the nature, and causes and effects, of social exclusion, the boundary between exclusion and inclusion is not fixed but fluid, and may be crossed several times. Moreover, inclusion may entail the recognition of mutual diversity (Young

1999, 2002). For example, research on the effectiveness of offending behaviour pro-grammes should consider how useful these are to particular groups and whether men and women, and different ethnic groups, would benefit from particular pro-grammes, or how they might be designed within and outside custody to accommo-date the needs of these groups. For example, if policies were subjected to ethnicity testing, we would need to take account of ethnic differences in prison and try to ameliorate disadvantages suffered by ethnic groups, and if we focus on social exclusion, we also need to focus on class.

The traditional social work ethos of the Probation Service, for example, has tended to individualise problems, focusing on the problems of clients as individual pathologies, rather than examining structural problems and the socio-economic context which may affect offending patterns, or the effects of racism (see Chapter 12, section 12.3). If the liberal ethos of social work is to treat people equally, then this might be construed as meaning no special treatment for black offenders. But if life experiences are different, punishment should take special account of this, as well as recognising the different contexts of male and female offending.

It is also important to keep in mind that the most striking feature of the prison population is its class membership. A focus on social exclusion may obscure the importance of class. Similarly the focus on cognitive behaviouralism, on individ-ual responsibility for managing individual risks, diverts attention from the signifi-cance of class and structural causes of crime and the social reaction to crime. The term social exclusion has superseded the use of the term 'underclass' which is now seen as pejorative (see Byrne 2005).

However, while social exclusion is primarily associated with class, it may also be experienced by some ethnic groups in inner-city areas and by women, in so far as women as a group are poverty-prone, and poverty in wealthy societies is now defined in terms of social exclusion (see Pantazis *et al.* 2006). Within the prison population we find ethnic-minority prisoners are over-represented relative to their proportions in the general population, which raises questions regarding the role of racism within the criminal justice system (see section 10.4 below).

In most discussions of social deprivation the focus is on poverty and class, but there are other areas of inequality we should consider which have implications for sentencing policy and treatment within prison (see Chapter 11), namely gender inequality and race inequality. We will therefore focus further on the experiences of women and ethnic minorities to explore some of these problems and conclude with a discussion of the problem of disability which may also contribute to social exclusion (see O'Grady *et al.* 2004).

10.3 Gender

10.3.1 Gender and justice

At first glance the most striking feature of the statistics for both crime and impris-onment is that women are under-represented. This has been seen by some as sug-gesting that women are treated more leniently than men. But it is not clear-cut. Within the prison population we find an over-representation of working-class women and a disproportionate number of ethnic-minority women, particularly foreign nationals.[7] So this suggests that a number of complex forces are operating which shape the structure of the prison population.

Research over the last ten years does not show women *generally* are treated more harshly. The Wedderburn Report found little evidence to show that women were treated more severely than men. In fact, a lower proportion of women than men were sentenced to immediate custody for indictable offences and the average sentence length was shorter (Prison Reform Trust 2000). In 2001, 41 per cent of women eligible for a home detention curfew were released under curfew compared to 24 per cent of eligible men (Councell and Olagundoye 2003). Women are more likely to be discharged or given a community sentence than men and less likely to be sentenced to custody (Home Office 2002h). Women serve shorter sentences than men, if we control for the type of offence and criminal history, but *some* women receive heavier sentences. There are also higher rates of remand for women than men where the outcome is a non-custodial sentence.

On the other hand, women are imprisoned for less serious offences than men and are also more likely to go to prison with fewer previous convictions than men. Approximately one-third of women in prison have no previous convictions compared to 15 per cent of men.

Women may be disadvantaged at the disposal stage because the options may be limited by restricted availability as well as by judgements about women's behaviour. Fewer hostels are available for women compared to men. Non-custodial alternatives may be seen as unsuitable for women with children, and sentencers may be reluctant to place women with dependent children on community punishment programmes if they think that it will be difficult for them to complete the programme. Some of the residential drug treatment programmes, for example, will not accept women with dependent children (Howard League for Penal Reform 2000).

Whilst some women will end up with a less severe sentence than men, others will end up with a harsher sentence than men, and individual women, particularly those who do not conform to gender roles, may be treated more harshly. For example, it has been argued that women perceived as bad mothers, or who already have children in care, are more likely to be given a custodial sentence, as are younger women who are perceived to be out of control (see Worrall 1990).

The question whether sentencers are more or less indulgent to women offenders was extensively researched throughout the 1980s and 1990s. Heddermann and Gelsthorpe (1997) found that magistrates saw women as troubled rather than troublesome, more in need of help than punishment, and saw probation as appropriate for a large proportion of female offenders. They were also reluctant to fine women if it would affect children adversely.

---

[7] Information on both groups is available from Ministry of Justice statistics, Offender Management Caseload Statistics and from the publications under s 95 of the Criminal Justice Act 1991, namely *Women and the Criminal Justice System* and *Race and the Criminal Justice System*; see Allwood (2008); Jones and Singer (2007).

10.3.2 **Differential treatment**

There is evidence of differential treatment and differential impact at a number of levels of the criminal justice system, in relation to women and ethnic minorities as offenders and as victims. It occurs at all stages of the criminal justice and penal processes: in policing, during the pre-trial process, at trial in the perceptions of juries and court officials, in the treatment of certain suspects and victims (for example, rape complainants) and post-sentence (see Hood 1992; Bowling and Phillips 2000; Carlen 2002) A key principle of punishment is to treat like cases alike. So when we talk of discrimination, or bias, we are talking about differential treatment based not on the specific circumstances of the crime, but on arbitrary characteristics of the defendant, such as the fact that the individual is female, black or working class. This bias can operate in an overt, direct way or unconsciously, and may operate indirectly or be institutionalised within the system, in its procedures and practices and within formal rules of law, for example, in the law of provocation, which has proved difficult to apply to women who kill abusive partners.

Section 95 of the Criminal Justice Act (CJA) 1991 requires the Home Secretary to publish information considered expedient to enable those involved in the administration of criminal justice to avoid discriminating against any person on the ground of race, sex, or any other improper ground. On the basis of this information and a number of empirical studies, we can construct a picture of the population to establish whether all offenders are treated equally or whether some groups are treated differently, although evidence of difference may not itself indicate unjust or unfair treatment. Differential treatment may arise from indirect discrimination if an apparently neutral rule impacts unfairly on a particular group. There are statutory duties under the Equality Act 2006 on public authorities to promote equality and to work towards the elimination of unlawful discrimination.

Here we focus specifically on issues of equality versus difference in relation to gender. Although the prison population is overwhelmingly male, the number and proportion of women prisoners is increasing and the treatment of women prisoners is therefore becoming more important (see section 11.2.2). We will therefore consider whether women prisoners should be treated equally, or whether and how difference should be acknowledged within the prison system. The particular problems women prisoners face at the point of imprisonment will be considered in Chapter 11.

10.3.3 **Equality versus difference**

Gender-specific policies raise the question of reconciling differential treatment with principles of equality, as well as the risk of ascribing inherent characteristics to women, that is, the problem of essentialism. The Committee on Women's Imprisonment, chaired by Dorothy Wedderburn, which visited 14 prisons, emphasised that applying principles of punishment in an equitable and non-discriminatory way does not entail equal treatment, but rather treatment as an equal (Prison Reform Trust 2000). It should take account of the fact that women are less dangerous than men, that the social costs of women's imprisonment are higher than men's and that different treatment for men and women within the penal system is justifiable: '[e]qual treatment...does not mean identical treatment, whether for women or for members of cultural or ethnic minorities' (Prison Reform Trust 2000: para 7.2). A similar approach is taken by the Corston Report (2007) and the Government has now moved some way towards recognising the need for gender-specific policies (see Chapter 11, section 11.5.4).

If we say that women should not be incarcerated because they are not dangerous, then one could argue that this should apply to non-dangerous men. Critics might claim that a regime which is accommodating to women, which gives women differential treatment, such as extra home leave to deal with their families, would be unfair to men who may also wish to enjoy such advantages, and would be met by similar demands from men. But this argument would not defeat a claim for differential treatment as it could feasibly be extended to men and is unlikely to open the floodgates as relatively few men are primary carers. Humanising the women's prison regime may also benefit male prisoners as good practice there may provide a model for men's prisons.

However, when reforms have been introduced in other jurisdictions, they have often been challenged by men arguing denial of their right to equality. In Canada, a male prisoner argued that his rights under the equality clause (Article 15) of the Charter had been breached, because he could be searched by female as well as male officers, but women could be searched only by women officers. His claim was rejected by the Supreme Court which argued that, within wider historical, biological and sociological contexts, the use of male officers in women's searches is potentially more threatening, so treating men and women differently in this context was not discriminatory.[8]

This issue of unfairness also arose in the South African Constitutional Court in *Hugo v President of the RSA* (1997) where, again, the Court rejected a claim of unfairness by a male prisoner. A female prisoner who had young children was released under an amnesty given by President Mandela but the amnesty was not extended to male prisoners. The majority of the court held that it was not unfair discrimination because young mothers were a vulnerable group and, even if it were seen as unfair, it could be justified because of the needs of young children.

The principle of equality is often cited as the reason for not improving the women's regime, as it would be unfair to treat men and women unequally. This rationalisation is also advantageous to the suppliers of punishment as many of the measures, such as more home leave, have cost implications.

A more controversial issue is whether a case can be made for differential sentencing of women, and particularly for using women's social and economic deprivation as grounds for mitigation of sentence (see Hudson 1998 and section 10.2 above). Support for the view that woman's role as the primary carer is a factor which should be taken into account in sentencing, along with factors such as mental illness, abuse, economic position, and the effect of a custodial sentence on others in the household, is also given by the Wedderburn Report (Prison Reform Trust 2000). If women suffer disproportionately greater poverty, or abuse, or if they develop drug or alcohol addictions as a result of this abuse and exclusion, should this be reflected in the sentencing process? Such a policy is unlikely to be accepted or to be popular for the reasons we have already discussed, but Pre-Sentence Reports

[8] *Weatherall v Canada* (1993).

and Sentence Planning could recognise these problems and consider how to deal with them, for example, by setting up special programmes to deal with the effects of violence, as used in Canadian women's prisons.

Moreover, the criminal justice system still accepts that a special programme is needed to deal with young offenders (see Chapter 8) so a special programme for women's justice, which recognises that there are also special factors leading to women's crime, could be introduced. However, this might militate against treating women as independent agents, rather than perpetuating ideas about the dependence and vulnerability of woman. Perhaps if such arguments were extended to male prisoners in similar circumstances, such as male carers, they would be more acceptable. So a man with dependent children should also be given consideration for additional home leave. Fair treatment would also demand a consideration of the effects of reducing a prisoner's status on the Incentives and Earned Privileges Scheme, for example, as this will affect entitlement to extra visits (see Chapter 9, section 9.4.4).

10.3.4 The merits and problems of a difference-based approach: empowerment in the context of coercion

Attempts were made in Canada in the 1990s to move away from a liberal feminist position of equality of provision for female offenders, which in practice usually used male standards, towards recognition of women's differences from men and the empowerment of women. A Task Force on Federally-Sentenced Women, which included feminist participants and which reported in 1990, generated the creation of five new regional facilities for women, including a Healing Lodge, replacing the former single federal penitentiary, the Prison for Women. The new regime included extended home visits, and culturally sensitive and feminist therapeutic programmes to deal with domestic violence and drugs. The effect of these changes was an overall improvement in the quality of life for women prisoners.

However, the feminist approach based on difference and applied in Canada, has been criticised on a number of grounds. The Canadian experience illustrates some of the problems with a 'difference-based' approach and highlights the problem facing feminist prison reformers, namely the conflict between feminist principles of empowerment and responsibility, on the one hand, and the reality of living in a coercive community like a prison, on the other hand, so that reforms will be neutralised. Hannah-Moffat (2002) argues that the ideas embodied in the Task Force programme in Canada have been eroded through lack of resources, and denial of basic rights. Despite the initial enthusiasm, the reforms were diluted with a move toward increased security and privatisation. Within a coercive context, the development of autonomy will inevitably be limited.

Similarly, Carlen (2002) argues that focusing on women's imprisonment, while of value and interest, can divert us from the impact of the power of the prison to punish, its retributivist function, which, she argues, has been overlooked by radical theories, including left criminology, and postmodern and feminist theories.

It is also questionable how progressive the Canadian reforms were as there is still a tendency to construe women's imprisonment as a consequence of their victimisation, treating women as passive victims, even if we call them survivors. Focusing on therapeutic programmes for individual prisoners essentially characterises the individual as an object of reform and sees the problem as the individual's mal-adjustment to society, rather than looking at the wider social structure. There is also a tendency in these Canadian programmes to focus on women as wives and mothers, which is reminiscent of the traditional view of women prisoners held by nineteenth-century reformers.

Focusing on reform *per se* also means that less attention will be given to alternatives to prison, particularly for those serving shorter sentences, and the use of imprisonment will go unchallenged. Bringing feminism into a system of correction can have the unintended effect of legitimising incarceration and, for this reason, some feminist groups in Canada have now distanced themselves from these projects (see Hannah-Moffat 2002). But this raises difficult issues as feminist-inspired programmes have led to better conditions and improved women's lives, and feminist therapeutic programmes have assisted women on their release. There are examples of gender-sensitive regimes in the USA which have been successful in reducing reoffending and, to some extent, in empowering women (see de Cou 2002; Poteat 2002). Similarly in the UK, while progressive measures are still part of a system of state incarceration and while their radical impact may be neutralised in a regressive political context, the alternative of doing nothing may be more damaging to those receiving punishment. Moreover the opportunity to participate within a therapeutic community may be empowering for women even if circumscribed by the prison context (see Parker 2006). In the light of these problems, we will consider in Chapter 11 the experience of women prisoners in England and Wales and ways in which women's imprisonment might be reformed and reduced.

10.4 A focus on race

10.4.1 Ethnic minorities and the criminal justice system

In the first part of this book, we considered the quest for justice in the context of theories of punishment and the notions of fairness in relation to proportionality, but fairness is also important in relation to the distribution of punishment. If there are racially disproportionate outcomes, then this may indicate *prima a facie* unjust treatment or discrimination and this needs to be investigated and strategies developed to deal with this.

Statistical data on the criminal justice system suggests there are differentials in the experience of ethnic minorities at all stages of the criminal justice process, in rates of stop and search, arrest, remands in custody before trial, and, importantly for our purposes, in rates of imprisonment.[9] The *British Crime Survey* research (Kershaw *et al.* 2000), and other studies, shows that ethnic minorities are also at a greater risk of victimisation than white people for violent and property offences, and are more likely to be victims of racially motivated offences. In 2005/6 there were 139,000 reported racially motivated incidents (see Jones and Singer 2007).

Statistics would suggest that, in the criminal process, from a police stop to prosecution and bail decisions, members of ethnic minorities are likely to be

---

[9] Statistics are published annually on *Race and the Criminal Justice System* under s 95 of the CJA 1991; see Jones and Singer (2007).

over-represented as suspects and defendants. Although there are wide regional variations, black people are more likely to be stopped and searched than white people and young black people are the most likely to be stopped and searched for drugs (Home Office 2002c). The study by Phillips and Brown (1998) also found that the numbers of African Caribbean people arrested is higher than would be expected. Further, black and South Asian people are over-represented in arrests for drugs, fraud, and forgery, and black people are over-represented in arrests for robbery.

The latest available statistics on *Race and the Criminal Justice System* published in October 2007, under s 95 of the 1991 Criminal Justice Act (Jones and Singer 2007) show that:

> [m]embers of our Black communities are seven times more likely than their White counter-parts to be stopped and searched, three and a half times more likely to be arrested, and six times more likely to be in prison.
>
> (ibid: ix)

This shows an increase since 1999/2000 when the number of black people arrested was four times higher than white people relative to their numbers in the general population. Arrest rates also vary between different areas and for different offences. Some differences may be due to objective factors, such as differences in offending patterns and social and economic factors which increase the risk of offending, for example, the relative youthfulness of ethnic minority populations and their concentration in inner-city areas. But there are also some indications that the police may be more willing to proceed against young black suspects on weaker evidence.

The suggestion that the police target ethnic minority populations has been supported by the fact that black and Asian defendants are more likely to have their case terminated by the Crown Prosecution Service (Barclay and Mhlanga 2000). This study also found higher acquittal rates for black and Asian defendants for some offences, in the magistrates' courts (ibid). This might be construed as suggesting a greater willingness to proceed initially with a weak case against ethnic minority defendants.

There are also differentials in cautioning with higher cautioning rates for white and Asian suspects than black suspects, which may reflect in part the fact that the latter are less likely to admit the offence (Home Office 2002c). Black suspects are less likely to be cautioned by the police, and research suggests they are more likely to be remanded in custody than to be given bail (Home Office 2002c).

Bail decisions are significant because defendants who are remanded in custody are statistically less likely to receive a non-custodial sentence at trial. This may be because being on bail makes it easier to keep a job and maintain a smart appearance for trial and also gives freer access to one's solicitor and case preparation. Phillips and Brown (1998) also found significant disparities in the refusal of police bail between different ethnic groups, when controlling for type of offence and previous convictions: 26 per cent of white suspects in their study were refused bail, compared to 34 per cent of black and 35 per cent of Asian suspects. Furthermore, there is evidence that bail decisions are affected by criteria such as homelessness and unemployment, and that these socio-economic factors disproportionately affect black defendants. Hood's (1992) study of Birmingham Crown Court found that African-Caribbean defendants were more likely to be remanded in custody and less likely to be given bail than white defendants because of the impact of these apparently neutral criteria. Figures from the Crown Court for 2005 also show that a greater proportion of white than black or Asian defendants were found guilty, but custodial sentences were given to a greater proportion of black than white or Asian defendants (Jones and Singer 2007).

Although the *British Crime Survey* (Kershaw *et al.* 2000) found that members of ethnic minorities were more likely than the rest of the population to think the criminal justice system was working well, in view of these statistics, it is perhaps not surprising that members of ethnic-minority groups express less confidence that they will be treated fairly as defendants by the criminal justice system (Mirrlees-Black 2001).

This sense of unfairness is exacerbated by the fact that within various parts of the criminal justice system ethnic minorities are over-represented as clients and under-represented as employees, relative to their numbers in the wider population. This disparity has implications for the legitimacy of the system as well as its efficiency and quality and there are targets for ethnic-minority recruitment for the Police Force, Probation Service and Prison Service (see Chapter 11, section 11.8.2).

It is in the composition of the prison population in England and Wales that the disproportionate presence of ethnic minorities is most striking. In June 2006, ethnic-minority prisoners accounted for 26 per cent of the male prison population and 28 per cent of the female prison population of England and Wales. There is also some evidence that black prisoners are more likely to be serving longer sentences than white or Asian prisoners (Jones and Singer 2007).

Some of the disparity in sentence length could be accounted for by differences in offences and, among women, a high number of foreign nationals are imprisoned for drug offences, but the differences are not so marked within the indigenous population. In trying to explain this differential, particularly as to whether social and economic disadvantage is a significant influence, we need to consider the earlier stages of the criminal justice process. The over-representation of ethnic minorities in prison can reflect the accumulation of past decisions which draw black suspects into the criminal justice process. We need to consider the reporting of crimes, the response of the police, and the making of bail decisions by the courts and, since the 1980s, criminological studies have been completed on a wide range of areas, although there are still some areas which need further investigation, including deaths in custody and the treatment of ethnic minorities within the Probation Service. Further, while successive governments have been slow to recognise discrimination in the criminal justice process, the provision in s 95 of the 1991 Criminal Justice Act which mandated the monitoring and publication of information about race has provided more information. All agencies in the criminal justice system have a duty to promote race equality under the Race Relations (Amendment) Act 2000 and also to monitor progress towards that goal.

Official crime statistics are generally seen as giving an incomplete indication of true levels of crime, but using self-report and victim studies we can construct a picture of the experiences of ethnic groups within the criminal justice system. However, official statistics can give an indication of patterns of decision making which may be significant in explaining differentials. A variety of other sources, including the *British Crime Survey*, police and Home Office statistics, and research studies, can give us a picture of the ethnic minority composition and treatment of the population of suspects, offenders and victims. We also need to bear in mind that the ethnic-minority population is not homogeneous. There are different rates of incarceration, distinct subcultures, including those which are age-based, white ethnic minority groups, and a substantial number of foreign-national prisoners, from a range of ethnic groups (see Chapter 11, section 11.7.6).

In Chapter 11 we will consider the experience of imprisonment and the way criminal justice agencies have sought to deal with racism. Reference to ethnicity/ ethnicities in the following discussion is used to mean the shared history, cultural heritage, and common experiences of distinct groups. Our sense of who we are will be shaped by this awareness of difference and diversity.

10.4.2 **Racism as ideology and practice**

Racism has been seen as an ideology and set of exclusionary practices based on assumptions about racial hierarchies. Racism attributes fixed characteristics to social groups which are then used to justify denial of access to resources. Racism may be conscious, or subconscious, operate at individual, sub-cultural, or institutional levels, and lead to direct and indirect discrimination. The available research suggests that racism may be found, for example, in employment strategies and the police treatment of black suspects and black offenders.

Racism may operate at the level of individual bias and prejudice or institutionally, being built into the culture of an organisation and embedded in its policies and practices (Macpherson 1999). The Macpherson Report highlighted the problem of institutional racism within the criminal justice system and its failure to protect ethnic minorities. By institutional racism Macpherson meant:

the collective failure of an organization to provide an appropriate and professional service to people because of their colour, culture, or ethnic origin. It can be seen or detected in processes, attitudes and behaviour which amount to discrimination through unwitting prejudice, ignorance, thoughtlessness and racist stereotyping which disadvantage minority ethnic people.

(Macpherson 1999: para 0.34)

Since that Report the Government has taken more interest in institutional racism and there has been some progress. Racial harassment is now a criminal offence and procedures dealing with racist incidents improved. The problems of racism within the Prison Service have also been addressed by the Prison Inspectorate (HM Inspectorate of Prisons 2005a) and the Mubarek Report (Keith 2006; see also Chapter 11, section 11.7.5 below).

10.4.3 **Research difficulties**

There are methodological problems in proving the influence of racism, in controlling for other variables, and isolating the socio-economic factors which might be the mechanisms for the production of differentials. Although there is a widely held perception in ethnic-minority communities of unfair treatment as suspects and offenders, the evidence of differential treatment is ambiguous. Ethnic-minority offenders are more likely, for example, to be released on parole and on home detention curfews than white offenders (Home Office 2001f) but they are also less likely to be fined and discharged and more likely to be given a community sentence (Home Office 2002c) which places them higher up the tariff.

However, many of the research studies have been fairly small-scale, so the numbers involved may be too small to draw firm conclusions. Although studies of particular courts during a limited time span have been conducted, there is no systematic monitoring of sentencing outcomes for different ethnic groups so there is a lack of clear data on this issue. While *some* judges and decisions in *some* courts may reflect racist assumptions, it is difficult to draw general conclusions or to infer racist bias on the part of sentencers who are constrained by a number of factors in the decisions they can make (see Chapter 2 on discretion). It may be difficult to extricate the impact of specific factors.

For example, there is some evidence that ethnic-minority defendants value jury trial because they believe it is less biased than a summary trial and any bias on the part of individual jury members will be offset by other jurors. A decision to elect for jury trial will mean that if convicted they face a more severe sentence and, if they plead 'not guilty' but are then convicted, they will not receive a sentence discount and so face a longer sentence. So this might be construed as a form of indirect discrimination, although offence profiles may account to some extent for these differentials (see Hood 1992).

There is, nevertheless, some evidence to suggest that black people are more likely to receive a custodial sentence even when we control for previous record, offence, and PSR recommendations. A study of Birmingham Crown Court found that African-Caribbeans were more likely to receive a custodial sentence for offences in the middle range of seriousness (Hood 1992). Hood found that about 80 per cent of the over-representation of black men in the prison population could be accounted for by their over-representation among those convicted in the Crown Court, by the types of crime and offences with which they are charged and convicted and by higher numbers presenting for sentencing. However, this meant that 20 per cent of the over-representation was due to differential treatment and other factors, such as not-guilty pleas. Hood's study has been criticised because it fails to address the issue of why so many black defendants elect trial by jury and for assuming that factors such as previous convictions are racially neutral (see Bowling and Phillips 2002).

A more recent study of ethnic-minority defendants in the Crown Court by Shute, Hood and Seemungal (2005) found that there had been improvements in attitudes towards these defendants so there was no evidence of overt racism. However, there was still a *perception* of unfairness on the part of many ethnic-minority defendants and their lawyers.

10.4.4 Racism and social deprivation

So what can we infer from the evidence available? Factors to consider in understanding the complex relationship between race and crime include the socio-economic characteristics of ethnic-minority communities, namely deprivation and unemployment, which affect black people disproportionately. There are also demographic issues. The majority of ethnic-minority communities are located in urban areas where there are higher-than-average levels of poverty, homelessness, crime and unemployment and this will also contribute to their higher victimisation rates. Because some ethnic-minority populations are younger than the ageing white population, this will affect the crime rate. There is also a geographical concentration in the more criminogenic urban areas, ethnic minorities have higher rates of homelessness, and many young black males under-achieve in education. There may also be sub-cultural differences within ethnic minorities in terms of how they deal with deprivation and racism. Ethnic groups are not homogeneous, but comprise diversities in culture, sources of identity and demographic structures whose experiences may differ substantially.

Over-representation has not only been attributed to racism at the level of individual decisions and differential treatment, but also to policies and practices which increase the speed with which black defendants move through the criminal justice system and move up the tariff. Racism may be a feature of individuals' beliefs as well as built into the policies of institutions. Some of the differentials may be due to factors such as offending patterns, while others reflect social and economic factors which increase the risk of offending.

If the profile of the prison population is strongly linked with social exclusion and social and economic deprivation, and if these problems are suffered by black communities and young black males are excluded from legitimate sources of status, then it may be unsurprising to find disproportionate numbers of black males in prison. Criminal activity may be an illegitimate means of social inclusion in providing the means to participate in a particular lifestyle. Criminality is strongly associated with social exclusion in so far as it links with poor social conditions. The experience of imprisonment may itself be seen as a further form of social exclusion, which reinforces housing and work problems on release.

So the marginalisation of ethnic minority communities needs to be addressed. However, others are sceptical of economic determinist and structural explanations, not least because many members of these groups may experience these problems without resorting to crime. In the current climate of increased punitiveness, these social disadvantages will be seen as less important than individual decisions to commit crimes, and it is unlikely that these disadvantages will be given serious consideration at the sentencing stage.

10.5 Disability

We have focused above on race and gender but, of course, these are not the only grounds of discrimination.[10] In recent years the Prison Service has become more aware of its obligations not to discriminate against staff or prisoners on grounds of sexual orientation and has set up a network for lesbian, gay, bisexual and transgender staff members. But the issue of disability is also important. The prison population may include a wide range of disabilities and illnesses. The ageing of the prison population will also increase the numbers of disabled prisoners (see Chapter 9, section 9.2.1).

---

[10] A single Commission for Equality and Human Rights has now been established by the Equality Act 2006 (Department of Trade and Industry 2004) to replace the Commission for Racial Equality, the Equal Opportunities Commission and the Disability Rights Commission.

Prisons must comply with the Disability Discrimination Act (DDA) 1995 which prohibits discrimination in the provision of goods, facilities and services on the basis of disability. So prisons, like other institutions, have to consider what reasonable adjustments and accommodation should be made to meet the needs of disabled prisoners as well as disabled staff, whose treatment is included in the equal opportunities regime. The DDA is premised on the assumption that equality equals differential treatment just as racial or sexual equality strategy may also use differential treatment to achieve equality.

New prisons have been built to comply with the DDA and refurbishments of older prisons have been undertaken to ensure compliance. Particularly, they need to make sure that prisoners are able to understand the Prison Rules and to provide an interpreter if necessary. Prisoners' needs should be taken account of in allocating cells and in ensuring access to work, education and physical education. Appropriate books should be provided in the prison library. Complaints can be made through the Complaints Procedure or to the Ombudsman, or civil proceedings could be initiated.

Prisoners could also use Article 14, if issues are raised within the ambit of other Articles of the European Convention. For example, Article 8 might be breached if disabled prisoners were allowed fewer family visits than other prisoners. Prisons have Disability Liaison Officers and the Prison Service has published guidelines for dealing with disabled prisoners. It has also formulated a Disability Strategy and set up a Disability Support Network for staff.

The PRT found that provision and support was variable and examples of good practice in some prisons were reported (Prison Reform Trust 2004b). As well as problems of access to facilities, because of the failure to incorporate disabled needs into prison design, there are problems of access to services, for example, for prisoners with visual and hearing impairments.

A new programme, *No One Knows*, to examine and publicise the experiences of people with learning difficulties and learning disabilities who come into contact with the criminal justice system has been initiated by the Prison Reform Trust, in view of the increasing numbers of disabled prisoners and in response to complaints of unequal access to activities and poor treatment, including examples of prisoners confined to their cells for long periods because of inadequate facilities for their needs (Loucks 2007). It is estimated that there are about 5,000 people with learning disabilities within the prison population (see Rack 2005). However, this group of prisoners has been under-researched and we have very little information on female or ethnic-minority offenders within this group.

Moreover, if their needs are not identified as they enter the criminal justice system, this could have serious implications for outcomes during interrogation. It could also mean that they will not benefit from special measures granted by the Youth Justice and Criminal Evidence Act 1999. Prisoners with learning difficulties may also find it difficult to comply with community punishments and if in custody may find it difficult to adapt to the regimented nature of prison life resulting in disruptive behaviour and segregation. The problems of identification and assessment, as Loucks (2007) points out, will be harder at times of overcrowding when prisoners are moved around the prison estate.

10.6 Conclusion

10.6.1 The limits of penal policy?

We have identified a number of important areas where it may be difficult to achieve equality of impact and have considered some of the problems which arise in implementing impact mitigation. As we have seen, there are problems in compensating offenders for the personal and social problems they experience. Expecting sentencers and penal policy to solve all the problems stemming from the structural and personal factors which affect the lives and punishment of offenders is unrealistic. It may be better to address the problems we have identified through social policies aimed at rectifying inequality, promoting social inclusion and providing support to individuals and communities. Some of the problems of reconciling criminal justice and social justice through notions of citizenship and human rights are explored by Cook (2006) with reference to recent developments in the UK. But, in relation to the particular problems experienced by particular groups within prison, then improvements in prison conditions and better support for prisoners to maintain contact with their families may be the best way forward. Some of these alternative solutions will be considered in Chapter 11.

10.6.2 Discussion question

Amy is a mother with four children under ten years of age. The children's father, Ben, has been in prison for two years. Amy has several convictions for theft, all preceding the period in which she went to live with Ben and had her children. Amy got into severe financial difficulties two years ago and agreed to deliver packages of drugs, on a regular basis, to distributers. She was caught, pleaded guilty on a charge of possession with intent to supply, and received a sentence of three years.

Ben's family have always rejected her; her own family consists of an ill and elderly mother and a sister who has two children. No one offers to look after her children and she agrees that they be voluntarily accommodated by the local authority. A recent review by the local authority noted the children's distress in their new homes (they cannot all be accommodated in the same foster family). Amy appeals her sentence.

1. How might it be possible—if at all—for the Court of Appeal to justify a decision to substitute a community order for Amy's custodial sentence?

2. What solutions to this type of situation—other than at the sentencing stage—can you suggest?

11

Experiencing imprisonment

SUMMARY

In Chapter 7, we examined the issues raised in achieving justice at the point of sentencing, by considering the differential impact of the prison regime on particular groups of prisoners and in Chapter 9 we considered the quest for justice within the prison context. In this chapter, we will consider another related aspect of justice in prison, by considering whether discrimination operates within the prison system, either directly or indirectly. We will examine this with specific reference to women and ethnic minorities, including foreign-national prisoners. We will also assess the impact of specific policies which aim to reduce the risk of unfair treatment to these groups, in the context of the empirical research.

11.1 Equality, discrimination and human rights

11.1.1 The Equality Act 2006

In Chapter 7, we considered the issue of equality and difference in punishment at the point of sentencing and highlighted some of the problems that arise in taking account of differences in personal circumstances, at the individual level, and their implications for the issue of impact mitigation. We also considered in Chapter 10 the limits of impact mitigation in relation to class, gender and race. We argued there that it was difficult to expect penal policy to solve social problems, and particularly the problem of social exclusion. However, recognising this does not preclude a concern with discrimination within the criminal justice system or with differences in the experience of punishment. We will therefore consider in this chapter the experience of imprisonment for two specific groups—women and ethnic minorities—and look at ways of addressing the problems posed by these different experiences.

As we shall see, the treatment of women and ethnic minorities is governed by a framework of legislation designed to promote equality and human rights. This is reflected in the Equality Act 2006 which establishes the new Commission for Equality and Human Rights, dissolving the Commission for Racial Equality, the Equal Opportunities Commission and the Disability Rights Commission. It also extends areas of discrimination to religious belief and sexual orientation. The aim of the new framework is to promote respect for human rights and equal opportunities and work towards the elimination of unlawful discrimination. The new 'gender equality duty' imposed by Part 4, s 84 of the Equality Act 2006 means that public authorities must take positive action to eliminate unlawful discrimination and harassment on grounds of sex and to promote gender equality, which may mean treating women differently. This means that they must be more pro-active in dealing with discrimination and devising gender-specific and gender sensitive regimes and policies and simple formal inequality will be insufficient. This provision came into force in April 2007. These duties will be enforced by the Commission for Equality and Human Rights. As the argument advanced by those involved with assessing penal regimes is that prison is disproportionately harsher for women than men, this may mean radically rethinking how to deal with deviant women.

Part 2 of the Equality Act also imposes a prohibition on discrimination on grounds of religion or belief. The Act also imposes a disability equality duty on authorities. NOMS is also setting out how the requirements of the gender equality duty will be met and providing guidance on implementing a Gender Equality Scheme, publishing an Equality and Diversity Implementation Plan. The Government's performance of its obligations under the duty will be monitored by the new Equality and Human Rights Commission. NOMS is also developing a National Service Framework for Women which will state the policy for commissioning services for women offenders; and working on Equality Impact Assessments in its Action Plan.

11.1.2 Domestic anti-discrimination law

Prison life is also governed by the framework of anti-discrimination law which provides a framework for race relations and race equality policies. The anti-discrimination law relevant to the treatment of prisoners includes s 95 of the Criminal Justice Act 1991, which imposes a requirement to obtain relevant information to avoid discrimination on grounds of race, sex and other improper grounds, but has no accompanying requirement to introduce anti-racist measures.

The Race Relations (Amendment) Act 2000 imposes on public authorities a statutory duty to promote race equality, which includes monitoring the adverse impact of policies, taking positive action to meet the needs of particular racial groups, and assessing the impact of any new policies on the promotion of race equality. Section 1 makes it unlawful for public authorities to discriminate in any of their functions. The reference to 'any of its functions' also means that cases other than those relating to access to employment, education or provision of services, may be brought. So it would cover any aspect of prison life, including, for example, decisions on the segregation, classification and transfer of prisoners. The Act requires public bodies to eliminate unlawful discrimination and promote equality of opportunity and good race relations between people of different groups. The Act encompasses direct and indirect discrimination. It requires authorities to take account of the impact of their services and policies on ethnic minorities and to establish Race Equality Schemes and to monitor their progress in relation to those schemes. The effect of the Act is to bring public services, including the Prison Service, the Probation Service, the Border and Immigration Agency and the police, within the ambit of anti-discrimination law. It amends s 76 of the RRA 1976, removing the exception for the police and other public authorities and acts which safeguard national security. Progress in the pursuit of equality will also be monitored by the new Equality and Human Rights Commission, established by the Equality Act 2006, which has abolished the Commission for Race Equality, transferring its role to the new Commission.

11.1.3 **European Convention and European Union law**

There have also been advances in both European Union law and European Convention law. In European Union law, Article 13 EC enacted by the Treaty of Amsterdam, introduced a general principle of non-discrimination which prohibits discrimination on sex, race and other grounds. One of the first measures to be introduced under Article 13 was the new Race Equality Directive which came into force at the end of 2003, and embodies the principle of equal treatment regardless of ethnic or racial origin. There is also a new Charter of Fundamental Rights of the European Union.

The European Court of Human Rights is also now more open to indirect discrimination claims brought under the European Convention on Human Rights (ECHR) than in the past. Moreover, with the Human Rights Act (HRA) 1998, the protection of prisoners' rights under the Convention has been strengthened. So if there is information available on disparities between ethnic minorities on issues such as transfer and segregation, where there is a duty to monitor, then there would be *prima facie* evidence of discrimination. The HRA makes it possible to bring an action in the domestic courts.

Cases on racism may also be brought under Article 3, the right not to be subjected to degrading treatment. In *Hilton v UK* (1976), the European Commission of Human Rights said that claims of racist abuse of a prisoner by an officer could raise an Article 3 challenge of degrading treatment.[1] An action could also be brought under Article 14, provided that the discriminatory act falls within the scope of another Convention right, that the complainant can show a difference of treatment compared to a person in an analogous situation and that the discrimination is not justifiable. If Protocol 12 were to be ratified, it would be easier to bring a discrimination claim under the Convention without engaging the other rights, but the UK government has said that it will not ratify Protocol 12.

Recent developments in Convention law have been more promising, with the recognition of indirect discrimination in *Abdulaziz, Cabales and Balkandali v UK* (1985) and positive discrimination in *Thlimmenos v Greece* (2000). If a black prisoner could show he was treated less favourably than a white prisoner in relation to home visits, for example, he could invoke Articles 8 and 14. However, qualifications to Article 8 might be used in the context of the needs of the prison and the public for security. But there would have to be reasonable and objective justification for differential treatment and the measure would have to be proportionate to its aims. A case might also be brought if it could be proved that ethnic minority offenders were sentenced disproportionately compared to white offenders.

With the HRA 1998 in force, it is expected that more cases may be brought under Articles 8 and 14 although, because of the absence of a free-standing discrimination provision, it may be preferable to bring a racism case under Article 3, to argue for degrading treatment. The Act also means that a wider range of types of discrimination can be challenged. For example, in *Hindawi* (2006) a challenge under Article 14 and Article 5 succeeded when the House of Lords held that it was discriminatory to exclude foreign-national prisoners from an early release scheme.

---

[1] See also *East African Asians* case (1981).

11.2 Women in prison

11.2.1 The rise in the female prison population

The number of women imprisoned in England and Wales increased rapidly during the 1990s, more rapidly than the number of male prisoners, although the latter also reached record levels. The number of women prisoners increased from 3.5 per cent of the total prison population in 1991 to 4.4 per cent in 1999, to 6.1 per cent in 2001 and in 2005 it was almost 6 per cent. The proportion now is about 5.5 per cent. On 14 March 2008 there were 77,418 men in prison and 4,447 women.

Despite the dramatic percentage increase, the number of women prisoners is still relatively low compared to the number of male prisoners and relative to the number of women in the population as a whole (51.3 per cent of the total population of England and Wales). There is a substantial literature explaining women's minimal presence in the crime statistics as well as a number of explanations for their deviance, which lie outside the scope of this book.[2]

The actual numbers cited in official statistics usually represent the count on a particular day, like a snapshot, but the number of receptions in prison throughout the year may be substantially higher. The increase in the 1990s has been attributed to several factors, including a general increase in the use of custody, an increase in average sentence length, as well as an increase in the numbers of women appearing before the courts, and increasing numbers of women convicted for drugs offences which attract longer sentences (see the research for the Home Office conducted by Woodbridge and Frosztega 1998). The majority of women are serving short sentences of under 12 months.

The change may also reflect a general increase in punitiveness and tougher sentencing of drugs-related crime, as well as the decline in the use of suspended sentences since 1991. The chance of receiving a custodial sentence increased for both male and female offenders in the 1990s as we saw in Chapter 9 (see Hough *et al.* 2003). So women are now more likely to receive custody for offences of theft, handling and fraud compared to the early 1990s. The numbers of women remanded in custody since the early 1990s have also increased, although over a half of women remanded in custody are not given a custodial sentence at trial.

Generally, we can say that women commit fewer and less serious crimes than men and that their criminal careers are shorter. While women are becoming more involved in violent crime and in drug crime as couriers, the attitudes of sentencers may also be changing. The most common offences for which women are imprisoned are drugs offences and property offences. In 2006 drug offenders constituted one-third of sentenced female prisoners and one-third of this group were foreign nationals. However, since 2002 the proportion of female foreign nationals in prison for drugs offences has fallen by one-third (Ministry of Justice 2007a: 8.12). This may be partly accounted for by the increased use of scanning devices at airports of departure. Although there has also been an increase in offences of violence against the person, fewer women than men are imprisoned for violence, and the majority of female prisoners do not present a danger to the public.

---

[2] See, for example, the review of the literature in Howden-Windell and Clark (1999).

The differences in offending patterns for the female and male sentenced prison population are illustrated by Figures 11.1 and 11.2. These graphs compare the figures for 2006 with a decade earlier in 1996. As these charts show, the most significant increase for female offenders has been in drugs offences.

It had been expected that the expansion of non-custodial penalties would benefit women. Instead, this had the unintended effect of net-widening and failed to counteract countervailing forces such as the increasing populist punitiveness

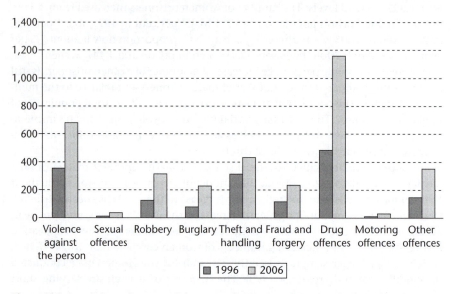

Figure 11.1 Female immediate custodial-sentenced prison population by offence group and year
Source: Ministry of Justice (2007a: 91)

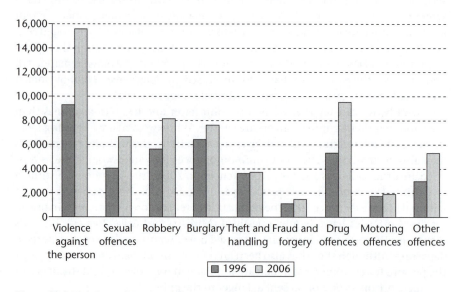

Figure 11.2 Male immediate custodial-sentenced prison population by offence group and year
Source: Ministry of Justice (2007a: 90)

of the 1990s and the application to women of the widely held view that 'prison works' (see Chapter 1). The use of both community sentences and custody has increased and a wide range of options may mean women move up the sentencing tariff more rapidly. As Player argues 'the Criminal Justice Act 2003...increases women's custodial eligibility by increasing their risk of breaching a court order, allowing their persistence to aggravate the severity of their sentence, while failing to inhibit their promotion up the sentencing tariff in pursuit of their welfare interests' (Player 2005: 434).

The number of women beginning community sentences increased by 22 per cent between 1996 and 2006 compared to 9 per cent for males (Ministry of Justice 2007a: para 3.4). Where women are given community orders they are more likely than men to have them terminated for positive reasons, for example, for successful completion or good progress (Ministry of Justice 2007a: para 5.5). Ironically, the expansion of community penalties and curfews may also disadvantage women in some respects as the home becomes the focus of attention of criminal justice agencies, subject to scrutiny and surveillance, which means that they will be observed as partners of male offenders. Indeed, the family is still seen as a *locus* of criminality with the emphasis on parental responsibility for young offending.

The current emphasis on risk management, defined for most offenders as risk of persistence rather than risk of dangerousness, has affected women as it means that more women are serving short sentences for lesser property offences. Furthermore a greater focus on community sentences, as embodied in the CJA 2003, may have mixed effects if conditions are attached to those sentences which women find difficult to meet. Women may be at greater risk of breaching conditions because of the problems of meeting both the requirements of supervision and the competing demands of child care, although guidance from the Sentencing Guidelines Council (2004c) encourages sentencers to take account of the offender's ability to comply with particular requirements. Nevertheless the Corston Report welcomed the shelving of Custody Plus specifically because it might increase the numbers of women in prison serving short sentences and being recalled to prison for breaches (2007: para 5.17). As noted in Chapter 9 a large number of receptions into custody are for breaches and this applies to women prisoners as well. According to the Corston Report, half of new receptions into Holloway prison are for breach. In some cases the breach in question may be a failure to meet an appointment which in some cases could be because of child care or transport problems (ibid: para 5.25). Moreover, as the majority of women are sentenced in the magistrates' courts, the increased powers of magistrates may mean an increase in the number and length of custodial sentences, moving women offenders into the 6–12 months range.

11.2.2 The typical woman prisoner

The typical woman prisoner, like the typical male prisoner, is likely to have had housing problems, low educational achievement, and problems with drugs, alcohol or mental illness before entering prison. However, unlike the typical male prisoner, she is much more likely to have experienced domestic violence and sexual abuse. The Corston Report found that over one-half of women in prison reported previous domestic violence (Corston 2007: para 2.3).

We noted in Chapter 1 public concern over the harm caused by sexual offenders, including paedophiles, but less attention has been paid to the long-term impact of this abuse in the context of women's imprisonment. Two-thirds of women entering custody require drug detoxification compared to one-half of men entering prison (Corston 2007: para 2.13).

We also noted in Chapter 9 the correlations between risk of imprisonment and social class, housing problems, and poverty and unemployment, which characterise the profile of the typical prisoner, and these correlations are stronger in relation to female imprisonment (see section 9.2.1). Women are less likely than male prisoners to have been in work before imprisonment, and more likely to be unemployed after imprisonment. Women prisoners also have more experience of being in care in the past, and there are a disproportionate number of mentally ill prisoners compared to male prisoners (Corston 2007). A higher proportion of women in prison had housing problems prior to imprisonment compared to male prisoners. Moreover, the loss of housing while in prison does not just pose problems for the individual, but means it may be harder for women to be reunited with their families. The Wedderburn Report argued that 'women represent the extremes of social exclusion' (Prison Reform Trust 2000: xv). Many women in prison have high levels of deprivation before conviction. In some respects women are more likely to be socially excluded because they are poverty-prone, because they live longer, have higher morbidity rates, and earn less than men. Social problems which existed before entering prison may also be exacerbated by prison. Women are also less likely than men to have accommodation waiting for them on release. About one-third of women prisoners lose their homes while in prison. The Social Exclusion Unit Report (2002) found that over 40 per cent of women in prison had not worked for at least five years before entering prison and only 39 per cent had any educational qualifications.

Women in prison have higher rates of mental and physical illness than women in the general population and high rates of learning disabilities. Of course women prisoners are not a homogeneous group; the female prison population includes black and other ethnic-minority prisoners, who make up about 28 per cent of the female prison population, foreign-national prisoners, who make up 19 per cent of the female prison population, women with disabilities and women with a range of health problems.

11.3 Life in women's prisons

11.3.1 The research base

Life in women's prisons has been under-researched until relatively recently. Before the 1980s there was relatively little interest in women's prisons in penal policy and few studies were conducted. However, during the 1980s the interest in women's imprisonment increased. At that time there were particular concerns over women with mental health problems and especially with the conditions then prevailing at Holloway prison. Research conducted since then showed that women prisoners have been marginalised within the penal system, in part because of their relatively low numbers compared to men. Moreover, because of their failure to 'react' to poor prison conditions in terms of violence other than against themselves, they may be seen as compliant and accepting of their conditions, when this could be a refusal to resort to male tactics. In any event this may contribute to their marginalisation, so the Woolf Report (1991), for example, said very little on women's prisons.

In recent years the concern has been with the expansion of the female prison population and whether gender-specific penal policies are needed. The interest of the public in women's imprisonment has also increased, not least because of the salacious interest of the media which has displayed in recent years a fascination with women prisoners, portraying them as either neurotic or tough and masculine.

There is now acceptance in penal policy that women prisoners deserve separate attention. The Government's strategy for women prisoners now is to take account of their special needs and of the specific factors which influence women's offending (Home Office 2000a, 2001e, see section 11.5.4 below). There is also now more information available on women's imprisonment and its impact. Several major studies of women's imprisonment have been undertaken. A review of women's imprisonment was undertaken in 1997 by the then Chief Inspector of Prisons, Sir David Ramsbotham (HM Chief Inspector of Prisons 1997b). The Review was critical of the management of women's prisons, the excessive security used in women's prisons, the lack of consistency on privileges across the women's prison estate, the treatment of juveniles, the holding of young offenders in prison establishments, the training of staff, allocation procedures, the handcuffing of women during labour and on ante-natal visits, reception procedures, training for staff conducting strip searches and using control and restraint techniques, access to phones, access to translators, induction programmes, visiting arrangements, healthcare provision, particularly for women with mental health problems, and educational provision. The Review made 160 recommendations, some of which have now been implemented. The Review was followed up four years later to assess progress (HM Chief Inspector of Prisons 2001). The Wedderburn Report on women's imprisonment, published in 2000, argued that women serving short sentences for less serious offences and women with mental health problems should be diverted from custody, while sentences could be shortened for those in prison and greater use could be made of temporary release (Prison Reform Trust 2000).

In addition, a major study of the physical and mental health of women prisoners, *The Health of Women in Prison*, was published in 2006 by researchers at Oxford University who interviewed 505 female remand prisoners over a period in 2004–5 (Plugge *et al.* 2006).

The most recent major review, the Corston Report, examined women with particular vulnerabilities in the criminal justice system, arguing that custody should be used only where necessary for public protection but that there are many women in prison for non-violent offences who could be dealt with differently (Corston 2007). This research for the Review included visits to six women's prisons, three women's community centres, and a medium-secure women's hospital. In examining 'vulnerabilities' the Report focused on issues such as domestic violence, child care issues, including being a single parent, and personal issues, including mental illness, substance misuse and eating disorders, as well as socio-economic factors such as poverty and unemployment (Corston 2007: para 14). Some of their recommendations have been partially accepted by the Government (see section 11.5.4 below and Ministry of Justice 2007b).

We therefore have far more information on the issues involved in women's imprisonment now and the prospects of a gender-specific penal policy are now much brighter, as the Government has increasingly accepted that women's offending may raise different issues to men.

11.3.2 The women's prison estate

The small size of the female prison population, and therefore the small size of the women's prison estate, means that women may be held far from home, making it difficult to organise visits or support for their families. Women are held on average further away from home than male prisoners. This also has implications for resettlement as it is harder to facilitate resettlement if they are accommodated far from their communities. There are large geographical areas, including the West Midlands and Wales without women's prisons and the problem has increased with the closure of Brockhill Prison at Redditch to women. Because of the increased need for additional places for women, some men's prisons have been converted to take women, including Buckley Hall, Downview and Morton Hall, and a new purpose-built women's prison, Bronzefield, opened in June 2004 at Ashford, Middlesex, run by UK Detention Services, with a mother and baby unit. But some women's prisons have been re-roled to take men which may mean women are held even further from home.

In March 2008 there were only 17 women's prisons. One-half of women prisoners are held over 50 miles from home and one-quarter are held more than 100 miles from home (Prison Reform Trust 2007a). From 1999–2004 the women's prison estate was managed separately by a special unit at Prison Service Headquarters but is now managed geographically, by Area Managers responsible for both men and women's prisons in their areas. A Women and Young People's Group in the Prison Service gives advice and support to prisons on women's issues and it has produced a Prison Service Instruction (PSI) on gender equality impact assessments (PSI 40/2007). This means that any changes in Prison Service policy or practice need to be assessed to consider their relevance for gender equality. It is also formulating Gender-Specific Standards which form part of the Government's response to the Corston Report.

Because there are fewer women's prisons, the women's prison estate is also less flexible in terms of catering for different types of prisoner with particular needs. This also means it may be harder to transfer disruptive women prisoners than male prisoners for whom more places are available. If difficult prisoners are transferred to an ordinary prison, the restrictions may mean regime changes for other prisoners and stricter control than is warranted. The small size of the estate also means less flexibility for providing appropriate accommodation for prisoners or the right level of supervision. There may be places available in closed but not open prisons and vice versa.

Women prisoners have been held in some of the worst conditions within the prison system. When the Chief Inspector of Prisons visited Holloway in 1995 he walked out in disgust because it was so dirty with sightings of rats and cockroaches reported and, in the 2003 league table, Holloway was still rated the worst prison, at level 1, although it is now at level 3. However, the most recent report of the Prison Inspectorate (HM Chief Inspector of Prisons 2008) found that the five women's prisons inspected were performing reasonably well with good relationships between staff and prisoners, although there remain variations between prisons.

11.3.3 Women prisoners and male penal policies

Until relatively recently women's imprisonment was largely subsumed within the male prison system and women were punished within a penal system designed for men. Because women constitute a minority, they were at a disadvantage as institutions will usually favour the interests of the majority for administrative convenience. This means that women may be adversely affected by policies based on the actions of male prisoners. If women are housed within the precincts of a men's prison, it may be difficult to guarantee their security at times of disorder and also may mean that they are subject to higher levels of security than is necessary, even in normal conditions.

The experience of the prison riots strongly influenced penal policy in the 1990s, but these were primarily male events, so the direction of penal policy was predicated principally on male experiences, leading to a stress on the need for security and control. This has meant that women's needs have been marginalised and subsumed within a system primarily defined by men and this may make the experience of prison for women more onerous. Even where the problem has been acknowledged, the focus is on accommodating women's needs within the male framework with some minor adjustments, rather than radically rethinking the question.

While the improvements in the prison regime in the immediate post-Woolf period benefited women, women also shared in the retrenchment of these benefits. Most notably they were subject to increased security after the Whitemoor and Parkhurst escapes. In this sense they were 'punished' disproportionately as the escapes, like the earlier riots, did not involve women's prisons or women prisoners. The Learmont and Woodcock Reports impacted disparately on women prisoners because they resulted in greater use of shackles on outside visits and cuts in home leave, although the cuts in temporary release imposed after the Learmont Report have now been relaxed. The response to the escapes also meant that there was an increase in the numbers of women held in closed prisons, even if they met the criteria for transfer to open prisons, where there is more access to home, their children and outside work.

During the late 1990s, security concerns and the war on drugs inside prison also disadvantaged women as they generated more intensive controls, including the use of Dedicated Search Teams, dressed in black combat clothes, to search prisoners' cells, and mandatory drug testing. In addition, visitors, including children, were subject to greater surveillance. Yet women are less likely to escape or to riot. If they do escape they are less likely to constitute a threat to the public, as they commit fewer offences of violence and may be easier to trace, as they are likely to contact their families. Mandatory drug-testing policies have been applied in men's and women's prisons even though there are fewer drugs-related incidents in women's prisons and the Chief Inspector of Prisons has argued that less stringent testing for drugs should be introduced in women's prisons (HM Chief Inspector of Prisons 1997b, 2001). Women are generally less dangerous than men, both on official statistics and self-report studies and are less likely to abscond, yet they were subjected to similar levels of security. In fact, the issue during the riots was rather how best to protect women prisoners from male prisoners if a riot occurred at a shared site. Women have also been subjected to routine strip- or full-searching as it is now known, despite the fact they pose lower security risks. In its latest report the Prison Inspectorate notes that at Peterborough prison where women on Imprisonment for Public Protection sentences were accommodated, although the regimes for men and women were managed separately, the ethos, policies, procedures and systems in key areas such as safer custody were those of a male prison (HM Chief Inspector of Prisons 2008: 44).

11.4 Women prisoners and the pains of imprisonment

Women prisoners deserve special attention because, it has been argued, they experience the pains of imprisonment more intensely than their male counterparts, for a number of reasons, the principal one being that women with children are most likely to be the primary carers and therefore experience greater anxiety at separation from their children. In some cases, the women may not even know who is looking after their children. Disquiet in recent years has been expressed over the problems for women prisoners of maintaining contact with their children and over the presence of male officers in women's prisons. There is also concern over the large numbers of children who have a parent in custody. It is estimated at present that 160,000 children a year are affected.

11.4.1 Women as carers

Women prisoners may have particular concerns about childcare, caring for elderly relatives, and anxieties about declining fertility, which will not affect men to the same extent. Women prisoners are concerned at losing contact with their children and their greatest fear is that their children may be taken into care while they are serving their sentence. Babies are permitted to stay with their mothers for a maximum of 18 months and places in mother and baby units are limited. Trying to deal with family crises while inside prison is a major problem for women prisoners. Women usually remain responsible for family decisions and find it hard to co-ordinate arrangements from prison. If they are detained for a long period of time they may lose their home, which will make it harder to keep their children. While the wife of a male prisoner may struggle to keep family life going, for women who are the main carers, prison will have a more significant impact on the structure of home life.

Women are more likely than male prisoners to have dependent children and less likely than male prisoners to have a partner caring for their children. The Corston Report found that only 5 per cent of the children of women prisoners remained in their own home (Corston 2007: para 2.9): 12 per cent are in care or with foster or adoptive parents, 25 per cent are with grandmothers, and 29 per cent are with other family members or friends. A higher proportion of children of women prisoners end up in care compared to children of male prisoners.

So although women may have a similar social profile to men in terms of social exclusion, this may be exacerbated by the fact of being the primary carer. As women may be allocated to prisons far from their homes, there may be problems in organising regular visits from their families as children have to be escorted. Although there is a means-tested allowance for close family members to visit, this is limited and long-distance visits may be very expensive. Many prisons are located in rural areas with inadequate bus services. The costs of visits may be a problem especially as it means time off work for the person escorting the children, given the distance from home for many prisoners. Longer visits which last all day would be better for women with children as would cheap transport to the nearest railway station. Women may avoid having their children visit them because they think they would be distressed by the surroundings or being searched, although visiting facilities in women's prisons are usually superior to those in men's prisons.

The pains of imprisonment may be greater because of these anxieties regarding family obligations which do not face male prisoners to the same extent but deal only with disruptions in their working lives. Anxieties about families was a major issue for women interviewed in the Oxford study of remand prisoners. Their concerns focused on their children and the plight of elderly relatives (Plugge *et al.* 2006).

11.4.2 Privacy and prison conditions

Women also experience prison more severely than men in so far as they find intrusions of privacy more painful, in part because, unlike their male counterparts, they usually have less experience of communal life, through sports and activities. Because of this, open prisons, paradoxically, may seem more repressive, if it means sharing a dormitory. In addition, control in open prisons may be based more heavily on compliance with rules, rather than physical barriers, with adverse disciplinary consequences. Women may also find the physical conditions more distressing because women usually have more health awareness as the family member who is most likely to take responsibility for family health. They are therefore more concerned with hygiene and may be more upset by having to eat in their cells, by the limited number of showers, and by poor hygiene standards. The Corston Report found that there were still instances of slopping out because of a failure to provide 24-hour access to facilities, or queuing to use the toilet at night which prisoners find humiliating and degrading (Corston 2007: para 3.16).

Concerns over privacy may be exacerbated by the presence of male officers. Women prisoners do not like men entering their rooms; they do not like to be observed while washing, especially if they have previously been abused, and find providing samples for drug testing, for example, quite intrusive. Although using male officers in women's prisons was initially intended as an equal opportunities measure for staff, the policy has not been welcomed by prisoners. As large numbers of women prisoners have experienced violence from men in the past, this has made it especially difficult for them, but most women find the presence of male officers difficult to deal with. The Chief Inspector of Prisons has argued that there should be a minimum of 75 per cent female staff in women's prisons (HM Chief Inspector of Prisons 1997b). But in practice women's prisons are mostly staffed by male officers, which generates a masculinist occupational culture. Working at women's prisons may be unpopular because it is seen as low-status work and women officers may find it difficult to transfer because of staff shortages.

11.4.3 **Expectations of women prisoners' behaviour**

Officers' expectations of women's behaviour are more demanding in the sense that women are more likely than men to be reprimanded for petty offences such as swearing or other behaviour which is seen as unfeminine (Carlen 1998). In 2006 there were 136 proven offences against prison discipline for each 100 prisoners, for males and females combined, the most common offences being disobedience or disrespect. For males the figure is 131 per 100 prisoners, but for females the rate is 204 per 100 prisoners and a similar pattern is found over the past ten years. Female prisoners have a higher offence rate than male prisoners for all offences except for escapes or absconding. Women prisoners also had a higher punishment rate with 315 punishments per 100 of the female prison population compared to 225 for men. The figures indicate women have higher punishment rates for loss of privileges, loss of earnings and additional days awarded (Ministry of Justice 2007a: paras 9.3, 9.4).

Devlin (1998) argues that women are more likely to be punished for minor disciplinary matters and are subject to more intensive discipline and surveillance. Women prisoners are seen by officers as more argumentative than male prisoners and less able to accept discipline. Women may find it hard to adjust to prison for the reasons considered above. Because women may have had greater autonomy in running their own homes, they may also find it harder to adjust to a regime which essentially treats them like children in many ways. As women's prisons are smaller, women prisoners may be subject to greater scrutiny, so disciplinary infractions are more likely to be noticed. Women with mental health problems are more likely to be charged with disciplinary offences and may react badly to being held on a segregation unit or on cellular confinement (O'Brien *et al.* 2001). The disciplinary regime is used to control women's behaviour and to contain mentally ill women. While women prisoners who are dissatisfied with their treatment have access to the range of remedies and the complaints procedure available to male prisoners, like them they may be reluctant to complain if they think it may cause more problems for them.

11.4.4 **Women prisoners' health needs**

Women's healthcare in prison is an important issue because women prisoners have higher rates of mental illness and prescription drug use than male prisoners (Prison Reform Trust 2003; Social Exclusion Unit 2002). A survey of female prisoners in 1997 found that 40 per cent had received treatment for mental health problems before entering prison and about one-half of women prisoners had some drug dependency prior to prison (Singleton *et al.* 1998; O'Brien *et al.* 2001). Two-thirds of women prisoners suffer from some form of mental health problem such as depression and anxiety and about one-half are taking prescription psychotropic drugs. A higher proportion of women than male prisoners enter prison with mental health problems which may be exacerbated in prison, by worries about family and housing. Women also often feel unsafe in prison and may experience victimisation, theft of property and threats of violence. The use of medicines increases in prison and many women take prescription psychotropic drugs for the first time while in prison. Substantial volumes of sleeping pills and tranquillisers are consumed. However, counselling is becoming more available (see Prison Reform Trust 2003). Outside prison women have higher morbidity rates than men and this is also reflected inside prison, and these health problems may add to the stresses of imprisonment. But while many women prisoners have emotional and social problems, the number of disturbed and difficult prisoners with severe and untreatable problems is relatively small. While recognising the health problems, we need to avoid over-emphasising the therapeutic needs of women, or medicalising women's deviance, which perpetuates the popular perception of women as unstable.

The Oxford study found that the health status of the women who entered prison was poorer than for women in the general population and problems included both physical and mental health, which meant considerable demands were made on the health services within prison (Plugge *et al.* 2006). Women prisoners were five times more likely to have a mental health problem than women in the general population; over half had used illegal drugs before going into prison. Interestingly, the research found that the health status of some women actually improved in prison, because they did *not* have access to drugs and alcohol, but they did have regular meals, healthcare and protection from abusive relationships. However, many reported becoming unfit with lack of exercise and the researchers argue that more attention should be given to support for healthcare in prison, especially as health issues may be linked to offending behaviour, and that improving health should be a key performance indicator. The prisoners interviewed emphasised that they wanted more access to exercise and healthier food rather than high-carbohydrate food. The authors' recommendations include more research on health needs of foreign-national prisoners, and on measures to help women sleep to avoid the use of sleeping pills, more support for prisoners who witness suicides or self-harm, more access for prisoners to cleaning materials, more help to disabled prisoners, more support for improving physical health, for example, hepatitis B vaccinations, better training for staff to improve delivery of healthcare, and access to in-cell sanitation at all times.

Many women prisoners have drug or alcohol problems which require treatment but an unintended effect of mandatory drug testing is that some prisoners are switching from cannabis to heroin, because the latter is harder to detect. The Chief Inspector of Prisons was critical of the lack of therapy and detoxification programmes in women's prisons and, in the follow-up to the Thematic Review, expressed concern 'that the health care needs of women might be swamped by those of the majority male prisoner population' (HM Chief Inspector of Prisons 2001). In its recent review of mental health in prisons, the Prison Inspectorate found that female prisoners reported the highest levels of psychological and emotional disorder and distress and were on high levels of medication when they might have benefited more from counselling (HM Inspectorate of Prisons 2007b).

There are also high levels of attempted, threatened and successful suicide in the female prison population. In 2003, 14 of the 94 suicides in prison (15 per cent) were committed by women. However, the numbers have fallen since then, with 13 female suicides in 2004, 4 in 2005 and 3 in 2006, but the number increased to 8 out of 92 in 2007. High-risk factors for suicide include neuroses, drug and alcohol misuse, and being in care as a child, all of which are present in both the female and male prison populations.

Self-harming is also much higher in the female prison population and particularly amongst women under 21. Women account for nearly half of recorded self-harming incidents. Self-harm may have been used as a way to deal with stress before imprisonment, although they may be more likely to engage in self-harm in response to poor conditions, while men may be more likely to direct violence against others or to damage property in such cases.

The Report by the Prison Reform Trust, *Troubled Inside* (2003), considered the mental health needs of women prisoners and raised the issue of whether prisons should be used as psychiatric hospitals and whether, given the numbers of women with mental health problems and the number of attempted suicides, it would be better to focus on the mental health needs of offenders rather than simply incarcerating them (see Peay 2007).

These difficulties may be compounded by the fact that the standards of health care in prison, particularly for mentally ill prisoners, fall well below those in the National Health Service outside prison, in terms of the services available and quality of care (see Reed and Lyne 2000). The demands on health services in prison are greater than in the community, because of the higher rates of mental disorder, drug misuse, and self-harming in prison. Responsibility for healthcare has been transferred from the Prison Service to the National Health Service and responsibility for funding has moved from the Home Office to the Department of Health. This has had a beneficial effect on health service provision but there are still problems given the demand for services. Training, particularly training in mental health care, needs improving. The burden on prison medical staff and on officers and other prisoners would be reduced if more facilities were available to divert mentally ill offenders from prison and if mental health care and drug treatment programmes within the community were improved.

Women with serious mental health problems do need access to an appropriate therapeutic regime. Until recently a proper therapeutic community for women, comparable to Grendon for male prisoners, was not available. A women's annexe at Winchester Prison, West Hill, was converted to a therapeutic centre but it closed in 2004 to make room for male prisoners. However, a therapeutic unit for 40 women is now available at HMP Send in Surrey.

The standard of care for prisoners with severe mental health problems is also dependent on facilities in the wider community. Where problems are severe and transfer to hospital is necessary, it may take several months to find a suitable hospital bed (Corston 2007: para 12). Also, because of problems within the NHS, it may take considerable time for medical staff to provide reports requested by sentencers which may delay provision of appropriate methods of disposal for women.

However, these problems not only present huge demands on the prison, but also reflect social problems which it would be unreasonable to expect the prison system to solve. As the Corston Report concluded: 'the Prison Service cannot and should not be expected to solve social problems' (para 7.24). As we argued in Chapter 10, what are needed are social policies to address these social problems which will include greater provision for support within the community. Expecting prison staff to redress these problems may be unrealistic.

11.4.5 **Constructive regimes for women**

Because of the smaller size of women's prisons, it is difficult to provide the full range of education and training opportunities available in men's prisons. Until the 1970s women's training was mainly domestic work with limited opportunities for serious vocational or academic work. The focus was also on 'feminine' skills, such as taking pride in one's appearance, reflecting the view that adjusting to the gender role is part of the rehabilitation process. Although it has been criticised for this reason, courses such as hairdressing do at least offer a prospect of self-employment on release. Domestic work also forms a large part of male prison work, of course, as much of the work is servicing the prison.

In the 1970s vocational courses were introduced, although often in subjects like home economics. The situation now is much improved with some light industrial work for women in prison such as manufacturing clothes and furniture, printing and desktop publishing, and a wider range of educational and training courses (see Simon 1999). Improving the provision of work and training is crucial to strengthening women's position in the labour market when they return to the community. Women prisoners have much lower literacy and numeracy skills than the wider population.

Given that most women are serving short sentences, they need intensive training for work. Although many jobs in prison are in housekeeping or cleaning, to meet the needs of the prison, this could be tied to a National Vocational Qualification, as it is crucial to improve access to the job market. A survey of women's work and training experiences in prison and on release found that while the majority of women had access to work while in custody, they also found that employment of very little value to them in finding work on release (see Hamlyn and Lewis 2000).

Efforts are being made to ensure greater consistency in educational provision and greater co-ordination between different prison establishments. Prisoners are now being used to assist with the teaching of PE and other educational activities. The provision of offending behaviour programmes in women's prisons should also take account of women's needs, and programmes specially designed for women offenders are now being developed and introduced. However, women offenders generally prefer and benefit from individual client-centred counselling and treatment approaches, but cognitive behavioural programmes are more likely to be accredited. Some of the issues which arise in working with women offenders as well as alternatives to imprisonment are considered by Sheehan *et al.* (2007) who draw on ideas in other jurisdictions.

The Corston Report (2007) has also emphasised the need for training in very basic life skills, such as cooking healthy meals, and organising family life, for women whose lives have been chaotic and these should be given a higher priority. So a woman-centred approach should be applied to work, training and education, but this means that issues such as life skills and building self-esteem, the Report argued, should be addressed as a priority and a prerequisite for benefiting from vocational or educational courses. For those with more advanced skills, a course offering women help and advice in setting up small businesses, such as that offered at Holloway, would be useful and could be extended further.

11.4.6 **Black women prisoners**

In 2006, 28 per cent of women prisoners were from black and other ethnic minorities. However, the experiences of this group have been under-researched so relatively little information has been available until recently. Black women enmeshed in the criminal justice system have to negotiate the multiple hazards of class, gender, and ethnicity. Black women receive custodial sentences at earlier stages in their criminal careers than white women and are over-represented in prison. Some of the reasons for this were discussed in Chapter 10. Explanations have focused on the role of racism in these decisions, but the impact of poor housing and social exclusion also needs to be considered.

Black women and women from ethnic minority groups may face additional problems within the justice system because they are subject to racist and patriarchal attitudes and stereotypes. Racism may shape the experience of imprisonment in a number of ways, in the allocation of resources and in treatment and attitudes, issues considered in the second part of this chapter, and for black women this will overlay and may exacerbate the problems considered above (see Chigwada-Bailey 2003 and also section 11.7 below). The review of progress by HM Chief Inspector of Prisons in 2001 found that 'while there were some examples of positive initiatives, comparatively little proactive race relations work was taking place in female establishments. This should be a priority across the women's estate' (2001: para 2.72). However, as we shall see, this is now given much greater emphasis and will be considered below. In recent studies, black and ethnic-minority women were found to be less negative about their treatment than black and ethnic-minority men, and generally, relations between staff and prisoners seem to be better in female prisons (HM Chief Inspector of Prisons 2008). However, one group of female prisoners, foreign-national prisoners—who account for 19 per cent of the female prison population—may experience particular problems and a recent study found that family and immigration problems were major concerns for these women (HM Inspectorate of Prisons 2006).

11.4.7 **Women's relative advantages in the prison regime**

So far the disadvantages experienced by women have been highlighted, but in some respects women would seem to benefit under the current prison regime. Generally women's prisons have better visiting facilities than men's prisons. Female prisoners also spend higher than average hours in purposeful activities than men, longer outside their cells, and more hours in education and skills training.

Women are also allowed to have their babies with them in a Mother and Baby Unit (MBU) up to the age of 18 months (or 9 months in two of the units). There are currently seven such units. Under Prison Rule 9(3) a pregnant woman can apply for transfer to an MBU. Mothers' rights to retain their babies have been strengthened by using Article 8 of the ECHR, as separation may breach Article 8. The blanket policy of the Prison Service to remove a child at 18 months was successfully challenged under the Human Rights Act in *R (P, Q & QB) v Secretary of the State for the Home Department* (2001). Here, the Court of Appeal said that prisoners retain the right to respect for family life while in prison. In considering whether the state's grounds for interfering with the right are justified, the court will take account of the need for security in prison, the need to avoid discrimination, and whether the rule was appropriate in the individual case, and the more serious the interference, the more compelling the justification would need to be. If the policy stemmed from the welfare of the child and if, in a particular case, the effect on the child was very adverse, the court could intervene in an exceptional case.

There are also indications that women's prisons have better relations between staff and prisoners than men's prisons. The Prison Inspectorate's Annual Report found that three-quarters of women in their survey thought staff treated them with respect (HM Chief Inspector of Prisons 2008).

11.5 Gender-specific penal reform and ameliorative justice

11.5.1 A gender-specific policy?

As we have seen, the current regime has been subject to criticism on a number of grounds and a number of proposals for reform have been made by the Chief Inspector of Prisons, the Prison Reform Trust, and other campaigning groups. However, the views of prisoners and prison officers of appropriate treatment for women prisoners have received less attention. The campaigning and support group, Women in Prison, founded in 1983 by ex-prisoners, has consistently argued that we need a national strategy for the care of women prisoners.[3] Most campaigners have argued for a *gender-specific* policy which takes account of the differing needs and circumstances of women prisoners outlined above, to achieve substantive equality rather than formal equality.

Carlen (1998) has also argued for a coherent and holistic policy for women's prisons, and for all new measures introduced to be gender and ethnicity tested, to see whether they impact differentially on female or ethnic minority prisoners. Different regimes for men and women may be justified, she says, on the principle of 'ameliorative justice'. This principle 'assumes that as women (and black women in particular), because of their different social roles and relationships and other cultural difference, are likely either to suffer more pains of imprisonment than men, or to suffer in different ways, the prison authorities are justified in running different regimes for women to make up for (or ameliorate) the differential pains of imprisonment attributable to gender or ethnic difference' (ibid: 10–11). Gender testing means 'asking whether biological or ideological differences in gender identity will require proposed regime innovations to receive differential implementation in the men's and women's prisons' (ibid: 134).

11.5.2 Changing the women's prison regime

A gender-specific penal policy should, in particular, acknowledge women as primary carers and recognise that women in prison receive far less support than male prisoners from their partners. It would also demand a more sensitive drugs policy,

---

[3] See http://www.womeninprison.org.uk.

allowing women more control over clothes and food, increasing the use of women officers in women's prisons, increasing gender awareness training for staff, to meet needs of female offenders, and making use of women officers' experience in devising future strategies.

An increased number of assisted visits would help, as would easing restrictions imposed on mothers in their contact with their children. Temporary release, weekend leave, and weekend visits from children, perhaps lodging with local families and visiting their parents in the day, would also assist prisoners with children. Incoming calls would enable prisoners to maintain contact with their families. The resettlement of women should also take into account the need for women to move away from their home areas to escape violent relationships. Women want more privacy so they would value more single-cell accommodation. They also want more choice in how to spend their association time, whether to stay in their cell, to take part in activities, or to be on their own. They also want more freedom to cook for themselves, more female doctors, and better healthcare. Privacy issues could be helped by using scanning machines, which are now highly sophisticated, instead of full searching. Women also need more help with drug problems, and access to gender-appropriate treatment programmes inside and outside prison. A frequent criticism of the Mandatory Drug Testing programme is that it is punitive rather than constructive and does not address the source of the problem. Drug treatment and testing orders also need to be geared towards women, and improved community-based services provided for women with mental health problems who are at risk of offending. More attention should be given to improving access to health, education, and support on release into the community, although resettlement is now a Prison Service Key Performance Target. Housing is also a major concern for women prisoners who want to be reunited with their families.

While housing women within the perimeter of men's prisons would increase their chance of being housed nearer home, it will usually mean additional unnecessary security. Although the Woolf Report (1991: para 11.65) thought women could be held in the same establishments as men, provided that they were in separate blocks on a shared site—ideally in community prisons near the main centres of population—most reformers advocate holding women in separate institutions. NACRO favours community houses where women could live, and perhaps have their children living with them under supervision. If more hostels were available for women, it might be possible to transfer women there mid-sentence, or use them as alternatives to custody. The Wedderburn Report (Prison Reform Trust 2000) favoured replacing existing women's prisons with geographically dispersed custodial centres, and a network of supervision, rehabilitation and support centres. It advocated a reductionist programme on the grounds that women's patterns of offending are different and because the social costs of women's imprisonment are greater than the costs of men's imprisonment. The Corston Report (2007) recommended replacing women's existing prisons with small, multi-functional centres, geographically distributed to allow women to be located nearer their home. It also proposed a new Commission for women who offend or are at risk of reoffending, which would be cross-departmental and incorporate the Women's Offending Reduction Programme and provide strong leadership for implementing change and addressing issues which lead to female criminality.

But larger prisons are more popular with governments and the Prison Service because they are perceived to be more cost effective in achieving economies of scale. The Carter Report (Carter 2003) argued that unsuitable prisons, including those in the women's prison estate, should be replaced with more cost-effective institutions. The Government, in response, has said that it will close some smaller prisons and replace them with new larger prisons (Home Office 2004b). But this overlooks the disadvantages of larger institutions and means that it will be harder for prisoners to be housed nearer home.

The Corston Report (Corston 2007) emphasises the need for a woman-centred approach which will focus on the needs of the individual women and bring together a range of services to address health, abuse, drug and alcohol misuse in community-based centres. Although this might seem expensive, by cutting the use of imprisonment this would free up prison places. Moreover, a considerable amount of expenditure has been earmarked for prison expansion and some of this could, and should, be used for reforming the facilities available for women. Moreover with the new commissioning arrangements being organised by NOMS, there are more opportunities for commissioning innovative provision of community centres and community programmes to divert female offenders from custody. Those women who do need secure custody should be housed in small secure custodial units (Corston 2007: para 3.34). But Corston warns that there is a danger of gender-specific agendas being diluted without a strong central structure and this is why she argues for the appointment of a Commissioner for Women to provide direction and leadership. The example is given of the situation in relation to youth justice in the 1990s when there was a lack of integration and little strategic overview (see Audit Commission 1998). However, the Youth Justice Board has since provided leadership and coherence in Youth Justice and similar reforms are needed to provide justice for women. An imaginative use of women's work on community schemes suggested by Corston is training women to renovate properties which could be used to provide accommodation for women on bail or on release (2007: 5.15). The existing women's prison estate could then be transferred to the male prison estate to reduce over-crowding there. The Corston Report does raise the possibility of a separate sentencing framework for women but acknowledges that now is not the appropriate time (ibid: 4.11); however that the Sentencing Guidelines Council should consider the gender aspect in formulating guidelines and it is now including specific gender questions in its consultations (ibid: 5.18). The Corston Report recommends that defendants who are primary carers of young children should be remanded in custody only after considering a probation report on the likely impact on the children (Corston 2007: 9). The Howard League has argued for a Director General for Women Prisoners. The Wedderburn Report advocated setting up a National Women's Justice Board but this has not yet happened.

11.5.3 Reducing the number of women in prison

Carlen (1998: viii) argues that women's imprisonment in England and Wales is 'excessively punitive; totally inappropriate to the needs of the women being sent to prison; and ripe for abolition in its present form'. Her conclusions are based on a study of nine closed and three open women's prisons between December 1996 and October 1997, interviewing officers and 39 prisoners and ex-prisoners, and governor-grade staff, probation officers, education staff, members of the Board of Visitors, as well as those working with penal reform groups. Carlen proposes as a starting point a five-year experiment to release women offenders and deal with them outside prison. Prison should be reserved for the few women who commit serious crime, or the alternative is likely to be further deterioration of the women's prison estate, more overcrowding and faster staff turnover. Carlen argues that stronger constraints on sentencers are needed.

As noted above, the Wedderburn Report recommended establishing a National Women's Justice Board to set up a network of support services linked to the custodial units and, until then, to take responsibility for the existing prisons (Prison Reform Trust 2000). The Committee argued that pre-sentence reports should be used in all cases involving women offenders where there is a prospect of a custodial or community sentence. It should not be assumed by the courts that some penalties are unsuitable for women, because of their domestic circumstances, or because they involve manual work (see Hedderman and Gelsthorpe 1997). But community punishments could be made more suitable for women offenders if childcare provision were available (Prison Reform Trust 2000: para 5.15).

Given that the UK has a wide range of alternatives to prison, the scope for reductionism is greater than in most other European societies. Even if a fully reductionist policy is not adopted, the regime could be ameliorated for those within prison. Women should not be separated from their babies, unless there are exceptional circumstances. Healthcare and drug treatment programmes could be improved. HM Chief Inspector of Prisons (1997b) has argued that lower security in women's prisons is feasible because the women are unlikely to abscond.

An abolitionist approach for women prisoners is unlikely to be formally adopted in the present political climate, and because it would be seen as unfair to male prisoners. However, a step towards decarceration was evident in the recommendations of the Halliday Report and the greater emphasis on community punishment in the 2003 Criminal Justice Act. There has also been a decline in the numbers being imprisoned for non-payment of fines since 1995 (see Chapter 7, section 7.3). There is now greater recognition of the need to provide differential regimes and the Government has formulated a strategy for women prisoners which recognises this (Home Office 2001e, 2004b; also section 11.5.4 below).

Although the Carter Report (2003) did not specifically focus on women prisoners, some of its recommendations, which include greater use of fines, curfews, and satellite tracking and use of conditional cautions for adults, might benefit women. It also favours more demanding community sentences. However, this also increases the risk of breach and therefore custody if fines are unpaid or conditions not met. For this reason the Corston Report recommended that we need more attention to be paid to gender-specific sanctions and disposals. Community sentences could be used more widely for women, the Report argues, and made more effective. One proposal is for a 'prostitution referral order' which would be delivered by a supervisor with particular expertise on working with women involved in prostitution. Using curfews and electronic monitoring more widely would also enable some women to be dealt with in the community. The Report is critical of sentencers who impose a custodial sentence for the women's own good, or own safety, or give access to services like detoxification when these services would be better provided in the community.

The Report also welcomes the jettisoning of intermittent custody, arguing that going into prison at weekends would be very disruptive for women with children, and more importantly that if the public do not require protection from women during the week, then they do not need to be locked up at weekends (para 5.17). Although intermittent custody was seen by the Government as particularly effective for women, there is also the danger that it might have a 'net-widening' effect, by being used on women who might not have received a custodial sentence.

A network of community centres for women could supervise community sentences and provide a range of support for offenders, including health resources, to address the underlying causes which contribute to offending behaviour. The Report made 43 recommendations on ways of improving the treatment and intervention in relation to women offenders. One proposal is that sentencers who give non-custodial community orders could review compliance, which might enhance sentencers' confidence in those sentences and would also benefit offenders themselves. More use could also be made of suspended sentences. The Report also argues that the government needs to increase public awareness of the costs of women's imprisonment. It emphasises that the indications are that the public might be less punitive towards non-violent female offenders if they are made aware of the context of offending and the impact of imprisonment and what is involved in community punishments (ibid: para 6.3.4). Campaigns to air these issues in the media have been initiated by Smart Justice for Women. The Corston recommendations are also endorsed by the Carter Report on Prisons (Carter 2007).

11.5.4 The Government's policy on women offenders

The Government published its strategy for women offenders in 2000. It emphasised the importance of improving women's access to health services and support for those using drugs, focusing on women's housing, education and employment needs, and strengthening family relationships. It accepted that 'the current system does impact differently on women and men, because women are usually the primary carer for their children, and because their small numbers in the system can mean prison places further from home' (Home Office 2000a: 1). It acknowledged the links between women's offending and social exclusion and that women offenders may be victims of abuse. It engaged in a consultation process which was published in its Consultation Report in 2001 (Home Office 2001e), following which it announced a new Women's Offending Reduction Programme (WORP) to divert women from custody. The aim was to co-ordinate efforts to deal with women's offending including efforts to deal with work, training and healthcare.

The main focus of the programme is on community-based provision for female offenders and the use of custody as a last resort. The Annual Review published in 2005 indicated that priority areas were to focus on drug misuse and mental health problems of women offenders. It noted that some progress is being made in improving the provision of women-only hostels and community-based mental health services for women, as well as improving mental health facilities for women in prison. New offending behaviour programmes for women are also being developed. More research is now being undertaken on 'what works' for women (see Sheehan *et al.* 2007). The strategy of allocating prisoners as close to home as possible continues, but obviously is limited by the small size of the estate. Young women aged 15–16 have now been removed from prison accommodation and foreign-national prisoners have been allocated to specific prisons so they will be held together and appropriate resources can be provided for them. In its *Five-Year Strategy for Protecting the Public and Reducing Re-offending* (Home Office 2005b), the Government stated that offenders who are not dangerous, violent or seriously persistent should be punished in the community. But at the same time, new prisons for women have been opened to deal with expansion of the female population and the number of women in prison has not fallen.

WORP involves several agencies and aims to reduce offending and to promote equality of treatment and access to provision drawing on the work of a range of government departments, and from the public and voluntary sectors. Its goals, as set out in the Action Plan, have included increasing opportunities to deal with offending in community programmes for women, setting up links with the National Drug Strategy and focusing on women with mental health problems, and designing accredited offending behaviour programmes specifically for women. It has also reviewed the accommodation of women with children in bail hostels and probation facilities.

A Together Women Programme was also launched in 2005 to evaluate whether a multi-agency approach to female offenders within the community could be developed, to avoid using custodial sentences for women offenders. This assessment will be concluded in 2009, but it seems likely that this route will be developed further as well as the use of women's centres for offenders and those at risk of offending. The Government will be looking at this in the light of the experience and success of these one-stop women's centres discussed in the Corston Report and in the study of community provision by Gelsthorpe *et al.* (2007) for the Fawcett Society. These centres provide a range of services and support on issues including substance abuse and domestic violence and their scope could be expanded further to incorporate work and training skills. The female prison population could also be reduced by cutting the number of remand prisoners through better bail provision, including hostels for women and children. A shift away from custody for women would also represent a substantial saving as community sentences are much cheaper. It would be consistent with the Government's wider strategy to make greater use of community sentences and to reserve custody for dangerous and highly persistent offenders.

In the past few years there have also been improvements in the management of women prisoners and a move towards recognising the specific needs of women prisoners. There is now a Women's Policy Group at Prison Service Headquarters. Offending behaviour programmes are now being designed specifically for women. There have also been improvements in temporary release and in healthcare, for example, improved therapeutic provisions and better training for staff in mother and baby units. The CARAT scheme (counselling, arrest, referral advice, and through-care services) for drug users is now in operation in all prisons and there are also intensive drug treatment programmes. Gender-specific standards are being established. Underpinning these programmes is the duty to promote gender equality, and this may have immediate practical benefit to women. For example, the implementation of Gender-Specific Standards will include access to showers, and other measures to improve hygiene.

Women prisoners may also benefit from the Human Rights Act 1998 if they are able to use Article 8 to increase access to their families and protect their right to privacy, and Article 14 if they are treated differently to male prisoners. To prove differential treatment, the applicant has to show that she was treated less favourably than others on the basis of a personal characteristic and that the person to whom he or she is comparing herself is in an analogous situation. In *Lockwood v UK* (1993) it was made clear that the relevant comparator here would be other prisoners within the prison population rather than an ordinary citizen in the community. So if women prisoners are treated differently to male prisoners in relation to other Convention rights, then they could bring a case under Article 14. For example, it could be argued that Article 8, the right to family life, is breached if women's home visits are stopped because of assumptions based on male prisoners' behaviour.

In reviewing women's imprisonment we should not lose sight of the aims of imprisonment discussed in Part A of this book. From the retributivist standpoint we should ask whether women's imprisonment in current conditions is proportionate and non-degrading. If imprisonment entails the loss of one's home and loss of contact with children as well as loss of liberty, it is arguably disproportionate and hard to justify on retributivist grounds. The Corston Review emphasised that for many women 'prison is both disproportionate and inappropriate' (Corston 2007: 1). The loss of privacy, the use of male officers and the indignities of imprisonment such as strip-searching, as we have seen, may add to the humiliation and degradation of punishment well beyond the actual loss of liberty demanded by retributivism. Given that large numbers of women entering prison have suffered physical and sexual abuse, the use of full searching is particularly upsetting. It is also hard to justify the increased use of imprisonment on grounds of incapacitation or social protection, given the fact that the majority of women are not dangerous and serve short sentences and so could be incapacitated in the community by electronic monitoring and curfews. The deterrent value of women's imprisonment is also questionable as women tend to have shorter criminal careers, although in 2002 women's reoffending rates reached the same levels as men, which raises questions about prison's deterrent value (see Chapter 4 above and Home Office 2003f). The Prison Ombudsman, Stephen Shaw, has also said that 'the current use of imprisonment reflected in Styal, Holloway and other women's prisons is disproportionate, ineffective and unkind' (Shaw 2005: 60).

Rethinking women's imprisonment and transferring women to community centres, for example, would also allow more prison places to be available for men's prisons and thereby reduce overcrowding. It would also cut the costs of imprisonment which are substantial, particularly when the ancillary costs of support to women's families are added to the calculation. There would also be longer-term benefits if supporting families prevented children being taken into care which, as we have seen, strongly correlates with future offending. The impact on children is now receiving more attention as we saw in Chapter 10. Providing more family-friendly opportunities to undertake community sentences within school hours and making arrangements for paying fines would be appropriate steps in this direction.

The most recent policy statement on women prisoners is the Government's response to the Corston Report in December 2007 (Ministry of Justice 2007b). It announced it will set up a Reducing Re-offending Inter-Ministerial Group (IMG) to provide governance to further the Corston recommendations, and a cross-departmental unit for women and criminal justice in the Ministry of Justice, to co-ordinate and monitor work undertaken to implement the Corston recommendations. It will include representatives from the Department of Health and the new Government Equalities Office. There will also be a designated ministerial 'champion' for women, Maria Eagle MP, at the Ministry of Justice who will be responsible for issues relating to women and criminal justice. Part of the strategy will be to develop community-based services and particularly women's community centres, for women who do not need to be in custody. For those who do need a secure setting, better ways of dealing with these women will be explored and particularly the recommendation regarding smaller custodial units for women. The Government accepts that custody for women should be reserved for serious and violent offenders, that community punishment should normally be used for non-violent female offenders, and that community provision should be appropriate to women's needs. It also plans to introduce gender-specific standards for women in prison in 2008, to review the future of the women's estate, to examine the merits of smaller custodial units for women, closer to home, and to set up a pilot unit. It also plans to ensure that the SGC guidelines on seriousness and drug couriers address issues relevant to the sentencing of women.

The needs of women offenders will also be considered as part of the Reducing Re-Offending Strategic Plan to be launched in Spring 2008 and published at the end of 2008. The Government accepts that custodial remands should be reduced, for example through use of tagging and the new Bail Accommodation and Support Scheme, to ensure that accommodation and support services are available for women, but it does not accept that the Bail Act should be amended, so that custodial remand should never be used in cases where it is unlikely to result in a custodial sentence. It also rejects the Corston proposals for a separate probation report on the impact of custody on dependent children, on the grounds that there are already processes in courts for this information to be provided, but will examine whether there are any gaps in providing this information. It accepts the need to improve access to drug services in the community. It has said that it will take account of the Corston Report in responding to the Carter Report (2007). The Government proposes to study whether mandatory full searching, as it is now known, is necessary in women's prisons. Women's organisations will be involved in developing policies and plans. There is a new offender management training programme for dealing with women offenders being developed by NOMS and there is also a training package being developed by the Prison Service Women and Young People's Group for staff working with women in prison.

So at a policy level, there has been considerable progress on the issue of women prisoners since the first edition of this book was published. But the Government is clear that no additional resources are currently available to implement these proposals, so it remains to be seen how rapidly or whether some of these measures will be implemented. A recent debate in the House of Lords expressed the concern of all those involved with prison reform at the slow response to the Corston Report despite accepting nearly all its recommendations (Hansard, 31 January 2008, col. 796–825). It is also hard to see why further study of the merits of smaller units is necessary when research on this is already available. There seems to be a discrepancy between the commitment to reducing offending and imprisonment of women and the commitment to strategies, including sentencing reforms, which may well increase the use of imprisonment for women as well as men. So the WORP has not been integrated with other policies currently operating in the criminal justice arena. There is also the concern that the Government's quest for cost-effective prisons will mean that secure custody centres for women will be located within the larger-scale prisons rather than closer to women's homes and on separate sites.

11.6 Black and ethnic-minority prisoners

The outcome of the processes discussed in Chapter 10, section 10.4 above is that ethnic minorities are over-represented in the prison population, relative to their proportions in the population as a whole, and this over-representation is highest in the remand population and in the female population. This is illustrated by Table 11.1.

Ethnic monitoring of the prison population began in 1984 and since then the number of ethnic-minority prisoners has steadily increased, the rate of increase being faster for black and South Asian prisoners than white prisoners. Black prisoners tend to be younger than white prisoners and in 2001 more were imprisoned for robbery and drug offences (51 per cent) compared to a third of Asian prisoners and a quarter of white prisoners (Home Office 2003f). Black prisoners are more likely to have been sentenced to longer sentences as we can see from Table 11.2.

The latest available figures show that there were 12,180 black and minority ethnic (BME) prisoners in England and Wales. They comprised 19 per cent of the

Table 11.1 Population in prison establishments by self-identified ethnic group, gender, British nationals and all nationalities, 30 June 2006

England and Wales	Ethnicity of prisoner						Total
	White	Mixed	Asian or Asian British	Black or Black British	Chinese or Other ethnic group	Not known	
British Nationals							
Males	50,645	1,723	3,092	6,653	143	460	62,715
% of total males	81	3	5	11	0	1	100
Females	2,849	141	68	344	14	30	3,445
% of total females	83	4	2	10	0	1	100
TOTAL	53,494	1,864	3,159	6,997	157	490	66,160
% of total	81	3	5	11	0	1	100
All Prisoners							
Males	53,972	2,108	5,010	10,923	873	632	73,519
% of total males	73	3	7	15	1	1	100
Females	3,165	191	107	883	81	36	4,463
% of total females	71	4	2	20	2	1	100
TOTAL	57,137	2,299	5,117	11,806	954	668	77,982
% of total	73	3	7	15	1	1	100

Source: Jones and Singer (2007: 89).

Table 11.2 Prison population by ethnic group, type of prisoner, age group, offence group and sentence length, 30 June 2006

| | Ethnicity of prisoner | | | | | | | | | | | | | |
| | White | | Mixed | | Asian or Asian British | | Black or Black British | | Chinese or Other | | Not Known | | Total | |
	N	%	N	%	N	%	N	%	N	%	N	%	N	%
Total	57,137	100	2,299	100	5,117	100	11,806	100	954	100	668	100	77,982	100
Total remand	8,837	15	454	20	1,050	21	2,327	20	211	22	189	28	13,067	17
Untried	5,295	9	291	13	699	14	1,504	13	135	14	139	21	8,064	10
Convicted unsentenced	3,541	6	162	7	350	7	822	7	76	8	51	8	5,003	6
Immediate custodial sentenced	47,892	84	1,791	78	3,736	73	8,933	76	590	62	462	69	63,404	81
Age group (sentenced)														
Aged 15–17	1,400	3	108	6	90	2	255	3	9	1	4	1	1,865	3
Aged 18–20	4,479	9	271	15	334	9	818	9	55	9	30	6	5,987	9
Aged 21–24	7,427	16	343	19	793	21	1,438	16	94	16	67	15	10,163	16
Aged 25–29	8,701	18	374	21	989	26	1,801	20	113	19	77	17	12,056	19
Aged over 30	25,885	54	695	39	1,530	41	4,621	52	318	54	284	61	33,333	53
Total	47,892	100	1,791	100	3,736	100	8,933	100	590	100	462	100	63,404	100
Offence group														
Violence against the person	12,627	26	454	25	915	24	1,937	22	129	22	154	33	16,215	26
Sexual offences	5,502	11	100	6	334	9	575	6	44	8	43	9	6,598	10
Robbery	5,945	12	355	20	466	12	1,549	17	42	7	57	12	8,415	13
Burglary	6,828	14	183	10	160	4	546	6	23	4	50	11	7,791	12
Theft and handling	3,477	7	100	6	174	5	312	3	23	4	39	8	4,125	7
Fraud and forgery	826	2	36	2	291	8	469	5	61	10	9	2	1,692	3
Drug offences	6,274	13	390	22	890	24	2,874	32	165	28	54	12	10,647	17
Motoring offences	1,535	3	39	2	141	4	181	2	5	1	19	4	1,920	3
Other offences	4,539	9	124	7	350	9	453	5	95	16	34	7	5,594	9
Not recorded	338	1	11	1	14	0	38	0	3	1	3	1	408	1
Total	47,892	100	1,791	100	3,736	100	8,933	100	590	100	462	100	63,404	100

Table 11.2 *Continued*

	White		Mixed		Asian or Asian British		Black or Black British		Chinese or Other		Not Known		Total	
	N	%	N	%	N	%	N	%	N	%	N	%	N	%
Sentence length														
Young offenders														
Less than 1 year	1,594	3	75	4	85	2	162	2	26	4	8	2	1,949	3
I year or more	4,731	10	336	19	377	10	1,004	11	41	7	31	7	6,521	10
All young offenders	6,325	13	411	23	462	12	1,165	13	68	11	39	8	8,470	13
Adults														
Less than 1 year	5,176	11	131	7	419	11	664	7	96	16	51	11	6,536	10
1 year but less than 4 years	13,780	29	402	22	955	26	1,798	20	104	18	143	31	17,181	27
4 years or more	22,610	47	848	47	1,901	51	5,306	59	322	55	229	50	31,217	49
All adults	41,567	87	1,380	77	3,274	88	7,768	87	522	89	423	92	54,934	87
Total	47,892	100	1,791	100	3,736	100	8,933	100	590	100	462	100	63,404	100

Source: Jones and Singer (2007: 90).

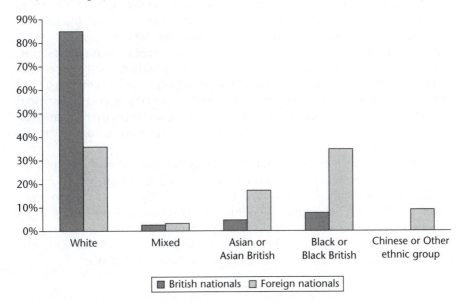

Figure 11.3 Immediate custodial-sentenced receptions by nationality and percentage ethnic group, 2006
Source: Ministry of Justice (2007a: 78)

British National population: 11 per cent black or black British, 5 per cent Asian or Asian British and 3 per cent mixed ethnic group (Ministry of Justice 2007a: 2).

Taking a snapshot of prisons in England and Wales on 30 June 2006, 26 per cent of the prison population came from ethnic groups other than white (Jones and Singer 2007: 90), 11,806 prisoners were black or black British, which amounted to 15 per cent of the total prison population, 5,117 (or 7 per cent) were Asian or Asian British, and 2,922 (4 per cent) were from the mixed ethnic group (ibid).

In June 2006 black and minority ethnic groups were 26 per cent of the male prison population and 28 per cent of the female prison population (ibid: xvii). Foreign nationals comprised 15 per cent of the male prison population and 23 per cent of the female prison population but 40 per cent of the BME prison population (ibid: 87). There were also higher proportions of all minority ethnic groups than white groups held on remand. The statistics also show variations in sentence length for different ethnic groups. Examining the figures for adult offenders, we find 59 per cent of black offenders, 55 per cent of Chinese/other offenders, 51 per cent of Asian offenders and 47 per cent of both white and mixed offenders were serving sentences of 4 years or more. This reflects to some extent differences in types of offence and their seriousness. So 32 per cent of black prisoners, 28 per cent of Chinese/Other, 24 per cent of Asian prisoners, and 14 per cent of white prisoners were serving sentences for drugs offences which attract longer sentences (ibid: 88).

A large proportion of ethnic minority prisoners are foreign nationals, defined as non-UK passport holders. In 2006, 9,380 foreign-national prisoners were received under immediate custodial sentence, which represents a 186 per cent increase since 1996. In the early 1990s the largest group was Nigerian nationals, but now the largest single group is Jamaican nationals (25 per cent of the group). Over half of the group are from six countries, Jamaica, the Irish Republic, Nigeria, India, Pakistan, and Turkey. The total group includes 168 nationalities. The group also includes Western Europeans, including large numbers of Dutch nationals, involved in the higher levels of the drugs trade, whereas the female foreign-national prisoners are mostly drug couriers. 47 per cent of foreign-national prisoners are imprisoned for drug offences, mainly drug trafficking, 43 per cent of foreign-national men and 79 per cent of foreign-national women, compared to 13 per cent of British-national sentenced men, and 29 per cent of British sentenced women. 60 per cent of foreign nationals are serving sentences over 4 years. The foreign national prison population includes children under the age of 18 and remand prisoners.

As well as ethnic diversity, we find a wide range of religious beliefs held by prisoners. About 33 per cent of prisoners have no religious affiliation, 30 per cent are Anglicans, 17 per cent are Catholic and 11 per cent are Muslim. The prison population also includes adherents of Buddhism and Paganism. 71 per cent of Asian prisoners are Muslim and the issues raised by their imprisonment are now receiving more attention. More research is now being undertaken on the particular problems of Muslim prisoners (see Spalek 2002, Beckford *et al.* 2005).

11.7 **The experience of imprisonment**

11.7.1 **Less favourable treatment?**

Of course the Prison Service has no part in sentencing decisions, so it cannot control the numbers entering prison, but it has a duty to ensure that ethnic minority prisoners do not receive less favourable treatment on grounds of race or ethnic origins and to ensure justice inside prisons. The Statement of Purpose of the Prison Service declares a commitment to promoting diversity and equality of opportunity, and combating unlawful discrimination. Yet it has been argued that black and minority ethnic groups in prison have been subject to a racist bias in the allocation of work, training and education, in the type of work allocated, in terms of promotion of inmates to positions of responsibility, in their treatment by officers, and that they continue to experience racial abuse and harassment. The lowest provision of work and education is in remand prisons where ethnic minorities are a sizeable proportion of the population. Both the former and current Director General of the Prison Service have acknowledged that the Prison Service is institutionally racist and has pockets of blatant racism (HM Prison Service 2004: Appendix 5, 15). This also features in prisoners' reports of their experiences in prison (see HM Inspectorate of Prisons 2005a; section 11.9.2 below). These issues also affect ethnic minority staff and ethnic minorities are under-represented in prison staff and on Independent Monitoring Boards.

Research on racism in prisons was undertaken in the 1980s by Genders and Player (1989) as well as by Chigwada (1989) and McDermott (1990) and in the 1990s by Fitzgerald and Marshall (1996). However, the Woolf Report said virtually nothing on racism, and referred only to the erratic compliance of establishments with the race relations policy, the need for more progress, and the failure of some prisoners to monitor race relations properly. Recent studies and investigations have been completed by NACRO (2000a, 2003g), the Commission for Racial Equality (2003), HM Inspectorate of Prisons (2005a, 2006), Cheliotis and Liebling (2005), the Prison Reform Trust (2006) and the Mubarek Inquiry (Keith 2006), all of which have highlighted continuing areas of concern and made recommendations for improvement.

Racism may be direct and overt, expressed in attitudes and behaviour. Areas of discretion within the administration of the prison regime allow more opportunity for racism to be activated expressly in decisions by officers. Racism may also be indirect in failing to take account of the social context of factors which may be relevant to offenders' behaviour in prison, and overlooking the disparate effect of apparently neutral policies. It may be institutionalised in the sense that it is embedded in the culture and practices and policies of institutions and agencies. Earlier studies of racism in prisons have found evidence of direct racism but recent work suggests that racism may be more subtle covert racism or be embedded in the culture and practices of the institution, that is, institutional racism.

11.7.2 **Work, training and discipline**

The allocation of work is an area where discretion may be exercised by supervisors. Twenty years ago Genders and Player (1989) interviewed staff and prisoners and observed prison life. They found prison officers using negative racial stereotypes and expressing negative comments about race relations policies whilst the majority of ethnic-minority prisoners interviewed thought that there was a problem of racism in prison, even if they had not experienced problems themselves. The researchers highlighted various practices used by work supervisors to circumvent formal procedures and to exercise discretion and concluded that 'racial discrimination is intrinsic to the social organisation of prisons' (Genders and Player 1989: 131). For example, they found differential treatment in the allocation of work in the prisons, based on racial stereotypes. White prisoners were more likely to be found in the better jobs while ethnic minorities were over-represented in the least popular jobs and more likely to be unemployed. Their research suggested a use of stereotypes, with black prisoners seen as unsuitable for education and training because of a negative attitude to authority and to work.

Genders and Player (ibid) also found differences in assessment reports on those prisoners reported for disciplinary offences. They found evidence of some prison officers demonstrating high-level racist assumptions. A common assumption among white officers was that black prisoners were lazy, arrogant, hostile and paranoid about racism, while Asian prisoners were seen as well-behaved and submissive. Genders and Player found that officers were more likely to take disciplinary action against black prisoners and that they saw black prisoners as harder to manage because they were hostile to authority.

Genders and Player concluded that racist attitudes were part of the occupational culture of officers, reflecting their isolation and the dangerousness of the occupation, which makes such occupations vulnerable to stereotyping. Other researchers at that time found similar problems. Chigwada (1989) interviewed black women in prison who believed that they were treated differently on account of their race in relation to the allocation of work and access to education, where priority was given to white women, and who thought that they were more likely to have their privileges withdrawn for minor matters. There was also an assumption amongst officers that black women need more supervision, because they were trouble makers and harder to control, which had implications for their treatment.

McDermott (1990), in a study of five male adult prisons in the period 1985–9, found no statistically significant differences in access to education and vocational training programmes, in fact ethnic minorities were over-represented in these programmes and viewed them favourably. But they were under-represented in 'trusted' jobs such as prison orderlies. She also found that the black prisoners in her sample were more likely to be the subject of disciplinary charges and for the vaguer offences of disobeying orders or being disrespectful. They believed racism was a significant factor in these decisions. The perception of some officers was that black prisoners are anti-authority and disruptive.

These studies were undertaken some time ago but more recent studies, such as that undertaken by NACRO (2000a), found that black prisoners were the least satisfied regarding access to work, compared to Asian and white prisoners, but were happier than white prisoners over access to education. Black prisoners also complained that black visitors were more likely to be searched than others. A study of prisoners' perceptions of race relations in prison was also conducted by Cheliotis and Liebling (2005), using surveys of 4,860 prisoners in 49 establishments in England and Wales, and large proportions of the ethnic minority groups thought they were subject to unfair treatment compared to the white majority.

Since the late 1980s, the level of awareness on the part of the prison management of the problem of racism in prison has increased with various race relations policies being formulated (see section 11.8 below). Following the case of *Alexander v Home Office* in 1988 the ruling was circulated in all prisons and the case discussed in training. The court found that Alexander had been unlawfully discriminated against when he applied for work in the prison kitchen at Parkhurst and that he was refused work on racist grounds. The decision to allocate work was based on a report containing negative and racist comments. This was the first successful reported case brought by a prisoner under the Race Relations Act (RRA) 1976.

Today there is more scope to bring an action as a case can now be brought under the Human Rights Act 1998 (see Chapter 9, section 9.6.3) and the RRA 1976 has itself been amended and its scope broadened (see section 11.1.2 above). It is made clear in the latest Prison Service Orders and Instructions that allocation to accommodation, work, training and education must be made on a non-discriminatory basis.

The Prison Inspectorate conducted a review of race relations in prison, which was published in December 2005 (HM Inspectorate of Prisons 2005a). Their findings were based on a review of survey material from 5,500 prisoners from all ethnic groups and consultations with white and visible-minority staff, governors, managers and prisoners, including black, Asian and mixed-race prisoners, women, young offenders and juveniles and foreign-national prisoners, in 18 prisons. The Review found that, instead of a shared understanding of race issues within prisons, there are a series of 'parallel worlds' with different groups of staff and prisoners having quite different views and experiences. Prisoners were asked about direct experiences of racism. Visible-minority prisoners were more negative than white prisoners across the four key areas of safety, respect, purposeful activity and resettlement. Most thought that racism existed, particularly in relation to differential access to the prison regime and treatment by staff, for example the way in which they were spoken to or searched, the way requests were dealt with or how long they waited for things that they needed. However, young black prisoners were more positive than adult black prisoners. However, in one area of prison life, education and training, black and Asian prisoners were more likely to positively value education than white prisoners. This was confirmed in their most recent report (HM Chief Inspector of Prisons 2008). This report also found prisoners continuing to refer to covert racism in the form of 'favouritism' and 'subtle prejudice' (ibid: 27).

11.7.3 Racial harassment

A further problem highlighted in recent studies is the problem of racial harassment by both staff and other prisoners. If a prisoner wants to complain about racism, he or she can use the ordinary complaints procedure, the special local incident form, or can complain directly to the Commission for Equality and Human Rights (the Commission) who can advise and support complainants, and also the prisoner could complain to the Ombudsman. The definition of a racist incident is 'any incident which is perceived to be racist by the victim or any other person', as used in the Macpherson Report (Macpherson 1999). However, despite the formal procedures available, prisoners may be reluctant to complain for fear of being seen as trouble-makers or causing trouble for themselves or because they do not believe that their complaint will be taken seriously (see NACRO 2000a; HM Inspector of Prisons 2005a; Keith 2006).

A report on Brixton in 2000 by the Race Relations Advisor was very critical of the bullying and harassment of ethnic-minority prisoners, the fact that punishment was used disproportionately against black prisoners, without the knowledge of senior managers, and the bullying of ethnic-minority staff and prisoners. Clements (2000) found evidence of racial harassment, abuse and racist language.

In other prisons, ethnic-minority prisoners have been the target of racist abuse and violence and there are some indications that these incidents of harassment have been under-reported, because of concerns that they will not be taken seriously or that complainants will be seen as troublemakers. Racist abuse in Wormwood Scrubs was the subject of a report in 1999 and the CRE has investigated racism at Brixton, Parc and Feltham. It conducted a full investigation into racism in the Prison Service, with reference to the need to eliminate unlawful racial discrimination and the need to promote equality of opportunity. The CRE examined the nature and frequency of incidents of racial discrimination, the way they are investigated and the circumstances leading to the murder of Zahid Mubarek. It examined events between mid 1991 and July 2000 in Brixton Prison, between 1998 and July 2000 in Parc Prison, and between January 1996 and November 2000 in Feltham Young Offenders Institution, in the light of reports and evidence suggesting acts of discrimination. The CRE was very critical of the Prison Service's failure to protect Mubarek and its failure to eliminate discrimination.

The CRE found the Prison Service guilty of racial discrimination at Feltham, Parc and Brixton (Commission for Racial Equality 2003). The Report made 17 findings of unlawful racial discrimination against the Prison Service, most of which relate to individual cases. These findings related to the general atmosphere of the prison, the treatment of staff and prisoners, access to goods, services, and facilities; control of the use of discretion, disciplinary matters, and the Incentives and Earned Privileges Schemes; access to work, investigation of complaints, protection from victimisation, and management procedures. Although it has the power to issue a non-discrimination notice, instead the CRE entered into a dialogue with the Prison Service to develop an Action Plan, *Implementing Race Equality: A Shared Strategy for Change,* to deal with these problems (see section 11.8 below, HM Prison Service/ CRE 2003). It also published a review of race relations in prison in December 2005. The CRE has been monitoring the progress of the initiatives in the Action Plan. It is hoped that the Commission for Equality and Human Rights will take on this role. A new Prison Service Order on Race Equality was issued in 2006 to further the pursuit of race equality and to implement the race equality duty (PSO 2800).

The Prison Rules include new disciplinary offences of racially aggravated assault and racially aggravated damage to or destruction of any part of prison or other property, and insulting behaviour. They are directed at the behaviour of prisoners rather than staff or visitors. If an offence is committed in prison and there is clear evidence of racial motivation, then the case for referral to the police is strengthened or if the victim requests a police investigation (*Discipline Manual*: Appendix 3, para 7). Racially aggravated and racist offences, which include assault, damage or destruction of property, threatening, abusive or insulting racist words or behaviour, and displaying any threatening, abusive or insulting racist material, are specified in the *Prison Discipline Manual* (HM Prison Service 1995b: 6.9997, 6.9998, see also PSI 51/2000). If an offence is racially aggravated, this will be reflected in the punishment. It will be deemed to be racially aggravated if the offender demonstrates towards the victim a hostility based on the victim's membership of a racial group, or is motivated by hostility to members of a racial group, based on membership of that group.

In addition a violence reduction strategy has been introduced by the Prison Service with all individual prisons now obliged to develop local strategy to reduce violence and create a culture of non-violence amongst prisoners (PSO 2750) as well as an anti-bullying strategy (PSI 51/1999) so there are procedures to deal with bullying when perpetrators have been identified, although the issue in the Mubarek case was the failure to identify the risk.

Victimisation, racism and harassment are problems which affect ethnic minority officers as well as prisoners. Because of their numbers, they may feel isolated and may be more likely to suffer victimisation and harassment (McDermott 1990). Some black staff in McDermott's sample found that the other white officers caused them more problems than the prisoners, and they found it difficult when white staff were making racist comments to prisoners in front of them, making them feel both visible and invisible. A lukewarm approach to dealing with racist incidents gives a message that black officers have to learn to deal with racism rather than expecting the authorities to eliminate racism.

A new support network, RESPECT, was set up in 2001 to improve working conditions of black and minority ethnic staff and to support staff who have been victims of racism. The Prison Reform Trust (2006) surveyed and interviewed members of RESPECT in 2004–6 and found that 61 per cent of the staff interviewed believed that they had experienced racial discrimination including isolation, harassment, verbal abuse, and mostly from their colleagues rather than from prisoners or managers. Their respondents reported that they thought that blatant overt racism was becoming less common but covert racism and institutional racism were more serious problems. Two-thirds of the BME staff in the PRT survey thought that institutional racism remained a problem, particularly in relation to career development and promotion and grievance procedures, with promotion hindered by subtle discrimination. There was also a lack of confidence among BME staff in procedures for dealing with complaints about racism: covert racism may be harder to prove and investigators are likely to be senior white officers. It may be that a less formal and less legalistic procedure, such as mediation, may be more effective especially as this would mean complainants take a more active role in proceedings. This study also highlights the problem with lack of adequate training in diversity and cultural racism.

11.7.4 Deaths in custody

There have also been instances of murders by other prisoners where there is a clear racist motive. Zahid Mubarek was murdered in Feltham Young Offenders Institution in March 2000. While sleeping he was clubbed into a coma by his cellmate, Robert Stewart, using part of the furniture in his cell, and died later in hospital. Prior to the murder Stewart had written racist letters and threatened to kill his cellmate. It was clear that Stewart had a personality disorder and deeply entrenched racist beliefs and had already been charged, under the Protection from Harassment Act 1997, with racially motivated malicious communications. The conditions in Feltham had also been criticised by the then Chief Inspector of Prisons, David Ramsbotham.

The Formal Investigation of the Commission for Racial Equality into the murder of Mubarek was highly critical of failures on the part of the prison to spot the potential risk and to protect Mubarek from Stewart, or to follow up warnings in Stewart's file, as well as failures to follow Prison Service Orders and failures by senior managers to give priority to race issues (Commission for Racial Equality 2003). It found 20 areas of failure which, it argued, allowed Stewart to progress to murder; if any of them had been dealt with, it would have prevented Mubarek's death. It was clear from Stewart's letters what would happen, yet these were either not read or, if read, not acted upon. A public inquiry on the Mubarek case, chaired by Mr Justice Keith, set up in May 2004 and reported in 2006, focused attention on the wider culture and practice of the Prison Service, just as the Macpherson Inquiry highlighted problems within the police.

In its submission to the second phase of the Mubarek Inquiry, the CRE reviewed the progress of the Prison Service in achieving the goals in the Action Plan. A Race and Equalities Action Group in the Prison Service has been set up to oversee the implementation of the Action Plan and to ensure proactive promotion of race equality, and to take account of any possibility of discrimination in those policies. Areas for immediate attention were identified and incorporated in the Prison Service Race Equality Scheme for 2005–8.

The Prison Service has developed procedures for carrying out race equality impact assessments and introduced performance targets for race equality including staff recruitment. There are also training schemes for staff carrying out impact assessments, and a new system of consultation with prisoners, staff and local communities on race equality issues.

In its submission the CRE acknowledged the efforts being made to address the problems highlighted by the death of Zahid Mubarek but found that there was still evidence of poor practice. For example, it expressed concern about the procedures for complaints and reporting of racist incidents and noted that prisoners said they felt inhibited in making complaints because their reports were read by officers.

A later study by the Prison Inspectorate (2005a) found this was still the case. So while the formal policies to promote race equality and challenge racism were certainly evident, they were not always being implemented and managers needed to be aware of what was actually happening on the wing (Commission for Racial Equality 2005). An inquiry was set up to examine the measures which need to be taken to prevent the recurrence of such a tragedy and the Report was published in 2006. There has also been a further similar incident, namely the murder of an Asian prisoner, Shahid Aziz, by his white cellmate, Peter McCann, in HMP Leeds in 2004. McCann had been classified as low risk, but the inquest was critical of the failure to pass on relevant information to the prison.

In addition to the issues raised by the deaths of Shahid Aziz and Zahid Mubarek, there is concern over deaths in custody following the use of physical restraints, and whether such deaths are properly investigated, for example, the Alton Manning case referred to earlier (Chapter 9, section 9.5.1).[4] As well as deaths from excessive restraint, there have been instances of deaths arising from inadequate medical treatment or failure to recognise or diagnose a medical condition. Deaths in custody now fall within the remit of the Prisons and Probation Ombudsman. They may also form the basis of an Article 2 [EHR] claim against the Prison Service.

[4] See *R v DPP ex p Manning* (2001).

11.7.5 **The Report of the Mubarek Inquiry**

The Mubarek Report was published in June 2006 and reflected similar concerns to the CRE Report (Keith 2006). Although it focused on Feltham, where the murder occurred, many of the issues raised apply across the prison estate. The Inquiry investigated whether the events which led to Stewart and Mubarek sharing a cell, despite what was known about Stewart, were attributable to a collective organisational failure which was informed by the institutional racism of Feltham. The two major issues raised were the problems with enforced cell sharing and the failure to pass on information which might have prevented the attack. The Report argues for an end to enforced cell sharing to reduce the risk of prisoner-on-prisoner attacks, that a date should be set for achieving this goal and extra funds provided from government for this purpose. Single cells would prevent tensions escalating between prisoners as well as increasing privacy. While sharing might be desirable, for example, where there is a risk of suicide or self-harm, in most cases it should be avoided. There should also be published guidelines for officers to use in allocating prisoners to shared cells and for dealing with requests to share with particular individuals, and prisoners should be interviewed to explain any preferences for the type of prisoner with whom they would prefer to share. Moreover, the suitability of particular prisoners for sharing should be reviewed regularly in consultation with the prisoners' personal officers.

The other major issue in the failure to prevent the attack was the failure to pass on information about Stewart to Feltham, and within the prison, particularly about his racism, his possible involvement in a murder at another YOI, and his disruptive behaviour in other institutions. The Report recommends that information on the facts of offences or charges should be stored on the new national database for offenders, the National Offender Management Information System (NOMIS). Cell-sharing risk assessments should also be added to the online database, so that prisoners who might constitute risks to others, because of their racist views or other issues, can be clearly identified. Reasons should also be given if prisoners are transferred so that prisons can be warned if there are any problems and files should be transferred with prisoners. If a prisoner arrives without a copy of the cell-sharing risk assessment form, then he should be placed in a single cell until it is found, or a new one is completed. Risk assessments of prisoners should be reviewed regularly involving representatives from the prisoner's wing, healthcare and from the team responsible for implementing the prison's violence reduction strategy. The emphasis in the Report is on closer scrutiny and assessment of all prisoners, using OASys.

Mr Justice Keith recommended a review of training to improve and develop interpersonal skills. It is also noted that some of the establishments visited in the course of the inquiry did not have a full Personal Officer Scheme in place because of a lack of resources, with a landing officer instead taking on the role. Other recommendations in the Mubarek Report include the suggestion that the cell-searching policy be reviewed to increase the chance of finding concealed weapons in cells as it was clear that in Feltham full cell searches were not taking place on the unit. The Report also found that the care of prisoners suffering from mental health problems at the time of Mubarek murder was poor (see Chapter 7).

What emerges clearly from the Report is that attacks on prisoners in their cells by other prisoners are more likely to happen in prisons which are not functioning well and the concern is, as he points out, that 'population pressures and understaffing can combine to undermine the decency agenda and compromise the Prison Service's ability to run prisons efficiently' (Keith 2006: para 63.7). One important recommendation made is that diversity training for officers should emphasise the need for staff to put themselves in the position of black and minority ethnic prisoners and give them techniques to do so. The Mubarek inquiry and other studies (HM Inspectorate of Prisons 2005a; Prison Reform Trust 2006) have found a lack of insight on the part of officers into how a black or Asian prisoner might feel about sharing a cell with a white racist. The Report also recommended that the Prison Service, the Chief Inspector of Prisons and the CRE should consider whether there is a need for complaints of racism or other serious complaints to be dealt with by an independent body, or by introducing an independent element. Moreover, Race Relations Liaison Officers (RRLOs) could also be recruited from outside the prison services, from specialists in equality and diversity.

The Government has accepted many of the recommendations in the Mubarek Report in full or in part and they have been incorporated within the Race Equality Action Plan (Home Office 2006c). By the time the Report was published many of the issues had already begun to be addressed, for example issues relating to the flow of information, and the broader issues of race equality have been moved forward by the Race Equality Plan. The Government accepted in principle that enforced cell sharing should end but has said that it will continue for some time due to population pressures and that diverting resources to this objective would have an adverse effects on other efforts to improve prison standards. Since 2006, of course, the problem of cell sharing has persisted with the prison population reaching record levels. The Government also accepts in part that there should be an independent element built in to investigations of complaints of racism and that RRLOs should be recruited from outside as well as within the Prison Service and such appointments have already been made in some prisons.

11.7.6 Foreign-national prisoners

As well as considering the experience of women and ethnic-minority prisoners, we also need to consider the position of foreign-national prisoners who constitute 14 per cent of prisoners in England and Wales. The percentage of sentenced male and female foreign nationals broken down by region is given in Figures 11.4 and 11.5.

As can be seen, a large percentage of male foreign-national receptions in 2006 were from Europe (36 per cent), 26 per cent from Africa and 18 per cent from Asia. The distribution of female foreign-national receptions in prison in 2006 was 34 per cent from Africa, 28 per cent from Europe and 19 per cent from Asia.

The increase in the number of foreign-national prisoners is not confined to the UK, but is found throughout Western Europe, where there are increasing numbers of foreign-national prisoners, sentenced for migration-related and drug-trafficking crimes. The percentage of foreign-national prisoners in the prison population as a whole has increased from 7.8 per cent in 1993 to 14 per cent in 2007. About a quarter of foreign-national prisoners are serving sentences for drugs offences which attract longer sentences, even for first convictions, compared to 12 per cent of UK national prisoners. In the UK, asylum seekers who have not committed offences are no longer held in prison. However, convicted prisoners who have ended their

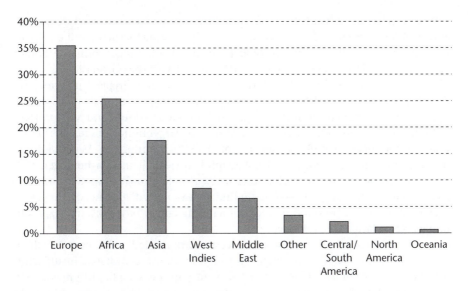

Figure 11.4 Percentage of male foreign nationals receiving immediate custodial-sentenced receptions by region, 2006

Source: Ministry of Justice (2007a: 79).

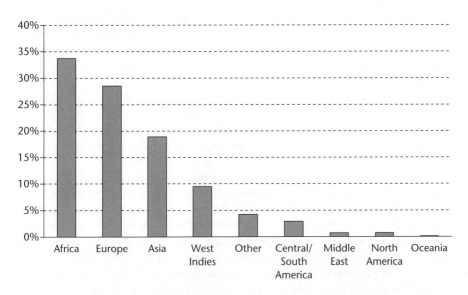

Figure 11.5 Percentage of female foreign nationals receiving immediate custodial-sentenced receptions by region, 2006

Source: Ministry of Justice (2007a: 79).

sentences may be held in prison rather than immigration detention centres, while they await deportation or decisions on asylum or their immigration status, with limited access to telephones and lawyers. The number of prisoners from the Caribbean has fallen with heavier scanning at airports there, but the number from West Africa is increasing.

Foreign nationals constitute a large proportion of women prisoners in the UK and experience real problems of isolation and of providing for their families. These women experience deprivations through problems of obtaining information about visiting rights in their own language, and problems with the prison diet.

The policy now is to concentrate foreign-national prisoners in particular prisons, principally Bullwood Hall and Canterbury, while foreign nationals make up 60 per cent of the population in the Verne, an adult men's prison, and Morton Hall holds female foreign-national prisoners. While the larger minorities may be better provided for, there are problems for the smaller ethnic minorities. As with ethnic minority prisoners generally, it is not helpful to treat them as a homogeneous group when they represent a diverse range of people, drawn from 172 different groups, with a wide range of needs including, for example, dietary needs. However, they may also share common problems, including family problems, immigration problems and language problems.

There are particular concerns over access to translation facilities (HM Chief Inspector of Prisons 2001) and their low use when they are available. Insufficient information in their own language and difficulty in speaking English may affect access to work and participation in offending behaviour programmes which will also have implications for parole, or in resettlement programmes, and mean problems in accessing lawyers or understanding the English legal system, or negotiating immigration.

The Prison Service does provide information in 22 languages but this does not extend to minority languages within the foreign-national population. A Foreign National Prisoners Handbook is given to prisoners at induction. Foreign nationals may be isolated by language problems, they may also have problems arranging legal representation and difficulties contacting home. There have been some improvements with better arrangements to make cheap calls home, but better access to airmail letters is needed. The basic entitlement is still only a free 5-minute phone call once a month and any additional calls are very expensive. When prison resources are stretched because of the increasing demands for prison places, considered earlier, their needs may be less likely to be addressed.

Many of the problems faced by women prisoners, such as separation from their families, considered above, are exacerbated for foreign-national prisoners, especially for those serving long sentences, who find it difficult to keep in contact with their families and, if they do, have to deal with family problems from a distance by phone (Caddle and Crisp 1997; HM Inspectorate of Prisons 2006). Many suffer from mental and physical health problems, especially as some foreign-national prisoners have experienced abuse and torture abroad, and these health problems may be affected by their isolation. The Wedderburn Report (Prison Reform Trust 2000) recommended that there should be a review of policy issues raised by foreign national women prisoners serving long sentences. There is currently no specific Prison Service policy for these prisoners.

There have been some recent improvements—for example, a new scheme to deport prisoners earlier, subject to risk assessments, in line with arrangements under the home detention curfew for UK nationals, was introduced in June 2004. Foreign-national prisoners are now being concentrated in fewer prisons to improve the management and care of these prisoners. Further improvements to the lives of these prisoners could be achieved by several measures, for example, increasing cultural awareness of their particular needs and problems. Their lives could also be improved by greater access to letters and telephone calls, especially for those with no contacts in the UK.

What is also needed is a distinct policy strategy for the treatment and provision of services for foreign-national prisoners in each prison, separate from race relations policies, as each raises different issues. A separate policy for foreign-national prisoners would be better able to achieve equality for them. Improved training of staff, better provision of information and more appropriate programmes are also recommended. Some reformers favour a review of sentencing guidelines for drug couriers, to take account of the welfare of the prisoners' dependent children. A new Prison Service Order setting out standards and requirements for treatment and how they will be monitored is also recommended. A new PSO on Foreign National Prisoners Liable to Deportation has been issued but it is primarily concerned with improving procedures rather than general conditions (PSO 6000 28/2006). Greater use could be made of electronic monitoring to cut the numbers on remand, or to deal with those awaiting immigration decisions.

While special treatment for foreign-national prisoners might raise concerns that British-national prisoners will be disadvantaged, the purpose of these measures would be to place them in the same position as British-national prisoners in their access to services and resources, rather than giving preferential treatment, although this argument might currently carry little weight.

A review of foreign-national prisoners was undertaken by the Prison Inspectorate in 2006, focusing on prisons outside London (HM Inspectorate of Prisons 2006). At the time of their research there were approximately 10,000 foreign-national prisoners, 13 per cent of the prison population as a whole, drawn from 172 different countries, but with Jamaicans and Nigerians constituting the largest groups. They found that foreign-national prisoners' key concerns related to family matters, particularly maintaining family links, language problems and immigration issues. Those prisoners who did not speak English experienced the greatest problems in access to resources. Although the staff they interviewed also recognised that these were the key areas, they did not consider them as serious as the prisoners interviewed did, and they were unsure how to respond to the problems. Language problems were a particular issue for prisoners from Vietnam, China, the Middle East and Eastern Europe, while family and immigration problems were a particular issue for women prisoners.

Prisoners also experienced racism, negative stereotyping and disrespectful treatment, and resettlement problems, and had less contact with personal officers. Negative perceptions of women offenders as negligent mothers may be focused on foreign-national women who have left their children behind to carry drugs. The problems often overlapped as prisoners dealing with immigration issues may lack the language skills to obtain the necessary information from appropriate sources or to access resources within the prison. Foreign-national prisoners receive fewer visits than other prisoners. Black and minority ethnic foreign-national prisoners reported worse experiences than white foreign-national prisoners, particularly in relation to racism and religious observance. All staff interviewed wanted more training and guidance on foreign-national issues.

The Review also found low awareness of available services, for example interpreters, outside agencies or FNP (foreign-national prisoners) co-ordinators. Although

Hibiscus and the Citizens Advice Bureau gave some general information to prisoners, there was insufficient independent specialist advice on individuals' immigration problems. There was a marked lack of co-ordination between the Immigration and Nationality Directorate (now the Border and Immigration Agency, BIA) and the Prison Service which meant that some prisoners were still in prison after completing their sentence, despite a revised PSO intended to improve liaison between them, and adding to the problem of overcrowding. There was considerable confusion and ignorance among staff on how to support or inform prisoners awaiting deportation. There was also very little contact with home countries on resettlement issues, despite the current emphasis on end-to-end offender management. However, they did find examples of good practice in some prisons, for example the support given by the pressure group Hibiscus, now part of the Female Prisoners' Welfare Project, which helps prisoners in the UK and liaises with contacts overseas, but there were no consistency or co-ordination between the Prison Service and other agencies.

The Review therefore strongly recommended that NOMS and the Prison Service introduce national standards for treatment of foreign-national prisoners, and a national strategy and policy for their treatment and support, which prioritises the issues of family contact, immigration and language. Better procedures are needed for identification of foreign-national prisoners, better support regarding these key needs of family links, immigration and language. It argues that foreign-national strategies should be embedded within a wider diversity strategy and diversity training should include awareness of the needs of and attitudes towards foreign national prisoners. Although they may share common problems, they are also a diverse group with important differences within the group. The Review advocates better links with the immigration service and better support inside prison and on departure from prison to enable speedier decision making. Each prison should have a named immigration officer to whom inquiries could be directed. In addition, prisoners could be given more practical support to maintain contact with their families and make greater use of telephone interpreting services, for example.

As we saw in Chapter 1 the issue of foreign-national prisoners has moved up the political agenda and there have been some recent changes. The SGC Guidance on drug couriers will be taking account of particular issues raised by female offenders. There is now a Prison Transfer Agreement between the UK and Jamaica, so some low risk prisoners may be returned to Jamaica to serve their sentence and negotiations are ongoing with Nigeria and Ghana to set up similar arrangements. A Facilitated Returns Scheme was also set up in October 2006 to provide financial assistance for prisoners liable to deportation home. In addition, following the criticism of delays in handling deportation cases before prisoners' release dates, this process has now been accelerated.[5] The focus has been on dealing with these prisoners primarily as an immigration issue and setting up targets for removal from the UK. But there is still no specific policy or strategy for the treatment of these prisoners within prison. A follow-up study by the Prison Inspectorate in January 2007 found continuing problems. As political pressures on the government to locate 'missing' prisoners and speed up deportation intensified, there was also increased anxiety

---

[5] The procedures relating to immigration and foreign nationals in prison were revised in PSO 4630, 17/07/2006 and PSI 21/2007.

amongst prisoners over their future and a higher incidence of self-harm. Prisoners were being moved from open to closed conditions and there were still delays in processing because of the pressure on the immigration authorities dealing with these cases (HM Inspectorate of Prisons 2007a). In 2007 23 foreign-national prisoners committed suicide, a large proportion of 92 suicides in that year.

Although fewer foreign nationals have been held in prison after completing their sentences, and many have been moved to Immigration Removal Centres (IRCs), the problems they face persist and the IRCs have experienced their own problems of disorder. However, the Inspectorate did find some improvement in immigration casework in 2007 (HM Chief Inspector of Prisons 2008). They also found that the majority of prisons inspected (80 per cent) did have a foreign-national strategy—a dramatic increase compared to a few years ago—but often lacked an implementation strategy and still lacked national or regional guidance.

11.8 Race relations policies in the Prison Service

11.8.1 Guidance and compliance

As we have seen, a number of problems facing black and minority ethnic prisoners and staff have been identified. Various designed to address some of these issues have been introduced. The Prison Service was one of the first criminal justice bodies to collect data on ethnic minorities and the first to develop a race relations policy, although it has been criticised for failing to develop an effective anti-racist strategy. It was also the first public sector organisation to impose a ban on staff affiliated with known racist groups, such as the British National Party, and operates a strict policy of intolerance and dismissal for unacceptable behaviour. In 2003–4, 26 of these cases proceeded to formal disciplinary hearings, 7 of which led to dismissal and 15 to other outcomes, including written warnings (HM Prison Service 2004).

The Home Office instituted a review of prison race relations work in 1981, then issued a Circular on Race Relations to all establishments which said race relations problems were rare, but this was an area of sensitivity and gave advice on race relations work, emphasising the need to obtain more information on ethnic minorities and the importance of equal treatment. Governors were required to appoint Race Relations Liaison Officers (RRLOs) to provide and collect information.

McDermott (1990) examined the impact of the race relations policy in the late 1980s. She found that the majority of prisoners in her sample saw relationships between staff and prisoners as good, although ethnic minorities were more likely to see staff as unfair, racist and disrespectful. The staff interviewed were more positive than the prisoners about staff–prisoner relations. Very few thought their colleagues were racist, although this was perceived as more of a problem in prisons with larger proportions of ethnic-minority prisoners. One-third of staff wanted more race relations training, others were resistant to this, not seeing it as necessary, but rather as reverse discrimination. The ethnic-minority officers in McDermott's study felt isolated and marginalised by both staff and prisoners, and said that black prisoners see them as part of the establishment, while white prisoners see them as having 'a chip on their shoulder'.

The Woolf Inquiry received complaints of discrimination, and complaints have been made regularly to the CRE. The Woolf Report said little on race relations but commented that they were an insidious problem for the Prison Service of which it is aware: 'But there are still grounds for concern. The evidence suggests that the compliance by prison establishments with the race relations policies is erratic. The monitoring returns from prisons indicate that there remains a significant proportion of prisons which fails to provide adequate details of equal opportunity provisions' (Woolf and Tumim 1991: para 12.140).

The *Race Relations Manual* for the Prison Service was first published in 1991 and subsequently amended. The Manual published more detailed guidance and policies on matters including responsibility for implementing the race relations policy, measuring progress, and training. Pocket books were issued to all staff. Research carried out by the CRE and Prison Service in 1995 led to a revised Prison Service Order on race relations and a new Manual in 1997. An Advisory Group on Race was set up and met outside bodies such as the CRE and NACRO and, following their advice, strengthened the role of Race Relations Liaison Officers (RRLOs) and Race Relations Management Teams (RRMTs).

A further study was undertaken by NACRO in the late 1990s (NACRO 2000a). Prisoners and staff in a variety of public and private prisons, including Holloway and the Wolds, as well as Dartmoor, Belmarsh, and young offender institutions, were interviewed and the sample also included remand and women prisoners, white and ethnic-minority staff and prisoners. The researchers specifically asked how their interviewees saw race relations in prison in 1998 and 1999, following the new Race Relations Instruction to Governors from the Prison Service. Using interviews and questionnaires, they found that, although there was a commitment to race equality on the part of the Director General of the Prison Service, there was still a long way to go and a continuing perception of unfairness. Staff were aware of the new Race Relations Order and white staff were more aware than black staff. Some staff were critical of 'too much political correctness' but the majority of those who had received race relations training had found it useful. The majority were in favour of ethnic monitoring, although critical of the amount of paperwork involved. Of the prisoners interviewed, about three-quarters knew that there was a Race Relations Policy, but fewer know what the policy covered.

A higher proportion of ethnic-minority prisoners thought that relations with staff were poor. Prisoners from ethnic minority groups were less likely to assess race relations as good and more likely to assess them as poor. Respondents did not think that more black officers would help. The researchers found that verbal and racial abuse were still common, and there were still incidents of physical abuse from other prisoners, but few reported these incidents, because they thought that there was no point, nothing would be done and it would just cause more trouble. The NACRO research found that racist incidents between prisoners and staff were still occurring. They found that black prisoners felt isolated if held in a prison with mostly white prisoners, especially if situated in a white rural area, and would therefore benefit from community prisons located near large towns. Few prisoners in the survey had contact with community groups outside. But there are now black prisoner support groups.

To sum up their findings, although the Race Relations Policy has a high profile in the Prison Service, it was not working well at a day-to-day level, the policy was not fully understood, and the training was not equipping staff to deal fairly with colleagues or prisoners. The RRLOs were still overworked. Many staff were happy to leave it to the RRLOs and not to take responsibility themselves for providing regimes which do not discriminate. A follow-up study (NACRO 2003g) found that, while there had been some progress, there was still a long way to go.

But while there is a commitment to racial equality in the Prison Service, it is still very hard to control discriminatory behaviour at a micro-level. Despite a well-established Race Relations Policy operating throughout the Prison Service, there are still incidents of racist abuse and harassment and a failure to protect prisoners from such incidents (Commission for Racial Equality 2003). The CRE Report has highlighted the survival of racist attitudes despite two decades of progressive legislation.

11.8.2 Recent initiatives

RESPOND (Racial Equality for Staff and Prisoners) was launched in 1999, following the Macpherson Report, to confront racial harassment and discrimination, support ethnic-minority staff, and ensure equal opportunities for ethnic-minority prisoners. The Prison Service has appointed a Race Equality Advisor to develop the RESPOND initiative further. The strategies in RESPOND are backed up by targets, for example to assist recruitment of ethnic minorities, to set up an ethnic-minority network to support ethnic-minority staff, to review complaints procedures, to improve racial equality training for senior management, and to monitor the numbers of complaints and incidents and the career progress of staff from ethnic minorities. A Diversity and Equality Group has also been established. It will identify policies and standards to ensure that they address the specific problems identified by the CRE and to assess policies to consider their potential negative impact on grounds of race. RRLOs are now required to spend one day a week on their duties and at larger prisons RRLOs are full-time appointments.

The most significant development is the Action Plan designed by the Prison Service with the CRE (HM Prison Service/CRE 2003). It covers a five-year period and identifies key areas of work and relevant time scales. It is designed to ensure that policies are assessed for their impact on different groups. It includes the following:

- a heavier weighting for race equality within the performance management system
- revisions to the procedures for ethnic monitoring of prisoners to include a range of factors such as privilege levels, complaints, segregation, adjudication, and access to activities
- revisions to the Racist Incident Reporting Form
- increased ethnic monitoring of staff to include grievances, promotion and leavers
- a review of intervention strategies and treatment of racial complaints
- a review of Race and Diversity training to ensure staff meet the requirements of the Race Relations (Amendment) Act 2000 and that more information is provided to staff and prisoners
- clarification of the role of RRMTs which will include prisoner representatives and representatives from external community groups.

Action has been taken to implement the CRE recommendations. A report on race equality work is now included in the Annual Report of the Prison Service. There is now a policy of intolerance and dismissal for unacceptable behaviour. A Race Equality Working Group is acting as an advisory body and a Diversity and Equality web site provides information to assist in promoting equality. Guidelines on conducting race relations impact assessments are given in PSI 37/2005. The Prison Service Order on Race Equality (PSO 2800) has been revised to take account of the Race Relations (Amendment) Act 2000. It makes the Governor responsible for race equality and requires him to establish a Race Equality Action Team of senior managers, to set out and deliver the race equality action plan. It shifts the focus away from an anti-racist focus towards promoting good race relations, towards a more proactive role and also integrates the pursuit of race equality into prison management.

Efforts have also been made to broaden the social composition of officers with a higher number of ethnic-minority officers. Increased recruitment of ethnic-minority staff is desirable on grounds of fairness, but it would also assist in the smooth running of the prison as it would legitimise the authority of prison officers and reduce tensions. Several recruitment campaigns have been conducted, with limited success. Employees of the Prison Service are still mostly white. It is also hard to retain ethnic-minority staff so success in attracting staff may be offset by the turnover of staff. The employment of ethnic-minority staff in the Prison Service with the aim of achieving racial equality is now a Key Performance Target. The aim is to have a level of ethnic-minority staffing which reflects the ethnic composition of the wider society. In 2006–7 it just missed the target of 5.9 per cent, but this was an increase from 4.6 per cent in 2005–6 (HM Prison Service 2007a). The Prison Service is also trying to recruit more Muslim staff, to reflect the increase in Muslim prisoners. However, there was no increase in ethnic-minority staff at governing positions, but there was an increase in the number of ethnic-minority staff in senior operational managerial positions, to 3.17 per cent. Promotions will be monitored under the Action Plan. A new unit at the Home Office, the Criminal Justice System Race Unit, has been set up as part of the Office for Criminal Justice Reform, to identify and disseminate good practice across criminal justice agencies, and to increase the confidence on the part of ethnic minorities that they are treated fairly in the criminal justice system. Monitoring schemes have been expanded to take account of the Race Relations (Amendment) Act 2000 and the Action Plan. Within prisons the measurement of developments in race equality is a performance target.

The Prison Inspectorate now has a specialist race relations adviser and specialists in race relations are included in inspection teams and non-BME and BME prisoners are interviewed separately and carry out their own ethnic monitoring. In its latest Annual Report (HM Chief Inspector of Prisons 2008) it reports that 'structures for monitoring and overseeing race equality in prisons, are, in general, more robust. Most race equality officers were full time appointments, though many still reported that they had insufficient time to cover their duties' (ibid: 26). Another positive development is the establishment of a National Body of Black Prisoner Support Groups, which will collect information and act on behalf of support agencies working with black prisoners.

11.9 Challenging racism

11.9.1 Policy into practice

Several initiatives would help in promoting racial equality, including greater awareness and understanding on the part of staff of the impact of institutional discrimination and the differential impact of the criminal justice system on black and minority ethnic groups, greater awareness of the race relations policy, and the production of a simplified version of the racial equality strategy and race relations policy for prisoners. Greater effort is needed to make staff understand the value of ethnic monitoring so that they are able to meet the needs of all ethnic minorities, not just the larger minorities. Staff also need more information on making outside community contacts which would help prisoners during sentence and on release. Prisoners should also be involved in discussions on how to achieve equal access to prison facilities and how to reduce racial incidents. Reporting of such incidents should be encouraged and prisoners should be able to feel confident that they will be dealt with properly. Ethnic monitoring of adjudications would be helpful to examine differences in the use of disciplinary procedures.

Many of these issues are covered in the new Prison Service/CRE Action Plan and when the Action Plan has been fully implemented, this will be an important step forward. Greater consistency in recording decision making between criminal justice agencies would also assist in tracking the progress of black and minority defendants through the system. This would further our understanding of the processes relevant to explaining the over-representation of black and ethnic-minority groups in the prison population (see NACRO 2004d).

While there has been a shift in policy towards greater awareness of the problems facing ethnic-minority prisoners at a managerial level, the difficulty remains of how to ensure that ameliorative measures are applied in practice. With the substantial increase in the prison population since 1994, the increased concern with security overshadowed concern with racism for several years. However, the Mubarek case brought the issue of race equality to the forefront of penal policy again and race equality is given a high priority at the formal policy level. In its response to the Carter Review, the Government has stressed the need to 'eliminate any aspects within the correctional services which expose offenders to danger or discrimination. In particular racism will not be tolerated' (Home Office 2004b: 23). The generally reductionist shift may also benefit ethnic-minority suspects if greater use is made of electronic monitoring and of community sentences, to divert offenders from custody. But the Carter Report did not refer to problems of racism and race relations in prison, nor did it refer to the importance of social exclusion which, as we saw in Chapter 10, is relevant to understanding the relationship between race, crime and imprisonment. The leader of the Prison Officers' Association, Colin Moses, is strongly committed to challenging the culture of racism within this occupational group. While it might be unrealistic to expect one agency to deal with the problems of racism generated in the wider society, nonetheless the Prison Service can contribute to a climate of anti-racism and play a pivotal role in dealing with the effects of racism in an arena of vulnerability, where racist abuse can have considerable effect. The promotion of equal opportunity and non-discrimination is also beneficial to the good order of the prison as racial conflict is a source of tension within prisons.

11.9.2 *Parallel Worlds*

However, the thematic study of black and ethnic minority (BME) prisoners by the Prison Inspectorate, *Parallel Worlds*, which considered the views of staff and prisoners on race relations in prison and possible problems, and examined the effectiveness of monitoring and complaints procedures, found a gap between formal policy initiatives and the experience of different groups of staff and prisoners. So they found that governors and white RRLOs were the most optimistic regarding race relations, thinking that the regime was operating fairly while acknowledging that more needs to be done. But ethnic-minority staff were less likely to think that their prison was tackling race relations effectively, although they accepted some progress had been made. There were references to overt and subtle racism from colleagues, and they also felt they had insufficient support from managers in applying for promotion. White staff, however, tended to see racism as an issue between prisoners rather than a issue for staff, and did not seem aware of the extent to which their visible minority colleagues had experienced discrimination. Some minority staff felt isolated and that they were being overlooked for promotion.

As regards the prisoners, the overall finding was that black and minority ethnic prisoners felt they receive worse treatment than white prisoners. Safety was the major concern for Asian prisoners, with between one-third and one-half saying they felt unsafe, particularly women and young adults. Asian prisoners were more likely to report bullying; black prisoners were more concerned than Asian about the lack of respect they felt in their treatment from staff, but felt safer than Asian prisoners. However, the most recent report of the Chief Inspector of Prisons made similar findings on both safety and respect for Asian and black prisoners (HM Chief Inspector of Prisons 2008: 27). Results were also analysed by religion and Muslim prisoners gave more negative responses than non-Muslim prisoners in terms of feeling unsafe and lack of respect.

In the *Parallel Worlds* study, both black and Asian prisoners were also less positive about healthcare and the reviewers found that providers of healthcare did not recognise specific needs of ethnic-minority communities, for example in relation to sickle cell anaemia. BME prisoners are also under-represented at the therapeutic prison, Grendon, the reasons for which are considered by Sullivan (2007). The outcomes of complaints of racist incidents were also examined in *Parallel Worlds*. Most of the complaints related to prisoner-on-prisoner complaints. Although investigations were undertaken properly, it was difficult for RRLOs to follow through complaints against staff as it was hard to get staff to report colleagues. Complaints against staff were responded to less effectively than complaints against prisoners. So minorities lacked confidence in the complaints system. There were variations in the number of racist incident complaints between prisoners. Complaints about prisoners were upheld more often than complaints against staff and the outcomes were more severe for prisoners than staff.

The Report found that 'race relations management teams were operating effectively in less than half of the fieldwork establishments visited' (HM Inspectorate of Prisons 2005a: para 6.37). For example, meetings were irregular and poorly attended which suggests that race relations were not a key management priority. The Report also questioned whether the race equality duty was satisfied in contracted-out prisons. The Report was critical of the quality of ethnic monitoring which was often inaccurate and not sufficiently disaggregated to show variations between experiences of different minority groups. Also, about a quarter of governors were negative about the CRE Report and seemed unsure how to progress further in the pursuit of race equality.

However, the researchers found that the prisons with the best practice were those where race and diversity was given a high priority and sufficient support from senior managers. Examples of good practice included establishment of the 'Parva against Racism' movement at Glen Parva YOI, which involved workshops, sport and debates, the use of mediation to deal with complaints at Huntercombe, and contact with relevant outside bodies at Styal and Forest Bank.

The Report also questioned the sufficiency of training in equipping managers, governors and officers for their responsibilities in promoting race equality. At the time of the research, in-service race awareness training was no longer given and, instead, the very limited diversity training does not focus specifically on race and the Report argues that race relations training should be both mandatory and separate from diversity training.

Parallel Worlds found that while, on the one hand, non-BME governors and RRLOs thought the regime was operating fairly, while acknowledging that more needs to be done, very few of the BME staff thought that enough was being done, although they accepted that there had been some progress. Similarly amongst prisoners, the majority of BME prisoners think racism is still evident in so far as they are treated differently by staff and in terms of access to facilities, and waiting for requested items. Black prisoners felt safer in prison than Asian prisoners, but fewer black than Asian prisoners thought staff treated them with respect. Both had worse experiences than non-BME prisoners in terms of issues of resettlement, purposive activity, safety and respect. The Report also found that meetings of RRMTs were erratic, poorly attended and not fully representative and there was little evidence of actions being generated or followed up. RRLOs were conscientious but were overstretched and not given enough support, time or training.

Most complaints of racism were about other prisoners, followed by the discriminatory impact of decisions by staff. But many prisoners would not make a complaint either because they thought it would not be taken seriously or were worried about repercussions. BME prisoners were less likely than non-BME prisoners to believe that complaints would be dealt with fairly and clearly, if they feel it is unfair, they may be unlikely to complain at all. Furthermore, prisoners serving shorter sentences may feel it is not worth complaining.

Parallel Worlds makes depressing reading, given that it is reviewing the situation after Mubarek and after the CRE Report. Although many of the issues raised are addressed in the Action Plan, it shows that after 20 or so years of formal changes to reduce racism, problems remain. In their most recent report, the Prison Inspectorate found that the quality of investigations into racist incidents was still 'variable and often poor' (2008: 26). Staff investigating complaints were untrained and there were often delays. Moreover, black and ethnic-minority prisoners were still more negative regarding their treatment than white prisoners in their answers to over half of the questions in the survey. This was most marked in male local prisons.

Cheliotis and Liebling (2005) also found considerable differences between prisons and their research confirmed earlier studies in finding that ethnic minority prisoners rated race relations more unfavourably than white prisoners. Interestingly female prisoners and adult prisoners were more likely than males or younger prisoners to rate the quality of race relations more favourably. Perceptions of race relations correlated with other key areas of treatment including fairness, respect, humanity, relationships with staff and safety. White prisoners had a more positive view of race relations than ethnic-minority prisoners. In fact membership of an ethnic group was the main determinant of the perceived quality of race relations.

11.10 Conclusion

11.10.1 Justice, equality and difference?

Just as women have been marginalised both within criminology and the criminal justice system, so the needs and experiences of black and minority ethnic groups have also been marginalised until relatively recently. In debates on penal reform and policy, the voices of women and minority ethnic prisoners and officers have been muted. However, conceptualising women within the penal system raises questions about equality and difference which also arise in relation to black and minority ethnic groups. We considered in Chapter 10 the problems of construing issues in terms of difference or equality and the problems of essentialism. Similar problems arise in relation to ethnic minorities. The research also shows that surveys of all prisoners may not sufficiently reflect the different experiences of different groups. There is also the question of whether the goal is formal equality—equal treatment which treats all individuals the same—or whether the focus should be on equal opportunity, to look at the conditions which prevent ethnic minorities from competing with others fairly, or equality of outcome which considers the results of policies and programmes to see if they are disproportionate in their outcomes, in order to achieve justice in sentencing and punishment. As we have seen, there have been substantial policy changes over the last five years, the equality duty is having an impact on the governance of prisons and the issue of diversity is receiving more attention. At a formal level, procedures and strategies are in place to prevent discrimination on grounds of race, sex or other grounds but perceptions of prison life on the part of BME prisoners remain more negative than those of white prisoners. Progressive measures have been introduced and are having an impact on penal policy. But the success of these measures depends in part on available resources, the issue of overcrowding, and the impact of other expansionist penal policies including the move towards large-scale prisons and acceptance of high levels of imprisonment.

11.10.2 **Discussion questions**

In revising the issues raised in Chapter 11 you may wish to reflect on the following questions:

1. Is it fair to say that the current prison regime impacts more harshly on some groups of prisoners than others? If so, consider the ways in which equality of impact might be achieved.
2. Are women punished differently from men and should they be?
3. Is there any empirical evidence to suggest that the experiences of ethnic minorities in prison differ from those of non-minorities?
4. How has the Prison Service responded to the problem of racism in prisons?
5. What are the main problems to be tackled if race equality within prisons is to be achieved?

Guidance on dealing with these questions is given in the Online Resource Centre.

online resource centre

12

Just punishment in the community

SUMMARY

The focus of this chapter is the supervision and punishment of offenders who are sentenced to a community order, or who are serving a custodial sentence and are released from prison to Probation Service supervision. The chapter examines the policy aim of reducing reoffending through the use of requirements to control and rehabilitate the offender in the community, and discusses the theory and practice of rehabilitation which underpins these initiatives. Having reviewed changes in the theory and practice of probation work, the chapter reviews the debate on what counts as just punishment in the community.

12.1 Introduction

12.1.1 Custodial penalties

'Custodial penalties' may appear as an inappropriate side-heading to begin a chapter about community punishment. Yet it would be wrong to think that only those offenders given non-custodial penalties spend time being punished in the community. The provisions governing early release from prison mean that most offenders spend part of their sentence in prison and the remainder in the community (see section 12.2.4 below and also Chapter 5). The Criminal Justice Act (CJA) 2003 provides a not-yet-implemented structure for this in relation to sentences of 51 weeks or less and gives increased possibilities for the court to impose or suggest the content of rehabilitative programmes for prisoners on release. The aim is to have 'seamless' sentencing. Indeed, in current policy, post-custody supervision and treatment is at least as important as community supervision as a penalty in its own right.

The context for these developments in law and policy is a desire for what the Home Office has called more 'flexible' sentences and the Halliday Report (2001) was set up to 'identify and evaluate' new flexible frameworks 'which join up custodial and community sentences' (see Chapter 4, section 4.1.1). There are several reasons why this approach was, and still is, seen as attractive. There was disappointment with the apparent failure of the Criminal Justice Act (CJA) 1991 to effect a long-term reduction in imprisonment, concern at the amount of discretion accorded to the judiciary, and frustration at the ineffectiveness of short prison sentences in reducing offending. As David Blunkett, the former Home Secretary put it, 'it is crackers to put people in jail for a short time without any measures to change them or any plan for when they come out' (quoted in Ellis and Winstone 2001/2: 20). The White Paper, *Criminal Justice: The Way Ahead*, noted that in 1999 the 42,000 adult males who had served a prison term of less than 12 months (47 per cent of the total discharges) would have had no opportunity of engaging in rehabilitation programmes post-release (Home Office 2001a: para 2.73).

The Halliday Report proposed the 'custody plus' scheme for short prison sentences to address the concern to develop more effective risk management programmes with offenders (2001: paras 3.10 and 3.11), and to provide a cost-effective way of reducing conviction rates (ibid: paras 2.74–2.75). The trend is that 'the boundary between custodial and community sentences is becoming more fluid', making essential more effective collaboration between the Prison and Probation Services over arrangements for the post-prison care of offenders (Raynor and Vanstone 2002: 107). To this end the Prison and Probation Services became part of the National Offender Management Service (NOMS) in 2004 with the dual aims of punishing offenders and reducing offending: see *Reducing Crime, Changing Lives* (Home Office 2004b: para 25).

The policy aim in 2003 was, then, that 'plain' custody should not be an option for sentences of immediate imprisonment for a term of less than 12 months[1] but the replacement 'custody plus' (CJA 2003 s 181(1)) and intermittent custody orders will probably not be implemented, as we noted in Chapter 3, because of the lack of resources to fund and staff the extra community supervision required. The custody plus sentence, a split custody and community sentence modelled on the detention and training order introduced in 2000 for young offenders, would have entailed custody for 2–12 weeks, plus supervision in the community for 6 months or more. The custodial part of sentences passed under s 181 can also be suspended, there being the power to activate the custodial part of the sentence if the requirements for the community part are not met (see ss 189–190).

The intermittent custody order (see Chapter 3, section 3.1.3), based on the so-called 'weekend prison' sentences available in some other jurisdictions (for example, the Netherlands), would have allowed the court to specify periods of temporary release on licence (ss 183–184). The licence periods of intermittent and suspended sentences, together with those of custody plus sentences, would be subject to the requirements imposed by the sentencing court (see Roberts 2003). These can be one or more of the requirements listed (with similar lists in ss 182 and 190). The details of these requirements are found in ss 199–213 (with details of the attendance centre order for those aged under 25 in s 214) and are the same as those that are available for community orders (see s 177). The requirements include unpaid work (as in the community service order), curfew or exclusion, drug rehabilitation or alcohol treatment, attendance at a specified activity or programme, and supervision. The intermittent custody order was piloted in 2004–6 in courts feeding into two intermittent custody centres (HMP Kirkham for males and HMP Morton Hall for females) using 40-place units located outside the main residential area of each prison but on Prison Service property. The pilots showed that the level of compliance among offenders was 'exceptionally high' (Probation Service 2006) and 'judges who were interviewed were enthusiastic advocates of the disposal for cases

---

[1] The Halliday Report had also recommended that 'plain custody' should continue but only for the exceptions to 'custody plus' where the offender was not assessed as likely to reoffend or where supervision would be 'not worthwhile' because the offender would fail to comply with the requirements (2001: paras 3.20–3.25).

involving serious "one-off" offences committed by offenders with jobs or childcare responsibilities' (Penfold *et al.* 2006).

In the last decade, there has also been a focus on the release of long-term 'dangerous' prisoners to managed rehabilitation programmes in the community. Those convicted of specified offences of sex and violence can be given 'extended sentences' where the extended part of the custodial sentence is served in the community (see Chapter 5, section 5.4.4). Offenders are assessed to determine their risk level, and the content of the community programme is tailored to addressing the offender's risk factors effectively.

The Halliday Report (2001: Chapter 4) proposed increasing the post-release supervisory periods of all prison sentences of 12 months or more to a norm of one half, with more detailed planning by all agencies before the offender is released. The Report argued that, 'these steps would make visible to the offender, the public, and the prison and probation services, what the court expected of the sentence, in terms of efforts to prevent re-offending' (2001: para 4.15). These ideas have also been incorporated in the CJA 2003 (see Chapter 5) and implemented since April 2005. Release to Probation Service supervision is automatic at the half-way stage (s 244, but see s 247), and the courts are empowered to make a recommendation to the Home Secretary—who must consider it—of conditions to be included in the licence on release. The Home Secretary, when giving directions to the Parole Board, must have regard to the need not only to protect the public but also to rehabilitate the offender (s 239(6)).

The overall effect of these new provisions is that the court has more 'say' over what happens to an offender on release from custody and the offender is subject to more structured programmes of rehabilitation and control in the community.

12.1.2 **Community penalties**

In a parallel policy proposal the White Paper asked for 'more flexible and effective community sentences' (Home Office 2001a: para 2.69) which give the courts 'a menu of options to choose from, providing elements of punishment, crime reduction and reparation, to fit both the offender and the offence' (ibid: para 2.70). The CJA 2003 does this by replacing the existing orders with a single community order, and by providing in s 177, as noted above, the range of specified requirements which courts can impose (see also section 12.2.2 below).

Despite this high policy profile for community penalties, they are of relatively recent origin. Until the end of the nineteenth century the only non-custodial penalties were the forerunner of the conditional discharge, binding-over powers whose origins lie in the Justice of the Peace Act 1361, and fines (Worrall 1997: 7). The Probation of Offenders Act 1907, the Criminal Justice Act 1948, and the Criminal Justice Act 1972 introduced probation, attendance centre orders, and community service orders, respectively, with compensation orders becoming sentences in their own right in 1988 (ibid: 8). Before the CJA 1991 the disposals with a severity level above fines and below custody were usually referred to as 'intermediate sanctions'—between fines and prison—or 'alternatives to custody' to stress the legitimacy of their use instead of prison. However, the use of such orders was varied and inconsistent and there was pressure for clarification as to when to use them rather than custody or fines.

Table 12.1 The use of non-custodial penalties as a percentage of all sentences[a]

	1978	1983	1988
Fines	Over 50%	–	Under 40%
Community Service + Probation Orders	8	14	17
Custody	14	16	17

[a] Based on sentences given for indictable offences.

Source: Figures taken from the White Paper (Home Office 1990a: para 4.2).

There was also a need for changed attitudes to 'alternatives' to custody. As the 1990 White Paper noted, 'there seems to be an assumption that custody is the only "real" punishment' (Home Office 1990a: para 4.1). Certainly the use of probation orders and community service orders had fallen before the 1990s (see Table 12.1).

With the economic imperatives to reduce the use of custody that we discussed in Chapter 1, Government strategy by the end of the 1980s was to 'market' the top end of community penalties as sufficiently tough to be used instead of custody. The Consultation Paper, *Punishment, Custody and the Community* (Home Office 1988a), had asked for suggestions as to how to make probation more 'intensive' and how to develop new forms of surveillance such as tracking. At the same time, the document aimed specifically at the Probation Service, *Tackling Offending: An Action Plan*, urged 'tougher' probation orders (Home Office 1988b), and *Supervision and Punishment in the Community* (Home Office 1990b) discussed new 'control' aims for probation.

Consequently, the 1990 White Paper gave a high profile to community penalties (itself a new term), arguing that prison was ineffective in reducing offending and that deterrence often did not work (Home Office 1990a: paras 2.6–2.9). It stressed that 'just deserts' would be the guiding principle even when punishment took place in the community (ibid: para 4.3; see also Chapter 2). 'Restrictions on liberty would become the connecting thread in a range of community penalties as well as custody' (ibid: para 4.5). The resulting CJA 1991 incorporated this tandem policy of discouraging the use of custody (see Chapter 3) and encouraging the use of non-custodial penalties. The aim was that non-custodial penalties should stand in their own right, not be seen simply as (inadequate) alternatives to custody.[2] That was still the aim when the CJA 2003 was passed with plans to revitalise community punishment (see below).

12.1.3 Why 'community'?

'Community' is now a key word in policy documents and is used to describe the new penalties introduced in 1991 and in 2003. It is easy to chart its incidence and use through a series of criminal justice policy papers, including for example, *Punishment, Custody and the Community* (Home Office 1988a) and *Strengthening Punishment in the Community* (1995a). 'Community'—now 'an all-pervasive rhetoric'

---

[2] For a review of theories and projects around 'alternatives to custody' see Bottoms *et al.* (2004).

in policy discourse (Garland 2001b: 124)—is another instance of how quickly we take for granted the use of new words and concepts (ibid: 1). Arguably it is now 'one of the most promiscuous words in contemporary political usage' (Worrall 1997: 46). It was certainly a key term in policy documents of the 1980s and 1990s in regard, not only to criminal justice, but also to child protection, care of the old and the mentally ill. Worrall argues that 'it is prefixed to innumerable "feel good" words, such as care, centre, home, school, health, provision, transport, crime prevention, service, and, of course, punishment' (ibid).

What the word 'community' was meant to signify in 1990, and does signify now, is not so easy to establish. It may be referring to a set of shared values or to a place and there is ambiguity in the juxtaposition of 'the community' and 'punishment'. Three possible and different relationships between the two concepts have been posited, echoing Stan Cohen's statement in relation to crime control generally: 'communities can be the agents, *locus* or beneficiaries of crime control' (Nelken 1994: 249).

The community as a site

In several policy areas, notably those relating to offenders, the mentally ill and the old, *in* the community means the *locus* of the intervention is somewhere that is not an institution. So, for example, 'care in the community' means care in the home or family, punishment in the community means punishment imposed elsewhere than the prison setting.

The community as agent

The idea of punishment *by* the community was evident in *Partnership in Dealing with Offenders in the Community* (Home Office 1990c) which made suggestions for participation 'by the community' in providing punishment in partnership. What this implied was an element of privatisation, with the Probation Service providing the managers and co-ordinators for partnership with commercial and charitable projects. Chapter 10 in *Supervision and Punishment in the Community* (Home Office 1990b), devoted to 'The Voluntary and Private Sectors', further argued that the greater involvement of the independent sector could 'help achieve the objectives of protecting the public, reducing offending and securing value for money' (ibid: para 10.2). In particular the Government hoped that partnership with the voluntary sector would 'involve the community at large much more in work with offenders' (ibid: para 10.4).

The community as beneficiary

Community service orders had been introduced for reasons that included the provision of reparation to the community. Punishment in the community became important symbolically as punishment *for* (the benefit of) the community.

Nelken makes the point that these three possibilities reflect very different conceptions of crime; they could also reflect different conceptions of what is meant by punishment in the community. Although he notes it 'would be unwise to belabour the message that prepositions can alter propositions' (Nelken 1994: 250), in the rhetoric of 'partnership in the community' punishment does become 'by and for' the community. Since the Crime and Disorder Act (CDA) 1998, the Probation Service has been part of the network of preventative projects 'which dominate the law and order landscape' (Raynor and Vanstone 2002: 107; see also Crawford 1997).

The 1990 White Paper also linked the discourse of community with that of individual and parental responsibility which underpinned several pieces of legislation at that time: 'reforming offenders is always best if it can be achievable...this needs self-discipline and motivation...The probation service tries to make offenders face up to what they have done to give them a greater sense of responsibility and to help them resist pressure from others to take part in crime' (Home Office 1990a: para 2.6).

Lacey and Zedner focus on the idea of responsibility from a different angle. Their starting point is 'the apparent disjuncture between the demise of community and the growth of its rhetorical appeal' (1995: 301). They try to answer two questions (ibid 302): how do you explain the use of 'community' to render policies attractive when the community is breaking down, and why is 'community' referred to so often despite criticism of the concept? They point to two different histories of community as a concept. The first is the political rhetoric of welfarism after the Second World War and the development of community studies to discover the spatial entity in which these welfare interventions can be implemented.[3] The second is one where community is the site of a conservative or moral majoritarian political discourse. Lacey and Zedner argue that these appeals to community in the 1980s were used to reallocate responsibility, ideas of community being invoked and evoked both to explain and to cure social disorder (1995: 301). The strength of this discourse consequently legitimised a diversion of responsibility for crime from the government to family and community.

Nelken also notes that 'community responsibility is here conceived as an individual responsibility in the aggregate' (Nelken 1994: 266), and he expresses fears that this facilitates greater social control through a 'dispersal of discipline'. Rather than diminishing social control by diverting offenders from custody, punishment in the community can increase it: discipline permeates into society's informal networks (see Brownlee 1998b: 180–2). There is a diffusion of control with a lighter touch but the impact is more pervasive, with new forms of discipline supplementing, but not replacing, the prison system (Cohen 1985).

Probation practice, as established at the beginning of the twentieth century, has been seen as a tool for this new form of social control, designed not just to prevent law breaking but also to inculcate specific norms and attitudes. According to Garland, 'probation, supervision, after care—all of these represent an extension and multiplication of the judicial gaze, and of the consequent range of intervention' (1985: 239). Probation practice in the community means that such normalisation can be exercised 'without disrupting those disciplines already provided by the home, the school, the work place, etc' (ibid).

Wasik and colleagues (1999: 69–83) argue that the focus on community as local involvement is part of a need to increase the legitimacy of the criminal justice system. With law and order policies not perceived by the public as 'working', local crime prevention schemes, such as Safer Cities and Neighbourhood Watch, are encouraged, and so provide at least the appearance of action. Daly (2003) also

---

[3] See, for example, Hillery (1955) for a discussion of the different meanings of community in the mid-twentieth century.

focuses on legitimacy, taking an analysis of the concept of governance as her starting point. She argues that its central focus on power 'enables us to understand and locate changes in governance as stemming from, in some respects anyway, what states have to do to build or regain legitimacy. Because the state no longer occupies a privileged position of power, much of the push towards partnership can be understood as a search for legitimacy' (ibid: 123). Partnership practices and policies can be constructed as consensual and so acceptable (ibid). So important is the aim of legitimacy through holding the community and individual more responsible for crime prevention that, she argues, 'the delivery of outcomes through partnership take precedence over efficiency and reduced expenditure' (ibid: 121).

This notion of 'responsibilisation' is important in current policy analysis. Kemshall examines social policies aimed at citizen 'remoralisation' (see also Chapter 8, section 8.4.2) and argues that the Probation Service has been a key agency in the control and exclusion of the irresponsible citizen (Kemshall 2002: 41). We will return to her arguments later in this chapter: the debate on whether community punishment is a means of greater, not lesser, social control is still very much alive.

12.2 **The legal framework**

12.2.1 **Seriousness and liberty**

As we saw in Part A of this book, seriousness and restrictions on liberty are important concepts in sentencing. The 1990 White Paper proposed that the new statutory rationale of just deserts would operate in community sentences as 'graduated restrictions on liberty, which are related to the seriousness of offending' (1990a: para 4.7). The sentencing framework introduced by the CJA 1991 incorporated these ideas and the CJA 2003 has largely repeated this approach (see Chapter 3), notwithstanding the emphasis on persistence and on risk. Just as with custodial sentences, a statutory hurdle was enacted for community sentences in s 6 of the CJA 1991 (now CJA 2003, s 148; see also Chapter 3, Table 3.1). The court may pass a community sentence only if it is of the opinion 'that the offence, or the combination of the offence and one or more offences associated with it' is 'serious enough to warrant such a sentence'.

The pre-2003 scheme

A just deserts rationale theoretically means that sentencers do not have the discretion to choose deterrence, rehabilitation, psychiatric treatment, or social work 'help' as the primary sentencing aim in relation to 'intermediate' sentences. The scheme proposed in the 1990 White Paper and incorporated in the CJA 1991 was that the court should make the initial sentencing decision on retributivist principles, and then consider other aims of sentencing when choosing the particular community penalty to impose. Depending on whether, for example, the offender was seen to need advice and training or be under a duty to make some reparation to the community, a probation order or community service order could be made (Home Office 1990a: para 4.8), with the 'amount' made proportionate to seriousness. In other words, desert determines the size of the penalty, and suitability dictates its form (Rex 1998: 383). The vexed question of ranking community punishments was not tackled in 1990–1.

The Criminal Justice Act 1993 made amendments to community sentencing in line with those to custodial sentencing (see Chapter 3), and the Crime (Sentences) Act 1997 extended the possible use of the community service order, the attendance centre order, and curfew orders for fine default. The resulting legislative framework for community sentences was re-enacted in the Powers of Criminal Courts (Sentencing) Act (PCCSA) 2000 (ss 33–62) and new names for existing orders were introduced by the Criminal Justice and Court Services Act (CJCSA) 2000. The new names stressed punishment and rehabilitation as a focus for the community service order and the probation order respectively. The CJCSA 2000 also introduced a range of new requirements that could be added to a community rehabilitation order including a drug abstinence or exclusion requirement. In line with the continuing focus on deprivation of liberty in the community, the CJCSA 2000 provided a curfew condition which could be added to community orders to require the offender to remain for specified periods in specified places, between 2 and 12 hours a week.

To summarise briefly, the scheme set up by the CJA 1991 and continued in the PCCSA 2000 had the following elements:

- 'community orders' covering a range of existing penalties which became 'sentences of the court' rather than alternatives to punishment
- fines as the presumptive sentence with legislative hurdles to discourage inappropriate use of community (and also custodial) penalties
- a primary sentencing decision on the basis of seriousness as to whether to impose a community penalty, plus subsequent decisions on the type of community penalty and the commensurate 'amount' of the community penalty (PCCSA 2000, ss 35(3)(a) and (b))[4]
- punishment and rehabilitation as the aims of probation supervision.

The CJA 2003

The CJA 2003 heralded, it was said, a new utilitarian approach to community sentences as indicated by the title of the Halliday Report (2001), *Making Punishments Work*. According to Jack Straw, the former Home Secretary, 'it was time to make the sentence fit the offender, rather than the offence' (quoted in Lacey 2002: 26; see also Chapter 3, section 3.3.1). The Halliday Report proposed a new single community punishment order with 'ingredients' specified by the court instead of the existing community penalties which consisted of the following orders: community rehabilitation, community punishment, curfew, community punishment and rehabilitation, drug treatment and testing, attendance centre (under 21), exclusion and drug abstinence (2001: para 6.6). The specified elements, it proposed, would be chosen from compulsory programmes aimed at changing offending behaviour, compulsory work, restrictions and requirements such as a curfew or electronic monitoring, reparation, and supervision to support resettlement and enforce the sentence (ibid).

---

[4] See CJA 1991, s 8(1), then PCCSA 2000, s 41 for probation aims, and CJA 1991 s 11—then PCCSA 2000, s 51(3)—for combination order aims.

The ambiguity of rationales is again evident in that para 6.6 points out that 'the punitive weight' should determine how much should be done to reduce the risks of reoffending and make reparation. There is an echo here of a much earlier consultation paper where it was stated that every penalty should have three elements: deprivation of liberty, action to reduce offending, and recompense to the victim and/or public (Home Office 1988a: para 1.5).

The report pointed out that the punitive weight might be difficult to measure in some instances, but suggested an outline 'tariff' for the ingredients making up the new punishment order and set this out in relation to a bottom tier, a middle tier and a top tier. In each tier there is a selection of specified elements which are bracketed together with the suggestion to the sentencer that these can be taken alone or in combination (ibid: para 6.8). The White Paper endorsed this approach (2001: para 2.70) and guidance on the CJA 2003 is framed in relation to three sentencing ranges (low, medium and high), although flexibility is urged (Sentencing Guidelines Council 2004c). The Act has simply empowered the courts to make a community order imposing on the offender 'any one or more' of the specified requirements (s 177(1)).

In Chapter 3 we noted that the two-stage decision approach to community sentencing is continued by the CJA 2003. The problem of choice remains.

12.2.2 Choosing the community punishment

In Part B of this book we have been looking primarily at how punishment operates in practice in the UK. In regard to community sentences, probation officers must provide—or buy in—the supervision and programmes as specified by the court, though how they do so is a matter for the Probation Service. It has been argued, however, that a clear, principled sentencing framework had not been achieved in practice, due partly to the lack of guidance, in particular as to how the court might balance proportionality with 'suitability' (Rex 1998: 384).

Writing before the 1991 Act, Wasik and Hirsch had considered various models for applying desert principles to the choice of non-custodial penalties. They argued that the key issue was how much substitution amongst such penalties was possible, arguing for a 'partial substitution' model (1988: 561). The vexed question of establishing the comparative severity of a sanction could be done in various ways, including by opinion poll (ibid: 563–5) but probation fits uneasily into a desert model unless conditions are added to probation to constitute the punishment (ibid: 568–9). The thrust of Wasik and Hirsch's argument was that the punishment component, commensurate to seriousness, must take precedence, and utilitarian aims could only determine the substitution issue. Morris and Tonry, using practice in the United States, argued for much more interchangeability of punishment than this limited substitution model (1990: 10). When drafting what became the CJA 1991, the Government apparently took on board the suggestions of theorists such as Wasik and von Hirsch (Rex 1998: 383; Ashworth 1992: 247), rather than Morris and Tonry. These issues remain (see Harrison 2006).

There is also the difficulty of calculating the amount of deprivation of liberty, a factor which Rex believes explains the greater use of community service orders and combination orders (community service with probation supervision) immediately after the implementation of the CJA 1991, because calculating punishment in hours was easier for sentencers (Rex 1998: 387–8). The upward trend in the proportion of probation orders with additional requirements after 1996 is harder to explain.[5] It could signal that the ironic consequence of 'legislation intended to bring home the fact that community orders contain restrictions, seems to have been to increase the restrictions imposed on offenders' liberty' (ibid: 390).

In practice, argues Rex, 'the result has been a scheme which may have been intended to resemble the desert based model proposed by Wasik and Von Hirsch (1988), but which in fact had much more in common with the looser arrangements recommended by Morris and Tonry' (1998: 385). Arguably, the CJA 2003, s 166(2), which allows the court to pass a community sentence even if the seriousness criterion for custody has been met, does remove the clear 'in/out' demarcation line which Tonry and Morris criticised. In terms of justice for offenders, both schemes are problematic. To increase the amount of rehabilitation imposed because of proportionality requirements rather than what is required to prevent reoffending might not seem sensible, but rehabilitation divorced from offence seriousness could lead to punitive levels of intervention (see section 12.4.3 below).

A Probation Circular (Home Office 2005c) provided guidance on the implementation and use of the new community order including a table (see Table 12.2 below) which gives detailed suggestions on hours and purposes for different levels of seriousness in relation to each main requirement.

The Circular provides many more complicated charts and 'Model combinations of Requirements' (ibid: 12) but, as Mair et al. (2007) point out, 'not only are the model combination types inadequately differentiated from each other but sentencing can also take account of several purposes' (ibid: 13). They go on to say that 'in addition to the possibilities for confusion and tension between probation officers and sentencers, another key potential problem with both of the new orders is requirement overload. Sentencers, especially magistrates, tend to believe that more is almost certainly better' (ibid), although they point out that figures for the first year of use did not reveal overload, with most orders having only one or two requirements attached (ibid: 18). They found that the unpaid work requirement was becoming increasingly popular and that half of the available requirements had not been used or had been used 'very rarely' (ibid: 31).[6]

Whether the most recent changes will be sufficient, together with the new requirement that community penalties must be used only if the offence is punishable by imprisonment, will make such penalties more attractive to sentencers and the public—so that they become alternatives to custody rather than to fines—is still open to doubt. As Worrall (1997) pointed out, there is a continuing lack of legitimacy of community punishment in the eyes of the public, due perhaps to the tenacious legacy of the Victorian principle of less eligibility, under which the offender's punishment must be seen as approximating to a poorer standard of life than that of the poorest respectable citizen (ibid: 13).

---

[5] This trend continued until at least 2002 (see Criminal Statistics 2003).
[6] For further reading on community punishment, see Lewis et al. (2005) (focusing on issues around race) and Worrall and Hoy (2005). See also National Offender Management Service (2006a) for policy on 'Working with Probation to Protect the Public and Reduce Re-offending'.

Table 12.2 Criminal Justice Act 2003—requirements

Requirement	Level of Seriousness	Length	Report	Main Purpose(s)
Unpaid work	Low	40–80 hours*	'Fast Delivery'	punishment
	Medium	80–150 hours*	'Fast Delivery'	reparation
	High	150–300hours*	'Fast Delivery'	rehabilitation
Supervision	Low	up to 12 months	'Fast Delivery'	rehabilitation
	Medium	12–18 months	'Standard'	
	High	12–36 months	'Standard'	
Programme (Accredited)	Medium	stated number (or	depends on	rehabilitation
	High	range) of sessions	programme	
Drug rehabilitation Offender must consent	Low	6 months	• see footnote	rehabilitation
	Medium	6–12 months	'Standard'	
	High	12–36 months	'Standard'	
Alcohol treatment Offender must consent	Low	6 months	• see footnote	rehabilitation
	Medium	6–12 months	'Standard'	
	High	12–36 months	'Standard'	
Mental health treatment Offender must consent	Medium	up to 36 months	'Standard'	rehabilitation
	High			
Residence	Medium	up to 36 months	'Standard'	rehabilitation
	High			protection
(specified) Activity	Medium	20–30 days*	'Fast Delivery'	rehabilitation
	High	up to 60 days*		reparation
Prohibited Activity	Low	up to 24/36 months	'Fast Delivery'	punishment
	Medium	for SSO/CO		protection
	High			
Exclusion	Low	up to 2 months	'Fast Delivery'	punishment
	Medium	up to 6 months*		protection
	High	up to 12 months*		
Curfew typically up to 12 hours/ day	Low	up to 2 months	'Fast Delivery'	punishment
	Medium	2–3 months*	'Fast Delivery'	protection
	High	4–6 months*	'Fast Delivery'	
Attendance centre	Low	12–36 hours	'Fast Delivery'	punishment

Notes:

* Length = in line with Sentencing Guidelines Council Guidelines.

Report = the minimum level of Report which should be used when proposing the Requirement (but the court may be able to make the Requirement without considering such a Report—see Section 2).

• A 'Fast Delivery' Report may be sufficient where a current treatment plan is already available.

** Purpose = indicates NPD's interpretation of the main purpose of the Requirement. All Requirements are presumed to meet the purpose of the reduction of crime, either through rehabilitation, or by deterrence through their punitive impact. See Section 4.3.

Source: Home Office (2005c: 8).

12.2.3 **Enforcement**

Absenteeism—non-attendance at community service requirements—is a major problem and one with which the Government, through its inspectorates, is currently concerned (HM Inspectorate of Probation *et al.* 2007). There are two opposed schools of thought on how best to manage this. Eadie and Willis (1989) pointed to the different attitudes of community service supervisors and organisers with and without a social work qualification. Those without such a qualification tended to adopt an industrial model where absenteeism, if repeated, warrants dismissal; those with such training were inclined to give defaulters the benefit of the doubt and take a 'second chance' approach (ibid: 412). As early as 1988 the first draft of the new National Standards made clear to the Probation Service that they must take a tougher line and start breach proceedings after two failures to attend without acceptable explanation. This may be more palatable to the new generation of probation officers whose training is not based in social work (see below).

However, it is 'one thing to promise uncompromising discipline, but another thing to deliver it': offenders who are given probation and community service are often the ones who require that particular disposal in order to help them become more disciplined in terms of time management (Eadie and Willis 1989: 414). Early return to the courts for breach then means that their treatment cannot be successful. Ellis *et al.* found that enforcement practice varies, with 'pockets of poor practice', and that in all five areas researched failure to attend at the required time was the most common form of non-compliance (1996: 52). Farrall (2002) examined long-term absences from probation supervision and found that the number of breaches increased during the 1990s although the percentage was quite small: 2 per cent in 1988 had their orders terminated early for failing to comply with the requirements compared with 3 per cent in 1993 and 6 per cent in 1999 (ibid: 264). Financial problems, drug usage and depression were commonly associated with the absenteeism of probation offenders (ibid: 267–8). The CJCSA 2000, in effect, created a statutory warning to reinforce the new National Standards which provided that offenders would be issued with a maximum of one warning for an unacceptable failure to comply with a community sentence in any 12-month period. Previously there had been two possible warnings. Section 53 of the Act—although never implemented—'marks a major departure from the current situation where breach is regulated by guidance in the form of National Standards' (NACRO 2001a: 4). Schedule 8 of the CJA 2003 now provides similar requirements although if a breach is proved the court is no longer mandated to impose a custodial sentence. See the Online Resource Centre for further information.

online resource centre

Further evidence of this more punitive trend can be found in s 62 of the Child Support, Pensions and Social Security Act 2000. This allows social security benefits to be removed or reduced for up to 26 weeks as a result of a breach of a community service order (see McKeever 2004).

12.2.4 Release on licence

About 30 per cent of those offenders who are currently being supervised in the community are on a period of licence supervision as part of their custodial sentence.[7] In section 12.1.1 above we reviewed the not-yet-implemented arrangements for prisoners given sentences of less than 51 weeks under the CJA 2003, s 181 as well as the new provisions for longer sentences which mean their all prisoners are released to the supervision of the Probation Service. In Chapter 5 we reviewed arrangements for longer-term prisoners which also have resource

---

[7] See http://www.probation.homeoffice.gov.uk: 'National Probation Service: About Us', accessed 10 January 2005 and 17 March 2008.

implications. This will increase further the importance—for the Probation Service workload and for Government policy—of early release supervision.

As we saw in Chapter 5, for most of the history of custodial punishment there has been a possibility of release before the end of the custodial sentence specified. The policy reasons for early release have varied from time to time, but all reasons have been based on utilitarian principles and cut across retributivist sentencing principles. Currently the focus is the use of early release in order to mandate the involvement of offenders in post-release programmes. However, whilst assessment for discretionary release and for the tailoring of post-release programmes is based on risk assessments, for most offenders the result is a programme which addresses their persistence in reoffending rather than their potential danger to the public. The Probation Service is again being forced to focus on rehabilitating ex-prisoners.

12.3 The development of probation practice

12.3.1 The history of the Probation Service until the 1970s

Probation is central to the history and current implementation of community sentences. According to the web page of the National Probation Service (NPS), 'each year the probation service commences the supervision of some 175,000 offenders. The case load on any given day is in excess of 200,000.' As a sentencing disposal, probation developed essentially as 'the practice of releasing certain people from court with some kind of condition that they behave themselves in the future' (Raynor and Vanstone 2002: 11), a practice originating in America and Britain in the nineteenth century. The first stage in the history of the Probation Service has been referred to as the 'special pleading phase'. The essential purpose was to provide information on the offender with the intention that it would mitigate the severity of the sentence imposed. In the development of probation work, the concept of the recognisance—a surety for good behaviour—was influential, as was the involvement of religious societies in what was seen as essentially 'missionary work' to the courts (Raynor and Vanstone 2002: 12–16). This practice ethos continued from the 1870s to the 1920s, beginning with the Police Court Mission and survived the establishment of a statutory Probation Service by the Probation of Offenders Act 1907.

This 'orthodox history' of the humanitarian origins of probation underestimates the influence of social and political ideas on policy, notably concern about the 'moral degeneration' of the working class (ibid: 16–19). The writings of probation officers at the beginning of the twentieth century revealed an 'increasingly pseudo-psychological and eugenic tone', a 'kind of moral extemporising in the guise of theory', which prompted early pressure for their education and training (ibid: 32–5). At the same time, the development of the positivist school of criminology in the last quarter of the nineteenth century provided a theory of crime causation which focused on environmental factors and which, therefore, validated a treatment approach to dealing with offenders (see Brownlee 1998b: Chapter 3; Cavadino and Dignan 2002: 49–50).

The next phase of development between the 1930s and 1970s, categorised as the 'diagnosis' phase, evidenced a move towards professionalism and rehabilitative aims in probation. Social work training, based on a medical model, became a requirement. Consequently, the Probation Service was heavily involved in the 'treatment ideal' with various practice approaches. Criticism of the prevalent casework approach began as early as the 1950s (Raynor and Vanstone 2002: 41–4) but it was the emergence of the 'nothing works' orthodoxy which seriously challenged the Probation Service. Until then the Service had depended for its authority on the rehabilitative ethos and the utilitarian aim of probation to improve in some way the life of the offender and/or decrease his criminality. By the end of the 1970s the Probation Service was in crisis, split over ideals and aims.

12.3.2 Changing the Probation Service

A scrutiny of the articles in the *Probation Journal* at the end of the 1970s reveals quite starkly the increasing *angst* of the Service in relation to the aims and public expectations of its work. The loss of identity for the Service, resulting not simply from the demise of rehabilitation but also from the tension in managing the care and control aspects of their work, without an overall operational aim, led to ideological conflicts. One of these can be located in the wider debate between genericism and specialism in social work (Worrall 1997: 67–9), another in the different attitudes to the role and nature of the National Association of Probation Officers. These conflicts related to the wider question of the search, in the 1970s and 1980s, for an acceptable response by the Probation Service to the apparent demise of rehabilitation. In this period, referred to as the phase of pragmatism, three schools of thought—the radical, the personalist and the managerial—emerged. Although the dominant ethos of the Probation Service is now different (see section 12.3.4), these various strands are still present in debate (see, for example, Mantle and Moore 2004).

The radical approach

A minority of officers criticised the traditional counselling and casework role of probation officers because they held ideas about the structural rather than personalised causes of offending. Some campaigned to refuse to write reports in 'not guilty' pleas and to withdraw from staffing Prison Welfare Departments because they believed the chances of an offender being given a custodial sentence were too heavily stacked against disadvantaged offenders (Worrall 1997: 70). The radical approach was wary of counselling practice, based as it is on the assumption that the fault lies with an individual offender and not with society.

The personalist approach

This paradigm—or theory of practice—was based on the belief that the treatment model contributed to injustice through coerced treatment (see Raynor and Vanstone 2002: 44–5). Bottoms and McWilliams (1979) voiced these concerns and proposed a separation of the surveillance and casework functions of probation work. They suggested that the Probation Service should concentrate on the empowerment of the offender, an approach which would enable the Probation Service to operate without the medical and discriminatory aspects of the treatment model. Harris (1980) also justified what in practice probation officers had been spending much of their time doing, notably giving practical help to offenders in arranging housing, jobs and medical care. Others emphasised the professionalism involved in this: 'to give help in a probation context requires skill of the highest order' (Celnick and McWilliams 1991: 166), and an R v R programme (reasoning and rehabilitation), for example, was developed to provide life skills training (see Raynor and Vanstone 1994).

The managerialist approach

Like the radical approach, the managerialist approach is also not concerned with the individual offender *per se*. Its focus is the management of groups of offenders in cost-effective ways and in the 1980s the Probation Service was increasingly subject to what was then New Managerialist thinking. The clearest evidence of its increasing importance can be found in the promulgation of National Standards—a significant development in the move to a nationally regulated Probation Service.

The Home Office issued the Statement of National Standards and Objectives for the Probation Service (SNOP) in 1984. Some probation officers viewed it as a major threat (see Mair 1997); some chief probation officers—given the responsibility to ensure that their services were cost efficient—embraced it (Raynor and Vanstone 2002: 78). McLaughlin and Muncie (1994) argue that the key to this shift lay in the managerialist aims of having quantifiable outcomes for probation practice: to 'advise assist and befriend' is not readily quantifiable but is, instead, an 'expensive and unaccountable ideal' (ibid).

National Standards, revised since, prescribe a series of objectives in which the functions of the Probation Service are redefined: to divert high-risk offenders away from prison, to reduce the incidence of crime, and to deploy resources in the most cost-effective fashion. Social work-based tasks were subordinated to the role of controlling and containing offenders in the community, a focus necessary to ensure the 'loss of liberty' element of community penalties post-CJA 1991. The managerialist focus also underpinned the development of the use of commercial and voluntary providers of Probation Service projects so that the Probation Service became a manager, not only of its own work, but also of the work of providers (see below).

The demise of the rehabilitative ideal had forced the Probation Service to rethink its practice. The rebranding, in the CJA 1991, of probation and other community penalties as first and foremost punishments which involved control and loss of liberty forced a further rethink. The argument is that in the 1990s the third strand became dominant and probation officers turned into penal managers or correctional officers in the community.

12.3.3 Penal 'managers' in and since the 1990s

The 1990s saw a stronger focus in probation practice on the delivery of punishment, on cost-effective and outcome-monitored management, on working in partnership, and on actuarial risk assessment (see Chapters 5 and 13). The new requirements for probation officer training were also a sign of a different government approach to the practice of probation itself. In 1995 the Home Office published *New Arrangements for the Recruitment and Qualifying Training of Probation Officers* (Home Office 1995b, implemented in the Probation (Amendment) Rules 1995, Statutory Instrument 1995 No. 2622) which proposed that the requirement that probation officers hold the Diploma in Social Work, or its equivalent, be abolished. Aldridge and Eadie point out that the Home Office had pushed through this change despite opposition from nearly all the other players in the criminal justice system (1997: 111). The issue of probation training apparently found itself 'at the intersection of several Conservative preoccupations', including a negative view of probation as 'advocating rehabilitation and embodying the hated "political correctness"' (ibid: 122). It is also possible that the Government saw probation work as a source of employment for redundant military personnel (ibid).

The designation of the (then) probation order as a punishment to be imposed proportionate to seriousness caused difficulties. Until 1948 probation had been used instead of a conviction, and instead of a sentence until 1991. Whatever their practice approach, probation officers had conceptualised their work as an alternative to punishment and criticised the change. Some officers argued in favour of a non-punitive paradigm in probation work.[8] However, a viable opposition was difficult to mount.[9]

The policy trend to a greater use of probation–private partnerships was also evident. Ring-fenced probation budgets—with money that could only be spent on partnership projects—meant that, with no increased resources, some forms of community penalties and rehabilitative projects could be provided only by projects part-funded and perhaps wholly run by voluntary or commercial agencies. As we have seen (section 12.1.3), several documents had proposed and encouraged partnership, not a new idea but the scale proposed was of a different order. The development necessitated the probation officer becoming a manager and fundholder with a key role in partnerships.

This led Drakeford (1993) to ask 'who will do the work?', raising the issue that the statutory responsibilities placed on the probation officer are being carried out by voluntary bodies, and that professional skills are being downgraded. It also raises the issue of accountability (see the discussion in Chapter 9 in relation to prison privatisation) and the potential incompatibility of the aims and interests of the Probation Service and those voluntary or private organisations with which they are partners.[10] As we shall see below, the trend towards 'out-sourcing' has now been taken much further.

12.3.4 A National Probation Service

Despite these concerns, and despite substantial cuts in funding in the mid-1990s, the Probation Service is now 'centre stage' in the criminal justice system because of its key role in Government policies (Raynor and Vanstone 2002: 82), and has apparently adapted its practice to risk management and punishment-oriented policies (see also Chapter 5, section 5.4.4). New thinking about rehabilitation (see, for example, Burnett and Roberts 2004; Harper and Chitty 2005; see also section

---

[8] Stopard (1990), for example, argued that the Probation Service has traditionally viewed control of an offender as a means to the end product of help or treatment so that the offender would learn self control (see also Singer, 1991; and Home Office 1990b: para 7.3).

[9] See, for example, McWilliams and Pease who were at pains to distinguish rehabilitation from reformation, arguing that rehabilitation is essentially the restoration of the rank and rights of the offender and may not involve reform as such (1990: 19).

[10] See, for example, Smith *et al.* (1993: 33–4); see also Bretherton (1991) for the difficulties of putting partnership into practice in relation to one particular project.

12.4.2 below) and, in particular, the use of cognitive behaviourism from psychology (see Home Office 2003d), together with actuarial methods, which have been developed in relation to the New Penology, have given the Probation Service the resources to pursue the new policy focus on managing risk with the dual aim of control and rehabilitation.

The Probation Service has also been subject to reorganisation into a national body. The National Probation Service (NPS) for England and Wales was set up by the CJCSA 2000, with the following aims, as set out in s 2: the protection of the public, the reduction of reoffending, the proper punishment of offenders, ensuring offenders' awareness of the effects of crime on the victims of crime and the public, and the rehabilitation of offenders. Section 1(1) sets out the tasks of the NPS as giving assistance to the courts 'in determining the appropriate sentences to pass, and making other decisions, in respect of persons charged with or convicted of offences', and as providing the supervision and rehabilitation of such persons. Section 1(2) makes clear that these functions extend in particular to giving effect to community orders, supervising persons released from prison on licence, and providing accommodation in approved premises. Section 3 makes the NPS directly accountable to the Home Secretary. Section 41 of the PCCSA 2000 re-enacted[11] the aim of probation (rehabilitation) orders as that of securing the offender's rehabilitation or protecting the public from harm from him or preventing the committing by him of further offences.

The CJCSA 2000 also changed the regional structure of the Service into 42 local areas, each coterminous with the local Police Service area (replacing the existing 54 Probation Services). The explanatory notes to the Bill referred to the proposals of the Consultation Paper *Joining Forces to Protect the Public* (Home Office 1998a) for greater Prison and Probation Service collaboration, arguing that the 54 separate Probation Services set up by the Probation Service Act 1993 'were not conducive to the efficient and successful achievement of this aim'. In a parallel reorganisation of the Family Court Welfare Services, the duty of the Probation Service to provide social work reports to the courts in private-law children cases was transferred to the new Children and Family Court Advisory and Support Service (CAFCASS), an umbrella organisation for welfare reports to the courts on children.

Revised National Standards (Home Office *et al.* 2000) also came into force in April 2000. They have been analysed as 'part of a wider development that devolves to the Probation Officer increasing responsibility for punishment beyond the walls of the prison', but this opens up the risk of probation practice becoming too open to individual officer interpretation (Sparrow *et al.* 2002: 33). National Standards act as reassurance for the government: '[t]he reframing of the Probation Service (and the work of the probation officers) is increasingly and explicitly set through the central apparatus of the Home Office' (ibid). This central control had also been facilitated by a range of management initiatives such as the new public management and financial management initiative (ibid). If a decision is to be taken that will depart from the standards then it has to be endorsed by a designated line manager, a requirement seen as evidence of further de-professionalisation of officers in the Probation Service (ibid). A further revision of the National Standards was implemented in 2005.

---

[11] Section 41(1) was largely a re-enactment of the revised s 2 of the 1973 Act.

The Probation Service has, then, been subject to considerable organisational and target-driven change. As a recent review of these changes notes, 'our overall impression has been that a period of stability, reflection and objective analysis would be beneficial for the probation service. We are doubtful that this is likely to be the case' (Oldfield and Grimshaw 2008: 5; see also the Online Resource Centre).

online
resource
centre

12.3.5 The Offender Management Act 2007

As noted above, the Prison and Probation Services became part of the National Offender Management Service in 2004. Faulkner (2005) argued that issues around accountability and responsibility should have received more attention in the original proposals for the establishment of NOMS but provisions in the Offender Management Act (OMA) 2007 bring these issues to the fore.

In 2005 the Government published a Consultation Paper, *A Five-Year Strategy for Protecting the Public and Reducing Re-offending.* Under the heading 'A vibrant system which values its staff', the paper argued that 'we need to make sure that the way our system is designed helps us bring in the best possible people and organisations to support every offender' (Home Office 2005b: 8) and proposed a system of commissioning. The paper reasoned that if those who buy services for offenders are separated out from the providers of those services 'there is no incentive to deliver services that do not work' (ibid).[12] Consequently, the Government introduced in November 2006 the Offender Management Bill which received the Royal Assent on 27 July 2007.

Part 1 of the OMA 2007 concerns new arrangements for the provision of probation services, including the abolition of local probation boards and the establishment of probation trusts (ss 11 and 5 respectively). Section 1(1) of the Act defines 'probation purposes', in effect the remit of the probation trusts, as

(a) courts to be given assistance in determining the appropriate sentences to pass, and making other decisions, in respect of persons charged with or convicted of offences;

(b) authorised persons to be given assistance in determining whether conditional cautions should be given and which conditions to attach to conditional cautions;

(c) the supervision and rehabilitation of persons charged with or convicted of offences;

(d) the giving of assistance to persons remanded on bail;

(e) the supervision and rehabilitation of persons to whom conditional cautions are given;

(f) the giving of information to victims of persons charged with or convicted of offences.

Section 3(2) of the Act gives the Secretary of State the power to 'make contractual or other arrangements with any other person for the making of the probation provision' and the first NOMS 'Commissioning Framework' was published in 2007.[13] The Foreword to this document includes the following statement:

As we move to a needs based commissioning system, commissioners will make judgements about what type of service is needed to manage offenders effectively and to reduce reoffending. These judgements need to be based on the best available evidence about what is working

---

[12] See also National Offender Management Service (2006b) regarding *Public Value Partnerships.*

[13] National Offender Management Service (2007): see http://noms.justice.gov.uk/news-publications-events/news/commissioning-framework/.

and what isn't, what the priorities for improvement are, where and with whom resources should be invested.

(National Offender Management Service 2007: 1)

A 'contestability prospectus'—a five-year strategy—aimed at the public, voluntary and private sector suppliers and specifying the type, length and value of contracts available was published before the OMA 2007 was passed (National Offender Management Service 2006b). The National Association of Probation Officers criticised this as containing 'a whole range of unproven assertions' (NAPO 2006: 2).

Taken together, these changes alter the work and ethos of the Probation Service. The NPS was moved closer to prison and police work and further away from social work. The provisions for more severe penalties for breach of community orders and the introduction of curfew orders further emphasise the control function of the NPS. By 2000, the onerous task had been placed on the NPS of preventing reoffending in relation to offenders on community and custodial sentences, and also in relation to joint crime-prevention projects with the police force. The NOMS web site now explains that 'the concept of end-to-end offender management ensures that offenders are offered the best possible opportunity to change their offending behaviour'[14] and the Prison Service web site states that 'NOMS is the system through which the highest quality correctional services and interventions are commissioned and provided to protect the public and reduce re-offending'.[15] It became imperative for the Service to discover 'what works', with a policy emphasis on evidence-based practice. The next section will, therefore, look at new theories of rehabilitation and their practical effects.

12.4 Rehabilitation: old and new

12.4.1 Introduction

The aim of rehabilitation is to reduce the crime rate by reforming and rehabilitating the individual, so he is less likely to reoffend. This approach was popular in the 1950s and early 1960s which is usually seen as the high point of the rehabilitative ideal.

As we have seen, rehabilitation is an important element of community sentences and the licence period of custodial sentences, as well as a key factor in parole decisions. Imprisonment also offers an opportunity to reform and rehabilitate the offender, giving him skills to survive outside while also changing his attitude towards offending (see Chapter 9). Rehabilitation is utilitarian in the sense that it is forward-looking and consequentialist: its objective is for the individual to contribute to society at the end of the period of rehabilitation and thereby add to the maximisation of happiness as well as enhancing his own happiness. In Bentham's model prison, the individual would be expected to undertake useful work and learn how to contribute to society in future by developing his skills and rationality. In the twentieth century the rehabilitative ethos focused on individualised

---

[14] See http://noms.justice.gov.uk/managing-offenders/end-to-end/; see also National Offender Management Service (2006a).

[15] See http://www.hmprisonservice.gov.uk/abouttheservice/noms/.

treatment of the offender, developing the treatment appropriate to him, rather than simply reflecting the severity of the offence. Proportionality then is less important as indeterminate sentences provide for treatment for as long as is necessary to rehabilitate the offender.

The rehabilitative ideal declined in popularity in the 1970s and 1980s, confronted by high levels of recidivism, but within the penal system there was still a commitment to it, albeit on a small scale in therapeutic programmes rather than at a macro-level. The rehabilitative approach has been beneficial in so far as it has encouraged the development of new programmes within the Prison and the Probation Services, stimulated the search for alternatives to incarceration, and widened the range of options. At its height the rehabilitative model was seen as much more progressive than retributivism, which as we have seen, has been (wrongly) associated with revenge and harsh punishment.

However, an attack on rehabilitation was mounted from two directions. First, it was challenged on the ground that offenders regularly reoffend despite undergoing rehabilitative programmes. Second, it has been argued that the approach is flawed in principle because of the rights violations permitted by it. Both these criticisms will be considered.

12.4.2 Does rehabilitation 'work'?

Nothing works

A key landmark in the assault on the rehabilitative ethos was Martinson's 1974 paper 'What works?'. Martinson reviewed the results of 231 research studies of a range of programmes aimed at rehabilitation in the period 1945–67, which suggested that various therapies and regimes which had been tried at that time, as well as different types of sentence, were ineffective in preventing reoffending. At best all they could do was reduce the adverse effects of imprisonment on offenders. The programmes included counselling, individual and group work, and a range of different therapeutic environments. Martinson concluded that 'with few and isolated exceptions, the rehabilitative efforts that have been reported so far have had no appreciable effect on recidivism' (ibid: 25). Similar conclusions were drawn from other studies in that period, such as Brody's (1976) review of UK sentencing policies which found no evidence to suggest that a particular type of sentence was more effective than others in preventing reoffending. Martinson's conclusions were endorsed by a National Research Panel on Rehabilitative Techniques, set up in the US in 1977, which commissioned papers on the issue and concluded that 'Lipton, Martinson, and Wilks were reasonably accurate in their appraisal of the rehabilitation literature' (Sechrest *et al.* 1979).

Martinson's paper was widely and mistakenly interpreted as suggesting 'nothing works', but Martinson himself was not so pessimistic (see Allen 1981). All Martinson was saying is that no one has yet proved conclusively that something works. Moreover, subsequent studies have been more promising. But the willingness to embrace a pessimistic view should also be seen in the context of the retreat from welfare in that period (see Pitts 1992b).

In the wake of Martinson's paper, the rehabilitation movement lost support and this contributed to the loss of political will to deal with the underlying social and economic problems or to develop a socio-economic approach to crime prevention (see Allen 1981). Instead, as we saw in Chapter 1, from the mid-1980s the UK government tried to fashion a cost-effective justice system. In addition, the decline of the rehabilitative model undermined support for rehabilitation-oriented practices like remission for good behaviour and early release mechanisms, predicated on the presumption of rehabilitation. After Martinson there were arguments—similar to those we have already encountered in our earlier discussions of deterrence and incapacitation—over the methodologies employed to prove or disprove the value of rehabilitative programmes. Opponents claimed that contrary evidence was obscured by the way the research was conducted and, given the broad time scale of Martinson's review, many of the studies cited in his paper were out of date by the mid-1970s. Large-scale studies of reoffending do not tell us enough about *which* individuals were helped by *which* programmes, and the individual who is helped may be overlooked in data on those who were not.

But it would be absurd to infer from this that nothing works; rather what evidence we now have suggests that *some* programmes are effective in reducing reoffending for *some* offenders and not others. Rehabilitative programmes are expensive so it is important to target specific programmes at those most likely to benefit.

A range of approaches has been used to study the effectiveness or ineffectiveness of rehabilitation programmes, including statistical analysis, interpretive studies, and meta-analyses. Of course it is difficult when measuring reoffending to know whether the offender did reoffend but was not caught, or alternatively, that he would not have reoffended anyway for some other reason. Rutherford (1992), for example, argues that juvenile offenders may mature and 'grow out of crime'. So a viable research study needs to control for these variables.

There is also the problem of the time lag for such studies. Expecting a particular programme to prevent reoffending may be unrealistic because the reasons for offending and desistance from offending are so complex and may include a range of factors including drugs and alcohol. Figures may also conceal whether the offence in question was committed before completing the programme.

As Rubin (2003) points out, in evaluating the rehabilitative ideal we should not assess it in terms of the complete reformation of the offender, but rather assess its value and effectiveness against alternatives, such as incapacitation, or warehousing, of offenders.

What works?

The major reviews of work on treatment programmes and reoffending were assessed by McGuire and Priestley who found that the effect of treatment showed on average a reduction in recidivism rates of between 10 per cent and 12 per cent (McGuire and Priestley 1995: 9). This is the average figure but in some of the programmes the figures were much higher: for example, Lipsey's (1992) review of programmes for young offenders also found treatment had a positive effect in reducing reoffending in 64.5 per cent of the experiments he examined.

Many studies focus on whether the respondents reoffend and, if we find high numbers do reoffend, then the programme is deemed ineffective. But Wilson (1985) argues it is better to focus on the frequency of reoffending and using this we find the results are more encouraging. He refers to studies of delinquents in Chicago by Murray and Cox (1979) who found that those programmes with stronger supervision had the greatest effect on the rate of recidivism. Restrictiveness and supervision appear to be important, whether the programme is deployed in the community or custody. Wilson notes that various studies suggest that some types of offender are easier to change than others and further research on this is needed. Young, verbal, intelligent, and neurotic offenders seem to be more amenable to therapy. A programme might be deemed a partial success if it leads to offenders committing less serious offences than the one for which they were originally convicted.

It is also difficult, as Walker (1991) notes, to draw firm conclusions because if we select any group of offenders, some of them may not respond to any form of corrective treatment, others may have responded better to another regime than the one tried, and there may be some who did respond positively to a particular regime, but they are swamped by a large number of failures. The successful outcome of a particular regime may also be affected by the individuals administering it, making it more difficult to assess the results than say, drugs trials. So to say 'nothing works' is an overstatement: some things work with some offenders but not with most or not for long and it may be hard to identify the cases in which they did work.

Something works

Considerable research has been undertaken in recent years to establish which type of regime works best in preventing reoffending. Numerous research studies have investigated the most effective practical programmes in the USA, Canada and Europe (see McGuire 1995). Since the late 1990s the 'nothing works' philosophy has been replaced by the view that 'something works' and some things work for some offenders.

Research suggests that cognitive-behavioural methods, rather than psychoanalytic or psychotherapeutic approaches or counselling which address deep-seated causes of crime, are the most effective in teaching new ways of thinking and behaving. These include teaching practical skills to cope with personal and social problems, using a range of methods of treatment, depending on participants' abilities and levels of risk, encouraging offenders to empathise with victims and to think about the effects of their actions. The aim is to enhance problem-solving skills so that individuals can control themselves and their environments to avoid exposing themselves to high-risk situations. Cognitive-behavioural treatment is very popular but some programmes combine a variety of modes of treatment.

A recent Home Office study (2002d) on cognitive-behavioural treatment programmes in England and Wales found that reconviction rates fell after cognitive skills treatment. The rates for treatment groups were up to 14 per cent lower than for control groups who did not receive treatment. If this were quantified in terms of numbers expected to complete cognitive skills programmes in 2002–3, this would amount to nearly 21,000 crimes prevented. There is now more optimism regarding the value of offending-behaviour programmes and in this sense the rehabilitative ideal has gained ground.

The available research on evidence-based crime prevention, including cognitive behaviour treatment (CBT) and other interventions, in a range of contexts, is reviewed by Welsh and Farrington (2006) and Sherman *et al.* (2006). Although, there have been positive results, there have been concerns that CBT can be less successful in relation to women offenders, not least because women may have different learning styles and different therapeutic needs. As we saw in Chapters 10 and 11, most of the findings on the rehabilitation of offenders have been drawn from research studies of male offenders. However, more work is now being undertaken on female offenders and there is more interest in developing gender-appropriate courses. Women may benefit more from small-group therapeutic approaches, but it may be harder to 'sell' these in the prison context because of the weight given to risk-based models. 'What works' in relation to female offenders is considered by Sheehan *et al.* (2007) and Blanchette and Brown (2006).

Given that the yardstick for rehabilitation and change is primarily in terms of recidivism, recent studies have been more favourable. Greatest improvements are made by those who complete at least 18 months of therapy. A number of studies have been undertaken of HMP Grendon, the therapeutic category B medium-security prison which opened in 1962, which have been quite promising. Marshall's study in 1997 showed lower reconviction rates for those who went to Grendon than for those who elected for Grendon but did not go, and there were similar findings by Taylor (2000). This suggests that the Grendon regime does make a significant impact on reconviction rates despite high levels of psychopathy, dangerousness and psychological disturbances among the population there.

Wilson and McCabe (2002) considered how Grendon 'works' from the prisoners' perspectives. They sat in on therapy groups, interviewed inmates, and sought prisoners' own views and used prisoners' autobiographical materials. At Grendon, inmates meet in small groups of up to eight people three to five times per week. Wilson and McCabe found that treatment takes time and new behaviours need to be constantly strengthened by other prisoners and key staff members, and having a personal 'champion' on the staff was very important. Other prisoners played a key role in the therapy groups and the emphasis was on involving prisoners in community life so they experienced social inclusion rather than exclusion. The quality of life at Grendon was also significant, affecting how prisoners viewed the therapeutic process. Officers were polite, called prisoners by their first name, and treated them respectfully as human beings, which also assisted in this process of inclusion.

The attack on rehabilitation from the standpoint that 'nothing works' has therefore been strongly challenged in recent years. However Pitts (1992b) is sceptical regarding the renaissance of the 'something works' doctrine. Referring to the DHSS Intermediate Treatment Initiative which did contribute to a reduction in juvenile imprisonment in the period 1979–89, he points out that the evidence suggests that 60 per cent of those who took part in Initiative Projects were reconvicted within two years. He argues that the evidence does not suggest that we have something which works, but rather the emergence of a 'something works doctrine' which serves a useful political role in legitimising government efforts to promote an alternative non-custodial sentencing tariff. For it to be effective as an ideology it needs to seem to be supported by carefully designed research.

12.4.3 The critique of rehabilitation: the demand for justice

A more compelling critique of the traditional rehabilitative model is from the rights-based perspective. It argues that the rehabilitative ideal, when applied in practice, may lead to rights violations, to injustice and unfairness, and to excessive punishment (see American Friends Services Committee 1971). It treats the offender as the passive recipient of treatment, rather than as a freely consenting subject. The decline of the rehabilitative model can be attributed in part to the attack from civil libertarians and to their efforts to reassert due process rights in the late 1970s and early 1980s, particularly in response to indeterminate and individualised sentencing in the United States. It was the reaction to these concerns which stimulated the revival of retributivism.

The demands for justice and fairness, the importance of treating like cases alike, increased the pressure for determinate sentences and specific sentences for specific crimes rather than individualised sentences, in both the UK and the USA. Rehabilitation has also been strongly associated with indeterminate sentences and for allowing too much discretion to sentencers, leading to inconsistency and extended sentences. However, the attack on discretionary sentencing met with more success in the USA than the UK because attempts to curtail or limit sentencing discretion have been strongly resisted by sentencers in the UK. The revival of retributivism also occurred later in the UK, as we have seen, in the CJA 1991. New desert theory is hostile to predictive sentencing which would be acceptable on a rehabilitation model. Rehabilitative regimes may also allow the use of invasive treatments, such as drug therapies, to control behaviour.

The rehabilitative model was criticised from both left and right; from the left for failing to get to grips with the underlying social inequalities and problems which may generate crime and for treating the individual without addressing social causes. Probation practice influenced by the rehabilitative ideal has been criticised on the same grounds, that it individualises fundamental social problems which are linked to social factors such as poverty and racism. But it met with criticism from the right, because it appeared to deny individual responsibility for crime, and also for the cost of apparently wasteful programmes. The extreme form of the rehabilitative model sees the task of the criminal justice system as to cure the errant individual rather than to punish him if he is not responsible, because it would be unjust to punish if the person is not responsible because of an illness which precipitates offending.

Yet at the time of its ascendancy rehabilitation was seen as a progressive theory and anti-punitive. Moreover, its fall from popularity was followed not by a rediscovery of the social context of criminality, but rather by increased punitiveness. The decline of rehabilitation created space for incapacitation and populist punitiveness to flourish. The importance of law and order as a key political issue in turn made it difficult for rehabilitation programmes to find support and funding.

Sentencing systems with judges strongly committed to the rehabilitation model, such as Canada and the United States in the 1980s, tended to generate longer and harsher sentences on average than retributivist justice, creating further problems of prisoners' institutionalisation. Such systems usually give substantial discretion to sentencers and because protecting society from dangerous individuals is a priority, their release will be undertaken cautiously. There may be problems in determining whether and when someone has been rehabilitated. It may be hard for applicants to know what criteria are used which will lead to frustration. From the prisoners' standpoint, indeterminate sentences are the sentences most feared. Moreover within a therapeutic environment, the offender feels under constant observation and strong surveillance can mean the impact of the prison goes deeper, affecting one's sense of self, rather than as being experienced as simply 'doing time'.

12.4.4 **The New Rehabilitationism**

In response to these criticisms, rehabilitationism has adapted. Hudson (1993) refers to the strong meaning of rehabilitation as preventing reoffending, and prison should be oriented towards this. The new rehabilitationists demand something more positive than humane containment and minimum standards, prison should be a positive rather than a negative experience. The New Rehabilitationism, she argues, does not entail indeterminate sentencing; rehabilitative progress is not the criterion for sentence length. Hudson argues that in cases of low culpability, rehabilitation should be the prime objective and punishment kept to a minimum. If imprisonment is imposed then it should not exceed the sentence pronounced by the court. This raises issues regarding the right of the offender to refuse participation but many would argue the offender should be obliged to take part in offending behaviour programmes.

Paradoxically, although the attack on the rehabilitative ideal was launched from a rights-based perspective, in recent years the revival of rehabilitation in the late 1990s was itself associated with a rights-based approach in the USA, particularly in the work of Rotman (1990). Rotman argues that the right of the state to punish and the right of the criminal not to be punished unduly, are best protected by rehabilitation being offered within a determinate sentence, fixed by considerations of desert and dangerousness. The obligation of the state is to provide basic physical standards in the prison and rehabilitative facilities sufficient to ensure that the offender is not damaged by the effects of incarceration. He cites the case of *Laaman v Helgemoe*, in which the United States Supreme Court said that '[p]unishment for one crime, under conditions which spawn future crime and more punishment, serves no valid legislative purpose and is so totally without penological justification that it results in the gratuitous infliction of suffering in violation of the Eighth Amendment' (see Rotman 1990: 81–2).

In the UK the issue has arisen in relation to whether the Secretary of State is under a duty to provide sufficient offending behaviour programmes to enable prisoners to prepare themselves for consideration for release. The provision of constructive regimes is a key element in the prisoner's rehabilitation. Several first instance cases found that the issue was not justiciable but in *R (Cawser) v Secretary of State for the Home Department* (2003), the Court of Appeal found it would be irrational to have a policy of making release dependent on the completion of such courses without making reasonable provision for those courses. Since then, challenges have been brought by IPP prisoners who have argued that the failure to provide sufficient courses constitutes a breach of Article 5 of the Convention, when they are detained beyond the minimum term because of this failure. As we saw in Chapter 9, section 9.3.3, there are still insufficient offending behaviour courses to meet the demand so that prisoners are being detained longer than necessary after completing the minimum term of their sentence. In the most recent test case, *Secretary of State for Justice v Walker and James* (2008), the Court of Appeal found that the Secretary of State had acted unlawfully in failing to provide appropriate access to courses to allow IPP prisoners to demonstrate to the Parole Board that their detention was no longer necessary to protect the public, and that their continued detention for this reason could breach Article 5(4). However the Court set aside an order for James's release and the parties are now seeking leave to appeal.[16]

Rotman (1990) distinguished the rights-based model of rehabilitation from the earlier penitentiary model, which seeks to reform through contemplation and submission to the regime, and from the therapeutic and social learning models. As we have seen the latter are problematic because it is questionable whether the individual does engage in such contemplation, or whether such regimes are effective or rather coercive. The New Rehabilitationism emphasises justice rather than treatment, so the offender's due process rights are respected and he is protected from coercive treatment. It treats the individual as possessing rights and as capable of making choices but also as having a positive right to appropriate treatment to prevent reoffending. In the New Rehabilitationism the emphasis is on non-coercive training and treatment. The New Rehabilitationism may also be seen as part of restorative justice which seeks to reintegrate the offender within the community, using treatment programmes as part of this process, while also respecting the human rights of both offender and victim (see Chapter 6). At the same time, efforts have been made to 'rehabilitate' the rehabilitative ideal in the face of the extensive criticisms made during the 1970s and 1980s. Rubin (2003) rejects the association of rehabilitation with coercion, pointing out that it is absurd to dismiss this approach on the basis of its abuse by some regimes and institutions. In any event, historically rehabilitation can also be associated with progressive policies which, at the time, provided an alternative to more repressive penal practices. Moreover, within the modern American prison context, he argues, it provides the most humane way of structuring prison life: 'the rehabilitative ideal, together with the insistence on regularized, bureaucratic governance, remains the principal source of decent and humane correctional practices' (ibid: 82). He also rejects the inevitable association of rehabilitation with the use of indeterminate sentences, pointing out that such sentences can also be found in contexts where no efforts are made to rehabilitate offenders. Rehabilitation, he argues, could also impose more restraint on prison expansion, or what he describes as the 'incarcerative frenzy' in the United States, than rival theories of punishment. Given current concerns over that expansion, the political climate may now be more favourable to rehabilitation.

12.5 Conclusions

12.5.1 The survival of rehabilitation

Although we find numerous references to the decline of rehabilitation in commentaries on penal policy, nonetheless the commitment to rehabilitation remains an element of UK penal policy. It survived the negative reaction to Martinson's paper, in specific programmes for offenders within prison and in work with young offenders and with specific groups such as sex offenders, rather than in mainstream penal policy. As Zimring and Hawkins (1995) have observed, rehabilitation generated far more discussion than incapacitation in penological research in

---

[16] See the Online Resource Centre for updates on this case.

**online
resource
centre**

the 1980s. It also remained a rationale of the work at Grendon Underwood and now underpins offending behaviour programmes in contemporary prisons (see Chapter 9). Although the CJA 1991 referred to it only in relation to probation work, it is emphasised in the Halliday Report. That report advocated more investment in preparing prisoners for return to society, with a new Custody to Work Programme, and recommended that the prisons should be made more accessible.

Rehabilitation is clearly back on the political agenda. It was a feature of the White Paper, *Criminal Justice: The Way Ahead* (Home Office 2001a) which aims to reduce reoffending by improving the education and vocational qualifications of prisoners so they leave prison better prepared to re-enter society. The focus is more on sentence outcomes, looking at what works for which type of offender. It is concerned to improve the funding for prison service offending behaviour programmes as well as practical skills courses, more drug programmes, and the custody plus sentence. It stresses that prison is not just for punishment and incapacitation but should help prevent reoffending, by providing a humane regime, and adequate training, because there is a strong link between unemployment, homelessness and reoffending. It emphasises the need to put more money into resettlement of prisoners, to address the problems of social exclusion. These issues have also been considered by the Social Exclusion Unit (2002).

In practice there is also still a strong concern with rehabilitation amongst probation officers. The recognition of the individual's capacity to change exists alongside the obligation to manage risk and this is reflected in the conflict between care and control in the Probation Service that we have summarised. In the Prison Service too we find offending behaviour programmes which are concerned with rehabilitation and which have achieved some success. The difficulty is, as we shall see in the next section, that there is debate as to whether the New Rehabilitationism is 'really' rehabilitation.

12.5.2 **Rehabilitation or risk control?**

2001 saw the publication of the mission statement for the (then) new National Probation Service, *A New Choreography* (Wallis 2001). At that time Nellis asked, very aptly in relation to a policy statement so strangely entitled, whether the NPS was indeed 'dancing to a new tune' (2002: 369). The point he was making is that different interpretations can be placed on what is known about the delivery of community punishments.

That delivery can now be conceptualised in (at least) two ways. First, it could be a later version of the 'normalising' sector of the modern penal complex (Garland 1985: 238ff; see section 12.1.3), delivering a 'soft' version of discipline and rehabilitation by instilling values and helping the offender to establish a 'normal' lifestyle. Second, it could be perceived as an important element of a (new) late modern or postmodern penality that focuses on the actuarially-based management of risk. The first alternative implies that community punishment is still part of the penal–welfare complex originating a century ago, in which probation practice adds to social welfare rather than reduces it (ibid: 240). On the other hand, the practice of community punishment may now be a firm part of the risk management machine we discussed in Chapter 5 (see also Robinson 2002: 5).

In addition, there are the duties relating to the enhanced role of the victim which we discussed in Chapter 6, and successive revisions to National Standards have shown an increased emphasis on the rights and experiences of victims within supervision programmes as well as a greater emphasis on risk assessment at each stage of the supervision process. In the context of restorative justice ideas, Duff has asked whether 'altruism should be engaged in punishment' (2003).[17] He argues against the 'merely punitive' punishment, by which he means those punishments intended or administered solely as retribution or as deterrents, or which seek to exclude and stigmatise offenders. Instead the Probation Service should treat the offender as a member of the normative community, should include censure in supervision but incorporate in that censure the restorative justice value of integration (ibid: 186). In other words, the Probation Service should engage in what he refers to as constructive or communicative punishment (ibid: 185). All this still leaves the Probation Service with an ambiguous role.[18]

In recent years there have been attempts to analyse risk management and rehabilitation in practice to determine whether they are in fact radically different. Parts of this project would appear to be a genuine attempt to delineate the nature of both of those two approaches in more empirical and conceptual detail, but at times the exercise appears more as an attempt to heal the rifts in the Probation Service by the use of words which paper over the cracks. So, for example, Gwen Robinson has argued that risk management and rehabilitation are not radically different approaches, it is largely a question of words and methods (1999; see also Fitz Gibbon 2007 for concerns about assessment skills). Hutchinson (2006), in an article entitled 'Countering catastrophic criminology', has also analysed the continuities rather than the ruptures in modern penalty and penal practice.

It could be argued, however, that the conflation of risk management with rehabilitation conceptualises modern rehabilitation in a much narrower way. An example given of the practical integration of risk management and rehabilitation is the evolution of 'third-generation assessment instruments'. The level of service inventory, for example, measures both the likelihood of reconviction and information about the personal characteristics and the offender's social life which increase his chances of reconviction (see Robinson 1999: 429; see also Chapter 13, section 13.2.1 for information on assessment of young offenders).

Robinson also conducted empirical research to determine whether probation practice could now be located in the postmodern form of penality to which we referred above. Traditional individual rehabilitative case work is taken to equate to a 'modern' categorisation, practice methods based in actuarial risk assessment equate to postmodern, and so Robinson focused on establishing how effective had been the attempt to institute a risk-based approach in probation supervision. Her findings reveal some ambivalence. Officers were still using clinical judgements for classification, for example, which does not fit into statistical risk assessment and other tools of the New Penology, but Robinson concluded also that normalisation, 'the disciplinary individual based processes of modern penality, dependent on personal interactions between the probation officer and the offender, is no longer at the heart of probation practice' (2002: 5).

---

[17] In fact the title reads 'Should Al Truism Be Engaged in Punishment'.
[18] See, for further earlier comment, May (1990) and Sheppard (1990).

The report of an inspection in 1997 also endorsed a focus on individual offenders rather than categories of offender: 'potentially dangerous offenders do not necessarily have anything in common except the likelihood that they may seriously harm someone else. A key to effective supervision is therefore to approach each case individually and tailor supervision to its particular needs, bearing in mind the overall objective of public protection' (HM Inspectorate of Probation 1997: 252–3). Robinson argues that this individualised risk-management model was given further impetus by the legislation pertaining to the registration of sex offenders (2002: 9).

These developments could then be seen as evidence of probation retaining its sense of transformative or rehabilitative optimism, but Hudson sees other developments as evidence that the Probation Service is moving away from risk management to what she calls risk control (2001). Robinson points to the increasing importance of actuarially based assessment instruments, noting the above report's acknowledgement that 'even the best practice cannot guarantee a person will not seriously harm someone else... the aim is to reach a defensible position—one which would stand up to scrutiny if the handling of the case were to be investigated' (HM Inspectorate of Probation 1997: 231, 245 in Robinson 2002: 10). She concludes that it is now 'clear that rehabilitation is no longer understood as an all-purpose prescription, even in the relatively limited context of probation supervision': the scope of rehabilitation has been narrowed and the character is different in that it focuses on offending behaviour rather than the offender (Robinson 2002: 16).

The managers of correctional policy[19] in the community do not endorse this ambiguity about what constitutes community punishment. We noted that National Standards were a crucial tool for 'modernising' the Probation Service: opposition to their use has 'consisted—and still consists in isolated pockets of antediluvian officers—of two main strands', staff dislike of being told what to do and distrust attempts to impose consistency. This was the view of Hopley (2002: 298) who led the team that revised the 1995 National Standards. His statement clearly individualises and denigrates opposition to values underpinning the new correctional services and it ignores the intense debate about the value base of probation work, evident in the middle of the 1990s in a series of articles in the *Howard Journal* (see James 1995, Nellis 1995, Masters 1997 and Spencer 1995).

Paul Boateng, the then Minister of Home Affairs, was equally clear: 'we are a law enforcement agency. That is what we are. That is what we do' (quoted in Hopley 2002: 303). Noting that offenders should be worried about the tougher new approach, Hopley also explains that there is a great potential benefit for offenders: 'for those who do not want a life of crime, it is an advantage that the work the Probation Service will do with them is based on something that is proven to work, rather than on whatever interests the probation officer responsible for their supervision' (ibid: 305–6). The new focus on value-for-money preventative programmes provided as a result of competitive tender and the closer links between probation, prison and the police may well be speeding up the development of a very different community corrections service.

---

[19] An increasingly used phrase: see, for example, Home Office (1999c) *The Correctional Policy Framework*.

12.5.3 **Justice in community punishment**

What counts as justice in the context of community punishment is also a contested area. Harding (2000), writing as a Chief Probation Officer, argued that putting into practice the restorative concepts of penance, making amends, and the involvement of the community and victim are essential aspects of 'just' practice. However, whilst arguing for communicative community punishment, Duff acknowledges that its preconditions are unlikely to be met within existing political societies, given that punishment is currently meted out to a group who have already suffered disadvantage and exclusion (2003: 192–4). Communicative and rehabilitative approaches which treat the individual offender will have limited effect unless the social context in which offending occurs is also addressed. A Home Office study of offenders found that, in their sample, 49 per cent said they had or expected to have long-term health problems or disabilities, 70 per cent had rented their accommodation from a local authority or housing association (compared with 25 per cent of the general population), 35 per cent had problems with debt, 54 per cent were signing on as unemployed, and there were high levels of educational under-achievement (Mair and May 1997). The result is that the risk factors which are predictive of offending are also descriptive of the caseloads of probation officers: young offenders are most likely to come from particular neighbourhoods and schools with particular factors in their background (Lacey 2002: 29–30). In custodial settings, too, the emphasis is now on providing constructive regimes which try to combat social exclusion by offering education and training programmes (see Woolf and Tumim, 1991; Simon 1999). This is not simply to prevent rioting and disorder in prisons but because it facilitates reintegration and rehabilitation.

Further, the sought-after 'flexibility' in community sentencing has 'the potential for arbitrariness and discrimination' in deciding how much 'treatment' offenders need in the community; 'flexibility' might be the opposite of justice (Raynor and Vanstone 2002: 106). Recent research found male/female variations in the use of requirements and a wide variation between probation areas with regard to the number and type of requirements used in orders (Mair *et al.* 2007: 31; see also Chapter 11, section 11.2.1 for other gender differences). Research on the 'old' community order had also found issues of gender (McIvor 1998; Bowen *et al.* 2002), including issues of childcare provision, and also race discrimination (Denny 1992). Resource constraints may also affect the provision of community penalties differentially: if a particular community punishment scheme is not in operation in a particular area, it is not available to the courts.

Arguably, then, the goal of 'fair punishment' is being lost and a stronger human rights culture is needed in relation to community punishment (Hudson 2001). Nonetheless, the greater use of community penalties is to be welcomed.

Given what we know (or think we know) about other advantages of punishment in the community, such as its lower costs, its general tendency to be less dehumanising than custody and to drive fewer of those who endure it to self-harm and suicide, the lack of any demonstrable superiority on the part of institutional sentencing in controlling recidivism should mean that it is the use of *custody* not community sentencing that has to be justified and defended.

(Brownlee 1998b: 180)

12.5.4 **Discussion questions**

Below are questions which raise important issues. There is further reading, and also guidance on thinking about these issues, in the Online Resource Centre.

1. Is what is known about the practice of assessment and supervision of offenders in the community evidence that it operates within a postmodern penality?

2. In what ways is the sentencing framework established by the Criminal Justice Act 2003 for imposing those penalties which are between fines and prison a 'better' framework than the one it replaced?

3. How does the New Rehabilitationism differ from earlier forms of rehabilitation?

13

....

Punishing young offenders

SUMMARY

This chapter examines the current practices and policy trends in relation to both community and custodial penalties for young offenders. It focuses on issues arising from the policy concern with risk and anti-social behaviour and highlights the continuing deficiencies in the care of young people detained in Prison Service establishments. It also reviews developments in the use of supervision orders. Finally, it examines the advantages and limitations of using rights conventions to ensure more appropriate treatment of children and young people who commit offences.

13.1 Pre-'punishment' court orders

13.1.1 Civil orders

As we saw in Chapter 8 (section 8.4.3), policies of diversion from prosecution and to preventative programmes have been accompanied by other policy agendas which focus on controlling children and their families through a range of new civil orders and, as we shall see, contracts and agreements. These new tools for responding to anti-social and criminal behaviour through the civil justice system—or by using 'voluntary' contracts—are aimed at delaying the 'criminalisation' of children or preventing further offending and are not technically punishments (although there is debate as to whether ASBOs are 'a measure of first or last resort': see NACRO 2007c: 3). In practice these developments, part of the 'Respect' and 'Safer Communities' agendas, have drawn more children and young people within the ambit of state surveillance and, as we shall see, may hasten entry into the criminal justice system. Further, there are other concerns because of the context for these new initiatives. Cleland and Tisdall (2005) have noted that the traditional 'triangle of relationships between the state, parents and children' should now be replaced with a square, because of a fourth 'side' which is now very important— the community—but, they go on to argue, the values represented by that fourth element are 'profoundly worrying' because they encourage punitive treatment of children engaging in anti-social behaviour (ibid: 413; see also Chapter 12, section 12.1.3 for a discussion of 'community'). There are also rights issues raised by these developments. For all these reasons we have, therefore, decided to include a discussion of these orders in a book on sentencing and punishment.

Anti-social behaviour orders

Anti-social behaviour orders (ASBOs) and child safety orders were the first new orders introduced in 1998. The common criterion is that the child or adult has acted 'in a manner that caused or was likely to cause harassment, alarm or distress' to one or more persons outside the family (Crime and Disorder Act (CDA) 1998, ss 1(1) (a) and 12(3)(c)). The ASBO must last for not less than two years whilst the maximum period for a child safety order is three months (exceptionally twelve months). ASBOs can be awarded by magistrates in their civil jurisdiction or, with the implementation of the provisions in the Police Reform Act 2002 (and the Criminal Procedure (Scotland) Act 1995) can be imposed by the criminal courts against individuals convicted of a criminal offence. These orders are sometimes referred to as CRASBOs. The number of such orders now exceeds the numbers imposed as a result of 'stand-alone' applications under s 1 of the Crime and Disorder Act 1998. If applications for ASBOs are made under s 1 in the magistrates' courts and the person on whom the order is being sought is under 18, then the magistrates should be ones who are also youth court magistrates (*Practice Direction on the Composition of Benches* (2006); see also NACRO (2007c) for further detailed information on ASBOs relating to children and young people). Child safety orders, on the other hand, are a little-used family jurisdiction supervision order.

The Anti-Social Behaviour Act (ASBA) 2003 incorporated the proposals in *Respect and Responsibility* (Home Office 2003b) by widening the scope and use of ASBOs (s 85). Sections 85–86 of the Act increase the range of the 'relevant authorities' who can apply for an ASBO to include county councils and Housing Action Trusts as well as the local authority with housing responsibility, the police and registered social landlords. The ASBA 2003 also introduced a presumption that a parenting order will be made with an ASBO (s 85, amending the CDA 1998, s 9), whilst the CJA 2003 (s 322 amending the CDA 1998 s 1) added a further presumption that an ISO (individual support order) will be made alongside an ASBO for the under 18s.[1] The ISO adds a positive requirement 'in the interests of preventing any repetition of the kind of behaviour which led to the making of the anti-social behaviour order'—as opposed to the negative requirement of the ASBO—and can be imposed for a period up to six months. Further, Part 2 of the ASBA 2003 amends housing legislation to allow landlords to make applications to the court on the basis of anti-social behaviour by the tenant. If successful, such applications have serious implications for security of tenure and residence, implications which extend to the tenant's children, whether or not they have been involved in the anti-social behaviour.

The ASBA 2003 also provides the police with controversial new powers to disperse groups in 'designated areas' and to remove from that area individuals who do not live there. These powers relate to all ages but, in addition, there is the power to return home an under-16-year-old (ss 30–36) but this power was challenged in *R (W) v Commissioner of Police of the Metropolis and Another* (2005) which held that s 30(6) did not give the police the power to use reasonable force to return a child home (see Hollingsworth 2006).

The Government had originally expressed its unwillingness to use ASBOs with juveniles, explaining that they were aimed at adults, but then stated that they would be used only for those over 12, before reducing the lower age to 10 (see Burney 2005: 97–8). The result was that, by the end of 2004, 52 per cent of orders had been given to 10–17-year-olds. Further, statistics collated by the Home

[1] The Criminal Justice and Immigration Act 2008 ss 124–5 makes amendments concerning ISOs end parenting orders: see the Online Resource Centre for updates.

Office revealed that, after initial reluctance to use the orders, there was an alarming rise in the use of ASBOs for young people aged 10–17 inclusive in the period 2001–4: a total of 185 were imposed in England and Wales in 2001, 515 in 2003, and 1,077 in 2004.[2] Statistics also suggest that there is 'injustice by geography' in that some areas impose considerably more orders than others and research done for the Youth Justice Board (2006a) found that a disproportionate number of the sample—22 per cent—of the sample were from black and ethnic minority groups. Generally, the whole sample comprised a highly disadvantaged group although they note that their sample was obtained from youth offending teams (YOTs) and so might be more reflective of young people already known to the youth justice system than of those on ASBOs more generally (ibid).

It is local authorities and the police who apply for ASBOs but some commentators have pointed to the role of the judiciary in their increasing use. Donoghue states that 'it is the judiciary who primarily define their legitimacy, their purpose and scope, and their function in law' (Donoghue 2007: 428) and Bateman accuses magistrates of giving insufficient attention to the legal requirement to impose an order only if it is 'necessary', assuming—wrongly—that alternatives have been tried already (Bateman 2007: 313–20). Further, in the *McCann* (2003) case in relation to Article 6 of the ECHR—the right to a fair trial and the issue of the standard of proof—the Court of Appeal decided, albeit not unanimously, that 'these restrictions are imposed for preventative reasons not punishment' (*per* Lord Hope). In Scotland, however, there is no curfew or 'naming and sharing' (see below) available for use with under-18s (see NACRO 2007c: 7); see also MacDonald and Telford (2007) for a discussion of the use of ASBOs in Scotland).

ASBOs can include various constraining requirements. Donoghue maintains that 'the potential for ASBOs on conviction to be issued inappropriately by the courts is clear: not only is there no statutory requirement for proof of prior interagency consultation, but there is also the possibility that the order will contain inappropriate conditions' (2007: 426). The YJB research noted above includes the following findings:

Geographical 'exclusions' and 'non-association' with anti-social peers were regarded on all sides as the most problematic prohibitions in terms of compliance. Young people and their parents/carers reported that being prohibited from associating with friends in familiar local territories resulted in a serious—and in some cases counter-productive—restriction of normal daily activities. The qualitative data confirmed that the majority of breach cases centred on failure to comply with these types of prohibition.

(Youth Justice Board 2006a: 8)

ASBOs are ineffective if the number of breaches of prohibitions is an indicator of failure: the Audit Office found that over half of those in their sample group—46 per cent of whom were under 18—breached their order, and a third did so on two or more occasions (Home Office 2006f: paras 5b and 5h of the Executive Summary). A breach is dealt with by the criminal courts and, because breaches have provided the sentencing courts with a growing body of work for the courts, the Sentencing Advisory Panel (SAP) has issued advice on the sentencing of young offenders for breach (2007a: para 78ff).

---

[2] See http://www.crimereduction.gov.uk/.

There is another issue raised by the practice of ASBOs and that is the issue of the 'naming and shaming' of those given orders, which may be seen as an element of what Cobb describes as the incremental reduction in anonymity rights for minors over the last decade (Cobb 2007: 360–1). Yet *Stanley v Metropolitan Police* (2004) did not declare the publicity practices to be in breach of Article 8(1) of the ECHR (see Burney 2005: 96–7; see also Taylor 2006), although the practice of 'aggressive publication of ASBOs, through, for instance, the door-step distribution of leaflets containing the names and addresses of children subject to ASBOs' has been criticised by a Commissioner on Human Rights (Gil-Robles 2005: 37; see also Donoghue 2007: 420–1). The Judicial Studies Board justifies the procedure because 'it is in the community interest that any order will be enforced in order to protect the community. Unless the nuisance is extremely localised, enforcement of the order will normally depend upon the general public being aware of the order and of the identity of the person against whom it is made' (undated: section 3.6). The Children and Young People's Act 1933 s 39, as amended by the Youth Justice and Criminal Evidence Act 1999, gives the court a discretion to forbid identification in any civil or criminal proceedings, but the courts have justified over-riding the child's anonymity under this provision by taking account of the deterrent effect of publicity on the young defendant. Brown LJ argued in *Winchester Crown Court* (2000) that 'these deterrents are proper objectives for the court to seek' because the effect is beneficial in reducing the young person's offending (at para 13).

Parenting orders

Parenting orders, as introduced by ss 8–11 of the CDA 1998, are triggered if the child or young person is subject to a range of orders, is convicted of a criminal offence, or fails to comply with a school attendance order.[3] Section 8(1) lists the relevant orders as a child safety order, an anti-social behaviour order, and a sex offender order (now sexual offences prevention order), these orders being created, respectively, by ss 11, 1 and 2 of the CDA 1998. Parenting orders can last up to 12 months and can specify particular requirements if that would be desirable to prevent further anti-social behaviour or offending. Parents must also attend for a concurrent period not exceeding three months and not more than once a week, parenting classes or counselling as determined by the responsible officer.[4] In *R (M) v Inner London Crown Court* (2003) the court concluded that a parenting order did not breach either Articles 6 or 8 of the European Convention for the Protection of Human Rights and Fundamental Freedoms (ECHR). In this case a mother sought judicial review of the decision of the Crown Court to dismiss her appeal against the imposition of a 12-month parenting order following her daughter's conviction for wounding. The court found that a fair trial was not undermined by the wide discretion given to magistrates to evaluate the need for an order, and that a parenting order is not disproportionate, given the pressing social need to address the problems created by juvenile crime and the early research on such orders.[5]

---

[3] Under the Education Act 1996, ss 443–444: CDA 1998, s 8(1)(d).

[4] The Anti-Social Behaviour Act 2003, s 18 amends s 8 so that the parenting class or counselling requirement is discretionary if the specified parent/s has already attended a programme. The 'responsible officer' is defined in the CJA 2003, s 197.

[5] In fact the order was quashed in this case because the magistrates' decision to impose the order in relation to a neighbour dispute was seen as irrational: see [2003] Fam Law 477–8.

The ASBA 2003 also widened the scope of parenting orders (ss 18, 20–24, 26–29), and included detailed provisions in relation to parenting contracts (ss 19 and 25). The latter were developed as voluntary agreements between youth offending teams and parents of children referred to them but s 27 of the Act mandates the court, when deciding whether to make a parenting order under s 26, 'to take into account (amongst other things) –

(a) any refusal by the parent to enter into a parenting contract under section 25 in respect of the child or young person, or

(b) if the parent has entered into such a parenting contract, any failure by the parent to comply with the requirements specified in the contract.'

A professionally developed tool is thereby brought within the scrutiny of the court and so given a quasi-legal status in that there are ramifications for non-participation or non-compliance. Further, the Act extends the use of parenting orders in cases of exclusion from school (s 20) and allows for a penalty notice, in effect an 'on the spot' fine, to be served on a parent who could otherwise be convicted of an offence under s 444 of the Education Act 1996 on account of the child's irregular attendance at school (s 23). By s 18(3), parenting orders made in these circumstances or any other situation may include attendance at a residential course as part of the requirement to attend a guidance programme. This amounts to a serious restriction on liberty which is not a result of a conviction for an offence and is, therefore, vulnerable to challenge as contrary to ECHR rights.

Parental compensation orders

The parental compensation order (PCO) was introduced by the Serious and Organised Crime and Police Act 2005 (s 144 and Schedule 10) which inserted ss 13A–13E into the Crime and Disorder Act 1998. The orders have been piloted in ten local authority areas since July 2006[6] in conjunction with Targeted Youth Support Pathfinders. A Magistrates' Court may make a PCO on application from a local authority when it is satisfied that the child (who must be under 10) has taken, or caused loss of or damage to property in the course of committing an act which, 'if he had been aged 10 or over, would have constituted an offence; or acting in a manner that caused or was likely to cause harassment, alarm or distress to one or more persons not of the same household as himself; and that it would be desirable to make the order in the interests of preventing a repetition of the behaviour in question'. Tony McNulty MP, the Minister for Policing, Security and Community Safety, explained their purpose: 'By requiring the parent(s) or guardian(s) to pay compensation, the PCO is designed to provide compensation to those affected and to prevent further behaviour by the child of the type which caused the order to be made. The PCO will therefore encourage parents and their children to understand their responsibilities and to take responsibility for behaviour'.[7]

In this section we have reviewed a diverse range of orders which affect parents, and indeed the whole family, of children who engage in criminal and anti-social behaviour. Some of them would appear to be disproportionate to the behaviour which triggers them and would appear to punish family members who might have

---

[6] See, for information on the pilots being run by selected local authority children's trusts, http://www.everychildmatters.gov.uk/deliveringservices/targetedyouthsupport/pathfinder/.

[7] Hansard, HC 20 July 2006, Cols 44–45WS.

little influence on the actions of other family members. They evidence a very grey area in current policy which has been driven by ideology and media interest, and they may not achieve their aims. Rather, they may create further problems for parents and their children. They also conflict with retributivist principles in so far as they may impose 'punishment' on third parties (see Chapter 2 section 2.5).

13.1.2 Referral orders

The referral order is another relatively recent new order which has a somewhat ambivalent status. It is a criminal order, imposed by a youth court, but it diverts the offender from the court to a Panel to agree a programme of preventative or restorative activities rather than to impose punishment. It is a compromise which has its roots in the 1960s.

In 1964 a Labour policy report, *Crime: A Challenge to us All*, advocated family courts geared to achieving agreement with the offender as to what should be done to prevent his offending (see Harris and Webb 1987: 23), but, as we saw in Chapter 8, substantial legislative change was not achieved at that time in England and Wales. However, the new method of dealing with first-time offenders at the youth court by the use of referral orders (see section 8.1.3), introduced by the Youth Justice and Criminal Evidence Act 1999 Part I (now in the PCCSA 2000, ss 16–18) could be said to have established something similar to the approach envisaged 40 years ago, and implemented in Scotland in Children's Hearings.

The referral order can be for 3–12 months and amounts, then, to a new form of diversion, that of diversion from any other order that could have been imposed by the court. The Youth Offender Panel (YOP), to which the young offender is referred, includes lay members. The young offender is expected to help negotiate and agree a contract of activities, individualised preventative measures to address his or her offending. Failure to agree or comply can mean referral back to the youth court. If the contract is successfully 'signed off' the conviction is regarded as spent. By the end of the first 18 months of operation, referral orders accounted for 30 per cent of youth court orders (Home Office 2003c: para 16).

As originally passed, this provision for offenders under 18, who pleaded guilty to all offences charged and who had no previous convictions or bind-overs, mandated a referral order, with two exceptions.[8] If the court considered the offence to be very serious, a custodial penalty could be imposed; if the court considered the offence to be sufficiently minor, an absolute discharge could be given. The intent was to remove the discretion of the youth court to 'punish' young offenders on a first prosecution, provided they pleaded guilty. Discretion to use the referral order or not remained where the young offender pleaded guilty to only some of the charges.

However, the referral conditions have been amended in response to several pressures. First, there was evidence of a rise in the number of apparently tactical 'not guilty' pleas in order to be given a referral order rather than risk a harsher sentence. There was also a rise in the use of absolute discharges by youth courts, possibly because of concern by magistrates that the resources of the Youth Offender Panel

---

[8] PCCSA 2000, ss 16 and 19. The only other exception allowed by these provisions is if the Mental Health Act 1983 is applicable and a hospital order is made.

and the preventative programmes were being 'unnecessarily' expended on referral orders for trivial offences (NACRO 2003b). Further, whilst some magistrates appeared to view referral as too heavy-handed, others were critical of the loss of their discretion to impose more punitive orders (Ball 2000). Whether the fact that, for example, not all previous convictions for very minor offences have been recorded, and so a referral order is 'wrongly' made (Newburn *et al.* 2002: 20–2), and that magistrates do not believe a three-month period of YOP supervision is necessary (see Greenhow 2003: 267), should constitute successful pressure for change, is another question.

Since August 2003, the compulsory referral conditions have the additional condition that the offence being dealt with must be an imprisonable one whilst the court has discretion to impose the order on the same conditions (in addition to the existing conditions) if the offence is not imprisonable (s 17(1A) of the PCCSA 2000).[9] The Criminal Justice and Immigration (CJI) Act 2008 will make further changes by amending s 17(1A) and (2) so that the court would have a discretion to make a referral order if the offender had been dealt with by a court on one previous occasion and, exceptionally, even if he had been referred to a Youth Offender Panel.[10]

Referral orders and (final) warnings may in practice require the young offender to engage in a form of restorative justice under which meetings are organised with the attendance where possible of the victim and significant others in the life of the young offender. These may take the form of, for example, family group conferences, victim–offender mediation, or restorative cautioning which were discussed in Chapter 6 (section 6.3.2). Restorative theories and practices are currently of crucial importance in setting agendas for change although, as we saw in Chapter 6, it is clear that initiatives are being seen as developments which must prove their worth.

The scheme is open to the criticism, however, that the young offender is perhaps wrongly assumed to be sufficiently mature to engage in negotiating a package of activities and to be able to understand fully the implications of breaking the terms of the 'contract' (see Wonnacott 1999). Using words such as contract for the outcome of this process has been criticised as 'an abuse of contractual language' which hides 'too much executive discretion in respect of the contents of the order' (Ashworth 2000: 332–3). Home Office research on the first two years of operation would suggest, however, that some of the concerns have not materialised, with positive comments being made by parents and young offenders (Newburn *et al.* 2002).[11] Further, the profile of the volunteer members of the youth offender panels is, encouragingly, more akin to that of the general population than to that of the lay magistracy. For example, 37 per cent of the panel members are under 40 years of age, as opposed to around 4 per cent of magistrates, and 7 per cent of panel members are 'black' compared to 2 per cent of magistrates (Audit Commission 2004: 24).[12]

---

[9] Referral Orders (Amendment of Referral Conditions) Regulations SI 2003/1605. The accompanying guidance suggests that a fine, conditional discharge or reparation order will normally be appropriate if a referral order is not used for first-time offenders (NACRO 2003b: 1).

[10] Section 35; see also ss 36–7.

[11] There are concerns, however, that victims are not involved as extensively as planned (Newburn *et al.* 2002: Executive summary: viii): see also Chapter 6.

[12] This may be partly the result of a lower minimum age (18) for panel members as opposed to the 27-year-old minimum for the magistracy.

At the National Referral Order Conference organised by the YJB in March 2008 Bill Kerslake, Head of Effective Sentences at the YJB, gave figures for the disposals made in relation to the total of children and young people who had been given a reprimand or warning or a criminal court order in 2005–6. Of these the pre-court options amounted to 45 per cent of the total and the 'first tier' disposals (discharges, fines and compensation, referral and reparation orders) comprised 35 per cent (community penalties accounting for 17 per cent and custody for 3 per cent), with referral orders themselves being the most used of all court orders at 24 per cent of the total of orders.[13] He also reported that referral contracts included direct victim involvement in 10 per cent of contracts, and in 25 per cent if indirect contact was included. A reconviction rate of 45 per cent after 1 year was given, compared with 70 per cent for other higher-tariff community sentences and 78 per cent for custody (ibid).

online resource centre

In 2005 the number of referral orders made accounted for almost half of all community sentences on 10–17-year-olds (Home Office 2007c: Table 3.7) and the CJI Act 2008 includes amendments to widen their use (see the Online Resource Centre for updates). These changes draw on the thinking in *Youth Justice: Next Steps* proposed that the court should be allowed to impose a referral order on a second conviction, for example where it was not available on first conviction because of a not guilty plea (Home Office 2003c: para 16). Whilst it is too soon to draw conclusions on the benefits and drawbacks of referral orders, there would seem to be some optimism that they are effective in reducing offending rates and diverting from more penal options.

13.2 Community programmes

It is worth reminding ourselves at this stage of the range of possible responses to juvenile offending which are available to professionals in the youth justice system and, specifically, to the youth court: see Chapter 8 (section 8.1.3) and Figure 13.1 below (which excludes CJI Act 2008 changes). You might also wish to look at the Online Resource Centre for a list of acronyms used in the youth justice system.

online resource centre

13.2.1 Assessment and information

In our review of protective sentencing in Chapter 5 we noted the importance of risk assessment (of reoffending and of harm to others) in decision making. In Chapter 12 we examined assessment in relation to the imposition of requirements in community sentences and in supervision by the Probation Service of offenders on release from a custodial sentence. In particular we focused on rehabilitation as an aim in community supervision, and the 'what works' approach to choice of prevention programmes to be used. Minors are not exempt from all these trends and concerns.

---

[13] See http://www.yjb.gov.uk/NR/rdonlyres/ABA6B736-A43E-4743-A953-A7BB067C860B/0/National ReferralOrderConference2008.ppt#268,8. Referral orders priorities for action: an overview—challenges and opportunities.

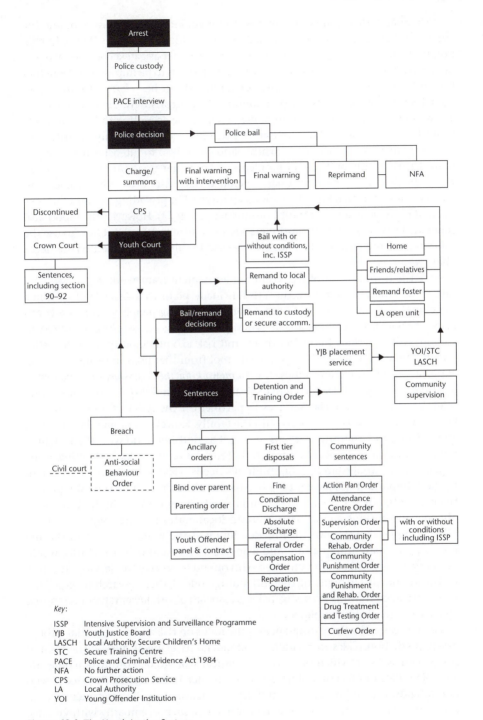

Figure 13.1 The Youth Justice System

Note: This chart is for general guidance only. Some details have been omitted, such as the limitation of certain options to certain age groups.

Source: Audit Commission (2004: Exhibit 2).

In Chapter 8, for example, we referred to the importance of assessment and the use of Asset as the assessment tool used by Youth Offending Teams (YOTs) in relation to the final warning scheme. Such assessments act as gatekeepers; they determine what form and quantity of intervention, if any, is to be imposed and whether the child or young person—or his/her family—is to be referred to any other agencies for more specialist help or support. Not surprisingly the importance of assessment has been flagged up in policy documents: according to *Misspent Youth* it 'allows a degree of flexibility in both sentencing and constructing the intervention plan on a [proposed] final warning' and could lead to intensive intervention to deal with family and school problems at an earlier stage (Audit Commission 1996: 69). A more recent report has concluded that Asset is usually completed to an acceptable standard and 'is a major step forward in providing a comprehensive risk and needs assessment' (Audit Commission 2004: 73). However, the report also concluded that some YOT practitioners 'are not entirely clear about how to use the information' and that Asset is 'not always used to full effect' in identifying needs (ibid: 74–5).

Since the introduction of the 'common assessment framework' for use in relation to all children's services, the YJB has made plain that Asset 'will continue to be used as the primary tool for assessment of young people within the youth justice system' because, inter alia, it 'is designed to focus on assessing risk of reconviction, risk of serious harm to others, and risk of vulnerability' (Youth Justice Board 2006d: 2). Asset is, then, a separate tool from that used in relation to local authority child protection duties, the *Framework for the Assessment of Children in Need and their Families* (Department of Health 2000), but the YOT can refer a young offender to the local Social Services Department if the Asset assessment reveals behaviour attributable to harm within the family. However, few members of YOTs attend *Framework* training, perhaps 'seeing it as nothing to do with them', which might indicate a professional approach that focuses on the risk of offending at the expense of an understanding of children's needs (Calder 2003: 29). This is particularly important in relation to 'looked-after' children[14] whose offending rate is treble the offending rate of other children, and 50 per cent of children in young offender institutions are, or have been, in local authority care (NACRO 2003c). NACRO argues that training in child development and welfare 'is vital for sharing the corporate parenting culture and associated aims and objectives' that would be necessary for looked-after children who offend to receive the services and care which are effective in reducing their offending. Indeed, their research suggests that access to shared training across agencies is associated with lower rates of offending by looked-after children (ibid: 5).

A major reason for these differences is the focus on risk and on actuarial, group-based, prediction scales in relation to offenders. Assessment questionnaires and scales such as Asset, which produce a numerical score to determine outcome, are a visible indicator of 'actuarial justice' (see Chapter 1). For a child 'in need'[15] who also offends, the end product, even with the inclusion in the assessment checklists of new factors referred to as 'dynamic' factors, such as empathy with victims,

---

[14] 'Looked-after children' are children voluntarily accommodated by, or in the care of, the local authority (under ss 20 and 31 respectively of the Children Act 1989).

[15] This is a term used in s 17 of the Children Act 1989 to refer to children whose health or development requires or will require the provision of services by the local authority.

might, it is argued, be an intervention which is inappropriate to the child's needs or disproportionate to the offending (Hudson 2003: 49–50). However, research completed for the YJB on the reliability and validity of *Asset* concluded that, whilst there was an 'acceptable' level of consistency between individual assessors (referred to as inter-rater reliability), there were significant divergences and the report suggested some YOT staff 'may be allocating ratings on the basis of perceived problems rather than the extent to which these were associated with the likelihood of further offending' (Baker *et al.* 2005: 6; see also 53).

For minors, as for adults, the court has required a pre-sentence report (PSR) since the CJA 1991 with the purpose, according to the White Paper (Home Office 1990a), of providing the court 'with detailed information about how the offender could be punished in the community, so that option can be fully considered'. Research for the YJB suggested that there is a correlation between the quality of PSRs and levels of custodial sentencing with, for example, more than 40 per cent of PSRs being assessed as unsatisfactory or poor in high custody areas (NACRO 2000b: 2–3). Whilst the proportion of reports recommending custody or giving no clear proposal varied, it was as high as 32 per cent in one high-custody area (ibid: 3). There is also a suggestion of racial discrimination in operation via PSRs. A review by HM Inspectorate of Probation (2000) of adult defendants found that, while 60 per cent of reports on white defendants were satisfactory, the equivalent for African or African-Caribbean defendants was 49 per cent. The quality and nature of information before the sentencing court is, then, very important.

13.2.2 Community orders

It is quite difficult to keep up with the ever-changing nomenclature of community punishment (see section 8.1.3) and there is still a different range of options for minors before and after their 16th birthday. The situation is complicated because some provisions have not been implemented whilst new orders will be introduced by the CJI Act 2008.

16–17-year-olds

Orders which were defined as community penalties for those over 16, and so including 16- and 17-year-olds, were renamed by the Criminal Justice and Court Services Act (CJCSA) 2000 (ss 43–45: see Chapter 12) and are replaced by the 'community order' introduced by the CJA 2003. However, although s 177 of the CJA 2003—which deals with community orders—was implemented in April 2005 the entry into force of the provision (and also ss 179–180) was delayed for 16–17-year olds until 4 April 2009.[16] Those aged 16–17 are, therefore, currently in the same position as before. If the community order had been implemented for 16–17-year-olds (but see below), the court would have been able to impose one or more of the requirements[17] from the list of 12 options in s 177 (see Chapter 12). The drug rehabilitation requirement (see also s 209(2)) would have replaced the drug

[16] See SI 2005/950 Art. 2(2) as amended by SI 2007/391 Art. 2.
[17] SI 2003/3282 brought several of the provisions of the Act relating to the requirements into force. Community sentences for offenders *over* 18 have been in force since April 2005.

treatment and testing order introduced by the CDA 1998 (re-enacted as PCCSA 2000, ss 52–58). The court must specify a period (up to three years) for completion of all the requirements. In addition other non-custodial penalties continue to be available in the 'first tier' of penalties: discharges, fines, compensation orders, reparation orders, together with referral orders (see section 13.1.2 above).

10–15-year-olds

For those under 16 the CJA 2003 s 147(2) renamed the community orders in existence before 1998, as well as those subsequently added, as a generic new 'youth community order'. The community orders are the following (the relevant sections of the PCCSA 2000 are given): a curfew order (s 163), an exclusion order (s 40A(1), introduced by the CJCSA 2000), an attendance centre order (s 163), a supervision order (s 63(1)), and an action plan order (s 69(1), introduced by the CDA 1998).[18] The reparation order (introduced by the CDA 1998, ss 67–68) continues as a penalty that is not a community order. The distinction is of significance because, since the CJA 1991, there has been a statutory hurdle for the imposition of a community penalty on minors and adults, that the offence is 'serious enough to warrant such a sentence' (see Chapter 3).

Youth Justice—Next Steps proposed to replace all nine non-custodial sentences for 'juveniles' (see Figure 13.1 above) with one sentence, 'a broader Action Plan Order to run for 1–12 months with 1–3 interventions from a comprehensive menu' which includes fines, reparation and mentoring (Home Office 2003c: paras 7 and 17). This proposal was endorsed in a later policy document (DfES 2004: para 4.21). What is now being proposed is a similar order, but for all minors and with a different name—the youth rehabilitation order.

Youth Rehabilitation Orders

Part 1 of the CJI Act 2008 will introduce youth rehabilitation orders (YROs) which the courts will be able to impose—subject to conditions—on any convicted offenders under 18 years old. It will be a new generic community sentence allowing the court to impose one or more of 15 requirements on a list—a 'menu'—similar to that available for courts when imposing a community order on an adult offender under s 177 of the CJA 2003. The order can last up to three years. The order can also include an electronic monitoring requirement and, providing the offence in question is punishable by custody and the seriousness threshold for custody has been satisfied (together with a persistence criterion for those aged less than 15), the YRO could be an order with intensive supervision and surveillance or with fostering.[19]

ISSP

Another important development has been the introduction of 'tougher' and more controlling forms of non-custodial punishment or 'treatment' for minors. The supervision order (PCCSA 2000, ss 63–68) has been the vehicle for many of these initiatives. The CDA 1998 provided for the imposition of a reparation condition in a supervision order and widened the criteria for making a residence requirement

---

[18] Exclusion, action plan, and curfew orders are also available for 16- and 17-year-olds.
[19] Section 1 and Schedule 1; see also ss 2–7.

(s 71). An intensive supervision and surveillance programme (ISSP)—which can be part of a supervision order or community rehabilitation order—was introduced by the YJB in 2001. It is aimed at 15–17-year-old offenders who have been charged or warned at least four times in the previous 12 months and so are at high risk of (further) imprisonment (see Leigh 2001/2). The ISSP—which can also be a condition of community supervision in the second half of a detention and training order (see below)—uses a combination of electronic and other forms of tracking, with staff sent to deal with non-compliance as soon as possible. In addition there are 25 hours of compulsory educational or other activities, such as reparation or offending behaviour programmes, per week. Since the programme started in July 2001, up to the end of March 2006, 19,037 persistent young offenders have been referred to an ISSP.[20] This requirement makes sense in the context of the strong link between educational attainment and offending (ibid; see also Moore 2004; Waters 2007).

More recently, s 88 of the ASBA 2003 empowers the court to require that a child or young person lives with a local authority foster parent for a period up to 12 months as part of the supervision order, and extends the length of the intensive supervision stage of the order from 3 months to 6 months (implemented September 2004). One research study found that reconviction rates were unaffected by the intervention but that there was a 30–50 per cent reduction in the volume of crime committed by ISSP participants (Little *et al.* 2004). The Government hopes to establish the ISSP 'as the main response to serious and persistent offending' (Home Office 2003c: para 20).

Other orders

Curfew, disqualification and exclusion orders, all introduced in the last decade, are also evidence of the more restrictive nature of requirements and orders. For example, curfew orders, introduced by the CDA 1998, were extended to children under 16 years of age by s 48 of the Criminal Justice and Police Act 2001, and the CJCSA 2000 (ss 26–38) introduced disqualification orders. These can be imposed on adults and minors as an additional penalty where the offender is sentenced by the Crown Court for offences against children (as defined in Schedule 4 of the Act). If the offender is a minor, the court must make such an order if it is satisfied 'having regard to all the circumstances, that it is likely that the individual will commit a further offence against a child' (s 29(4)). The effect of the order is to prohibit the young offender from working with children in the future and a breach of the order constitutes a criminal offence. There are rights issues here, given the use of civil orders where the proceedings are not subject to the same safeguards as orders imposed in criminal proceedings (see section 13.1.1).

Whilst the names of orders are changing, it is becoming clear that the trend is to give courts more flexibility in constructing a programme of intervention. It would also appear that the proposed programmes may become increasingly more intensive. This approach puts a premium on there being adequate resources and training for those delivering the programmes, and for suitable 'education' of magistrates

---

[20] See http://www.yjb.gov.uk/en-gb/yjs/SentencesOrdersandAgreements/IntensiveSupervisionAndSurveillanceProgramme/.

and judges. The fear is that the negative images of young offenders as youths combined with the possibilities for imposing more restrictive requirements in community orders may not lead to the intended reduction in punishment levels.

13.3 **Detention**

13.3.1 **New statutory provisions 1998–2003**

Despite the policy aim of reducing the use of custody for young offenders the last decade or so has witnessed the introduction of several new provisions to allow the courts to impose detention. Some of these provisions were enacted at the same time as very similar provisions for adults, again raising the question as to the extent to which children and young people who offend are being treated differently.

Detention and training order

The CJA 1991 repealed the relevant sections of the Criminal Justice Act 1982 so that minors and adults were subject to the same statutory criteria for the imposition of custodial and community penalties (see section 8.1.3). Subsequent legislation has re-enacted this all-age approach and the change made by the CJA 2003 in relation to the weight to be given to previous offences in calculating seriousness applies to minors as well as adults. The 'normal' custodial sentence provided by the CJA 1991—for all but the most serious of offences—was detention in a youth offender institution for those aged 15, 16 or 17,[21] but legislation from 1994–8 significantly extended the custodial options for sentencers. The Criminal Justice and Public Order Act (CJPOA) 1994, ss 1–4, lowered the age at which a child could be detained by introducing secure training orders for 12–14-year-olds. This was continued in the CDA 1998 which combined the two forms of detention into 'detention and training orders' (s 73). It lowered the minimum age to 10 (though there are currently no designated institutions for the 10- and 11-year-olds under this order) and raised the maximum length of the order to 24 months (the minimum length being 4 months). These changes have been referred to as a 'legislative clampdown on children and young people' (Scraton and Haydon 2002: 314). The provisions in s 73 were re-enacted in the PCCSA 2000.

The CDA 1998 enacted or re-enacted additional criteria for imposing custody on the lower age groups: for those under 15 the minor must be a 'persistent' offender; in addition for those under 12 the order must be necessary to protect the public (now PCCSA 2000 s 100(2)). In 2003 the Government proposed to remove the 'persistence' condition for 12–14-year-olds on the ground that it had 'proved complex in practice' (Home Office 2003c: para 21) but this has not been done. In *R v TTG* (2003), a case concerning a 14-year-old boy who had two previous convictions, the Court of Appeal restricted the scope of the term by stating that this did not amount to persistence 'given the ordinary meaning of the term'. Arguably, the

---

[21] In fact the sentence of detention in a young offender institution was also applicable to 18–20-year olds until that sentence was abolished by s 61 of the CJCSA 2000. This means that all offenders of 18 years of age and above are treated as adults for the purpose of custodial sentences.

'complexities' the Government refers to have arisen only because of a desire by sentencers to 'get round' the wording of the statute and impose detention on this age group.

In contrast to the previous order, the detention and training order may be served in a variety of penal and local authority establishments at the discretion of the Home Secretary, theoretically giving more flexibility to address the needs of the young offender. Half the length of the order is served in an institution, the remainder is spent on supervision in the community, breaches leading to further detention. However, provided the offender has behaved and made progress in detention, the presumption since 2002 has been to release the young offender one to two months earlier than the half way stage (unless the conviction was for a serious violent or sexual offence), possibly with an electronic monitoring requirement (see NACRO 2007d).[22]

Orders for public protection

The CJA 2003 introduced new protective sentences for both adult and juvenile 'dangerous' offenders (see Chapter 5) which means that, for all offences committed since April 2005, the courts have available two new sentences for offenders under 18: the sentence of detention for public protection and the extended sentence of detention. If the conviction of the young offender is for a 'serious' specified offence and the court believes that there is 'a significant risk to members of the public' that the young offender will cause them serious harm 'by the commission by him of further specified offences' then there are two options under s 226. For this part of the Act a 'specified offence' is one of the many sexual or violent offences listed in Schedule 15 to the Act whilst a 'serious offence' is a sub-category of specified offences for which the maximum penalty for an adult would be life or 10 years. If the young offender would otherwise have been eligible for a sentence of detention for life under the PCCSA 2000, s 91 (see section 13.3.2 below) and the offence seriousness justifies it, the court *must* impose that sentence. This then is not a new sentence but one with an extra set of criteria within the CJA 2003. If the offender was not so eligible, and the new extended sentence under s 228 would not be adequate to protect the public, then the court is mandated—until s 14 of the CJI Act 2008 is in force—to impose the new sentence of detention for public protection. This is an indeterminate sentence, with a minimum tariff period set by the court, which could last beyond the maximum which would otherwise be available. The amended s 226(3) will give the court discretion to impose this sentence only if the minimum period is at least two years.

The YJB issued guidance for YOTs in 2006 (Youth Justice Board 2006c), updating guidance issued in 2005. The guidance for the Crown Prosecution Service states that the youth specialist CPS officer should take into account '[t]he need, in relation to those under 18, to be particularly rigorous before concluding that there is a significant risk of serious harm by the commission of further offences: such a conclusion is unlikely to be appropriate in the absence of a pre-sentence report following assessment by a young offender team'.[23] However, NACRO's first *Youth*

---

[22] See PCCSA 2000 s 102 and guidance issued by the Youth Justice Board in 2000 and 2002: see NACRO (2003a).

[23] See: http://www.cps.gov.uk/legal/section4/chapter_b.html#32.

Crime Briefing on the dangerousness provisions noted that the determination of 'dangerousness' is crucial for the young person and yet assessment of risk is difficult and prone to inaccuracy. The Asset assessment tool, it contends, is 'something of a compromise between clinical and actuarial approaches to assessment' but 'does not provide any easy answers' (NACRO 2005: 4; see also NACRO 2006; section 13.2.1 above).

As NACRO has pointed out, some of the specified offences for the purposes of these new provisions would not otherwise permit a sentence of long-term detention (2004c: 7). They require the youth court to consider, when deciding on jurisdiction, whether the criteria are likely to be made out and, if so, to commit the young person for trial at the Crown Court. It may also commit to the Crown Court for sentence, having received more information in the course of the trial.

The trigger for an extended sentence is a conviction for a specified offence and a finding that the significant risk condition is met, as in s 226. The extended sentence is mandatory in these circumstances. It is also available where the offence is a 'serious' offence but does not warrant detention under s 226. It is not a new order, being a custodial sentence where the licence period has extended. For the under-18s the custodial period must be at least 12 months and the extension period cannot exceed, for adults and minors, 5 years (for violent offences) or 8 years (for sexual offences). Section 229 introduces clarification as to how to assess 'dangerousness'.[24]

There are clearly no government plans to discontinue these sentences and the much older sentences of detention which are now in ss 90 and 91 of the PCCSA 2000 (see below): 'the most serious offences are no less damaging to victims and the community, and the most dangerous offenders are no less of a threat, because they involve under-18-year-olds' (Home Office 2003c: para 22).

13.3.2 Older provisions: murder and serious crimes

The PCCSA 2000, ss 90–91, largely re-enacted legislation first passed in the Children and Young Persons Act 1933, s 53 to provide longer periods of detention to cater for what was anticipated as the exceptional circumstance of a minor committing murder (s 53(1), now PCCSA 2000, s 90) or a 'grave' crime (s 53(2), now PCCSA 2000, s 91). Both sets of provisions now apply to all minors above the age of criminal responsibility. The murder provision had always so applied but the minimum age for the grave crimes provision was 14, until s 16 of the CJPOA 1994 lowered it to 10. There are, however, some offences which trigger s 91 only for 14–17-year olds, notably causing death by dangerous driving.

Until the Criminal Justice Act 1961, only murder, attempted murder, manslaughter, and wounding with intent to do grievous bodily harm could trigger the orders for detention at Her Majesty's pleasure (s 90) or for a specified period (s 91). In 1961 the definition of grave crimes was extended to those where the offence carried a maximum penalty of 14 years for an adult. Since then legislation has inadvertently extended the scope of the grave—now serious—crimes provision by the addition of offences with a 14-year maximum. Most recently the CJA 2003 and the Sexual Offences Act 2003 have provided further relevant maxima which are already in force (see NACRO 2004c: 2). The scope of s 91 has also been extended by the

---

[24] Most of the issues relating to these new orders are dealt with more fully in Chapter 5 above.

addition of specific offences for which the provision applies, for example, in relation to indecent assault since the CJPOA 1994 (see PCCSA 2000, s 91(1) and (2)).

In addition there is a new set of provisions in the CJA 2003 (ss 289–293), already in force, which import into the grave/serious crimes provision another means by which this longer sentence can be imposed on 16- and 17-year-olds at the Crown Court. The CJA 2003, s 287 provides for minimum sentences for listed firearm-related offences if the offence is committed when the offender is 18 years old or over.[25] Whilst the prescribed minimum for adults is 5 years, for an offender under 18 in England and Wales, or under 21 in Scotland, the minimum is 3 years. If the conditions are met—unless 'exceptional circumstances' apply—the courts must impose on the minor a sentence of detention 'of at least that term' (new s 91(5)). This provision would appear to over-ride the requirement in s 91(3) that the courts must be 'of the opinion that none of the other methods in which the case may legally be dealt with is suitable'.

The penalty for murder is mandatory—in effect a life sentence—and this has raised issues of rights in relation to the length of time spent in detention for murder. The most important and high-profile case was that of the two boys, Thompson and Venables, who were given sentences of detention at Her Majesty's pleasure for their murder of James Bulger when they were 11 years old.[26] They challenged, first by judicial review, the raising by the Home Secretary of the minimum period to be served in detention before release is considered (the tariff element of the sentence). This case went through the English appeal system and ultimately to the European Court of Human Rights where the Home Secretary's power to set a minimum detention period was deemed to be contrary to Articles 5(4) and 6(1) of the ECHR because such decisions should be made and reviewed by a judicial body (*V and T v UK* (2000)).[27] The sentencing court must now set the tariff period and *Smith* (2005) and *Dudson* (2005) concerned the proper procedure for review of the minimum period, taking into account the child's welfare. This decision is now also affected by s 269 and Schedule 21 of the CJA 2003 which require the court to have regard to a 'starting point' of 12 years in setting the tariff for a minor. This is higher than the 8 years set for Venables and Thompson by the European Court.

Whilst there has been no noticeable trend in the number of murders by 10–17 year-olds for whom a sentence under s 90 must be imposed (with total annual figures varying from 10–25 cases in 1989–99: Figure 13.2 below), the use of the grave/serious crimes provision has greatly increased over the years. Compared with only 6 sentences made under s 53(2) (or, later, s 91) in 1970, 65 were made in 1980, 315 in 1993, and 607 by 1999 (see Figure 13.3 below). A steady rise therefore became a steep rise in the 1990s.

This trend can only partly be explained by the factors noted above and, instead, it has been argued that a major factor was increased punitiveness on the part of youth court magistrates: an increased numbers of cases, including property

[25] This compares with the requirement that the offender is over 16 in relation to the mandatory minimum sentences for a third drug trafficking or domestic burglary offence (PCCSA 2000, ss 110 and 111). However, the CJA 2003, s 291 gives the Secretary of State the necessary powers to increase to 18 the minimum age for the new firearms provisions.

[26] For discussion of the moral panic which this case provoked, see Chapter 8 (section 8.3.3).

[27] For a detailed discussion of the tariff element and this mandatory sentence more generally, see McDiarmid (2000).

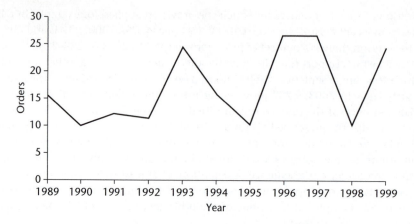

Figure 13.2 Convictions for murder 1989–1999
Source: NACRO (2001c).

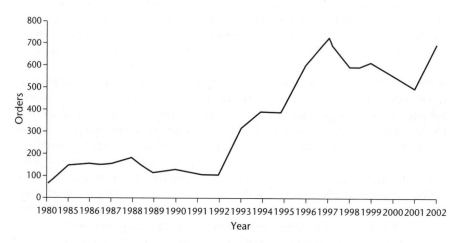

Figure 13.3 Sentences under section 91 (1980–2002)
Source: NACRO (2004e).

offences that might not have been so transferred earlier, were sent to the Crown Court for trial (NACRO 2001/2: 8).[28] This is despite the fact that, inadvertently or otherwise, the provisions for secure training orders, and then the detention and training order which replaced them, raised the maximum custodial sentence available to the youth court for a single offence from six months to two years. The 'attractiveness' of the s 91 provision for judges had, however, been increased by *Mills and related appeals* (1998) which instituted a continuum between detention and training orders and detention under s 91. This means that, if the maximum period for a detention and training order is held not to be commensurate with seriousness, then the court can impose a s 91 sentence just above that maximum if it

---

[28] Although the general power to commit 15–17-year-olds to the Crown Court for sentence was repealed by the CDA 1998, with effect from 31 May 2000.

so wishes. Previously, the courts had attempted to discourage the use of the 'grave crimes' provision by establishing a gap of a year between the maximum period that could be imposed for a detention and training order and the minimum period that could be imposed for a s 91 order.

A problem—in the eyes of magistrates in youth courts—has been the restrictive nature of the criteria for imposing detention and training orders on offenders under 16 years of age. Their 'solution' was to decline jurisdiction so that the Crown Court could impose detention under s 91(3) 'if the court is of the opinion that none of the other methods in which the case may legally be dealt with is suitable'. This tactic was not immediately successfully appealed but *R v Manchester City Youth Court* (2002) saw a change in thinking, and in *R (on the application of W) v Thetford Youth Court* (2002) the Divisional Court made clear that justices could not decline jurisdiction when they had no power to impose a custodial sentence simply because they felt custody was warranted. In the *Thetford* case the young offender was an 11-year-old and the circumstances of his offending could not meet the statutory criteria for a detention and training order. The Divisional Court stated that Parliament's intention to restrict the use of custody in relation to those under 14 should be upheld. In *C v Balham Youth Court* (2003) the court similarly confirmed this reasoning in relation to a 14-year-old, stating that cases which came within the s 91 provision should not be transferred to the Crown Court unless a sentence of more than 2 years was envisaged.

The Divisional Court has, therefore, been a useful tool to rein in the punitiveness of youth court and Crown Court sentencers. It is regrettable that this is necessary. Nevertheless, on one day at the end of 2007 there were 348 children in detention under ss 90 and 91,[29] as well as those children sentenced under the new dangerousness provisions.

13.3.3 Conditions in detention

Although the Government's policy now is to try to reduce the number of young offender places, the result of the increased use of custodial measures over the last decade has meant that there are still large numbers of young people in custody. A survey on 12 March 2004 found there were 10,515 male young offenders and 504 female young offenders in detention, in the 15–21-year-old age group (Prison Reform Trust 2004a).[30] The majority of these offenders were in the 18–21 age range though the number of 15–17-year-olds in custody has doubled over the last decade. In 2002 young people under 21 constituted 16 per cent of the population in custody, the majority of them in prison for non-violent offences. On 14 March 2008 the Howard League gave a figure of 2,639 boys and 207 girls (i.e. under 18) in custody. Almost two-thirds of these children were serving a detention and training order but 536 were on remand whilst 44 were on indeterminate sentences. The YJB web site shows that the juvenile secure-estate population peaked in 2002 but is still higher than in 2000–1 (see Figure 13.4 below).

---

[29] On 28 December 2007: see http://www.howardleague.org/index.php?id=561.
[30] Where not otherwise specified, statistics in the remainder of this section are from the Prison Reform Trust (2004).

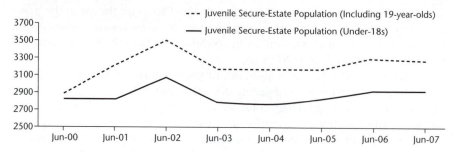

Figure 13.4 Secure estate population trend 2000–2007

Note: The solid line represents the total under-18 population. The dashed line includes 18- and 19-year-olds.

Source: Youth Justice Board web site: http://www.yjb.gov.uk/en-gb/yjs/Custody/CustodyFigures/.

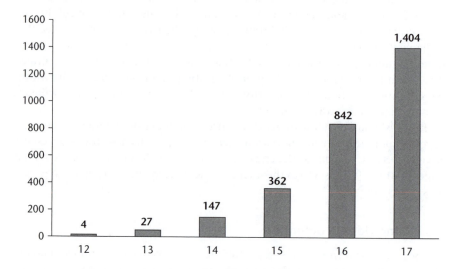

Figure 13.5 Under-18 secure-estate population by age, December 2007

Source: Youth Justice Board Custody Statistics, December 2007

About half of the under-18-year-olds in custody are aged 17, the rest are 12–16 years old (see Figure 13.5).

'Injustice by geography' also continues in that there are wide regional variations in the use of sentences of detention. Figures released by the YJB in November 2003 showed a low custody rate of 7.2 per cent for the south-east (excluding London) and a higher rate of 10.5 per cent in Wales, these figures not correlating with gravity factors. The latest information from the YJB suggests continuing regional differences (see Figure 13.6).

The detention and training order allows for the allocation of 12–17-year-olds to any part of the juvenile secure establishment, notably young offender institutions (YOIs), secure training centres, and local authority secure units. Since 2000, the YJB has been responsible for the allocation strategy. The presumption is that 15–17 year-olds will be placed in YOIs, whether open or closed institutions, whilst 10–14 year-olds will be accommodated outside the Prison Service, although vulnerability

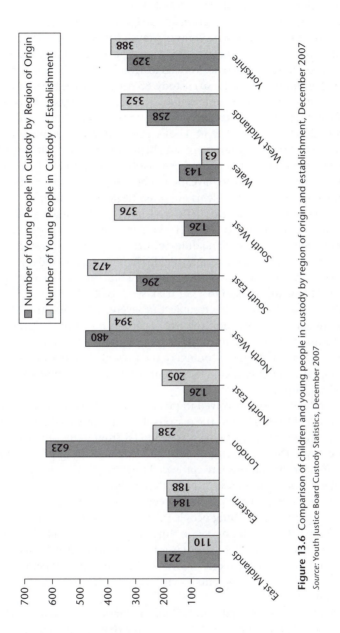

Figure 13.6 Comparison of children and young people in custody by region of origin and establishment, December 2007

Source: Youth Justice Board Custody Statistics, December 2007

and gender may allow for different placements. In practice, discretionary place-ment outside the Prison Service is difficult because the majority of the secure juvenile estate is still to be found in Prison Service establishments. This trend to greater, not less, use of such prison accommodation for minors sentenced to long-term detention has been criticised (NACRO 2001c: 6).

'The shift in the pattern of placements is significant in the context of the typical characteristics of children who commit grave crimes' (ibid). As with adult prison-ers, many young offenders have a history of social exclusion, including unemploy-ment—in relation to those over 16 years to age—and also exclusion from school. A recent survey found that, prior to custody, 83 per cent of the boys and 65 per cent of the girls had been excluded from school, whilst 37 per cent of the boys and 43 per cent of the girls had been accommodated by the local authority (HM Inspectorate of Prisons 2004). Those in the 14–17 age group often have experience of being in care, poor educational achievement, and behavioural and mental health problems, including drug and alcohol abuse (see Chapter 8, section 8.2.1). Young offenders are three times more likely to have mental health problems than other young peo-ple, yet those with such problems are often neglected (Walker and Beckett 2003: 98). In 2000, of 15–20-year-olds in Prison Service establishments, 90 per cent had a diagnosable mental health problem (Lyon *et al.* 2000) whilst prisoners in the 18–20 age group are more likely than adults to suffer from mental health problems and more likely to commit, or attempt, suicide than younger or older prisoners (Lader *et al.* 2000). NACRO is also concerned about mental capacity in relation to the right of the child or young person to a fair trial (see NACRO 2007e).

Conditions in YOIs have been subject to severe criticism, particularly the treat-ment of remand prisoners and the use of certain forms of restraint with all pris-oners. Goldson (2006), examining the treatment and death of children in Prison Service establishments in the context of the current United Nations concern about violence against children, concludes that what occurs is 'tantamount to institu-tional child abuse'.

Young offenders were involved in prison riots and disturbances in 1990 at Glen Parva and Pucklechurch, and the reasons they gave included discontent over con-ditions and overcrowding, being placed too far from home, and the fact that they simply enjoyed the excitement of rioting (Woolf and Tumim 1991). Inspections of youth offender institutions have provided numerous examples of poor practice in keeping good order and preventing bullying and assaults on young inmates, and several recent reports have pointed to continuing significant weaknesses in pro-vision for children and young people in custody. A Report by HM Inspectorate of Prisons (2004) found that over one-third of those 15–18-year-olds surveyed had felt unsafe at some time whilst in custody (including all the 15-year-old girls), a quarter said they had not received any visitors, and only 30 per cent of boys said it had been easy for their parents to visit. Being held too far from home is clearly still a problem.

In 2005 the YJB published a draft Code of Practice 'for managing the behaviour of the troubled and troublesome young people that are cared for in secure accom-modation'. It covered elements such as 'a planned approach for managing individ-ual behaviour', 'diversion, de-escalation and diffusion processes', 'a fair system of rewards' and 'processes for consulting with children'. The final version was issued in 2006 (Youth Justice Board 2006b). However, the situation is proving resistant to radical change. For example, Group 4's privately run Medway Secure Training Centre (STC) for 12–14-year-old persistent offenders was severely criticised after an inspection in 1999 for its use of restraints and dangerous neck locks, for using unqualified staff who lacked experience of working with children, and for the absence of procedures for dealing with bullying. Yet, despite a better report after an inspection in 2003 (Social Services Inspectorate 2004), problems remained and other STCs have since been subject to criticism. The most recent example concerns Oakhill STC, a privately run centre, which the Chief Inspector of Prisons, Anne Owers, recommended be closed because of the 'staggering levels of use of force by staff' (see HM Inspectorate of Prisons 2008). Statistical information is not collected centrally about injuries, rather than death, sustained by minors in custody although the Howard League gives a figure of 298 young people injured over a 22-month period during the use of restraint and control measures. The YJB has protocols on the use of physical restraint under review[31] and, on 20 March 2008, Justice Minister David Hanson announced that the report of the review of the use of restraint in juvenile secure settings, set up in October 2007, would be delayed until June in order to allow time for the National Children's Bureau to collect evidence on the use of restraint in secure children's homes for which there is 'no central prescription of techniques'.[32]

Government policy has for some time acknowledged the shortcomings in the treatment of young offenders in custodial institutions. In particular the YJB has indicated that there needs to be 'a greater emphasis on safeguarding arrangements to protect children from suicide, self-harm, bullying and harm from staff and other adults' (see NACRO 2003d: 1). The propensity to suicide is higher amongst prisoners, including minors, than among the population outside: 25 boys aged 15–17 hanged themselves while in custody in the period 1990–2003. Since April 2004 the Prisons and Probation Ombudsman has had the responsibility for investigating all deaths in custody. Sadly, cases of death by injury or suicide involving minors hit the headlines with depressing regularity. The death in 2004 of 15-year-old Gareth Myatt did so because he 'is believed to be the youngest person in living memory to die not by their own hand in a British penal institution' (Travis 2004). Gareth died after losing consciousness whilst being restrained by staff at the Rainsbrook Secure Centre. Liam McManus, a 15-year-old boy serving a six-week sentence for breach of a supervision order, was found hanged in his cell on 29 November 2007 at Lancaster Farms Young Offenders' Institution. He is the thirtieth juvenile to die in custody since 1990 and the fifth 15-year-old.[33]

Whilst the majority of young detainees are boys and their conditions are a source of grave concern, there are also problems specific to girls. Howard League research (2004) gives a figure of 90 girls under 18 in prison on any given day and points out that, unlike the situation for boys, there are no prisons that are solely for girls. Sentenced girls are therefore held in four designated prisons where they may be placed on a separate wing for juveniles or on wings which also hold women over 18. As we saw in Chapter 11, extensive criminological research has documented forms of disadvantage to female adult offenders on custodial regimes and

---

[31] Paul Coggins, HC Col 605W, 14 May 2004.
[32] See http://www.justice.gov.uk/news/announcement200308a.htm (accessed 21 March 2008). See the Online Resource Centre for further developments.
[33] Reported in the *Guardian*, 30 November 2007 on p 15.

**online
resource
centre**

community orders but there has been little on gender differences in juvenile justice until very recently (see Piper 2005, 2006b). Most research stemmed from the 1970s and 1980s when a more welfare-focused system operated. However, *Girls in Prison* (Ofsted 2004) and a report by the Howard League for Penal Reform (2004), *Advice, Understanding and Underwear*, have provided evidence of what amounts to discriminatory treatment of girls in custodial establishments, stemming from the much smaller numbers of young female detainees and from their different needs. There appear to be insufficient staff trained to deal with the specific problems of vulnerable (young) females and, with only four institutions, there is a greater likelihood of being placed far from home. The Ofsted Report (2004) surveyed girls completing a detention and training order. It found the majority had poor educational histories and low self-esteem but that they appreciated the educational opportunities in custody. The comments by the girls on the community part of their sentence—which they felt was too risky for them—and on the standard of resettlement support, were more negative.[34]

There are also issues of racial discrimination for young offenders as for adults (see Chapter 11), with black children over-represented in custodial establishments. Wilson's ethnographic research on a small group of group of 16–17-year-old young black men in a young offender institution found that they 'knew nothing of the penal system's formal processes for dealing with complaints of a racial nature'. Further, the collection of data about race in prison 'was at best a managerial process that did not trouble the lives of the young black prisoners about whom the statistics were being kept and the reports were about' (Wilson 2003: 422). Yet, for this group at least, 'the Govs [the staff] were universally perceived to be able to "get away with more" than the police in the community' in regards to racist behaviour (ibid: 423).

It would appear that the welfare of minors in custody is not yet a high enough priority, and that too many children are suffering to no good purpose. Youth custody is also a waste of money. Reconviction rates are very high for this age group and 'there appears to be an inverse correlation between age and reoffending following a custodial sentence' (NACRO 2003e: 1–2). In 1999, 80 per cent of 14–17 year-olds discharged from prison were reconvicted within two years. Research on a two-year follow-up of offenders who had experienced the new intensive regimes running at Thorn Cross YOI and Colchester Military Corrective Training Centre since 1996–7 found no significant differences between the two cohorts in terms of reconvictions but the YOI sample took longer to reoffend and committed significantly fewer crimes (Farrington *et al.* 2002: 1). This meant that at least £5 was saved for every £1 expended on the programme at Thorn Cross as opposed to a loss at Colchester. Whilst the ethos in both regimes was of 'discipline' and 'hard work', the emphasis on physical activities at Colchester was not effective in reducing offending; the education and mentoring aspects at Thorn Cross probably were effective. Nevertheless, despite this relative success, the reconviction rate for the Thorn Cross sample was still 65.1 per cent as opposed to the 75.6 per cent rate for the control group, which had been matched for a similar predicted reconviction rate using actuarially produced tables (ibid: 4). The Howard League currently gives a figure of a 70 per cent rate for reconviction within one year.

---

[34] See also Douglas and Plugge (2007) for a review of their research on young women in custody.

The Howard League has, therefore, taken a policy decision in recent years to use the courts, particularly since the implementation of the Human Rights Act 1998, to challenge government policies on the treatment of young offenders (Crook 2003). We have already referred to the case which successfully challenged the interpretation in Prison Service Order (PSO) 4950 of the duty of the local authority to children in need in a custodial establishment in that area (see Chapter 8, section 8.2.1). A Further case, that of *R (on the application of BP) v Secretary of State for the Home Department* (2003), concerned a 17-year-old who had been in what amounted to solitary confinement for over 23 hours a day during 2 periods of 5 and 4 days, in the segregation unit of a young offender institution. He claimed breaches of Articles 3 and 8 of the ECHR. The court ruled that the rules of the institution had been breached and that insufficient regard had been had to the young man's known vulnerability but did not expressly forbid the use of segregation. More recently the Howard League brought another successful case—*R (K) v Manchester City Council* (2006)—in relation to assessing whether a child in custody would be 'in need' on release. Mr Justice Lloyd Jones decided against the argument that the YOT was the 'agency best suited to meeting the needs of K... The defendant authority is required itself to carry out an assessment. It is not entitled to delegate that function.' He further stated that YOTs can, and should, refer children to children's services, both under s 47 for a child at risk and under s 17 for child welfare.

13.4 The role of rights for young offenders

13.4.1 The utility of rights conventions

As we saw above, the law, and particularly rights-based jurisprudence, can be used successfully to improve the lives of young offenders. Not only are there rights applying to all age groups, notably for the UK, the Human Rights Act 1998 and the jurisprudence of the ECHR, to which we have referred elsewhere, but there are several conventions applying exclusively to minors. The United Nations Convention on the Rights of the Child (CRC) is the best known and the most influential statement of principle on children's rights generally but there are associated conventions which focus on juvenile justice: the Beijing Rules 1985 (the UN Standard Minimum Rules for the Protection of Juvenile Liberty), the Riyadh Guidelines 1990 (UN Guidelines for the Prevention of Juvenile Delinquency), and the Tokyo Rules 1990 (the UN Standard Minimum Rules for Non-Custodial Measures). The CRC has also recently published a General Comment (No. 10, 2007) on 'Children's rights in juvenile justice'.

Yet the use of rights as a tool for improving the lives of children, whether as offenders or not, can produce problems. Their employment can produce different approaches to children's welfare and their utility has often been questioned.[35] Further, the debates on rights do not take place in a political or social vacuum: 'they

---

[35] For a useful review of the different theoretical perspectives and of the sources of international rights, see Fortin (2003: Part One). For a detailed and spirited discussion specifically in relation to young offenders see Chapter 18 of that volume: we will draw heavily on its insights. For a theoretical critique of reliance on rights to achieve improvements for children, see King (1997a).

are informed, mediated and—to an extent—regulated by the historical and contemporary contexts in which they arise' (Scraton and Haydon 2002: 314; see also Chapters 9 and 11 for rights in relation to adult prisoners).

Article 40(2)(b) of the CRC enjoins governments to ensure in particular that '[e]very child alleged or accused of having infringed the penal law has at least the following guarantees' which include being presumed innocent until proven guilty, having access to information and legal advice, being dealt with 'without delay by a competent, independent and impartial authority', with access to review of a penal decision, and to having his or her privacy respected. We have already noted that Article 40 also promotes separate and different treatment and it would appear that the youth court is sufficiently separate to comply with this (Fortin 2003: 563). The CRC does not give any direct remedy for infringements, however. Those jurisdictions which have ratified the CRC are deemed to have promised to amend and operate the laws of the country to bring them in line with the CRC. The (only) sanction is the international and national censure when the Committee on the Rights of the Child publicly concludes on the extent of a government's compliance with the CRC's principles. The UK government has suffered criticism in response to its first two Reports to the Committee. For example, the Committee asked the UK in 1995 to give 'serious consideration' to raising the age of criminal responsibility (Committee on the Rights of the Child 1995: para 36); in 2002 it was more critical (Committee on the Rights of the Child 2002: para 59) given the lack of a positive response and the negative change of abolishing the presumption of *doli incapax*. (The UK government submitted its consolidated third and fourth report to the UN Committee on the Rights of the Child on 15 July 2007.)

For individuals and for pressure groups supporting young offenders, the ECHR may provide a surer remedy. Since October 2002 children, as people, have been able to complain directly to the domestic court that their rights under the ECHR are being infringed. Several Articles, notably Article 3, no inhuman or degrading treatment, Article 6, the right to a fair trial, and Article 7, no punishment without law, are of potential utility for children as for adult defendants and offenders. However, the courts have ruled that the lack of legal representation for minors in Children's Hearings in Scotland, though civil proceedings, has infringed the child's rights under Article 6 (*S v Principal Reporter and the Lord Advocate* (2001)). Failing to warn a young person that an admission of guilt regarding a sexual assault—as part of the process of giving a reprimand or warning—will result in their being placed on the sex offenders' register has also been acknowledged as a breach of Article 6.[36] However, Hollingsworth (2007b) argues, in the light of recent jurisprudence, for a lack of judicial consistency in relation to children's rights under the ECHR.

The procedures adopted by the youth courts are generally compliant with the ECHR and magistrates have recently been encouraged to make further changes to improve communication between magistrates and young offenders (Home Office 2001b). The same cannot be said of the Crown Court's compliance, the court to which, as we saw in section 13.3.2 above, minors are transferred in relation to particular crimes and outcomes. Around 5 per cent of young defendants are currently tried in the Crown Court, either because of the nature of the alleged offences

---

[36] *R (U) v Comr of Metropolitan Police; R (U) v Chief Constable of Durham Constabulary* (2002): see Fortin (2003: 562–3).

or because of the age of their co-defendants (Home Office 2003c: para 12). The high-profile trial of Venables and Thompson, aged 11, brought this issue to public attention. The formal setting, the relentless publicity, their relative isolation and the length of the proceedings were at odds with the requirement under the CRC Article 40(1) that they be treated 'in a manner consistent with the promotion of the child's sense of dignity and worth', and the requirement of the Beijing Rules that the proceedings 'be conducted in an atmosphere of understanding' where the juvenile can properly participate (r 14.2). More importantly it was argued to the European Court that it infringed Articles 3 and 6 of the ECHR. Whilst the claim under Article 3 was rejected, an infringement of Article 6—the right to a fair trial— was upheld because they had been unable to participate fully in a trial pitched at the level of understanding of adult participants.

This case (*V and T v United Kingdom* (2000)) did not prohibit the use of the Crown Court for minors, although it led to a direction by the Lord Chief Justice (*Practice Note (trial of children and young people)* 2000) requiring a variety of practical changes to make the court room and process more conducive to the participation of minors. The result is, in relation to the Crown Court, that 'children are still required to sit in a dock, stared at by a jury, and cross-examined by barristers' (Fortin 2003: 565).

Of perhaps most importance, given the problems we have reviewed in the previous section, is the extensive use of detention for young offenders by the courts in England and Wales. Article 37 of the CRC states that it should be 'a measure of last resort' and the Committee on the Rights of the Child has criticised the UK for the earlier ages at which detention is now used, as well as the greater numbers being detained, the longer sentences available, and the unacceptable conditions in young offender institutions (Committee on the Rights of the Child 2002: paras 59–62).

However, as Scraton and Haydon (2002) have argued, it is too easy for the government to hide a lack of attention to the rights of minors behind a rhetoric of rights. In reference to the UK's Second Report to the Committee on the Rights of the Child (UK Government 1999), they make the following comment: 'Using a discourse of "rights" and "responsibilities", the punitive potential of the [1998] Act is reconstructed as enabling, supportive welfare intervention. In an ironic interpretation of Article 3, the Report states: "It is in the interests of children and young people themselves to recognise and accept responsibility, and to receive assistance in tackling criminal behaviour"' (Scraton and Haydon 2002: 321). Similarly they point out that the Report justified the abolition of the presumption of *doli incapax* as a means of ensuring that the courts are able to address offending behaviour by children in the 10–14 age group (UK Government 1999: 17) and the changes to the right to silence—allowing adverse inferences to be drawn—as a 'common sense' change, so that the child is not deprived of his or her responsibility to provide 'an innocent explanation' (ibid: 180).

Scraton and Haydon consequently argue for a proper rights-based approach in youth justice which they distinguish from a just deserts approach, on the basis that the former can legitimately differentiate treatment between adults and minors; it can 'mitigate' for age and maturity in a way that is currently lacking and can focus on the child's welfare without relying on an image of the child as weak and dependent (ibid: 324–5). This is a compelling argument which challenges the concern that a rights-based approach might mean that adults and minors are treated (inappropriately) alike.

Other commentators have recently suggested that the discourse has now moved away from rights. For example, Williams is concerned about the effect of the 'Every Child Matters' policies, with a focus on outcomes and the potential of children when adults:

Every Child Matters, *Youth Matters* and the Children Act 2004 all suggest a deliberate decision to eschew both the language and the concept of children's rights in favour of the pursuit of New Labour's 'five outcomes'. The result is that deficiencies in human rights awareness, and the suppression of rights-based reasoning, in decisions concerning children may be about to get worse, at least in England.

(Williams 2007: 263).

Currently the lack of a clear rights-based approach means that young offenders may be treated more harshly, as researchers concluded in relation to developments in Northern Ireland: 'Overall, in relation to the sentencing of juveniles, the evidence shows that very often they are disadvantaged in comparison to adults. They are disproportionately more likely to receive up-tariff sentencing options such as community sentences and custody, and are more likely to receive immediate custody for less serious and property related offences than adults' (O'Mahoney and Deazley 2000: 58).

The 'clarification' of Articles 37 and 40 of the UN CRC in the recent General Comment on rights in juvenile justice (Committee on the Rights of the Child 2007) should give pause for thought. It points out, for example, that Article 3 should be heeded in relation to young offenders: the best interests of the child should be a 'primary consideration' but we saw in Chapter 8 that even the weak welfare test in s 44 of the 1933 Children and Young Person's Act is being downgraded in importance. So, on the one hand, we have welfare being 'trumped' by the aim of preventing offending and, on the other, as we have seen, rights can become a meaningless rhetoric. So rights constitute a problematic discourse in relation to children and young people who offend and, on their own, are not the answer to achieving a lower use of custody and better conditions within custody. However, as, Kilkelly and Lundy (2006) argue, the CRC can be used as an 'auditing' tool to assess the extent of compliance or non-compliance within policy and practice. Yet, publicity about the shortcomings will always be insufficient. As Drakeford and Butler (2007) have recently pointed out, conditions and suicides in youth prisons have not led to a national 'scandal' in the same way that some other child deaths do: Victoria Climbié was portrayed as a victim, Gareth Myatt was not. The pressures on politicians to 'talk tough', to respond to perceived public opinion, and not to challenge negative images of young people make it very difficult to successfully implement either the welfare or the rights of young offenders.

13.4.2 **Youth justice as experiment?**

At the beginning of Chapter 8 we noted the concern that the separateness of the juvenile justice process and outcomes is under threat and that minors are increasingly being treated like adults. However, there is, arguably, an opposite trend: that penal measures have increasingly been piloted on minors. Using children and young people as a testing ground for policies is not new and not necessarily deleterious. For example, the rehabilitative approaches used with children in the nineteenth century were adopted in the adult system in the first half of the twenti-eth century whilst the hurdles for the imposition of custody enacted for minors in the 1980s were extended to adults in the CJA 1991. More recently, the Youth Justice and Criminal Evidence Act 1999 applied to a range of 'vulnerable adults' some of the witness protection afforded children, and conditional cautions—in the form of voluntary cautioning plus and now the final warning programme for juveniles—have been introduced for adults by the CJA 2003, with the objective of (a) facili-tating the rehabilitation of the offender, or (b) ensuring that he makes reparation for the offence (s 22(3)). Similarly the linked custodial punishment and commu-nity supervision in the detention and training order has, in effect, been rolled out for adults with the new early release provisions (see Chapter 12, section 12.2.4).

All these examples augur less punitive and more effective responses—*provided that* they are used to decrease the use of custody—and it is a plus for minors that they are available to them earlier than to adults. We are aware that the youth jus-tice system is chosen as the site for experimentation because it is easier to introduce and implement legislation relating only to that section of the population in which it is seen as legitimate to compulsorily control, educate and reform individuals. Nevertheless, there can be no problem *per se* with extending to adults the benefits of policies pioneered with minors, of 'civilising' punishment up through the age range.

Concern stems, rather, from the fact that youth justice policies now encourage more intervention—often punitive—in the lives of young offenders, and are based on particular images of children which legitimise more punitive responses. The benefits for young offenders of experiencing 'cutting edge' and enlightened practi-cal ideas can easily be outweighed by the drawbacks of being guinea pigs for puni-tive products such as curfews and intensive behaviour modification programmes.

Publicity is currently more often given by the Government to the provisions which indicate a 'tough' or 'new' approach to dealing with children who commit offences or who might progress from anti-social behaviour to criminality. For two reasons it is a pity that this more 'audible' strand of youth justice policy is punitive and underpinned by images of minors which focus on near-adult and 'dangerous' aspects. First, it obscures the fact that there are positive new approaches in juven-ile justice and developments in other areas of government policy which take into account what is known about the multiple causality of offending and which aim to respond to social deprivation and need. Their lower priority precludes a wider debate about young offenders. Second, the dominant and often negative images of children and young people which underpin policy are powerful: they can legitim-ise practices which may not be in the child's best interest and may not even reduce offending.

13.4.3 A deferred conclusion?

We noted in Chapter 8 that policy developments for young offenders are often presented as 'new', a break with the past, and self-evidently better than past prac-tice. This is misleading. All is not new and commentators have pointed this out (for example, Fionda 1999). This again precludes useful debate where parallels can be drawn with past practices and their effectiveness or drawbacks used to inform pre-sent practice and policy. We have discussed restorative justice elsewhere (Chapter

6) and simply repeat the point that, in youth as in adult justice, it needs to be accomplished with a proper sense of its validating principles.

So what *is* justice for 10–17-years-olds? As Weijers points out, there is a double paradox in relation to juvenile justice. There is the paradox stemming from 'the search for a compromise between deserved punishment and useful punishment' when there are 'centrifugal forces' pushing the two justifications apart (2002: 138): the theme which runs through this book. However, there is also the paradox that in dealing with minors the criminal justice system 'will always have to take account of the dilemma that, while they are developing towards responsibility, they are presumed to be dependent and not yet fully responsible' (ibid: 139). Duff suggests that we should question whether the punishment meted out to minors should be different from that meted out to adults, taking account of the effect and meaning of punishment for juveniles. He concludes that 'the obvious candidate' as an inappropriate punishment for juveniles is imprisonment (2002: 132).

Developments in children's services around 'safeguarding' and the links made across youth justice, child protection and children's services by the administrative changes that have been introduced by the Children Act 2004, might help to put more focus on the welfare of young offenders. However, whilst Chapter 6 of the *Second Joint Chief Inspectors' Review of Children's Safeguards* (Commission for Social Care Inspection *et al.* 2005) focused on children and the justice system and brought to light that 10 per cent of YOT employees or volunteers had not been CRB-checked (ibid: para 6.32), it was not comprehensive. Inspectors' reports in the past have been another tool for putting the spotlight on shortcomings and these reports may well increase in importance.

We would argue that rights could be more important in resolving at least some of the conditions and processes identified as unacceptable. A rights approach does not mean minors are necessarily treated the same as adults. Children and young people should be treated by known procedures and by measures which are not disproportionate to what they have done but, equally, substantive and procedural law needs to be enacted and implemented on the basis of conceptions of children which acknowledge their state of both being and becoming. That would allow minors to be accorded respect for their abilities and concerns, but would acknowledge, where appropriate, their inability to be held fully responsible where their stage of maturity and life experience would make it unjust to do so.

13.4.4 **Case study**

online resource centre

Below is a case study which covers material in Chapter 8 as well as this chapter. There is guidance in the Online Resource Centre to help you advise these two young people.

Jay, aged 13, and his cousin Kate, aged 17, were arrested whilst in a video warehouse which they had entered by prising open a small window. They were taken to the local police station where, in the presence of a solicitor and an appropriate adult, Jay confessed to burglary. Jay had been reprimanded the previous year.

You are the solicitor:

1. Explain to Jay what decision the police are likely to make about him.
2. Explain to Jay what would happen if the police decided to give him a warning.

Then:

Kate was found to have stolen and hidden a quantity of videos before the arrival of the police. Kate, who had been warned for an offence a year previously, was prosecuted for the offence of burglary of commercial premises (Theft Act 1968, s 9) for which the maximum penalty is ten years. She decided to plead guilty.

3. Explain to Kate what options are open to the youth court and which option they are most likely to choose.

4. Explain to Kate whether the options would be different if she had committed burglary of a residential property (for which the maximum penalty is 14 years).

Consider this alternative scenario:

Assume that Jay and Kate confess to having jointly committed the offence of having possession of a Class B drug with intent to supply (Misuse of Drugs Act 1971, s 5(3)—for which the maximum penalty is 14 years' imprisonment). The youth court decides that a custodial sentence is the only appropriate sentence for both of them.

5. Explain to Jay and Kate how and where might such a sentence be imposed and on what criteria. (Jay is still 13 and Kate is still 17.)

14

Future directions

In this book we have reviewed a wide range of issues concerning the law, policy, and practice of sentencing and punishment and have examined the main philosophical justifications for the state's responses to those adjudged by the courts to be criminals. However, there are themes in criminology and penology, and in penal policy and practice, which cut across the chapters in this book, and which allow us to identify trends in sentencing and punishment in the late twentieth and early twenty-first centuries. In our concluding comments we will simply highlight these issues.

14.1 The role of punishment

14.1.1 The decreasing importance of sentencing?

A recurring theme of this book has been the changes in thinking on various aspects of sentencing and punishment policy and practice since the 1970s. We also find, during this period, a growing recognition, in the light of socio-legal and criminological research, that the penal sanction has limited usefulness (see our discussions on deterrence, incapacitation, and rehabilitation in Chapters 4, 5 and 12 respectively). The knowledge that few crimes are reported, that even fewer are successfully prosecuted to the point of sentence, and that punishments which ensure the offender does not reoffend are rare, undermines the value of academic and professional investments in this area of public life.

Furthermore, recent developments in what has been referred to by Crawford (2003) as the 'contractual governance' of deviant behaviour would seem to diminish further the importance of those legal provisions and punishment practices with which this book has been concerned. Crawford's argument is that 'the ultimate symbol of state sovereignty—the penal sanction—itself is in crisis' and is being supplanted as a social control mechanism by a complex mesh of localised contracts in policy areas as diverse as housing, education and community safety (2003: 480). For Crawford, new contractual forms of government, notably crime prevention partnerships, reflect a new 'future-focused logic of crime prevention, risk minimization and insurance' which suggests 'a very different idea of justice, one that is more instrumental than moral, more consequential than symbolic and more utilitarian than retributive' (ibid: 486).

A good example of the declining influence of penal measures and the increasing use of civil or 'voluntary' measures is the repertoire of new tools for controlling anti-social behaviour. Not only is there the anti-social behaviour order (ASBO) which we discussed in the last chapter (section 13.1.1) but there are also now agreements and contracts whose use has shown a huge increase since they were introduced. The Respect Task Force reported in November 2006 that in 2003–4, 3,948 acceptable behaviour contracts (ABCs) were signed, in 2004–5, 6,901 and in 2005–6, 7,500.[1] Updated guidance on ABCs and anti-social behaviour agreements was issued by the Home Office's Anti-Social Behaviour and Alcohol Unit in 2007 (Home Office 2007d). The guidance, noting that 'the flexible nature of ABCs means that they can be used incrementally', gives a range of increasingly interventionist options which could be used (ibid: 2). It further points out that 'the prospect of a more formal, legal intervention can provide an added incentive to adhere to the contract' (ibid). There is, then, a whole new system of behaviour control which is operating outside the formal criminal justice system but making use of the shadow of the law.

There is also a trend towards the greater use of fixed penalty notices—those fines which are outside of sentencing courts and imposed administratively, not judicially. In addition, with the increase in the number of civil orders for which the police can apply, the role of the police in punishing offenders has increased, with a corresponding decrease in the role of the sentencing court.

We now have a plethora of civil orders relating to a wider range of offences and offenders, including violent offenders, which encroach on freedom of movement. The effect of these changes has also had implications for the prison population, as in some cases, breaches of those orders have, led to custodial sentences.

There is also another trend which, though not decreasing the role of sentencing courts, is evidence of greater control of the sentencer. Indeed, the desire on the part of the Government for efficiency and effectiveness has led to greater central control of the agents of community punishment as well as those who deliver sentences. We saw in Chapter 2 the types of constraint progressively placed on judges and magistrates in exercising their discretion in sentencing. Whilst clearer and much-needed detailed advice has been produced by the Sentencing Advisory Panel, and guidelines are increasingly being produced by the Sentencing Guidelines Council (SGC), this development also presages increasing control of sentencing guidance from outside the judiciary through the relationship between the SGC and the Secretary of State (Criminal Justice Act (CJA) 2003 s 170; now referring to the Secretary of State for Justice). The SGC also has appointed 'non-judicial' members who must have experience of policing, criminal prosecution, criminal defence, and the promotion of the welfare of victims of crime, although the Chair must be the Lord Chief Justice (CJA 2003, s 167).

On the one hand, these developments are to be welcomed if they contribute to greater clarity of sentencing guidance and more consistency of sentencing practice, and to the reduction of injustice by geography in the provision of the best quality programmes to help and 'correct' the diverse population of offenders subject to community and custodial penalties. On the other hand, this trend causes unease. It is not to be welcomed if it ensures—through a greater use of management tools such as monitoring, standardisation, rigid line management, and budget control—a country-wide level and form of practice at the expense of professional expertise and a sense of doing justice on an individual basis.

Yet these changes do not diminish the importance of sentencing and punishment. In policy terms, as we saw in Chapter 1, and in our review throughout this

---

[1] See http://www.crimereduction.gov.uk/crimereduction009.htm.

book of the major legislative innovations of 1991, 1997, 1998, 2000 and 2003, sentencing and punishment remain very high on the agenda of both the Government and the public. The law and order issue dominated elections in the 1990s, and was an important issue in the 2005 election. It remains an essential item on party manifestos, and is likely to figure in future general elections. Paradoxically, the importance of the visible, sanctioning institutions of the courts and prisons increases as the state's capacity to control crime becomes more limited.

14.1.2 **The increasing importance of social policy?**

The 'Third Way' criminal justice policy developed by the Labour governments since 1997 aimed at finding a viable alternative to the welfare-based social democracy of much of the nineteenth century and the neo-liberalism dominant in the Conservative governments of Mrs Thatcher (see Giddens 1998, 2000). New Labour thinking recognises that there are links between social exclusion (caused by socio-economic factors) and crime, but retains a stress on the importance of personal and family responsibility. Whilst the problem is viewed as at least partly structural ('tough on the causes of crime'), the solution is individual ('tough on crime').

However, the social and penal policies most likely to be effective in reducing criminality and anti-social behaviour are also likely to take some time to show results. Investments in early years' family support, better designed communities, and programmes to remedy educational deficits and other forms of disadvantage can never produce quick results. Newburn argued that the New Labour modernisation project, because of the tensions in its emergence and its role in electoral success, 'has at its heart a concern with image management...It is here that the tensions between short-termism and the longer-term modernisation project have perhaps been clearest...Harsher punishment and impatience with civil liberties can also be seen as part of a strategy of claiming that "something is being done" about crime' (2001–2: 5). The longer-term, perhaps sounder, policy achievements are 'masked by, and occasionally undermined by, knee-jerk policy-making and populist, short term rhetoric' (ibid).

The political imperative to appear punitive not only hides more effective, longer-term reforms but may also hinder their effectiveness. Tough speaking—encouraging the public's punitiveness—can undermine the longer-term effects of positive social policies, for example when children are repositioned as hardened criminals (see Chapters 8 and 13). Consequently, Sparks and Taylor noted in 2001, 'the demonization of "yobs" contrasts vividly with the more rounded work on issues for young people from the Social Exclusion Unit' (2001/2: 6) and this continues to be the case. It is an encouraging sign, however, that one Cabinet Minister has said that, 'one of the things we have to do as a government is talk about young people in a much more positive fashion...and not to give the impression that most young people are about to commit acts of antisocial behaviour (Ed Miliband, quoted in Wintour 2007: 1).

A further example of policy conflict can be found in the goal of reducing the use of custodial penalties. This was a consistent policy imperative before the major sentencing legislation of 1991 and 2003, and yet was rarely publicised as such. But the reductionist aim will never be achieved, as many commentators have observed, whilst governments aim also to be seen as the toughest (see Hough *et al.*

2003; Sparks and Taylor 2001/2). As Sanders and Loveday pointed out following the publication of the Auld and Halliday reports, 'without identifying mass imprisonment ("punitive segregation") as the problem (rather than the solution), is not all the rest mere tinkering—just a re-arrangement of the deck-chairs on the Lab–Con's Titanic criminal justice system?' (2001–2).

However, in the face of mounting pressure on the prison system, the highest levels of the prison population on record, and the associated costs of incarceration, the Government has been encouraged to explore possible reductionist policies as we have seen, if only in relation to specific offender groups. This shift reflects the view that prison may not 'work' for all groups, and that, in some cases, alternatives may need to be considered. These reductionist trends lie uneasily alongside the commitment to 'rebalance the criminal justice system' in favour of the law-abiding majority by dealing robustly with crime and anti-social behaviour, and a move towards large-scale prisons.

14.2 The influence of rights jurisprudence

14.2.1 The European Convention on Human Rights

In examining developments in penal policy, we have drawn attention to the influence on government policy and sentencing guidelines of judgments from the European Court of Human Rights and, since the implementation of the Human Rights Act 1998, from the domestic courts. At the time of writing, however, there are many relevant cases which are in the process of appeal and which might mandate further changes in policy. So far, we have noted—although we have not had the space to do so comprehensively—ECHR cases which have led to significant changes, for example, to the setting of minimum terms for life sentences, and the processes and criteria for release after the minimum term, for both adults and minors. Rights-driven change is also now enshrined in statute to make the sentencing decision more 'open'. For example, s 174 of the CJA 2003 imposes a duty on the sentencer to give reasons for a sentence in open court and explain 'in ordinary language' the effect of the sentence. Specifically, the sentencer must state the aggravating and mitigating factors considered and, if moving outside the guidelines, he or she must explain why. We have also identified a number of areas of prison life in which rights have been given effect and it seems that future litigation on prison life will continue to be framed within the rights discourse of the ECHR. As we have seen, rights have been a significant influence on both the theory and practice of punishment in recent years and continue to provide a means of raising standards in the criminal justice process, particularly within the context of custody, and to provide a counter to demands for penal austerity.

14.2.2 The United Nations Convention on the Rights of the Child

Whilst the above shifts in policy are to be welcomed, it is a cause for concern that rights-based change has not gone far enough in relation to children and young people who offend and that the UN Convention on the Rights of the Child has not had as much impact as many commentators would wish. Over half of the number of ASBOs issued have been imposed on children aged 10–17 and the use of publicity in relation to such orders has incurred public criticism by a Commissioner for Human Rights (Gil-Robles 2005). Indeed, current constructions of citizenship in relation to young people within the context of 'Third Way' values are particularly problematic for children (see Piper 2008: Chapter 8). As Gray argues, the focus in current social and penal policy on responsibilisation and 'the individualisation of social risks' has 'done little to either boost young offenders' sense of social worth or change their material circumstances' (Gray 2007: 410). If children make 'wrong' choices or 'fail' to make any positive choices then various forms of discipline or punishment are triggered but, argues Childright, whilst it 'is perfectly legitimate to promote responsibility...it is not equally legitimate to withhold rights until a young person can demonstrate that responsibility' (Childright 2005: 3).

The sentencing framework for children and young people is also not sufficiently different from that relating to adult offenders. The CJA 2003 has continued the use of statutory criteria for all age groups for the imposition of custodial and community sentences which means that the test for custody, 'so serious that neither a fine alone nor a community sentence can be justified', therefore applies to anyone above 10 years old, the age of criminal responsibility. That the dividing line is set at 10 for the purposes of criminal proceedings is itself a cause for concern. Further, whilst there are orders specified for use with children under 16, adult community orders are currently available (s 177) for young people aged 16–17. The Criminal Justice and Immigration Act 2008 will seek to introduce a new order for all offenders aged 10–17 although it is based on that currently available for adults. The CJA 2003 has not, therefore, brought all provisions into line with the recommendations of the UN Convention on the Rights of the Child that there should be different processes and outcomes for those under 18. Further, the 18–20-year-old age group continues to be neglected and, as we saw in the last chapter, conditions in detention institutions for young people are still far from ideal and with totally unacceptable methods of restraint being used (Howard League for Penal Reform 2007).

14.2.3 The European Union framework

The directives and frameworks emerging from the European Union should not be classified as rights jurisprudence and placed in this section but we have done so because they are an external source of regulation of English criminal justice and sentencing which often draws its ideas from victims' rights approaches. We have mentioned in the book several measures which have been influenced by decisions of the European Union and amongst these are the Framework Decision on the Standing of Victims in Criminal Proceedings and the European Convention on the Compensation of Victims of Violent Crime. However, the orders freezing property or evidence under Council Framework Decision 2003/577/JHA are within a more managerialist crime-control paradigm. In addition, the Criminal Justice and Immigration Act 2008 Part 6 includes new measures to implement European Framework Decision 2005/214/JHA on the mutual recognition of financial penalties, to promote 'international co-operation in relation to criminal justice matters'.

These developments focus on the enforcement of orders, the recovery of fines and property, the making of compensation and the standing of victims. We would expect these developments to continue and intensify.

14.3 The role of courts

14.3.1 Informal justice

A further trend, addressed at several points in this book, is that of the increasing importance of informal justice processes. The most significant is the use of mediation and conferencing in relation to restorative justice. This leads to a need to reconceptualise the relationship between informal justice and formal processes. Roche has focused in particular on how accountability can be introduced into these new informal processes, an urgent matter given our knowledge of the powerful criticisms of informal justice made in the 1970s and 1980s, when such processes were last in the forefront of policy and professional practice (Roche 2003: 24).

Informal justice has many advantages, particularly its ability to produce tailor-made outcomes and to encourage more positive relationships after the disruptions, harm and anger caused by offending. Yet these advantages are not automatic and if not achieved can cause further distress or outcomes which do not do justice to all those involved. Just as happened with community justice in the 1970s and family mediation in the 1980s, there is now a similar tendency with victim–offender mediation and conferences, to see only the 'good' through the lens of enthusiasm. A more critical forensic gaze is also required to avoid injustice.

14.3.2 'Community' and 'therapeutic' courts

Community courts and therapeutic courts are related developments which draw on the use of informal procedures but, unlike the above processes, aim to increase the role of the court. There is now an International Network on Therapeutic Jurisprudence, set up by David Wexler, who coined the phrase, whose web site explains the approach as follows:

Therapeutic Jurisprudence concentrates on the law's impact on emotional life and psychological well-being. It is a perspective that regards the law (rules of law, legal procedures, and roles of legal actors) itself as a social force that often produces therapeutic or anti-therapeutic consequences. It does not suggest that therapeutic concerns are more important than other consequences or factors, but it does suggest that the law's role as a potential therapeutic agent should be recognized and systematically studied.[2]

Therapeutic courts are multi-disciplinary in that they draw on, or refer to, a range of associated services such as drug treatment or anger management courses, housing and welfare agencies and family support services but also use the authority of the court to ensure regular attendance at the required services. Such courts have been pioneered mainly in the USA and Australia[3] but in the UK domestic violence

---

[2] See http://www.law.arizona.edu/depts/upr-intj/.
[3] See, for example, the special issue, 'Therapeutic Jurisprudence', of the journal *Law in Context* (2003) Vol 20(2).

courts (see Burton 2006) and drug courts have been piloted (see Harwin and Ryan 2007). The former are criminal courts, the latter have been set up either in criminal courts or in civil courts with a child protection remit. Jack Straw, Minister for Justice, announced in March 2008 that four more drugs courts would be set up. Community courts have also been established in Liverpool and Salford, using the same multi-agency model and with a particular focus on drugs offences but with an emphasis on using a more 'user-friendly' building, for example a converted school.[4] The use of one judge through a case and the readier access to rehabilitative and welfare services is a development to be welcomed and copied.

There is some concern, nevertheless, that the pressure for encouraging change in the lives of the people before the courts—be they drug users, perpetrators of domestic abuse or minority rights violations, tax evaders, or any of the other offenders who are the focus of specialist courts worldwide—might undermine their rights to due process. Plotnikoff and Woolfson (2005) in their review of research on problem-solving courts in other jurisdictions, for the Department for Constitutional Affairs, have pointed to the importance of involving lawyers conversant with and supportive of the new approaches. It is to be hoped, however, that they do not simply become social workers with a law degree because, as we have seen in relation to children in detention (Chapter 13, section 13.3.3), the use of courts in their traditional role can still be effective.

14.4 Organisational changes in managing crime and disorder

In the criminal justice system we have seen major changes in the administration of criminal justice, with the breaking up of the Home Office and the arrival and departure of several Home Secretaries. Indeed, ministerial responsibility for crime and justice might now be seen as a 'poisoned chalice' for ministers given the problems we have highlighted. These upheavals have resulted in the creation of the Ministry of Justice and the transfer of key areas of criminal justice policy and management, including offender management, to the Ministry of Justice.

In a recent policy document (Home Office 2007a) the Home Secretary emphasised that the Government would be taking a 'more rounded view of tackling crime, from prevention through to rehabilitation' and that this would also mean less direct control, allowing professionals greater flexibility, and also stronger partnerships with business and industry (see also Home Office 2007b). We have seen the continuing rise of the market in recent years with contestability extended to a wider range of criminal justice functions including community punishment. The role and status of the Probation Service have also changed: it is now a national body, under direct central control and subject to National Standards and the detailed statutory provisions of the CJA 2003. It has also become part of the larger National Offender Management Service in a merger with the Prison Service.

We are also seeing a tension between central control and local autonomy on issues of crime and disorder and between central and local government and local

---

[4] See http://www.justice.gov.uk/news/sp260308a.htm.

communities and corporate interests. The tensions between central government and corporate interests on the one hand, and local communities, the police and local government on the other, over the governance of crime in public and private space, are explored by Hadfield (2006) in *Bar Wars*. What his study of the night-time economy in city centres shows is that, despite a commitment to rebalancing the criminal justice system in favour of the law-abiding majority, the Government's relaxation of regulatory constraints on the alcohol industry has contributed to a context in which anti-social behaviour has flourished.

14.5 Terrorism and security

The first edition of this book was conceived and written after the events of 11 September 2001. In this political climate, as Zedner notes, the 'language of security is increasingly supplanting that of crime control' (2003: 151). Certainly events of recent years have seen policing—nationally and internationally—dominated by terrorist threats and actions. Internationally as well as nationally, politicians perceive a need to be seen to be firm, decisive and punitive in the 'battle' against a new and immensely more harmful form of criminality. If these attitudes and the over riding concerns with security were to influence attitudes to lesser forms of risk and to criminality in general, then this would reduce the chances of success of reductionist policies. In the national context, the fears expressed regarding the use of the more draconian sections of the CJA 2003 would be justified.

Since the first edition of this book, we have seen terrorist attacks closer to home with the 7 July 2005 bombings, and terrorism and national security have assumed further importance in the crime control agenda. This has shaped domestic criminal justice policy in so far as the fight against terrorism worldwide has become focused on threats from within, which has added to a sense of insecurity, and has been used to legitimise increases in police powers. We have seen further extensions to anti-terrorism law in the Prevention of Terrorism Act 2005 and the use of Control Orders. We have also seen increasingly a conflict between the Government and civil libertarians and professionals over this agenda, which has been framed by the UK's continued participation in two major military engagements overseas.

14.6 The quest for justice

The subtitle of this book is 'The Quest for Justice' and this has been a recurring theme throughout our review of sentencing and penal policy. Justice appears as a neutral word—the 'pure' end product of a positive moral process. The even-handed figure with the scales, the 'avenging angel' of Miss Marple in Agatha Christie's *Nemesis*, the wise Judge Solomon: all are symbols of justice dealt out above the everyday ambiguities and complexities of life.

Yet in practice justice is inextricably linked with money. According to retributivist principles, justice is done only if punishment is seen by all concerned as commensurate with seriousness. When the public's and sentencers' perception of seriousness is heightened then, without restraint, the system will lead to harsher sentences. More intensive supervision or (longer) prison sentences mean that the cost rises. Restorative justice is not immune from the link between money and justice, despite the principle that it pays back and restores. If what has been damaged, be it property or person, is seen by those at a restorative conference as a great harm, the procedures to ensure adequate reparation may themselves be costly.

Utilitarian principles are seemingly more economic in so far as the principle of parsimony demands that intervention should be the minimum necessary to achieve the outcome. But implementing 'what works', although cheaper than 'blanket' solutions, is still expensive and success is not guaranteed. Incapacitation is clearly expensive and deterrence requires a high level of publicity and education to be effective.

The variables which influence what counts as justice are not independent and can all be manipulated:

- the selection of agreed justifying principles and an agreed notion of the inalienable components of justice
- the selection of concepts of what counts as serious and dangerous and the different levels of seriousness and dangerousness
- the amount of money the electorate is prepared to spend on achieving justice in sentencing and punishment.

If these variables, and their operation in the dispensing of justice in sentencing and punishment, could be openly debated, some progress might be made. Currently, the climate of populist punitiveness, the sense of international, national and personal insecurity, and the lack of an ethical consensus on dealing with 'evil' and 'deviance' preclude proper debate. We hope that this book will contribute to the likelihood of such a debate taking place.

BIBLIOGRAPHY

Abel, R. (1982) *The Politics of Informal Justice*. New York, Academic Press.

Adler, R. (1985) *Taking Juvenile Justice Seriously*. Edinburgh, Scottish Academic Press.

Advisory Council on the Penal System (1977) *The Length of Prison Sentences*, Interim Report. London, HMSO.

Advisory Council on the Penal System (1978) *The Review of Maximum Sentences*, Final Report. London, HMSO.

Aertsen, I., Daems, T. and Robert, L. (eds) (2006) *Institutionalizing Restorative Justice*. Cullompton, Willan.

Aldridge, M. and Eadie, T. (1997) 'Manufacturing an Issue: The Case of Probation Officer Training' *Critical Social Policy* Vol 17(1), 111–24.

Alldridge, P. and Mumford, A. (2005) 'Tax Evasion and the Proceeds of Crime Act 2002' LS Vol 25(3), 353–73.

Allen, F. (1981) *The Decline of the Rehabilitative Ideal*. New Haven, CT, Yale University Press.

Allen, R. (1996) *Children and Crime*. London, Institute for Public Policy Research.

Allwood, Z. (2008) Statistics on Women and the Criminal Justice System 2005/06. London, Ministry of Justice.

Althusser, L. (1971) *Lenin and Philosophy*. London, New Left Books.

American Friends Services Committee (1971) *Struggle for Justice: A Report on Crime and Punishment in America*. New York, Hill and Wang.

Amos, M. (2004) '*R v Secretary of State for the Home Department ex parte Anderson*—Ending the Home Secretary's Sentencing Role' MLR Vol 67, 108–23.

Andenaes, J. (1974) *Punishment and Deterrence*. Ann Arbor, University of Michigan Press.

Archard, D. (1993) *Children, Rights and Childhood*. London, Routledge.

Armstrong Kelly, G. (1969) *Idealism, Politics and History*. Cambridge, Cambridge University Press.

Ashworth, A. (1975) 'Sentencing in Provocation Cases' Crim LR, 553–63.

Ashworth, A. (1983) *Sentencing and Penal Policy*. London, Weidenfeld and Nicolson.

Ashworth, A. (1984) 'Techniques of Guidance on Sentencing' Crim LR, 519–30.

Ashworth, A. (1986) 'Punishment and Compensation: Offender, Victim and State', OJLS vol 6, 86–122.

Ashworth, A. (1987) 'Disentangling Disparity' in C. Pennington and S. Lloyd-Bostock (eds) *The Psychology of Sentencing*. Oxford, Oxford Centre for Socio-legal Studies, Wolfson College, Oxford University, 24–7.

Ashworth, A. (1992) 'Non-Custodial Sentences' Crim LR, 242–51.

Ashworth, A. (1993) 'Victim Impact Statements and Sentencing' Crimi LR, 498–509.

Ashworth, A. (1995) *Sentencing and Criminal Justice* (2nd edn). London, Butterworths.

Ashworth, A. (1998a) 'Structuring Sentencing Discretion' and 'Four techniques for reducing sentencing disparity' in A. von Hirsch and A. Ashworth (eds) *Principled Sentencing: Readings on Theory and Practice* (2nd edn). Oxford, Hart Publishing, 212–19, 227–39.

Ashworth, A. (1998b) *The Criminal Process* (2nd edn). Oxford, Clarendon Press.

Ashworth, A. (2000) *Sentencing and Criminal Justice* (3rd edn). London, Butterworths.

Ashworth, A. (2002a) 'Sentencing' in M. Maguire *et al.* (eds) *The Oxford Handbook of Criminology* (3rd edn). Oxford, Oxford University Press, 1076–1112.

Ashworth, A. (2002b) 'Responsibilities, Rights and Restorative Justice' *British Journal of Criminology* Vol 42, 578–95.

Ashworth, A. (2003) 'New Sentencing Proposals for England and Wales', *Sentencing Observer*, No. 2, 9.

Ashworth, A. (2004) 'Criminal Justice Act 2003: Part 2: Criminal Justice Reform—Principle, Human Rights and Public Protection' Crim LR, 516–32.

Ashworth, A. (2005) *Sentencing and Criminal Justice* (4th edn). Cambridge, Cambridge University Press.

Ashworth, A. and Player, E. (1998) 'Sentencing, Equal Treatment and the Impact of Sanctions' in A. Ashworth and M. Wasik (eds) *Fundamentals of Sentencing Theory*. Oxford, Clarendon Press.

Ashworth, A. and Player, E. (2005) 'The Criminal Justice Act 2003: The Sentencing Provisions' MLR Vol 68(5), 822–38.

Ashworth, A. and von Hirsch, A. (1997) 'Recognising Elephants: The Problem of the Custody Threshold' Crim LR, 187–200.

Asquith, S. (2002) 'Justice, Retribution and Children' in J. Muncie, G. Hughes and E. McLaughlin (eds) *Youth Justice, Critical Readings*. London, Sage, 275–83.

Audit Commission (1996) *Misspent Youth: Young People and Crime*. London, Audit Commission.

Audit Commission (1998) *Misspent Youth, '98: The Challenge for Youth Justice*. London, Audit Commission.

Audit Commission (2004) *Youth Justice 2004*. London, Audit Commission.

Auld, Lord Justice (2001) *Review of the Criminal Courts of England and Wales*. London, The Stationery Office.

Bagaric, M. (2001) *Punishment and Sentencing: A Rational Approach*. London, Cavendish.

Bailey, W. C. (1980) 'Deterrence and the Celerity of the Death Penalty: A Neglected Question in Deterrence Research' *Social Forces* Vol 58, 1308–33.

Bailey, W. C. and Peterson, R. D. (1997) 'Murder, Capital Punishment and Deterrence: A Review of the Literature' in H. Bedau (ed) *The Death Penalty in America: Current Controversies*. New York, Oxford University Press, 135–61.

Bailin, A. (2002) 'The Inhumanity of Mandatory Sentences' Crim LR, 641–45.

Baker, E. (1993) 'Dangerousness, Rights and Criminal Justice' MLR Vol 56, 528–47.

Baker, E. and Clarkson, C. M. V. (2002) 'Making Punishments Work? An Evaluation of the Halliday Report on Sentencing in England and Wales' Crim LR, 81–97.

Baker, K., Jones, S., Merrington, S. and Roberts, C. (2005) *Further Development of Asset*. London, Youth Justice Board.

Ball, C. (1995) 'Youth Justice and the Youth Court—The End of a Separate System?' *Child and Family Law Quarterly* Vol 7(4), 196–208.

Ball, C. (2000) 'The Youth Justice and Criminal Evidence Act 1999 Part I: A Significant Move towards Restorative Justice or a Recipe for Unintended Consequences?' Crim LR, 211–22.

Ball, C. (2004) 'Youth Justice? Half a Century of Responses to Youth Offending' Crim LR, 167–80.

Bandalli, S. (1998) 'Abolition of the Presumption of *Doli Incapax* and the Criminalisation of Children' *Howard Journal* Vol 37(2), 114–23.

Bar Council, The (2006) *Guide to Sentences for Serious Crimes*. http://www.criminalbar.com/210/redirect/SentencingNov06.pdf.

Barclay, G. and Mhlanga, B. (2000) *Ethnic differences in Decisions on Young Defendants Dealt With by the Crown Prosecution Service*, Home Office Section 95 Findings 1. London, Home Office.

Barker, J. (1985) 'Some Problems in Sentencing Juveniles' Crim LR, 759–63.

Barry, M. (2005) *Youth Policy and Social Inclusion*. London, Routledge.

Bateman, T. (2007) 'Ignoring Necessity: The Court's Decision to Impose an ASBO on a Child' *Child and Family Law Quarterly* Vol 19(3), 304–21.

Beccaria, C. (1767) *On Crimes and Punishments and Other Writings*, ed. R. Bellemy (1995). Cambridge, Cambridge University Press.

Beck, U. (1992) *The Risk Society: Towards a New Modernity*. London, Sage.

Beckett, K. and Western, B. (2001) 'Governing Social Marginality: Welfare, Incarceration and the Transformation of State Policy', in D. Garland (ed) *Mass Imprisonment*. London, Sage, 35–50.

Beckford, J. A., Joly, D. and Khosrokhavar, F. (2005) *Muslims in Prison: Challenge and Change in Britain and France*. London, Palgrave.

Bedau, H. (1997) 'Prison Homicides, Recidivist Murder and Life Imprisonment' in H. Bedau (ed) *The Death Penalty in America: Current Controversies*. New York, Oxford University Press, 176–82.

Beinart, S., Anderson, B., Lee, S. and Utting, D. (2002) *Youth at Risk? A National Survey of Risk Factors and Problem Behaviour among Young People in England, Scotland and Wales*. London, Communities that Care.

Bennett, J., Crewe, B. and Wahidin, A. (eds) (2007) *Understanding Prison Staff*. Cullompton, Willan.

Bentham, J. (1789) *Introduction to the Principles of Morals and Legislation*, ed J. L. Burns and H. L. A. Hart (1996). Oxford, Clarendon.

Bentham, J. (1843) 'Anarchical Fallacies' in J. Bowring (ed) *The Works of Jeremy Bentham*. Edinburgh, William Tait.

Beyleveld, D. (1980) *A Bibliography on General Deterrence*. Farnborough, Saxon House.

Black Committee (1979) Report of the Children and Young Persons' Review Group. Belfast, HMSO.

Blagg, H. (1985) 'Reparation and Justice for Juveniles' *British Journal of Criminology* Vol 25(7), 267–79.

Blanchette, K. and Brown, S. L. (2006) *The Assessment and Treatment of Women Offenders: An Integrative Perspective*. Chichester, John Wiley.

Block, B. (1993) 'A Fine Mess' *Justice of the Peace*, 16 May, 308.

Blumstein, A., Cohen, J. and Nagin, D. (1978) (eds) *Deterrence and Incapacitation*. Washington, DC, National Academy of Sciences.

Boin, A. and Rattray, W. A. (2004) 'Understanding Prison Riots: Towards a Threshold Theory' *Punishment and Society* Vol 6(1), 47–66.

Bonger, W. (1916) *Criminality and Economic Conditions*. Boston, Little Brown.

Boswell, G. (1991) *Section 53 Offenders: An Exploration of Experience and Needs*. London, The Prince's Trust.

Bottoms, A. (1985) 'Justice for Juveniles 75 years on' in D. Hoath (ed) *75 Years of Law at Sheffield 1909–84*. Sheffield, University Printing Unit.

Bottoms, A. (1995) 'The Philosophy and Politics of Sentencing' in C. M. V. Clarkson and R. Morgan (eds) *The Politics of Sentencing Reform*. Oxford, Clarendon.

Bottoms, A. (2002) 'On the Decriminalisation of English Juvenile Courts' in J. Muncie, G. Hughes and E. McLaughlin (eds) *Youth Justice, Critical Readings*. London, Sage, 216–27.

Bottoms, A. and McWilliams, W. (1979) 'A Non-Treatment Paradigm for Probation Practice' *British Journal of Social Work* Vol 9(2), 159–202.

Bottoms, A., Rex, S. and Robinson, G. (eds) (2004) *Alternatives to Prison, Options for an Insecure Society*. Cullompton, Willan.

Bowden, P. (1996) 'Violence and Mental Disorder' in N. Walker (ed) *Dangerous People*. London, Blackstone, 13–27.

Bowen, E., Brown, L. and Gilchrist, E. (2002) 'Evaluating Probation-based Offender Programmes for Domestic Violence Perpetrators: A Pro-feminist Approach' *Howard Journal* Vol 41(3), 221–36.

Bowling, B. and Phillips, C. (2002) *Racism, Crime and Justice*. London, Longman.

Boyle, M. H. and Lipman, E. (2002) 'Do Places Matter? Socioeconomic Disadvantage and Behavioral Problems of Children in Canada' *Journal of Consulting and Clinical Psychology* Vol 70(2), 378–89.

Braithwaite, J. (1989) *Crime, Shame and Reintegration*. Cambridge, Cambridge University Press.

Braithwaite, J. (2000) *Regulation, Crime, Freedom*. Aldershot, Ashgate.

Braithwaite, J. (2002) *Restorative Justice and Responsive Regulation*. Oxford, Oxford University Press.

Braithwaite, J. (2003) 'Principles of Restorative Justice' in A. von Hirsch, J. Roberts, A. Bottoms, K. Roach and M. Schiff (eds) *Restorative Justice and Criminal Justice, Competing or Reconcilable Paradigms?* Oxford, Hart Publishing, 1–20.

Braithwaite, J. and Pettit, P. (1990) *Not Just Deserts: A Republican Theory of Criminal Justice*. Oxford, Clarendon Press.

Brasse, G. (2003) 'Money Laundering—Who's Been Taken to the Cleaners?' *Family Law*, 492–6.

Bretherton, H. (1991) 'Partnership in Practice', *Probation Journal*, 132–5.

Britton, B., Hope, B., Locke, T. and Wainman, L. (1988) *Policy and Information in Juvenile Justice Systems*. London, NACRO/Save the Children Fund.

Brody, S. (1976) *The Effectiveness of Sentencing*, Home Office Research Study No. 35. London, HMSO.

Brody, S. and Tarling, R. (1980) *Taking Offenders out of Circulation*, Home Office Research Study, No. 64. London, HMSO.

Brooks-Gordon, B. and Bainham, A. (2004) 'Prisoners' Families and the Regulation of Contact' *Journal of Social Welfare and Family Law* Vol 26, 263.

Brown, A. (2004) 'Anti-Social Behaviour, Crime Control and Social Control' *Howard Journal* Vol 43(2), 203–11.

Brown, M. (1998) 'Serious Violence and Dilemmas of Sentencing: A Comparison of Three Incapacitation Policies' Crim LR, 710–22.

Brown, M. (2002) 'The Politics of Penal Excess and the Echo of Colonial Penality' *Punishment and Society* Vol 4(4), 403–23.

Brown, S. (1991) *Magistrates at Work*. Buckingham, Open University Press.

Brownlee, I. (1998a) 'New Labour—New Penology? Punitive Rhetoric and the Limits of Managerialism in Criminal Justice Policy', *Journal of Law and Society* Vol 25(3), 313–35.

Brownlee, I. (1998b) *Community Punishment*. London, Longman.

Bui, H.S. (2004) 'Criminal Justice and Mental Health' *Probation Journal* Vol 51(3), 260–1.

Búrca, G. and de Witte, B. (2005) (eds) *Social Rights in Europe*. Oxford, Oxford University Press.

Burnett, R. and Roberts, G. (eds) (2004) *What Works in Probation and Youth Justice: Developing Evidence-Based Practice*. Cullompton, Willan.

Burney, E. (1985) 'All Things to All Men: Justifying Custody under the 1982 Act' Crim LR, 284–93.

Burney, E. (2002) 'Talking Tough, Acting Coy: What Happened to the Anti-Social Behaviour Order?' *Howard Journal* Vol 41(5), 469–84.

Burney, E. (2003a) 'Using the Law on Racially Aggravated Offences' Crim LR, 28–36.

Burney, E. (2003b) Book review. *Howard Journal* Vol 42(4), 405–6.

Burney, E. (2005) *Making People Behave: Anti-social Behaviour, Politics and Policy*. Cullompton, Willan.

Burney, E. and Pearson, G. (1995) 'Mentally Disordered Offenders: Finding a Focus for Diversion' *Howard Journal* Vol 34, 291–313.

Burton, M. (2006) 'Judicial Monitoring of Compliance: Introducing "Problem Solving" Approaches into Domestic Violence Courts in England and Wales', *International Journal of Law, Policy and Family* Vol 20(3), 366–78.

Byrne, D. (2005) *Social Exclusion* (2nd edn). London, Sage.

Caddick, B. and Watson, D. (1999) 'Rehabilitation and the Distribution of Risk' in P. Parsloe (ed) *Risk Assessment in Social Care and Social Work*. London, Jessica Kingsley Publications, 53–68.

Caddle, D. and Crisp, D. (1997) *Imprisoned Women and Mothers*, HORS 162. London, Home Office.

Calder, M. (2003) 'The Assessment Framework: A Critique and Reformulation' in C. Calder and S. Hackett (eds) *Assessment in Child Care: Using and Developing Frameworks for Practice*. Lyme Regis, Russell House Publishing, 3–60.

Campbell, S. (2002) *A Review of Anti-Social Behaviour Orders*. HORS No. 236. London, Home Office.

Campbell, T. (1983) *The Left and Rights: A Conceptual Analysis of the Idea of Socialist Rights*. London, Routledge & Kegan Paul.

Campbell, T. (2001) *Justice* (2nd edn). London, Macmillan.

Carlen, P. (1983) *Women's Imprisonment*. London, Routledge.

Carlen, P. (1989) 'Crime, Inequality and Sentencing' in P. Carlen and D. Cook (eds) *Paying for Crime*. Milton Keynes, Open University Press, 8–28.

Carlen, P. (1998) *Sledgehammer: Women's Imprisonment at the Millennium*. London, Macmillan.

Carlen, P. (ed) (2002) *Women and Punishment: The Struggle for Justice*. Cullompton, Willan.

Carlile Report (2006) *The report of an independent inquiry into physical restraint, solitary confinement and forcible strip searching of children in prisons, secure training centres and local authority secure children's homes*. London, Howard League for Penal Reform.

Carlisle, Lord (1988) *The Parole System in England and Wales*, Report of the Review Committee. London, HMSO.

Carter, Lord (2007) *Securing the Future: Proposals for the Efficient and Sustainable Use of Custody in England and Wales*. London, Ministry of Justice.

Carter, P. (2003) *Managing Offenders, Reducing Crime: A New Approach* (The Carter Report). London, The Stationery Office.

Cavadino, P. (1988) 'Sentencing Variations in Magistrates' Courts' *Crime UK,* 31.

Cavadino, M. and Wiles, P. (1994) 'Seriousness of Offences: The Perceptions of Practitioners' Crim LR, 489–98.

Cavadino, M., and Dignan, J. (2002) *The Penal System* (3rd edn). London, Sage.

Cavadino, P. and Dignan, J. (2006) *Penal Systems: A Comparative Approach*. London, Sage.

Celnick A. and McWilliams W. (1991) 'Helping, Treating and Doing Good' *Probation Journal* Vol 39, 164–70.

Centre for Reviews and Dissemination (1999) *Systematic Review of the International Literature on the Epidemiology of Mentally Disordered Offenders,* CRD Report 15. York, York University.

Chalmers, J., Duff, P. and Leverick, F. (2007) 'Victim Impact Statements, Can Work Do Work, for Those Who Bother to Make Them' Crim LR, 360–79.

Cheliotis, L. K. and Liebling, A. (2005) 'Race Matters in British Prisons: Towards a Research Agenda', *British Journal of Criminology* Vol 46, 286–317.

Chigwada, R. (1989) 'The Criminalisation and Imprisonment of Black Women' *Probation Journal,* Vol 37, 100–5.

Chigwada-Bailey, R. (2003) *Black Women's Experience of Criminal Justice: A Discourse on Disadvantage* (2nd edn). Winchester, Waterside.

Childright (2005) 'Which Youth Matters? Comments on the Government Green Paper' *Agenda*. Colchester, Children's Legal Centre, University of Essex.

Christie, N. (1977) 'Conflicts as Property' 23 *British Journal of Criminology* 289, reprinted in E. McLaughlin, R. Ferguson, G. Hughes and L. Westmarland (2003) *Restorative Justice, Critical Issues*. Milton Keynes, Open University Press and London, Sage. Chapter 1.

Christie, N. (2007) 'Restorative Justice: Answers to Deficits in Modernity' in D. Downes, P. Rock, C. Chinkin, and C. Gearty (eds) *Crime, Social Control and Human Rights*. Cullompton, Willan.

Clancy, A., Hough, M., Aust, R. and Kershaw, C. (2001) *Crime, Policing and Justice: The Experience of Ethnic Minorities from the 2000 British Crime Survey*. HORS 223, London, Home Office.

Clarke, J. (2002) 'Whose Justice? The Politics of Juvenile Control' in J. Muncie, G. Hughes and E. McLaughlin (eds) *Youth Justice, Critical Readings*. London, Sage, 284–95.

Clarkson, C. (1997) 'Beyond Just Deserts: Sentencing Violent and Sexual Offenders' *Howard Journal* Vol 36(3), 284–92.

Cleland, A. and Tisdall, K. (2005) 'The Challenge of Anti-social Behaviour: New Relationships between the State, Children and Parents' *International Journal of Law, Policy and the Family* Vol 19(3), 395–420.

Clements, J. (2000) *Assessment of Race Relations at HMP Brixton*. London, Prison Service.

Clemmer, D. (1940) *The Prison Community*. New York, Holt, Rhinehart and Winston.

Cobb, N. (2007) 'Governance through Publicity: Anti-social Behaviour Orders, Young People, and the Problematization of the Right to Anonymity' *Journal of Law and Society* Vol 34(3), 342–73.

Cobley, C. (1997) 'Keeping Track of Sex Offenders—Part 1 of the Sex Offenders Act 1997' MLR vol 60, 60–9.

Codd, H. (2004) 'Prisoners' Families: Issues in Law and Policy' *Amicus Curiae* Vol 55, 2.

Codd, H. (2008) *In the Shadow of Prison: Families, Imprisonment and Criminal Justice.* Cullompton, Willan.

Cohen, J. (1978) 'The Incapacitative Effect of Imprisonment' in A. Blumstein, J. Cohen and D. Nagin *et al.* (eds) *Deterrence and Incapacitation: Estimating the Effects on Crime Rates,* Washington, National Academy of Sciences, 187–243.

Cohen, S. (1985) *Visions of Social Control.* Cambridge, Polity Press.

Cohen, S. (1994) 'Inside the System' in N. Lacey (ed) *A Reader in Criminal Justice.* Oxford, Oxford University Press, 278–30.

Commission for Racial Equality (2003) *A Formal Investigation by the CRE into HM Prison Service, England and Wales, Part I, The Murder of Zahid Mubarek; Part II, Racial Equality in Prisons.* London, CRE.

Commission for Racial Equality (2005) *Submission to the Zahid Mubarek Inquiry.* London, CRE.

Commission for Social Care Inspection, Office for Standards in Education, HM Chief Inspectorate of Constabulary, HM Crown Prosecution Service Inspectorate, HM Inspectorate of Probation, HM Inspectorate of Prisons, the Healthcare Commission, and HM Inspectorate of Court Administration (2005) *Safeguarding Children, The Second Joint Chief Inspector's Report on Arrangements to Safeguard Children.* London, HMICI.

Committee on the Rights of the Child (1995) *Concluding Observations of the Committee on the Rights of the Child: United Kingdom of Great Britain and Northern Ireland.* CRC/C/15/Add 34. Geneva, Centre for Human Rights.

Committee on the Rights of the Child (2002) *Concluding Observations of the Committee on the Rights of the Child: United Kingdom of Great Britain and Northern Ireland.* CRC/C/15/Add 188. Geneva, Centre for Human Rights.

Committee on the Rights of the Child (2007) *General Comment No. 10 (2007), Children's Rights in Juvenile Justice.* CRC/C/GC/10. Geneva, Centre for Human Rights.

Cook, D. (1989) 'Fiddling Tax and Benefits' in P. Carlen and D. Cook (eds) *Paying for Crime.* Milton Keynes, Open University Press, 109–27.

Cook, D. (2006) *Criminal and Social Justice.* London, Sage.

Cope, N. (2003) 'It's No Time or High Time: Young Offenders' Experience of Time and Drug Use in Prison' *Howard Journal* Vol 42(2), 158–75.

Corbett, C. (2000) 'The Social Construction of Speeding as Not "Real Crime"' *Crime Prevention and Community Safety* Vol 2(4), 33–46.

Corbett, C. (2003) *Car Crime.* Cullompton, Willan.

Corbett, C. and Caramlau, I. (2006) 'Gender Differences in Responses to Speed Cameras: Typology Findings and Implications for Road Safety'. *Criminology and Criminal Justice* Issue 4, 411–33.

Corston, J. (2007) *The Corston Report: A Report by Baroness Jean Corston of a Review of Women with Particular Vulnerabilities in the Criminal Justice System.* London, Home Office.

Councell, R. and Olagundoye, J. (2003) *The Prison Population in 2001: A Statistical Review.* Home Office Findings 195. London, Home Office.

Councell, R. and Simes, J. (2002) 'Projection of Long Term Trends in the Prison Population to 2009' *Home Office Statistical Bulletin.* London, Home Office.

Council of Europe (1987) European Prison Rules, adopted 12 February 1987. Strasbourg, Council of Europe.

Council of Europe (1991) *Report to the United Kingdom Government on the Visit to the United Kingdom Carried out by the European Committee for the Prevention of Torture and Inhuman or Degrading Treatment or Punishment from 29 June 1990 to 10 August 1990.* Strasbourg: Council of Europe.

Coyle, A. (2005) *Understanding Prisons: Key Issues in Policy and Practice.* Milton Keynes, Open University Press.

CPS (1988) Annual Report 1987–8. London, HMSO.

CPS (1991) Annual Report 1990–91. London, HMSO.

CPS (1994) *The Code for Crown Prosecutors* (3rd edn). London, Director of Public Prosecutions.

CPS (2000) *The Code for Crown Prosecutors* (4th edn). London, Director of Public Prosecutions.

Cracknell, S. (2000) 'Anti-Social Behaviour Orders' *Journal of Social Welfare and Family Law* Vol 22(1), 108–15.

Crawford, A. (1997) *The Local Governance of Crime.* Oxford, Oxford University Press.

Crawford, A. (2000) 'Justice de Proximité—The Growth of "Houses of Justice" and Victim/ Offender mediation in France: A Very UnFrench Legal Response?' *Social & Legal Studies* Vol 9(1), 29–53.

Crawford, A. (2003) 'Contractual Governance of Deviant Behaviour' *Journal of Law and Society* Vol 30(4), 479–505.

Crawford, A. and Enterkin, J. (2001) 'Victim Contact Work in the Probation Service: Paradigm Shift or Pandora's Box?' *British Journal of Criminology* Vol 41, 705–25.

Crawford, A. and Newburn, T. (2002) 'Recent Developments in Restorative Justice for Young People in England and Wales' *British Journal of Criminology* Vol 42, 476–95.

Crawford, A. and Newburn, T. (2003) *Youth Offending and Restorative Justice.* Cullompton, Willan.

Crawley, E. and Sparks, R. (2005) 'Hidden Injuries: Researching the Experience of Older Men in English Prisons' *Howard Journal,* Vol 44(4), 345–6.

Crawley, E. and Sparks, R. (2008) *Age of Imprisonment.* Cullompton, Willan.

Creighton, S. and King, V. (2000) *Prisoners and the Law* (2nd edn). London, Butterworths.

Criminal Justice: The Way Ahead (2001) Cm 5074. London, Stationery Office.

Croall, H. (1992) *White Collar Crime.* Milton Keynes, Open University Press.

Crofts, T. (2002) *The Criminal Responsibility of Children and Young Persons: A Comparison of English and German Law.* Aldershot, Ashgate.

Crook, F. (2003) 'Children in Prison: Advocating for the Human Rights of Young Offenders' *Criminal Justice Matters* No 54, 24–25.

Cross, R. (and Ashworth, A.) (1981) *The English Sentencing System.* London, Butterworths.

Crow, I. (1996) 'Employment, Training and Offending', in M. Drakeford and M Vanstone (eds) *Beyond Offending Behaviour.* Aldershot, Arena, 51–67.

Crow, I. and Simon, F. (1987) *Unemployment and Magistrates' Courts.* London, NACRO.

Crow, I., Richardson, P., Riddington, C. and Simon, F. (1989) *Unemployment, Crime and Offenders*. London, Routledge.

Crowley, A. (1998) *A Criminal Waste: A Study of Child Offenders Eligible for Secure Training Centres*. London, The Children's Society.

Cummins, I. (2006) 'A Path Not Taken? Mentally Disordered Offenders and the Criminal Justice System' *Journal of Social Welfare and Family Law* Vol 28 (3–4), 267–81.

Cunliffe, J. and Shepherd, A. (2007) *Re-offending of Adults: Results from the 2004 Cohort*. London, Home Office.

Cuppleditch, L. and Evans, W. (2005) *Re-offending of Adults: Results from the 2002 Cohort*, Home Office Statistical Bulletin. London, Home Office.

Da Silva, N., Cowell, P., Chinegwundoh, V., Mason, T., Maresh, J. and Williamson, K. (2007) *Prison Population Projections 2007–2014, England and Wales*. London, Ministry of Justice.

Daly, M. (2003) 'Governance and Social Policy' *Journal of Social Policy* Vol 32(1), 113–28.

Davies, P. Francis, P. and Jupp, V. (2003) *Victimisation, Theory, Research and Practice*. Basingstoke, Palgrave Macmillan.

Davis, G. (1992) *Making Amends: Mediation and Reparation in Criminal Justice*. London, Routledge.

Davis, G., Boucherat, J. and Watson, D. (1988) 'Reparation in the Service of Diversion: The Subordination of a Good Idea' *Howard Journal* 27(2), 127–33.

Davis, K. C. (1969) *Discretionary Justice: A Preliminary Inquiry*. Baton Rouge, Louisiana State University Press.

Davis, M., Takal, J-P, and Tyrer, J. (2004) 'Sentencing Burglars and Explaining the Differences between Jurisdictions', *British Journal of Criminology* Vol 44, 741–58.

Davis, R., Lurigio, A. and Skogan, W. (eds) (1997) *Victims of Crime* (2nd edn). Thousand Oaks, CA, Sage.

Day Sclater, S. and Piper, C. (1999) 'The Family Law Act 1996 in Context', in S. Day Sclater and C. Piper (eds) *Undercurrents of Divorce*. Ashgate, Aldershot.

Day Sclater, S. and Piper, C. (2000) 'Re-moralising the Family? Family Policy, Family Law and Youth Justice' *Child and Family Law Quarterly* Vol 12(2), 135–51.

DCSF (Department for Children, Schools and Families) (2007) *The Children's Plan: Building Brighter Futures*, Cm 7280. London, The Stationery Office.

de Cou, K. (2002) 'A Gender-wise Prison: Opportunities for, and Limits to, Reform' in P. Carlen (ed) *Women and Punishment: The Struggle for Justice*, Cullompton, Willan, 97–109.

Dear, G. E. (2006) *Preventing Suicide and Other Self-Harm in Prison*. London, Palgrave.

Denny, D. (1992) *Racism and Anti-Racism in Probation*. London, Routledge.

Department for Constitutional Affairs (2006) *Your Choice to Have a Voice in Court*. London, Office for Criminal Justice Reform.

Department of Health (1999) *Review of the Mental Health Act 1983*. London, Department of Health.

Department of Health (2000) *Framework for the Assessment of Children in Need and their Families*. London, HMSO.

Department of Health (2005) *Government Response to the Report of the Joint Committee on the Draft Mental Health Bill 2004*, Cm 6624. London, The Stationery Office.

Department of Health and Home Office (1992) *Review of Mental Health and Social Services for Mentally Disordered Offenders and others Requiring Similar Services*, Vol 1: Final Summary Report, Cm 2088. London, HMSO.

Department of Health/Home Office (2000) *Reforming the Mental Health Act: Part II High Risk Patients*. Cm 5016-II. London, The Stationery Office.

Department of Trade and Industry (2004) *Fairness for All: A New Commission for Equality and Human Rights*, Cm 6185. London, The Stationery Office.

Devlin, A. (1998) *Invisible Women*. Winchester, Waterside Press.

DfES (Department for Education and Skills) (2003) *Every Child Matters* Cm 5860. London, The Stationery Office.

DfES (Department for Education and Skills) (2004) *Every Child Matters: Next Steps*. London, The Stationery Office.

DfES (2005) *Youth Matters* Cm 6629. London, The Stationery Office.

DfES (2007) *Every Parent Matters*. London, DfES.

Dicey, A. V. (1885) *Introduction to the Study of the Law of the Constitution*. London, MacMillan.

Diduck, A. (1999) 'Justice and Childhood: Reflections on Refashioned Boundaries' in M. King (ed) *Moral Agendas for Children's Welfare*. London, Routledge.

Dignan, J. (1999) 'The Crime and Disorder Act and the Prospects for Restorative Justice' Crim LR, 48–60.

Dignan, J. and Lowey, K. (2000) *Restorative Justice Options for Northern Ireland: A Comparative Review*. Belfast, Criminal Justice Review Group.

Dignan, J. and Marsh, P. (2001) 'Restorative Justice and Family Group Conferences in England: Current State and Future Prospects' in A. Morris and G. Maxwell (eds) *Restorative Justice for Juveniles: Conferencing, Mediation and Circles* Oxford, Hart Publishing, 85–101.

Dingwall, G. (1998) 'Selective Incapacitation after the Criminal Justice Act 1991: A Proportional Response to Protecting the Public?' *Howard Journal* Vol 37(2), 177–87.

Dingwall, G. (2006/7) 'From Principle to Practice: Reconstructing the Nature of Sentencing Guidance' *Contemporary Issues in Law* Vol 8(4), 293–318.

Ditchfield, J. (1976) *Police Cautioning in England and Wales*, Home Office Research Study 37. London, HMSO.

Dobash, R. P., Dobash, R. E., Cavanagh, K. and Lewis, R. (1999) 'A Research Evaluation of British Programmes for Violent Men' *Journal of Social Policy* Vol 28(2), 205–34.

Dodd, M. (1999) '*R v Central Criminal Court ex parte S*. Privacy and the Press—The Latest Stage in the Battle' *Child and Family Law Quarterly* Vol 11(2), 171–81.

Domanick, J. (2004) *Cruel Justice: Three Strikes and the Politics of Crime in America's Golden State*. Berkeley, University of California Press.

Donoghue, J. (2007) 'The Judiciary as a Primary Definer on Anti-Social Behaviour Orders' *Howard Journal*, Vol 46(4), 417–30.

Donohue, J. J. and Wolfers, J. (2006) 'Uses and Abuses of Empirical Evidence in the Death Penalty Debate', 58 *Stanford Law Review,* 791–846.

Donzelot, J. (1980) *The Policing of Families*. London, Huchinson.

Dorling, D., Rigby, J., Wheeler, B., Ballas, D., Thomas, B., Fahmy, E., Gordon, D. and Lupton, R. (2007) *Poverty, Wealth and Place in Britain, 1968 to 2005*. Bristol, Policy Press.

Douglas, N. and Plugge, E. (2007) 'The Health of Young Women in Custody: Emerging Concerns and a Case for Advocacy' *Childright* CR 238, 14–17.

Downes, D. (1988) *Contrasts in Tolerance*. Oxford, Clarendon Press.

Downes, D. (2001/2) 'Four Years Hard: New Labour and Crime Control' *Criminal Justice Matters* Vol 46, 8–9.

Downes, D., Rock, P., Chinkin, C. and Gearty, C. (eds) (2007) *Crime, Social Control and Human Rights*. Cullompton, Willan.

Drakeford, M. (1993) 'But Who Will Do the Work?' *Critical Social Policy* Vol 3(2), 64–76.

Drakeford, M. and Butler, I. (2007) 'Everyday Tragedies: Justice, Scandal and Young People in Contemporary Britain' *Howard Journal* Vol 46(3), 219–35.

Duff, A. (2001) *Punishment, Communication and Community*. Oxford, Oxford University Press.

Duff, A. (2002) 'Punishing the Young' in I. Weijers and A. Duff (eds) *Punishing Juveniles, Principle and Critique*. Oxford, Hart Publishing, 115–34.

Duff, A. (2003) 'Probation, Punishment and Restorative Justice: Should Al Truism be Engaged in Punishment?' *Howard Journal* Vol 42(2), 181–97.

Dunbar, I. and Langton, A. (1998) *Tough Justice, Sentencing and Penal Policies in the 1990s*. London, Blackstone Press.

Dupont, C. and Zakkour, P. (2003) *Trends in Environmental Sentencing in England and Wales*. London, Department for Environment, Food and Rural Affairs.

Dworkin, R. (1977) *Taking Rights Seriously*, London, Duckworth.

Dworkin, R. (1986) *A Matter of Principle*. Oxford, Oxford University Press.

Dyson, S. and Boswell, G. (2006) 'Sickle Cell Anaemia and Deaths in Custody in the UK and USA' *Howard Journal* Vol 45(1), 14–28.

Eadie, T. and Willis, A. (1989) 'National Standards for Discipline and Breach Proceedings in Community Service: An Exercise in Penal Rhetoric?' Crim LR, 412–19.

Easton, S. (2001) 'Punishing Sex Offenders: Discrimination or Justifiable Treatment?' *International Journal of Discrimination and the Law* Vol 5, 71–97.

Easton, S. (2002) 'Feminist Perspectives on the Human Rights Act: Two Cheers for Incorporation' *Res Publica* Vol 8(1), 21–40.

Easton, S. (2006) 'Electing the Electorate: The Problem of Prisoner Disenfranchisement' MLR Vol 69(3), 443–52.

Easton, S. (ed) (2008a) *Marx and Law*. Aldershot, Ashgate.

Easton, S. (2008b) 'Marx's Legacy' in S. Easton (ed) *Marx and Law*. Aldershot, Ashgate.

Easton, S. (2008c) 'Dangerous Waters: Taking Account of Impact in Sentencing' Crim LR, 2, 105–20.

Editorial (2000) Crim LR, 209–10.

Edwards, I. (2001) 'Victim Participation in Sentencing: The Problems of Incoherence' *Howard Journal* Vol 40(1), 39–54.

Edwards, I. (2002) 'The Place of Victims' Preferences in the Sentencing of "Their" Offenders' Crim LR, 689–702.

Edwards, I. (2004) 'An Ambiguous Participant: The Crime Victim and Criminal Justice Decision-making' *British Journal of Criminology* Vol 44, 967–82.

Edwards, I. (2006) 'Restorative Justice, Sentencing and the Court of Appeal' Crim LR, 110–23.

Ehrlich, I. (1975) 'The Deterrent Effects of Capital Punishment: A Question of Life or Death' *American Economic Review*, Vol 65, 397–417.

Einat, T. (2004) 'Criminal Fine Enforcement in Israel' *Punishment and Society* Vol 6(2), 175–94.

Elkins, M. and Olagundoye, J. (2001) *The Prison Population in 2000: A Statistical Review*. Home Office Findings No. 154. London, Home Office.

Ellis, T. and Winstone, J. (2001–2) 'Halliday, Sentencers and the National Probation Service' *Criminal Justice Matters* No 46 Winter, 20.

Ellis, T., Hedderman, C. and Mortimer, E. (1996) *Enforcing Community Sentences: Supervisors' Perspectives on Ensuring Compliance and Dealing with Breach*, Home Office Research Study No. 158. London, Home Office.

Engels, F. (1843) 'Outline of a Critique of Political Economy'. *Marx and Engels: Collected Works* Vol 3, London, Lawrence & Wishart (1975), 418–43.

Erez, E. (1999) 'Who's Afraid of the Big Bad Victim? Victim Impact Statements as Victim Empowerment and Enhancement of Justice' Crim L R, 545–56.

Etzioni, A. (1993) *The Spirit of Community: Rights, Responsibilities and the Communitarian Agenda*. New York, Crown Publishers.

Evans, R. (1991) 'Police Cautioning—The Young Adult Offender' Crim LR, 598–609.

Evans, R. (1994) 'Cautioning: Counting the Cost of Retrenchment' Crim LR, 566–75.

Evans, R. and Wilkinson, C. (1990) 'Variations in Police Cautioning Policy and Practice in England and Wales' *Howard Journal* Vol 29(3), 155–76.

Exworthy, T. and Gunn, J. (2003) 'Taking another Tilt at High Secure Hospitals' *British Journal of Psychiatry* Vol 182, 469–71.

Family Law (2005) 'Case Reports: Contempt of Court—Sentencing' *Family Law*, 532–34.

Farrall, S. (2002) 'Long term Absences from Probation: Officers' and Probationers' Accounts' *Howard Journal* Vol 41(3), 263–78.

Farrall, S. and Maltby, S. (2003) 'The Victimisation of Probationers' *Howard Journal* Vol 42, 32–54.

Farrington, D. (1997) 'Human Development and Criminal Careers' in M. Maguire *et al.* (eds) *The Oxford Handbook of Criminology* (2nd edn). Oxford, Oxford University Press, 361–408.

Farrington, D. (2002a) 'Developmental Criminology and Risk-Focused Prevention' in M. Maguire, R. Morgan and R. Reiner (eds) *The Oxford Handbook of Criminology* (3rd edn). Oxford, Oxford University Press, 657–701.

Farrington, D. (2002b) 'Understanding and Preventing Crime' in J. Muncie, G. Hughes and E. McLaughlin (eds) *Youth Justice, Critical Readings*. London, Sage, 425–30.

Farrington, D. (2007) 'Childhood Risk Factors and Risk-focused Prevention' in M. Maguire, R. Morgan and R. Reiner (Eds) *The Oxford Handbook of Criminology* (4th edn). Oxford, Oxford University Press, 602–40.

Farrington, D. and Bennett, T. (1981) 'Police Cautioning of Juveniles in London' *British Journal of Criminology* Vol 21(1), 123–35.

Farrington, D. and Morris, A. (1983) 'Sex, Sentencing and Conviction', *Journal of Criminology* Vol 23(3), 229–48.

Farrington, D. and Painter, K. (2004) *Gender Differences in Offending: Implications for Risk-focused Prevention*. London, Home Office Online Report 09/04.

Farrington, D., Ditchfield, J., Howard, P. and Jolliffe, D. (2002) *Two Intensive Regimes for Young Offenders: A Follow-up Evaluation*, RDSD Findings 163. London, Home Office.

Farrington, D., Langan, P. and Wikstrom, P.-O. (1994) 'Changes in Crime and Punishment in America, England and Sweden between the 1980s and the 1990s', *Studies in Crime Prevention* Vol 3, 104–31.

Faulkner, D. (2005) 'Relationships, Accountability and Responsibility in the National Offender Management Service' *Public Money and Management* Vol 25(5), 299.

Fazel, S., Benning, R. and Danesh, J. (2005) 'Suicides in Male Prisoners in England and Wales, 1978–2003, *The Lancet* Vol 366(9493), 1301–2.

Feeley, M. and Simon, J. (1992) 'The New Penology: Notes on the Emerging Strategy of Corrections and its Implications' *Criminology*, Vol 30 (4), 449–74.

Feinberg, J. (1994) 'The Expressive Function of Punishment' in A. Duff and D. Garland (eds) *A Reader on Punishment*. Oxford, Oxford University Press, 71–91.

Feldman, M. (1992) 'Social Limits to Discretion' in K. Hawkins (ed) *The Uses of Discretion*. Oxford, Clarendon, 164–83.

Fenwick, H. (1997) 'Procedural "Rights" of Victims of Crime: Public or Private Ordering of the Criminal Justice Process?' MLR Vol 60(3), 317–33.

Field, S. (2007) 'Practice Cultures and the "New" Youth Justice in (England and) Wales' *British Journal of Criminology* Vol 47, 311–30.

Findlay, M. and Henham, R. (2005) *Transforming International Criminal Justice: Retributive and Restorative Justice in the Trial Process*. Cullompton, Willan.

Fionda, J. (1999) 'New Labour, Old Hat: Youth Justice and the Crime and Disorder Act' Crim LR, 36–47.

Fitzgerald, M. and Marshall, P. (1996) 'Ethnic Minorities in British Prisons: Some Research Implications', in R. Matthews and P. Francis (eds) *Prisons 2000: An International Perspective on the Current State and Future of Imprisonment*. London, Macmillan, 139–62.

FitzGibbon, D. (2007) 'Risk Analysis and the New Practitioner' *Punishment and Society* Vol 9(1), 87–97.

Flaherty, P. (2006/7) 'Sentencing the Recidivist: Reconciling Harsher Treatment for Repeat Offenders with Modern Retributivist Theory' *Contemporary Issues in Law* Vol 8(4), 319–36.

Fletcher, G. (1982) 'The Recidivist Premium', *Criminal Justice Ethics* Vol 1(2), 54–9.

Flood-Page, C. and Mackie, A. (1998) *Sentencing Practice: An Examination of Decisions in Magistrates' Courts and the Crown Court in the mid-1990s*, Home Office Research Study 180. London: Home Office.

Flood-Page, C. et al. (2000) *Youth Crime: Findings from the 1998/99 Youth Lifestyles Survey*, Home Office Research Study 209. London, Home Office.

Floud, J. (1982) 'Dangerousness and Criminal Justice' *British Journal of Criminology* Vol 22(3), 213–28.

Fortin, J. (2003) *Children's Rights and the Developing Law* (2nd edn). London, Lexis Nexis.

Foucault, M. (1977) *Discipline and Punish: The Birth of the Prison*. London, Allen Lane.

Fox, D., Dhami, M. and Mantle, G. (2006) 'Restorative Final Warnings: Policy and Practice' *Howard Journal* Vol 45(2), 129–40.

Freiberg, A. (2000) 'Guerillas in our Midst? Judicial Responses to Governing the Dangerous' in M. Brown and J. Pratt (eds) *Dangerous Offenders*. London, Routledge, 51–69.

Garafalo, R. (1914) *Criminology*. Boston, MA, Little, Brown.

Garland, D. (1985) *Punishment and Welfare: A History of Penal Strategies*. Aldershot, Gower.

Garland, D. (1990) *Punishment and Modern Society: A Study in Social Theory*. Oxford, Clarendon Press.

Garland, D. (1991) 'Sociological Perspectives on Punishment', in N. Morris and M. Tonry (eds) *Crime and Justice* Vol 14. Chicago, University of Chicago Press.

Garland, D. (1996) 'The Limits of the Sovereign State' *British Journal of Criminology* Vol 36(4), 445–71.

Garland, D. (1999) 'Sociological Perspectives on Punishment' in A. von Hirsch and A. Ashworth (eds) *Principled Sentencing, Readings on Theory and Policy*. Oxford, Hart Publishing, 381–93.

Garland, D. (2001a) 'The meaning of mass imprisonment', in D. Garland (ed) *Mass Imprisonment*. London, Sage, 1–3.

Garland, D. (2001b) *The Culture of Control*. Oxford, Oxford University Press.

Garland, D. (ed) (2001c) *Mass Imprisonment*. London, Sage.

Garland, D. (2002) 'Penal Strategies in a Welfare State' in J. Muncie, G. Hughes and E. McLaughlin (eds) *Youth Justice, Critical Readings*. London, Sage, 197–215.

Gelsthorpe, L. (1992) *Social Inquiry Reports: Race and Gender Considerations*, Research Bulletin 52. London, Home Office.

Gelsthorpe, L. (1999) 'Parents and Criminal Children', in A. Bainham, S. Day Sclater and M. Richards (eds) *What Is a Parent? A Socio-Legal Analysis*. Oxford, Hart Publishing.

Gelsthorpe, L. (2002) 'Recent Changes in Youth Justice Policy in England and Wales' in I. Weijers and A. Duff (eds) *Punishing Juveniles: Principle and Critique*. Oxford, Hart Publishing, 45–66.

Gelsthorpe, L. and Morris, A. (1999) 'Much Ado About Nothing—A Critical Comment on Key Provisions Relating to Children in the Crime and Disorder Act 1998' *Child and Family Law Quarterly* Vol 11(3), 209–21.

Gelsthorpe, L. and Morris, A. (2002) 'Restorative Youth Justice: The Last Vestiges of Welfare?' in J. Muncie, G. Hughes and E. McLaughlin (eds) *Youth Justice: Critical Readings*. London/Milton Keynes, Sage/Open University Press, 238–54.

Gelsthorpe, L. and Padfield, N. (eds) (2003) *Exercising Discretion, Decision-making in the Criminal Justice System and Beyond*. Cullompton, Willan.

Gelsthorpe, L., Sharpe, G. and Roberts, J. (2007) *Provision for Women Offenders in the Community*. London, Fawcett Society.

Genders, E. (2003) 'Privatisation and Innovation—Rhetoric and Reality: The Development of a Therapeutic Community Prison' *Howard Journal* Vol 42(2), 137–57.

Genders, E. and Player, E. (1989) *Race Relations in Prison*. Oxford, Clarendon Press.

Genders, E. and Player, E. (1995) *Grendon: A Study of a Therapeutic Prison*. Oxford, Clarendon Press.

Genders, E. and Player, E. (2007) 'The Commercial Context of Criminal Justice: Prison Privatisation and the Perversion of Purpose' Crim LR, 513–29.

Genn, H. (1988) *Hard Bargaining: Out of Court Settlement in Personal Injury Actions*. Oxford, Clarendon Press.

Genn, H. (1999) *Paths to Justice: What People Do and Think about Going to Law*. Oxford, Hart Publishing.

Gesch, C. B., Hammond, S. M., Hampson, S. E., Eves, A. and Chowder, M. J. (2002) 'Influence of Supplementary Vitamins, Minerals and Essential Fatty Acids on the Antisocial Behaviour of Adult Prisoners: Randomised, Placebo-controlled Trial' *British Journal of Psychiatry* Vol 181, 22–8.

Gibson, B. (1990) *Unit Fines*. Winchester, Waterside Press.

Giddens, A. (1990) *The Consequences of Modernity*. Cambridge: Polity Press.

Giddens, A. (1998) *The Third Way*, Cambridge. Cambridge, Polity Press.

Giddens, A. (1999) 'Risk and Responsibility' MLR Vol 62(1), 1–10.

Giddens, A. (2000) *The Third Way and its Critics*. Cambridge, Polity Press.

Gill, M. and Spriggs, A. (2005) *Assessing the Impact of CCTV*, Home Office Research Study 292. London, Home Office.

Giller, H. (2000) *Final Warning Interventions*. London, Youth Justice Board.

Gil-Robles, A. (2005) *Report by the Commissioner for Human Rights on his Visit to the UK.* Strasbourg, Council of Europe.

Goldson, B. (1999) 'Youth (In)Justice: Contemporary Developments in Policy and Practice' in B. Goldson (ed) *Youth Justice: Contemporary Policy and Practice.* Aldershot, Ashgate, 1–27.

Goldson, B. (2000a) 'Wither Diversion? Interventionism and the New Youth Justice' in B. Goldson (ed) *The New Youth Justice.* Lyme Regis, Russell House Publishing, 35–7.

Goldson, B. (2000b) 'Children "in Need" or "Young Offenders"? Hardening Ideology, Organisational Change and New Challenges for Social Work with Children in Trouble' *Child and Family Social Work* Issue 5, 255–65.

Goldson, B. (2006) 'Damage, Harm and Death in Child Prisons in England and Wales: Questions of Abuse and Accountability' *Howard Journal* Vol 45(5), 449–67.

Graham, J. and Bowling, B. (1995) *Young People and Crime*, Home Office Research Study 145. London, Home Office.

Gravett, S. (2003) *Coping with Prison.* London, Sage.

Gray, C. and Elkins, M. (2001) 'Projections of Long Term Trends in the Prison Population to 2008', *Home Office Statistical Bulletin* 8/01. London, Home Office.

Gray, P. (2007) 'Youth Justice, Social Exclusion and the Demise of Social Justice' *Howard Journal* Vol 46(4), 401–16.

Greene, J. (1998) 'The Unit Fine: Monetary Sanctions Apportioned to Income' in A. von Hirsch and A. Ashworth (eds) *Principled Sentencing: Readings on Theory and Policy.* Oxford, Hart Publishing, 268–71.

Greenhow, J. (2003) 'Referral Orders: Problems in Practice' Crim LR, 266–8.

Greig, D. (2002) *Neither Bad nor Mad: The Competing Discourses of Psychiatry, Law and Politics.* London, Jessica Kingsley.

Gullick, M. (2004) 'Sentencing and Early Release of Fixed Term Prisoners' Crim LR, 653–62.

Haas, H., Farrington, D., Killias, M. and Sattar, G. (2004) 'The Impact of Different Configurations on Delinquency' *British Journal of Criminology* Vol 44, 520–32.

Hackler, J. and Garapon, A. (1986) *Stealing Conflicts in Juvenile Justice: Contrasting France and Canada*, Discussion Paper 8, Centre for Criminological Research, Edmonton, Alberta, University of Alberta.

Hadfield, P. (2006) *Bar Wars.* Oxford, Oxford University Press.

Hagell, A. and Newburn, T. (1994) *Persistent Young Offenders.* London, Policy Studies Institute.

Hall, S., Clarke, J., Crichter, C., Jefferson, T. and Roberts, B. (1978) *Policing the Crisis: Mugging, the State and Law and Order.* London, Macmillan.

Halliday Report (2001) *Making Punishments Work: Review of the Sentencing Framework for England and Wales.* London, Home Office.

Hamilton, J. and Wisniewski, M. (1996) *The Use of the Compensation Order in Scotland*, Crime and Criminal Justice Research Findings No 14. Edinburgh, The Scottish Office.

Hamlyn, B. and Lewis, D. (2000) *Women Prisoners: A Survey of their Work and Training Experiences in Custody and on Release.* HORS No 208, London, Home Office.

Hannah-Moffat, K. (2002) 'Creating Choices: Reflecting on Choices' in P. Carlen (ed) *Women in Punishment: The Struggle for Justice.* Cullompton, Willan, 199–219.

Hannah-Moffat, K. and O'Malley, P. (eds) (2007) *Gendered Risks.* London, Routledge-Cavendish.

Harding, J. (1994) 'Youth Crime: A Relational Perspective' in J. Burnside, and N. Baker (eds) *Relational Justice*. Winchester, Waterside Press, 104–13.

Harding, J. (2000) 'A Community Justice Dimension to Effective Probation Practice' *Howard Journal* Vol 39(2), 132–49.

Harding, L. (1996) *Family, State and Social Policy*. London, Macmillan.

Harper, G. and Chitty, C. (eds) (2005) *The Impact of Corrections on Re-offending: A Review of 'What Works'* (3rd edn) Home Office Research Study 291. London, HORDSD.

Harris, M. K. (1998) 'Reflections of a Skeptical Dreamer: Some Dilemmas in Restorative Justice Theory and Practice' *Contemporary Justice Review* Vol 1, 57–69.

Harris, R. (1980) 'A Changing Service—The Case for Separating Care and Control in Probation Practice' *British Journal of Social Work* Vol 10(3), 163–84.

Harris, R. (1992) *Crime, Criminal Justice and the Probation Service*. London, Routledge.

Harris, R. and Webb, D. (1987) *Welfare, Power and Juvenile Justice*. London, Tavistock.

Harrison, K. (2006) 'Community Punishment or Community Rehabilitation: Which is the Highest in the Sentencing Tariff?' *Howard Journal* Vol 45(2), 141–58.

Hart, H. L. A. (1968) *Punishment and Responsibility: Essays in the Philosophy of Law*. Oxford, Oxford University Press.

Harvey, C. W. (1984) 'Hegel's Theory of Punishment Reconsidered' *Dialogos*, 43, 71–80.

Harwin, J. and Ryan, M. (2007) 'The Role of the Court in Cases Concerning Parental Substance Misuse and Children at Risk of Harm' *Journal of Social Welfare and Family Law*, Vol 29 (3 and 4), 277–92.

Hawkins, K. (ed) (1992) *The Uses of Discretion*. Oxford, Clarendon.

Hawkins, K. (2002) *Law as Last Resort*. Oxford, Oxford University Press.

Hay, C. (1995) 'Mobilisation through Interpellation—James Bulger, Juvenile Crime and the Construction of a Moral Panic' *Social and Legal Studies* Vol 4(2), 197–223.

Hay, D., Linebaugh, P. and Thompson, E. P. (1975) *Albion's Fatal Tree*. London, Allen Lane.

Hayes, M. and Williams, C. (1999) ' "Offending" Behaviour and Children under 10', *Family Law*, 317–20.

Hedderman, C. (1990) 'The Effect of Defendants' Demeanour on Sentencing in the Magistrates' Courts', Home Office Research and Development Research Bulletin No 29, 32–6.

Hedderman, C. and Gelsthorpe, L. (1997) *Understanding the Sentencing of Women*. HORS No 170. London, HMSO.

Hedderman, C. and Hough, M. (1994) *Does the Criminal Justice System Treat Men and Women Differently?*, HORS 10. London, HMSO.

Hegel, G. W. (1832) *Hegel's Philosophy of Right*, trans. T. M. Knox, 1952. Oxford, Clarendon Press.

Heidensohn, F. (ed) (2006) *Gender and Justice: New Concepts and Approaches*. Cullompton, Willan.

Henham, R. (1995) 'Sentencing Policy and the Role of the Court of Appeal' *Howard Journal* Vol 34(3), 218–27.

Henham, R. (1997) 'Anglo-American Approaches to Cumulative Sentencing and the Implications for UK Sentencing Policy' *Howard Journal* Vol 36(3), 263–83.

Henham, R. (2001) 'Sentencing Dangerous Offenders: Policy and Practice in the Crown Court' *Crim LR*, 693–711.

Hetherington, A. (1996) 'The Legitimacy of Capital Punishment in Hegel's' *Philosophy of Right'*, *Owl of Minerva* Vol 27, 167–74.

Heyman, S. J. (1996) 'The Legitimacy of Capital Punishment in Hegel's *Philosophy of Right*: A Comment', *Owl of Minerva*, 27, 175–80.

Hillery, G. (1955) 'Definitions of Community: Areas of Agreement' *Rural Sociology* Vol 20(2), 111–23.

Hinchman, L. P. (1991) 'On Reconciling Happiness and Autonomy: An Interpretation of Hegel's Moral Philosophy', *Owl of Minerva* Vol 23, 29–48.

Hine, J. (2007) 'Young People's Perspectives on Final Warnings' 2 Web JCLI (available at: http://webjcli.ncl.ac.uk/2007/issue2/hine2.html).

HM Chief Inspector of Prisons (1997a) *Young Prisoners: A Thematic Review*. London, HMSO.

HM Chief Inspector of Prisons (1997b) *Women in Prison: A Thematic Review*. London, Home Office.

HM Chief Inspector of Prisons (1998) *Report on an Unannounced Short Inspection of HMP Woodhill 14–16 July 1998*. London, HMCIP.

HM Chief Inspector of Prisons (2001) *Follow up to Women in Prison: A Thematic Review*. London, Home Office.

HM Chief Inspector of Prisons (2002) *Annual Report of HM Chief Inspector of Prisons for England and Wales 2000–2001*. London, The Stationery Office.

HM Chief Inspector of Prisons (2004) *Annual Report of HM Chief Inspector for England and Wales 2002–2003*. London, The Stationery Office.

HM Chief Inspector of Prisons (2005) *Report on an Unannounced Inspection of HMP Rye Hill, 11–15 April 2005*. London, HMIP.

HM Chief Inspector of Prisons (2006a) *Annual Report England and Wales* 2004–2005. London, The Stationery Office.

HM Chief Inspector of Prisons (2006b) *Report on an Unannounced Full Follow-up Inspection of HMP Pentonville, 7–16 June 2006*. London HMCIP.

HM Chief Inspector of Prisons (2007) *Annual Report England and Wales 2005–2006*. London, Stationery Office.

HM Chief Inspector of Prisons (2008) *Annual Report England and Wales 2006/07*. London, The Stationery Office.

HM Government (2005) *Statutory Guidance on Inter-agency Co-operation to Improve the Wellbeing of Children: Children's Trusts*. London, DfES.

HM Inspectorate of Prisons (2004) *Juveniles in Custody*. London, HMIP.

HM Inspectorate of Prisons (2005a) *Parallel Worlds: A Thematic Review of Race Relations in Prison*. London, HMIP.

HM Inspectorate of Prisons (2005b) *Recalled Prisoners*. London, HMIP.

HM Inspectorate of Prisons (2006) *Foreign National Prisoners: A Thematic Review*. London, HMIP.

HM Inspectorate of Prisons (2007a) *Foreign National Prisoners: A Follow-up Report*. London, HMIP.

HM Inspectorate of Prisons (2007b) *The Mental Health of Prisoners: A Thematic Review of the Care and Support of Prisoners with Mental Health Needs*. London, HMIP.

HM Inspectorate of Prisons (2008) *Report on an Announced Inspection of the Management, Care and Control of Young People at Oakhill Secure Training Centre*. London, HMIP.

HM Inspectorate of Prisons in conjunction with the Youth Justice Board (2004) *Juveniles in Prison: A Unique Insight into the Perceptions of Young People Held in Prison Service Custody in England and Wales*. London, The Stationery Office.

HM Inspectorate of Probation (1995) *Dealing with Dangerous People: The Probation Service and Public Protection*. London, Home Office.

HM Inspectorate of Probation (1997) 'Risk Management Guidance' *in Management and Assessment of Risk in the Probation Service*. London, Home Office.

HM Inspectorate of Probation (2000) *Towards Race Equality: A Thematic Inspection*. London, HMSO.

HM Inspectorate of Probation (2004) *Towards Race Equality: Follow Up Inspection Report*. London, Home Office.

HM Inspectorate of Probation (2006a) *An Independent Review of a Serious Further Offence Case: Anthony Rice*. London, Home Office.

HM Inspectorate of Probation (2006b) *Working to Make Amends*. London, HMIP.

HM Inspectorate of Probation, HM Inspectorate of Courts Administration, HM Inspectorate of Constabulary (2007) *A Summary of Findings on the Enforcement of Community Penalties from Three Joint Area Inspections*, Thematic Inspections Report. London, Home Office.

HM Prison Service (1995a) *Report of the Review of Sentence Planning 1994/5*. London, HMSO.

HM Prison Service (1995b) *Prison Discipline Manual*. London, HM Prison Service.

HM Prison Service (2002a) *Suicide and Self-Harm Prevention*, Prison Service Order 2700. London, HM Prison Service.

HM Prison Service (2002b) *Safer Custody Report for 2001: Self-inflicted Deaths in Prison Service Custody*. London, HM Prison Service.

HM Prison Service (2003) *Corporate Plan*. London, HM Prison Service.

HM Prison Service (2004) *Annual Report 2003–4*. London, HM Prison Service.

HM Prison Service (2007a) *Annual Report and Accounts April 2006–March 2007*, No 0717 2006–07. London, The Stationery Office.

HM Prison Service (2007b) *Business Plan 2006–2007*. London, NOMS.

HM Prison Service/CRE (2003) *Implementing Race Equality in Prisons: A Shared Agenda for Change*. London, HM Prison Service.

Hobbes, T. (1651) *Leviathan*, ed. J. Plamenatz (1962). Glasgow, Collins.

Hodgson Committee (1984) *The Profits of Crime and Their Recovery*. Aldershot, Gower.

Holdaway, S. and Desborough, S. (2004) *The National Evaluation of the Youth Justice Board's Final Warning Projects*. London: Youth Justice Board.

Holdaway, S., Davidson, N., Dignan, J., Hammersley, R., Hine, J. and Marsh, P. (2001) *New Strategies to Address Youth Offending—The National Evaluation of the Pilot Youth Offending Teams*, RDS Occasional Paper 69. London, Home Office.

Hollingsworth, K. (2006) 'R(W) v Commissioner of Police for the Metropolis and Another— Interpreting Child Curfews: A Question of Rights?' *Child and Family Law Quarterly* Vol 18(2), 253–68.

Hollingsworth, K. (2007a) 'Judicial Approaches to Children's Rights in Youth Crime' *Child and Family Law Quarterly* Vol 19(1), 42–59.

Hollingsworth, K. (2007b) 'Responsibility and Rights: Children and their Parents in the Youth Justice System' *International Journal of Law, Policy and the Family* Vol. 21(2), 190–219.

Home Office (1951) *Sixth Report on the Work of the Children's Department*. London, HMSO.

Home Office (1968) *Children in Trouble*, Cmnd 3601. London, HMSO.

Home Office (1984) *Statement of National Standards and Objectives for the Probation Service*. London, Home Office.

Home Office (1985) *The Cautioning of Offenders*, Circular 14/1985. London, Home Office.

Home Office (1988a) *Punishment, Custody and the Community* Consultation Paper, Cm 424. London: HMSO.

Home Office (1988b) *Tackling Offending: An Action Plan*. London, HMSO.

Home Office (1988c) *Private Sector Involvement in the Remand System*, Cm 434. London, HMSO.

Home Office (1990a) *Crime, Justice and Protecting the Public: The Government's Proposals for Legislation*, Cm 965. London, HMSO.

Home Office (1990b) *Supervision and Punishment in the Community*, Cm 966. London, HMSO.

Home Office (1990c) *Partnership in Dealing with Offenders in the Community*, London, HMSO.

Home Office (1991) *Custody, Care and Justice: The Way Ahead for the Prison Service in England and Wales*, Cm 1647. London, HMSO.

Home Office (1994a) *Monitoring of the Criminal Justice Acts 1991 and 1993—Results from a Special Data Collection Exercise*, Home Office Statistical Bulletin Issue 20/94. London, Home Office.

Home Office (1994b) *Revised Standards: The Cautioning of Offenders*. London, Home Office.

Home Office (1995a) *Strengthening Punishment in the Community*, Cmnd 2780. London, HMSO.

Home Office (1995b) *New Arrangements for the Recruitment and Qualifying Training of Probation Officers*. London, Home Office.

Home Office (1996a) *Protecting the Public: The Government's Strategy on Crime in England and Wales*, Cm 3190. London, HMSO.

Home Office (1996b) 'The Prison Population in 1995' *Home Office Statistical Bulletin* Issue 14/96. London, Home Office.

Home Office (1997a) *No More Excuses: A New Approach to Tackling Youth Crime in England and Wales*, Cm 3809. London, The Stationery Office.

Home Office (1997b) *Rights Brought Home: The Human Rights Bill*, Cm 3782. London, The Stationery Office.

Home Office (1998a) *Joining Forces to Protect the Public: Prisons–probation*. London, Home Office.

Home Office (1998b) *Bind Overs: A Power for the 21st Century*, Cm 3908. London, Home Office.

Home Office (1999a) *Managing Dangerous People with Severe Personality Disorder. Proposals for Policy Development*. London, Home Office.

Home Office (1999b) *Statistical Bulletin*, Issue 21/99. London, Home Office.

Home Office (1999c) *The Correctional Policy Framework*. London, Home Office.

Home Office (2000a) *The Government's Strategy for Women Offenders*. London, Home Office.

Home Office (2000b) *The Victim Perspective: Ensuring the Victim Matters*. Thematic Inspection Report, HM Inspectorate of Probation. London, Home Office.

Home Office (2001a) *Criminal Justice: The Way Ahead*. Cm 5074. London, HMSO.

Home Office (2001b) *Victim Personal Statements*, Circular 35/2001. London, Justice and Victims' Unit, Home Office.

Home Office (2001c) *The 2001 British Crime Survey. First Results England and Wales*, Home Office Statistical Bulletin 18/01. London, Home Office.

Home Office (2001d) *The Youth Court 2001: The Changing Culture of the Youth Court, Good Practice Guide*. London, Home Office.

Home Office (2001e) *The Government's Strategy for Women Offenders: Consultation Report*. London, Home Office.

Home Office (2001f) *Prison Statistics, England and Wales 2000*. London, The Stationery Office.

Home Office (2002a) *Justice for All*, Cm 5563. London, The Stationery Office.

Home Office (2002b) 'Falconer—Clear and Effective Sentencing Policy', Press Release: 257/2002. London, Home Office.

Home Office (2002c) *Statistics on Race and the Criminal Justice System*, 2000, *A Publication under s 95 of the Criminal Justice Act 1991*. London, Home Office.

Home Office (2002d) *An Evaluation of Cognitive Behavioural Treatment for Prisoners*. London, Home Office.

Home Office (2002e) *Prison Statistics, England and Wales 2001*. London, The Stationery Office.

Home Office (2002f) *Proceeds of Crime Act—Guidance Published on Investigation Powers*. London, Home Office.

Home Office (2002g) *Press Release 274/2002*. London, Home Office.

Home Office (2002h) *Statistics on Women and the Criminal Justice System: A Home Office Publication under Section 95 of the Criminal Justice Act 1991*. London, Home Office.

Home Office (2003a) *Restorative Justice: The Government's Strategy*, Consultation Paper. London, Home Office.

Home Office (2003b) *Respect and Responsibility—Taking a Stand against Anti-social Behaviour*, Cm 5778. London, Stationery Office.

Home Office (2003c) *Youth Justice—The Next Steps*. London, Home Office.

Home Office (2003d) *A New Deal for Victims and Witnesses*. London, Home Office.

Home Office (2003e) *Valuing the Victim—An Inspection into National Victim Contact Arrangements*, Thematic Inspection Report, HM Inspectorate of Probation. London, Home Office.

Home Office (2003f) *Prison Statistics: England and Wales 2002*, Cm 5996. London, The Stationery Office.

Home Office (2003g) *Statistics on Race and the Criminal Justice System: A Home Office Publication under Section 95 of the Criminal Justice Act 1991*. London, Home Office.

Home Office (2003h) *Criminal Statistics, England and Wales 2002*, Cm 6054. London, The Stationery Office.

Home Office (2004a) *Compensation and Support for Victims of Crime*, A Consultation Paper. London, Home Office.

Home Office (2004b) *Reducing Crime—Changing Lives*. London, The Stationery Office.

Home Office (2005a) *OASys Implementation and its Development*, Probation Circular 14/2005. London, Home Office.

Home Office (2005b) *A Five Year Strategy for Protecting the Public and Reducing Re-offending*, Cm 6717. London, The Stationery Office.

Home Office (2005c) *Probation Circular 25/2005: Criminal Justice Act 2003: Implementation on 4 April*. London, Home Office.

Home Office (2006a) *Rebalancing the Criminal Justice System in Favour of the Law Abiding Majority: Reducing Reoffending and Protecting the Public*. London, Home Office.

Home Office (2006b) Press release @ http://press.homeoffice.gov.uk/press-releases/8,000-new-prison-places.

Home Office (2006c) *Zahid Mubarek Inquiry: The Government's Full Response to the Report*. London, Home Office.

Home Office (2006d) *Improving Prison and Probation Services: Public Value Partnerships*. London, Home Office.

Home Office (2006e) *Statistics of Mentally Disordered Offenders 2005 England and Wales*, Home Office Statistical Bulletin 05/07. London, Home Office.

Home Office (2006f) *Tackling Anti-Social Behaviour*, National Audit Office 'Value for Money' Report by the Comptroller and Auditor General, HC 99 2006–7.

Home Office (2007a) *Cutting Crime: A New Partnership*. London, Home Office.

Home Office (2007b) *Bringing Offenders to Justice: Criminal Justice Penalties and Sentencing*. London, Home Office.

Home Office (2007c) *Sentencing Statistics 2005 England and Wales*, Home Office Statistical Bulletin 03/07. London, Home Office.

Home Office (2007d) *Guidance on the Use of Acceptable Behaviour Contracts and Agreements*. London: Home Office.

Home Office (2008) *Working Together to Protect the Public: The Home Office Strategy 2008–11*. London, Home Office.

Home Office, Department of Health and Welsh Office (2000) *National Standards for the Supervision of Offenders in the Community*. London, The Stationery Office.

Home Office, Welsh Office, DHSS (1980) *Young Offenders*, Cmnd 8045. London, HMSO.

Home Office/Youth Justice Board (2002) *Final Warning Scheme, Guidance to the Police and Youth Offending Teams*. London, Home Office.

Home Secretary, Lord Chancellor and Attorney General (2006) *Making Sentencing Clearer: A Consultation and Report of a Review*. London, Home Office.

Hood, R. (1962) *Sentencing in Magistrates' Courts*. London, Tavistock.

Hood, R. (1992) *Race and Sentencing*. Oxford, Clarendon Press.

Hood, R. and Hoyle, C. (2008) *The Death Penalty: A World-wide Perspective* (4th edn). Oxford, Clarendon.

Hood, R. and Shute, S. (1996) 'Protecting the Public: Automatic Life Sentences, Parole and High Risk Offenders' Crim LR, 788–800.

Hood, R., Shute, S., Feilzer, M. and Wilcox, M. (2002) *Reconviction Rates of Serious Sex Offenders and Assessments of their Risk* HORS 164. London, Home Office.

Hopley, K. (2002) 'National Standards: Defining Service' in D. Ward, J. Scott and M. Lacey (eds) *Probation: Working for Justice* (2nd edn). Oxford, Oxford University Press.

Hough, M. and Roberts, J. (1998) *Attitudes to Punishment: Findings from the British Crime Survey*, Home Office Research Study, No 179. London, HMSO.

Hough, M. and Roberts, J. (2005) 'Sentencing Young Offenders: Public Opinion in England and Wales', *Criminal Justice* Vol 5(3), 12–32.

Hough, M., Jacobson, J. and Millie, A. (2003) *The Decision to Imprison: Sentencing and the Prison Population*. London, Prison Reform Trust.

Howard League for Penal Reform (2000) A *Chance to Break the Cycle, Women and the Drug Treatment and Testing Order*, Briefing Paper. London, Howard League for Penal Reform.

Howard League for Penal Reform (2004) *Advice, Understanding and Underwear: Working with Girls in Prison*. London, Howard League for Penal Reform.

Howard League for Penal Reform (2007) *Children in Prison: An Independent Submission to the United Nations Committee on the Rights of the Child*. London, Howard League for Penal Reform.

Howard, D. and Christophersen, O. (2003) *Statistics of Mentally Disordered Offenders 2002*. RDS 14/03. London, Home Office.

Howden-Windell, J. and Clark, D. (1999) *Criminogenic Needs of Female Offenders: A Literature Review, Report to Women's Policy Group*. London, Home Office.

Howse, K. (2003) *Growing Old in Prison—A Scoping Study of Older Prisoners*. London, Prison Reform Trust.

Hoyle, C. and Young, R. (eds) (2002) *New Visions of Crime Victims*. Oxford, Hart.

Hoyle, C., Young, R. and Hill, R. (2002) *Proceed with Caution: An Evaluation of the Thames Valley Police Initiative in Restorative Cautioning*. York, Joseph Rowntree Foundation.

Hucklesby, A. and Hagley-Dickinson, L. (eds) (2007) *Prisoner Resettlement: Current Policy and Practice*. Cullompton, Willan.

Hudson, B. (1993) *Penal Policy and Social Justice*. London, Macmillan.

Hudson, B. (1998) 'Mitigation for Socially Deprived Offenders' in A. von Hirsch and A. Ashworth (eds) *Principled Sentencing: Readings on Theory and Policy*. Oxford, Hart, 205–8.

Hudson, B. (2001) 'Human Rights, Public Safety and the Probation Service: Defending Justice in the Risk Society', *Howard Journal* Vol 40(2), 103–13.

Hudson, B. (2001/2) 'The Halliday Report: Opening or Closing the Revolving Door?' *Criminal Justice Matters* No 46, 7–8.

Hudson, B. (2003) *Justice in the Risk Society*. London, Sage.

Hutchinson, S. (2006) 'Countering Catastrophic Criminology' *Punishment and Society* Vol 8(4), 443–67.

Hutton, N. (2005) 'Beyond Popular Punitiveness?' *Punishment and Society* Vol 73(3), 243–58.

Impalox Group (2007) *Evaluation of the Assessment Procedure at Two Pilot Sites in the DSPD Programme*. London, Home Office.

Ingleby Report (1960) *Report of the Committee on Children and Young Persons* Cmnd 1190. London, HMSO.

Inquest (1998) *Report on the Death in Prison Custody of Alton Manning*. London, Inquest.

International Centre for Prison Studies (2007) *World Prison Brief*. King's College London, www.kcl.ac.uk/deptsa/rel/icps/worldbrief/europe.html.

Jackson, E. (2007) 'Prisoners, their Partners and the Right to Family Life' *Child and Family Law Quarterly* Vol 19(2), 239–46.

Jackson, J. (2003) 'Justice for All: Putting Victims at the Heart of Criminal Justice' *Journal of Law and Society* Vol 30(2), 309–26.

Jackson, S. (1999) Family Group Conferences and Youth Justice' in B. Goldson (ed) *Youth Justice: Contemporary Policy and Practice*. Aldershot, Ashgate.

Jacobson, J. and Hough, M. (2007) *Mitigation: The Role of Personal Factors in Sentencing*. London, Prison Reform Trust.

Jago, R. and Thompson, E. (2001) 'Private Prison Contractors', *The Prisons Handbook*. Winchester, Waterside Press, 253–56.

James, A. (1995) 'Probation Values for the 1990s—and Beyond?', *Howard Journal*, Vol 34(4), 326–43.

James, A. and James, A. L. (2008) 'Changing Childhood in England: Reconstructing Discourse of "Risk" and "Protection" in Children's Best Interests' in A. James and A. L. James (eds) *European Childhoods: Culture, Politics and Participation*. Basingstoke, Palgrave Macmillan.

James, A. L., Bottomley, A. K., Liebling, A. and Clare, E. (1997) *Privatizing Prisons: Rhetoric and Reality*. London, Sage.

Jeffrey, C.R. (1965) 'Criminal Behaviour and Learning Theory', *Journal of Criminal Law, Criminology and Police Science* Vol 56, 294–300.

Jenks, C. (1996) *Childhood*. London, Routledge.

Jewkes, Y. (ed) (2007) *Handbook on Prisons*. Cullompton, Willan.

Jewkes, Y. and Johnston, H. (eds) (2006) *Prison Readings*. Cullompton, Willan.

Johnstone, G. (2000) 'Penal Policy Making: Elitist, Populist or Participatory?' *Punishment and Society* Vol 2 (2), 161–80.

Jones, A. and Singer, L. (2007) *Statistics on Race and the Criminal Justice System—2006*. London, Ministry of Justice.

Jones, D. (2001) '"Misjudged Youth": A Critique of the Audit Commission's Reports on Youth Justice' *British Journal of Criminology* Vol 41, 362–80.

Jones, K. (2003) 'Coping with Complexity' *Mediation Matters* Issue 75, 8.

Judicial Studies Board (undated) Reporting Restrictions: Magistrates' Courts http://www.jsboard.co.uk/publications/rrmc/index.htm (accessed 12 September 2007).

Junger-Tas, J. (1994) 'The Changing Family and its Relationship with Delinquent Behaviour', in C. Henricson (ed) *Crime and the Family*, Family Policy Studies Centre Occasional Paper 20. London, Family Policy Studies Centre, 18–25.

Junger-Tas J. (2002) 'The Juvenile System: Past and Present Trends in Western Society' in I. Weijers and A. Duff (eds) *Punishing Juveniles, Principle and Critique*. Oxford, Hart, 23–44.

JUSTICE (1998) *Victims in Criminal Justice*, Report of the JUSTICE Committee on the Role of the Victim in Criminal Justice. London, JUSTICE.

Kant, I. (1785) *Fundamental Principles of the Metaphysic of Ethics*, trans. T. K. Abbott, 1969. London, Longmans.

Kant, I. (1796–7) *The Metaphysics of Morals*, trans. Mary Gregor (1991). Cambridge, Cambridge University Press.

Keith, B. (2006) *Report of the Zahid Mubarek Inquiry*, HC 1082. London, The Stationery Office.

Kelly, D. P. and Erez, E. (1997) 'Victim Participation in the Criminal Justice System' in R. C. Davis, A. J. Lurigio and W. G Skogan (eds) *Victims of Crime* (2nd edn). Thousand Oaks, Sage, 211–30.

Kempf-Leonard, K. and Peterson, E. (2000) 'Expanding the Realms of the New Penology' *Punishment and Society* Vol 2(1), 66–97.

Kemshall, H. (2002) 'Effective Practice in Probation: An Example of "Advanced Liberal" Responsibilisation?' *Howard Journal* Vol 31(1), 41–58.

Kemshall, H. (2003) *Understanding Risk in Criminal Justice*. Oxford, Oxford University Press.

Kennedy, L. (1990) *On the Borders of Crime, Conflict Management and Criminology*, New York, Longmans.

Kershaw, C., Budd, T., Kinshott, G., Mattinson, J., Mayhew, P. and Myhill, A. (2000) *The 2000 British Crime Survey*, HO Statistical Bulletin, 18/00. London, Home Office.

Kershaw, C., Goodman, J. and White, S. (1999) *Reconvictions of Offenders Sentenced or Discharged from Prison in 1995 in England and Wales*. Home Office Statistical Bulletin 19/99. London, Home Office.

Kilbrandon, Lord (1964) *Children and Young Persons, Scotland*. Edinburgh, Scottish Home and Health Department.

Kilkelly, U. and Lundy, L. (2006) 'Children's Rights in Action in Using the UN Convention on the Rights of the Child as an Auditing Tool' *Child and Family Law Quarterly* Vol 18(3), 331–50.

Killias, M. (2003) *European Sourcebook of Crime and Criminal Statistics*. Cullompton, Willan.

King, M. (1997a) *A Better World for Children? Explorations in Morality and Authority*. London, Routledge.

King, M. (1997b) 'The James Bulger Trial: Good or Bad for Guilty or Innocent Children' in M. King, *A Better World for Children*. London, Routledge.

King, M. (ed) (1999) *Moral Agendas for Children's Welfare*. London, Routledge.

King, M. and Piper, C. (1989) *La Prise en Charge de la Délinquance Juvénile*. Report to the Ministry of Justice, Paris.

King, M. and Piper, C. (1995) *How the Law Thinks about Children* (2nd edn). Aldershot, Arena.

King, R. and Morgan, R. (1980) *The Future of the Prison System*. Aldershot, Gower.

Knock, K. (2002) 'The Police Perspective on Sex Offender Orders: A Preliminary Review of Policy and Practice', *Police Research Series Paper 155*. London, Home Office.

Koffman, L. (2006) 'The Rise and Fall of Proportionality: The Failure of the Criminal Justice Act 1991' Crim LR, 281–99.

Koffman, L. (2008) 'Holding Parents to Account: Tough on Children, Tough on the Causes of Children?' *Journal of Law and Society* Vol 35(1), 113–30.

Koffman, L. and Dingwall, G. (2007) 'The Diversion of Young Offenders: A Proportionate Response?' *Web JCL*, 2, I.

Labour Party (1964) *Crime—A Challenge to Us All*. London, Labour Party.

Lacey, M. (2002) 'Justice, Humanity and Mercy' in D. Ward, J. Scott and M. Lacey *Probation, Working for Justice* (2nd edn). Oxford, Oxford University Press, 25–38.

Lacey, N. (1988) *State Punishment*. London, Routledge.

Lacey, N. (1998) 'Punishment and Community' in A. von Hirsch and A. Ashworth (eds) *Principled Sentencing: Readings on Theory and Policy*. Oxford, Hart, 394–408.

Lacey, N. and Zedner, L. (1995) 'Discourses of Community in Criminal Justice' *Journal of Law and Society* Vol 22(3), 301–25.

Lader, D., Singleton, N. and Meltzer, H. (2000) *Psychiatric Morbidity among Young Offenders in England and Wales*, Report by the ONS (Office for National Statistics) for the Department of Health. London, ONS.

Laing, J. (1999) 'Diversion of Mentally Disordered Offenders: Victim and Offender Perspectives' Crim LR, 805–19.

Landau, S. (1981) 'Juveniles and the Police—Who Is Charged Immediately and Who Is Referred to the Juvenile Bureau?' *British Journal of Criminology* Vol 21(1), 27.

Le Grand, J. (1998) 'The Third Way Begins with CORA' *New Statesman* 6 March.

Lea, J. and Young, J. (1984) *What Is to Be Done about Law and Order?* Harmondsworth, Penguin.

Learmont, J. (1995) *Review of Prison Service Security in England and Wales and the Escape from Parkhurst Prison on Tuesday 3rd January 1995*, Cm 3020. London, HMSO.

Leigh, A. (2001/2) 'Keeping on the Right Track' *Safer Society* Winter, 25–6.

Lemert, E. (1967) *Human Deviance, Social Problems and Social Control*. Englewood Cliffs, NJ, Prentice Hall.

Levi, M. (1989) 'Suite Justice: Sentencing for Fraud' Crim LR, 420–34.

Levi, M. and Pithouse, A. (2000) *White Collar Crime and its Victims*. Oxford, Clarendon.

Lewis, S., Raynor, P., Smith, D. and Wardack, A. (eds) (2005) *Race and Probation Alternatives to Prison, Alternatives to Prison*. Cullompton, Willan.

Lianos, M. and Douglas, M. (2002) 'Dangerization and the End of Deviance' *British Journal of Criminology* Vol 40(3), 264–78.

Liberty (2006) *Renewing the Prevention of Terrorism Act 2005: Submission to the Joint Committee on Human Rights*. London, Liberty.

Liberty (2007) *Briefing on the Criminal Justice and Immigration Bill*. London, Liberty.

Liebling, A. and Maruna, S. (eds) *The Effects of Imprisonment*. Cullompton, Willan.

Liebmann, M. (2000) 'A Survey of RJ in Custodial Settings' *RJ* Issue 3, 1.

Light, R. and Bryony Campbell (2006) 'Prisoners' Families: Still Forgotten Victims?' *Journal of Social Welfare and Family Law* Vol 28 (3–4), 297–308.

Lippke, R. L. (2007) *Rethinking Imprisonment*. Oxford, Oxford University Press.

Lipsey, M. W. (1992) 'The Effect of Treatment on Juvenile Delinquents: Results from Meta-analysis' in F. Losel, T. Bliesener and D. Bender (eds) *Psychology and Law: International Perspectives*. Berlin, de Gruyter.

Little, M., Kogan, J., Bullock, R. and van der Laan, P. (2004) 'An Experiment in Multi-Systemic Responses to Persistent Young Offenders Known to Children's Services' *British Journal of Criminology* Vol 44, 225–40.

Littlechild, B. (1997) 'Young Offenders, Punitive Policy and the Rights of Children' *Critical Social Policy* Vol. 17(3), 73–91.

Livingstone, S. (2000) 'Prisoners' Rights in the Context of the European Convention on Human Rights', *Punishment and Society* Vol 2(3), 309–24.

Livingstone, S. (2003) *Prison Law* (3rd edn). Oxford, University Press.

Livingstone, S., Owen, T. and Macdonald, A. (2008) *Prison Law* (4th edn). Oxford, Oxford University Press.

Locke, T. (1988) 'Policy, Information and Monitoring Juvenile Crime and Justice' in B. Britton, B. Hope, T. Locke and L. Wainman (eds) *Policy and Information in Juvenile Justice Systems*. London, NACRO/Save the Children.

Loucks, N. (2007) *No One Knows: The Prevalence and Associated Needs of Offenders with Learning Difficulties and Learning Disabilities*. London, PRT.

Lukács, G. (1975) *The Young Hegel*. London, Merlin Press.

Lyon, D. (ed) (2006) *Theorizing Surveillance: The Panopticon and Beyond*. Cullompton, Willan.

Lyon, J. (2003) 'The Cost of a Broken Promise' *Criminal Justice Matters* Vol 54, 28–9.

Lyon, J., Dennison, C. and Wilson, A. (2000) *Tell Them so They Listen: Messages from Young People in Custody*. HORS Study 201. London, HMSO.

MacDonald, S. and Telford, M. (2007) 'The Use of ASBOS against Young People in England and Wales: Lessons from Scotland' LS Vol 27(4), 604–29.

Mackie, A., Raine, J. W., Burrows, J., Hopkins, M. and Dunstan, E. (2003) *Clearing the Debts: The Enforcement of Financial Penalties in Magistrates' Courts*. Home Office On-Line Report 09/03. London, Home Office.

Macpherson, W. (1999) *The Stephen Lawrence Inquiry, Report of an Inquiry by Sir William Macpherson of Cluny, Advised by Tom Cook, The Right Revd. Dr John Sentamu and Dr Richard Stone*, Cm 4262–1. London, Home Office.

Magistrates' Association (1997, 2003) *Magistrates' Court Guidelines*. London, The Magistrates' Association.

Maguire, M. (2002) 'Crime Statistics' in M. Maguire, R. Morgan and R. Reiner (eds) *The Oxford Handbook of Criminology* (3rd edn). Oxford, Oxford University Press, 322–75.

Maguire, M. and Shapland, J. (1997) 'Provision for Victims in an International Context' in R. Davis, A. Lurigio and W. Skogan (eds) *Victims of Crime* (2nd edn). Thousand Oaks, CA, Sage, 211–28.

Maguire, M., Morgan, R. and Reiner, R. (2002) *The Oxford Handbook of Criminology* (3rd edn). Oxford, Oxford University Press.

Mair, G. (1997) 'Community Penalties and Probation' in M. Maguire, R. Morgan and R. Reiner (eds) *The Oxford Handbook of Criminology* (2nd edn). Oxford, Clarendon Press, 1195–1232.

Mair, G. (ed) (2004) *What Matters in Probation*. Cullompton, Willan.

Mair, G. and May, C. (1997) *Offenders on Probation*, HORS 167. London, Home Office.

Mair, G., Cross, N. & Taylor, S. (2007) *The Use and Impact of the Community Order and the Suspended Sentence Order*. London, Centre for Criminal Justice Studies.

Mantle, G. and Moore, S. (2004) 'On Probation: Pickled and Nothing to Say' *Howard Journal* Vol 43(3), 299–316.

Marcuse, H. (2002) *One-Dimensional Man*. London, Routledge.

Marquart, J. W., Ekland-Olsen, S. and Sorensen, J. R. (1989) 'A National Study of *Furman*-Commuted Inmates: Assessing the Threat to Society from Capital Offenders', *Loyola of Los Angeles Law Review*, Vol 23(1), November, 5–28.

Marshall, P. (1997) *A Reconviction Study of HMP Grendon Therapeutic Community*. London, Home Office.

Marshall, T. (1985) *Alternatives to Criminal Courts*. Aldershot, Gower.

Marshall, T. (1992) Seminar, 21 January, Law Department, Brunel University.

Marshall, T. (1997) 'Seeking the Whole Justice' in S. Hayman and M. Wright (eds) *Repairing the Damage: Restorative Justice in Action*. London, ISTD.

Marshall, T. H. (1950) *Citizenship and Social Rights*. Cambridge, Cambridge University Press.

Martin, J. and Webster, D. (1971) *The Social Consequences of Conviction*. London, Heinemann.

Martinson, R. (1974) 'What Works? Questions and Answers about Prison Reform', *The Public Interest* (Spring), 22–54.

Marx, K. (1853) 'Capital Punishment', first published in *New York Daily Tribune*, February 17 and 18, reprinted in *Marx and Engels: Collected Works*, Vol 11, London, Lawrence and Wishart (1979), 495–501.

Marx, K. and Engels, F. (1845) 'The Holy Family' in *Marx and Engels: Collected Works*, Vol 4 (1975), London, Lawrence and Wishart (1975), 5–211.

Mason, T. and Mercer, D. (1999) A *Sociology of the Mentally Disordered Offender.* London, Longman.

Masters, G. (1997) 'Values for Probation, Society and Beyond' *Howard Journal* Vol 36(3), 237–47.

Matthews, R. (1988) *Informal Justice.* London, Sage.

Matthews, R. (1999) *Doing Time.* Basingstoke, Palgrave.

Matthews, R. (ed) (1989) *Privatising Criminal Justice.* London, Sage.

Mattinson, J. and Mirrlees-Black, C. (2000) *Attitudes to Crime and Criminal Justice: Findings from the 1998 British Crime Survey,* Home Office Research Study 200. London, Home Office.

Mauer, M. (2001) 'The Causes and Consequences of Prison Growth in the United States' in D. Garland (ed) *Mass Imprisonment.* London, Sage, 4–14.

Mauer, M. and Huling, G. (1995) *Young Black Americans and the Criminal Justice System.* Washington DC, The Sentencing Project.

May Committee (1979) *Report of the Committee of Inquiry into the United Kingdom Prison Services,* Cmnd 7673. London, HMSO.

May, M. (2002) 'Innocence and Experience: The Evolution of the Concept of Juvenile Delinquency in the Mid-nineteenth Century' in J. Muncie, G. Hughes and E. McLaughlin (eds) (2002) *Youth Justice, Critical Readings.* London, Sage, 98–114.

May, T. (1990) *Probation: Politics, Policy and Practice.* Milton Keynes, Open University Press.

McAlinden, A-M (2007) *The Shaming of Sex Offenders: Risk, Retribution and Reintegration.* Oxford, Hart.

McBride, W. L. (1975) 'The Concept of Justice in Marx, Engels and Others', *Ethics,* 85, 204–18.

McDermott, K. (January 1990), 'We Have No Problem: The Experience of Racism in Prison', *New Community,* 213–28.

McDiarmid, C. (2000) 'Children Who Murder: What Is Her Majesty's Pleasure?' Crim LR, 547–63.

McDonald, I. (2006) 'The "Respect Action Plan": Something New or More of the Same?' *Journal of Social Welfare and Family Law* Vol 28(2), 191–200.

McEvoy, K., Mika, H. and Hudson, B. (2002) 'Practice, Performance and Prospects for Restorative Justice' *British Journal of Criminology* Vol 42, 469–75.

McGhee, J. Waterhouse, L. and Whyte, B. (2002) 'Children's Hearings and Children in Trouble' in J. Muncie, G. Hughes and E. McLaughlin (eds) *Youth Justice, Critical Readings.* London, Sage, 228–37.

McGuire, J. (ed) (1995) *What Works? Reducing Reoffending.* Chichester, John Wiley.

McGuire, J. and Priestley, P. (1995) 'Reviewing "What Works": Past, Present and Future', in J. McGuire (ed) *What Works? Reducing Reoffending.* Chichester, John Wiley, 3–34.

McIvor, G. (1998) 'Jobs for the Boys? Gender Differences in Referral to Community Service' *Howard Journal* Vol 37(3), 280–90.

McKeever, G. (2004) 'Social Security as a Criminal Sanction' *Journal of Social and Welfare Law* Vol 26(1), 1–16.

McLaughlin, E., Ferguson, R., Hughes, G. and Westmarland, L. (2003) *Restorative Justice, Critical Issues.* Milton Keynes, Open University Press and London, Sage.

McLaughlin, E. and Muncie, J. (1994) 'Managing the Criminal Justice System' in J. Clarke, A. Cochrane, E. McLaughlin (eds) *Managing Social Policy.* London: Sage.

McLaughlin, E., Muncie, J. and Hughes, G. (2001) 'The Permanent Revolution: New Labour, New Public Management and the Modernization of Criminal Justice' *Criminal Justice* Vol 1(3), 301–18.

McRobbie, A. and Thornton, S. (2002) 'Rethinking "Moral Panic" for Multi-mediated Social Worlds' in J. Muncie, G. Hughes and E. McLaughlin (eds) *Youth Justice: Critical Readings*. London, Sage, 68–79.

McWilliams, W. (1990) 'Probation Practice and the Management Ideal', *Probation Journal* Vol. 37(2), 60–7.

McWilliams, W. and Pease, K. (1990) 'Probation Practice and an End to Punishment', *Howard Journal* Vol. 29(1), 14–24.

Miers, D. (1989) 'The Compensation Provisions' Crim LR, 32–42.

Miers, D. (1990) *Compensation for Criminal Injuries*. London, Butterworths.

Miers, D. (2004) 'Situating and Researching Restorative Justice in Great Britain' *Punishment and Society* Vol 6(1), 23–46.

Miers, D., Maguire, M., Goldie, S., Sharpe, K., Hale, C., Netton, K., Doolin, S., Uglow, S., Enterkin, J. and Newburn, T. (2001) *An Exploratory Evaluation of Restorative Justice Schemes*. Crime Reduction Research Series Paper 9. London, Home Office.

Mill, J. S. (1861) *Utilitarianism*. Oxford, Oxford University Press, 1998.

Ministry of Justice (2007a) *Offender Management Caseload Statistics 2006*. London, Ministry of Justice.

Ministry of Justice (2007b) *The Government's Response to the Report by Baroness Corston of a Review of Women with Particular Vulnerabilities in the Criminal Justice System*, Cm 7261. London, The Stationery Office.

Ministry of Justice (2007c) *Penal Policy—A Background Paper*. London, NOMS, Home Office.

Ministry of Justice (2007d) *Statistics of Mentally Disordered Offenders 2006, England and Wales*, Statistical Bulletin. London, Ministry of Justice.

Ministry of Justice (2007e) *Sentencing Statistics 2006 England and Wales*, Statistical Bulletin. London, Ministry of Justice.

Mirrlees-Black, C. (2001) *Confidence in the Criminal Justice System: Findings from the 2000 British Crime Survey*. Home Office Research Findings No 137. London, Home Office.

Moloney Report (1927) *Report of the Departmental Committee on the Treatment of Offenders*. Cmnd 2381. London, HMSO.

Monaghan, G., Moore, S. and Hibbert, P. (2003) *Children in Trouble: Time for Change*. Barkingside, Barnardo's.

Moore, M., Estrich, S., McGillis, D. and Spellman, W. (1985) *Dealing with Dangerous Offenders: The Elusive Target of Justice*. Cambridge, MA, Harvard University Press.

Moore, R. (2003a) 'The Use of Financial Penalties and the Amounts Imposed: the Need for a New Approach' Crim LR, 13–27.

Moore, R. (2003b) 'Executing Warrants against Fine defaulters: The Continuing Search for Effectiveness and Efficiency' Crim LR, 595–606.

Moore, R. (2004) 'Intensive Supervision and Surveillance Programmes for Young Offenders: The Evidence Base so Far' in R. Burnett and C. Roberts (eds) *What Works in Probation and Youth Justice: Developing Evidence-based Practice*. Cullompton, Willan.

Morgan, P. (1996) 'Family Crisis Affects Us All', in C. Donnellan (ed), *Marriage and Divorce: Issues for the Nineties*. London, Independence Educational Publishers.

Morgan, R. (2000) *The Judiciary in the Magistrates' Courts*, Home Office RDS Occasional Paper No 66. London, Home Office.

Morgan, R. and Liebling, A. (2007) 'Imprisonment: An Expanding Scene', in M. Maguire *et al., The Oxford Handbook of Criminology* (4th edn). Oxford, Oxford University Press, 1100–39.

Morris, A. and Gelsthorpe, L. (1990) 'Not Paying for Crime: Issues in Fine Enforcement' Crim LR, 839–51.

Morris, A. and Giller, H. (1987) *Understanding Juvenile Justice*. Beckenham, Croom Helm.

Morris, A. and Maxwell, G. (2001) 'Implementing Restorative Justice: What Works?' in A. Morris and G. Maxwell (eds) *Restorative Justice for Juveniles: Conferencing, Mediation and Circles*. Oxford, Hart, 267–81.

Morris, A., Wilkinson, C., Tisi, A., Woodrow, J. and Rockley, A. (1995) *Managing the Needs of Female Prisoners*. London, Home Office.

Morris, N. (1974) *The Future of Imprisonment*. Chicago, University of Chicago Press.

Morris, N. and Miller, M. (1985) 'Predictions of Dangerousness', in M. Tonry and N. Morris (eds) *Crime and Justice: An Annual Review of Research*, Vol 6. Chicago, University of Chicago Press, 1–50.

Morris, N. and Tonry, M. (1990) *Between Prison and Probation*. Oxford, Oxford University Press.

Mountbatten, Lord (1966) *Report of the Inquiry into Prison Escapes and Security*, Cm 3175. London, HMSO.

Moxon, D. (1993) *The Use of Compensation Orders in Magistrates' Courts*, Home Office Research Bulletin. London, Home Office.

Moxon, D., Corkery, J. M. and Hedderman, C. (1992) *Some Developments in the Use of Compensation Orders in Magistrates' Courts since 1988*, Home Office Research Study 126. London, HMSO.

Mulcahy, L. (2000) 'The Devil and the Deep Blue Sea? A Critique of the Ability of Community Mediation to Suppress and Facilitate Participation in Civil Life' *Journal of Law and Society* Vol 27(1), 133–50.

Muncie, J. (1999) 'Institutionalised Intolerance: Youth Justice and the 1998 Crime and Disorder Act' *Critical Social Policy* Vol 19(2), 147–75.

Muncie, J. (2000) 'Pragmatic Realism? Searching for Criminology in the New Youth Justice' in B. Goldson (ed) *The New Youth Justice*. Lyme Regis, Russell House Publishing, 14–34.

Muncie, J. (2004) *Youth and Crime: A Critical Introduction* (2nd edn). London, Sage.

Muncie, J. (2006) 'Repenalisation and Rights: Explorations in Comparative Youth Criminology' *Howard Journal* Vol 45(1), 42–70.

Muncie, J. and Hughes, E. (2002) 'Modes of Youth Governance: Political Rationalities, Criminalization and Resistance' in J. Muncie, G. Hughes and E. McLaughlin (eds) *Youth Justice: Critical Readings*. London, Sage, 1–18.

Muncie, J., Hughes, G. and McLaughlin, E. (eds) (2002) *Youth Justice: Critical Readings*. London, Sage.

Munro, V. (2002) 'The Emerging Rights of Imprisoned Mothers and their Children' *Child and Family Law Quarterly* Vol 14, 303.

Murphy, J. G. (1973) 'Marxism and Retribution' *Philosophy and Public Affairs* Vol 2, 217–43.

Murphy, K. and Harris, N. (2007) 'Shaming, Shame and Recidivism' *British Journal of Criminology* 47(6), 900–17.

Murphy, T. and Whitty, N. (2007) 'Risk and Human Rights in UK Prison Governance' *British Journal of Criminology* Vol 47(5), 798–816.

Murray, C. and Cox, L. (1979) *Beyond Probation: Juvenile Corrections and Chronic Delinquent.* Beverly Hills, CA, Sage.

NACRO (1985) *Juvenile Crime*, Juvenile Crime Briefing. London, NACRO.

NACRO (1986) *Cautioning and Diversion of Juvenile Offenders*, Juvenile Crime Briefing. London, NACRO.

NACRO (1989) *Diverting Juvenile Offenders from Prosecution*, Juvenile Crime Policy Paper 2. London, NACRO.

NACRO (1993) 'Supplementary Guidance on Cautioning' NACRO Briefing, December. London, NACRO.

NACRO (1997) 'A New 3Rs for Young Offenders'. London, NACRO.

NACRO (2000a) *Race & Prisons*. London, NACRO.

NACRO (2000b) *Pre-Sentence Reports and Custodial Sentencing*. NACRO Briefing, December. London, NACRO.

NACRO (2000c) *Some Facts about Young Offenders*. NACRO Briefing. London, NACRO.

NACRO (2001/2) 'Children Who Commit Grave Crimes' *Safer Society* Winter, 8–9.

NACRO (2001a) *The Criminal Justice and Court Services Act 2000, Youth Justice Implications*, NACRO Briefing. London, NACRO.

NACRO (2001b) *Public Opinion and Youth Justice*. Youth Crime Briefing. 12/01. London.

NACRO (2001c) *The Grave Crimes Provision*. Youth Justice Briefing. London, NACRO.

NACRO (2001d) *Appeals within the Youth Justice System Part 2*. NACRO Briefing. London, NACRO.

NACRO (2002a) *Some Facts about Young People who Offend—2000*, Youth Crime Briefing. London, NACRO.

NACRO (2002b) *Proportionality in the Youth Justice System*. London, NACRO.

NACRO (2002c) *Women Who Challenge: Women Offenders and Mental Health Issues*. London, NACRO.

NACRO (2003a) *Detention and Training Order Early Release—The Revised Guidance and Use of Electronic Monitoring*, Youth Crime Briefing, March. London, NACRO.

NACRO (2003b) *Youth Crime, Section Update, September 2003*. London, NACRO.

NACRO (2003c) *Looked After Children Who Offend: The Quality Protects Programme and YOTS*, Youth Crime Briefing. London, NACRO.

NACRO (2003d) *Youth Crime, Section Update, December*. London, NACRO.

NACRO (2003e) *Counting the Cost: Reducing Child Imprisonment*. Summary. London, NACRO.

NACRO (2003f) *Family Group Conferencing and Youth Justice*, Youth Crime Briefing. London, NACRO.

NACRO (2003g) *Race and Prisons: Where Are We Now?* London, NACRO.

NACRO (2004a) *Some Facts about Young People Who Offend—2002*, Youth Crime Briefing. London, NACRO.

NACRO (2004b) *Anti-social Behaviour Orders and Associated Measures (Part 2)*, Youth Crime Briefing. London, NACRO.

NACRO (2004c) *New Legislation—Impact on Sentencing*, Youth Crime Briefing. London, NACRO.

NACRO (2004d) *Barriers to Equality: Challenges in Tracking Black and Minority Ethnic Defendants through the Criminal Justice System*. London, NACRO.

NACRO (2004e) *The Grave Crimes Provision*, London, NACRO.

NACRO (2005) *Dangerousness and the Criminal Justice Act 2003*, Youth Crime Briefing, June. London, NACRO.

NACRO (2006) *Managing Risk in the Community in the Youth Justice System*, Youth Crime Briefing, September. London, NACRO.

NACRO (2007a) *Effective Practice with Children and Young People Who Offend—Part 2*, Youth Crime Briefing, March. London, NACRO.

NACRO (2007b) *Naming and Shaming—Publicity for Children and Young People Involved in Anti-social or Offending Behaviour*, Youth Crime Briefing. London, NACRO.

NACRO (2007c) *Further Developments in Measures Related to Anti-social Behaviour*, Youth Crime Briefing, March. London, NACRO.

NACRO (2007d) *The Detention and Training Order*, Youth Crime Briefing, June. London, NACRO.

NACRO (2007e) *Mental Capacity and Related Issues in the Youth Court*, Youth Crime Briefing, June. London, NACRO.

NACRO (2007f) *Some Facts about Children and Young People Who Offend—2005*, Youth Crime Briefing. London, NACRO.

NACRO (2008) *Some Facts about Children and Young People Who Offend—2006*, Youth Crime Briefing. London, NACRO.

NAPO (2006) *News*, Issue 182, 15 September.

Nash, M. (1992) 'Dangerousness Revisited' (1992) *International Journal of the Sociology of Law*, Vol 20, 337–49.

National Offender Management Service (2006a) *Working with Probation to Protect the Public and Reduce Re-offending*. London, Home Office.

National Offender Management Service (2006b) *Improving Prison and Probation Services: Public Value Partnerships*. London, Home Office.

National Offender Management Service (2007) *Commissioning Framework, National Commissioning Plan 2007–8*. London, Home Office.

Nelken, D. (1994) 'Community Involvement in Crime Control' in N. Lacey (ed) *A Reader in Criminal Justice*. Oxford, Oxford University Press, 247–77.

Nellis, M. (1995) 'Probation Values for the 1990s' *Howard Journal* Vol 34, 19–44.

Nellis, M. (2002) 'Probation Partnership and Civil Society' in D. Ward, J. Scott and M. Lacey (eds) *Probation, Working for Justice* (2nd edn). Oxford, Oxford University Press, 356–74.

Netten, A., Saunders, R., Sharpe, K. and Uglow, S. (2002) *The Introduction of Referral Orders into the Youth Justice System, Final Report*. HORS 242. London, Home Office, Development and Statistics Directorate.

Newburn, T. (1988) *The Use and Enforcement of Compensation Orders in Magistrates Courts*, Home Office Research Study 102. London, HMSO.

Newburn, T. (1995) *Crime and Criminal Justice Policy*. London, Longmans.

Newburn, T. (1996) 'Back to the Future? Youth Crime, Youth Justice and the Rediscovery of "Authoritarian Populism"' in J. Pilcher and S. Wagg (eds) *Thatcher's Children, Politics, Childhood and Society in the 1980s and 1990s*. London, Falmer Press, 61–76.

Newburn, T. (2001–2) 'Modernisation, New Labour and Criminal Justice Policy' CJM No 46 Winter, 4–5. London, Centre for Crime and Justice Studies, Kings College.

Newburn, T., Crawford, A., Earle, R., Goldie, S., Hale, C., Hallam, A., Masters, G., Netten, A., Saunders, R., Sharpe, K. and Uglow, S. (2002) *The Introduction of Referral Orders into the*

Youth Justice System: Final Report. Home Office Research Study 242. London, Home Office.

Nicholas, S., Kershaw, C. and Walker, A. (2007) *Crime in England and Wales 2006/07*, London, Home Office Statistical Bulletin, 11/07.

Nicholson, P. (1982) 'Hegel on Crime' *History of Political Thought* Vol 3, 103–21.

Norrie, A. (1998) 'The Limits of Legal Ideology' in A. von Hirsch and A. Ashworth (eds) *Principled Sentencing: Readings on Theory and Policy.* Oxford, Hart, 369–80.

Nozick, R. (1974) *Anarchy, State and Utopia*, Oxford: Blackwell.

NPS (National Probation Service) (2003) *OASys: The New Offender Assessment System: Important information for Sentencers*, Briefing note Issue 3. London, National Probation Service.

O'Brien, M., Mortimer, L., Singleton, N. and Meltzer, H. (2001) *Psychiatric Morbidity among Women Prisoners in England and Wales*, London, Office for National Statistics.

O'Grady, A., Pleasance, P., Balmer, N. J., Buck, A. and Genn, H. (2004) 'Disability, Social Exclusion and the Consequential Experience of Justiciable Problems' *Disability and Society* Vol 19(3), 259–72.

O'Mahoney, (2004) 'Restorative Justice and Youth Conferencing—Transforming Youth Justice in Northern Ireland' Paper presented at the SLSA Annual Conference April, Glasgow University.

O'Mahoney, D. and Deazley, R. (2000) *Juvenile Crime and Justice*, Review of Criminal Justice in Northern Ireland, Research Report 17. Belfast, Northern Ireland Office.

O'Mahoney, D. and Doak, J. (2004) 'Restorative Justice—Is More Better? The Experience of Police-led Restorative Cautioning Pilots in Northern Ireland' *Howard Journal* Vol 43(5), 484–505.

O'Malley, P. (2000) 'Risk Societies and the Government of Crime' in M. Brown and J. Pratt (eds) *Dangerous Offenders.* London and New York, Routledge, 17–33.

O'Shea, N., Moran, I. and Bergin, S. (2003) *Snakes and Ladders' Mental Health and Criminal Justice.* London, Revolving Doors Agency.

Office for National Statistics (2000) *Psychiatric Morbidity among Young Offenders in England and Wales*, London, Office for National Statistics.

Ofsted (Office of Standards in Education in consultation with HM Chief Inspector of Prisons) (2004) *Girls in Prison, The Education and Training of Under-18s Serving Detention and Training Orders.* London, HM Inspectorate of Prisons.

Oldfield, M. and Grimshaw, R. (2008) *Probation Resources, Staffing and Workloads 2001– 2008.* London, Centre for Crime and Justice Studies, King's College, in association with NAPO.

Olson, S. and Dzur, W. (2004) 'Revising Informal Justice: Restorative Justice and Democratic Professionalism' *Law and Society Review* Vol 38(1), 139–76.

Orton, S. and Vennard, J. (1988) 'Minor Offences and the Fixed Penalty: A Survey in England and Wales' in N. Walker and M. Hough (eds) *Public Attitudes to Sentencing.* Aldershot, Gower, 160–77.

Owen, T. (2007) 'Culture of Crime Control: Through a Post-Foucauldian Lens' *Internet Journal of Criminology* at http://www.internetjournalofcriminology.com

Padfield, N. (2002) 'Tariffs in Murder Cases' Crim LR, 192–204.

Padfield, N. (2007) 'Distinguishing the Unlawful from the Unjustifiable in the Rules on Early Release from Prison' CLJ Vol 66(2), 255–8.

Pantazis, C., Gordon, D. and Levitas, R. (2006) *Poverty and Social Exclusion: The Millennium Survey*. Bristol, Policy Press.

Park, I. (2000) *Review of Comparative Costs and Performance of Privately and Publicly Operated Prisons 1998–9*, Home Office Statistical Bulletin, 6/00. London, Home Office.

Parker, M. (2006) (ed) *Dynamic Security: The Democratic Therapeutic Community in Prison*. London, Jessica Kingsley.

Parole Board (2006) *Annual Report 2005–06*. London, Parole Board.

Parole Board (2007) *Annual Report and Accounts 2006/07*. London, Parole Board.

Pashukanis, E. B. (1978) *Law and Marxism: A General Theory*. London, Inklinks.

Paton, L. (2003) 'Anti-social Behaviour: The Government's Solution' *Childright* Vol 196, 4–6.

Patterson, A. and Thorpe, K. (2006) 'Public Perceptions' in A. Walker, C. Kershaw and S. Nicholas (eds) *Crime in England and Wales 2005/2006*, Home Office Statistical Bulletin 12/06. London, Home Office.

Pearson, G. (2002) 'Youth Crime and Moral Decline: Permissiveness and Tradition' in J. Muncie, G. Hughes and E. McLaughlin (eds) *Youth Justice, Critical Readings*. London, Sage, 45–9.

Peay, J. (2002) 'Mentally Disordered Offenders, Mental Health and Crime' in M. Maguire, R. Morgan and R. Reiner (eds) *The Oxford Handbook of Criminology* (3rd edn). Oxford, Oxford University Press, 746–91.

Peay, J. (2007) 'Mentally Disordered Offenders, Mental Health and Crime', in M. Maguire, R. Morgan and R. Reiner (eds) *The Oxford Handbook of Criminology* (4th edn). Oxford, Oxford University Press, 496–527.

Penal Affairs Consortium (1996) *The Imprisonment of Women: Some Facts and Figures*. London, Penal Affairs Consortium.

Penfold, C., Hunter, G. and Hough, M. (2006) *The Intermittent Custody Pilot: A Descriptive Study*, Home Office Findings 280. London, Home Office.

Pettit, P. with Braithwaite, J. (1998) 'Republicanism in Sentencing: Recognition, Recompense and Reassurance' in A. von Hirsch and A. Ashworth (eds) *Principled Sentencing: Readings on Theory and Policy*. Oxford, Hart, 317–30.

Phillips, C. and Brown, D. (1998), *Entry into the Criminal Justice System: A Survey of Police Arrests and their Outcomes*, Home Office Research Study 185. London, Home Office.

Phillips, Lord (2007) 'Issues in Criminal Justice—Murder' Speech, University of Birmingham, March 8.

Pinchbeck, I. and Hewitt, M. (1973) *Children in English Society: From the 18th Century to the Children Act 1948*, Vol 2. London, Routledge & Kegan Paul.

Piper, C. (1999) 'The Crime and Disorder Act—Child or Community Safety?' MLR Vol 62, 397–408.

Piper, C. (2000) 'Assumptions about Children's Best Interests' *Journal of Social Welfare and Family Law* Vol 22(3), 261–76.

Piper, C. (2001) 'Who Are These Youths? Language in the Service of Policy' *Youth Justice* Vol 1(2), 30–9.

Piper, C. (2004) 'Assessing Assessment' *Family Law* Vol 34, 736–40.

Piper, C. (2006a) 'Punishment, Penance and Impact: The Vagaries of Sentencing Policy', *The Barrister*, October.

Piper, C. (2006b) 'Feminist Perspectives on Youth Justice' in A. Diduck and K. O'Donovan, *Feminist Perspectives on Family Law*. London, Routledge Cavendish.

Piper, C. (2007) 'Should Impact Constitute Mitigation? Structured Discretion versus Mercy' Crim LR, 141–55.

Piper, C. (2008) *Investing in Children: Policy, Law and Practice* in Context. Cullompton, Willan.

Piper, C. and Easton, S. (2006/7) 'What's Sentencing Got to Do with It?' *Contemporary Issues in Law* Special Issue: Current Issues in Sentencing Policy, Vol 8(4), 356–76.

Pitts, J. (1988) *The Politics of Juvenile Justice.* London, Sage.

Pitts, J. (1992a) 'Juvenile Justice Policy in England and Wales' in J. Coleman, and C. Warren-Adamson, (eds) *Youth Policy in the 1990s.* London, Routledge, 172–88.

Pitts, J. (1992b) 'The End of an Era' *Howard Journal* Vol 31(2), 133–49.

Pitts, J. (2000) 'The New Youth Justice and the Politics of Electoral Anxiety' in B. Goldson (ed) *The New Youth Justice.* Lyme Regis, Russell House.

Platt, A. (1969) *The Child Savers: The Invention of Delinquency.* Chicago, University of Chicago Press.

Player, E. (2005) 'The Reduction of Women's Imprisonment in England and Wales', *Punishment and Society* Vol 7(4), 419–39.

Plotnikoff, J. and Woolfson, R. (2005) *Review of the Effectiveness of Specialist Courts in Other Jurisdictions*, DCA Research Series 3/05. London, Department for Constitutional Affairs.

Plugge, E., Douglas, N. and Fitzpatrick, R. (2006) *The Health of Women in Prison.* Oxford, Department of Public Health, University of Oxford.

PMSU (Prime Minister's Strategy Unit) (2007) *Building on Progress: Families.* London, Cabinet Office.

Poteat, S. (2002) 'The Women at Risk Programme' in P. Carlen (ed) *Women and Punishment: The Struggle for Justice.* Cullompton, Willan, 125–37.

Pratt, J. (1986) 'Diversion from the Juvenile Court' *British Journal of Criminology* Vol 26(3), 212–33.

Pratt, J. (1996) 'Governing the Dangerous: An Historical Overview of Dangerous Offender Legislation' *Social and Legal Studies* Vol 5(1), 21–36.

Pratt, J. (1998) 'Towards the "Decivilizing" of Punishment?' *Social and Legal Studies* Vol 7(4), 487–515.

Pratt, J. (2000) 'Dangerousness and Modern Society' in M. Brown and J. Pratt (eds) *Dangerous Offenders.* London, Routledge, 35–48.

Prins, H. (2005) *Offenders, Deviants and Patients.* London, Routledge.

Prison Reform Trust (2000) *Justice for Women: The Need for Reform.* London, Prison Reform Trust.

Prison Reform Trust (2003) *Troubled Inside: Responding to the Mental Health Needs of Women in Prison.* London, Prison Reform Trust.

Prison Reform Trust (2004a) *Briefing Paper.* London, Prison Reform Trust.

Prison Reform Trust (2004b) *Disabled Prisoners.* London, Prison Reform Trust.

Prison Reform Trust (2004c) *Response of the PRT to Managing Offenders, Reducing Crime and Reducing Crime, Changing Lives*, London, Prison Reform Trust.

Prison Reform Trust (2004d) *Forgotten Prisoners—The Plight of Foreign National Prisoners in England and Wales.* London, Prison Reform Trust.

Prison Reform Trust (2005) *Private Punishment: Who Profits?* London, Prison Reform Trust.

Prison Reform Trust (2006) *Experiences of Minority Ethnic Employees in Prisons.* London, Prison Reform Trust.

Prison Reform Trust (2007a) *Bromley Briefings: Prison Fact File*. London, Prison Reform Trust, December.

Prison Reform Trust (2007b) *Indefinitely Maybe? How the Indeterminate Sentence for Public Protection Is Unjust and Unsustainable*. London, Prison Reform Trust.

Prison Reform Trust (2007c) *Private Punishment: Who Profits?* London, Prison Reform Trust.

Prisons and Probation Ombudsman for England and Wales (2007) *Annual Report 2006–2007*, Cm 7163. London, HMSO.

Probation Service (2006)*: Intermittent Custody: Withdrawal of Authority to Supervise Offenders*. National Probation Service Bulletin Issue 41, 084/06.

Quirk, H. (2006) 'Review of "Proportionate Sentencing" by Andrew von Hirsch and Andrew Ashworth' *British Journal of Criminology,* Vol 46(5), 955–9.

Rack, J. (2005) *The Incidence of Hidden Disabilities in the Prison Population*. Egham, The Dyslexia Institute.

Raine, J., Dunstan, E. and Mackie, A. (2004) 'Financial Penalties: Who Pays, Who Doesn't and Why Not?' *Howard Journal* Vol 43(5), 518–38.

Rawlings, P. (1999) *Crime and Power: A History of Criminal Justice 1688–1998*. London, Longman.

Rawls, J. (1971) *A Theory of Justice*. Cambridge, MA, Harvard University Press.

Raynor, P. and Vanstone, M. (1994) 'Probation Practice, Effectiveness and the Non-treatment Paradigm' *British Journal of Social Work* Vol 24, 387–404.

Raynor, P. and Vanstone, M. (2002) *Understanding Community Penalties, Probation Policy and Social Change*. Buckingham, Open University Press.

Reece, H. (2005) 'From Parental Responsibility to Parenting Responsibly' *Current Legal Issues,* Vol 8, 459–83.

Reed, J. L. and Lyne, M. (2000) 'In-patient Care of Mentally Ill Prisoners; Results of a Year's Programme of Semi-structured Inspections', *British Medical Journal* Vol 320, 1031–34.

Reeves, H. (1989) 'The Victim Support Perspective' in M. Wright and B. Galaway (eds) *Mediation and Criminal Justice*. London, Sage, 44–55.

Renaud, Mr. Justice G. (2007) *Les Misérables on Sentencing: Valjean, Fantine, Javert and the Bishop debate the Principles*. Melbourne, Sandstone Academic Press.

Respect Task Force (2006) *Respect Action Plan*. London, Home Office.

Respect Task Force (2007) *Tools and Powers to Tackle Anti-social Behaviour,* London, Home Office.

Rex, S. (1998) 'Applying Desert Principles to Community Sentences: Lessons from Two Criminal Justice Acts' Crim LR, 381–91.

Reynolds, F. (1985) 'Magistrates' Justifications for Making Custodial Orders on Juvenile Offenders' Crim LR, 294–98.

Rhode, D. (1989) *Gender and Justice*. Cambridge, MA, Harvard University Press.

Richards, M. (1998) *Censure without Sanctions*. Winchester, Waterside Press.

Rickford, D. and Edgar, K. (2005) *Troubled Inside: Responding to the Mental Health Needs of Men in Prison*. London, Prison Reform Trust/King's Fund.

Rivera Beiras, I. (2005) 'State Form, Labour Market and Penal system: The New Punitive Rationality in Context' *Punishment and Society* Vol 7(2), 167–82.

Roberts, J. (2002) 'Alchemy in Sentencing: An Analysis of Sentencing Reform Proposals in England and Wales' *Punishment and Society* Vol 4(4), 425–42.

Roberts, J. (2003) 'Evaluating the Pluses and Minuses of Custody: Sentencing Reform in England and Wales' *Howard Journal* Vol 42(3), 229–47.

Roberts, J. and Hough, M. (2005) 'The State of the Prisons: Exploring Public Knowledge and Opinion', *Howard Journal* Vol 44(3), 286–306.

Roberts, S. (1979) *Order and Dispute*. Harmondsworth, Penguin.

Robinson, G. (1999) 'Risk Management and Rehabilitation in the Probation Service: Collision and Collusion', *Howard Journal* Vol 38(4), 421–33.

Robinson, G. (2002) 'Exploring Risk Management in Probation Practice' *Punishment and Society* Vol 4(1), 5–25.

Robinson, P. (2001) 'Punishing Dangerousness: Cloaking Preventive Detention as Criminal Justice' *Harvard Law Review* Vol 114(5), 1429–55.

Robinson, P. and Darley, J. M. (2004) 'Does Criminal Law Deter? A Behavioural Science Investigation', OJLS Vol 23(2), 173–206.

Roche, D. (2003) *Accountability in Restorative Justice*. Oxford, Oxford University Press.

Rock, P. (2002) 'On Becoming a Victim' in C. Hoyle and R. Young (eds) *New Visions of Crime Victims*. Oxford, Hart, 1–11.

Rose, N. (1987) 'Beyond the Public/Private Division: Law, Power and the Family' *Journal of Law and Society* Vol 14, 61–76.

Rose, N. (1990) *Governing the Soul: The Shaping of the Private Self.* London, Routledge.

Rose, N. (2000) 'Government and Control' *British Journal of Criminology* Vol 40, 321–39.

Ross, H. L. (1973) 'Deterrence Regained: The Cheshire Constabulary's Breathalyzer Blitz', *Journal of Legal Studies* Vol 2, 1–78.

Ross, H. L. (1992) *Confronting Drunk Driving*. New Haven, CT, Yale University Press.

Rossi, P., Waite, E., Bose, C. E. and Berk, R. E. (1974) 'The Seriousness of Crime: Normative Structure and Individual Differences', *American Sociological Review*, Vol 39, 224–37.

Rotman, E. (1990) *Beyond Punishment: A New View of the Rehabilitation of Offenders*. Connecticut, Greenwood Press.

Rousseau, J.-J. (1743) *The Social Contract*. ed M. Cranston (1968) Harmondsworth, Penguin.

Royal Commission on Capital Punishment (1953) *Report* Cmnd 8932. London, HMSO.

Royal Commission on Criminal Justice (1993) *Report* (Chair: Lord Runciman) Cm 2263. London, HMSO.

Royal Commission on Criminal Procedure (1981) *Report*, Cm 8092. London, HMSO.

Rubin, E. (2003) 'Just Say No to Retribution', *Buffalo Criminal Law Review* Vol 7(1), 17–83.

Rusche, G. and Kirchheimer, O. (1939) *Punishment and Social Structure*. New York, Russell and Russell.

Rutherford, A. (1992) *Growing out of Crime: The New Era*. Winchester, Waterside Press.

Rutter, M. and Giller, H. (1983) *Juvenile Delinquency: Trends and Perspectives*. Harmondsworth, Penguin.

Ryberg, J (2005) 'Retributivism and Multiple Offending' *Res Publica* Vol 11(3), 213–33.

Salmon, S. (2004) 'Children with a Prisoner in the Family' *Childright*, 203.

Salter, M. and Twist, S. (2007) 'The Micro-Sovereignty of Discretion in Legal Decision-Making: Carl Schmitt's Critique of Liberal Principles of Legality' *Web Journal of Current Legal Issues* Vol 3.

Sanders, A. (1985) 'Class bias in prosecutions' *Howard Journal* Vol 24(3), 176–99.

Sanders, A. (2001) *Community Justice: Modernising the Magistracy in England and Wales*. London, IPPR.

Sanders, A. (2002) 'Victim Participation in an Exclusionary Criminal Justice System' in C. Hoyle and R. Young (eds) *New Visions of Crime Victims*. Oxford, Hart.

Sanders, A. (2003) Book review, MLR Vol 66(1), 160–7.

Sanders, A., Hoyle, C., Morgan, R. and Cape, E. (2001) 'Victim Impact Statements: Don't Work, Can't Work' Crim LR, 447–58.

Sanders, A. and Loveday, B. (2001–2) Editorial, CJM No 46 Winter. London, Centre for Crime and Justice Studies, Kings College.

Sanders, A. and Young, R. (2000) *Criminal Justice* (2nd edn). London, Butterworth.

Sanders, A. and Young, R. (2006) *Criminal Justice* (3rd edn). Oxford, Oxford University Press.

Sarat, A. (1976) 'Public Opinion, the Death Penalty and the Eighth Amendment', *Wisconsin Law Review* Vol 17, 171–206.

Sayles, G. (1950) *The Medieval Foundations of England* (2nd edn). London, Methuen.

Schichor, D. (1995) *Punishment for Profit: Private Prisons, Public Concerns*. Thousand Oaks, CA, Sage.

Schofield, P. (2007) 'Jeremy Bentham. The French Revolution and Political Radicalization' in F. Rosen (ed) *Jeremy Bentham*. Aldershot, Ashgate, 535–8.

Scottish Executive (1999) *A Review of the Research Literature on Serious Violent and Sexual Offenders*. Edinburgh, Scottish Executive.

Scottish Executive (2001) *Scottish Strategy for Victims*. Edinburgh, Scottish Executive.

Scottish Executive (2002a) *Victims in the Scottish Criminal Justice System, The EU Framework Decision on the Standing of Victims in Criminal Procedure*. Edinburgh, Scottish Executive.

Scottish Executive (2002b) *Youth Justice in Scotland—A Progress Report for All those Working for Young People*. Edinburgh, Scottish Executive.

Scraton, P. and Haydon, D. (2002) 'Challenging the Criminalization of Children and Young People' in J. Muncie, G. Hughes and E. McLaughlin (eds) *Youth Justice: Critical Readings*. London, Sage, 311–28.

Sechrest, L. B., White, S. O., and Brown, E. D. (1979) *The Rehabilitation of Criminal Offenders*. Washington DC, National Academy of Sciences.

Seddon, T. (2006) *Punishment and Madness*. London, Routledge.

Sentencing Advisory Panel (2000) *Advice to the Court of Appeal—4. Racially Aggravated Offences*. London, Home Office.

Sentencing Advisory Panel (2002) *Minimum Terms in Murder Cases: The Panel's Advice to the Court of Appeal*. London, Home Office.

Sentencing Advisory Panel (2003a) *Driving Offences—Causing Death by Driving: The Panel's Advice to the Sentencing Guidelines Council*. London, SAP.

Sentencing Advisory Panel (2003b) *Annual Report 2002–3*, Summary. London, Home Office/LCD.

Sentencing Advisory Panel (2004) *Domestic Violence and Sentencing Consultation Paper*. London, SAP.

Sentencing Advisory Panel (2007a) *Consultation Paper on Breach of an Anti-Social Behaviour Order*. London, SAP.

Sentencing Advisory Panel (2007b) *Consultation Paper on Sentencing for Fraud Offences.* London, SAP.

Sentencing Advisory Panel (2008) *Advice to the Sentencing Guidelines Council, Driving Offences—Causing Death by Driving.* London, SAP.

Sentencing Guidelines Council (2004a) *Overarching Principles: Seriousness.* London, SGC.

Sentencing Guidelines Council (2004b) *Reduction in Sentence for a Guilty Plea.* London, SGC.

Sentencing Guidelines Council (2004c) *New Sentences: Criminal Justice Act 2003.* London, SGC.

Sentencing Guidelines Council (2005) *Guideline Judgments Case Compendium.* London, SGC.

Sentencing Guidelines Council (2006) *Overarching Principles: Domestic Violence.* London, SGC.

Sentencing Guidelines Council (2007a) *Definitive Guideline on the Reduction in Sentence for a Guilty Plea.* London, SGC.

Sentencing Guidelines Council (2007b) *Dangerous Offenders: Guide for Sentencers and Practitioners.* London, SGC.

Sentencing Guidelines Council (2007c) *Sexual Offences Act 2003, Definitive Guideline.* London, SGC.

Sentencing Guidelines Council (2008a) *Assault and other Offences against the Person. Definitive Guideline.* London, SGC.

Sentencing Guidelines Council (2008b) *Overarching Principles: Assaults on Children and Cruelty to a Child.* London, SGC.

Sentencing Guidelines Council (2008c) *Causing Death by Driving, Consultation Guideline.* London, SGC.

Shapland, J. (1981) *Between Conviction and Sentence: The Process of Mitigation.* London, Routledge & Kegan Paul.

Shapland, J. (2003) 'Restorative Justice and Criminal Justice: Just Reponses to Crime?' in A. von Hirsch, J. Roberts, A. Bottoms, K. Roach and M. Schiff (eds) *Restorative Justice and Criminal Justice: Competing or Reconcilable Paradigms?* Oxford, Hart, 195–218.

Shapland, J., Atkinson, A., Atkinson, H., Chapman, B., Dignan, J., Howes, M., Johnstone, J., Robinson, G. and Scorsby, A. (2007a) *Restorative Justice: The Views of Victims and Offenders— The Third Report from the Evaluation of Three Schemes.* Ministry of Justice Research Series 3/07. London, Ministry of Justice.

Shapland, J., Atkinson, A., Atkinson, H., Colledge, E., Dignan, J. Howes, M., Johnstone, J., Robinson, G. and Scorsby, A. (2007b) 'Situating Restorative Justice within Criminal Justice' *Theoretical Criminology* Vol 10(4), 505–32.

Shaw, C. R. (1930) *The Jack-Roller: A Delinquent Boy's Own Story.* Chicago, University of Chicago Press.

Shaw, S. (2005) *The Death in Custody of a Woman and a Series of Deaths in HMP/ YOI Styal August 2002–August 2003.* London, Prisons and Probation Ombudsman.

Sheehan, R., McIvor, G. and Trotter, G. (eds) (2007) *What Works with Women Offenders.* Cullompton, Willan.

Sheppard, G. (1990) 'Management: Short of Ideals?' *Probation Journal* Vol 37(4), 176–9.

Sherman, L. W. and Berk, R. A. (1983) 'The Specific Deterrent Effects of Arrest for Domestic Assault: Preliminary Findings', Unpublished Paper, Police Foundation, Washington.

Sherman, L. W., Farrington, D. P., Leyton MacKenzie, D. and Welsh, B. C. (eds) (2006) *Evidence-Based Crime Prevention*. London, Routledge.

Sherman, L. W., Strang, H., Newbury-Birch, D. and Bennett, S. (2007a) *Key Indicators of Effective Practice in Restorative Justice (KEEP)*. London, Youth Justice Board.

Sherman, L. W. and Strang, H., with Barnes, G., Bennett, S., Angel, C. M., Newbury-Birch, D., Woods, D. J., Gill, C. E. (2007b) *Restorative Justice: The Evidence*. London, Smith Institute.

Sherman, L. W., Strang, H., Newbury-Birch, D. and Bennett, S. (2007c) *Systematic Review of Recent Research Undertaken Regarding Restorative Justice, Reparation and Victims*. London, Youth Justice Board.

Shute, S. (2004a) 'The Sexual Offences Act 2003 (4) New Civil Preventative Orders: Sexual Offences Prevention Orders, Foreign Travel Orders; Risk of Sexual Harm Orders', Crim LR, 417–40.

Shute, S. (2004b) 'Punishing Murderers: Release Procedures and the "Tariff", 1953–2004' Crim LR, 873–95.

Shute, S., Hood, R. and Seemungal, F. (2005) *A Fair Hearing? Ethnic Minorities in the Criminal Courts*. Cullompton, Willan.

Simon, F. (1999) *Prisoners' Work and Vocational Training*. London, Routledge.

Simon, J. (1995) 'The Boot Camp and the Limits of Modern Penality', *Social Justice* Vol 22(2), 25–48.

Simon, J. (1998) 'Managing the Monstrous: Sex Offenders and the New Penology', *Psychology, Public Policy and the Law* Vol 4(1), 1–16.

Singer, L. (1991) 'A Non-punitive Paradigm of Probation Practice: Some Sobering Thoughts', *British Journal of Social Work* Vol 21, 611–26.

Singh Bhui, H. (2004) 'Developing Effective Practice and Policy with Foreign National Prisoners', unpublished.

Singleton, N., Meltzer, H., Gatward, R., Coid, J. and Deasy, D. (1998) *Psychiatric Morbidity among Prisoners*. London, HMSO.

Smart, J. J. C. and Williams, B. (1973) *Utilitarianism: For and Against*. Cambridge, Cambridge University Press.

Smith, A. (1998) 'Psychiatric Evidence and Discretionary Life Sentences' *Journal of Forensic Psychiatry* Vol 9(1), 17–38.

Smith, B. and Hillenbrand, S. (1997) 'Making Victims Whole Again' in R. Davis, A. Lurigio and W. Skogan (eds) (1997) *Victims of Crime* (2nd edn). Thousand Oaks, CA, Sage, 245–56.

Smith, D., Blagg, H. and Derricourt, N. (1988) 'Mediation in South Yorkshire' *British Journal of Criminology* Vol 28(3), 378–95.

Smith, D., Paler, I. and Mitchell, P. (1993) 'Partnerships between the Independent Sector and the Probation Service' *Howard Journal* Vol 32(1), 25–39.

Social Exclusion Unit (2002) *Reducing Re-Offending by Ex-Prisoners*. London, Social Exclusion Unit.

Social Services Inspectorate (2004) *Inspection of Medway Secure Training Centre, Kent*. London, Department of Health.

Spalek, B. (ed) (2002) *Islam, Crime and Criminal Justice*. Cullompton, Willan.

Sparks, C. and Taylor, M. (2001/2: 6) 'Challenging Times' CJM No 46, Winter, 6–7. London, Centre for Crime and Justice Studies, Kings College.

Sparrow, P., Brooks, G. and Webb, D. (2002) 'National Standards for the Probation Service: Managing Post-Fordist Penality' *Howard Journal* Vol 41(1), 27–40.

Spencer, J. (1995) 'A Response to Mike Nellis: Probation Values for the 1990s' *Howard Journal* Vol 34(4), 344–9.

Stamen, D. (2007) *Reconsidering Incarceration: New Directions for Reducing Crime.* New York, The Vera Institute of Justice.

Stanton, J. M. (1969) 'Murderers on Parole' *Crime and Delinquency* Vol 15, 149–55.

Steen, S. and Bandy, R. (2007) 'When the Policy Becomes the Problem: Criminal Justice in the New Millennium', *Punishment and Society* Vol 9(1), 5–26.

Stein, P. (1984) *Legal Institutions: The Development of Dispute Settlement.* London, Butterworths.

Steiner, E. (2003) 'Early Release for Seriously Ill and Elderly Prisoners: Should French Practice Be Followed?' *Probation Journal*, Vol. 50(3), 267–76.

Stewart, S. (1998) *Conflict Resolution: A Foundation Guide.* Winchester, Waterside Press.

Stockdale, E. and Devlin, K. (1987) *Sentencing* (1st edn). London, Waterlow Publishers.

Stopard, P. (1990) 'Punishment and Probation: The Rhetoric and Reality of the White Paper' *Probation Journal* Vol 3(3), 123–6.

Strang, H. (2003) *Repair or Revenge.* Oxford, Oxford University Press.

Strang, H. (2007) 'Institutionalizing Restorative Justice' *British Journal of Criminology* Vol 47(4), 704–6.

Straw, J. (1996) *Tackling Disorder, Insecurity and Crime.* London, Labour Party.

Sullivan, E. (September, 2007) 'Straight from the Horse's Mouth', *Prison Service Journal* 173, 9–14.

Tak, P. J. P. (2003) *The Dutch Criminal Justice System: Organization and Operation.* Den Haag, Boom Juridische Uitgevers.

Talbot, J. (2007) *No One Knows: Identifying and Supporting Prisoners with Learning Difficulties and Learning Disabilities: The Views of Prison Staff.* London, Prison Reform Trust.

Talbot, J. and Riley, C. (2007) 'No One Knows: Offenders with Learning Difficulties and Learning Disabilities', *British Journal of Learning Disabilities* Vol 35 (3), 154–61.

Tarling, R. (1979) 'The "Incapacitation" Effects of Imprisonment', *Home Office Research Bulletin*, No. 7, 6–8. London, Home Office.

Tarling, R. (1993) *Analysing Offending: Data, Models and Interpretations.* London, HMSO.

Tarling, R. (2006) 'Sentencing Practice in Magistrates' Courts Revisited' *Howard Journal* Vol 45(1), 29–41.

Tauri, J. and Morris, A. (2003) 'Reforming Justice: The Potential of Maori Processes' in E. McLaughlin, R. Ferguson, G. Hughes and L. Westmarland (eds) *Restorative Justice, Critical Issues.* Milton Keynes, Open University Press and London, Sage, 44–53.

Tavares, C. and Thomas, G. (2007) *Crime and Criminal Justice: Statistics in Focus: Population and Social Conditions*, 15/2007. Brussels, Eurostat.

Taylor, R. (2000) *A Seven Year Reconviction Study of HMP Grendon Therapeutic Community*, London, Home Office.

Taylor, R. (2006) '*Re S (A Child) (Identification: Restrictions on Publication)* and *A Local Authority v W*: Children's Privacy and Press Freedom in Criminal Cases' *Child and Family Law Quarterly* Vol 18(2), 269–86.

Teubner, G. (1989) 'How the Law Thinks: Towards a Constructive Epistemology of Law' *Law and Society Review* Vol 23(5), 727–56.

Thomas, D. (1979) *Principles of Sentencing* (2nd edn). London, Heinemann.

Thomas, D. (1995) 'Sentencing Reform in England and Wales' in C. Clarkson and R. Morgan (eds) *The Politics of Sentencing Reform*. Oxford, Clarendon Press.

Thomas, D. (2002) 'The Sentencing Process' in M. McConville and G. Wilson (eds) *The Handbook of the Criminal Process*. Oxford, Oxford University Press, 473–86.

Thomas, D. (2006a) 'Sexual Offences Prevention Orders: Grounds for Making an Order', Crim LR, 364–7.

Thomas, D. (2006b) 'The Sex Offenders Act 1997: Notification Requirements' Crim LR, 553–58.

Thomas, D. (2006c) 'The Sexual Offences Act 2003: Notification Requirements' Crim LR, 1085–87.

Thomas, D. (2007) 'Case Commentary: *Thomas* [2006] EWCA Crim 2036' Crim LR, 171–2.

Thompson, E. P. (1977) *Whigs and Hunters: The Origin of the Black Act*. Harmondsworth, Penguin.

Tickell, S. and Akester, K. (2004) *Restorative Justice: The Way Ahead*. London, JUSTICE.

Tilt, R., Perry, B., Martin, C., *et al.* (2000) *Report of the Review of Security at the High Security Hospitals*. London, Department of Health.

Titmuss, R. (1968) *Commitment to Welfare*. London, Allen and Unwin.

Toch, H. (ed) (1976) *Living in Prison: The Ecology of Survival*. Maryland, American Psychological Association.

Tombs, J. (2004) *A Unique Punishment: Sentencing and the Prison Population in Scotland*. Edinburgh, Scottish Consortium on Crime and Criminal Justice.

Tombs, J. and Jagger, E. (2006) 'Denying Responsibility: Sentencers' Accounts of their Decision to Imprison' *British Journal of Criminology*, Vol 46, 803.

Tonry, M. (1993) 'Proportionality, Interchangeability and Intermediate Punishments' in R. Dobash, A. Duff and D. Marshall (eds) *Penal Theory and Penal Practice*. Manchester, Manchester University Press.

Tonry, M. (1996) *Sentencing Matters*. Oxford and New York, Oxford University Press.

Travis, A. (2004) 'Jailed Teenager Died after Being Restrained' *Guardian* 23 April, 7.

UK Government (1999) *Second Periodic Report to the United Nations Committee on Rights of the Child* (CRC/C/83/Add.3).

Umbreit, M (1994) *Victim Meets Offender: The Impact of Restorative Justice and Mediation*. Monsey, NY, Criminal Justice Press.

Umbreit, M., Coates, R. and Vos, B. 'Victim Impact of Meeting with Young Offenders' in A. Morris and G. Maxwell (eds) (2001) *Restorative Justice for Juveniles: Conferencing, Mediation and Circles*. Oxford, Hart, 121–44.

Vail, J., Wheelock, J. and Hill, M. (eds) (1999) *Insecure Times*. London and New York, Routledge.

Valier, C. (2003) 'Minimum Terms of Imprisonment in Murder, Just Deserts and the Sentencing Guidelines' Crim LR, 326–35.

van den Haag, E. (1981) 'Punishment as a Device for Controlling the Crime Rate' *Rutgers Law Journal* Vol 33, 706.

van den Haag, E. (1985) 'The Death Penalty Once More', *University of California Davis Law Review* Vol 18, Summer, 957–72.

van Zyl Smit, D. (2000) 'Mandatory Sentences—A Conundrum for the New South Africa?' *Punishment and Society* Vol 2(2), 197–212.

van Zyl Smit, D. and Ashworth, A. (2004) 'Disproportionate Sentences and Human Rights Violations' MLR Vol 67(4), 541–60.

Vaughan, B. (2000) 'The Government of Youth: Disorder *and* Dependence?' *Social and Legal Studies* Vol. 9(3), 347–66.

Victim Support (2002) *New Rights for Victims of Crime*. London, Victim Support.

von Hirsch, A. (1976) *Doing Justice: The Choice of Punishments*. New York, Hill and Wang.

von Hirsch, A. (1986) *Past or Future Crimes: Deservedness and Dangerousness in the Sentencing of Criminals*. Manchester, Manchester University Press.

von Hirsch, A. (1993) *Censure and Sanctions*. Oxford, Clarendon.

von Hirsch, A. (1998) 'Selective Incapacitation: Some Doubts' in A. von Hirsch and A. Ashworth (eds) *Principled Sentencing: Readings on Theory and Practice*. Oxford, Hart, 121–6.

von Hirsch, A. (1999) *Criminal Deterrence and Sentence Severity*. Oxford, Hart.

von Hirsch, A. and Ashworth, A. (1996) 'Protective Sentencing under Section 2(2)(b): The Criteria for Dangerousness' Crim LR, 175–83.

von Hirsch, A. and Ashworth, A. (2005) *Proportionate Sentencing: Exploring the Principles*. Oxford, Oxford University Press.

von Hirsch, A. and Roberts, J. (1997) 'Racial Disparity in Sentencing: Reflections on the Hood Study', *Howard Journal* Vol 36(3), 227–36.

von Hirsch, A. and Ashworth, A. (eds) (1998) *Principled Sentencing: Readings on Theory and Practice* (2nd edn). Oxford, Hart.

von Hirsch, A. and Roberts, J. (2004) 'Legislating Sentencing Principles: The Provisions of the Criminal Justice Act 2003 Relating to Sentencing Purposes and the Role of Previous Convictions' Crim LR, 639–52.

von Hirsch, A., Ashworth, A. and Shearing, C. (2005) 'Restorative Justice: A "Making Amends" Model?' in A. von Hirsch and A. Ashworth, *Proportionate Sentencing*. Oxford, Oxford University Press, 110–30.

von Hirsch, A., Bottoms, A. E., Burney, E. and Wikstrom, P.-O. (1999) *Criminal Deterrence and Sentence Severity*. Oxford, Hart.

von Hirsch, A., Roberts, J., Bottoms, A., Roach, K. and Schiff, M. (eds) (2003) *Restorative Justice and Criminal Justice: Competing or Reconcilable Paradigms?* Oxford, Hart.

Wacquant, L. (2001a) *Prisons of Poverty*. Minneapolis, University of Minnesota Press.

Wacquant, L. (2001b) 'Deadly Symbiosis: When Ghetto and Prison Meet and Mesh', *Punishment and Society* Vol 3(1), 95–133.

Wacquant, L. (2007) *Urban Outcasts: A Comparative Study of Advanced Marginality*. Cambridge, Polity Press.

Wahidin, A. (2004), *Older Women in the Criminal Justice System*. London, Jessica Kingsley.

Walgrave, L. (1995) 'Restorative Justice for Juveniles: Just a Technique or a Fully Fledged Alternative?' *Howard Journal* Vol. 34(3), 228.

Walker, N. (1985) *Sentencing: Theory, Law and Practice*. Oxford, Oxford University Press.

Walker, N. (1991) *Why Punish?* Oxford, Oxford University Press.

Walker, N. (1999) *Aggravation, Mitigation and Mercy in English Criminal Justice*, Oxford, Blackstone.

Walker, N. (ed) (1996) *Dangerous People*. London, Blackstone Press.

Walker, S. and Beckett, C. (2003) *Social Work Assessment and Intervention*. Lyme Regis, Russell House.

Walklate, S. (2004) 'Justice for All in the 21st Century: The Political Context of the Policy Focus on Victims' in E. Cape (ed) *Reconcilable Rights?* London, Legal Action Group, 27–36.

Wallis, E. (2001) 'A New Choreography—An Integrated Strategy for the National Probation Service for England and Wales' *Strategic Framework 2001–2004*. London, Home Office.

Walmsley, R., Howard, L. and White, S. (1992) *The National Prison Survey 1991: Main Findings*, Research Study 128. London, HMSO.

Walton, A. S. (1983) 'Hegel, Utilitarianism and the Common Good' *Ethics* Vol 93, 753–71.

Warr, M. (1989) 'What Is the Perceived Seriousness of Crimes?' *Criminology* Vol 27(4), 795–821.

Ward, D., Scott, J. and Lacey, M. (2002) *Probation, Working for Justice* (2nd edn). Oxford, Oxford University Press.

Wargent, M. (2002) 'The New Governance of Probation' *Howard Journal* Vol 41(2), 182–200.

Wasik, M. (1983) 'Excuses at the Sentencing Stage' Crim LR, 450–65.

Wasik, M. (1999) 'Reparation: Sentencing and the Victim' Crim LR, 470–80.

Wasik, M. (2001) 'The Vital Importance of Certain Previous Convictions' Crim LR, 363–73.

Wasik, M. (2004) 'Going Round in Circles? Reflecting on Fifty Years of Change in Sentencing' Crim LR, 253–65.

Wasik, M., Gibbons, T. and Redmayne, M. (1999) *Criminal Justice, Text and Materials*. London, Longman.

Wasik, M. and Turner, A. (1992) 'Sentencing Guidelines for the Magistrates Courts' Crim LR, 345–56.

Wasik, M. and von Hirsch, A. (1988) 'Non-Custodial Penalties and the Principles of Desert' Crim LR, 555–71.

Wasik, M. and von Hirsch, A. (1990) 'Statutory Sentencing Principles: The 1990 White Paper' MLR, Vol 53, 508–17.

Wasik, M. and von Hirsch, A. (1994) 'Section 29 Revisited: Previous Convictions in Sentencing' Crim LR, 409–18.

Waters, I. (2007) 'The Policing of Young Offenders' *British Journal of Criminology* Vol 47(4), 635–54.

Watson, S. and Rice, S. (with prisoners at HMP Wolds) (2004) *Daddy's Working Away*. London, Care for the Family.

Weijers, I. (2002) 'The Moral Dialogue: A Pedagogical Perspective on Juvenile Justice' in I. Weijers and A. Duff (eds) *Punishing Juveniles: Principles and Critique*. Oxford, Hart, 135–54.

Weijers, I. and Duff, A. (2002) 'Introduction: Themes in Juvenile Justice' in I. Weijers and A. Duff (eds) *Punishing Juveniles: Principles and Critique*. Oxford, Hart, 1–21.

Weitekamp, E. and Kerner, H-J. (eds) (2002) *Restorative Justice: Theoretical Foundations*. Cullompton, Willan.

Welsh, B. C. and Farrington, D. P. (2002) *Crime Prevention Effects of Closed Circuit Television: A Systematic Review*, Home Office Research Study 252. London, Home Office.

Welsh, B. C. and Farrington, D. P. (eds) (2006) *Preventing Crime: What Works for Chidren, Offenders, Victims and Places*. New York, Springer.

Welshman, J. (2007) *From Transmitted Deprivation to Social Exclusion: Policy, Poverty and Parenting*. Bristol, Policy Press.

Whittacker, C. and Mackie, A. (1997) *Enforcing Financial Penalties*. HORS No 165. London, Home Office.

Wilcox, A., Young, R., and Hoyle, C. (2004) *An Evaluation of the Impact of Restorative Cautioning: Findings from a Reconviction Study*, Home Office Findings 255. London, Home Office.

Wilkinson, C. and Evans, R. (1990) 'Police Cautioning of Juveniles—The Impact of Circular 14/1985' Crim LR, 165–76.

Williams, B. (1999) 'The Victims Charter: Citizens as Consumers of the Criminal Justice Service' *Howard Journal* Vol 38(4), 384–96.

Williams, F. (1989) *Social Policy*. Cambridge, Polity Press.

Williams, J. (2007) 'Incorporating Children's Rights: The Divergence in Law and Policy' LS, Vol 27(2), 261–87.

Wilson, D. (2003) '"Keeping Quiet" or "Going Nuts": Some Emerging Strategies Used by Young Black People in Custody at a Time of Childhood Being Re-constructed' *Howard Journal* Vol 42(5), 411–25.

Wilson, D. and McCabe, S. (2002) 'How HMP Grendon Works in the Words of Those Undergoing Therapy' *Howard Journal* Vol 41(3), 279–91.

Wilson, J. Q. (1985) *Thinking about Crime* (2nd edn). New York, Vintage Books.

Windzio, M. (2006) 'Is There a Deterrent Effect of Pains of Imprisonment? The Impact of "Social Costs" of First Incarceration on the Hazard Rate of Recidivism', *Punishment and Society*, Vol 8(3), 341–64.

Wintour, P. (2007) 'Time to Stop Knocking the Young' and 'Miliband: "I want the Buzz Back in the Manifesto"' *Guardian* 23 July, 1 and 10.

Witte, A. D. (1980) 'Estimating the Economic Model of Crime with Individual Data', *Quarterly Journal of Economics* Vol 94, 57–84.

Wolpin, K. I. (1978) 'An Economic Analysis of Crime and Punishment in England and Wales, 1894–1967', *Journal of Political Economy*, Vol 86, 815–40.

Women's Offending Reduction Programme (2005) *Annual Review 2004–2005*. London, NOMS, Home Office.

Wonnacott, C. (1999) 'The Counterfeit Contract—Reform, Pretence and Muddled Principles in the New Referral Order' *Child and Family Law Quarterly* 271.

Wood, A. (1972) 'The Marxian Critique of Justice', *Philosophy and Public Affairs* Vol 1(3) 244–82.

Wood, A. (2004) *Karl Marx* (2nd edn). London, Routledge.

Wood, D. (1988) 'Dangerous Offenders and the Morality of Protective Sentencing' Crim LR, 424–33.

Wood, J. and Kemshall, H. (2007) *The Operation and Experience of Multi-Agency Public Protection Arrangements*, Home Office Findings 285. London, Home Office.

Woodbridge, J. and Frosztega, J. (1998) *Recent Changes in the Female Prison Population*, London, Home Office.

Woodcock, J. (1994) *The Escape from Whitemoor Prison on Friday 9th September 1994*, the *Woodcock Enquiry*, Cm 2741. London, HMSO.

Woolf, H. and Tumim, S. (1991) *Prison Disturbances April 1990*. Report of an Inquiry, Cm 1456. London, HMSO.

Woolf, Lord (2003) Speech, Perrie Lecture Awards, June 6.

Woolford, A. and Ratner, R. S. (2007) *Informal Reckonings: Conflict Resolution in Mediation, Restorative Justice and Reparations*. London, Routledge-Cavendish.

Worrall, A. (1990) *Offending Women: Female Law-breakers and the Criminal Justice System*. London, Routledge.

Worrall, A. (1997) *Punishment in the Community*. London, Addison Wesley Longman.

Worrall, A. and Hoy, C. (2005) *Punishment in the Community* (2nd edn). Cullompton, Willan.

Wright, M. (1996) *Justice for Victims and Offenders* (2nd edn). Winchester, Waterside Press.

Young, J. (1999) *The Exclusive Society*. London, Sage.

Young, J. (2002) 'Crime and Social Exclusion', in Maguire, M., Morgan, R. and Reiner, R. (eds) *The Oxford Handbook of Criminology* (3rd edn). Oxford, Oxford University Press, 457–90.

Young, P. (1989) 'Punishment, Money and a Sense of Justice' in P. Carlen and D. Cook (eds) *Paying for Crime*. Milton Keynes, Open University Press, 46–65.

Young, P. (1997) *Crime and Criminal Justice in Scotland*. Edinburgh, Stationery Office.

Young, R. (1989) 'Reparation as Mitigation' Crim LR, 463–72.

Youth Justice Board (2001) *Youth at Risk? A national survey of risk factors, protective factors and problem behaviour among young people in England, Scotland and Wales*, London, YJB.

Youth Justice Board (2004) *Restorative Justice in the Juvenile Secure Estate*. London, YJB.

Youth Justice Board (2006a) *Anti-social Behaviour Orders (Summary)*. London, YJB.

Youth Justice Board (2006b) *Managing Children and Young People's Behaviour in the Secure Estate: A Code of Practice*. London, YJB.

Youth Justice Board (2006c) *Dangerousness and the New Sentences for Public Protection: Guidance for Youth Offending Teams*. London, YJB.

Youth Justice Board (2006d) *Common Assessment Framework, Draft Guidance for Youth Offending Teams*. London, YJB.

Zedner, L. (2003) 'The Concept of Security: An Agenda for Comparative Analysis' LS Vol 23(1), 151–76.

Zehr, H. (1985) 'Retributive Justice, Restorative Justice' *New Perspectives in Crime and Justice* Vol 4. Akron, PA: MCC Office of Crime and Justice.

Zehr, H. and Mika, H. (1998) 'Fundamental Concepts of Restorative Justice' (1998) *Contemporary Justice Review* Vol 1, 47–55.

Zimring, F. (2001) 'Imprisonment Rates and the New Politics of Criminal Punishment' in D. Garland (ed) *Mass Imprisonment*. London, Sage, 145–9.

Zimring, F. (2005) *American Juvenile Justice*. New York, Oxford University Press.

Zimring, F. and Hawkins, G. (1986) *Capital Punishment and the American Agenda*. New York, Cambridge University Press.

Zimring, F. and Hawkins, G. (1995) *Incapacitation: Penal Confinement and the Restraint of Crime*. New York, Oxford University Press.

INDEX